Worldly Shakespeare

For Dominique Goy-Blanquet
Brave des Braves

Worldly Shakespeare

The Theatre of Our Good Will

Richard Wilson

EDINBURGH
University Press

© Richard Wilson, 2016

Transferred to digital print 2016

The Tun – Holyrood Road, 12(2f) Jackson's Entry, Edinburgh EH8 8PJ

www.euppublishing.com

Typeset in 10/12pt Goudy Old Style by
Servis Filmsetting Ltd, Stockport, Cheshire, and
printed and bound in Great Britain by
CPI Group (UK) Ltd, Croydon, CR0 4YY

A CIP record for this book is available from the British Library

ISBN 978 1 4744 1132 5 (hardback)
ISBN 978 1 4744 1133 2 (webready PDF)
ISBN 978 1 4744 1134 9 (paperback)
ISBN 978 1 4744 1135 6 (epub)

The right of Richard Wilson to be identified as the author of this
work has been asserted in accordance with the Copyright, Designs and
Patents Act 1988, and the Copyright and Related Rights Regulations
2003 (SI No. 2498).

Contents

Acknowledgements

A n earlier version of Chapter 2 was published in *Forgetting Faith: Religious Pluralism in Early Modern Europe*, ed. Tobias Döring *et al.* (Berlin: de Gruyter, 2011); and of Chapter 10 in *Between Shakespeare and Cervantes: Trails Along the Renaissance*, ed. Zenon Luis-Martinez and Luis Gomez Canseco (Newark: Juan de la Cuesta, 2006). A portion of the Epilogue appeared in *Approches critiques du 'Conte d'hiver' de Shakespeare*, ed. Yan Brailowsky and Anny Crunelle (Nanterre: Presses universitaires de Paris Ouest, 2011). A shorter version of Chapter 3 was originally published in *Poetica*, 36 (2004); of Chapter 5 as the 2006 Shakespeare's Globe Fellowship Lecture (London: Globe Education, 2006); of Chapter 6 in *Shakespeare*, 4 (2008); of Chapter 7 in *Shakespeare*, 6 (2010); of Chapter 8 in *Shakespeare Survey*, 66 (2013); and of Chapter 9 in *Shakespeare*, 9 (2013).

Note on Texts

All quotations from Shakespeare are from *The Norton Shakespeare*, based on the Oxford edition, edited by Stephen Greenblatt, Walter Cohen, Jean Howard and Katharine Eisaman Maus (New York: Norton, 2007).

Introduction:
No Offence in the World

'If we offend, it is with our good will', explains Peter Quince, in the Prologue Shakespeare gave him to speak for the actors in A Midsummer Night's Dream, insisting 'we come not to offend/But with good will' [5,1,108–9]. This wily auto-reference introduces 'our good Will' in terms of the inoffensiveness contemporaries reported, and that colours all his self-portraits, as 'obedient, hat-in-hand', 'good William' [As You, 5,1,53] protests that if we are offended, we should 'Think but this, and all is mended:/That you have but slumbered here' [Dream, Epi.,1–3].[1] Worldly Shakespeare is a book about the right 'our good Will' thereby claims, to offend with good will, and of the tolerance this demands, of an offence not given except with good will. In a previous study, Free Will: Art and Power on Shakespeare's Stage, I analysed the strategy by which this repeat offender spoke truth to power in a display of mock innocence.[2] By staging his own inhibition, as a 'tongue-tied unlettered clerk' hesitating at the door, while with 'dumb thoughts, speaking in effect' [Sonnet 85], 'Our bending author' [Henry V, Epi.,2] became, on this view, 'the major master of ellipsis in the history of theatre', as Harold Bloom puts it.[3] Thus, Shakespeare perhaps dramatised his situation when he had a messenger ask the Queen to 'Take no offence that I would not offend you for what you bid me do' [Antony, 2,6,100]. For 'thy sweet Will' [Sonnet 135] outfaced all forms of sovereignty, in this account, with a self-abjection that was in fact an inverted form of 'repressive tolerance'. With Worldly Shakespeare: The Theatre of Our Good Will, I extend consideration of this power to offend to Shakespeare's staging of toleration itself, and examine how his theatre presents itself as a model for 'a world made of diversity, including disparity and opposition', founded precisely on the right to give, but not to take, offence.[4]

Shakespeare is said to be the 'soul the world', and to promote 'global Shakespeare' as a figure for a world of difference has become a liberal cliché.[5] A running theme of this book is therefore that it was not by chance that this dramatist wrote for a theatre called the Globe. But Worldly Shakespeare asks what it means to be so 'worldly'. In The Tempest, for example, Prospero has acquired his power precisely by 'neglecting worldly ends' [1,2,89]. Here, and every time Shakespeare uses the term, it is as an antonym of 'unworldly', a usage shaped by the Old English woruldlic, meaning 'earthly' or 'mortal'. Thus, Henry VI turns from 'worldly solace' to a life of prayer [2 *Henry VI*, 3,2,151]; Richard III pretends that 'no worldly suits' would make him leave his 'divine meditation' [*Richard III*, 3,7,63]; Titus inters his slain sons 'Secure from worldly chances' [*Titus*, 1,1,152]; Richard II counts his kingdom but 'a worldly loss' [*Richard II*, 3,2,90]; a sick Henry IV senses his 'worldly business makes a period' [2 *Henry IV*, 4,3,358]; and Cassius plans suicide as one 'weary of worldly bars' [*Julius*, 1,3,95]. In all these instances, however, otherworldly transcendence is contradicted by the *worldliness* of the plays themselves, which always return to that 'ground of worldly *dogmata*' Thomas Hobbes addressed when he 'demoted the absolute claims of belief and conscience, with their recourse to a transcendent sphere, to the relativism and worldliness of opinion'.[6] Such a worldliness is stark in Claudio's *cri de coeur*, when told to prepare to die, that the 'most loathed worldly life . . . is a paradise/To what we fear of death' [*Measure*, 129–31]. So, although the mourners chant 'Thou thy worldly task has done' at her presumed graveside in *Cymbeline*, Innogen lives on, in reality, to face 'the furious winter's rages' [4,2,260–1].

Worldly Shakespeare is a study of how, in a world without access to the otherworldly, Shakespeare embraces the contradictions of 'the furious winter's rages'. His plays and poems remain current, I propose, because, more than any other literary works, they have shaped the worldliness that depends on the vital modern distinction drawn by Hobbes, between believing *someone* and believing *something*. The philosopher explained that trust 'can be had in any person', even if 'they do not believe the Doctrine of the Creed'; but that 'whereas the latter creates the idea of absolute authority, the former remains conditional'.[7] Likewise, 'worldly pleasure' displaces what flies 'Above the reach and compass of thy thought' [2 *Henry VI*, 1,2,45] on this stage, where Titus learns 'we worldly men' have 'mad, mistaking eyes' [*Titus*, 5,2,65]; Richard III revels in 'worldly things' [2,2,88]; and Richard II is proved to be deluded to think 'worldly men cannot depose' a king [*Richard II*, 3,2,52–3]. In this theatre Proteus can betray his friend for 'worldly good' [*Two Gentlemen*, 3,1,9]; and Othello destroy his wife because they share so little 'worldly matter' [*Othello*, 1,3,298]. Another reason these texts are destined to remain with us, *Worldly Shakespeare* therefore suggests, is that they foretell the concern of our political theorists about the 'impasses of the public sphere' when otherworldly sanction is disputed. In particular, their worldliness provokes the question that has lately returned with a vengeance, of what happens 'in a society divided by religious beliefs . . . in which each side fabricates arguments about what it can do to others based on its own faith'.[8]

In *Worldly Shakespeare* I understand *worldliness* as the right to give, without taking, offence, or the form of ironic tolerance that today's political philosophers describe as 'living together *in conflict*'.[9] This conflictual *agôn* speaks to 'the question of the neighbourhood' for thinkers like Alain Badiou, where people 'cannot be linked as neighbours, but only asserted as being in the same neighbourhood', and far from being universal a neighbourhood is merely 'an open space in the world'.[10] So, how did this dramatist become synonymous with the universalism of 'our good will', I ask, when his professional interest lay in heightening such conflict, by intensifying cultural, ethnic and religious divides? For, when introducing outsiders, Shakespeare always exaggerates their difference from his audience's norms.[11] Thus, if his works are so hospitable, this accent on gratuitous offence generates an awkward squad of anti-theatrical figures who ruin the dream of universality, starting with the pious ladies of Paris who dash the naïve ecumenical hopes of the lords of Navarre 'like a Christmas comedy' [Love's, 5,2,462], spoilsports like the sinister 'pale companion' Theseus bars from the games [Dream, 1,1,12], or party-poopers who, because they are not 'for dancing measures' [As You, 5,4,182], think 'there shall be no more cakes and ale' [Twelfth, 2,3,104].

Noticing how, by refusing to enter into the spirit of the play, Shakespeare's 'lean and hungry' [Julius, 1,2,195] indignados undermine their creator's authorial pose of peasant-like compliance, in Secret Shakespeare I keyed these naysayers to what I took to be the primal Shakespearean scene of a loyalty test – like the Elizabethan 'Bloody Question', about whether you would side with the Pope or the Queen – in which some sovereign or seducer demands a performance of submission, and the refusenik protests: 'I have that within which passes show' [Hamlet, 1,2,85], 'I cannot heave/My heart into my mouth' [Lear, 1,1,90], or 'There's beggary in the love that can be reckoned' [Antony, 1,1,15]. Born into an age of oaths, a traumatised post-Reformation world of violent confessional extremes, this writer made a song and dance out of resisting such resisters, I inferred in Secret Shakespeare, by soliciting toxic sectarian interpretations of his plays, as he did sexual ones in his Sonnets, but then placing these offending meanings under erasure. So the management of those conscientious objectors who will not collaborate with the stage by turning politics into culture in this way, 'for any man's persuasion' [Measure, 4,3,52], becomes the mainspring of his dramaturgy, I concluded, until his Prospero finally surrenders the dream of universal reconciliation, and concedes that they 'shall be themselves' [Tempest, 5,1,32].

On Shakespeare's agonistic stage, where the oracles are reduced to 'crooked smokes' [Cymbeline, 5,6,477], 'there is no justice', it is often felt.[12] This renunciation of closure has been connected by Stephen Orgel to the fact that the only time the dramatist ever airs the Aristotelian doctrine of cathartic drama, when Hamlet says 'The play's the thing/Wherein I'll catch the conscience of the king' [Hamlet, 2,2,581–2], 'Claudius refuses the catharsis'.[13] Of course, Shakespeare was deeply interested in the pharmakon principle of 'poison in jest' [3,2,214]: that a therapeutic purging may make 'The appetite . . . sicken and so die' [Twelfth, 1,1,3]. But as Jan Kott saw, this type of conflict drama 'brings no catharsis whatsoever'.[14] The philosopher Peter Sloterdijk has proposed a grand immunological theory that puts this refusal of catharsis in a truly global context, when he describes how the age-old sacrificial logic of a world purged of difference under a sheltering sky was shattered by the Reformation schism, when Europeans 'broke away from the Catholic-philosophical dream of a unified message to move towards multilinguality'. Sloterdijk's thesis explains why post-Reformation Europe pictured its sudden 'immune deficiency' with respect to confessional multiplicity as another fall of the Tower of Babel.[15] In Worldly Shakespeare I am therefore interested in how these plays react to that 'immunological crisis' by presaging a polity based not on confessional or ideological uniformity, but on incommensurable difference, an agonistic rather than therapeutic regime, that acknowledges the adversarial struggle of divided subjects as its condition of existence and, in generating *offensiveness as its own solution*, becomes like nothing so much as one of Shakespeare's jarringly unfinished plays:

> BIRON: Our wooing doth not end like an old play.
>   Jack hath not Jill. These ladies' courtesies
>   Might well have made our sport a comedy.
> KING: Come, sir, it wants a twelve-month and a day,
>   And then 'twill end.
> BIRON: That's too long for a play.
>
> [*Love's*, 5,2,851–5]

Too long for a play, let alone a game, Shakespeare's agonistic theatre presents itself as an *event* more real than any 'comedy' or 'sport', because it is without catharsis or conclusion. So *Worldly Shakespeare* interprets this turn away from therapy in the context of the historical events that the effort to give offence 'but with good will' appears to reflect, or that shaped the English political imaginary: the compromise 1598 Edict of Nantes, proclaiming freedom of worship for Protestants in their French heartlands, followed by the assassination of its promulgator, the Catholic convert King Henri IV, at the hands of a Jesuit *manqué* in 1610, with, between these turning-points, the long-awaited accession of James VI of Scotland to Elizabeth's throne in 1603, pre-empted by the 1601 Essex Rebellion, and darkened by the 1605 Gunpowder Plot of Catholics disappointed by the failure of this self-styled *Rex Pacificus* to emulate his French counterpart's Gallican system of religious toleration. I am here following recent critics inspired by the theories of Jacques Lacan, who propose that if the example of French tolerance and intolerance loomed large for Shakespeare's generation, both as a warning and as an incitement, it was as a mirror of English fears and aspirations, in which recognition of the self in the other precipitated a realisation of insatiable *lack*, the 'continual evanescence, or present-absence, of that which purports to be the universal object of desire: peace'.[16]

Much has been written after 9/11 about how, by becoming 'all things to all men' (1 Corinthians 9: 22), Shakespeare was following in the steps of St Paul, the tentmaker from Tarsus currently in favour for his universalism, in crafting symbolic shelters, so as to 'gather under a single roof', in Jacques Derrida's emotive phrase, 'the disordered plurivocality' of a multi-faith society.[17] Just as Badiou salutes in Paul the capacity to envision a universe constituted out of difference, so in this latest critical turn Shakespeare calls us to a universalism that is opposite to the 'simulacrum' of liberal universalism, one in which not only are there differences, but 'there is nothing else'.[18] As I myself argued in a 2007 study, *Shakespeare in French Theory: King of Shadows*, by such lights this poet of 'commodious thresholds' becomes, with his 'exits and [his] entrances' [*As You*, 2,7,140], a gatekeeper of Europe's benighted universalism. But my theme there was Derrida's qualification that while 'Open, waiting for the event as justice', this hospitality is absolute only if it keeps vigilant watch 'over its own universality'.[19] And in *Worldly Shakespeare* I traverse Shakespearean drama in the context of the religious politics of his own age, to explore a sense in which these non-cathartic plays are premised on a recognition that such universality is an impossibility, a peace that truly 'passes all understanding' (Philippians 4: 7), albeit one around which all our particular human desires must be formed. Thus, the time is always 'out of joint' [*Hamlet*, 1,5,189] in these plays, I accept; yet this very disarticulation is embraced with something like the *worldliness* Hannah Arendt thought was required because 'men, not Man, live on the earth and inhabit the world'. 'The human condition of work is worldliness', the worldly philosopher proposed.[20] So, though Shakespeare himself alluded to the Globe as 'this wide and universal theatre' [*As You*, 2,7,136], his theatre might more justly be called a *worldly stage*, I therefore conclude.

It has become reassuring to describe Shakespeare's plays as 'conversation pieces' which prefigure Hans-Georg Gadamer's hermeneutics and his genial idea that 'the experience of conversation' is premised on an understanding of 'what always remains to be said'.[21] In *Worldly Shakespeare*, however, I instead consider Shakespearean theatre as an agonistic drama of deliberate offence masked as good will, rather than of such mutual understanding, and a premonition of the realisation that what Rousseau would teach Enlightenment thinkers to consider the 'general will' must always be an act of faith, because there can be no inter-subjective communication without compulsion. A discursive context of this study is therefore the recent return of faith to Shakespeare studies, especially via the critical interest in political theology, the belief that the sovereign is God's representative on earth. For, inspired by a cult of the Catholic and Fascist jurist Carl Schmitt, with his infamous diktat that 'Sovereign is he who decides the exception', research on sacred kingship has lately been deployed to revive an old myth of Shakespeare as mystic monarchist, a theocrat whose plays propagandise the 'high Christian royalism' which might *impose* such a universal *Pax Romana*.[22] The Shakespearean playhouse operated as a kind of propaganda machine, in this analysis, for the Schmittian idea that 'the traditional state meant a sovereignty capable of the decision to end civil war': Hamlet's monarchic 'dying voice' [*Hamlet*, 5,2,335], for instance, exercised to nominate Fortinbras the inheritor of the realm.[23] According to this Schmitt-inspired reading, 'political representation is almost always a catastrophe for Shakespeare's "people"', who prefer the dictatorial decision of some present prince to the palaver of parliamentary representation.[24] Long associated with World War II flag-bearers E. M. W. Tillyard and G. Wilson Knight, Shakespeare's paradoxical royalism has therefore been given a fresh populist spin as a result of recent reappraisals of the monarchic vestiges in modern democracies like the United States, such as Eric Nelson's *The Royalist Revolution* and Eric Santner's *The Royal Remains*:

> Shakespeare's theatre has been an indispensable resource in allowing its audiences to work through the structural interregnum, the turbulent void at the heart of (early) modernity. But some of the radical implications of that interregnum did not become fully clear – remained latent – until it passed from the court into the very heart of the People . . . who became those in whose voice the death of the 'dying voice' silently resonates. . . .[25]

Schmitt's importance for Shakespeare criticism lies in his perception that because there was no division in the Elizabethan playhouse between the time of the playgoers and that of the play, 'Society too was on stage', and that this existential experience of theatre as event substantiated the myth of the real presence of the King. When he wrote his own study of the dramatist, 'Hitler's crown jurist' therefore de-Hamletised *Hamlet* and, noticing how for one minute at the end of his life Hamlet acts with authority as King, reinvented the great tragedy of indecision as a drama about dictatorial *decision* and an assertion of the sovereign exception grounded in the 'sacred blood right'.[26] In an earlier book, *Will Power: Essays on Shakespearean Authority*, shadowed by Michel Foucault, I likewise pointed to the kingly 'quality of mercy' [*Merchant*, 4,1,182] privileged in these plays to abrogate the law.[27] Yet theatre historians remind us how, despite their royal patent, Shakespeare's King's Men owed their profits to public performances, and were thereby 'able to pit different discourses against each other with far greater freedom than could courtly literature'.[28] So, in a series of critiques that factor in Arendt's civic republicanism, Julia Lupton has set the undoubted embarrassment that Shakespeare's stage is 'sundered by the lightning bolt of the monarch's caprice' against his prefiguration of citizenship, community and consent, stressing how these dramas also look forward to social norms, 'to equity, equality, and equivalence – opposites to the sovereign exception', and mark 'the occasion when personal sovereignty transforms into its opposite: as citizenship'.[29] Thus, as Schmitt's own antagonist, Ernst Kantorowicz, showed in his study of political theology, *The King's Two Bodies*, the reason Charles I pondered *Richard II* before his beheading was that this play foretold how a system that replaced the monarch's real presence with the puppetry of royal representation would make 'sovereignty a slave,/Proud majesty a subject' [4,1,241–2].[30] For according to such readings, the King was already becoming for Shakespeare what Slavoj Žižek terms him, after Hegel, the 'subject *par excellence*', whose self-subjection subjectified the state:

> The state without the monarch would still be a *substantial* order. The monarch represents the point of its subjectivization – but what precisely is his function? Only 'dotting the i's' in a formal gesture of taking upon himself (by putting his signature on them) the decrees proposed to him. . . . As soon as he concerns himself with questions of positive content, he crosses the line separating himself from his councillors, and the State regresses to the level of substantiality.[31]

All my work has concerned not only 'the complicity of a lethal politics and the configuring will of great art', but also 'the possible innocence of an art that escapes the will to contour it'.[32] So, in *Free Will* I explored how Shakespeare studies pivot on the question of whether this theatre substantiated sovereignty, as Schmitt held, or negotiated its transfer, as Kantorowicz countered, from the body of the king to the body of the people. Did this theatre envision a system of 'kings without monarchy' or one of 'monarchy without kings'?[33] In *Worldly Shakespeare* I pick up these debates, but with the twist that here it is in the irreconcilability of rival claims of citizen or sovereignty, equality or freedom, norm or exception, presence or representation, that

Shakespeare's agonistic drive is found. Everyone is familiar, for instance, with the classic observational equivalence that these plays are liable to both Christianising and secularising appropriation, and can be read as either sacred or profane, being 'haunted by rituals and beliefs that have been *emptied out*', in Stephen Greenblatt's formula, to the extent that, as Eric Mallin urges, we can 'entertain the notion of a godless Shakespeare'.[34] In *Secret Shakespeare* I pleased no one when I deduced the dramatist was born into a world of Catholic *ultras*, whom, by keeping vigilant guard against such universalism, like Montaigne, he *reacted against* in his plays. For the default response to this structural agonism is to resort to a bland Kantian critique, reasoning that if his texts are 'saturated in religious discourse', and 'alive to religious precedent', Shakespeare's creative practice is always to trump politics with culture, and 'to subordinate religious matter to the aesthetic demands of the work in hand'.[35]

Competing forms of Christianity, or other religions, become, in the frankly banalising synthesis authorised by the Shakespeare editorial establishment, 'raw material like anything else', that the genius 'draws on, but does not concede to', for as 'religion and aesthetics start pulling apart', in his staging of plural concepts of the good, all are 'subsumed to the specific demands of the literary artefact'.[36] That this liberal humanist idealisation of aesthetic closure and creative disinterest had its own Renaissance ideological roots, however, in the *politique* neutralism of Catholics such as Montaigne, was my theme in *Free Will*. Like Odysseus in the account by Theodor Adorno and Max Horkheimer, I argued there, Shakespeare saved his own creative life 'by denying himself under the name of Nobody'.[37] And the aesthetic ideology that has a 'Protean' Shakespeare subsuming political conflict and religious violence to his disinterested artistic neutrality collapses for the same reason that its constitutional counterpart, liberal democracy, is riven by contradiction, when, for all its tentativeness about reviving the worship of a single author in an age of theory, this aggrandisement of the Bard's sovereignty falls back on the insidious authoritarian notion that his art *compels*, albeit 'it compels towards tolerance and the acknowledgement of different voices'.[38]

In liberal humanist accounts, a plurivocal or 'Protean' Shakespeare can be made to presage the normative rationality of deliberative democracy. As Jonathan Dollimore points out, such a false humanism involves the wilful repression 'of what it is to be fully human'.[39] More specifically, such recuperative readings are purposely oblivious to the *performativity* of this theatre writing. For if these texts were as humane in their intentions as the official marginalia on Shakespeare and religion holds, they would not be plays. But as Henri IV learned to his cost, not even a present prince can *compel* the toleration of conflicting voices; so when Shakespeare wrote a comedy about a French king attempting to enforce cohabitation, the happy-ever-after denouement of *All's Well That Ends Well* unravelled due to the absence of mutual consent. Shakespeare may have been a pragmatist who staged the negotiability of all belief.[40] But the writer who gave Mercutio the dying curse 'A plague o' both your houses' [*Romeo*, 3,1,101], after Romeo causes his fatal wound by *coming between* him and his foe, or who entitled his final history, about the Reformation Henry VIII, '*All* is true', was no naïve campaigner for Third-Way comity, whether in religion, politics, or art, as the dramatist in Strindberg saw in a flash:

This play was produced in 1613 under the title *All Is True*; the Prologue hints at
that, too: 'Such as give/Their money out of hope they may believe,/May find
here truth' [7–9]. How is one to find any meaning in that? In the world of the
poet, in which before a higher court one can plead both-innocent-and-guilty,
there it can be true *and* false. Everything contains a yes and a no. Everything is
born of its opposite.[41]

As Strindberg understood, culture never triumphs over politics in Shakespeare's
plays, which instead continuously assert their antecedence to the modern ideology
of the aesthetic, as performances enmeshed in their own conflicted power relations
and material conditions. Thus Shakespeare does not simply caricature the negativity
of the enemies of theatre after the fashion of his rivals, with puritanical stereotypes
such as Shylock, Cassius and Malvolio. As Tom Betteridge has remarked in one of
the most stimulating of the recent Lacanian critiques, Shakespeare's plays are tormented by 'the fear that theatre is all its critics said it was', but the dramatist then
makes this very fear 'the fulcrum around which he simultaneously mounts a defence
and critique of his art'.[42] Thus, by incorporating its enemies into his work, as representatives of the resistance to the culturalisation of politics, the excluded ones who,
precisely by their exemption from the grand project of universal toleration, become
what Badiou calls 'vectors of humanity as a whole', Shakespeare renders the anti-
theatrical prejudice a constitutive and motivating element of his dramaturgy, with
a long line of protagonists who insist that their very roles are parts that they 'must
blush in acting' [*Coriolanus*, 2,2,141].[43]

A universalist Shakespeare inoculates his 'Protean' works of art against the religious condemnation coming from Protestant polemicists and Counter-Reformation
Catholics, it is conventionally proposed, when he absorbs their attacks on blasphemy, disorder, idolatry, pornography and transvestism in such mimetic ways. But
something more complex than homoeopathy, and less traditional than catharsis,
is going on when he echoes the visceral repugnance of Elizabethan moralists like
Stephen Gosson. For unlike the humanist defenders of the stage, Shakespeare
appears to have grasped that such antagonism had the advantage of 'actually taking
account of the radical potentiality of the theater'.[44] So, by having Caesar's assassins
decry the 'stinking breath' of 'the tag-rag people' down in the playhouse pit [*Julius*,
1,2,245–58]; Hamlet disintegrate 'this most excellent canopy', the 'majestical roof'
of the tiring-house, into 'a foul and pestilent congregation of vapours' [*Hamlet*,
2,2,290–3]; Lear despair at 'this great stage of fools' [*Lear*, 4,6,177]; or Macbeth
denigrate 'the poor player/That struts and frets his hour upon the stage' in 'sound
and fury, signifying nothing' [*Macbeth*, 5,5,23–7], he performs his own thesis about
causing offence with good will, and riskily tests the limits of empathy, or the extreme
boundaries of toleration, within his own house.

By minimising the cultural offensiveness of Shakespeare's plays, liberal criticism
'has obscured their antagonistic intensity', Ewan Fernie has objected, when these
titanic struggles between 'mighty opposites' [*Hamlet*, 5,2,63] are 'more liberal than
liberalism, which cannot allow for the kind of overriding commitment that threatens liberal freedoms. They are also more compellingly involving'. The politically

correct version makes Shakespeare's supposed 'liberal tolerance look like indifference', as Fernie rightly observes.[45] Yet in contrast to such tolerance, Catherine Belsey finds antagonism, and 'the antipathy that accompanies love', to be the motor even of Shakespeare's Sonnets, whose rhetorical mode, she notes, is consistently agonistic. For 'to speak is to fight', she explains, after Jean-François Lyotard, since *all* speech acts 'fall within the domain of a general agonistics'.[46] Thus, in awarding the anti-theatrical aversion of his avowed enemies legitimacy inside the Globe, the dramatist not only lives out the *agôn* in his crisis scenario of tolerating the intolerable, when a guest outstays the welcome and threatens to destroy the host, but offers his worldly stage as a virtual model for the kind of agonistic society towards which his writings seem to aspire. These plays and poems thereby prepare us, I will argue in *Worldly Shakespeare*, for what the philosopher Michael Walzer identifies in his book *On Toleration* as 'the central and most difficult issue' confronting our multi-cultural societies, as we struggle to create the political arrangements that will enable people from mutually offending ethnic, national, religious and sexual groups to coexist with a modicum of good will, namely, the problem of 'tolerating the intolerant'.[47]

That an audience might empathise with Brutus when he demurs he is 'not gamesome' [*Julius*, 1,2,30]; with Ulysses when he derides the 'strutting player' who thinks 'it rich/To hear the wooden dialogue and sound/'Twixt his stretched footing and the scaffoldage' [*Troilus*, 1,3,153–6]; with Isabella when she despises the antic performing 'such fantastic tricks before high heaven/As makes the angels weep' [*Measure*, 2,2,124–5]; or with Cordelia when she deplores the 'glib and oily art' of acting itself [*Lear*, 1,1,225], only goes to show that what Shakespeare is about in these plays is not the sublimation of difference in Kantian works of art, safely sealed from history, nor the substitution of politics in culture, but their counterpointing in 'the ever-present possibility of antagonism'. A running theme of *Worldly Shakespeare* is in fact that 'by bringing to the fore the inescapable moment of decision – in the sense of having to decide within an undecidable terrain', and thereby revealing 'the limit of any rational consensus' in 'our good will', the radical negativity of this worldly theatre strikingly anticipates the recent agonistic approach to politics that 'forecloses the possibility of a society beyond division and power'.[48] By contrast with the now commonplace critique of his universality, I wish, in particular, to probe how Shakespeare's antinomian strategy 'to offend/But with good will' has affinities with the 'agonistic pluralism' that has been projected out of the deconstructionism of Derrida, as well as the existentialism of Schmitt, by the Belgian political theorist Chantal Mouffe:

> From the point of view of 'agonistic pluralism', the aim of democratic politics is to construct the 'them' in such a way that it is no longer perceived as an enemy to be destroyed, but as an 'adversary', that is, somebody whose ideas we combat but whose right to defend those ideas we do not put into question. This is the real meaning of liberal-democratic tolerance, which does not entail condoning ideas that we oppose, or being indifferent to standpoints that we disagree with, but treating those who defend them as legitimate opponents. . . . An adversary is an enemy, but a legitimate enemy.[49]

Schmitt notoriously reduced politics to the distinction between enemy and friend, and an insistence on the irreducibility of antagonism, of 'dialectic without synthesis', has been the distinguishing mark of Žižek's contrarian provocations.[50] But no doubt mindful of the surreal proportionality of the Belgian-style 'monarchy without kings' Schmitt reviled, with its maxim that *le roi règne, mais il ne gouverne pas*, Mouffe finesses this 'ethics of dis-harmony' by proposing that the aim of a pluralistic politics is to transform the enemy into an adversary, *antagonism* into *agonism*, so that democracy's creative tension inheres in 'the recognition and legitimation of conflict and the refusal to suppress it by imposing an authoritarian order'.[51] To give offence 'with good will': there is a precedent for this opening to the enemy-as-friend in a reflection of the Jewish theologian Jacob Taubes – that Schmitt teaches that the enemy must be opposed but not destroyed, because to destroy the enemy who defines us is to lose a sense of self.[52] True democracy will therefore resist the moralisation of politics by absolutism, however liberal. The question this prompts, of course, is one that haunts Shakespeare's stage, and that comes back in each chapter of *Worldly Shakespeare*: how, in the absence of some Hegelian monarch or Schmittian Caudillo, are 'disagreements . . . actually dealt with in a regime of "agonistic pluralism"?'[53]

In *Shakespeare's Imaginary Constitution*, actor and attorney Paul Raffield argues that 'the ideal constitution envisaged by Shakespeare was predicated on the classical principle of the *pactum*: the equitable social contract between magistrate and citizen', which he understood as 'a flexible juridical framework within which the intricacy and vibrancy of society could be expressed'.[54] But as Etienne Balibar has pointed out, the philosopher of Dutch toleration, Spinoza, was not the first to grasp that 'consensus on the need for a social pact only exists when the state is not corrupt or, as Spinoza would say, "violent"'. So Shakespearean theatre thrives on the Spinozan awareness that no social order can overcome the necessity of antagonism, I want to argue, because 'antagonism is at once a barrier to society's realization, and its very condition of possibility'.[55] The disputatiousness of Shakespeare's imagined polity therefore explodes the playful ideal of *serio ludere* in Renaissance Platonism, the dialectic of *Discordia concors* that is often said to make him 'a consummate rhetorician of unification'.[56] But, then, without such comity, how *in the world* is 'our good will' ever to be negotiated? Mouffe answers that we can learn from Wittgenstein that what matters is that adversaries agree not on the substance but on the form of their opinions, that 'they agree in the *language* they use', and in the semiotic rules of the democratic game. Agreement to *play the game* according to the same language and rules is itself a type of consensus, this political theorist concedes. But it is a 'conflictual consensus', and not at all the Kantian 'good will' that for Gadamer inheres in the will to understand. Instead, it is a kind of Cold War that remains frozen in the double bind of mimetic rivalry, and the fact that, as René Girard has always stressed, 'the same movement that brings human beings together in their common desire for the same objects is also at the origin of their antagonism'.[57]

In contrast to the vision of the universal church that would be resumed in France with Louis XIV's revocation of his grandfather's edict, and inherited in the coercive totalitarian *laïcité* of the French Republic, Mouffe's distinctly 'Belgian' slant on the agonistic dialectic of mutually assured destruction, the Wittgensteinian perception that 'it is *acting* which lies at the bottom of the language-game' echoes post-Reformation doctrinal debates about *adiaphora*, the matters of indifference on which relaxed or latitudinarian Christians could *agree to differ*.[58] The inclusive logic of *adiaphora* has lately become of great interest to agonistic thinkers such as Badiou, as 'an indifference' which not only 'tolerates differences', but that actively seeks to generate 'new differences, new particularities'.[59] And in her study of the play-acting of the so-called 'Church Papists' who purported to conform to the Church of England, the historian Alexandra Walsham has reminded us that an entire theological science of casuistry was being elaborated across Europe in Shakespeare's time, like a system of method acting for a practice not of overt religious toleration, but of reluctant cohabitation, which inculcated a pragmatics of such deflecting language games as tactical feints, to mediate 'the mitigating circumstances that could make forbidden behaviour permissible'. This was the performative approach Locke would refine into a liberal paradigm of toleration; but with the difference that here there is no expectation of ever agreeing on 'the true and fundamental part of religion'.[60]

   The clerical permissiveness analysed by revisionist Tudor historians reflected the tide of pressure around 1600 for some Gallican or, as it would come to be termed, Anglican national compromise, which was being exerted by increasing numbers of laity, who were 'understandably hesitant to embrace a stance involving harassment and hardship'.[61] Shakespeare's contemporaries were, it seems, evolving something like the 'toleration in conflict' identified by political thinkers such as Walzer and Rainer Forst as the precondition of modern democracy: a tolerance that does not involve assimilation, but allows opposed communities to 'learn to live *as if* they possessed they possessed this virtue': to offend with good will.[62] So current philosophical interest in the performativity of 'agonistic pluralism' has obvious resonances with Shakespeare, the grandest master of this equivocating language game, who at the time of the Edict of Nantes, which was also the year prior to the move to the Globe, likewise represented his rules of conflict for the emergent system of pluralistic politics in ludic terms, when he had his clown Touchstone analyse the endless deferral of sectarian violence in the copycat craze of the French duel as a 'quarrel in print, by the book', proceeding towards a pragmatic acquiescence in live-and-let-live through the absurdist rule-making of seven degrees of offence:[63]

> All these you may avoid, but the Lie Direct; and you may avoid
> that too, with an 'if'. I knew when seven justices could not take up a
> quarrel but when the parties were met themselves, one of them
> thought but of an 'if', as 'If you said so, then I said so', and they
> shook hands and swore brothers. Your 'if' is the only peace-
> maker; much virtue in 'if'.
>
> [*As You*, 5,4,81–6]

'Far from the theatre of war', Elisabeth Roudinesco concurs, the duellists Touchstone admires 'never combat the contemptible odious *enemy*, but the *adversary*', who thus becomes 'one like them'.[64] So, Shakespeare's faith in the big 'if' of this agonistic game is not the same as the Machiavellian performance of 'politic religion' that permits Marlowe's characters to count *all* religion 'but a childish toy'.[65] This commendation of the 'quarrel in print' instead anticipates the Wittgensteinian point that without tacit prior agreement 'there would be no possibility of disagreement'.[66] And it is itself a playfully agonistic professional intervention that performs its own thesis, as it follows one of Shakespeare's most wounded auto-representations, when the bumpkin William is commanded by this supercilious court fool, who has stolen his girl, to 'Tremble, and depart' [*As You*, 5,2,53]. For an Elizabethan author to name himself 'in print, by the book' was highly unusual; and critics detect animus towards the self-inflated Ben Jonson in these exchanges in which a pretentious philosophiser preaches to a rustic simpleton.[67] But by turning personal grievance into a public demonstration of how to offend with good will, by being 'politic with my friend, smooth with mine enemy' [5,4,44], at the conclusion of a play about enmity between warring brothers that is ostensibly set in the eye of Europe's religious storm, on the fault-line between Catholic and Protestant communities in the Forest of Ardennes, 'our good Will' has overtly aligned his own equivocating 'language game' with the Gallican spirit of détente.

Critics make light of the 'Belgian' setting of *As You Like It*. Yet its agonistic spirit is in accord with the stand-off which the artist Velázquez would depict some years later in his painting of the exigencies of toleration in the Low Countries, *The Surrender of Breda*, also pointedly known, from the way in which the old enemies move to embrace surrounded by the very weaponry that they will soon see redeployed, as *The Lances*. There is no actual disarmament of offensive weapons in this famous picture of good will. The artist knows this truce will not hold, that the conflict we call the Thirty Years War has long to run, because by the time the picture was completed the roles of the victor and vanquished had been reversed. So what he depicts on the faces of the combatants is their good intent. And the provisional moratorium of Shakespeare's comedy hangs on the armistice of a similarly big 'if', when the boy-player charged with negotiating the Epilogue asserts that 'If I was a woman I would kiss as many' of the men in the audience 'as had beards that pleased me'. Kissing between men and boys has been the stuff of this story; but now the young actor is sure that 'as many as have good beards, will for my kind offer . . . bid me farewell' [Epi.,14–18]. Nor was Touchstone's sporting handshake any more likely than the promiscuous kiss of peace to disarm the vicious religiously motivated duels of Elizabethan exiles in the actual Forest of Ardennes.

With its sexual tropes 'of futurity, expectation, anticipation, fortune, and above all . . . truth', Shakespeare's stage has been called a 'theatre of intention'; and *As You Like It* shows how much it strove to be a theatre of *good intent*.[68] Yet, like Velázquez, Shakespeare foresaw how Europe's marriages of convenience would prove *wishful thinking*, procedural devices of accommodation, encoded in Wittgensteinian casuistry, like the fool's 'If you said so, then I said so'. So as a corrective, for the first time on his stage, and possibly as a later interpolation for the Jacobean court, he was tempted to intrude an all-powerful Baroque *deus ex machina*, Hymen, androgynous god of marriage, who, unlike the fractious Elizabethan fairies of *A Midsummer Night's Dream*, is supernaturally equipped to 'bar confusion', impose uniformity and transform antagonism to agonism by compelling earthlings to embrace liberty, equality and fraternity, in a state of exception where they are 'at one' and 'even' [5,4,97–9]. Hymen's surprise divine intervention is like some allegorical ceiling by the artist-diplomat Rubens, and a dramaturgical equivalent of the contemporary absolutist doctrine of *cujos regio, ejos religio*: 'whoever rules the state decides its religion'. But being equal and united will still require of inveterate foes a token demonstration of *atonement*, in the punning religious dispensation of this *Discordia concors*. So, for a play likely first acted in the months leading up to the passage of the decree of toleration into Parisian law on 25 February 1599, Shakespeare's 'Belgian' comedy remains in the end coolly realistic about the offensiveness of the very *good will* that is a precondition for such a 'conflictual consensus':

> Who doth ambition shun,
> And loves to lie i' th' sun,
> Seeking the food he eats,
> And pleased with what he gets,
> Come hither, come hither, come hither,
>   Here shall he see
>   No enemy
> But winter and rough weather.

> [*As You*, 2,5,32–9]

It may be pure chance that the courtier who sings about turning enmity to adversity in the Globe's founding song is named after the town in the Ardennes whose capture from the Catholic ultras had just enabled Henri to proclaim his edict of toleration. But the 'ragged' [2,5,13] lyrics Amiens 'warbles' [2,5,31] are a choric statement of the anti-Platonist thrust of the play, that there is no escaping the power of 'usurpers, tyrants' [2,1,61], even in the pastoral government the survivors desire, unless 'ambition' is renounced. With a worldly acceptance, instead, of living together in adversity, or an agreement to differ that is as elemental to politics as 'the winter to foul weather' [5,4,125], and that will so often carry its characters from comedy to tragedy, by highlighting the moment of decision Shakespearean drama pre-empts all such fantasies of the impossible 'fullness and universality of society'.[69] So *As You Like It* concludes with the satirist Jacques stubbornly pursuing the born-again Duke Frederick into an evangelising 'religious life', adamant that 'Out of these convertites / There is much matter to be heard and learned' [5,4,170–1], as though, despite the god of concord, the conditional ending of this play is registering in yet another unlikely religious conversion the impasse that Henri's last-minute change of heart had actually brought about.

Critics of *As You Like It* often misinterpret its surprise royal conversion as a sign of reconciliation. But then, one of the few historians to grasp how the Edict of Nantes in fact stalemated the crusade for a universal church in *deliberate divisiveness* was Roland Mousnier, a right-wing diehard follower of the excommunicated Archbishop Lefebvre. He acutely described the stand-off the play seems to record, however, when he noted that 'Protestants and Catholics alike regarded this "religious peace" as no more than a painful necessity, in that both sides considered the "religious division" a blemish on the state. Protestants bowed to the inevitable, hoping their "religion" would spread; Catholics were equally convinced they would shortly convert the Protestants'.[70] Such partisans 'might have seen the deal as not exactly a liberation, more a containment', concurs Diarmaid MacCulloch in *Reformation*, his survey of 'Europe's House Divided'.[71] For the warring Christian tribes of 1598 had simply agreed to differ in the same language, according to this historiography, and thereby to continue to offend each other, 'But with good will'. And so, resigned to the disillusion that 'All the world's a stage' [2,7,138], *As You Like It* concludes on such a big 'if' because its hostile 'winter and rough weather' symbolise the irremediable tear in the fabric of the resulting pluralistic society that we have inherited, for better or worse: the agonistic *dissensus* that a theorist such as Jacques Rancière applauds, in preference to the tyranny of any universalising consensus, as the true 'essence of politics', the paradox of two worlds in one.[72]

Far from vindicating universalism by the fiat of some all-powerful peacemaker, the epochal statute of toleration was perceived as shocking proof of princely powerlessness in a monarchy without kings, an abdication of the sovereign's sacred duty to impose uniformity, to make society 'at one' and 'even', by unilaterally abolishing differences in religious belief and behaviour. And in *Shakespeare's Tribe* Jeffrey Knapp has keyed the hospitality of these plays to their creator's similar 'doctrinal minimalism', his anti-cathartic refusal to impose any authoritarian order. If such an abjuration helped the playwright to escape the censor, Knapp suggests, so too did his pilgrim posture of 'barefoot' lowliness, his evident faith 'in plays as performing humble religious functions'. In opposition to the modern compulsion to elevate the author into a godlike Proteus, and worship his play-texts as holy scripture for some new secular religion, as Bloom would prefer, this account instead stresses all the signs that Shakespeare 'worried he might be posing as a churchman for his greater glory and profit', and so returned repeatedly to the canny Prince Hal story, 'of a weak ruler made strong by theft of godlike power', to ward off any such presumption of universality.[73]

The Christ-like 'willingness to stoop low amounted to more for Shakespeare than the modesty Jonson lacked', Knapp conjectures, for 'it may be that he kept his distance from higher powers in order to avoid the partisan view' of religion to which more preachy writers succumbed.[74] In *Free Will* I related this Shakespearean cringe to the depersonalisation of the substantial state through the abdication of the monarch his plays so often describe. This drama takes on new richness, I proposed, in light of current interest in the concept of the sovereign who 'reigns but does not rule', the theme of the *roi mehaigné*, or 'fisher king', that Giorgio Agamben tracks to the pseudo-Aristotelian treatise *On the World*, where God has absconded, like the Great King of Persia hidden inside his palace.[75] Now, with *Worldly Shakespeare*, I aim to extend these insights to the entire trajectory of the dramatist's career, to explore how his dramas register the moment of the Globe not as a high noon of either Western universality or authorial sovereignty, but as the dawn of an epoch of worldliness; and to consider how, by staging toleration in conflict, these 400-year-old play-scripts continue to provide us with pretexts for our globalised yet multifaceted communities, in these paradoxical times of Facebook and *fatwa*, of internet and *intifada*, when it is more than ever necessary 'to offend / But with good will'.

In *Worldly Shakespeare* I propose that the coincidence of the Globe with the invention of religious toleration was not accidental, but that the inauguration of the playhouse marked not the climacteric of Christian, still less Anglo-Saxon, universalism, so much as the dawn of an era of decentred interpretation, of offence with good will. The philosopher Gillian Rose spoke of abiding in 'the broken middle' between abstract universalism, with its discourse of rights, and postmodern particularism, with its language of difference, as an agonistic way of securing a justice that is 'good enough', and this worldly thinking sounds eminently Shakespearean.[76] For rather than subsuming his global politics into some 'Protean' art, Shakespeare subjected his art to a global politics, I contend in *Worldly Shakespeare*. So, at this moment when Jean Bodin's ecumenical dialogue *Colloquium* could culminate with a Calvinist, Catholic, Jew, Lutheran and Muslim singing polyphonically 'how good it is for brothers to live together' by 'the sweet power of music' [*Merchant*, 5,1,78], yet still send each off to defend his particular faith 'with his life', Shakespeare's anti-Platonist drama drew its force from the 'conflictual consensus' of just such an 'agonistic pluralism'.[77] Confronted by the murderous mayhem of the Wars of Religion, Shakespeare shared Bodin's acceptance, I suggest, of the cosmopolitan preaching of St Paul, that if 'instruments, such as the flute or the harp, do not give distinctive notes, how will anyone know what is being played?' (1 Corinthians 14: 7).

Although Derrida objected that 'if nothing is good except good will . . . this way of speaking belong[s] to a particular epoch, namely that of a metaphysics of the will', European thinkers of 1600 seem to have fully anticipated our Pauline revelation that, as Badiou asserts, 'differences *carry the universal*', for differences, 'like instrumental tones, provide us with the recognizable univocity that makes up the melody of the True'.[78] My opening chapter therefore focuses on the actual name of Shakespeare's playhouse in light of these Renaissance and modern debates about the difference between mere globalisation and the true conflictual worldliness that agonistic philosophers like Badiou and Jean-Luc Nancy call *mondialisation*.[79] What was in a name, I ask in 'A Globe of Sinful Continents', when the performers entitled their playing space a theatre of the world? And contrary to those, like the organisers of the 2012 British Museum exhibition 'Shakespeare Staging the World', who imagine that this name trumpeted English pride in conquest and exploration, as a symbol of the false universality flagged up by the global reach of Anglo-American capitalism or even of the BBC, the chapter argues that for the dramatist the earthy roundness of 'the great Globe' [*Tempest*, 4,1,149] signalled England's own particularity in its belatedness, imitativeness and dependency upon 'a world elsewhere' [*Coriolanus*, 3,3,139].

The British Museum placed Shakespeare's Globe at the still centre of a restless world, and together with its souvenir merchandise, like the director's accompanying book, the 2012 show was the most blatant attempt to date to co-opt the plays to the false universality of the global shopping arcade that beguiles postmodern museology. In fact, Shakespeare mockingly put that Marlovian will to universal consumption into the mouth of an egotistical rogue like Pistol, who does not care 'A foutre for the world and worldlings base', when he speaks 'of Africa and golden joys' [2 *Henry IV*, 5,3,92–3]. For as Badiou objects, 'all true universality is devoid of a centre'; and distinguishing globalisation from *mondialisation*, in *Worldly Shakespeare* I infer that Shakespeare's earthly image of his playhouse figured instead the ex-centring of the British Isles that went with the discovery of ideology, the revelation of the contingency of all the 'devices, traditions, ceremonies' that, as Robert Burton inveighed in 1621, the priests invent 'to keep men in subjection'.[80] Sloterdijk describes this experience of confessional difference as 'an immunological catastrophe'.[81] Yet happy to be counted himself among 'worldlings base', the dramatist's worldly wisdom that 'there's livers out of Britain' [*Cymbeline*, 3,4,139] can also be interpreted as an expression of relief at the escape from the murderous messianic dream of universal empire. So, in my second chapter I start from the famously conflicted denouement of Shakespeare's most topical work, when the lovers of *Love's Labour's Lost* postpone the universalist vision of some non-conflictual 'world-without-end bargain' [5,2,771], in sober recognition that the time it will take for each side to learn to love the other is 'Too long for a play' [855].

With its characters given the names of the leaders in the French civil wars, Shakespeare's counter-factual 'civil war of wits' [2,1,225] is a remorseful rewind to Renaissance Europe's '9/11', the 1572 St Bartholomew's Day Massacre of Protestants at the wedding of the turncoat king of toleration, Henri of Navarre, to 'La Reine Margot', Marguerite de Valois. The royal joker may have been the personification of worldliness; but this very big fictional 'if' struggles to turn the clock back, and make good his promise 'To force the pained impotent to smile' [831], by paying lip-service to the ceremonies of love. 'Paris is worth a Mass', Henri had laughed; and *Love's Labour's Lost* seems to respond by asking 'What if' the marriage of convenience between sworn enemies had been consummated, only to dash such fantasies 'like a Christmas comedy' [5,2,462]. For henceforth the challenge Shakespeare's agonistic theatre faces will be to prevent such ideal or pure communities 'from ever coming into existence', as Harry Levin put it, 'or to prevent existing communities from ever becoming ideal'.[82] Yet this theatre will become anti-utopian in this way without renouncing faith in the act of faith itself, this chapter concludes, for the 'great feast of languages' [3,1,34] in Shakespeare's Navarre sets it in a new performative direction, which points towards the future of religion in our own ironic 'age of interpretation', by echoing those very hardliners who complained that 'the King's conversion had not been sincere', precisely because it was all only an act.[83]

Though Puck promises 'Jack shall have Jill' and 'Nought shall go ill' [*Dream*, 3,3,46], Shakespearean drama will differ from 'an old play' precisely because its Jack hath not Jill, and it will be on that frustrating absence that its good will must come to depend. Shakespeare becomes Shakespeare, I thus propose in 'Too Long For a Play: Shakespeare and the Wars of Religion', only when his writing starts to articulate the fallen world of its historical reality, where 'a truce, and not a peace', is all a polarised Europe can achieve, and what matters is that implacable enemies can agree to differ 'In their own fashion, like a merriment' [766].[84] In his earliest plays the dramatist gave the great dream of a union of the human race a chance, by endorsing the Christian vision of 'One feast, one house, one mutual happiness' [*Two Gentlemen*, 5,4,170], which he was even prepared to identify with the Tudor project to 'unite the white rose with the red' [*Richard III*, 5,8,19]. The humanist fantasy that since 'We came into this world like brother and brother', we can still 'go out hand in hand, not one before the other' [*Comedy*, 5,1,426], was stretched to breaking point, however, when the survivors vowed to heal society's wounds, 'and wipe away her woe', after the 'direful slaught'ring' of *Titus Andronicus* [5,3,143–7]. In fact, that hope of unity hangs on a reversion to the closed system of human sacrifice, when the moor Aaron is buried alive in the foundations of the Capitol, for traditional culture feeds off violence and intolerance, this tragedy attests, and our universalist Western civilisation is literally grounded in the barbarism that was Rome.

Valuing the worldly above the universal, I propose, Shakespeare understood as well as the Lacanian critics of 'the democratic paradox' how the language of universalism is itself authoritarian, as 'it is only through the intervention of a master signifier that a consistent field of meaning can emerge'.[85] Thus the violently coercive preconditions of uniformity are laid bare at the end of *The Taming of Shrew*, Shakespeare's comedy about enforced conversion, when Petruchio's browbeaten bride declares that she is ashamed that subjects 'offer war when they should seek for peace,/Or seek for rule, supremacy, and sway/When they are bound to serve, love, and obey' [5,2,166–8]. As with the real religious conversions of the 1590s, the sincerity of Kate's improbable change of heart in this unlikely homily on obedience will be endlessly disputed by audiences and critics. But in Chapter 3 of *Worldly Shakespeare* I suggest that after these fraught beginnings Shakespeare's Elizabethan career can be regarded as a similarly ludic submission to coercive uniformity, when he takes the official prohibitions on portraying the Virgin Queen so literally the very act of performing monarchy becomes a calculated snub. This Shakespeare who writes in hate incorporates Gloriana's Protestant lunar symbol in a negative dialectic, I infer, which turns enmity on itself, to assert his adversarial yet constitutive relations with the detested figure reflected as the Elizabethan 'moonshine' of a guttering candle, soon to be 'in snuff' [*Dream*, 5,1,241]. In Schmitt's terms, Shakespeare's aesthetic power originated from this tactical elision of the power of his sovereign, which thus became the founding historical precipitate of his stage: the 'mute rock upon which the play' *as mere play* founders, sending 'genuine tragedy rushing to the surface'. Elizabeth, according to this antagonistic thesis, was Shakespeare's essential 'enemy/friend'.[86]

For proponents of agonistic pluralism the only thing that mutual offenders need agree upon is the *performance* of their good will. Going through the motions, even of offensiveness, becomes, in this thinking, more important than agreement itself. So in Chapter 4 I return to the play that announces by its title the agreement to differ, on which such conflicted consensus is based. Like other ideological critics of the 1990s, in my book *Will Power* I unpacked *As You Like It* as Shakespeare's bitter arcadia, in which the Robin Hood scenario prescribed the counter-revolutionary logic of carnival and pastoral, that if 'All the world's a stage', men and women are *merely* players. Dressed as 'merry men', the outlaws of this story of brothers and others turned the world upside down to restore the status quo, in this suspicious reading, as liberty crushed equality and fraternity.[87] But over twenty years on, the spiritual turn in Shakespeare studies has made it possible to revalue the role-play in the forest as a 'Romany' disguise that affiliates these roving players with religious wanderers. Now the gypsy cant invoked 'To call fools into a circle' [2,5,53] sounds like a conjuration to those of all faiths and none to convene 'Under the greenwood tree' [1] of the Globe, so as to mobilise their enmities to agonistic ends. Thus, rather than a cause of disillusion about the impossibility of 'earthly things made even' being 'at one together' [5,4,99], the 'big "if"' of Shakespeare's 'rogue state', pitched in the epicentre of Europe's wars of religion, is the constitutive lack, on this view, around which a future society of 'co-mates and brothers' [2,1,1] can be dreamed.

If the agonistic idea that no final closure is possible or desirable draws on the tradition of deferral and undecidability invoked at the end of As You Like It, the play still cannot tell us how to resist the moralisation of politics by an irreconcilable such as Jacques, whose parting shot is to maintain, 'To see no pastime I' [5,4,184]. So Chapter 5 surveys Shakespeare's developing dramatisation of the challenge posed by the solitary exception that most pushes the limits of toleration with intolerance, the religious militant. In Elizabethan England this meant the politicised Catholic who signed up to the Jesuit campaign of terrorist violence that began with assassination attempts on the Queen, and ended in the 1605 plot to exterminate the entire political establishment. Taking its cue from the historian Emmanuel Le Roy Ladurie's insight that modern Islamist militancy had its roots in the spiritualised politics of this Catholic Counter-Reformation, and that Ayatollah Khomeini's ancestors were the 'hysterical preachers of the 1580s', 'Fools of Time: Shakespeare and the Martyrs' parallels the martyr complex of the modern suicide bomber with the annihilating Manichean zeal of Hamlet, Shakespeare's most terroristic protagonist.[88] Critics have long viewed this Black Prince as a mouthpiece for Baroque theological controversies about the Apocalypse, Purgatory and Doomsday. But in Worldly Shakespeare I propose that this eschatological discourse takes on far more sinister meaning after 9/11, since when Hamlet has become a play about 'self-slaughter' [1,2,32] as a form of holy terror, and its most famous soliloquy, 'To be or not to be' [3,1,56], a deeply disturbing meditation on the absolute antagonism of the jihad.

The occult affiliation of al Qaeda with the Society of Jesus compels us to reassess the apocalyptic sacrificial language that fires Shakespeare's Jacobean tragic protagonists, and that inflates them with self-righteous fury, like Lear's, or self-pity, like Macbeth's. Shakespeare's biographical connections to the Gunpowder Plotters have always made it seem as if his works were written just a wall away from the secret cells of Catholic treason. But our appreciation of what it would mean to exterminate 'so many princes at a shot' [Hamlet, 5,2,311] makes these plays seem ever more timely in addressing the non-negotiability of sectarian violence. Where rival European dramatists wrote tragedies revelling in cathartic revenge, or Trauerspiele mourning martyrdom, Shakespeare, I propose, created a drama out of an agonistic 'tarrying with grief', in Judith Butler's formulation, rather than by advancing any such decisive resolution.[89] And this anticipation of the antinomies of our own pluralistic society is never more prophetic than in the Shakespearean premonition of one of the defining issues for modern multiculturalism, the question of the veil. Today's commentators often conceive of the veil as an obstruction of Enlightenment; but Chapter 6, 'Veiling an Indian Beauty: Shakespeare and the Hijab', looks at the ways in which the silk masks and other facial coverings which play such conspicuous parts in these dramas in fact mediate 'good will', and function not simply as concealments, but means of causing offence with good intentions, the mimetic signals of a provocation, and in particular of a confessional otherness, that *hides in plain view*.

The eyes are the only part of the person visible in a mask; and with its rhetorical question, 'Hath not a Jew eyes?' [3,1,50], *The Merchant of Venice* is often thought to offer a 'frame of reference allowing a place for racial and ethnic tolerance', a moot lesson in 'self-intolerance and other-tolerance'.[90] Such readings generally overlook the ways in which this unsettling comedy finesses the religious antagonisms that, in the effective absence of Jews in Elizabethan London, its audiences would project into the history of Christian bigotry.[91] In *Worldly Shakespeare*, however, I infer that Bassanio's suspicion of the 'beauteous scarf/Veiling an Indian beauty' [3,2,99] is *itself* an Islamophobic cover for a Christian subtext, which we can appreciate anew in light of 'the sorry affair of the *foulard*'.[92] For the scarf image is keyed to an orientalist discourse in which the 'Dark Lady' figures the impenetrability of global trade to occidental unmasking, a *travailing* of 'sails and veils' that Shakespeare sees materialised, as does Derrida, in the secretion of silk, the most disgusting yet desirable of oriental imports. In a culture craving the transparency of eye-to-eye contact, his texts thus valorise the 'visor effect' of masked desire as a means to insert private faces into public spaces, I argue, and insinuate the silk 'vizard' as a symbolic form of ritualised aggression, a screen like the hijab, that mimes confrontation by putting the offending *secrecy on display*. The Moorish Catholic subtext of *The Merchant of Venice* thereby helps construct an agonistic public sphere in place of antagonistic religious violence, as a forum for an ironic 'qualified intolerance', I conclude, when the overdetermined Muslim veil is worn in spite of its blood-stained traces of cultural suspicion and sectarian hate.

'It is almost morning', sighs Portia in the last lines of *The Merchant of Venice*, 'And yet I am sure you are not satisfied/Of these events' [5,1,294–6]; and there is indeed no text of Shakespeare's that more evidently foreshadows the agonistic political thinking which holds that 'Society never manages to be society, because everything in it is penetrated by its limits, which prevent it from constituting itself as an objective reality'.[93] That the dramatist continues to place antagonism at the centre of his political vision in this way is the theme of Chapter 7, which takes as its starting point the use made of Shakespearean references to Shah Abbas of Persia in a 2009 exhibition to underwrite the British Museum's project of validating its collections by presenting the world's empires as successive steps in the march of global capitalism. Nothing better exemplifies the culturalisation of politics than this triumphal march of glittering empire expositions in the heart of cosmopolitan London. Visitors were, however, appalled by the sacrificial instruments on display as the imperial procession reached the Aztecs; and in 'When Golden Time Convents: Shakespeare and the Shah' I maintain that, in common with the play's editors and critics, the curators equally effaced the intolerable religious violence of both the

Shah's Persia and Shakespeare's England when they signposted their Abbas show with quotations from *Twelfth Night*.

What the museologists ignore when they mobilise the idea that Shakespeare is 'not for an age, but for all time' for modern multiculturalism is the irony that *Twelfth Night* is *itself* a dramatisation of the origins of their dream of universality in bloody sectarian strife.[94] The allusions to the Shah that punctuate Shakespeare's text point in fact to the play's sponsors being leaders of the 1601 Essex Revolt, the disastrous attempt to force 'a solemn combination of our dear souls' [5,1,370], by precipitating the accession of King James of Scotland to the English throne, in a *coup d'état* meant to see 'These sovereign thrones' decisively 'supplied, and filled with one self king' [1,1,37]. So what the Shah show suppressed was Shakespeare's insistence on 'the wind and the rain' [5,1,376]: the elemental antagonism that precludes any such universality. More specifically, the opportunistic appropriation of *Twelfth Night* at the British Museum effaced what these quotations encode: the sectarian violence that literally underwrote the prospects for a 'golden time' [369] of religious toleration, through a Catholic conspiracy, worthy of the Iran–Contra operation in the Reagan White House, to divert the silk suits exchanged for weapons in Persia to fund the insurgency at home.

With its epiphany scenario of waiting the arrival of 'wise men' from the East [1,5,75], *Twelfth Night* seems written in fulfilment of Viola's mission: 'I hold the olive in my hand. My words are as full of peace as matter' [1,5,185–6]. But if these plays are structured around the expectation that 'The time of universal peace is near' [*Antony*, 4,6,4], in *Worldly Shakespeare* I suggest that such universality-to-come is posited here as an absence or lack that has its focus, its veritable *objet petit a* or 'foolish thing' [*Twelfth Night*, 5,1,378] in the 'blank' [2,4,109] sexuality of Cesario: the young page whose avatar, the 'fencer to the Sophy' [3,4,247] who haunts the text, was the go-between, held as surety by Shah Abbas, on whose amorous suit the entire scam, and funding for the play, had come to depend. The in-joke about travel assurance, that this Robert Sherley and his brother will be paid '*Shahly*' [3,4,246], thereby registers how Shakespeare's professional anxiety about waiting on the great as a form of emasculation was driven to a pitch by the plight of the hostage in Isfahan, where the Shah took pleasure in castrating his favourites with his own scimitar. Far from being innocent instruments of global trade, the 'rapier, scabbard and all' [3,4,244] that overshadow *Twelfth Night*, as they did the exhibition, should then be viewed, this chapter concludes, as figuring the *lack* of the universal peace that we desire, and its violently disabling conditions of possibility, or the unintended consequences of 'what you will'.

Instead of welcoming the 'golden time' of toleration *surely*, the New Year comedy with which Shakespeare ushered in a new century looked forward in wariness that 'What's to come is still unsure' [2,3,45]. And when James did succeed to the English throne, the poet voiced this unsureness in one of his most leery sonnets, in which the good news that 'peace proclaims olives of endless age' is undercut by the irony that 'with the drops of this most balmy time' 'Incertainties now crown themselves assured' [Sonnet 107]. To salute a new era when 'Peace puts forth her olive every-where' [*2 Henry IV*, 4,3,87] as a 'crowned uncertainty' was perverse; but Chapter 8 turns to a drama that practically predicts Schmitt's objection that 'A world in which the possibility of war is utterly eliminated, a completely pacified globe, would be a world without distinction of friend and enemy, and so a world without politics'.[95] That is the philosophy outlined by the politician Ulysses in *Troilus and Cressida*, a play that dates from the interim between Essex's execution and James's coronation, in which the chaos of the Trojan war unfolds as a textbook warning of how 'when degree is shak'd' [1,3,101], by the neutralising of antagonistic differences in consensus, 'The wise and fool, the artist and unread,/The hard and soft seem all affined and kin' [24–5], until 'Each thing meets/In mere oppugnancy', or bestial antagonism, and 'this solid globe' melts into the unintended consequence of a world consumed by war:

Then everything includes itself in power,
Power into will, will into appetite;
And appetite, an universal wolf,
So doubly seconded with will and power,
Must make perforce an universal prey,
And last eat up himself.

[*Troilus*, 1,3,110–15]

Troilus and Cressida is Shakespeare's most Schmittian dramatisation of the problem posed by the fact that the representative procedures of deliberative parliamentarianism permit no place for the antagonism that instead subverts them in outright violence. For in this play war is mediated into a 'pale and bloodless emulation' [1,3,134], an agonistic contest said to be 'Like an Olympian wrestling' [4,7,78]. Thus, when Greeks and Trojans fight, it is to see who can rank beside the all-time Olympic wrestling champion, 'Bull-bearing Milo' [3,1,233], but even this bloodless 'maiden battle' [4,6,89] is halted by the referee before it becomes too real. Shakespeare's most studied evocation of ancient Greece thus turns out to be an excavation of the origins of 'our good will', the Olympic spirit of 'fair play' that frames its 'dull and long continued truce' [1,3,259], and ensures that whenever enemies fall, 'in the fan and wind of your fair sword,/You bid them rise and live' [5,3,39–43]. It is in accord with this ethical turn that the Trojan War here becomes a harmless game stalled in the 'time of pause' [5,3,34] that is orchestrated by the go-between Pandarus, a personification of undifferentiating 'Love, love, nothing but love' [3,1,105]. So, like paintings of the time that depict swords suspended over prostrate victims, such as Rembrandt's *The Sacrifice of Isaac*, the picture of Hector with his 'sword i'th'air,/Not letting it decline on the declined' [4,7,72–3], stands, I propose, for the neutralising of politics by culture in the 'strutting play' [1,3,153], with which Europe's leaders hoped to convert religious violence into mutual 'good will' by deflecting their 'pelting wars' [4,7,151] through the 'stickler-like' [5,9,18] rules of mere 'good sport' [1,1,109].

Shakespeare's Troy story is a representation of representative government at the point when a post-monarchical constitutionalism 'attempts to reduce antagonism to an agonism in which political actors struggle but ultimately defer to the victor'.[96] One of the discursive contexts of this monarchy without kings, I therefore infer, was the Olympic revival initiated in the 1590s by *politique* Catholics, whose rulebook, *Agonisticon*, appears to have inspired the author's neighbours to establish 'Grecian Games' as a sporting substitute for religious conflict in the Elizabethan Cotswolds. This was the pacifist and pastoral Olympic tradition movingly invoked at the opening of the 2012 London Games. But in his darker Olympian history, Shakespeare never forgets that Milo, the greatest Olympic medallist, was himself devoured by a wolf. For here the 'universal wolf' of sacrificial violence that, as Sloterdijk reminds us, stalked the ancient games, is unleashed when Achilles disdains Hector's 'fool's play' [5,3,44], and the *agôn* reverts to the antagonism of bare life, in which the beast and sovereign are one and the same, because instead of the chivalrous Milo, 'The bull has the game' [5,8,2].[97] Thus, *Troilus and Cressida* projects a scenario Shakespeare had never before envisioned: the power vacuum created as elemental adversaries like the 'seas and winds, old wranglers' take a truce [2,2,72], and the 'big "if"' of the representative state is instituted, followed by the catastrophe when the antagonism repressed after 'degree is shak'd' returns 'In beastly sort' [5,11,5], with the irruption of the enemy who truly 'decides on the exception'.

Troilus and Cressida is here read as a premonition, staged in the interregnum between regimes, of the 'democratic paradox' that worries political thinkers, that unless antagonism is safeguarded in a system of agonistic pluralism, it will 'manifest itself in the emergence of fascism, which has its appeal in open avowal of antagonism'.[98] This realism elevates the play above the puerile aestheticism of the plays that it contains. But the constitutional breakdown it dramatises is still represented as a Hobbesian nightmare, when Hector's mutilated corpse is dragged about 'the shameful field' [5]. That atrocity thus makes it all the more surprising that in one of Shakespeare's next works the dictatorial figure of a great decider looks set to be welcomed, when *Measure for Measure* closes with the Duke of Vienna imposing a Baroque absolutist solution critics often hear as a fanfare for the coronation of King James. Nothing in Shakespeare is more supportive of the notion that the poet became a pious apologist for divine right than the Duke's sermon, half way into this tragicomedy, about the holiness of 'He who the sword of heaven will bear' [3,1,480]. But in Chapter 9, 'As Mice by Lions', I infer that the problematic contradiction between this political theology and the early characterisation of the Duke as like the 'o'ergrown lion in a cave,/That goes not out to prey' [1,3,23], is in fact a telltale result of co-authorship, and that the decisiveness of the denouement of the *Measure for Measure* we possess is the absolutist signature of Thomas Middleton, the Protestant hardliner who succeeded Shakespeare as chief dramatist of the King's Men.

Evidence that Middleton revised *Measure for Measure* after Shakespeare's death, and reoriented the Duke's soliloquy about divine right to extol the coronation sword of justice, rather than the sword of mercy, throws into relief the play's initially far sharper interrogation of absolutism. The updating of the story to the Central Europe of a Duke of Vienna and 'King of Hungary' [1,2,2] during the Thirty Years War allows conservative critics to decrypt this composite text as a homage to the monarch as 'he who decides on the exception'. But such readings ignore the development its plot seems to trace, up to the Duke's soliloquy, whereby a constitutional monarchy represents the Žižekian point where the state subjectifies itself, a self-effacement of sovereign violence here enacted in the sacrifice of sacrifice itself, when royalty renounces its right to capital punishment. The acephalic comedy Shakespeare himself devised about 1603 reflected the indecisiveness of the Presbyterian system James endured in Scotland, I therefore deduce, in its sequencing of the endless substitutions in the kind of headless polity the King had recently complained about at his Hampton Court conference of Puritan leaders. But in tune with all his reca-pitulations of Shakespeare, Middleton's forced ending instead sounds the 'terrible approach' [*Timon*, 5,5,2] of the providential despotism the younger writer moralised. The Middletonian figure of the omniscient king without monarchy, presiding 'in this state' as its 'looker-on' [*Measure*, 5,1,314], chillingly predicts the famous frontis-piece of Hobbes's *Leviathan*, with its picture of the 'mortal god' who oversees peace and security, I conclude. But that panoptic *heading* only goes to show how much of the problematic text of *Measure for Measure* is not the product of 'our good will'.

For Puritans like Middleton, English identity was defined by antagonism to the enemy of Catholic Spain, an existential hatred Schmitt admired in Cromwell, who orated how 'the first lesson of Nature' was that 'our National Being' depended on war with 'the Spaniard', 'the providential enemy' whose 'enmity is put into him by God'.[99] Shakespeare's difference from Middleton is thus never clearer than in *All's Well That Ends Well*, a truly worldly comedy that was planned, I infer, as a diversion during the 1604 peace conference with Spain, yet which turns not on reconciliation, but on the hope that 'young Chairbonne the puritan and old Poisson the papist, howsome'er their hearts are severed in religion, their heads are both one, they may jowl horns together like any deer i' th' herd' [1,3,46–8]. The text finds a prompt for this jousting in the name of the King himself, which was also that of the patron saint of Spain and of the well Catholics venerated at Compostela. For when he has the heroine pretend she is 'Saint Jaques' pilgrim, hither gone' [3,4,4], Shakespeare not only aligns the King's coronation on the Feast of St James, 25 July, with Santiago, but affiliates the Jacobean court of St James with the Catholic cult of healing wells that had been the thaumatological reason for its location at St James's Spring, where kings had 'touched' to cure. This pilgrimage reverses the rite, however, when instead of being healed, Helena touches the King, a modernisation that chimes with James's aversion to the ceremony as popish superstition. Thus, in *All's Well That Ends Well*, 'they say miracles are past'; yet this play about a forced marriage seems to want to antagonise 'our philosophical persons' [2,3,1] by insisting on the need to throw a coin in the fountain to make a superstitious wish for 'all being well'.

From the body of a dying king to the body of a pregnant subject, or well to welfare, as it transfers healing from the court to the clinic *All's Well That Ends Well* registers more than any other Shakespeare drama the biopolitics that Foucault and his suc-cessors describe, when sovereignty migrated from the flesh of the prince to the body of the people. When its title is taken literally, I propose in Chapter 10, this well-wishing romance about wellbeing, perhaps acted before royalty in Bath during an epidemic of plague, accurately predicts the evolution of the well from sacred spring to thermal spa. As a doctor's daughter, Helena thus begins by wishing 'That wishing well had not a body in it' [1,1,168], in reference to the incarnational theology that induced Catholic zealots to fortify the healing waters with saints' relics; but she ends practising the type of 'popish imposture' Protestants identified with the Jesuit 'exorcist' [5,3,302]. Shakespeare's closest examination of the power of biopolitics thereby prefigures the theme of theorists like Santner, that after their representational protocols have ensured that 'The King's a beggar' [Epi.,1], 'post-monarchical societies are faced with the problem of *securing the flesh* of the new bearer of the principle of sovereignty, the People'.[100] So *All's Well* ends by including the remnants of the old Catholic carnality in the new representational order as provocatively 'incensing relics' [5,3,25], just as the playhouses annexed the ruins of friaries, and modern arts festivals overlap with medicinal spas, to become what Santner terms the *extimate* dimension of the aesthetic, 'inside it yet only partially incorporated', and essential to its *agôn*.[101]

In *All's Well That Ends Well* Shakespeare returns to the literal wellsprings of cathartic drama in the *pharmakon*, the poison that cures. Yet here the inclusion of the 'providential enemy' of Catholic Spain proves only an 'incensing' incitement, when Helena diverts to Italy, as if, by offending with good will, the cathartic content administered by the dramaturge in tolerating the intolerant is limited to an innocuous placebo. So Shakespeare's Jamesian comedy is 'religion lite', its worldliness reduced to the minimal morality that 'There's place and means for everyman alive' [4,3,316]. This anti-catharsis spoke to disillusion with the toleration edicts of the actual King of France, Henri IV, which his counterpart voices when he regrets how 'on our quick'st decrees time / Steals, ere we can effect them' [5,3,41]. But the stand-off in the shot-gun marriage the play stages also accords with the sensation that pervades Shakespeare's Jacobean work of an antagonism 'which any print of goodness will not take' [*Tempest*, 1,2,355], the incorrigible alienation put into the mouth of Iago, a Jesuitical traitor who shares the suspect name of the King: 'Demand me nothing. What you know, you know. / From this time forth I never will speak word' [*Othello*, 5,2,309]. In the Epilogue of *Worldly Shakespeare* I therefore turn to a work that foregrounds the dramatist's relations with his own best 'enemy friend', Robert Greene, who died cursing the 'upstart crow' for stealing his ideas, but whose *Pandosto*, about a paranoid king, the great survivor unashamedly plagiarised, sixteen years later, for the plot of *The Winter's Tale*.[102]

Shakespeare's antagonist excoriated him as a lying and thieving conman, 'beautified' from the illicit swag of his 'playing fardel'.[103] Recent critics have justified these aspersions of illegitimacy and plagiarism in light of the culture of print, with its patriarchal notions of authorial intention and intellectual property. Yet in the romance Shakespeare spun out of his rival's 'sad tale' [*Winter's*, 2,1,27] of jealousy and suspicion, he happily owned up to the offensive imputations, by personifying his craft in the pedlar Autolycus, 'a snapper-up of unconsidered trifles' [4,3,25], whose traffic in foul sheets and leaky condoms metonymises the playwright's puncture of proprietary protection. So, by intruding this mercurial charlatan into his filched fable, the bricoleur of *The Winter's Tale* also asks what it would mean if there were 'no truth at all' [3,2,138] in the sovereignty upheld in the story by the song of Apollo, or in art as therapy. What if the possessive ideology of the controlling author was itself an absolutist myth? Shakespeare never forgot the 'vile' accusation that he 'beautified' [*Hamlet*, 2,2,111] his stolen goods. But by now tolerating this intolerable offence, cheerfully admitting his non-cathartic art remained a bastard, 'like an old tale still' [*Winter's*, 5,2,55], and so welcoming enmity into his work, he presented this 'beautification' of old antagonisms as a model for an agonistic society: like the hybrid carnations 'some call nature's bastards', but which his characters learn to cultivate precisely for their offensive 'piedness' [4,3,82–7]. He thus offered his worldly theatre, with the flesh of its boy-player 'beautified' into the offensively Catholic statue of 'some great Mater' [5,2,94] by the blush of those same flowers, as the *incarnation* of 'our good will'.

Writing wryly about his mentor, the Renaissance scholar D. J. Gordon, Frank Kermode observed that a critic who chooses to celebrate absolutism in Shakespearean culture usually does so not only out of a 'taste for recondite and difficult scholarship', but because 'supreme authority' is 'something he would have liked himself'. Thus, as Kermode wickedly recalled, after Charles I stepped onto the scaffold from the Whitehall Banqueting House in January 1649, 'the world became altogether less satisfactory to Gordon. The Stuart courts combined sumptuary display with learned texts in support of absolute monarchy. The world outside encroached crudely, disastrously, on this magical realm, the spirit of which might be restored by great scholarship. To provide that was to join the greatness of which he had learned to speak'.[104] As someone who came to literary criticism at the University of York in the 1970s through the grandiose art-historical door Kermode described, I recognise the astuteness of his story of the academic illusion of power. In *Worldly Shakespeare: The Theatre of Our Good Will*, I have therefore set out to write against the political theology that identifies the dramatist with the universality that goes with the sovereignty of a modern literary author or divine-right king. The methodology I have preferred, in viewing these premodern works through a lens of postmodern political philosophy, aims instead to recover what Walter Benjamin called the 'critical violence' of the artwork, the *agôn* that resists *aesthesis*.[105] Thus, I have read Shakespeare's agonistic theatre as a collective act of offending with 'good will', being reassured that though Hamlet pretends to the King the play is cathartic, but 'poison in jest', with 'No offence in the world' [*Hamlet*, 3,2,214–15], he shows from the start how, for those ready to be offended, 'by Saint Patrick there is . . . And much offence, too' [1,5,140–1].

NOTES

1. Ben Jonson, 'To the memory of my beloved, the author', in Stephen Greenblatt et al. (eds), *The Norton Shakespeare* (New York: Norton, 2007), p. 3351; 'obedient, hat-in-hand': Maurice Hunt, 'The Warwickshire of Shakespeare's mind', *Connotations*, 7 (1997/8), 159–78, here 172. For the irony of Shakespeare's self-deprecating auto-representations, see also James Bednarz, *Shakespeare and the Poet's War* (New York: Columbia University Press, 2001), pp. 117 and 123; Phyllis Rackin, *Stages of History: Shakespeare's English Chronicles* (Ithaca: Cornell University Press, 1990), p. 244; and Meredith Anne Skura, *Shakespeare the Actor and the Purposes of Playing* (Chicago: Chicago University Press, 1993), p. 139.
2. Richard Wilson, *Free Will: Art and Power on Shakespeare's Stage* (Manchester: Manchester University Press, 2013).

3. Harold Bloom, *The Anatomy of Influence* (New Haven: Yale University Press, 2011), p. 55.

4. Herbert Marcuse, 'Repressive tolerance', in Robert Paul Wolff, Barrington Moore and Herbert Marcuse (eds), *A Critique of Pure Tolerance* (Boston: Beacon Press, 1969), pp. 95–137; 'a world made of diversity': Jean-Luc Nancy, *The Creation of the World or Globalization*, trans. François Raffoul and David Pettigrew (New York: State University of New York, 2007), p. 109.

5. Roger Scruton, *The Soul of the World* (Princeton: Princeton University Press, 2014), pp. 64–5 et passim.

6. Kirk Witters, *The Opinion System: Impasses of the Public Sphere from Hobbes to Habermas* (New York: Fordham University Press, 2008), pp. 1–2.

7. Thomas Hobbes, *Leviathan* (Harmondsworth: Penguin, 1968), I: 7, p. 132; Witters, *The Opinion System*, p. 152.

8. Wendy Brown and Rainer Forst, *The Power of Tolerance: A Debate* (New York: Columbia University Press, 2014), p. 29.

9. Ibid., p. 76.

10. Kenneth Reinhard, 'Toward a political theology of the neighbour', in Slavoj Žižek, Kenneth Reinhard and Eric Santner, *The Neighbour: Three Inquiries in Political Theology* (Chicago: Chicago University Press, 2013), p. 66; Alain Badiou, *L'etre et l'evenement* (Paris: Seuil, 1988).

11. See Walter Cohen, 'The undiscovered country: Shakespeare and mercantile geography', in Jean Howard and Scott Shershow (eds), *Marxist Shakespeares* (London: Routledge, 2001), p. 135.

12. David Wootton, 'No justice', *Times Literary Supplement*, 12 December 2014, 3–5, here 5. From the extensive secondary literature on Shakespeare's dramaturgy of conflict, see especially Joel Altman, *The Tudor Play of Mind: Rhetorical Inquiry and the Development of Elizabethan Drama* (Berkeley: University of California Press, 1978), pp. 34, 390–1 et passim; G. Beiner, *Shakespeare's Agonistic Comedy: Poetics, Analysis, Criticism* (Cranbury, NJ: Fairleigh Dickinson University Press, 1993); Stanley Boorman, *Human Conflict in Shakespeare* (London: Routledge, 1987); Carla Dente and Sara Soncini (eds), *Shakespeare and Conflict: A European Perspective* (Basingstoke: Palgrave, 2013); and Joseph Lowenstein, 'Plays agonistic and competitive: the textual approach to Elsinore', *Renaissance Drama*, 19 (1988), 63–96.

13. Stephen Orgel, 'The play of conscience', in *The Authentic Shakespeare, and Other Problems of the Early Modern Stage* (New York: Routledge, 2002), pp. 129–42, here p. 140. For a discussion of Shakespeare's abiding interest in the *idea* of theatrical catharsis, which does not detract from Orgel's argument, see Thomas Rist, 'Catharsis as "purgation" in Shakespearean drama', in Katharine Craik and Tanya Pollard (eds), *Shakespearean Sensations: Experiencing Literature in Early Modern England* (Cambridge: Cambridge University Press, 2013), pp. 138–56.

14. Jan Kott, *Shakespeare Our Contemporary*, trans. Boleslaw Taborski (London: Methuen, 1965), p. 132. Kott could find no mediation or reconciliation in Greek drama either: see *The Eating of the Gods*, trans. Boleslaw Taborski and Edward Czerwinski (New York: Random House, 1970).

15. Peter Sloterdijk, *Globes. Spheres II: Macrospherology*, trans. Wieland Hoban (Pasadena: Semiotexte, 2014), pp. 749–50.

16. Richard Hillman, *Shakespeare, Marlowe and the Politics of France* (Basingstoke: Palgrave, 2002), p. 122. See also Andrew Kirk, *The Mirror of Confusion: The Representation of French History in English Renaissance Drama* (New York: Garland, 1996), p. 5.

17. 'All things to all men': Julia Reinhard Lupton, *Thinking with Shakespeare: Essays on Politics and Life* (Chicago: University of Chicago Press, 2011), p. 219; 'gather under a single roof':

Jacques Derrida, *Specters of Marx: The State of the Debt, the Work of Mourning, and the New International*, trans. Peggy Kamuf (London: Routledge, 1994), p. 22.

18. Alain Badiou, *Saint Paul: The Foundations of Universalism*, trans. Tray Brassier (Stanford: Stanford University Press, 2003), pp. 98–9; Lupton, *Thinking with Shakespeare*, pp. 242–6.

19. 'Commodious thresholds': Robert Weimann, 'Shakespeare's endings: commodious thresholds', in *Author's Pen and Actors Voice: Playing and Writing in Shakespeare's Theatre* (Cambridge: Cambridge University Press, 2000), Chapter 8; Richard Wilson, *Shakespeare in French Theory: King of Shadows* (London: Routledge, 2007); Derrida, *Specters of Marx*, p. 168.

20. Hannah Arendt, *The Human Condition* (Chicago: University of Chicago Press, 1958), pp. 7–8. Arendt defines her sense of *worldliness* as the condition of human action, 'because we are all the same, that is, human, in such a way that nobody is ever the same as anyone else who ever lived, lives, or will live' (p. 8). For Shakespeare's 'Hegelian wit' in making us at home in the world, see also Jennifer Bates, *Hegel and Shakespeare on Moral Imagination* (Albany: SUNY Press, 2010), pp. 70–4.

21. Jean Grondin, *Hans-Georg Gadamer: A Biography*, trans. Joel Weinsheimer (New Haven: Yale University Press, 2003), p. 289.

22. Carl Schmitt, *Political Theology: Four Chapters on the Concept of Sovereignty*, trans. George Schwab (Chicago: University of Chicago Press, 1985), p. 5; Debora Shuger, *Political Theologies in Shakespeare's England: The Sacred and the State in 'Measure for Measure'* (Basingstoke: Palgrave, 2001), pp. 56–7.

23. Carl Schmitt, *Glossarium*, ed. Eberhard Freiherr von Medem (Berlin: Duncker and Humblot, 1991), p. 3, trans. and quoted in Jan-Werner Müller, *A Dangerous Mind: Carl Schmitt in Post-War European Thought* (New Haven: Yale University Press, 2003), p. 90.

24. Oliver Arnold, *The Third Citizen: Shakespeare's Theater and the Early Modern House of Commons* (Baltimore: Johns Hopkins University Press, 2007), p. 12.

25. E. M. W. Tillyard, *The Elizabethan World Picture* (London: Chatto and Windus, 1943); G. Wilson Knight, *The Sovereign Flower: On Shakespeare as the Poet of Royalism* (London: Methuen, 1958); Eric Nelson, *The Royalist Revolution: Monarchy and the American Founding* (New Haven: Harvard University Press, 2014); Eric Santner, *The Royal Remains: The People's Two Bodies and the Endgames of Sovereignty* (Chicago: University of Chicago Press, 2011), pp. 160–1.

26. Carl Schmitt, *Hamlet or Hecuba: The Intrusion of the Time into the Play*, trans. David Pan and Jennifer Rust (New York: Telos, 2011), pp. 39 and 56.

27. Richard Wilson, 'The quality of mercy: discipline and punishment in Shakespearean comedy', in *Will Power: Essays on Shakespearean Authority* (Hemel Hempstead: Harvester, 1993), pp. 118–57.

28. David Norbrook, '"What care these roarers for the name of king?": language and utopia in *The Tempest*', in Jonathan Hope and Gordon McMullan (eds), *The Politics of Tragicomedy: Shakespeare and After* (London: Routledge, 1992), pp. 21–54, here p. 35.

29. Julia Reinhard Lupton, *Citizen-Saints: Shakespeare and Political Theology* (Chicago: University of Chicago Press, 2005), p. 6; 'Introduction', in Graham Hammill and Julia Lupton (eds), *Political Theology and Early Modernity* (Chicago: University of Chicago Press, 2012), p. 2. See also Julia Lupton, *Afterlives of the Saints: Hagiography, Typology, and Renaissance Literature* (Stanford: Stanford University Press, 1996), and Lupton, *Thinking with Shakespeare*.

30. Ernst Kantorowicz, *The King's Two Bodies: A Study in Medieval Political Theology* (Princeton: Princeton University Press, 1957), pp. 24–41. For a more recent spin on this theme, see the influential essay by David Scott Kastan, 'Proud majesty made a subject: Shakespeare and spectacle of rule', *Shakespeare Quarterly*, 37 (1986), 460–75.

31. Slavoj Žižek, *The Sublime Object of Ideology* (London: Verso, 1989), pp. 221–2.

32. Alain Badiou, 'Philippe Lacoue-Labarthe (1940–2007)', *Pocket Pantheon: Figures of Postwar Philosophy*, trans. David Macey (London: Verso: 2009), p. 157.

33. 'Kings without monarchy': Nelson, *The Royalist Revolution*, p. 232. For an important account of the crucial difference between Kantorowicz and Schmitt as theorists of political theology, to which I am indebted, see Victoria Kahn, 'Political theology and fiction in *The King's Two Bodies*', *Representations*, 106 (2009), 77–101, especially 79–81.

34. Stephen Greenblatt, *Shakespearean Negotiations: The Circulation of Social Energy in Renaissance England* (Oxford: Clarendon Press, 1988), p. 119; Eric Mallin, *Godless Shakespeare* (London: Continuum, 2007), p. 5.

35. Alison Shell, *Shakespeare and Religion* (Arden Critical Companions) (London: A. and C. Black, 2010), p. 3

36. Ibid., pp. 2–3 and 19.

37. Theodor Adorno and Max Horkheimer, *Dialectic of Enlightenment* (Stanford; Stanford University Press, 2007), p. 60.

38. Shell, *Shakespeare and Religion*, p. 19.

39. Jonathan Dollimore, 'Then and now', *Critical Survey*, 36 (2014), 35.

40. See Lupton, '*All's Well That Ends Well* and the Futures of Consent', op. cit. (note 17), pp. 97–129, here pp. 118–19; and Lars Engle, *Shakespearean Pragmatism: Market of His Time* (Chicago: University of Chicago Press, 1993).

41. August Strindberg, *Letters to the Intimate Theatre*, trans. Walter Johnson (London: Peter Owen, 1967), pp. 217–18.

42. Tom Betteridge, *Shakespearean Fantasy and Politics* (Hatfield: University of Hertfordshire Press, 2005), pp. 83 and 86.

43. Badiou, *Saint Paul*, p. 20.

44. Michael Bristol, *Carnival and Theater: Plebeian Culture and the Structure of Authority in Renaissance England* (London: Methuen, 1985), p. 113. See also Thomas Cartelli, *Marlowe, Shakespeare, and the Economy of Theatrical Experience* (Philadelphia: University of Pennsylvania Press, 1991), p. 13; and Orgel, 'The play of conscience', p. 141: 'One of the most striking characteristics of the Elizabethan and Stuart stage is the degree to which its playwrights seem to share, and even to make capital out of, the prejudicial assumptions of their most hostile critics'.

45. Ewan Fernie, 'Introduction', in *Spiritual Shakespeares* (London: Routledge, 2005), pp. 7–8.

46. Catherine Belsey, *Shakespeare in Theory and Practice* (Edinburgh: Edinburgh University Press, 2008), pp. 73 and 85; Jean-François Lyotard, *The Postmodern Condition: A Report on Knowledge*, trans. Geoffrey Bennington and Brian Massumi (Manchester: Manchester University Press, 1984), p. 10.

47. Michael Walzer, *On Toleration* (New Haven: Yale University Press, 1997), p. 80.

48. Chantal Mouffe, *Agonistics: Thinking the World Politically* (London: Verso, 2013), pp. xi, 1 and 3.

49. Chantal Mouffe, *The Democratic Paradox* (London: Verso, 2000), pp. 101–2. For the standard critique of Shakespeare's 'universalism', see Jean Howard and Marion O'Connor, *Shakespeare Reproduced: The Text in History and Ideology* (London: Methuen, 1987), p. 4.

50. Carl Schmitt, *The Concept of the Political*, trans. George Schwab (Chicago: University of Chicago Press, 1996), p. 27; Slavoj Žižek, *The Puppet and the Dwarf: The Perverse Core of Christianity* (Cambridge, MA: MIT Press, 203), and *In Defence of Lost Causes* (London: Verso, 2008). For an acute analysis of Žižek's identification of politics with antagonism, see Todd McGowan, 'Hegel as Marxist: Žižek's revisionism of German idealism', in Jamil Khader and Molly Anne Rothenberg (eds), *Žižek Now: Current Perspectives in Žižek Studies* (Cambridge: Polity Press, 2013), pp. 31–53. 'Dialectic without synthesis' is Jonathan Culler's characterisation of the poetics of Paul de Man: *Framing the Sign: Criticism and Its Institutions* (Oxford: Basil Blackwell, 1988), pp. 112–13.

51. 'Belgian-style': Carl Schmitt quoted in Giorgio Agamben, *The Kingdom and the Glory: For a Theological Genealogy of Economy and Government*, trans. Lorenzo Chiesa and Matteo Mandarini (Stanford: Stanford University Press, 2011), p. 74; Mouffe, *The Democratic Paradox*, pp. 103 and 137–9.

52. See Jacob Taubes, *To Carl Schmitt: Letters and Reflections*, trans. Keith Tribe, ed. Mike Grimshaw (New York: Columbia University Press, 2013), p. xv et passim.

53. Jan-Werner Müller, *A Dangerous Mind: Carl Schmitt in Post-War European Thought* (New Haven: Yale University Press, 2003), p. 239.

54. Paul Raffield, *Shakespeare's Imaginary Constitution* (Oxford: Hart, 2010), p. 9.

55. Etienne Balibar, *Spinoza and Politics*, trans. Peter Snowdon (London: Verso, 2008), p. 119; McGowan, 'Hegel as Marxist', p. 32.

56. Margaret Healy, *Shakespeare, Alchemy and the Creative Imagination: The Sonnets and A Lover's Complaint* (Cambridge: Cambridge University Press, 2011), p. 198. For Shakespeare's supposed Platonism, see in particular Frances Yates, 'Shakespeare and Platonic tradition', in *Renaissance and Reform: The Italian Contribution: Collected Essays III* (London: Routledge and Kegan Paul, 1983), pp. 151–60; and Richard Cody, *The Landscape of the Mind: Pastoralism and Platonic Theory in Tasso's 'Aminta' and Shakespeare's Early Comedies* (Oxford: Oxford University Press, 1969).

57. Mouffe, *The Democratic Paradox*, pp. 67–8, 97–8 and 131; Hans-Georg Gadamer, 'Text and interpretation', trans. Dennis Schmidt and Richard Palmer, in *Dialogue and Deconstruction: The Gadamer–Derrida Encounter*, ed. Diane Michelfelder and Richard Palmer (Albany: SUNY Press, 1989), pp. 21–51; 'they agree in the *language*': Ludwig Wittgenstein, *Philosophical Investigations* (Oxford: Oxford University Press, 1953), vol. 1, p. 241.

58. 'It is our *acting*': Ludwig Wittgenstein, *On Certainty* (London: Collins, 1972), p. 204. For *adiaphora*, see James Alan Waddell, *The Struggle to Reclaim the Liturgy in the Lutheran Church: Adiaphora in Historical, Theological and Practical Perspective* (Lewiston: Mellen, 2005).

59. Badiou, *Saint Paul*, p. 99; and see Daniel Boyarin, 'Paul among the anti-philosophers, or, Saul among the sophists', in John Caputo and Linda Martin Alcoff (eds), *St Paul Among the Philosophers* (Bloomington: Indiana University Press, 2009), p. 111.

60. Alexandra Walsham, *Church Papists: Catholicism, Conformity and Confessional Polemic in Early Modern England* (Woodbridge: Boydell and Brewer, 1993), pp. 63–4; see also Henry Kamen, *The Rise of Toleration* (Toronto: McGraw Hill, 1961), and Joseph Lecler, *Toleration and the Reformation*, trans. T. L. Westow, 2 vols (New York: Association Press, 1960); John Locke, 'A letter concerning toleration', in *'A Letter Concerning Toleration' and 'Two Treatises of Government'* (New Haven: Yale University Press, 2003), p. 229. For Locke's refinement of the debate about *adiaphora*, see John Marshall, *John Locke: Resistance, Religion, and Responsibility* (Cambridge: Cambridge University Press, 1994), pp. 33–72; Alex Tuckness, *Locke and the Legislative Point of View: Toleration, Contested Principles, and the Law* (Princeton: Princeton University Press, 2002), pp. 17–25; and James Tully, *An Approach to Political Philosophy: Locke in Contexts* (Cambridge: Cambridge University Press, 1993), p. 48.

61. Walsham, *Church Papists*, p. 63.

62. Rainer Forst, *Toleration in Conflict*, trans. Ciaran Cronin (Cambridge: Cambridge University Press, 2013); Walzer, *On Toleration*, p. 81.

63. For a stimulating conspectus of current critical responses to the question of religious performativity, see Jane Hwang Degenhardt and Elizabeth Williamson (eds), *Religion and Drama in Early Modern England: The Performance of Religion on the Renaissance Stage* (Ashgate: Farnham, 2011).

64. Elisabeth Roudinesco, *Philosophy in Turbulent Times: Canguilhem, Sartre, Foucault, Althusser, Deleuze, Derrida*, trans. William McCuaig (New York: Columbia University Press, 2008), p. 152.

65. Christopher Marlowe, *The Jew of Malta*, Prologue, l. 14, in Frank Romany and Robert Lindsey (eds), *Christopher Marlowe: The Complete Plays* (London: Penguin, 2003), p. 248. See Chloe Preedy, *Marlowe's Literary Scepticism: Politic Religion and Post-Reformation* (London: Arden Shakespeare, 2014).

66. John Gray, *Liberalisms: Essays in Political Philosophy* (London: Routledge, 1989), p. 252; Mouffe, *The Democratic Paradox*, p. 64.

67. See Bednarz, *Shakespeare and the Poet's War*, pp. 122–3.

68. Luke Wilson, *Theaters of Intention: Drama and the Law in Early Modern England* (Stanford: Stanford University Press, 2000), p. 127.

69. Ernest Laclau, *Emancipations* (London: Verso, 1996), p. 53.

70. Roland Mousnier, *The Assassination of Henri IV: The Tyrannicide Problem and the Consolidation of French Absolute Monarchy in the Seventeenth Century*, trans. Joan Spencer (London: Faber and Faber, 1973), pp. 143–4.

71. Diarmaid MacCulloch, *Reformation: Europe's House Divided, 1490–1700* (London: Allen Lane, 2003), p. 472.

72. Jacques Rancière, *Dissensus: On Politics and Aesthetics*, trans. Steven Corcoran (London: Continuum, 2010), pp. 37–8.

73. Jeffrey Knapp, *Shakespeare's Tribe: Church, Nation, and Theater in Renaissance England* (Chicago: University of Chicago Press, 2002), pp. 54–5 and 176; Harold Bloom, *Shakespeare: The Invention of the Human* (London: Fourth Estate, 1999), pp. xvii and 716.

74. Knapp, *Shakespeare's Tribe*, p. 55.

75. Agamben, *The Kingdom and the Glory*, pp. 68–73.

76. Gillian Rose, *The Broken Middle* (Oxford: Blackwell, 1992). For a commentary, see Kate Schwick, *Gillian Rose: A Good Enough Justice* (Edinburgh: Edinburgh University Press, 2012).

77. Jean Bodin, *Colloquium of the Seven about Secrets of the Sublime*, trans. Marion Leathers Kuntz (Philadelphia: Pennsylvania State University Press, 2008), p. 489.

78. Jacques Derrida, 'Three questions to Hans-Georg Gadamer', in Michelfelder and Palmer (eds), *Dialogue and Deconstruction*, p. 53; Badiou, *Saint Paul*, p. 106.

79. Nancy, *The Creation of the World*.

80. 'All true universality': Badiou, *Saint Paul*, p. 19; Robert Burton, *The Anatomy of Melancholy*, 3 vols (London: Dent, 1932), vol. 3, p. 331.

81. Sloterdijk, *Globes. Spheres II*, p. 788.

82. Harry Levin, *The Myth of the Golden Age in the Renaissance* (London: Faber and Faber, 1970), p. 187.

83. 'Age of interpretation': Richard Rorty and Gianni Vattimo, *The Future of Religion* (New York: Columbia University Press, 2005), pp. 3–4; 'the King's conversion': Mousnier, *The Assassination of Henri IV*, p. 116.

84. 'A truce': Mousnier, *The Assassination of Henri IV*, p. 131.

85. Mouffe, *The Democratic Paradox*, pp. 137–8.

86. Schmitt, *Hamlet or Hecuba*, p. 45.

87. Wilson, 'Like the old Robin Hood: *As You Like It* and the enclosure riots', in *Will Power*, pp. 66–87.

88. Emmanuel Le Roy Ladurie, 'L'Iran de 1979 et le France de 1589', *Le Nouvel Observateur*, 22 January 1979, quoted and trans. in Janet Afary and Kevin Anderson, *Foucault and the Iranian Revolution: Gender and the Seductions of Islam* (Chicago: University of Chicago Press, 2005), pp. 104–5.

89. Judith Butler, *Precarious Life: The Powers of Mourning and Violence* (London: Verso, 2005), p. 30.

90. B. J. Sokol, *Shakespeare and Tolerance* (Cambridge: Cambridge University Press, 2008), p. 155.

91. A notable exception is Stephen Orgel's *Imagining Shakespeare* (Basingtoke: Palgrave, 2004), which argues that in the absence of any contemporary Jewish referent, 'Shylock can be seen as a kind of Puritan' (p. 154).

92. Badiou, *Saint Paul*, p. 8.

93. Ernesto Laclau and Chantal Mouffe, *Hegemony and Socialist Strategy: Towards a Radical Democratic Politics* (London: Verso, 1985), p. 127.

94. 'Not for an age': Jonson, 'To the memory of my beloved', p. 3352.

95. Schmitt, *The Concept of the Political*, p. 35.

96. McGowan, 'Hegel as Marxist', p. 38.

97. Sloterdijk, *Globes. Spheres II*, pp. 177–8, 307–8, 311.

98. McGowan, 'Hegel as Marxist', p. 38.

99. Schmitt, *The Concept of the Political*, pp. 67–8; Oliver Cromwell, Speech to Parliament, 17 September 1656, in Thomas Carlyle (ed.), *Oliver Cromwell's Letters and Speeches* (New York: Dutton, 1907), pp. 149–53.

100. Santner, *The Royal Remains*, p. xv.

101. Ibid., pp. 146 and 152.

102. Robert Greene, *A Groat's-worth of Witte, bought with a million of repentance* (1592); reprinted in Samuel Schoenbaum, *Shakespeare: A Documentary Life* (Oxford: Oxford University Press, 1975), p. 115.

103. Ibid.

104. Frank Kermode, *Not Entitled: A Memoir* (London: Harper Collins, 1996), pp. 181–2.

105. Walter Benjamin, 'On semblance' and 'Goethe's elective affinities', in *Selected Writings: I, 1913–1926*, ed. Marcus Bullock and Michael Jennings (Cambridge: Harvard University Press, 1996), pp. 224 and 341.

1 A Globe of Sinful Continents: Shakespeare Thinks the World

THE LAKE OF DARKNESS

What were Shakespeare and his fellows thinking when they called their play-house the Globe? How, in the dramatist's own proto-Hegelian expression, did they 'think of the world' [*Julius*, 1,2,301]? The name they attached in 1599 to 'This wide and universal theatre' [*As You*, 2,7,136] provokes this question, as much as it cries out to be revisited in the context of twenty-first-century debates about the competing claims of universalism and pluralism. Yet it has become so over-familiar that even Shakespeare scholars rarely give its significance much pause. Theatre specialists infer that in naming their house the Globe, its founders advertised 'a decorative scheme intended to foster an emblematic conception of the theatre as a microcosm, a theatre of the world'. But what remain strangely unexplored are the ways in which the ancient *topos* of the *Theatrum Mundi*, and the Pythagorean metaphor that 'All the world's a stage' [138], resonated in what Heidegger termed 'the age of the world picture', with Sir Francis Drake's circumnavigation of 1577–80, or Abraham Ortelius's cartographic 'theatre of the world', the 1570 atlas *Theatrum Orbis Terrarum*, displaying planispheres sectioned like some exotic fruit. And more importantly, the relation of the name of the people's palace erected on London's quayside to the contemporary shock of global religious multiplicity has rarely, if ever, been discussed.[1]

The first visitors to Shakespeare's playhouse were quick to notice its resemblance to Rome's circular amphitheatres, and to conclude that 'the theatre was constructed in the style of the ancient Romans', as a German tourist reported on 3 July 1600, because the Coliseum provided the classical architectural model for 'this great globe' [*Tempest*, 4,1,153].[2] But in the second part of *Globes*, his monumental history of globalisation, the radical philosopher Peter Sloterdijk has teased out the sinister implications of this roundness, the dark precedent that 'the Roman arena could advance to a metaphor for the world' only because 'the central tenet of ancient fatalism attained concretion in its construction: no one escapes this world alive'. For Sloterdijk, the lesson of the circus was therefore that 'a human life can never be more than a saving up to die', and the mass slaughters in the amphitheatre routi-nised the immune system that was otherwise stimulated in scapegoat rites, like the Lupercalia, or wolf game, aimed at cheating death. The *agôn* of the 'bloody ring of decision' was an auto-immunisation that generated the primal enmity, in this analy-sis, between those who die now and those who die later: 'Him or me, us or them: the fascism effect was invented in the gladiatorial games as the theatricalization of *diffé-rance*'.[3] And it was just this primordial antagonism haunting the shape of the theatre that Shakespeare confronted in his inaugural Globe play, *Julius Caesar*, where the Lupercalia is rerun within the 'course' [1,2,4] of a circular 'O world' [3,1,208] that is explicitly associated with the circuit where 'so many lusty Romans/Came smiling' [2,3,78] to feast their eyes on blood.

If Shakespeare associated the Globe with the Roman arena, it is certainly chill-ing that one of his only allusions to the Coliseum refers to its horror as the scene of martyrdom, and the sinister fact that the amphitheatre was built over the site of Nero's lake: 'Frateretto calls me', reports Poor Tom in *King Lear*, 'and tells me Nero is an angler in the lake of darkness' [3,6,6]. 'When the stadiums scream', writes Sloterdijk, in any case, 'the masses celebrate their success in postponing death'; and it is only when the Christians show that 'those who die sooner are not losers' that the repetition compulsion of the sacrifice enacted inside 'the lake of darkness' is broken. The philosopher locates an architectural figure for this rupture in 'the counter-arena' of St Peter's Square, 'a true anti-circus' that gave 'access to the community of love'.[4] But cued by the mimetic theory of René Girard, he also explains how the name of Shakespeare's Globe recorded an immunological crisis that was more fatal than even Christianity to the ancient inurement in the round, when Europeans grasped 'that they are contained or lost – which now amounts to virtually the same thing – somewhere in the boundless'. The icon for that exposure was the model of the earth as a terrestrial globe, which, starting with the Behaim Globe of Nuremberg of 1492, represented the world *from the outside*: 'the new "earth apple" – as Behaim called his globe – proclaimed to Europeans the topo-logical message of the Modern Age, that humans exist on the edge of an uneven round body whose whole is neither a womb nor a vessel, and offers no shelter'.[5] So, according to Sloterdijk, 'the immunological catastrophe of the Modern Age is not the "loss of the center", but the loss of the periphery'.[6] For what made the 'world picture' of the globe such a traumatic break with the morphological circularity of the theatrical arena was that it afforded European consciousness *no immunity* to its loss of differentiation:

In the earth's circumnavigated spaces, all points are of equal value. This neu-tralization subjected the spatial thought of the Modern Age to a radical change of meaning. The traditional situations that humans 'live and move and have their being' in regional orientations, markings and attractions was outdone by a system localizing any point in a homogeneous, arbitrarily divisible represen-tational space. . . . Humans can no longer remain at home in their traditional world interiors, and the phantasmal roundings-off of those interiors. They no longer dwell exclusively beneath their home-centred sky.[7]

The name of Shakespeare's Globe signalled the 'historical hyper-event of the earth's quantification', when Europe's sense of its own exception was shattered, according to this account of globalisation.[8] For along with the thought of the outside, 'a second abyss opens up in foreign cultures that demonstrate that everything we took to be the eternal order of things can be different'. When the 'plague ships of knowledge' returned to Europe, it was therefore with the news that 'every point on a circumnavigated orb can be affected by transactions between opponents, even from the greatest distance'. Sloterdijk's book is prompted, he explains, by the fact that 'Europeans managed to ignore, falsify and delay' this realisation for so long that globalisation hit them late in the twentieth century as a novel phenomenon, a disregard he identifies in particular with 'the last legitimist of European power', Carl Schmitt.[9] In the Nazi legist's study *The Nomos of the Earth* the exceptionalist doctrine that possession is nine-tenths of the law received its ultimate legitimation; but Sloterdijk traces Schmitt's 'metaphor-spawning' association of the terrestrial globe with the geopolitics of *Lebensraum* back to Shakespeare's *The Rape of the Lucrece*, where Tarquin eyes his victim's breasts 'like ivory globes circled with blue,/A pair of maiden worlds unconquerèd' [407]. As early as 1594, the philosopher comments, 'it was already sufficient for an object to appear round, desirable and asleep in order to become describable as a conquerable "world"'. Yet *Globes* concludes that Shakespeare already also foretold the rude wakening from this Eurocentric delusion, when 'unanalyzable Calibans declare their decolonization'.[10]

Pictures of the Coliseum and the London replica of Shakespeare's playhouse bookend *Globes*, to illustrate the immunological transformation it recounts, 'From the closed world to the open universe'.[11] On Bankside, 'The little O o'the earth' [*Antony*, 5,2,79] still incorporates a pillared tiring-house 'painted with unnumbered sparks' [*Julius*, 3,1,63], to symbolise the enfolding celestial sphere, augmented by 'Hercules and his load' [*Hamlet*, 2,2345], the Atlas figure who had propped up the sky in classical cosmography. But the first drama staged in this 'majestic world' [*Julius*, 1,2,132] concerns the impatience of Renaissance men at how the ornamented 'canopy most fatal' [5,1,87] of this 'disturbèd sky' [1,3,38] oppresses 'the narrow world/Like a Colossus' [1,2,157]; while it is now 'the foremost man in all this world' [4,2,74], and not the slave, who is hunted in the circular 'O world' [3,1,209] like some beast. 'This wooden O' [*Henry V*, Pro.,13] is therefore 'naughty' [*Julius*, 1,1,15], as poststructuralist critics point out, because here 'the sway of earth/Shakes like a thing infirm' [1,3,3–4] with 'the awl' [1,1,21] of undifferentiation that is personified by the punning Cobbler at the start of the opening play. Shakespeare's world is the disenchanted globe, in other words, of the age of circumnavigation; and the Bard of Bankside knows as well as any postmodern philosopher that 'the circumnavigated globe is not beautiful but interesting':[12]

> Every globe adorning the libraries and salons of educated Europe embodied the doctrine of the precedence of the outside, in which Europeans advanced as discoverers, merchants and tourists. . . . Celestial globes still continued . . . to promote the illusion of cosmic shelter for mortals beneath the firmament, but their function became increasingly ornamental. Nothing can save the physical

heavens from being disenchanted. What looks like a vault is an abyss perceived through a casing of air. The rest is displaced religiosity and bad poetry.[13]

THE THICK ROTUNDITY OF THE WORLD

Terrestrial globalisation terminated what Peter Sloterdijk terms 'the First Ecumene', because 'Christianity now had to be told of its own particularity'.[14] Yet although Shakespeare's Globe was built on the quayside of a tidal estuary, like a true cosmopolitan threshold or Thames-side window on the world, the liminal situation of this revolving 'planet' is seldom connected with the pluralist revelation of seventeenth-century thinkers like Robert Burton that 'Because God is infinite, he should be diversely worshipped', for it is 'impossible that one religion should be universal'.[15] Ortelius had styled his atlas a theatre, however, precisely because the Dutch mapmaker pictured 'the round earth's imagined corners' framing an unfolding spectacle within a classical arena like that of Andrea Palladio's contemporary Teatro Olimpico, a perspective scene in which all the diffuse acts of the global drama would be played according to the unities of time and space, as though, two centuries before universal clock time, contemporaneity was already understood as the temporality of a new planetisation.[16] So the frontispiece to *Theatre of the Lands of the World* figures a proscenium arch, crowned by twin hemispheres, from behind which 'will emerge the show of all the world's countries', as in a theatre 'the actors perform actions that add up to the play itself, an analogue for amassed knowledge'.[17] It is not necessary, then, to go so far as Frances Yates, who fantasised about the Globe as a cosmic memory theatre, to see how this planetary model for 'the idea that the events, features, and phenomena of the created world are infinitely many but all one', worked two ways, and how the circularity of Shakespeare's theatre and Ortelian cosmography were 'dialogically related':[18]

> The Globe Theatre would have been for Shakespeare the pattern of the universe, the idea of the Macrocosm, the world stage on which the Microcosm acted his parts. All the world's a stage. The words are in a real sense the clue to the Globe Theatre.[19]

Anne Barton noted that it was only at the time of the first terrestrial globes, in the mid-sixteenth century, 'that the image of the world as a stage entered English drama', a trope that Jean-Christophe Agnew also connects to 'England's new map of commodity circulation', with the emergence of a world market.[20] The topos of the theatre of the world would soon become ubiquitous in Baroque culture. But whereas the notion of the 'theatre state' served to reinforce social roles in countries like Spain, when Shakespeare has a character sigh 'I count the world but as. . . . A stage where every man must play a part' [*Merchant*, 1,1,77–8], it sounds as though this meta-theatricality is keyed to some personal disorientation at 'peering in maps for ports and piers and roads' [19]. On this world-stage an Antonio will discover he has to share the same space as his enemy Shylock: the corollary, Sloterdijk points out, of having investments 'not in one bottom trusted, /Nor in one place' [*Merchant*, 1,1,42–3].[21] For whether or not the Latin motto translated in *As You Like It*, the first Globe comedy – *Totus mundus agit histrionem* – was literally written up above its stage, the name of this circular house implied an entire philosophy of life as a unified play, a humanist concept that Ortelius's biographers connect to his membership of the Protestant sect the Family of Love. And in one of the rare critical accounts to grasp what was implied in such a name, John Gillies reminds us that, just as universal cartography gained prestige from the old idea of the world-as-theatre, so theatre acquired universality from associating with the cosmological picture of planetary cartography, allowing plays like *Henry V* and *Julius Caesar* to transmit 'the exhilaration of both dramatist and audience with the imagined conquest of geographic space'.[22]

Critics have long perceived that what distinguishes Elizabethan theatre, and above all Shakespeare, is the way in which this drama abolishes the representational difference between 'world and stage' by literalising the ancient philosophical cliché.[23] Thus, all Elizabethan plays were acted within what was effectively a world map in its own right, Gillies reminds us. Yet the moment of the Globe, which was the high noon of globe manufacture, was also the instant when the very concept of the earth's planetary roundness was delivering the unprecedented shock to Christian universality that Sloterdijk describes, as the persecution of Shakespeare's coeval Galileo testified.[24] So, when he had Puck promise to 'put a girdle round about the earth/In forty minutes' [*Dream*, 2,1,175], the dramatist registered how uncanny the idea of the earth's curvature, and Europe's relativity, must have appeared to a generation experiencing the literal *disorientation* entailed by the terrestrial sphere: 'that it was possible to travel in a straight-line course' yet return to the same place.[25] For East was West, or outside inside, according to the shape of the 'earth apple', as John Hale noted in his study *The Civilization of Europe in the Renaissance*. Hale's inference, that Europe's self-positioning within planetary space marked the point when inhabitants of this peninsular of Eurasia became 'civilised', has been criticised for ethnocentrism. But what the historian described was the loss of Europe's exceptionality, which, if it did not yet lead to toleration of the intolerable, was the *worldliness* that arose from cartographic exposure:

> Neither atlases nor maps showed any bias towards Europe. Devoid of indications of national frontiers, they were not devised to be read politically. In spite of the dramatic power games among countries of the West, the cartographers' *horror vacui* retained an even-handed deployment of information across the board. Neither cartographers nor traders thought in terms of an economically 'advanced' West and a 'backward' or marginally relevant East.[26]

In *Shakespeare's Restless World*, a hurried spin-off, via a BBC radio series, of a 2012 exhibition of late-Renaissance bric-à-brac, 'Shakespeare Staging the World', British Museum director Neil MacGregor relates the first English terrestrial globes, constructed for the Inns of Court by Emery Molyneux in 1592, to what he terms the sixteenth-century 'space race', and proposes that when such instruments 'went on triumphant public display' before Queen Elizabeth's courtiers, 'Shakespeare would almost certainly have been amongst them'. So, when Oberon boasts how 'We the globe can compass soon, / Swifter than the wandering moon' [4,1,95–6], according to this reading, 'Shakespeare's very English fairies are, in their whimsical, poetical way, restating the nation's pride' in England's triumphal rise from piracy to paramount position.[27] Such is the elision of nationalism with universalism in every populist celebration of the Bard. Evidently, MacGregor is deaf to the local anti-Elizabethan errancy of that 'wandering moon'. To be sure, the representation of space is never neutral, as Francis Barker remarked of Lear's cadastral map, for the 'chart of sovereign possession is always a field of struggle . . . the focus of power and danger, and site of powered or impotent linguistic performances. The map, and the land it obliquely represents, are caught up in a force-field of language and desire, as well as of possession'.[28] But the identification of Shakespeare's self-reflexive fairy 'roundel' [2,2,1] with the supremacism of Elizabethan imperialism, as if it is 'caught up in the new Protestant future of northern Europe', as imagined in the planetising charts of Drake's triumphal circumnavigation, misses what makes a drama like A Midsummer Night's Dream so destabilising, which is that it is precisely when Puck sets out to put 'a girdle round about the earth' that everything starts to go pear-shaped.[29]

MacGregor's book and exhibition comprise the most systematic bid thus far to annex Shakespeare to the merchandising bazaar of the postmodern museum. In Bloomsbury, the fact that Shakespeare was writing at the moment when Londoners got a first 'visual sense of the whole world, and in particular of the roundness of the world', was thus unashamedly used to affiliate the plays with 'the emerging role of London as a world city', and a globalisation that at the end of his book the director identified with the world mission of the BBC, as illustrated in Eric Gill's 1932 sculpture, above the portal of Broadcasting House, of Prospero and Ariel astride a revolving sphere.[30] The Bard was thus recruited to the museum's long-term project, attractive to its donors, of validating imperialism as a necessary phase in the march of global capitalism. As Michael Hardt and Antonio Negri explain in Empire, globalised capitalism is at once a deterritorialised set of 'open and expanding frontiers' and an 'apparatus of rule that incorporates the entire global realm' into a single system for effecting the privation of the world.[31] And such was the process of world privation to which the British Museum, by its institutional commitment, was appropriating Shakespeare.

Theorists of modernity like Fredric Jameson remind us how 'the very possibility of a new globalization' that derived from the worldwide expansion of capital in the age of empire depended on a productive revolution that made peasants into workers.[32] In fact, Shakespeare disavowed any such imperialist concept of the world by attributing to the deluded Richard II the pre-Copernican idea that the sun hides 'Behind the globe' as it 'lights the lower world' [Richard II, 3,2,34]. But if we want to learn how such a nomos of the earth was prefigured in English theatre, we need look no further than the stage of Shakespeare's precursor Marlowe, whose Tamburlaine operates like some cartographical maniac, with a perpetual motion across a thousand plateaus, and a drive to 'make the point' of the meridian himself, which annihilates geographical difference, 'as if to insist on the essential meaninglessness' of distance. Such homogenising of space, a register of 'transcendental homelessness', Stephen Greenblatt suggests, was doubtless keyed to the equalising effect of the planispheres Marlowe pondered in the bureau of his spymaster, Walsingham.[33] And the result is that his plays really do aspire to the spurious Anglocentric universality the British Museum mistakenly ascribes to Shakespeare, as they strive to prove that 'the essence of what it is to be restlessly human in a constantly restless world' is to speak and behave exactly like the playwright. For if Shakespeare would become the dramatist of the true worldliness that Jean-Luc Nancy terms *mondialisation*, Marlowe was a precocious genius of the possessive Schmittian drive of globalisation:[34]

> Look here, my boys, see what a world
> Lies westwards from the midst of Cancer's line,
> Unto the rising of this earthly globe,
> Whereas the sun declining from our sight,
> Begins the day with our antipodes:
> And shall I die with this unconquered?
>
> [2 *Tamburlaine*, 5,3,145–50]

It was his alertness to 'the key indicator of globalization, erosion of distance', that propelled Marlowe's projection of 'the mania for absolute power on the world-stage, carried out on a global, Tamburlaine scale'.[35] But a worldly Shakespeare surely caught the sound of this Marlovian ethnocentrism, as it mistook its own desires for universals, when he had the sociopathic Pistol spit 'like a man of this world', 'A foutre for the world and worldlings base!/I speak of Africa and golden joys' [2 *Henry IV*, 5,3,91]. On Marlowe's world stage, where all characters speak the same, and the globe is already a Romantic absolute, planetisation means colonisation, and 'the wind that bloweth all the world' is 'Desire of gold'.[36] For this political insider's privileged personal access to the map-room of Protestant empire clearly shapes the westward course of the *translatio imperii* in his America-directed imagination. 'Give me a map', his buccaneering Tamburlaine commands, 'then let me see how much/Is left to conquer of the world' [2 *Tamburlaine*, 5,3,123–4]. But though the cartographic revolution did give Europeans an intellectual edge, as the first 'to imagine the geographical space in which they lived' in terms of rational relations, this came at the cost of the relativity that contradicted their age-old assumptions of priority.[37] Thus, despite the will to 'Smite flat the thick rotundity of the world' [*Lear*, 3,2,8] with maps, historians insist that the mathematical projection of the earth unhinged, rather than reinforced, Eurocentric prejudices, hopes and fears. As the geographer Robert Kaplan remarks, far from confirming Europe's fond illusions about perpetual peace, individual freedom or human brotherhood, the advent of universal cartography during Shakespeare's lifetime in fact called time on the Renaissance dream of 'gentle concord in the world' [*Dream*, 4,1,140], for it was then that maps started to serve 'as a rebuke to the very notions of the equality and unity of mankind', and to register 'all the different environments of the earth that make men profoundly unequal and disunited in so many ways, leading only to conflict', a *dissensus* with which their realism is exclusively concerned.[38]

WHERE STOOD BELGIA?

To recent historians of the map, the image of 'this world's globe' [*2 Henry VI*, 3,2,406] is an emblem of the disenchantment of the world, a record of 'the collapse of the metaphysical immune system that had stabilized the imaginary of Old Europe', in Sloterdijk's terms, and the revenge of geography on political theology.[39] A modern sense of racial separation begins, they suggest, with Ortelius's frontispiece, where female icons of Europe, Asia, Africa and America embody incompatible potentialities.[40] According to this counter-intuitive historiography, the 'little O o' th' earth' [*Antony*, 5,2,79], 'the narrow world' [*Julius*, 1,2,135], would thereby figure for Shakespeare's generation of Europeans as its *objet petit a*, the entity that, in the terms of Jacques Lacan, is a cause rather than an object of desire, the signifier on whose account we desire and pursue the whole. And it is true that repeated meta-theatrical references in the plays to the gaping 'wooden O' as a 'naughty world' [*Merchant*, 5,1,91], an incomplete 'little world' [*Richard II*, 2,1,44; 5,5,9; *Lear*, 3,1,10], or hungry 'O without a figure' [*Lear*, 1,4,168], do sexualise, not to say feminise, its aporetic significance in ways that equate to the problematic depiction of the terrestrial sphere in late Renaissance art. In *Global Interests: Renaissance Art Between East and West*, Jerry Brotton and Lisa Jardine zoom in, for instance, on one of the best-known pictorial representations of a globe, lying between the French envoys in Holbein's double portrait of 1533, *The Ambassadors*, and argue that it has been turned to show Brazil to record an aspiration to French imperial power that is 'desperately counterpointed' with France's geopolitical marginality. So, far from the cultural triumphalism that Edward Said attributed in *Orientalism* to Europe's conceptualisations of its demonised other, Holbein's globe, alongside the haunting anamorphic skull, broken lute and other distracting symbols of failure and frustration, is an emblem of unsatisfied desire and intellectual defeat:

> In Holbein's *The Ambassadors* the aspiration towards imperial power figures as an absence or as a space between the participants portrayed . . . The possibility of filling the void at the centre of the composition depended on the outcome of events imminent at the time it was painted. . . And all of these outcomes were political failures.[41]

Holbein's globe functions as a *momento mori*, the cartographic equivalent of those impossible objects and mathematical puzzles which drive Dürer's Melancholia to despair, for it begs 'the question of the location of the middle, and consequently the identity and residence of the overlord'.[42] Indeed, as soon as Tamburlaine calls for a map, to show him the western hemisphere of 'this earthly globe', even Marlowe's terminator dies with 'this unconquered'. So, Marlowe's Tartar may bequeath his empire to his heirs, but he is never more of a disoriented Elizabethan than when yearning to 'win the world' by circumnavigating 'along the oriental sea . . . about the Indian continent:/Even from Persepolis to Mexico,/And thence unto the Straits of Jubalter' [*1 Tamburlaine*, 3,3,253–6]. For this was, of course, the global circuit, from Acapulco to Manila via Gibraltar, completed by those convoys of 'embarkéd traders', grown 'big-bellied' on 'the spiced Indian air' [*Dream*, 2,1,124–5], that Fernand Braudel termed the most complex trade cycle the world had ever known. And the historian of the Mediterranean went on to explain how this great rotating wheel of multilateral exchange reduced the Old World to the incidental position of a conduit, as between producing and accumulating countries, Europe and Islam came to function as intermediate transit zones, a fate, in particular, of decaying Venice.[43] In contrast to Marlowe's world conquerors, however, this very intermediacy is what seems to intoxicate a Shakespearean character like the truly piratical Falstaff, when he plans to traffic between two mistresses:

> Here's another letter to her. She bears the purse too. She is a region in Guiana, all gold and bounty. I will be cheaters to them both, and they shall be exchequers to me. They shall be my East and West Indies, and I will trade with them both.
>
> [*Wives*, 1,3,58–61]

Between Marlowe's map and Shakespeare's sphere, we already discern the contrast between what would become globalisation and the *mondialisation* or *worlding* of the rounded planet. For with his stress on the earthly, Shakespeare's worldliness seems always to bring the planet back to its 'rotundity'. Thus, 'She is spherical like a globe' is how Dromio describes the scullion Nell to his twin in *The Comedy of Errors*, with buttocks next to Irish bogs, and a face in the shape of America, 'embellish'd with rubies, carbuncles, sapphires, declining their rich aspect to the hot breath of Spain, who sent whole armadas of carracks to be ballast to her nose' [3,2,113–35]. Claiming to be the only geometer to compare 'the old imperfectly composed and the new lately reformed maps, globes [and] spheres', Richard Hakluyt had just promoted the first English globes in his 1589 *Voyages*, as 'collected according to the secretest and latest discoveries, both Spanish, Portuguese and English', when the play was acted at the Inns of Court in 1592, alongside the very globes it mocks.[44] Dromio's libidinous jest therefore confirms how rapidly the circular logic of a global economy became public property, but with it awareness of how intimately, in a system where what goes round comes about, the exotic and domestic are neighboured. As Harry Levin annotated it, the first Shakespearean reference to a terrestrial globe condenses the theme of this Pauline comedy, that the far and the near, home and away, have become uncannily interrelated: 'it embodies, on a miniature scale, the principal contrast of the play: on the one hand, extensive voyaging; on the other intensive domesticity'.[45] But the anxiety in the twin's gag about the hotspot of the Wars of Religion, 'Where stood Belgia, the Netherlands?' [3,2,136], makes this humour so much more than the projection of colonial acquisitiveness MacGregor makes it. For, as with Falstaff's tragicomic intercontinental trade, what we glimpse in the male insecurity about Nell's Arcimboldo-esque roundness is something more

Shakespearean, the auto-immune challenge analysed by Patricia Fumerton, that barbarism is to be discovered at home, in Antwerp or London, and that the worst enemy is the self:

> It was foreign trade, especially the East India Company's trade in spices, that supplied many of the ornaments, void stuff, and other trivia of the [English] aristocracy as well as an increasing proportion of its finances. What this underscored was that the trade that increasingly supplied the living of the aristocratic 'self' was also importing into that self an element so foreign to its self-image that it was conceptually 'savage'. More accurately, foreign trade exposed the fact that barbarousness had from the first been at the heart of the self.[46]

The stage of Shakespeare's Globe playhouse was wide, but in his worldliness it turns out to be not so universal. Hence it cannot be immaterial that though they glance at the globe a dozen times, his texts contain 350 references to the earth, with another fifty compounds such as 'earthlier happy' [*Dream*, 1,1,76] or 'earth-treading stars' [*Romeo*, 1,2,25]. No theatre, it seems, was ever more earthily *grounded*. For with their alertness to the interplay between the homely and outlandish, these dramas of complex causality 'are never merely ethnographic', observes Walter Cohen, as whenever the story is set in some faraway country, 'that land represents both itself and England' and, as a spatial analogue of anachronism, such reflexivity always exposes the limitations of *English* attitudes.[47] Characteristically, therefore, 'He does smile his face into more lines than is in the new map with the augmentation of the Indies' [*Twelfth*, 3,2,66], reports Maria of Malvolio's tragicomic efforts to 'revolve' [2,5,125] his personality; and the allusion to Hakluyt's travelogue, now 'augmented' with a rhumb-lined map of the East Indies, rather than being keyed to 'the triumph of English seafaring', as the museum asserts, reflects the hubris of such imperial pretensions back onto the pompous steward. Instead of heralding 'England's great success' in 'plunder and exploration, scientific inquiry and geopolitical manoeuvring', as MacGregor has it, Shakespeare's own 'revolving' on the new cartography truly brings the colonial project full circle in this way, by associating it, long before Jane Austen linked the slave trade to Mansfield Park, with the casual upstairs-downstairs cruelty of the English stately home, where it is in fact 'My lady' who is 'a Cathayan' [2,3,68].[48]

'I can hardly forbear hurling things at him', says Maria of the abused steward [2,5,69]; and Sir Andrew, 'I'd beat him like a dog' [2,3,126]. So, no wonder the author of these comedies relished Montaigne, for he clearly shared the Frenchman's sense that the atrocities of so-called cannibals were nothing compared with the barbarism 'we have not only read about, but seen ourselves in recent memory, not among savages or in antiquity, but among our fellow citizens and neighbours'.[49] A comedy like *Twelfth Night* will be full, then, of figures of speech drawn from fancy goods brought home by colonial exploration, the ginger [3,4,129] and pepper [2,3,105] that arrived like gifts of the Magi. But always there lurks Montaigne's verdict on these 'tradesmen's victories': 'So many millions put to the sword, and the most beautiful and richest part of the world shattered, on behalf of the pearls-and-pepper business!' 'Whoever else has ever rated trade and commerce at such a price?' Shakespeare seems to ask, with his French contemporary.[50] In *Twelfth Night* the violence that blows into Illyria with the 'notable pirate' Antonio, 'That took the *Phoenix* and her freight from Candy', and cost the duke's nephew Titus his leg [5,1,49–57], is more or less averted; but these comedic allusions to the piratical actuality of globalisation all foretell the tragic consciousness of dramas like *King Lear*, where, as Richard Marienstras wrote in *Le Proche et le Lontain*, 'at a time when newly discovered lands were providing a far distant setting for wild nature, Shakespeare's worldliness situates it within the bounds of civilised, indeed everyday life', and in every case, 'the near is more dangerous than the far':[51]

> This is most strange.
> That she, whom even but now was your best object,
> The argument of your praise, balm of your age,
> Most blest, most dearest, should in this trice of time
> Commit a thing so monstrous.
>
> [*Lear*, 1,1,214–18]

A DISH OF SOME THREE-PENCE

'What, in our house?' [*Macbeth*, 2,3,84]: Lady Macbeth's housewifely protest at the murder of Duncan is disingenuous, but this only intensifies the uncanny *homeliness* that haunts these plays, and that so offended Voltaire, where the domestic signifiers of tragedy are Gertrude's shoes or Othello's hanky. What Greenblatt calls the 'Machiavellian hypothesis' prompted by the shock of the New World, that 'custom is all in all', seems to be tested by this worldly writer, not on some stranger in a strange land, as it is by Marlowe, but on the audience, as Shakespeare takes what goes around seriously, and brings the global home.[52] For rather than projecting onto 'the barbarous Scythian' [*Lear*, 1,1,116] the certainty that 'Humanity must perforce prey upon itself, / Like monsters of the deep' [4,2,50–1], by locating the terror squarely 'in our house' this *revolutionary* thinking shatters the immunised and 'comfortable sense of Western or English selfhood in opposition to a unified "Otherness"'.[53] An authentically Shakespearean voice is therefore first heard when Tamora, the Queen of Goths, interrupts Titus's triumph on its way to the Coliseum to protest that the Roman immunological custom of human sacrifice is a 'cruel irreligious piety' [*Titus*, 1,1,130]. For in showing how the host turns hostile, in dramas where, as Gillies says, it is the alien who is in danger, and 'the exotic character who courts our sympathy', Shakespeare 'creates his own "heart of darkness"', not in Africa or the Indies, but in the European house.[54] *Housekeeping*, in the sense of the hospitality we owe the world that yet carries the risk of being consumed by it, appears indeed to be more of a concern here, in response to *circumspection* about the globe, than how much of it is left to conquer, as Julia Lupton infers. For 'whether it is in Capulet's bedroom, Brabantio's parlour, Macbeth's guest suite, or Timon's banqueting house, hospitality *chez Shakespeare*' sets the table for our own globalised debates about *polis* and *oikos*, norm and exception, the universal *versus* the particular.[55]

As the British Museum reminds us, Shakespeare keeps house in settings stuffed with luxury goods from across the world, like those husbanded by the tycoon Gremio in *The Taming of the Shrew*: 'Tyrian tapestry . . . Turkey cushions bossed with pearl,/Valance of Venice gold in needlework . . . and all things that belongs/To house or housekeeping' [2,1,341–8].[56] But in *Vermeer's Hat*, his dazzling book about the way the global economy penetrated Dutch interiors, Timothy Brook points out that these texts record the phase of *second contacts* in the evolution of a world market, the sequel when the first age of discovery trumpeted by Marlowe was over, and 'rather than deadly conflict, there was negotiation and borrowing; rather than triumph and loss, give and take; rather than the transformation of cultures, their interaction'.[57] Agonism replaced antagonism for the second global generation. Thus, after the great clash of civilisations, the seventeenth century would be a true worldly mercantilist era of tariffs and trade-offs, recounts Brook, a time for measurement, calculation, insurance and stocktaking that he finds punctually registered in the Shakespearean section of the judicial comedy *Measure for Measure*, dating from 1604, when Pompey derails the court with a bathetic Pinteresque monologue relating how the pregnant Mistress Elbow had an insatiable craving to consume stewed prunes:

> Sir, she came in great with child, and longing – saving your honour's reverence – for stewed prunes. Sir, we had but two in the house, which at that very distant time stood, as it were, in a fruit dish – a dish of some three-pence, your honours have seen such dishes; they are not china dishes, but very good dishes.
>
> [*Measure*, 2,1,82–6]

Sex, fruit, porcelain and a cheap imitation form a chain of signifiers, in this Lacanian tale of displaced 'longing', that not only recapitulates the play's theme of substitution, but enacts the endless extended supplementation and deferred gratification of all over-horizon global trade. No wonder the magistrate, Angelo, likens its stretched-out duration to 'a night in Russia,/When nights are longest there' [2,1,122–3]. China began arriving in Amsterdam only around 1600, and its cobalt blue and lustrous white colouring, with glassy transparent glaze created at a temperature of 1,300 degrees Celsius, instantly made this exorbitantly costly tableware a prime object of mimetic consumer desire. 'The first Chinese porcelain to reach Europe amazed all who saw or handled it. Europeans could think only of crystal when pressed to describe the stuff', and so seductive was its sensuous attraction that it instantly became 'synonymous with China itself'. Brook sees china, therefore, as a quintessential symbol of Shakespeare's agonistic age of *transculturation*, since it was, in fact, first manufactured as an intercultural crossover by Chinese ceramicists aiming to meet Persian aesthetic and Islamic religious demands. Soon 'everyone tried – and failed – to imitate the look and feel' of this deluxe product, and the 'bazaars were cluttered with second-rate imitations'. A decade later, however, the sinologist explains, the delayed pay-off of Pompey's shaggy-dog-story about frustrated satisfaction would not have been so excruciating, for by then Chinese porcelain was pouring into Europe's warehouses, and as its price plunged, so its transcendental place in the mimetic logic of the fashion system was superseded by carnations, and then, maniacally, by tulip bulbs.[58] By the time Wycherley wrote *The Country Wife* for Restoration London in 1675, 'china' had ceased to signify the exquisite unobtainable and become rakish slang for quick sex. But Shakespeare was writing at the moment of *measure* in the march of globalisation, when it was possible to know the value of everything, yet still to count the cost.

'Go to, go to, no matter for the dish', Judge Escalus interjects, during the testimony about Mistress Elbow's prunes. But though Pompey concedes its triviality – 'No, indeed, sir, not of a pin; you are therein in the right' [88] – in *Vermeer's Hat* we come to appreciate how the missing china dish might matter greatly to the audience at the Globe, as another circular *objet a*, an unattainable focus of a globalised mimetic lust. In 1604 *Measure for Measure* was so relevant to the hothouse society that was incubating the immunological disaster of the tulip mania, because its entire plot concerns absence, craving, displacement and the 'thirsty evil' of consuming 'Like rats that ravin down their proper bane' [1,2,109–10]. But if Shakespeare's plays are packed with such allusions to the imitative desire for fashion labels and imported luxuries, they are there not as Marlovian markers of colonial exploitation, imperial conquest, or what it is 'to be a king/And ride in triumph through Persepolis' [*1 Tamburlaine*, 2,5,53–4], but as signifiers of what René Girard calls the modern 'plague of undifferentiation'.[59] Here the gimcrack reproduction of the authentic and universal is as good as it will ever get. Like the museum curators, Lisa Jardine can discern 'the seeds of our own exuberant multiculturalism and bravura consumerism' in this Renaissance passion for 'worldly goods'.[60] Yet how to measure the value, and count the cost, of that absent but so desirable china dish, or why indeed it matters to the likes of Mistress Elbow and Master Froth, is, in a sense, a question that runs throughout these worldly plays.

'They are not china dishes, but very good dishes': Pompey sounds 'a tedious fool' [*Measure*, 2,1,70–120], apologising for the crockery supplied at Mistress Overdone's 'naughty house', 'the Bunch of Grapes', where Master Froth delights to sit 'in a lower chair', cracking 'the stones of the foresaid prunes', because 'it is an open room, and good for winter'. But this banal domestic scene has the suggestiveness of a genre painting of a Dutch interior. As Brook observes, 'Mistress Overdone did well enough as a procuress to be able to afford good dishes, but not Chinese porcelain'. So the type of vessel with which she served clients would have been faïence, pottery fired at 900 degrees and coated with tin oxide, a technique the Italians of Faenza learned from the Persians, 'who developed it to make cheap import substitutes that could compete with Chinese wares'. During Shakespeare's lifetime the most convincing of such copies were mass produced by Dutch tile-makers in Delft, and Delftware soon became 'the affordable substitute for ordinary people who wanted Chinese porcelain but could not dream of acquiring' the genuine article. Delftware has the deceptive appearance of porcelain, but lacks its thinness and translucence, and it is fatally liable to chip, which reveals the crude earthenware beneath the glaze of tin.[61] So, as symbols of the false promise of the fake, in a story about a viceroy whose flaws are exposed after 'some more test' is made of his 'metal' [1,1,48], Delftware dishes could hardly be more apt. But Pompey's admission that 'they are not china dishes' betrays a deeper anxiety, and the embarrassment that even the 'very good' that Europe produces is imitative or second rate. This was a disconcerting worldliness shared by Montaigne: 'When our artillery and printing were invented we clamoured about miracles: yet at the other end of the world in China men had been enjoying them for a thousand years'.[62] Thus, with the immunological shock of planetisation, and in place of its ethnocentrism, Europe was 'acquiring a new, humbler, perspective' on its undifferentiated place in a multipolar world, the historian William Bouwsma records in *The Waning of the Renaissance*:

> The whole earth could now be represented by a globe that could be held in one's hands. So a young man, on receiving the gift of a globe from his father, remarked: 'Before seeing it, I had not realized how small the world is'. Another blow to the self-image of Europe was implicit in the eschatological hopes of religious groups who looked forward to the onset of a new age. . . . Dissatisfaction with European ways was one source of favourable accounts of exotic cultures. Montaigne thought China 'a kingdom whose government and arts, without dealings with any knowledge of ours,' surpassed Europe in many ways. The Japanese were already being praised for their politeness, and for the intellectual quickness of their children. The non-European world was becoming a mirror in which to examine the blemishes of Europe.[63]

TARDY-APISH NATION

'If in Naples/I should report this now, would they believe me –/If I should say I saw such islanders?' exclaims Gonzalo in *The Tempest* of the 'people of the island', whose manners, he has discovered, 'are more gentle-kind than of/Our human generation you shall find/Many, nay, almost any' [3,3,28–34]. Editors connect his surprise with reports that American natives were 'gentle, loving, and faithful, void of all guile and treason, after the manner of the Golden Age'; and though the old lord is responding to a banquet laid out by Prospero's spirits, the inferiority complex he voices drives a story in which European castaways are garbed in garments acquired in Africa, 'at the marriage of the King's fair daughter Claribel to the King of Tunis' [2,1,69].[64] Along with almonds, sugar, and 'masses of gold', silk was in fact the main import into Jacobean England from North Africa; and if English writers scorned such fabrics as 'the materializations of oriental luxury and vice', they longed to produce the textiles themselves.[65] So an edgy mix of indebtedness and insecurity recurs whenever Shakespeare intrudes a character into an alien environment and the guest realises what 'a goodly city' his host inhabits [*Coriolanus*, 4,4,1]: from the instant in *The Comedy of Errors* when Antipholus of Syracuse goes to 'view the city' [1,2,31], and the misguided hospitality of the Ephesians means 'There's not a man I meet but doth salute me/As if were their well-acquainted friend. . . . Some tender money to me, some invite me,/Some other give me thanks for kindnesses' [4,3,1–5]. One of the plays in the genre set in the Ottoman Mediterranean that stage the temptation to 'turn Turk', this Shakespearean variant pushes the formula to its limit, by making the strangers the tourists' long-lost twins.[66] The fantasy parallels tall tales that native Americans spoke Welsh, and has analogues in fables of the gold of Eldorado or the treasury of Prester John, the legendary African king. But its libidinous consumerist drive will propel some of Shakespeare's most beguiling scenes:

> Be kind and courteous to this gentleman
> Hop in his walks, and gambol in his eyes.
> Feed him with apricots and dewberries,
> With purple grapes, green figs, and mulberries;
> The honey-bags steak from the humble-bees,
> And for night-tapers crop their waxen thighs
> And light them at the fiery glow-worms' eyes
> To have my love to bed and to arise. . . .

> [Dream, 3,1,146–53]

'Bottom's dream' [4,1,208] doubtless reflects the consumerist delirium of a London audience yearning to be 'translated' [3,1,105] to some Land of Cockaigne by shopping for 'worldly goods'; but the heady fantasy does seem to confirm the precocious sense of autonomy Londoners were developing through their trading relations with Asia, as discussed by Robert Batchelor in his study of John Selden's map of China.[67] Yet what this phantasmagoria does not assume is any immunised Anglocentrism, any more than does the Italianate 'flatt'ring dream' devised by the Lord in *The Taming of the Shrew* for the tinker Christopher Sly: 'Carry him gently to my fairest chamber,/And hang it round with all my wanton pictures' [Ind,1,40–1]. Instead, Shakespeare's plays seem to be agitated enough by 'Report of fashion in proud Italy/Whose manners still our tardy-apish nation/Limps after in base imitation' [*Richard II*, 2,1,23], to expose England's second-hand, substitute, tarnished underdevelopment, as an anachronistic latecomer on the provincial frontier of Renaissance civilisation.[68] In 1600 'the European Age' had not yet dawned, and 'the Indian economy was more productive than that of Europe'.[69] But it is difficult for us to grasp how peripheral England was even to continental Europe, as an undifferentiated margin on a margin, that was 'only just beginning to emerge from its status as the hinterland of Antwerp'.[70] In his own cameo textual appearances, however, Shakespeare always introduced himself as a cultural and geographical outsider, belated and outwitted like the Warwickshire yokel William. And what such gate-crashing tardiness evidently gave the dramatist was the untimeliness or 'view from afar' that Claude Lévi-Strauss considered to be the precondition of anthropology, but traced only as far back as Rousseau, a space of observation that permits not only an appreciation of the vulnerability of one's own lack of differentiation, but a *worldly* understanding of the context of the 'curiosity of nations' [*Lear*, 1,2,4], and thus a *toleration of the intolerable*:

> Cease to persuade, my loving Proteus
> Home-keeping youth hath ever homely wits.
> Were't not affection chains thy tender days

To the sweet glances of thy honoured love,
I rather would entreat thy company
To see the wonders of the world abroad
Than, living dully sluggardized at home,
Wear out thy youth in shapeless idleness.

[*Two Gentlemen*, 1,1,1–8]

In her cultural history of curiosity, Barbara Benedict keys the early modern European suspicion of travel to concern about the confessional relativism to which curiosity would lead, fears that were absorbed even by Montaigne, who came to deplore curiosity as an evil linked to the pride that 'makes us stick our noses into everything', because curiosity will not leave well alone: 'Montaigne's objection to curiosity expresses the period's anxiety about its power to swallow [religious] wonder and promote free thought'.[71] Curiosity killed the cat that played with me *too curiously*, appears to be the moral of this most curious of Renaissance thinkers, who thereby emerges as less *worldly* than Shakespeare. For from the start of his career, the dramatist's worldliness approximated to the 'anti-ethnocentrism' Lars Engle has described as the conceptual disorientation that comes from 'the imperative to avoid privileging one's own way of life'.[72] At a time when English satirists like Thomas Nashe were subjecting travellers to 'virulent criticism' in works like *The Unfortunate Traveller* and worrying about foreign travel precisely because they dreaded 'the commensurability of human beings, and therefore the capacity of the English to become like those they observed', Shakespeare seems instead to have shared Francis Bacon's culturalist philosophy, that 'Travel in the younger sort, is a part of education, and in the elder, a part of experience'.[73]

For a thinker whose fascination with religious multiplicity and cultural difference is often taken to be the foundation of ethnography, Montaigne was surprisingly critical of the curious. The emotional pull of Catholic universalism overrode his intellectual contextualism. In Shakespeare, too, the word 'curiosity' is invariably negative, and denotes pickiness, as when Timon is 'mocked for too much curiosity' in his clothes [*Timon*, 4,3,302]; 'curiosity in neither can make choice of either' of Lear's heirs [*Lear*, 1,1,5] or the dotard King blames his 'jealous curiosity' for his suspicions [1,4,59]. Likewise, 'curious' implies affected, as with the 'curious tale' a macho Kent brags he delights to 'mar in telling' [29]. Curiouser and curiouser, however, when Edmund declares he will permit neither custom nor 'The curiosity of nations' about his bastardy to stand in his way, because Mother Nature is his 'goddess' [1,2,1–4], the villain is paraphrasing Montaigne, who in his essay 'On a monster-child' mused that whatever is 'against custom we say is against Nature', yet 'nothing in Nature is unnatural'.[74] So it is the monster-child of this play who would sweep curiosity away. In *King Lear*, where Shakespeare out-Montaignes Montaigne for worldliness, curiosity, a capacity both to measure global differences and to make comparisons in a multipolar world, is thus reinstated as a name for what we might term anthropology. Thus, 'I do not like the fashion of your garments', the old King snaps, 'You will say they are Persian, but let them be changed' [3,6,73–4]. For cross-cultural comparisons are never here to the advantage of the English imitator:

Is man no more than this?
Consider him well. Thou owest the worm no silk, the beast no hide,
the sheep no wool, the cat no perfume. Ha! here's three on's are
sophisticated! Thou are the thing itself; unaccommodated man is no more
but such a poor, bare, forked animal as thou art.

[*Lear*, 3,4,94–9]

"Twere to consider too curiously to consider so', Horatio objects, when Hamlet likens the relics of Europe's highest achievers, Alexander and 'imperial Caesar', to Yorick's skull [*Hamlet*, 5,1,190–6]. The Christian prohibition of *curiositas* was motivated precisely by the aversion to seeing the great undifferentiation of death.[75] As Foucault observed, 'Curiosity is a vice stigmatized by Christianity, philosophy, and even science'. The philosopher therefore extolled curiosity as 'a passion for reality' that finds 'what surrounds us strange'.[76] And the curious Prince, who is anthropologist enough to know when a custom is 'more honoured in the breach than the observance' [1,4,18], and says he 'could be bounded in a nutshell', yet count himself 'a king of infinite space', has had the 'bad dream' of thinking 'this goodly frame the earth' nothing but 'a sterile promontory', and man, 'the beauty of the world, the paragon of animals', no more than a 'quintessence of dust' [2,2,248; 290–8]. The historian Bouwsma again: 'Curiosity, the cause and consequence of discoveries', triggered Spenglerian gloom about the decline of the West, with humanists like Ortelius's friend Justus Lipsius meditating that 'Once the East flourished: Assyria, Egypt, and Jewry excelled in war and peace. That glory was transferred into Europe, which now (like a diseased body) seemeth to be shaken. . . . And behold there ariseth elsewhere new people and a new world'.[77] Montaigne's scepticism was similarly sharpened by the sense that America was 'emerging into light when ours is leaving it'.[78] For as Hegel understood, the first age of globalisation was for Europe its twilight hour, the instant of greatest immunological exposure, when 'The increasing range of acquaintance with alien peoples under the pressure of necessity, as, for example, becoming acquainted with a new continent, had a sceptical effect upon the common sense of Europeans down to that time'.[79]

'What is a world? Or what does a "world" mean', asks Nancy in his anti-globalisation polemic *The Creation of the World*; and answers: 'a world is a totality of meaning. This amounts to saying that a worldview is indeed the end of the world as viewed, as digested, absorbed. . . . And this is why Heidegger in 1938, turning against Nazism, exposed the end of the age of the *Weltbilder*, of pictures of the world'. To create an interdependent worldliness, *mondialisation*, as opposed to globalisation, involves thinking a world without mastery, Nancy proposes: a thinking he identifies with art, which is 'a work opening beyond any meaning that is given'.[80] Likewise, for Badiou '*love* is the decision to create a new logic of the world, a new neighbourhood'.[81] And Shakespeare, whose wordplay on 'this solid globe' [*Troilus*, 1,3,113] suggests he was alive to the potential of 'this under globe' [*Lear*, 2,2,155], the scene of his own art, to become 'this world's globe' [2 *Henry VI*, 3,2,406], a paradigm for 'our good will', and was confident his particular worlding would 'the globe compass' as part of the planetary revolution, shared his audiences' fears about 'th'affrighted globe' [*Othello*, 5,2,109], 'this distracted globe' [*Hamlet*, 1,5,97], our *sullied* globe of undifferentiating globalisation, enough to be aware of the negativities of a 'globe of sinful continents' [*2 Henry IV*, 2,4,258]. He may not have shared Jonson's *Schadenfreude* at seeing 'the World's ruins', when in 1613 'the glory of the Bank' burned down.[82] But his 'brave new world' [*Tempest*, 5,1,186] turned out to be peopled with lechers, liars, murderers, rogues and fools. So, 'World, world, O world!' [*Lear*, 4,1,10] had been his tragic lament. Yet Shakespeare's final and surprisingly 'cheerful' [*Tempest*, 4,1,147] word on the name of his house, and on the entire metropolitan panorama of palaces and playhouses in which his works had been staged, was his most rounded, or truly worldly, 'view from afar':

> . . . the great globe itself,
> Yea, all which it inherit, shall dissolve;
> And, like this insubstantial pageant faded,
> Leave not a rack behind.
>
> [*Tempest*, 4,1,153–6]

NOTES

1. Peter Davidson, 'The iconography of the Globe', in J. R. Mulryne and Margaret Shewring, *Shakespeare's Globe* (Cambridge: Cambridge University Press, 1997), pp. 148–9; Martin Heidegger, 'The Age of World Picture', in *The Question Concerning Technology and Other Essays*, trans. William Lovitt (New York: Harper and Row, 1977), pp. 115–54.
2. 'Tuesday 3 July 1600': Anonymous Vatican MS, quoted in John Orrell, *The Human Stage: English Theatre Design, 1567–1640* (Cambridge: Cambridge University Press, 1988), p. 45.
3. Peter Sloterdijk, *Globes. Spheres II: Macrospherology*, trans. Wieland Hoban (Pasadena: Semiotexte, 2014), pp. 177–8, 307–8, 311.
4. Ibid., pp. 312, 318 and 320.
5. Ibid., pp. 774, 777 and 792.
6. Ibid., p. 788.
7. Ibid., pp. 783–4.
8. Ibid., p. 862.
9. Ibid., pp. 783, 788–90 and 870.
10. Ibid., pp. 876 and 890.
11. Ibid., p. 525.
12. Ibid., p. 771.
13. Ibid., pp. 792–4.
14. Ibid., p. 946.
15. Robert Burton, *The Anatomy of Melancholy*, 3 vols (London: Dent, 1932), vol. 3, p. 546.
16. 'Round earth's imagined corners': John Donne, 'Holy Sonnet 7', in C. A. Patrides (ed.), *The Complete English Poems of John Donne* (London: Dent, 1985), p. 438. For a magisterial account of the phenomenology of the time of globalisation, to which I am indebted throughout, see Peter Osborne, *The Politics of Time: Modernity and Avant-Garde* (London: Verso, 1995).
17. Paul Binding, *Imagined Corners: Exploring the World's First Atlas* (London: Review, 2003), p. 204.
18. Ibid., p. 206; Frances Yates, *Theatre of the World* (London: Routledge and Kegan Paul, 1969),

p. 189; 'dialogically related': John Gillies, *Shakespeare and the Geography of Difference* (Cambridge: Cambridge University Press, 1994), p. 70.

19. Juegen Schulz, 'Maps as metaphors: mural map cycles of the Italian Renaissance', in *Art and Cartography: Six Historical Essays* (Chicago: University of Chicago Press, 1987), pp. 97–122, here p. 112.

20. Anne Barton, *Shakespeare and the Idea of the Play* (London: Chatto and Windus, 1962), p. 61; Jean-Christophe Agnew, *Worlds Apart: The Market and the Theater in Anglo-American Thought, 1550–1750* (Cambridge: Cambridge University Press, 1986), p. 56.

21. Sloterdijk, *Globes. Spheres II*, p. 844.

22. Gillies, *Shakespeare and the Geography of Difference*, pp. 90–1.

23. See, for instance, the epilogue, 'The world stage', in Paul A. Kottman, *A Politics of the Scene* (Stanford: Stanford University Press, 2008).

24. Binding, *Imagined Corners*, p. 100.

25. Marshall McLuhan, *The Gutenberg Galaxy: The Making of Typographic Man* (Toronto: University of Toronto Press), p. 11.

26. John Hale, *The Civilization of Europe in the Renaissance* (London: Harper Collins, 1993), p. 20.

27. Neil MacGregor, *Shakespeare's Restless World* (London: Allen Lane, 2012), pp. 5–6. For an authoritative review, see Jean Wilson, 'Forks and shoes', *Times Literary Supplement*, 1 February 2013, p. 13, where the best-selling book is described as an 'airy nothing' that is 'old-fashioned' in its theatre history and 'confused' about religion, 'inaccurate in both picture captions and text', and the product of 'sloppy research and insufficient editorial control'.

28. Francis Barker, *The Culture of Violence: Tragedy and History* (Manchester: Manchester University Press, 1993), p. 1.

29. 'Caught up in the new Protestant future': MacGregor, *Shakespeare's Restless World*, p. 28.

30. 'Visual sense of the whole world': ibid., pp. 10 and 285–6, quoting Jonathan Bate; 'emerging role of London': British Museum, advertisement for its 'Shakespeare Staging the World' exhibition.

31. Michael Hardt and Antonio Negri, *Empire* (Cambridge, MA: Harvard University Press, 2000), p. xii.

32. Fredric Jameson, *The Cultural Turn: Selected Writings on the Postmodern, 1983–1998* (London: Verso, 1998), p. 67.

33. *Tamburlaine the Great, Part One*, 4,4,87, in Christopher Marlowe, *The Complete Plays*, ed. Frank Romany and Robert Lindsey (London: Penguin, 2003), p. 134; Stephen Greenblatt, *Renaissance Self-Fashioning From More to Shakespeare* (Chicago: University of Chicago Press, 1980), p. 195.

34. Jean-Luc Nancy, *The Creation of the World or Globalization*, trans. François Raffoul and David Pettigrew (New York: SUNY Press, 2007); MacGregor, *Shakespeare's Restless World*, p. 286.

35. Richard F. Hardin, 'Marlowe thinking globally', in Sarah K. Scott and M. L. Stapleton (eds), *Christopher Marlowe the Craftsman: Lives, Stage, and Page* (Farnham: Ashgate, 2010), pp. 23–32, here p. 28.

36. *The Jew of Malta*, 3,5,4–5, in Marlowe, *The Complete Plays*, p. 301.

37. Hale, *The Civilization of Europe*, p. 20.

38. Robert Kaplan, *The Revenge of Geography: What the Map Tells Us About Coming Conflicts and the Battle Against Fate* (New York: Random House, 2012), p. 28.

39. Sloterdijk, *Globes. Spheres II*, p. 559.

40. Francesco Bethencourt, *Racisms: From the Crusades to the Twentieth Century* (Princeton: Princeton University Press, 2014).

41. Lisa Jardine and Jerry Brotton, *Global Interests: Renaissance Art Between East and West* (Ithaca: Cornell University Press, 2000), pp. 56–7 and 61–2. Edward Said, *Orientalism* (London: Routledge and Kegan Paul, 1978).

42. Sloterdijk, *Globes. Spheres II*, p. 57.
43. Fernand Braudel, *The Wheels of Commerce*, trans. Sian Reynolds (London: Collins, 1982), p. 199.
44. Richard Hakluyt, *The Principal Navigations, Voyages, Traffics and Discoveries of the English Nation*, ed. John Masefield, 10 vols (London: Dent, 1927), vol. 6, pp. 242–4.
45. Harry Levin, 'Introduction', in William Shakespeare, *The Comedy of Errors* (New York: Signet, 1962), p. xxxii.
46. Patricia Fumerton, *Cultural Aesthetics: Renaissance Literature and the Practice of Social Ornament* (Chicago: University of Chicago Press, 1991), p. 173.
47. Walter Cohen, 'The undiscovered country: Shakespeare and mercantile geography', in Jean Howard and Scott Shershow (eds), *Marxist Shakespeares* (London: Routledge, 2001), p. 155.
48. MacGregor, *Shakespeare's Restless World*, pp. 6 and 10.
49. Michel de Montaigne, 'Of cannibals', in *The Complete Essays of Michel de Montaigne*, trans. M. A. Screech (Harmondsworth: Penguin, 1991), p. 236.
50. Ibid., 'On coaches', p. 1031.
51. Richard Marienstras, *New Perspectives on the Shakespearean World*, trans. Janet Lloyd (Cambridge: Cambridge University Press, 1985), p. 6.
52. Stephen Greenblatt, *Shakespearean Negotiations: The Circulation of Social Energy in Renaissance England* (Berkeley: University of California Press, 1988), pp. 26–33; 'custom is all in all': Burton, *The Anatomy of Melancholy*, p. 308.
53. David Vitkus, review of *Travel and Drama in Shakespeare's Time* (ed. Jean-Pierre Maquerlot and Michèle Willems), *Shakespeare Quarterly*, 50 (1999), 97–100, here 99.
54. Gillies, *Shakespeare and the Geography of Difference*, pp. 100–6.
55. Julia Reinhard Lupton, *Thinking with Shakespeare: Essays on Politics and Life* (Chicago: University of Chicago Press, 2011), p. 165.
56. See Cohen, 'The undiscovered country', pp. 133–5.
57. Timothy Brook, *Vermeer's Hat: The Seventeenth Century and the Dawn of the Global World* (London: Profile, 2008), p. 21.
58. Ibid., pp. 60, 63 and 73–4.
59. René Girard, *A Theater of Envy: William Shakespeare* (New York: Oxford University Press, 1991), pp. 162–3 et passim.
60. Lisa Jardine, *Worldly Goods: A New History of the Renaissance* (New York: Norton, 1998), p. 1.
61. Brook, *Vermeer's Hat*, pp. 61 and 78.
62. Montaigne, 'On coaches', pp. 1028–9.
63. William Bouwsma, *The Waning of the Renaissance, 1550–1640* (New Haven: Yale University Press, 2000), pp. 70 and 72–3, quoting Montaigne's essay 'On experience'.
64. 'Gentle, loving, and faithful': quoted by Bouwsma, *The Waning of the Renaissance*, p. 73.
65. T. S. Willan, *Studies in Elizabethan Foreign Trade* (Manchester: Manchester University Press, 1959), pp. 120–1 and 266–7; Peter Stallybrass, 'Marginal England: the view from Aleppo', in Lena Cowen Orlin (ed.), *Center and Margin: Revisions of the English Renaissance in Honor of Leeds Barroll* (Cranbury, NJ.: Associated University Press, 2006), pp. 27–39, here p. 31.
66. See Daniel Vitkus, *Turning Turk: English Theater and the Multicultural Mediterranean* (Basingstoke: Palgrave Macmillan, 2003), p. 39; and Goran Stanivukovic (ed.), *Remapping the Mediterranean World in Early Modern English Writings* (Basingstoke: Palgrave Macmillan, 2007), p. 10.
67. Robert Batchelor, *London: The Selden Map and the Making of a Global City, 1549–1689* (Chicago: University of Chicago Press, 2014).
68. For anxieties about 'apish' English imitativeness, see Mary Floyd-Wilson, *English Ethnicity and Race in Early Modern Drama* (Cambridge: Cambridge University Press, 2003), pp. 54–7.

69. Philip Curtin, *Cross-Cultural Trade in World History* (Cambridge: Cambridge University Press, 1984), p. 149.

70. Stallybrass, 'Marginal England, p. 31.

71. Barbara Benedict, *Curiosity: A Cultural History of Early Modern Inquiry* (Chicago: University of Chicago Press, 2001), p. 32; Montaigne, 'An apology for Raymond Sebond' and 'That it is madness to judge the true and the false from our own capacities', in *The Complete Essays of Michel de Montaigne*, pp. 204 and 555.

72. Lars Engle, 'Montaigne, Shakespeare, and anti-ethnocentrism', paper presented to the British Studies Seminar of the Hall Center for the Humanities, University of Kansas, cited in Hardin, 'Marlowe thinking globally', p. 28.

73. 'Virulent criticism': Sara Warneke, *Images of the Educational Traveller in Early Modern England* (Leiden: Brill, 1995), p. 7; 'the commensurability of human beings': Vitkus, *Turning Turk*, p. 9; Francis Bacon, 'Of travel', in *Essays*, ed. Michael Hawkins (London: Dent, 1972), p. 54.

74. Montaigne, 'On a monster-child', in *The Complete Essays of Michel de Montaigne*, p. 808. Jonathan Dollimore has argued that Montaigne's conception of 'custom' anticipated Louis Althusser's theory of ideology: *Radical Tragedy: Religion, Ideology and Power in the Drama of Shakespeare and His Contemporaries* (Brighton: Harvester, 1989), p. 18.

75. Sloterdijk, *Globes. Spheres II*, p. 317.

76. Michel Foucault, 'The masked philosopher', trans. Alan Sheridan, in *Politics, Philosophy, Culture: Interviews and Other Writings, 1977–1984*, ed. Lawrence Kritzman (London: Routledge, 1988), p. 328.

77. Bouwsma, *The Waning of the Renaissance*, pp. 69 and 73; Justus Lipsius, *Two Books of Constancy*, trans. Sir John Stradling (London, 1594), ed. Rudolf Kirk (New Brunswick, NJ: Rutgers University Press, 1939), p. 110.

78. Montaigne, 'On coaches', pp. 1028–9.

79. Georg Wilhelm Friedrich Hegel, 'Relationship of skepticism to philosophy, exposition of its different modifications and comparison to the latest form with the ancient one', in *Between Kant and Hegel: Texts in the Development of Post-Kantian Idealism*, ed. and trans. George di Giovanni and H. S. Harris (Albany: SUNY Press, 1985), p. 333.

80. Nancy, *The Creation of the World*, pp. 41 and 54.

81. Kenneth Reinhard, 'Toward a political theology of the neighbour', in Slavoj Žižek, Kenneth Reinhard and Eric Santner, *The Neighbour: Three Inquiries in Political Theology* (Chicago: Chicago University Press, 2013), p. 67; Alain Badiou, *L'etre et l'evenement* (Paris: Seuil, 1988).

82. Ben Jonson, quoted in E. K. Chambers, *The Elizabethan Stage*, 4 vols (Oxford: Oxford University Press, 1923), vol. 2, p. 422.

2 Too Long for a Play: Shakespeare and the Wars of Religion

Near the end of *Love's Labour's Lost* the young Lords of Navarre, who spend the play forgetting a puritanical faith that arms them against 'the huge army of the world's desires' [1,1,9], make a desperate appeal to the ladies from Paris to forget theirs, as Biron, who began this forgetfulness by arguing that 'If I break faith . . . I am forsworn on mere necessity' [1,1,151–2], protests that 'By being once false for ever to be true . . . falsehood, in itself a sin . . . purifies itself' [5,2,755–8]; and the King of Navarre, who had warned his friends 'You would for paradise break faith' [4,3,139], pleads with the French: 'Now, at the latest minute of the hour,/Grant us your loves'. The reply by the Queen of France is so uncompromising, however, that it sounds as if it signals the author's own admission of the impossibility of forgetting faith in the Wars of Religion to which all this confessional raillery alludes: 'A time, methinks, too short/To make a world-without-end bargain in' [5,2,68–71]. As its final song freezes spring to winter, *Love's Labour's Lost* therefore seems to confirm Perez Zagorin's opening remark in *How the Idea of Religious Toleration Came to the West*, that 'The sixteenth century was probably the most intolerant period in Christian history'.[1] The play that has worked so hard to prove 'Our loving lawful and our faith not torn' [4,3,281] is suspended instead in hard-line reassertion of fundamentalist faith, with love's labours towards a 'world-without-end bargain' of reconciliation and toleration now lost to the work of mourning in the absolutism of 'some forlorn and naked hermitage/Remote from all the pleasures of the world' [776–7], or a 'twelvemonth in an hospital' [848].

'That's too long for a play' [855]: the frustration of *Love's Labour's Lost* brings a sudden halt to Shakespeare's dramaturgy, when for the first time on his stage, 'Our wooing doth not end like an old play./Jack hath not Jill' [851–2]. If 'the vasty fields' [*Henry V*, Pro.,12] of France's civil wars had figured from the start as a mirror for his English audience to 'Look on thy country' by looking 'on fertile France', to see 'cities and the towns defaced', as Joan advises, the story so far had projected a cure for the 'pining malady' of these 'unnatural wounds' [*1 Henry VI*, 3,7,44–50] in 'a godly' and 'friendly peace', 'a knot of amity' to 'stop effusion of our Christian blood/And 'stablish quietness on every side' [5,1,5–38], like that eventually tied by Catherine and King Henry V in the only scene Shakespeare wrote entirely in French.[2] Thus, in *Titus Andronicus* the cannibalism of the Romans and atrocities of the Goths seem like the author's response to horrors 'we have not only read about, but seen', as Montaigne grieved, 'not in antiquity, but among our fellow citizens', in a France where Catholic fanatics did indeed cook and consume 'the tripe of Huguenots', just as Protestant vigilantes stuffed women they raped with gunpowder and set them alight.[3] Yet even here the carnage ceased amid plans to bind those 'By uproars severed' in 'one mutual sheaf,/These broken limbs again into one body' [*Titus*, 5,3,67–70]. *The Comedy of Errors* took due note of a France 'armed and reverted, making war against her heir', yet still cherished a hope that brothers might 'go hand in hand, not one before another' [3,2,122; 5,1,426]; *The Taming of the Shrew* culminated with Petruchio kissing Kate after she had disavowed revanchists who 'offer war when they should kneel for peace' [5,2,166]; and *The Two Gentlemen of Verona* closed in a 'penance but to hear/The story' of the exiles' return [5,4,167]. By contrast, the penance of 'frosts and fasts, hard lodging and thin weeds' that disrupts the happy ending of *Love's Labour's Lost* seems so harsh because this 'austere, insociable life' [5,2,781–3] is such an imposition of humourless faith upon the laughing faithlessness of the play:

> You shall this twelvemonth term from day to day
> Visit the speechless sick and still converse
> With groaning wretches, and your task shall be
> With all the fierce endeavour of your wit
> To force the painèd impotent to smile.
> BIRON: To move wild laughter in the throat of death?
> It cannot be, it is impossible.
> Mirth cannot move a soul in agony.
>
> [5,2,827–34]

At Easter 1594 the real King of Navarre began his penance to 'move wild laughter in the throat of death' by nursing the dying at the Hôtel-Dieu, washing the feet of the beggars of Paris, releasing prisoners and ritually fingering the suppurating ulcers of 660 sufferers of king's evil: lymphatic tuberculosis or scrofula. These thaumaturgical rituals key Shakespeare's comedy of faithlessness to the dizzy days after the 'perilous leap' of Henri of Navarre on 25 July 1593 when, draped in white, the Calvinist leader renounced his faith, and was then received into the Catholic Church, at a spectacular Mass in the abbey of St Denis outside Paris: conditions for entering the city and being crowned the King of France at Chartres. By choosing 'Virtue', Henri could now be portrayed as Hercules. But whether or not he did joke that 'Paris is worth a Mass', the bleak and inconclusive ending of Shakespeare's play seems to mark the hiatus when this apostate's new faith was tested by the terms issued in Rome, which demanded he not only 'seek the weary beds of people sick' [798], but establish a monastery in every province, say his rosary, keep fasts and obey all the Commandments, especially those 'forbidding fornication and adultery'.[4] Despite its naming of the historical Navarre, Biron, Longaville and de Mayenne, editors of *Love's Labour's Lost* detest the idea that it might refer to these events, since, as David Bevington huffs, 'to allude frivolously to these matters Shakespeare would have had to be contra-topical'.[5] This objection misses the point, however, that the 'contra-topicality' of such frivolity to the work of mourning may be the very theme of a *deliberately counter-factual play*, which knows full well 'The words of Mercury are harsh after the songs of Apollo' [5,2,904], but still refuses to 'forbear laughing' in the face of death [1,1,191]:

To see great Hercules whipping a gig,
And profound Solomon to tune a jig,
And Nestor play at pushpin with the boys,
And critic Timon laugh at idle toys!

[4,3,163-6]

It was Frances Yates who first suggested Shakespeare's staging of the Wars of Religion in *Love's Labour's Lost* was '*wilfully* frivolous'.[6] Thus, 'I will kiss thy royal finger and take leave' [5,2,859] says 'the magnificent Armado' [1,1,187], the play's knight of Spain whose penance of wearing Jaquenetta's dishcloth 'next his heart' [5,2,698] turns his Catholic faith to farce. Likewise, as the Spanish army marched peaceably out of Paris on the day of Henri's 'Joyous Entry', the fingering monarch 'watched them pass and when their ambassador saluted, raised his hat and bowed, saying, "My compliments to your King, go away in good time and don't come back"'.[7] Clearly, the laughing prince and playwright shared a precious capacity to see the funny side of 'the hot breath of Spain, who sent whole armadas of carracks' [*Comedy*, 3,2,134]; and critics connect the Archbishop's mad rigmarole in *Henry V* over 'the law Salic . . . in France' [1,2,11] to Henri's amusement at the claim to the French throne pushed by zealots on behalf of the Infanta of Spain.[8] The death cult of Shakespeare's intolerant sour-pusses, who don the 'black gown' of penitents to escort the Queen, as she shuts her 'woeful self up in a mourning house,/Raining tears of lamentation/For the remembrance' of her father's death [5,2,790–811], also seems to glance at the diehards of the Catholic League, with their Counter-Reformation penitential practices adopted from the Milan of Carlo Borromeo. Yet these extremist *dévotes* 'are clearly the winners of *Love's Labour's Lost*', notes Indira Ghose in *Shakespeare and Laughter*; and Yates admitted that if this comedy is read as 'a kind of sermon' against scientific enlightenment, its closing religiosity has the intolerance of 'a good Catholic'.[9] Indeed, processions of flagellants became more frenzied in Paris *after* the King's conversion, until they were outlawed as 'acts of sedition rather than piety'.[10] Shakespeare therefore neither underestimated the fury of the faith that will never be forgotten, nor the problem of tolerating the intolerant, even for a 'fair sweet honey monarch' [524]. But the challenge on which his comedy concludes, 'To force the painèd impotent to smile', hints how he could perceive that the frivolity of a jesting Gascon king and his laughing lords might yet help the faithful to forgive:

Oft have I heard of you, my Lord Biron,
Before I saw you; and the world's large tongue

Proclaims you for a man replete with mocks,
Full of comparisons and wounding flouts,
Which you on all estates will execute
That lie within the mercy of your wit. . .
Whose influence is begot of that loose grace
Which shallow laughing hearers give to fools.
A jest's prosperity lies in the ear
Of him that hears it, never in the tongue
Of him that makes it. Then if sickly ears,
Deafed with the clamours of their own dear groans,
Will hear your idle scorns, continue then,
And I will have you and that fault withal.
But if they will not, throw away that spirit,
And I shall find you empty of that fault,
Right joyful of your reformation.

[5,2,818–46]

Though the 'reformation' proclaimed by the title of Love's Labour's Lost implies the end of the Catholic belief in salvation by works, Rosaline's deferral of judgement to those 'Deafed with the clamours of their own dear groans' subjects this comedy to an even more laborious test than the one to which the actor kneels at the end of Shakespeare's other plays. For this stress on 'the fierce endeavour' of performance not only repeats the puritanical zeal with which the lords of Navarre 'mortified' themselves, when they swore to 'strict observances' of celibacy, poverty and seclusion. As recent critics observe, what is so unsettling about this additional twist is that Shakespeare here goes out of his way 'to recover notions of eremitism, of abstinence and of redeeming works' in terms that vengefully *exceed* the Protestant paradigm of the Huguenot-type conventicle with which the play began. Thus the ladies' appropriation of 'reform' makes this last conversion literally a *Counter-Reformation* act, for the measure of their 'reformation' will be the restoration of works as the 'yardstick' of faith. So it seems facile to interpret this superimposition of a Catholic paradigm of 'true austerity, abstinence and a rigid eremitism' as proof of the play's 'tolerant' Protestant inclusiveness. For if this 'complex amalgamation' of warring faiths is indeed 'a collective labour of love', its laughter in the dark is a truly agonistic confrontation that renders Shakespeare's confessional comedy as contrapuntal as its concluding avian cacophony of jarring Owl and Cuckoo.[11] As Drew Daniel writes, 'There is something manic-depressive about Love's Labour's Lost', which proceeds through a sequence of hysterical diversions that serves only to highlight this 'final, inevitable plunge into depression'.[12]

'Hence, hermit, then' [798]: at the end, the King's eremitic retreat segregates according to the very doctrine of salvation by works that the title of Love's Labour's Lost mocks: 'You that way, we this way' [904]. Shakespeare would return to the theme of a prodigal prince 'Redeeming time when men think least' with the 'reformation' of Prince Hal [1 Henry IV, 1,2,195], who some think was inspired by his namesake from Navarre.[13] And if Henri IV was indeed a model for this royal conversion from roué into ruler, that may explain why Henry V remains such a hermeneutic puzzle. For according to historians, the war of words over the sincerity of the turncoat's beliefs 'dominated public discourse as no other issue did in early modern France'.[14] Had he not been born to be a king, 'he would have been hanged as a thief,' Henri jested: like Hal.[15] But the great *politique* survivor had changed faith twice already before Shakespeare spun an entire play around the counter-intuition that 'It is religion to be thus forsworn' [Love's, 4,3,337]. *Love's Labour's Lost* therefore anticipates Catholic incredulity at this madcap's good works, when its Queen tells Navarre she values his change of heart 'As bombast', since it is no more 'devout' than a 'lining to the time' [5,2,563]. A sequence of textual repetitions reveals the dramatist himself stammering that 'your grace is perjured much,/Full of guiltiness. . . . You must be purged. . . . Your sins are rank./You are attaint with faults and perjury' [772–98]. This textual stutter suggests that even Shakespeare may not therefore have anticipated the theatrical panache with which the Calvinist from the Basque border country plunged into the histrionic chicanery of the royal healing and, as recounted in the famous study by Marc Bloch, ensured that far from being forgotten in the new order, 'the old belief in the supernatural gifts of royalty once more triumphed':[16]

> Paris had seen nothing of the kind since Henri III's flight in 1588; and the sick came forward in huge numbers. . . . Subsequently, Henri IV went on dispensing the grace of healing to the scrofulous, who always flocked to him in hundreds or even thousands on the four great festivals. . . . Like all the French kings, he administered the touch standing, and found it a tiring business; but he took good care not to avoid it. Desirous as he was of reconstructing the monarchy, he would surely not have neglected this part of the royal task.[17]

At the end of *Love's Labour's Lost* the King and his lords are resigned 'to choke a gibing spirit' [835] in a hospital. And in Paris too the crowned joker swallowed his scoffing as 'with his own hands, freshly anointed with the holy oil, he touched people . . . and God repeated for him the miracle granted to all kings of France: the scrofulous were healed'.[18] Medical experts tell us that the fistulas and tumours of lymphatic tuberculosis typically 'subside and then reappear giving the illusion of a cure'.[19] But Bloch notes how even in 'the age of faith' it was 'as clear as daylight that the effectiveness of the royal hand was liable to suffer eclipse', as so many 'came repeatedly for the laying on of hands – plain proof the first attempt had not been successful'; and how the last time a French king touched, in 1825, only five of 130 patients were even temporarily relieved. When sufferers failed to heal after Henri III touched them repeatedly, Jesuits declared the fiasco a sign of illegitimacy and cue for deposition. His successor's publicists therefore defied the factual evidence with Scripture, where 'the Apostles did not heal all', and by inventing a fresh tradition – that the royal gift originated when Clovis became the first king anointed with holy oil. As Bloch remarks, this fabrication is so patent the problem it poses is why people persisted in professing a faith in wonder-working monarchs when 'they did not in fact heal'.[20] And the question is moot with Shakespeare, whose recycling in *Macbeth* of the parallel tradition about Edward the Confessor's touching was recited to James I, a king who, unlike Henri, expressly asked to be excused a custom that disgusted him and that Calvinist faith taught him to scorn as 'sheer superstition':[21]

> There are a crew of wretched souls
> That stay his cure. Their malady convinces
> The great essay of art, but at his touch,
> Such sanctity hath Heaven given his hand
> They presently amend. . . .
>   'Tis called the evil –
> A most miraculous work in this good King. . . .
>   How he solicits heaven
> Himself best knows, but strangely visited people
> All swoll'n and ulcerous, pitiful to the eye,
> The mere despair of surgery, he cures,
> Hanging a golden stamp about their necks,
> Put on with holy prayers; and 'tis spoken,
> To the succeeding royalty he leaves
> The healing benediction.
>
>   [*Macbeth*, 4,3,141–57]

Considering James's deep physical revulsion from the touching rite, no one has answered Bloch's question about Shakespeare's 'eulogy of the wonder-working power': 'Was it discreet advice? Or ignorance of the hesitations shown by the last descendant of Banquo?'[22] When the Turkish ambassador asked James to touch his young son, however, 'the king laughed heartily' yet complied; and Bloch sees this as proof that James had learned 'not to take the matter seriously', having disappointed his first 'patients' by winking over their heads.[23] If he did not succeed in abolishing the rite he would still have agreed with William III, who, as he laid hands on his one and only sufferer, whispered 'God give you better health and more sense'.[24] But just as the infant Edward VI went through the motions, after 'his royal humour had prevailed over his evangelical doctrines', so James's sense of irony overcame his Calvinist logic that 'he could not see how he could heal the sick without a miracle, but miracles had ceased'.[25] He was torn, he explained, between 'performing an act that might be superstitious, or breaking an ancient custom', yet humorously 'resolved to give it a trial, but only by way of a prayer'; and with this artful play-acting, satisfied believers, while insulating himself against popish superstition by refusing to make the sign of the cross, and removing from the commemorative medallion any mention of a miracle.[26] The gift of a gold 'Angel' (a coin) had been a Tudor addition to the rite; but it is this new-minted tradition that Shakespeare highlights in *Macbeth*, where the medal bestowed on sufferers figures, according to an essay by Stephen Deng, the desacralisation and circulation of charisma from the mystical 'golden blood' [*Macbeth*, 2.3.109] of the monarch into the 'golden stamp' of monetary metal. Like the play's calculating Malcolm, by this account, James ended up performing the noxious business so convincingly precisely *because it was only an act*:

When he took the throne he knew that he needed to continue distributing angels in the ceremony of 'touching', despite his belief that 'the age of miracles is past', because he recognised an intimate connection between the gold coin and the health of the state. He could eschew concerns about idolatry because the healing coin connected more strongly to the *symbolic* economy of the state – riding on top of a magical or religious ceremony – than to the *mystical* prerogative of kingship. James discovered a potent form of charisma in the healing ceremony *despite his disbelief*. . . . If [he] did not believe that the ceremony actually cured individual patients, he at least believed that it contributed to the political strength of the state.[27]

'The Wisest Fool in Christendom' played the touching game without believing a word of it, but with the same make-believe as the King and lords accept the sentence in *Love's Labour's Lost*: 'A twelvemonth? Well, befall what befall,/I'll jest a twelvemonth in an hospital' [5,2,847]. This was not quite the politic performance based on an equal disbelief in *all* religions that Chloe Preedy has analysed in Marlowe's plays.[28] But like the real King from Navarre, the pawky Scot suspended his Calvinist faith to perform an act in which he did not believe, to pacify those who did, and thereby set them a play-acting example in *tolerating the intolerable*. So Bloch concludes that Shakespeare was a shrewd 'interpreter of the popular mind', because the faith of those who supported the monarchy was powerful enough to overrule the disbelief of the monarch himself.[29] Such suspension of disbelief, or give-and-take of opposing faiths, qualifies Stephen Greenblatt's suspicion that the theatricality of Shakespearean rulers, such as Hal, reveals how absolutism is built upon a Machiavellian 'hypocrisy so deep the hypocrites themselves believe it'.[30] But it also complicates the fashionable alternative, that, as Carl Schmitt wrote, all concepts of the state have been mere 'secularized theological concepts', ever since 'the absolute Prince stepped into the shoes of the Roman Pontiff'.[31]

The deliberate tomfoolery with which the Bourbon and Stuart successor sovereigns performed their sacerdotal roles as royal magicians in their newly united kingdoms throws doubt on Debora Shuger's claim in *Political Theologies in Shakespeare's England* that 'the haunting scenes when crowds of sick persons thronged to the defeated, dethroned Charles I to be healed by his touch' are evidence that throughout seventeenth-century Europe the mystique of sacred kingship 'seemed to need neither explanation nor defence'.[32] In fact we know that Henri, for one, agonised over betraying his Calvinist faith, and had to be persuaded by his Huguenot advisers, such as Sully, who urged him 'to let himself be converted for the sake of France'.[33] So, what we appear to witness in the *performance* of sacred monarchy by these sceptical monarchs is perhaps the kind of ritual that Peter Sloterdijk describes in his book *Globes* as the 'retroactive juridication of history', and that Jacques Derrida considered in *On Cosmopolitanism and Forgiveness*: the process by which newly installed regimes negotiate the embarrassment of their criminal origins, and the undeniable fact that 'All Nation-States are born and found themselves in violence'.[34] The deconstructionist philosopher was thinking of the South African Truth and Reconciliation Commission, as well as the apologies for American slavery or Vichy anti-Semitism. But in all such 'scenes of repentance, confession, forgiveness, or apology', he observed, 'hierarchies, sovereigns, and heads of state ask for "forgiveness"' on the ground that a clean break has supposedly now taken place, and 'This transformation structures the theatrical space in which the grand scene of repentance is played, sincerely or not':[35]

> The proliferation of scenes of repentance . . . signifies, no doubt, a *universal urgency* of memory. . . . [But] there are situations where it is necessary, if not to let the memory fade . . . at least to act as if, on the public scene, it was renounced. . . . The foundational violence is not only forgotten. The foundation is made *in order to* hide it; by its very essence it tends to organise amnesia under the celebration and sublimation of the grand beginnings.[36]

'There is always strategic calculation in the generous gesture of amnesty or reconciliation', cautions Derrrida.[37] Sure enough: 'Hyppolita, I wooed thee with my sword,/And won thy love doing thee injuries', admits Shakespeare's Theseus, 'But I will wed thee in another key –/With pomp, with triumph and with revelling'. So, from the Duke's command to 'Stir up the Athenian youth to merriments' [*Dream*, 1,1,16–19], to trumpet his annexation of Amazonia, and marriage to its queen, to the masque Prospero commissions for the betrothal of Ferdinand to Miranda that will unify Naples with Milan, this theatre keeps 'organising amnesia' for the 'grand beginnings' of newly amalgamated states. In *Nomos of the Earth* Carl Schmitt connects this work of compulsory forgetting to the *fait accompli* of plural monarchies, when 'Princely houses like the Hapsburg and the Bourbon aggregated various crowns under one power'. The maxim for the territorialising of religion then became *cujus regio, ejus religio*, 'whose is the territory, his is the religion', a doctrine that froze each piece of the German jigsaw into creedal uniformity after the Thirty Years War.[38] First set down in 1612, the formula was true to the state system Shakespeare auspicated with *The Winter's Tale* and other tragicomedies performed for the wedding of James's daughter Elizabeth and the Calvinist Frederick of the Palatinate, in which the 'great difference betwixt our Bohemia and your Sicilia' [1,1,3] was waved aside, in favour of the Protestant union James mistook for a first step to perpetual peace.[39] The real Bohemia would soon show Frederick the limits of the princely right to decide a state religion. But Shakespeare was already evolving an enlightened critique of this top-down religious uniformity: 'It is an heretic that makes the fire', Paulina lectures the tyrant Leontes, 'Not she which burns in it' [2,3,115–16].

The last executions for heresy in England took place just prior to the first performance of *The Winter's Tale*, in 1612, when two antitrinitarians were burned in London. So Shakespeare knew as well as Ernst Renan or Benedict Anderson why 'imagined communities' are constructed from memory.[40] What is notable, in fact, is how fraught the act of forgetting is on this stage, from the instant in *Love's Labour's Lost* when the death of the King of France appears to remind the lovers that the last time the real Navarre entered Paris was for his wedding to a French princess, which sparked the Bartholomew's Day Massacre, when the nuptial was 'a catastrophe', as Armado recalls: 'On whose side?/The King's – no, on both' [4,1,73–4].[41] So it is not only that Catholic and Protestant 'households, both alike in dignity . . . break into new mutiny' in these plays, causing peacemakers to cry 'A plague on both your houses' [*Romeo*, Pro.,1; 3,1,101], but that uniformity is sabotaged by iconoclasts like Rome's tribunes, zealous to 'Let no images / Be hung with Caesar's trophies' [*Julius*, 1,1,67–8]. Thus, in *Hamlet* Denmark's defeat of Norway makes it resemble 'Neptune's empire' [1,1,106], the Protestant confederation ruled by James's brother-in-law Christian IV, but it is haunted by a ghost calling from a Catholic Purgatory for revenge; while with Edgar impersonating the Jesuit 'Poor Tom' [2,3,20], *King Lear* is so 'cagey' about a united Britain that it can be decoded it as 'an anti-unionist drama', prophesying 'the division of the kingdom' [1,1,3] into its constituent parts.[42] Negotiating confessional conflict in Shakespeare's new united kingdoms is so problematic, then, because the very project of uniformity is so inimical to the toleration of difference.

When a Catholic ultra told Henri IV what was Caesar's had been rendered to Caesar, the King quipped that it was not rendered (*rendu*) but sold (*vendu*).[43] The joke underlines how it is too simplistic to see toleration as 'always on the side of the strongest, the good face of the sovereign', based on the right to decide the exception.[44] When, for instance, Theseus breaks the Athenian law on marriage, informing Egeus that 'I will overbear your will' [*Dream*, 4,1,150; 176], the variant texts disagree whether the bigoted father joins the feast. So, while Portia is astute to insist that 'The quality of mercy' is such that it 'becomes / The thronèd monarch better than his crown' [*Merchant*, 4,1,179–84], Isabella rebukes the judge that 'lawful mercy / Is nothing kin to foul redemption' [*Measure* 2,4,112]. Theseus is therefore careful to turn such 'melancholy forth to funerals', sensing 'The pale companion is not for our pomp' [*Dream*, 1,1,14]. But later plays are dogged by dissidents who bite the ruler's hand: malcontents like Don John, who would 'rather be a canker in a hedge than a rose in his grace' [*Much Ado*, 1,3,21]; conscientious objectors like the soldier Williams, who will not take the King's shilling [*Henry V*, 4,8,62]; separatists like Jacques, who are 'for other than dancing measures' [*As You*, 5,4,182]; or nihilists like Iago, whose motive is so blank he will never 'speak word' [*Othello*, 5,2,310]. In *Secret Shakespeare* I argued that, in an age of oaths, these plays all begin from this great refusal to 'heave my heart into my mouth', as Cordelia demurs [*Lear*, 1,1,90–1]; or to 'perform a part', as Coriolanus sneers, that 'never I will discharge' [*Coriolanus*, 3,2,105–9].[45] But Caesar surely speaks for the dramatist when he warns that 'such men are dangerous' because they 'love no plays' [*Julius*, 1,2,204–11]. A playwright cannot remain neutral when some anti-theatrical Malvolio threatens to 'be revenged on the whole pack', since it his own actors and audience who must 'entreat him to a peace':

When that is known, and golden time convents,
A solemn combination shall be made
Of our dear souls.

[*Twelfth*, 5,1,365–71]

A 'golden time', when 'a kind of Puritan' is entreated to a peace in which 'convents' are restored: this 'solemn combination' will take some negotiation. True, it is reported of Malvolio that 'The devil a Puritan he is, or anything constantly but a time-pleaser'; and the title *Twelfth Night* does promise New Year resolutions. But the prospects for a change of heart do not look good when Sir Andrew avers that if the steward were a Puritan, 'I'd beat him like a dog'. Asked the reason for this antipathy, the knight pronounces, 'I have reason good enough' [2,3,125–30]; and that determination speaks of the dramatist's sense of the non-negotiability of intolerance, like Shylock's aversion: 'As there is no firm reason/Why he cannot abide a gaping pig. . . . Why he a woollen bagpipe. . . . So I can give no reason, nor I will not,/More than a lodged hate and a certain loathing/I bear Antonio' [*Merchant*, 4,1,52–60]. Renaissance Venice was a model of religious coexistence; but in Shakespeare's city, the Jew insists, 'I will not eat with you, drink with you, nor pray with you' [1,3,31]. By contrast, in the fictive Bohemia a Puritan 'sings psalms to hornpipes' [*Winter's*, 4,3,41]; and the running gags about 'the man that hath no music' [*Merchant*, 5,1,82] key this festive world to the religious relaxation of carnival, which in England was a charade of hospitality, unlike the antagonistic *charivari*, shaped by the *agôn* of the New Year mumming ceremony of welcoming the stranger into the house.[46] So, if Henri's IV chicanery did set the scene for the Shakespearean conversion by which Hal is 'reformed', nothing better demonstrates that politic ruse of tolerating the intolerant than what is surely the finest example of the perversity of English humour: the transformation of the saintly idol of the Protestants, the martyr Sir John Oldcastle, into 'my old lad of the castle' [*1 Henry IV*, 1,2,37], Jack Falstaff, the most hypocritical of Puritans but loveable of rogues:

> Well, Hal . . . I am as melancholy as ... the drone of a Lincolnshire bagpipe . . .
> O, thou hast damnable iteration, and art indeed able
> to corrupt a saint. Thou hast done much harm upon me, Hal.
> God forgive thee for it. Before I knew thee, Hal, I knew noth-
> ing; and now I am, if a man should speak truly, little better
> than one of the wicked. I must give over this life, and I will
> give it over. By the Lord, an I do not, I am a villain.
>
> [*1 Henry IV*, 1,2,60–5]

Falstaff's conversion from Lollard martyr to laughing cavalier constitutes Shakespeare's most benign intervention in the politics of persecution and model for a negotiated religious peace. Gary Taylor and others have deduced that the writer was himself probably a 'church papist', or intermittent conformist to the Anglican Church, that 'he might have become a recusant' while commuting between London and Stratford, but that, like most Catholics, 'he had no appetite for martyrdom'.[47] If his heart did lie with the Old Religion, however, that makes it the more telling that, with a favourite pun, he should convert *gravity* to *gravy*, and the godly *grace* of the Lollard burned at Tyburn into the accommodating *grease* of the Fat Knight [*1 Henry IV*, 1,2,149]. Falstaff lives in dread of 'hell-fire' and Foxe's *Book of Martyrs*, with its engravings of 'burning, burning' [3,3,28], and can 'smell a fox' when the Justice calls him 'a candle, the better part burnt out' [1,2,142]. This carnival humour never lets us forget the ghastly body politics of martyrdom. But it serves an anodyne purpose in sublimating the Marian stake and Elizabethan scaffold into a safe symbolic sacrifice, a mimetic trivialisation that achieves catharsis when Falstaff is disguised as a witch, then purified 'With trial-fire' [*Wives*, 5,5,81] in a mock execution, and in Shakespeare's most localised play, the only one besides *Love's Labour's Lost* set in his own time, the horrors of Europe's *auto-da-fé* are harmlessly mimicked by Windsor's merry wives:

> Pinch him, and burn him, and turn him about,
> Till candles, and starlight and moonshine be out.
>
> [*Wives*, 5,5,98–9]

If *The Merry Wives of Windsor* closes with Shakespeare's most genial domestication of the flames of sectarian conflict, as the citizens of the Berkshire town wend home to 'laugh this sport over by a country fire, Sir John and all' [219], it opens with his most personal references to religious violence, as Falstaff vents animus against Sir Thomas Lucy, the Puritan persecutor of Midland Catholics, including the writer's Arden kin. Here sneers at 'lousy' Lucy and Oldcastle's powerful Brooke descendants, with Falstaff's unrepentant poaching of Justice Shallow's deer, are unusually raw allusions, and suggest the author's famous poaching exploit, at which they hint, was a sectarian riot, after Lucy had been instrumental in the execution of Edward Arden and his son-in-law for a plot to kill the Queen. Fifteen years on, Shakespeare's skimmington or *charivari* is turned into a hospitable feast, with 'hot venison pasty to dinner', and invitations to 'drink down all unkindness' [1,1,163–4]; but not before Europe's Wars of Religion have threatened to spread to Windsor Park. They do so in the person of the Frenchman Doctor Caius, whose paranoia and hostility to 'toys' of entertainment [1,4,38] mark him as a Huguenot refugee, presumably from Paris. The Massacre at Paris haunts the play, then, in more than one sense, when Caius, named after the Puritan Cambridge college, challenges the Welsh parson, Sir Hugh Evans, to a duel and, to steel himself, the clergyman sings the most celebrated verses of Marlowe, the poet lured to his death on some spying mission beside the Thames: '"To shallow rivers to whose falls – " God prosper the right! What weapons is he?' [*Wives*, 3,1,25–6].

Marlowe spooks Shakespeare's English comedy as the most unaccountable literary victim of Europe's sectarian wars, having been due to sail from Deptford on secret service for James in Scotland, where, 'when I last saw him', Thomas Kyd told the Privy Council, 'he meant to be'.[48] 'When a man's verses cannot be understood', or his code broken, Shakespeare mused, 'It strikes a man more dead than a great reckoning in a little room' [*As You*, 3,3,9]. But the surviving writer kept imagining spectral assignations, as if answering 'The Passionate Shepherd' in the verse that Evans sings, to reassure the 'dead shepherd' how 'now I find thy saw of might' [3,5,82]. Thus the dead poet stalks *Julius Caesar* when, 'for his bad verses', Cinna is murdered by the mob [3,3,30]: a rerun of the staging in *Massacre at Paris* of the killing of the Huguenot rhetorician Ramus, stabbed in his Sorbonne study by Catholic Leaguers as he frets over his text, 'To contradict which', jeers Guise, 'I say Ramus shall die'.

His biographer Charles Nicholl has recounted how Marlowe had visited Paris as 'Mr Merlin', an English courier for Navarre, so knew all about the city's 'thirty thousand sturdy student Catholics'. He may even have been personally present when one of them stabbed Henri III, and the Scots Guards proclaimed Henri IV 'our King and master!', since it was for doubling as an agent of the King of Scots that he was eliminated, Nicholl concludes.[49]

In *The Massacre at Paris* Marlowe appears to give himself a Mercurial cameo role in high politics as the 'Agent of England' whom the dying Henri III commands to tell Elizabeth 'Henry dies her faithful friend'.[50] So, if Nicholl is right, then it is the spectre of 'Mr Merlin' that rises from the buried subtext of his own play to cloud the happy end of *Love's Labour's Lost*, when the macabre Mercadé announces the death of the King of France. The words of this Mercury are indeed harsh after the songs of Apollo; and Marlowe's intrusive ghost may beckon hermetically to Shakespeare because at the time of his death the spy was reportedly 'persuading men of quality' to go with him over the water.[51] We cannot know how close he came to following this shadowy Hermes into the Underworld; but if *Love's Labour's Lost* reads like Apollo's answer to Mercury's *Massacre*, with the same cast converted from religious maniacs to would-be merry-makers, then *The Merry Wives of Windsor* is truly Shakespeare's exorcism:

> There will we make our peds of roses
> And a thousand fragrant posies.
> Mercy on me! I have a great dispositions to cry.
>
> [*Wives*, 3,1,17–19]

Under Windsor walls, Sir Hugh will be spared the fate of his literary hero, which is just as well if, as editors think, he is based on Shakespeare's Welsh Latin master Thomas Jenkins, who had studied at St John's, Oxford, with the Jesuit martyr Edmund Campion, and would be followed in his Stratford post by Simon Hunt, who also became a Jesuit, and then by John Cottam, whose brother, another priest, was hanged beside 'the old hermit of Prague' [*Twelfth*, 4,2,11], when Campion returned from Bohemia. With friends like these, it is no surprise Caius screams that he will 'kill de jack-priest', when he finds Sir Hugh's errand-boy hiding in his house. For, as the Massacre survivor reasonably demands: 'What shall de honest man do in my closet?' [*Wives*, 1,4,64; 102]. Windsor is in fact riddled with priest-holes, like the chimney up which Ford fires his guns hunting for Falstaff, being certain that 'There's a knot, a gang, a pack, a conspiracy against me' [4,244; 102]. So, with the Huguenot vowing 'the herring is no dead so I vill kill him' [2,3,10] and the popish priest itching to 'knog his urinals' [3,1,10], it is an act of true hospitality when the Host of the Garter Inn tramps Caius 'about the fields', when Evans sends for him 'old Windsor way and every way' [2,3,74; 3,1,5]. Puck led the boys a similar dance in the Athenian wood. But this Windsor feud is far more dangerous, since the French Doctor has imported 'your passes and staccados' [2,2,196], together with a rapier, from his homeland, where, as Stuart Carroll recounts in *Blood and Violence in Early Modern France*, the duelling frenzy spread at the time 'like an uncontrolled brush fire'.[52] Yet when 'Evans and Caius draw and offer to fight', according to the stage direction in the 1602 Quarto, the citizens step between the two, while by knocking heads together the Host executes Shakespeare's most deft annulment of sectarian hate:

Peace, I say, Gallia and Gaul, French and Welsh, soul-curer and body-curer. . . .
Peace, I say. Hear mine Host of the Garter. Am I politic? Am I subtle?
Am I a Machiavel? Shall I lose my doctor? No, he gives me the potions
and the motions. Shall I lose my parson, my priest, my Sir Hugh? No, he
give me the Proverbs and the No-verbs. Give me thy hand terrestrial –
so. Give me thy hand celestial – so. Boys of art, I have deceived you
both, I have directed you to wrong places. Your hearts are mighty, your
skins are whole, and let burnt sack be the issue. Come, lay their swords
to pawn. Follow me lads of peace, follow, follow, follow.

[3,2,81–94]

Antagonism turns to agonism in the Host's peace-making, which rehearses the climax of Henry VIII, where the King bullies the Catholic Archbishop Gardiner into tolerating the intolerant by embracing the Protestant Cranmer 'with a true heart / And brother-love' [5,3,204]. Such is the intransigence in his next comedy, As You Like It, that the god Hymen has to be enlisted to see that 'earthly things made even atone together' [5,4,98]. But Windsor's Host is a personification of such performativity, who, when the hoaxes are over, 'will to my honest knight Falstaff and drink canary with him' [3,3,73]. His politic strategy therefore makes this Machiavellian an English provincial Henri of Navarre, who schemes to marry Master Fenton to Anne Page because 'He dances, he capers, he has the eyes of youth; he writes verses, / he speaks holiday, he smells of April and May' [3,2,5–6]. Yet the ghost of Marlowe continues to menace his diplomacy, as Caius and Evans return the Host's good turn with a mean trick, pretending that 'three Doctor Faustuses' [4,5,56] from Germany have spirited away his horses. This horse-rustling 'Duke de Jamany' and his 'cozen Garmombles' [62–70] are said to mock a real Graf Mömpelgard; but they confirm how close its violent political unconscious comes to the surface of this fictional Windsor.

The citizens of Shakespeare's Windsor are far closer to Europe's Wars of Religion than they realise. In fact, there is a theory that the play was acted for Henri IV's investiture in the town as a Knight of the Garter; so it is tempting to imagine that, with the Host of the Garter as proxy, this relaxation of Huguenot history, 'with a posset for't at the latter end of a sea-coal fire' [1,4,6], reflects how the jovial monarch had pacified France.[53] It would thus be logical to infer that The Merry Wives of Windsor was the work listed by Francis Meres in September 1598 as Love's Labour's Won, and that this English comedy was the missing happy sequel to the French Love's Labour's Lost.[54] Then the context for its closing blessing – 'Heaven give you many, many merry days' [5,5,217] – would indeed be the Edict of Nantes, with which Henri had declared religious toleration in April of that year. But this drama has so many loose ends, and was revised so often, that it comes as no surprise that when, six years later, Shakespeare did bring a King of France on stage, to talk about his edicts, in *All's Well That Ends Well*, the unfinished project of tolerating the intolerant was still 'too long for a play':

> Not one word more of the consumèd time.
> Let's take the instant by the forward top,
> For we are old, and on our quick'st decrees
> Th'inaudible and noiseless foot of time
> Steals ere we can effect them.
>
>   [*All's Well*, 5,3,39–43]

All's Well That Ends Well was completed in time for the 1604 Somerset House conference that negotiated peace between Protestant England and Catholic Spain, at which Shakespeare and his fellows were paid to entertain the Constable of Castile. No play of his is more concerned with negotiating confessional difference, and its plot may even have been inspired by the Mountjoys, a firm of French milliners who were his landlords in London's Huguenot quarter of Cripplegate.[55] If this comedy was devised for the summit meeting, however, what is striking is how it turns the myth of sacred monarchy upside down, with a story about a doctor's daughter from Huguenot Languedoc who travels to Paris not to be touched, but to touch the King herself. In this version of the legend of the Fisher King, Shakespeare's King of France looks the image of the real one in his roving eye for 'those girls of Italy' [2,1,19], and his loyalty to his old friends from Narbonne. But he is ravaged by the kind of scrofulous fistula kings are supposed to cure. So, when Helena takes up the task of forcing 'the painèd impotent to smile', and administers her father's remedy for 'that malignant cause' with which his 'high majesty is touched' [2,1,109], it could not be clearer that this play's take on the touching rite, and on the entire mystery-mongering of sacerdotal kingship, is that the royal physician cannot heal anything by himself.[56]

'They say miracles are past', his lords exult when the King recovers to lead Helena 'a coranto' [2,3,1; 40]. But here miracles are not in the gift of the sovereign, who instead becomes one of a Shakespearean royal line, crowned by the senile Cymbeline, who will be forced by their subjects to declare that 'Pardon's the word to all' [*Cymbeline*, 5,6,423]. Without consent the King cannot make Bertram love Helena, any more than his real counterpart could coerce his Catholic subjects to embrace the Huguenots; for, as historians point out, the Edict of Nantes 'did not seem to Protestants to go far enough, while it drove many Catholics purple with rage'.[57] In its exhausted acceptance that 'The King's a beggar now the play is done' [Epi.,1], *All's Well That Ends Well* therefore marks its author's recognition that play-acting can only go so far, and that some things, such as religious toleration, are 'too long for a play'. Sheer 'tediousness and weariness' would instead eventuate in a 'tolerable reconciliation', rather than a 'consecrated union' between irreconcilables, wrote Sir Edward Sandys in his 1605 *State of Religion*, 'the first call for coexistence in Reformation Europe'.[58] And with its minimal morality – that 'There's place and means for every man alive' [4,3,316] – Shakespeare's almost exactly contemporary autumnal comedy seems wearily to concur:

Young Chairbonne the puritan and old Poisson the papist, howsome'er
their hearts are severed by religion, their heads are both one: they may jowl
horns together like any deer i' th' herd.

[1,3,45–7]

'When all Paris was prepared for joy, and pleased with its security, by the hand
of a dog this great, potent, and magnanimous Prince was murdered', Robert Cecil
informed the House of Commons after Henri was assassinated by the Jesuit-reject
Ravaillac on 3 May 1610, and he praised 'A King whom Catholics love and
Protestants admire for their freedom and liberty'.[59] In fact, as Roland Mousnier
objects in his study of the assassination, it had all been an act, since by 1610 a
Catholic like Ravaillac might 'be forgiven for supposing not one single promise had
been kept' by 'this false convert, a wolf in sheep's clothing'.[60] Shakespeare would
have been writing *The Tempest* at the time, where the irruption into the masque
of 'that foul conspiracy/Of the beast Caliban and his confederates' against his life
prompts Prospero's awareness that 'Our revels now are ended' [4,1,139–47]. So
perhaps it was the shocking news from France that provoked this greatest meditation on the performativity of peace and concord, as it seems the playwright had
always associated Henri with awareness that 'The King's a beggar'. *The Tempest*
would thus close not with the scenic illusion of absolute power, but with the sovereign's abjuration of this 'rough magic' [5,1,50], as he dissolves his claim to the
supremacy of his faith over that of others in empathetic acknowledgement of being
'One of their kind, that relish all as sharply/Passion as they' [23]. Ghosted by such
theological discourse, Shakespeare's last unaided drama has been a supreme work
of recollection of the 'dark backward and abyss' [1,2,50] of Europe's Christian past,
the ultimate conservation 'project' to gather history 'to a head' [5,1,1]. But now
its Epilogue ends in the total deconstruction of such metaphysical foundations,
with the silent translation of the departing *prayers* offered by Catholics for souls in
Purgatory into the '*praise* in departing' [3,3,38] that a believing audience grants 'our
actors' by applauding, with a similar combination of hands, as they vanish into 'thin
air' [4,1,148]:

> Now I want
> Spirits to enforce, art to enchant;
> And my ending is despair
> Unless I be relieved by prayer,
> Which pierces so, that it assaults
> Mercy itself, and frees all faults.
> As you from crimes would pardoned be,
> Let your indulgence set me free.
>
> [*Tempest*, Epi.,13–20]

If Shakespeare does not *quite* prefigure Slavoj Žižek's thesis that the essence of
Christian belief is that 'God does not believe in himself', he rounds off his work
of mourning with a humble inscription of the power-laden Christian language of

prayer, penitence and pardon into the performance of a player's professional plea for 'Gentle breath' and 'help of your good hands', as a way of reciprocating a faith 'Which is most faint' [3; 10–11].[61] To put this attenuated ascetic gesture into perspective, we might note how such faint 'praise' anticipates the weak belief that philosophers Richard Rorty and Gianni Vattimo describe in their dialogue *The Future of Religion* as not so much the forgetting of faith as its anamnesis, in a 'practical appeal to love, to charity'. According to this most faint form of religious thinking, from the time of the Wars of Religion, when 'Christian universalism discovered the idea of tolerance' in the toleration of the intolerant, the revelation that 'the truth of Christianity is the dissolution of the concept of universal truth itself' has entailed the paradox that *secularisation* has become 'the constitutive trait of authentic religious experience'.[62]

In the epoch of globalisation that the 'world ethos' of the Globe helped to inaugurate, Christian Europe has 'had to face being told of its own particularity'.[63] So, crown askew, like one of the broken clowns of Giacometti, Shakespeare's magus kneels before us at the end of the play praying for our most minimal prayers. Such a *performance* of faith *after* faith is very far from Weber's notorious thesis about disenchantment as the vehicle of modernity, since it is premised on a notion of religion as *post-* rather than anti-Christian. As Maurice Gauchet affirms, this sideways movement out of religion is *itself* Christian, since 'If we have gone from being within religion to being outside it. . . . It has not left us, and perhaps never will'.[64] Significantly, therefore, Rorty and Vattimo find their model for this 'transition from power to charity' in our 'age of interpretation' in the Western literary canon, precisely because its endless performativity makes it 'a model without foundations'. Just as Western literature 'would not be thinkable without Shakespeare', these two Gadamerian philosophers conclude, so 'our culture would not make sense if we were to remove Christianity from it'. But the 'baseless fabric' and 'insubstantial pageant' [151–5] of this 'faint' Shakespearean model means that, 'after the end of metaphysics', the goal of philosophy is no longer contact 'with something existing independently from us, but rather *Bildung*, the unending formation of oneself' in 'an ever-new self-description', an 'existential self-creation that replaces the ideal of handed-down knowledge' with 'appropriate irony'.[65] With such a ludic Shakespearean performance of faith, therefore, it truly is 'religion to be thus forsworn' [*Love's*, 4,3,337].

'Now, at the latest minute of the hour,/Grant us your loves' [5,2,768–9]: with his appeal for charity in place of power, Shakespeare inaugurated 'the age of interpretation' he found personified in a jovial King of France. Thus, a labour of love displaced the work of mourning for a faith that had brought catastrophe to Christians, and such *playfulness* can make this seem like a premonition of the religion for a secularised world that would shortly be known as the aesthetic. As Hugh Grady writes, when the Wars or Religion stalled in stalemate, 'it began to appear that art, not any specific faith, would have to provide a cultural community. The stage was set for the Enlightenment definition of the aesthetic in a divided but relatively tolerant Europe'.[66] In *Shakespeare's Tribe* Jeffrey Knapp likewise infers that Shakespeare believed that players could bridge confessional divides by the mere act of bringing enemies face to face.[67] Yet Svetlana Alpers reflects that by focusing on the effort required to do this, in a painting such as *The Surrender of Breda*, Velázquez instead depicts the agony of Catholic and Protestant, victor and vanquished, as *suspended*, rather than effaced. 'Smoke billows out over the battlefield. Soldiers mill about. The two former opponents engage in a courteous exchange. It does not have the appearance of the Spanish triumph that it was', and there is an entire ethics in this suspension: 'As Velázquez equalizes he refuses to take sides. Equality is an attribute of the people he depicts, impartiality is a matter of his view of them'.[68] By the time the picture was finished in 1635 Breda had been recaptured; so it is no wonder the Spanish artist gave its surrender such a human touch. Just that kind of human comedy was how enemies characterised Henri's histrionic *performance* of the rites of healing.[69] But by highlighting confessional differences in his unfinished plays, and tolerating the intolerant, this *agôn* is perhaps what Shakespeare imagined when he wrote about the sculpture gallery Paulina has converted into a 'chapel' so that she can take 'some great *mater* there in hand' [*Winter's*, 5,2,94; 5,3,86]: that rather than forgetting in a work of art, 'It is required/You do *awake* your faith' [94].

NOTES

1. Perez Zagorin, *How the Idea of Religious Toleration Came to the West* (Princeton: Princeton University Press, 2003), p. 2.

2. For a Lacanian study of 'the English gazing in the French "mirror"' to see 'what is to be avoided at all costs', and the marriage of Catholic France and Protestant England as a projection of 'the universal object of desire: peace', see Richard Hillman, *Shakespeare, Marlowe and the Politics of France* (Basingstoke: Palgrave, 2002), p. 122 et passim.

3. 'We have not only read about': Michel de Montaigne, 'On the cannibals', in *The Complete Essays of Montaigne*, trans. M. A. Screech (Harmondsworth: Penguin, 1991), p. 236; 'the tripe of Huguenots': Natalie Zemon Davis, *Society and Culture in Early Modern France* (Stanford: Stanford University Press, 1975), p. 324; setting women alight: Maximilien Béthune, duc de Sully, *Oeconomies Royales* (Paris: 1638), vol. 1, p. 35, quoted in Desmond Seward, *The First Bourbon: Henry IV of France and Navarre* (London: Constable, 1971), pp. 51–2.

4. Roland Mousnier, *The Assassination of Henri IV: The Tyrannicide Problem and the Consolidation of the French Absolute Monarchy in the Early 17th Century*, trans. Joan Spencer (London: Faber and Faber, 1973), pp. 115–16.

5. David Bevington, *Tudor Drama and Politics* (Cambridge, MA: Harvard University Press, 1968), p. 16. For the argument that there is 'an unmistakable parallel between Shakespeare's King of Navarre, who sets up a scholarly academy and takes a vow that he subsequently breaks, and the actual King of Navarre', however, see in particular Camille Wells Slights, *Shakespeare's Comic Commonwealths* (Toronto: Toronto University Press, 1993), pp. 74–7 et passim; and Hugh Richmond, 'Shakespeare's Navarre', *Huntington Library Quarterly*, 42 (1977), 193–216.

6. Frances Yates, *A Study of 'Love's Labour's Lost'* (Cambridge: Cambridge University Press, 1936), p. 3.

7. Seward, *The First Bourbon*, p. 104.

8. See Hillman, *Shakespeare, Marlowe*, pp. 190–1.

9. Indira Ghose, *Shakespeare and Laughter* (Manchester: Manchester University Press, 2008), p. 42; Yates, *A Study of 'Love's Labour's Lost'*, p. 199. Yates interpreted Berowne's attacks on intellectual pride as a Catholic response to Sir Walter Raleigh's 'School of Atheism', which

was strongly influenced by Shakespeare's own reading of the poetry of the Jesuit martyr Robert Southwell: pp. 198–202.

10. Mark Holt, *The French Wars of Religion, 1562–1629* (Cambridge: Cambridge University Press, 1995), pp. 125, 144 and 151; 'acts of sedition': Mousnier, *The Assassination of Henri IV*, op. cit. (note 4), p. 150.

11. Joan Curbet Soler, 'The theological contexts of *Love's Labour's Lost*', in *Lectures de 'Love's Labour's Lost' de William Shakespeare*, ed. Delphine Lemmonier-Texier and Guillaume Winter (Rennes: Presses Universitaires de Rennes, 2014), pp. 32–5.

12. Drew Daniel, *The Melancholy Assemblage: Affect and Epistemology in the English Renaissance* (New York: Fordham University Press, 2013), p. 68.

13. Hillman, *Shakespeare, Marlowe*, pp. 188–90.

14. Michael Wolfe, *The Conversion of Henri IV: Politics, Power, and Religious Belief in Early Modern France* (Cambridge, MA: Harvard University Press, 1993), p. 188.

15. Tallement de Réaux, 'Historiettes', 'Henry Quatriesme', p. 19; quoted in Seward, *The First Bourbon*, p. 61.

16. Marc Bloch, *The Royal Touch: Sacred Monarchy and Scrofula in England and France*, trans. J. E. Anderson (London: Routledge and Kegan Paul, 1973), p. 195.

17. Ibid., pp. 193–4.

18. Mousnier, *The Assassination of Henri IV*, p. 113.

19. Susan Wheeler, '*Henry IV of France Touching for Scrofula* by Pierre Ferens', *Journal of the History of Medicine*, 58 (2003), 79–81, here 79.

20. Bloch, *The Royal Touch*, pp. 193, 202–3, 238 and 240.

21. Ibid., p. 191.

22. Ibid., p. 192.

23. Ibid.

24. Quoted by Sigmund Freud, *Totem and Taboo: Some Points of Agreement Between the Mental Lives of Savages and Neurotics*, trans. James Strachey (London: Routledge and Kegan Paul, 1950), p. 42.

25. Bloch, *The Royal Touch*, p. 188.

26. 'Resolved to give it a trial', quoted by Stephen Deng, 'Healing angels and "golden blood": money and mystical kingship in *Macbeth*', in Nick Maschovakis (ed.), *'Macbeth': New Critical Essays* (London: Routlege, 2008), p. 167; Bloch, *The Royal Touch*, pp. 191–2; Keith Thomas, *Religion and the Decline of Magic: Studies in Popular Belief in Sixteenth- and Seventeenth-Century England* (Harmondsworth: Penguin, 1991), p. 197.

27. Deng, 'Healing angels', p. 177.

28. Chloe Preedy, *Marlowe's Literary Scepticism: Politic Religion and Post-Reformation* (London: Arden Shakespeare, 2014).

29. Bloch, *The Royal Touch*, p. 192.

30. Stephen Greenblatt, *Shakespearean Negotiations: The Circulation of Social Energy in Renaissance England* (Oxford: Clarendon Press, 1988), p. 55.

31. Carl Schmitt, *Political Theology: Four Chapters on the Concept of the Sovereignty*, trans. George Schwab (Chicago: University of Chicago Press, 2005), p. 36; 'stepped into the shoes': Ernst Kantorowicz, 'Mysteries of state', *Ernst Kantorowicz: Selected Studies* (New York: J. J. Augustin, 1965), p. 387.

32. Debora Shuger, *Political Theologies in Shakespeare's England: The Sacred and the State in 'Measure for Measure'* (Basingstoke: Palgrave, 2001), p. 57.

33. Sully, *Oeconomies Royales* (Paris: 1638), vol. 1, p. 176, quoted in Seward, *The First Bourbon*, pp. 96–7.

34. Peter Sloterdijk, *Globes. Spheres II: Macrospherology*, trans. Wieland Hoban (Pasadena: Semiotexte, 2014), p. 904; Jacques Derrida, *On Cosmopolitanism and Forgiveness*, trans. Mark Dooley and Michael Hughes (London: Routledge, 2007), p. 57.

35. Derrida, *On Cosmopolitanism*, pp. 28–9.
36. Ibid., pp. 29 and 56–7.
37. Ibid., p. 40.
38. Carl Schmitt, *Nomos of the Earth in the International Law of the 'Jus Publicum Europaeum'*, trans. G. L. Ulmen (New York: Telos Press, 2006), pp. 128–9.
39. See Frances Yates, *Shakespeare's Last Plays: A New Approach* (London: Routledge and Kegan Paul, 1975).
40. Ernst Renan, 'What is a nation?' Lecture at the Sorbonne, 11 March 1882, reprinted in Geoff Eley and Ronald Grigor Suny (eds), *Becoming National: A Reader* (Oxford: Oxford University Press, 1996), pp. 41–55; Benedict Anderson, *Imagined Communities* (London: Verso, 1983).
41. See Robert White, 'The cultural impact of the massacre of St Bartholomew's Day', in Jennifer Richards (ed.), *Early Modern Civil Discourses* (Basingstoke: Palgrave, 2003), p. 192; and Richard Wilson, '"Worthies away": the scene begins to cloud in Shakespeare's Navarre', in Jean-Christophe Mayer (ed.), *Representing France and the French in Early Modern English Drama* (Newark: Delaware University Press, 2008), pp. 93–109.
42. Philip Schwyzer, 'The Jacobean Union controversy and *King Lear*', in *The Accession of King James* (Basingstoke: Palgrave, 2006), p. 39.
43. Seward, *The First Bourbon*, p. 104.
44. 'The strongest': Jacques Derrida, 'Autoimmunity: real and symbolic suicides – a dialogue with Jacques Derrida', in Giovanna Barradori (ed.), *Philosophy in a Time of Terror: Dialogues with Jürgen Habermas and Jacques Derrida* (Chicago: University of Chicago Press, 2003), p. 127; J. W. Allen, *English Political Thought, 1603–1660* (London: Methuen, 1938), p. 12.
45. Richard Wilson, *Secret Shakespeare*.
46. See Richard Wilson, 'Making men of monsters: Shakespeare in the company of strangers', in *Shakespeare and French Theory: King of Shadows* (London: Routledge, 2007), pp. 242–60, esp. pp. 247–8; and Meg Twycross and Susan Carpenter, *Masks and Masking in Medieval and Early Tudor England* (Aldershot: Ashgate, 2002), pp. 78–100.
47. Gary Taylor, 'Forms of opposition: Shakespeare and Middleton', *English Literary Renaissance*, 24 (1994), 298.
48. Thomas Kyd quoted in David Riggs, *The World of Christopher Marlowe* (London: Faber and Faber, 2004), p. 139.
49. Charles Nicholl, *The Reckoning: The Murder of Christopher Marlowe* (London: Jonathan Cape, 1992), pp. 170–1 and 260–2.
50. Christopher Marlowe, *Massacre at Paris*, scene 9, 35–6, in *Christopher Marlowe: The Complete Plays*, ed. Frank Romany and Robert Lindsey (London: Penguin, 2003), p. 527; 'our King and master': Seward, *The First Bourbon*, p. 71.
51. Nicholl, *The Reckoning*, p. 260.
52. Stuart Carroll, *Blood and Violence in Early Modern France* (Oxford: Oxford University Press, 2006), p. 153. See also Richard Wilson, 'As bloody as the hunter: Shakespeare and the French duel', in *Shakespeare and French Theory*, pp. 202–25.
53. See William Green, *Shakespeare's 'The Merry Wives of Windsor'* (Princeton: Princeton University Press, 1962), pp. 36–7 and 168–9.
54. See J. M. Nosworthy, *Shakespeare's Occasional Plays: Their Origin and Transmission* (London: Edward Arnold, 1965), p. 88.
55. Charles Nicholl, *The Lodger: Shakespeare on Silver Street* (London: Allen Lane, 2007), pp. 28–34 and 263–70.
56. See Julia Reinhard Lupton, *Thinking with Shakespeare: Essays on Politics and Life* (Chicago: Chicago University Press, 2011), p. 112: 'High and low come into mysterious contact. The Royal Touch of magical kingship brushing against the feminine hands of a lay healer. . . .

Afflicted at least associatively with the very ailment his office is purported to cure, the royal physician cannot heal himself, and must open his sores to the ministrations of Helena'.

57. Mousnier, *The Assassination of Henri IV*, p. 148.

58. Sir Edward Sandys, *Europae Speculum, or a Relation of the State of Religion* (5th edn, London: 1632), p. 196, quoted in Theodor Rabb, *Jacobean Gentleman: Sir Edward Sandys, 1561–1629* (Princeton: Princeton University Press, 1998), pp. 33–4 and 36.

59. Quoted in G. B. Harrison, *A Second Jacobean Journal: Being a Record of Those Things Most Talked of During the Years 1607 to 1610* (London: Routledge and Kegan Paul, 1958), p. 194.

60. Mousnier, *The Assassination of Henri IV*, pp. 116 and 138.

61. Slavoj Žižek, *The Monstrosity of Christ: Paradox or Dialectic?*, ed. Creston Davis (Cambridge: MIT Press, 2009), pp. 48–9.

62. Richard Rorty and Gianni Vattimo, *The Future of Religion* (New York: Columbia University Press, 2005), pp. 14–15, 35 and 50–1.

63. Sloterdijk, *Globes. Spheres II*, p. 946.

64. Maurice Gauchet, *The Disenchantment of the World: A Political History of Religion*, trans. Oscar Burge (Princeton: Princeton University Press, 1997), p. 59.

65. Ibid., pp. 3–4, 53 and 60–1.

66. Hugh Grady, *Shakespeare and Impure Aesthetics* (Cambridge: Cambridge University Press, 2009), p. 21.

67. Jeffrey Knapp, *Shakespeare's Tribe: Church, Nation, and Theater in Renaissance England* (Chicago: University of Chicago Press, 2002), pp. 53–4.

68. Svetlana Alpers, *The Vexations of Art: Velázquez and Others* (New Haven: Yale University Press, 2005), p. 122. Cf. Joseph-Emile Muller, *Velázquez*, trans. Jane Brenton (London: Thames and Hudson, 1976), pp. 126–8: 'A victor can rarely have been depicted with such a total absence of arrogance. And the men assembled behind him have not a hint of triumph or scorn in their expressions. . . . The traces of the sky, the ravaged countryside, appear almost as a reminder of the past, and the calm sky has already forgotten all that has occurred'.

69. David Buisserat, *Henry IV* (London: George Allen and Unwin, 1984), p. 54.

3 Shakespeare in Hate: Performing the Virgin Queen

'He was not of an age, but for all time!': Ben Jonson's homage 'To the memory of my beloved, the Author, Mr William Shakespeare', has been so success-ful in creating the myth of the Bard as a timeless universal genius that we forget how Shakespeare's silence on his times must have offended contemporaries, and how much it might have been resented. The modern aesthetic that values art to the extent it subordinates its circumstances and defies its own time, originating without commission, was so alien to Renaissance culture, however, that we may suspect Jonson of special pleading when he insisted Shakespeare's work was never dictated by the headlines of 'the years'.[1] And this suspicion is confirmed by the fact that in the one year of his life when he might have been expected to comment on events it was precisely Shakespeare's silence that provoked hostile complaints. For in 1603, when, according to Thomas Dekker's eulogistic almanac of the 'wonder-ful year', the grieving poets of England 'rained showers of tears' over the body of Elizabeth,[2] Shakespeare's refusal to mourn became offensive as a result of the 'surge of royalist feeling which accompanied the queen's death'. Thus, within a month of her passing, the anonymous author of 'A mournful ditty entitled England's loss' was challenging 'You poets all, brave Shakespeare, Jonson, Greene,' to 'Bestow your time to write for England's Queen'.[3] The fact that Robert Greene had, in fact, himself died cursing Shakespeare as an 'upstart' Jesuitical 'crow' ten years before, made the call on the dead poet sound less like ignorance of his passing than a ghoulish rhyme, as someone pointed out, to shame two crypto-Catholic slackers by conjuring 'help of spirits in their sleeping graves,/As he that called to Shakespeare, Jonson, Greene,/To write of their dead noble Queen'.[4] So, the Protestant hack Henry Chettle must have known what he was doing when he sneered that Shakespeare's 'honied' smoothness was the reason why the pert 'Melicert', as he dubbed him, was so conspicuous by his absence, in the spring of 1603, from those writers grieving for their dead Queen:

Nor doth the silver-tongued Melicert
Drop from his honied muse one sable tear

To mourn her death that graced his desert,
And to his lays opened her royal ear.[5]

'He was not of an age': yet Shakespeare's obliviousness to contemporary affairs, his critics complained, was a deliberate antagonistic snub to a ruler who had 'graced his desert' and 'opened her royal ear' to patronise his career. As Michael Dobson and Nicola Watson recount in their hilarious history of this fantasy, the popular legend of Shakespeare as a protégé of Elizabeth (incarnated when Dame Judi Dench sweeps on stage in *Shakespeare in Love*) would reach its 'illogical end-point' in the delirious theory that 'Shakespeare' was, in fact, her pseudonym, and that the portrait in the Folio was a disguised likeness of the theatre-loving Queen.[6] Although Elizabeth was only ever once glimpsed 'at the play' (at the Blackfriars playhouse in 1601, for a Christmas performance by Paul's Boys) and Park Honan pointed out in his biography that the Queen gave no sign whatever that she cared for either the man or his works,[7] the myth of the monarch as a devoted fan, or even performer, of Shakespeare is one to which Jonson contributed, when he pictured the 'Sweet Swan of Avon' swooping to make 'those flights upon the banks of Thames,/That so did take Eliza'.[8] And this scenario of the stage-struck sovereign and supercilious scriptwriter is condensed in one of the most revealing of all anecdotes about the Bard, which actually has Gloriana making an importunate personal appearance on the boards.

The irresistible story of Gloriana's Globe benefit appearance was collected in his *Dramatic Table Talk* of 1825 by the bookseller and playwright Richard Ryan, and it tells how 'Queen Elizabeth was a great admirer of the immortal Shakespeare, and used frequently (as was the custom of persons of great rank in those days) to appear upon the stage before the audience, or to sit behind the scenes, when the plays of our Bard were performed'. F. E. Halliday, who pasted it into his *Shakespeare Companion*, mused that 'it would be pleasant to believe' the picturesque anecdote; though Samuel Schoenbaum dryly ironised that 'this heart-warming romantic encounter . . . is plausible enough' – aside from the 'trifling circumstances' that Shakespeare's 'stage afforded no scenery for eavesdroppers to conceal themselves', that 'the Queen did not expose herself to the multitude' and that she 'restrained from flirting publicly (or in private) with subjects of inferior station'.[9] Nonetheless, the theatre legend Ryan relayed in 1796, of the real monarch upstaged by the 'mimic monarch' of the boards, does encapsulate an essential truth about Shakespeare's usurpation from the old political order of an unprecedented new aesthetic sovereignty:

One evening, when Shakespeare himself was personating the part of a King, the audience knew of her Majesty being in the house. She crossed the stage when he was performing, and, on receiving the accustomed greeting from the audience, moved politely to the poet, but he did not notice it! When behind the scenes, she caught his eye, and moved again, but still he would not throw off his character, to notice her: this made her Majesty think of some means by which she might know whether he would depart, or not, from the dignity of his character while on the stage. Accordingly, as he was about to make his exit, she stepped before him, dropped her glove, and re-crossed the stage, which

Shakespeare noticing, took up, with these words, immediately after finishing his speech, and so aptly were they delivered, that they seemed to belong to it:

And though now bent on this high embassy
Yet stoop we to take up our Cousin's glove!

He then walked off the stage, and presented the glove to the Queen, who was greatly pleased with his behaviour, and complimented him upon the propriety of it.[10]

'Yet stoop we to take up our Cousin's glove': the tableau of the Queen of England dropping her glove, like the Marschallin in *Rosenkavalier*, to receive it back, when he finally deigns to acknowledge her, from a Shakespeare she allows to greet her as a cousin, clearly belongs to that genre of fables which register the birth of the modern cult of artistic genius, such as the polished anecdotes of Emperor Charles V kneeling in the studio of Titian to pick up the brush of the painter who works in a trance; Julius II and Michelangelo sitting together in a quarry to plan the Pope's tomb; or Cardinal Barberini holding a mirror up for Bernini as the boy-wonder models David on himself.[11] All these updatings of the legend of Apelles and Alexander, art historians observe, marked the moment of Mannerism, with its shift from royal command to the 'high embassy' of artistic self-sufficiency. Thus, the notion of Shakespeare belonging to a new type of performing monarchy impervious to political reality dates from tributes like that of John Davies in 1610, to 'good Will', who, if he had 'not played some kingly parts in sport', had been a fit 'companion for a King,/And been a King among the meaner sort'.[12] If Ryan's fantasy took such a hold despite its inherent implausibility, then, that was because the idea of a transfer of sovereignty between the poet and prince dated back to the seventeenth century, and the excitement of writers such as Dryden that the 'monarch-like' Shakespeare had usurped an older kind of sacred kingship: 'Shakespeare's pow'r is sacred as a King's'.[13]

Scholars infer from the salutes of his contemporaries that the dramatist himself acted the parts of monarchs such as Duncan, Henry IV and Henry VI; while another version of the romance of the surprise royal visit has him playing Oberon, the Fairy King, when Elizabeth – the 'Faerie Queen' herself – steps onto the stage and exclaims, 'Od's pittikins! Our Magnifico is cousin-german to all regal minds!'[14] For however unlikely the scenario, what these stories of the 'mimic monarch' who remains in character, in defiance of his real sovereign, but to the delight of his audience, all record is the symbolic revolution when theatre starts to arrogate the privilege of a calculated obliviousness towards its own contemporary context that critics mistake for a Kantian aesthetic. They suggest that rather than the cliché question about his relation to the Tudor monarchy, the truly historicist query about Shakespeare may concern his perverse *lack of relation to the Tudor state*. Thus, when the Queen was reported to have been 'so eager to see' Falstaff brought back to life in *The Merry Wives of Windsor* that (in the 1702 report of John Dennis) 'she commanded it to be finished in fourteen days, and was well pleas'd at the Representation', we could read this as a sign not of Shakespeare's readiness to salute the Order of the Garter, but of the desperation of the sovereign to get in on the act.[15] Unless prodded, Shakespeare did not recognise 'Good Queen Bess', we might infer, because he was only too happy to obey traditional interdictions against performing monarchy and to take the censors at their own word, by banishing any mention of contemporary politics from the stage. This would certainly accord with Carl Schmitt's theory that a Shakespearean drama like *Hamlet* draws its aesthetic force not from mirroring the real time of its own Elizabethan circumstances, but precisely by systematically representing that historical actuality as a taboo, a toxic or unspeakable scandal, and a secret never to be aired:

> The taboo can be explained precisely by the time and place of the origin and initial performance of Shakespeare's play, during the years 1600–1603 in London. This was the time in which all were expecting the death of the old Queen Elizabeth, these were the years of the utmost tension and uncertainty. . . . In her hand lay formidable political power. But she had no heirs and also delayed naming a successor. No one risked discussing this issue in public. One Englishman who had spoken of it had his hand cut off as punishment. The queen refused to hear the 'bells tolling' for her. But of course everyone talked about it in private. . . . These circumstances established the taboo of which we speak for the author of the tragedy *Hamlet*.[16]

For Schmitt, what we now read as Shakespeare's aesthetic power originated from his tactical elision of the power of his sovereign, which thus became the cathartic precipitate of his dramaturgy, the 'mute rock upon which the play' *as mere play* founders, sending 'genuine tragedy rushing to the surface'.[17] The poet's denegation of the Tudor and Stuart monarchy became, on this reckoning, a paradigm of theatre's dialectical relationship with its sovereign enemy. If this antagonistic theory holds, Shakespeare was therefore exploiting an inhibition inscribed into the very structure of the Elizabethan state. For within a year of her succession, in 1559 the Queen had decreed that no plays were permitted 'wherein matters of religion or the governance of the state . . . shall be handled or treated, being no mete matters to be written or treated upon . . . nor to be handled before any audience'.[18] And as her successor Charles I commented in 1625, this was taken to mean 'there was a commandment and restraint given against the representing of any modern Christian kings in those stage plays'.[19] The interdiction on the representation of any living monarch would be extended with the 1606 Act 'To Restrain Abuses of Players', to the mention 'in any stage play' of 'the holy name of God, or of Jesus Christ, or of the Holy Ghost, or of the Trinity'.[20] So it would seem to connect with those taboos on uttering the names of divinities, priests and kings, or imaging them, that have been collected by ethnologists. Thus, the 1563 proclamation forbidding any illustrator, except 'some special commission painter', to have any 'access to take the natural representation of Her Majesty', and prohibiting 'all manner of other persons to draw, paint, engrave, or portray Her Majesty's personage or visage', chimes suggestively with the repressions listed in *The Golden Bough* in support of Frazer's supposition that premodern societies 'believed portraits to contain the soul of the person portrayed'.[21]

Like the laws of other 'theatre states', such as Thailand and Korea, which as late as 1900 prohibited royal portraits from appearing on coins or stamps, since 'it would be an insult to the King to put his sacred face on objects that pass into the most vulgar hands and often roll on the ground in the dust or mud', the traitor's death inflicted in England for defacement of the Queen's head by counterfeiting is perhaps explained by what Frazer calls this 'civilised debt to the savage', and Jean Baudrillard 'the evil demon of images'.[22] As Martin Elsky recounts in *Authorizing Words*, his study of print culture, such anxieties inhibited the English language itself, which was conceived to be the personal property of the sovereign, as the Queen's English; or the King's, when distilled into the King James Bible.[23] Clearly, Mistress Quickly has cause to fear that should Caius blaspheme in royal Windsor, 'here will be an old abusing of the King's English' [*Wives*, 1,4,4], if to swear is to desecrate the Crown. The ancient Greeks sanctified their rulers by not only by refusing to pronounce their names, Frazer records, but by writing these on tablets that were then 'thrown into the deep waters' of the Aegean.[24] For language is haunted by the sacred, as Foucault explained, after Bataille, the void of death we must not name, yet 'from which we speak'.[25] Thus it is Freud who offers, in *Totem and Taboo*, the best insight into Shakespeare's acquiescence in the divinity that 'doth hedge a king' [*Hamlet*, 4,5,120], when he points to the fatal ambivalence of the 'royal touch', and the fact that disallowance of the monarch's likeness cuts both ways:

> The attitude of primitive peoples to their kings . . . is governed by two basic principles which seem to be complementary rather than contradictory. The ruler 'must not only be guarded, he must also be *guarded against*'. Both these ends are secured by taboo observances. We know why rulers must be guarded against. It is because they are the vehicles of a power which brings death and ruin to anyone who is not protected by a similar charge. Any contact with this dangerous entity is therefore avoided; and, if it cannot be avoided, some cer-emonial is devised to avert the dreaded consequences.[26]

When Elizabeth and her Stuart successors 'touched' to cure scrofula or 'king's evil', Freud theorised, whether or not they truly believed in what they were doing they were acting out the same rationale as the Nubas of East Africa who fear 'they die if they enter the house of the king', but that they can escape 'the penalty for the intrusion by baring their shoulder and getting the king to lay his hand on it'. The subjects' tuberculosis was a pretext, for what these monarchs were, in fact, absolv-ing was the crime of entering the royal presence, on the paradoxical principle that 'contact with the king is both remedy and protection against the dangers provoked by contact with the king'. Thus, the magic of the royal touch evaporated, Freud wryly notes, on the epoch-marking day when the English state no longer shrouded monarchy in inaccessibility, and as he laid on hands, the sceptical William of Orange whispered that he hoped his one and only 'patient' would be restored to sense as well as health.[27] According to the psychologist, court etiquette, like that which suffocated the Mikado of Japan, was devised more to insulate the subject from the sovereign than safeguard the latter, and what it expressed was intense hostility, in reality, towards the high and mighty parent: 'the ceremonial taboo of kings is *ostensibly* the highest honour, while *actually* it is the punishment for their exaltation'.[28] So, like the subjects of those Sultans chronicled by Frazer, who felt safe because their ruler 'never showed himself to his people, and only spoke to them from behind a curtain', Shakespeare's submission to the rule that the mystique of a 'crowned king' is kept 'fresh and new' by being stored 'like a robe pontifical –/Ne'er seen but wondered at' [*1 Henry IV*, 3,2,54–7] – by never mentioning the Queen by name – could be interpreted as his ironic playing along with what Freud diagnosed as the 'mass neurosis' of monarchy.[29] 'Our bending author', as he called himself, on one of the apologetic occasions, in the Epilogue of *Henry V* [Epi.,2], when he ate his own words – systematically cancelled his own topicality, and only ever referred to Elizabeth directly when he was exhausted, by his own account, and like some con-demned man on the scaffold, had literally nothing more to say:

> My tongue is weary; when my legs are too, I will bid you good
> night, and so kneel down before you – but, indeed, to pray for
> the Queen.
>
> [*2 Henry IV*, Epi.,28–30]

Like Edmund Campion praying for Elizabeth the instant before his grisly execution – or John Stubbs, in the episode that impressed Schmitt, raising 'his hat from his head with his left hand', after his right hand had been cut off, and crying, 'God save the Queen!' – at the end of his day this actor will not deny his sovereign her prayers.[30] When it suited him, Shakespeare was clearly not averse to putting power on display. But in an influential essay, 'Proud majesty a made subject', David Scott Kastan contends that by miming monarchy, and mixing kings with clowns, Shakespeare 'nourished the conditions that eventually permitted the nation to bring its king to trial'; and that by subjecting monarchs like Richard II to audience approval Shakespeare prepared for the time when, as Marvell wrote, the 'royal actor', Charles, 'The tragic scaffold might adorn:/While round the armed bands/Did clap their bloody hands'.[31] This was Ernst Kantorowicz's thesis in *The King's Two Bodies*; and Stephen Orgel concurs that 'making greatness familiar' by staging monarchy 'was potentially a revolutionary act – as Elizabeth was well aware'.[32] Such was the understanding the Queen herself expressed when she guessed, 'I am Richard II. Know ye not that?' and fumed that 'This tragedy was played forty times in open streets and houses', after the Essex rebels paid Shakespeare's troupe to act 'the killing of Richard II' the day before their *coup d'état*.[33] When the Earl had previously tried flattery, with an Accession Day masque saluting her as a goddess, Elizabeth declared that 'if she had thought there had been so much said of her' on stage, 'she would not have been there that night', and so stormed off to bed.[34]

From Privy Council orders against 'painting, engraving and printing of her Majesty's person and visage',[35] to the Queen's disgust that 'This is all against me', the one time when her marriage was debated in a play at court,[36] there is ample evidence for Kastan's thesis that 'Elizabeth understood it would not do to allow the Queen to be subject to the artist's vision; always it must be subject to the Queen's'.[37] Yet this was also a sovereign who exploited her 'privileged visibility', confident that 'We princes', as she told Parliament, 'are set on stages in the sight and view of all

the world'.[38] Although she sponsored only ninety court performances in the years
1590–1603, when Shakespeare was writing, compared with 300 James sponsored
between 1603 and 1616, Elizabeth was pleased to step from the throne to choose
a suitor for the May Queen of Sidney's *The Lady of May*, and receive the golden
apple George Peele awarded her in his *Arraignment of Paris*; for she grasped that
spectacular sovereignty 'depends on the effective control of the theatre space'.[39]
So, the question posed by the tale of the empress who had no fictive presence on
Shakespeare's stage is the one raised by his rivals: why, compared with those worshippers so eager, as Thomas Dekker enthused in *Old Fortunatus*, to 'travel to the
temple of Eliza'[40] by putting the Queen on show 'in various oblique and allegorical
guises',[41] did this player of monarchs act with such obliviousness towards his actual
sovereign, and maintain his theatrical decorum throughout her reign, as if she was a
figment or already dead?

   Through Shakespeare's reversal of her planetary imagery, Elizabeth appears
refracted on his agonistic stage as his essential enemy. Thus, 'Vouchsafe to show the
sunshine of your face', cry the courtiers who mistake Rosaline, masked as 'a moon,
and clouded', for the royal sun in *Love's Labour's Lost*, so proving that the dramatist
had an anthropological insight into how the lunar symbolism was 'moonshine in
the water', requiring similar atavistic practices to those of the Incas of Peru: 'That
we, like savages, may worship it' [5,2,200–7]. The next line of this text has been
censored, however. For like Feste's distancing of his performance from Countess
Olivia, 'I am not her fool' [*Twelfth*, 3,2,194], Shakespeare's elliptic relation to the
mythology of the Virgin Queen does look studied compared with the sycophancy
of other performers who entertained her as the goddess 'Diana'. Thus, in 1559
she had been welcomed into the City of London with pageants in which she saw
herself impersonated by a child, by 'one representing our dread sovereign Lady' as
a princess, and finally by 'a seemly and mete personage, richly apparelled, with a
sceptre in hand, as Queen'.[42] Performing monarchy to mirror the *implied* presence
of Elizabeth was a trick poets perfected, until, as Marlowe scoffed in *Dido, Queen of
Carthage*, they made 'the welkin howl,/And all the woods "Eliza" to resound!' with
their 'hideous echoes'.[43] In comedies that winked at the love life of the self-styled
Cynthia, such as *Sapho and Phao* and *Endimion*, John Lyly 'made it a speciality', while
dummies of the virginal Queen featured in municipal processions throughout her
reign; a cultic practice subversively parodied in 1602, however, with a puppet show
called *England's Joy*, which promised to present Elizabeth's apotheosis and triumphal
ascent into Heaven, but turned out to be a premature and wishful-thinking hoax.[44]

   Representations of Elizabeth grew ever more contrived as her day drew to its
close. Three years earlier, Jonson was perhaps guilty, therefore, not of *lèse-majesté*,
but of over-compensation for his own secret conversion to Catholicism, when he
broke the old taboo on impersonating the Queen in the theatre, by having a professional player 'boy her greatness' in the Globe presentation of *Every Man Out of His
Humour*. The device, in which the villain turns to good on seeing an 'actor portraying the Queen pass over the stage', had precedents, Jonson claimed, in 'diverse plays
and City Pageants'.[45] He was thinking of the Lord Mayor's shows, like the one in
1591 by George Peele that featured Astraea as a 'beauty fresh and sheen,/Shadowing

the person of our peerless Queen'; and dramas such as John Marston's *Histriomastix*, where the boy cast as the goddess of justice imitated Elizabeth.[46] Or he had in mind Munday's *Fidele and Fortunio*, where the author pleaded with the monarch in the hall to pardon his Catholic lapse. But these were civic or academic entertainments, gesturing to the 'virgin without compare' as an unseen spectator.[47] Thus, there was no trouble when Jonson saluted Elizabeth as Diana, 'Queen and huntress chaste and fair', and gave Cynthia a speaking part in *Cynthia's Revels*.[48] That was because the play was acted in private at Blackfriars. But if, as Jonson admitted, 'many seem'd not to relish it', when he made the Queen a character at the Globe, that might have been because he had done what Shakespeare was careful to avoid, by imposing monarchy on a free and democratic playhouse where there was supposed to be no such sovereign intrusion, 'no metadramatic social relations that sited the performance within the structures of rule'.[49] In fact, the incident reveals the extent to which other entertainers would go to ingratiate themselves with Gloriana; and it underlines their contrast to Shakespeare, whose stage depends instead, as Louis Montrose acutely remarks of A *Midsummer Night's Dream*, not 'upon her presence or intervention, but, on the contrary, her absence, her exclusion'.[50]

When the eighth muse approached Elizabeth as her 'lost sister' in a 1600 masque for the wedding of the heir of Shakespeare's patron, the Earl of Worcester, and declared she was Affection, '*Affection*', hissed the Queen, 'is false'.[51] She was referring to Essex, but what she displayed was how she ruled the stage. In the age of absolutism, as Louis Marin taught us, 'The king is only truly king, that is, monarch, in images. They are his *real presence*. Belief in the operativeness of his signs is obligatory, or else the monarch is emptied of his substance, because signs *are* the royal reality'.[52] Yet if Marin's thesis in *The Portrait of the King* – that power exists only in and through fields of representation – applies to Elizabethan England, what is so subversive about Shakespeare's theatre is how it is premised not on the 'real presence' of the monarch, as 'chief spectator or prime Subject of state and drama',[53] but on the evacuation of that presence, its banishment from the field of signification. Thus, in A *Midsummer Night's Dream* it is precisely the insignificance of Elizabeth's 'real presence', her abandonment of the realm of representation, which seems to be symbolised in one of the two undeniable Shakespearean allusions to her as a reigning monarch, Oberon's memory of the 'fair vestal, throned in the west', whose entire function is to disappear: 'But I might see young Cupid's shaft / Quenched in the chaste beams of the watery moon; / And the imperial votress passed on, / In maiden meditation, fancy free' [2,1,160–4]. For what is most telling is how Shakespeare sends 'the watery moon' off upon her royal progress, unseen by his characters except as a distant pale reflection.

If Shakespeare's 'moonshine' does mirror the Queen as his essential enemy, his *Dream* can be compared to contemporary pictures of the artist in the studio: like *Las Meninas* by Velázquez, where the artist paints himself gazing out of the frame to a place where we, in fact, now stand, but which is occupied by his models, who are dimly imaged, peering from a glass at the back, as the tired King and Queen. As Foucault comments, it is their *absent presence* that defines the point where art cuts free from patrons, and the doomed and faded world of princes to which art had hitherto referred.[54] In fact, Velázquez made sure we can never be certain what he is painting, and so called into doubt the material reality of the transient objects of his gaze, by having the arrival of a chamberlain in the background suggest that 'they are just passing through, as his responsibilities included opening and closing doors. Why then is Velázquez still painting? Perhaps he is painting *Las Meninas* itself.'[55] So Philip IV visits the artist in his studio, in this most mediated of all 'representations of representation', as Alexander waited upon Apelles, in the form of a fleeting if necessary illusion before the everlasting sovereignty of art. This was an age, Sir Thomas More observed, 'of kings' games, as it were stage plays, and for the more part played upon scaffolds'.[56] But like the Spanish court painter playing along with the Habsburgs out of necessity, Shakespeare seems to want to bring down the curtain on this tedious royal game, in overfamiliar and bored fatigue that 'I am aweary of this moon. Would he would change' [5,1,242].

'Shepherd, remember our Elizabeth,/And sing her rape, done by that Tarquin, Death': Chettle's remonstration with Shakespeare for failing to mourn the Queen confirms how suspect his aesthetic pose would have seemed to Protestants.[57] 'Supremely ill-judged' is how Peter Thomson rated this comparison of Elizabeth's death to the rape of Lucrece in *Shakespeare's Professional Career*.[58] But the graceless allusion hints at how its original readers must have regarded a poem which ends in an oath 'To rouse our Roman gods' [*Lucrece*, 1831] against Tarquin: as a picture of the Terror of the 1590s, when the regime was able, like the rapist, to 'give the watchword. . . . To draw the cloud that hides the silver moon' [370–1] and pretend the Queen was innocent. As Helen Hackett writes, lunar imagery became the sign for Elizabeth in her final decade, not only as an icon of immortality, but because 'the moon was dualistic, with a dark as well as a bright side, which enabled apparent celebration of the Queen to carry negative undertones'.[59] And as Frances Yates long ago noted, no one contributed more to this ambiguous symbolism than Shakespeare, whose imagery of a self-regarding moon – as when Titus shoots Virgo to pieces with arrows – was 'so remote from the stock-in-trade of the court poet' as to leave 'an eternal question-mark against his name'.[60] So, when Katherine is coerced by Petruccio into affirming that 'the moon changes even with your mind./What you will have it named, even that it is' [*Taming*, 4,6,21–2], the joke may well be on Elizabeth's Oath of Allegiance. Likewise, the warts and tears of Shakespeare's 'wat'ry moon' [*Dream* 2,1,162] seem to play with the melancholia of 'Water' Raleigh's poem 'The ocean's love to Cynthia', where, as the moon 'declines her beams. . . . All droops, all dies'.[61]

As Hackett comments, both Raleigh's poem and Shakespeare's *Dream* convey a *fin-de-siècle* sense that, due to female rule, the time is out of joint. They therefore belong to the covert oppositional 'discourse of disrespect and dissent' analysed by Philippa Berry, who shows how by comparing the intolerant Elizabeth to 'the dark face of the moon', texts like these 'uncover the "other" side of the Queen's courtly cult' and challenge her devotees by predicting her blackened eclipse, or implicating her with 'the lunar deity who was most difficult to idealise: Hecate, goddess of witchcraft, death, and the underworld'.[62] Such is the 'cloudy and forlorn' moon of *Venus and Adonis*, a 'life-poisoning' tyrant of 'mad mischance and . . . misery:/As burning fevers, agues pale and faint' [737–42]. And such, most strikingly, is the intolerant old moon of *A Midsummer Night's Dream*, who tyrannises, by control of the sea, a land robbed of its ancient Christian traditions, where 'the human mortals want their winter cheer' and 'No night is now with hymn or carol blessed' [*Dream*, 2,1,101–2]. This morbid, ill-omened and capricious moon is in fact based on a scandalous speech made by the Catholic martyr Campion himself, when he was the Oxford University Orator, in which he told the Queen to her face of the disasters she caused by flying too close to the earth and interfering in mortal affairs:[63]

> Therefore the moon, the governess of floods,
> Pale in her anger, washes all the air,
> That rheumatic diseases do abound.
> And thorough this distemperature we see
> The seasons alter. . . .
>
> [*Dream*, 2,1,103–7]

'But O, methinks how slow/This old moon wanes! She lingers my desires,/Like to a step-dame or a dowager,/Long withering-out a young man's revenue' [1,1,3–6]: the haggard crone of *A Midsummer Night's Dream*, who spies on lovers pretending a 'maiden meditation, fancy free' [2,1,164], shows how far from the clichés of *Shakespeare in Love* the toxic image of Elizabeth was in Shakespeare's mind, and how unlike the cult of 'the only phoenix of her age' was his insolent stage direction to the moon to 'take thy flight. Now die, die, die, die, die' [5,1,294].[64] No wonder, therefore, that Quince calculates that 'to bring moonlight into a chamber' is one of theatre's 'hard things', and can only be done through a glass darkly, as Bottom proposes throwing open the shutters of 'the great chamber window, where we play', so that 'the moon may shine in at the casement' [3,1,45–54]. For if this moon is, as editors assume, a refraction of Elizabeth in her Protestant guise as the cruel huntress Diana, the technical difficulty of presenting moonshine seems metonymic of the playwright's agonistic relation to power, and so of his entire euphemistic strategy 'to offend/But with good will' [5,1,108]. As they quiz the almanac to discover whether 'the moon doth shine that night we play', the actors acknowledge the Queen of Night as a structural necessity; but Starveling's efforts 'to disfigure . . . the person of Moonshine' with a guttering candle therefore come as close to *lèse-majesté*, or even to treason, as any actor surely dared.

In his agonistic theatre, Shakespeare plays along with the royal game in which he does not necessarily believe, by dutifully holding a mirror up to monarchy. More direct or literal attempts to 'find out moonshine' [3,1,41–53] are bound to be frustrated. And this is lucky, because Old Moonshine is here invested with savage despotic powers. She is the 'fruitless' [1,1,73], 'cold' [2,1,156], 'wand'ring moon' [4,1,98], who will be left at the end with Lion to 'bury the dead' [5,2,335]. Elizabeth's godson John Harington created vicious 'pen-caricatures of the Queen as a silly old woman', which expressed what was, in fact, her 'deep unpopularity amongst the common people' in her declining years.[65] But Shakespeare's scornful diminution of Elizabeth from the ominous power of 'the horned moon', to the 'small light' of a stinking and spitting candle, so pathetically 'in the wane' that 'in courtesy, in all reason, we must stay the time' [5,1,231; 240], is a staging of sovereignty so brutal in its demystifying desecration of Spenser's 'most royal Queen or Empress' that it had no analogue – until the day in 1603 when Cynthia at last appeared in her wax funeral effigy as she really was: shrivelled, wrinkled and decayed.[66] That final likeness would be crafted by tallow-chandlers; and as a figure predicting a death-mask, the melting wax of A Midsummer Night's Dream seems to be a representation that looks with a similar impudence, straight through Belphoebe's jewellery, wigs, cosmetics and eternally youthful disguise, to the skull beneath the skin.

'In her latter time, when she showed herself in public', recalled a courtier, after it was safe to do so, Elizabeth 'was always magnificent in apparel, supposing haply thereby, that the eyes of people, being dazzled by the glittering aspect of those accidental ornaments would not so easily discern the marks of age and decay'.[67] Shakespeare, however, appears to have been undeceived by this performance, since the wizened Old Moonshine of his play is sick, fading and shrunken, her days numbered at the start. She is a hate figure, therefore, for the 'political misogynism' which, according to Leah Marcus, also identified Elizabeth in the dramatist's 'Amazonian trull', the sexual 'puzzle', Joan [1 Henry VI, 1,3,83; 1,6,85; 3 Henry VI, 1,4,114], the monstrous Tamora, Queen of Goths, and even Lady Macbeth.[68] Andrew Hadfield infers that the unsettling misogyny implicit in these termagants is, in fact, the key to Shakespeare's anti-monarchist politics, for 'Republicanism was invariably cast as a masculine phenomenon' and 'established over the dead body of a woman'. With the 'animus against women' that marks the political plays he wrote under the Queen, this critic maintains, 'Shakespeare was seeing just how far he could push the historical links' between Elizabeth as the intolerant religious persecutor and earlier female tyrants.[69]

The recent reassessment of the 'republican moment' that began with the execution of Elizabeth's natural heir, Mary Stuart, in 1587, has led to a sharper critical awareness of the ways in which, far from sublimating religious and political controversy in some sterilising pre-Kantian aesthetic, Shakespearean drama emerged 'within a culture of political argument' and was itself 'an important form for advancing political debate, given that the key issue of sixteenth-century England, the succession, could not be discussed'.[70] The very oppressiveness of the Queen's power became a prime mover of Shakespeare's agonistic drama, according to this revaluation, and an opportunity for his negative capability, or capacity to thrive by tolerating the intolerable. Thus, 'Ill-met by moonlight' [Dream, 2,1,60], Shakespeare's lovers are irritated into responding to the waning moon as an obstacle to waxing masculine power. Its tenuousness is exactly like that of Elizabeth, indeed, in the only other definite Shakespearean glance at 'our gracious Empress', when she is upstaged in Henry V by Essex as the Londoners 'pour out' of the City to 'fetch their conquering Caesar in' on his return from Ireland [5,0,24–8]. Yet although 'already in snuff' at the start, the sinister old moon is still stubbornly malingering on Midsummer Night, and is last seen by Puck, well after 'The iron tongue of midnight' has chimed, as she is 'behowled' by the Irish wolf to the very end [Dream, 2,1,60; 5,1,240; 5,2,346; 355]. In this interregnum the aged moon survives in partial eclipse, therefore, as a cynically dialogic reflection of her superior and future conqueror:

> The moon's an arrant thief,
> And her pale fire she snatches from the sun.
>
> [*Timon*, 4,3,430–1]

Shakespeare's withered moon is a parasite on her own successor. She is thus a sitting target for the gynophobia that would later generate *Hamlet*, according to Steven Mullaney, where Gertrude resembles 'a degraded Elizabeth': the ageing female body, 'with its over-determined registers of sexuality and death', which reduces dependent men to melancholia by refusing to lie down and die.[71] So, 'let her paint an inch thick, to this favour she must come' [*Hamlet*, 5,1,179], rails her heir, as the whole community waits impatiently for the demise of its wicked stepmother, with her worn-out face squinting down upon a world of 'pacts and sects of great ones' [*Lear*, 5,3,18], whose fortune ebbs with hers. Contradicting the Queen's own motto, *Semper Eadam*, 'Swear not by the moon, th'inconstant moon/That monthly changes in her circled orb', Juliet had implored [*Romeo*, 2,1,151–2]. And Romeo's appeal to the 'fair sun' to 'Arise . . . and kill the envious moon/Who is already sick and pale with grief/That thou her maid art far more fair than she' [46–8] placed this lunar symbolism in the specific context of the Elizabethan court, thus anticipating the succession of feminine rule by a dawning masculine sun in terms that had irresistible dynastic implications.[72] Evidently, Shakespeare's facetious thanks to the 'Sweet moon . . . for thy sunny beams . . . thy gracious, golden, glittering gleams' [*Dream*, 5,1,261–3] were always intended to be double-edged. For this is a playhouse that puts itself under the influence of the waning moon, we see, not out of melancholy, but from provocatively dreaming of 'the next new moon', whose emphatically male, and phallic, succession will put an end to mourning, and bring 'The sealing day . . . For everlasting bond of fellowship' [1,1,83–5], with what looks like the assured ascent of James, the son of Elizabeth's great rival, the Queen of Scots:

> Four happy days bring in
> Another moon. . . .
> Four days will quickly steep themselves in night,
> And then the moon, like to a silver bow
> New bent in heaven, shall behold the night
> Of our solemnities.
>
> [*Dream*, 1,1,2–11]

The 1571 Treason Act, drafted by the author of *Gorboduc*, Thomas Norton, had made it high treason even to 'imagine' Queen Elizabeth's death.[73] So, what is startling about Shakespearean drama is how it circles, in the 1590s, around the question posed by Falstaff: 'Shall there be gallows' in the next reign for 'minions of the moon', the so-called 'men of good government' who time-serve their 'mistress the moon, under whose countenance [they] steal' [*1 Henry IV*, 1,2,23–52]? Thus, in *The Merry*

Wives, where 'a lower class woman copies England's "Fairy Queen"', if she does not actually impersonate her, the sovereign travestied by the ex-madam Mistress Quickly looks very much as if she is purifying Windsor Castle of 'something rotten', by pinching and burning Falstaff, to make it 'Worthy the owner' [5,5,57] who will succeed.[74] And when James I did at last arrive, and 'Elizabeth became a stick with which to beat the Stuart monarch', the dramatist, who was happy to reflect the new ruler in the mirror carried in Macbeth's masque of Stuart monarchs stretching 'to th'crack of doom' [4,1,133], pointedly refrained from the nostalgia for 'Good Queen Bess's golden days' that swept over the Jacobean stage, beginning in 1604 with the idealising of Elizabeth's life in Heywood's two-part *If You Know Not Me, You Know Nobody*, and glossing over her actual policies in Thomas Dekker's *The Whore of Babylon*, where she features as a Titania reluctant to strike, and including the macabre scene in *The Revenger's Tragedy* where the skull of one 'Gloriana' is used to poison the Duke who kisses it.[75]

The episode with Gloriana's poisonous skull is a caustic satire, it has been suggested, on James's embrace of Elizabeth's posthumous cult when he installed his predecessor's effigy in Westminster Abbey.[76] If so, what it confirms is how, 'as she passed into history and fiction', Gloriana became to Protestants such as Middleton 'an even more ethereal, mythical figure'.[77] But the only time Shakespeare ever represented Elizabeth explicitly on stage was at the very end of his career, and then in the most innocuous and minimal of forms: as a baby-doll, when in his final history, long after the old Queen had vanished, he collaborated with the Anglican John Fletcher in *Henry VIII* to chronicle the Tudor century, and so had finally to introduce the child of Anne Boleyn. What he then tactlessly decided to emphasise, even at the infant Elizabeth's christening, however, were the smoking ashes of she who 'must die –/She must' [*Henry VIII*, 5,4,59–60], to make way for a new living Elizabeth, the King's daughter, 'as great in admiration as herself', and also, it was insinuated, to cleanse the realm of the black, noxious and suffocating 'cloud of darkness' in which this Queen of executioners had lived:

> So shall she leave her blessedness to one,
> When heaven shall call her from this cloud of darkness,
> Who from the sacred ashes of her honour
> Shall star-like rise.
>
> [*Henry VIII*, 5,4,43–6]

In *Henry VIII*, Elizabeth is a two-faced figure, both 'loved and feared' for her 'terror', who divides 'her own' from 'her foes', who 'shake like field of beaten corn,/And hang their heads in sorrow' [30–2]. These words are usually taken to allude to foreign enemies, but the harvest was the favourite symbol for the Elizabethan Catholic community, and its waste here inverts the nurturing iconography Elizabeth had herself expropriated from the Virgin Mary.[78] Such an infanticidal mother evokes the fickle Cleopatra, whose luxuriousness, as 'She did lie/In her pavilion. . . . O'er-picturing' Venus, in what seems a recollection of Elizabeth in the state barge that 'Burned' upon the Thames [*Antony*, 2,2,197], likewise signifies a decadent sterility. For if the Egyptian 'strumpet' [1,1,13] does incorporate Elizabeth's dualistic character as 'at once the "popular" Queen and the demonized Whore of Babylon', it is with barrenness that *Antony and Cleopatra* concludes, in the macabre parody Nativity, when Cleopatra suckles her 'baby' asp [5,2,300].[79] So it is telling that in the only other Shakespeare scene where the Queen is explicitly named she is ridiculed for her sterile inability to achieve either religious or sexual congress. The hysterical mock trial in *King Lear*, cut from the Folio, regurgitates all the misogyny of the recusant caricature of Anne Boleyn's 'bastard' as a sexual monster; and it opens with the indictment of 'Madam' herself, who for once lacks 'eyes' in court or spies 'at trial'.

In *King Lear* 'Queen Bess' is summoned with the first line of a Protestant ballad, in which England hails her accession. But the Fool then completes the stanza by singing that because of venereal disease she is a 'leaky vessel', as unfit as her Church, and can never be England's bride. The gynaecological slander is close to Jonson's relish that 'she had a membrana on her which made her uncapable of man, though for her delight she tried many'.[80] But this was as near as the Bard ever came to penning an elegy for his late dead Queen: 'Come o'er the bourn Bessy, to me –/ Her boat hath a leak, / And she must not speak / Why she dares not come over to thee' [3,6,21–6]. In *King Lear* 'Bessy' is too malformed ever to 'come' to her suitor.[81] So, the jester's obscene jibe about what can never be spoken openly about Elizabeth's so-called 'virginity' suggests that Shakespeare's true picture of 'Sweet Bessy' may not have been far from the caricature of the lascivious and 'sick-thoughted' queen of *Venus and Adonis* [5], languishing in her erotic 'mishaps / As those poor birds that helpless berries saw' [603–5], the geriatric victim of her grotesque self-deceit that she could still 'like a fairy, trip upon the green' [146]:

> Were I hard-favour'd, foul, or wrinkled-old,
> Ill-nurtured, crooked, churlish, harsh in voice,
> O'erworn, despised, rheumatic and cold,
> Thick-sighted, barren, lean, and lacking juice,
> > Then mightst thou pause, for then I were not for thee;
> > But having no defects, why dost abhor me?
> Thou canst not see one wrinkle in my brow. . .
> My beauty as the spring doth yearly grow. . . .
>
> > > > [*Venus*, 133–41]

'How ended she?' Cymbeline asks of the deceased Queen; to be told that she met her end 'With horror, madly dying, like her life, / Which being cruel to the world, concluded most cruel to herself' [5,6,30–3]. As recent critics of *Cymbeline* emphasise, in this Jacobean tragicomedy England's reconciliation is made possible only by the extermination of the stepmother whose Protestant nationalism is as much a signifier of the Elizabethan system as her poisonings.[82] The nightmare end of *Cymbeline*'s dragon queen may therefore be Shakespeare's cool report on Elizabeth's demise, as she 'repented / The evils she hatched were not effected; so / Despairing died' [59–61]. For whether or not these lines refer to the macabre scene at Richmond, when Elizabeth lay 'forlorn on her cushions', before 'she turned her face to the wall and sank into a stupor', the relief does evoke the moment when, just before noon on 24 March 1603, the herald proclaimed the death of the old Queen on Tower Hill.[83] Earlier, in Cheapside, the response of Londoners had been 'silent joy for the succession of so worthy a king'. But the reaction of inmates of the Tower was far less muted, and on the leads of the roof Shakespeare's patron, the imprisoned Earl of Southampton, threw his hat up into the air so often and so high that it was finally blown clear over the walls, 'that all upon the Tower Hill might behold it'.[84] The liberated prisoners then took command of Queen Elizabeth's Bastille.

Shakespeare had imagined Elizabeth's Protestant moon as a bow 'new bent in heaven' into a potent masculine shape; and the inversion of the Reformation symbol suggests that he shared the optimism that an empowered James would not merely allow 'a Mass in a corner rather than lose a kingdom', as Catholics hoped,[85] but grant the freedom of conscience he appeared to offer, with his hints that he would 'never agree that any should die for error in faith'.[86] And for a few weeks the confidence of Shakespeare's backers did seem to be justified, when a delegation was assured that James 'would have no blood for religion, nor money for conscience, and would give order to clear the laws against Catholics'.[87] In May the Venetian envoy predicted that 'his Majesty would sooner or later restore England to the Roman cult', and in July recusancy fines were suspended, as the King astonishingly acknowledged 'the Roman Church to be our Mother'.[88] This was 'the high water of Catholic hopes', when Shakespeare responded to goading to mark the end of the era, however, with a sonnet that, far from weeping, celebrated the final eclipse of Old Moonshine in exactly the terms foretold in A Midsummer Night's Dream, as the removal of an obstruction to a young man's inheritance, and a joyous universal release:[89]

Not mine own fears nor the prophetic soul
Of the wide world dreaming on things to come
Can yet the lease of my true love control,
Supposed as forfeit to a confined doom.
The mortal moon hath her eclipse endured,
And the sad augurs mock their own presage;
Incertainties now crown themselves assured,
And peace proclaims olives of endless age.
Now with the drops of this most balmy time
My love looks fresh, and death to me subscribes,
Since spite of him I'll live in this poor rhyme
While he insults o'er dull and speechless tribes.
    And thou in this shalt find thy monument
    When tyrants' crests and tombs of brass are spent.

'I'll live': Sonnet 107 deserves to be known as the 'Dating Sonnet', since for all his cultivated reputation for topical reticence it is Shakespeare's most specific and unguarded statement on a contemporary event.[90] For Helen Hackett, in her authoritative Shakespeare and Elizabeth: The Meeting of Two Myths, this poem on 'the mortal moon' is unique in that 'it seems that for once Elizabeth is indeed the key to a work by Shakespeare'.[91] The survivor's celebration is also, however, one of the most over-determined texts ever composed, a fourteen-line riposte to Spenser's entire Faerie Queene, which in the previous sonnet is contemptuously dismissed as 'the chronicle of wasted time'. It is determined first of all by terror of a repeat of the St Bartholomew's Day Massacre, with rivers of blood in London streets. In 1603 those 'sad augurs' who feared such slaughter included the Venetian ambassador, who on the day Elizabeth died reported 'a capital gripped by dread of a Catholic revolt'.[92] The poet must himself have shared such worries, since he knew the militants were among those 'private friends' who read his Sonnets, such as Southampton. Shakespeare's images of his necessary enemy, as a wicked witch, lewd madam and stinking candle, had come dangerously close to the defiant contempt of the Earl's Catholic tutor, Swithun Wells, when he was challenged on the scaffold to disavow the Pope's bull excommunicating the Queen, and he scornfully joked, 'Better a roaring bull than a diseased cow'.[93] So this poem is also determined by the hate her enemies felt for Anne Boleyn's 'incestuous bastard', as 'that depraved, excommunicate, and heretic' whore.[94]

Shakespeare's long patience while the old moon waned made Sonnet 107 its author's most determined demonstration of the agôn of his dialectical dependency on power. But this 'survival sonnet' is determined too by the relief of a lucky escape, as the Earl, 'supposed as forfeit to a confined doom', is released, and in the pun on which the poem turns, the poet's 'true love' is granted a new lease. Certainly, this agonistic text is determined by pressure to mourn their 'Deborah' from those 'dull and speechless tribes' of Protestant hacks, whose crocodile tears Shakespeare transmutes into her successor's 'balmy' coronation oil. But it is also determined by 'the prophetic soul / Of the wide world dreaming on things to come': the hopes invested in James as a bringer of 'olives of endless age'. The irony of that expectation is that the poet had no more reason to credit dreams of 'things to come' than to believe the 'presage' now disproved by crowning 'incertain' James; or the moonshine of Elizabeth. And, indeed, within a year the King reinstated Catholic fines, quipping, 'Na, na, we's not need the papists noo'.[95] But this agonistic sonnet, which is so dialectically determined, is finally about freedom from determination. Whatever the poet's 'true love', he needs no 'lease' of limited toleration, he affirms. For it is death that now subscribes to art: 'I'll live in this poor rhyme'. Shakespeare, who throughout his career had been criticised for silence, had created an entire drama out of the refusal to speak. But during this caesura of 1603, in the brief interregnum of a moonless night, the time was free at last for his 'poor rhyme'. And the great survivor used his long-awaited instant of freedom to mark the limit of his toleration of the intolerable and, in the violence of his essential enmity, to spit upon the Tudor 'crests' and 'tyrant's tomb', making explicit for just this once the detestation for 'that ravenous tiger' [Titus, 5,3,194] that had always been implied:

No funeral rite nor man in mourning weed,
No mournful bell shall ring her burial;
But throw her forth to beasts and birds of prey.

Her life was beastly and devoid of pity,
And being dead, let birds on her take pity.

[195–9]

NOTES

1. E. K. Chambers, *William Shakespeare*, 2 vols (Oxford: Clarendon Press, 1930), vol. 2, pp. 207–9.
2. Thomas Dekker, 'Wonderful year 1603', in *The Non-Dramatic Works of Thomas Dekker*, ed. Alexander Grosart (London: privately printed, 1884), p. 88.
3. 'Surge of royalist feeling': Alexandra Walsham, '"A very Deborah?" The myth of Elizabeth I as a providential monarch', in Susan Doran and Thomas Freeman (eds), *The Myth of Elizabeth* (Basingstoke: Macmillan, 2003), p. 156; Chambers, *William Shakespeare*, p. 213.
4. Chambers, *William Shakespeare*, p. 212.
5. Henry Chettle, 'England's mourning garment', quoted in Chambers, *William Shakespeare*, p. 189.
6. Michael Dobson and Nicola Watson, *England's Elizabeth: An Afterlife in Fame and Fantasy* (Oxford: Oxford University Press, 2002), p. 137.
7. Dudley Carleton to John Chamberlain, 29 December 1601, *Calendar of State Papers Domestic, 1601–3* (London: HMSO, 1870), p. 374: 'I have just come from the Blackfriars, where I saw her at the play with all her *candidae auditrices*'; Park Honan, *Shakespeare: A Life* (Oxford: Oxford University Press, 1998), p. 296.
8. Chambers, *William Shakespeare*, p. 209.
9. F. E. Halliday, *A Shakespeare Companion, 1550–1950* (London: Duckworth, 1952), p. 188; Samuel Schoenbaum, *Shakespeare's Lives* (Oxford: Clarendon Press, 1970), p. 308.
10. Richard Ryan, *Dramatic Table Talk; or Scenes, Situations, and Adventures, Serious and Comic, in Theatrical History and Biography*, 2 vols (London: 1825), vol. 2, pp. 156–7.
11. Hugh Trevor-Roper, *Princes and Artists: Patronage and Ideology at Four Habsburg Courts, 1517–1633* (London: Thames and Hudson, 1976), p. 32; Alvin Kernan, *Shakespeare, the King's Playwright: Theater in the Stuart Court, 1603–1613* (New Haven: Yale University Press, 1995), pp. 159–60.
12. John Davies, quoted in Schoenbaum, *Shakespeare's Lives*, p. 55.
13. John Dryden, 'Prologue to *The Tempest, or the Enchanted Isle*', A4r, reprinted in C. E. Hughes, *The Praise of Shakespeare* (London: Methuen, 1904), p. 66.
14. Quoted in Dobson and Watson, *England's Elizabeth*, p. 127.
15. Quoted ibid., p. 122.
16. Carl Schmitt, *Hamlet or Hecuba: The Intrusion of the Time into the Play*, trans. David Pan and Jennifer Rust (New York: Telos Press, 2009), pp. 17–18.
17. Ibid., p. 45.
18. E. K. Chambers, *The Elizabethan Stage*, 4 vols (Oxford: Clarendon Press, 1923), vol. 4, p. 263.
19. Quoted in Virginia Crocheron Gildersleeve, *Government Regulation of the Elizabethan Drama* (New York: Columbia University Press, 1908), p. 119.
20. Chambers, *The Elizabethan Stage*, vol. 4, pp. 338–9.
21. *Tudor Royal Proclamations: The Later Tudors*, ed. Paul Hughes and James Larkin, 2 vols (New Haven: Yale University Press, 1969), vol. 2, p. 75; James Frazer, *The Golden Bough. Part II: Taboo and the Perils of the Soul*, 3rd edn (London: Macmillan, 1936), pp. 98–9.
22. Frazer, *The Golden Bough. Part II*, pp. 98–9; Jean Baudrillard, *The Evil Demon of Images* (Sydney: Power Institute, 1987).

23. Martin Elsky, *Authorizing Words: Speech, Writing and Print in the English Renaissance* (Ithaca: Cornell University Press, 1989), pp. 6 and 87–8.

24. Frazer, *The Golden Bough. Part II*, pp. 382–3.

25. Michel Foucault, 'Language to infinity', in *Language, Counter-Memory, Practice*, trans. Donald Bouchard and Sherry Simon (Ithaca: Cornell University Press, 1977), p. 53.

26. Sigmund Freud, *Totem and Taboo: Some Points of Agreement Between the Mental Lives of Savages and Neurotics*, trans. James Strachey (London: Routledge and Kegan Paul, 1950), p. 41. For the ambivalence of the sacred and therefore the danger of the 'royal touch' see the classic study by Mary Douglas, *Purity and Danger: An Analysis of the Concepts of Pollution and Taboo* (London: ARK Paperbacks, 1966), and the more recent reflections of Giorgio Agemben in *Homo Sacer: Sovereign Power and Bare Life*, trans. Daniel Heller-Roazen (Stanford: Stanford University Press, 1998).

27. Freud, *Totem and Taboo*, p. 42.

28. Ibid., p. 51.

29. Frazer, *The Golden Bough. Part II*, pp. 120–1; Freud, *Totem and Taboo*, p. 49.

30. John Neale, *Queen Elizabeth* (London: Jonathan Cape, 1934), p. 243.

31. David Scott Kastan, 'Proud majesty made a subject: Shakespeare and the spectacle of rule', *Shakespeare Quarterly*, 37 (1986), 459–75, esp. 460–1; Andrew Marvell, 'An Horatian ode upon Cromwell's return from Ireland', in *Andrew Marvell: The Complete Poems*, ed. Elizabeth Story Donno (Harmondsworth: Penguin, 1985), ll. 53–6, p. 56.

32. Ernst Kantorowicz, *The King's Two Bodies: A Study in Medieval Political Theology* (Princeton: Princeton University Press, 1957); Stephen Orgel, 'Making greatness familiar', in Stephen Greenblatt (ed.), *The Forms of Power in the English Renaissance* (Norman: Pilgrim Books, 1982), p. 45: 'the miming of greatness is highly charged because it employs precisely the same methods the crown was using to assert and validate its authority'.

33. First reported in John Nichols, *The Progresses and Processions of Queen Elizabeth*, 4 vols (London: John Nichols, 1823), vol. 3, p. 552; cited in Chambers, *The Elizabethan Stage*, vol. 2, p. 206.

34. Rowland Whyte, quoted in David Bevington, *Tudor Drama and Politics* (Cambridge, MA: Harvard University Press, 1968), p. 9.

35. Quoted in Kastan, 'Proud majesty', p. 461.

36. G. B. Harrison, *The Life and Death of Robert Devereux, Earl of Essex* (London: Cassell, 1937), p. 91.

37. Kastan, 'Proud majesty', p. 462. See also Fritz Levy, 'The theatre and the court in the 1590s', in John Guy (ed.), *The Reign of Elizabeth I: Court and Culture in the Last Decade* (Cambridge: Cambridge University Press, 1995), pp. 274–300: '"Staging" the queen was always a risky business since she and her officers were as well aware as modern scholars that the process, done too often or too badly, could easily derogate from royal authority' (p. 285).

38. Quoted in Stephen Greenblatt, 'Invisible bullets: Renaissance authority and its subversion, *Henty IV* and *Henry V*', in Richard Wilson and Richard Dutton (eds), *New Historicism and Renaissance Drama* (London: Longman, 1992), p. 108.

39. Kastan, 'Proud majesty', p. 466.

40. Thomas Dekker, *Old Fortunatus*, in *The Dramatic Works of Thomas Dekker*, ed. Fredson Bowers (Cambridge: Cambridge University Press, 1953), p. 1, Prologue, ll. 9–10.

41. Anne Barton, 'Harking back to Elizabeth: Jonson and Caroline nostalgia', in *Ben Jonson, Dramatist* (Cambridge: Cambridge University Press, 1984), p. 306.

42. John Nichols, *The Progresses and Public Processions of Queen Elizabeth* (London: Society of Antiquaries, 1823), vol. 1, pp. 33–54.

43. Christopher Marlowe, *Dido, Queen of Carthage*, 4,2,9–10, in *Christopher Marlowe: The Complete Plays*, ed. J. B. Steane (Harmondsworth: Penguin, 1969), p. 79.

44. Barton, 'Harking back to Elizabeth', p. 306. See also Frederick Boas, *Queen Elizabeth in Drama and Related Essays* (London: George Allen and Unwin, 1950), pp. 20–1.

45. Ben Jonson, *Every Man Out of His Humour*, ed. Helen Ostovich (Manchester: Manchester University Press, 2001), 'Apology for the original catastrophe', p. 373.

46. George Peele, *The Life and Works of George Peele* (New Haven: Yale University Press, 1952), p. 219.

47. R. Wilmot, *Tancred and Gismunda*, in W. C. Hazlitt (ed.), *Old English Plays*, 9 vols (London: Routledge, 1874), vol. 7, p. 49.

48. Ben Jonson, 'Hymn to Diana', from *Cynthia's Revels*, ed. George Burke Johnston (London: Routledge, 1954), p. 261.

49. Simon Shepherd, *Marlowe and the Politics of Elizabethan Theatre* (Brighton: Harvester, 1986), pp. 44–5.

50. Louis Montrose, '*A Midsummer Night's Dream* and the shaping fantasies of Elizabethan culture', in Richard Wilson and Richard Dutton (eds), *New Historicism and Renaissance Drama* (Harlow: Longman, 1992), p. 125. Lisa Hopkins, in *Writing Renaissance Queens: Texts by and about Elizabeth I and Mary, Queen of Scots* (Newark: University of Delaware Press, 2002), has also described Shakespeare's stance towards Elizabeth here and elsewhere as a 'strategy of avoidance': pp. 104–7; and Maurice Hunt, in 'A speculative political allegory in *A Midsummer Night's Dream*', *Comparative Drama*, 34 (2001), 423–53, considers that if, as he argues, Titania is a figure for the Queen, Shakespeare concealed the allusion from all but the initiated in the Essex faction, and was careful to maintain its 'deniability'. ·

51. Quoted in Roy Strong, *The Cult of Elizabeth* (London: Thames and Hudson, 1977), pp. 29–30.

52. Louis Marin, *The Portrait of the King*, trans. Martha Houle (Minneapolis: University of Minnesota Press, 1988), p. 8.

53. Shepherd, *Marlowe and the Politics of Elizabethan Theatre*, pp. 44–5.

54. Michel Foucault, *The Order of Things: An Archaeology of the Human Sciences*, trans. anon. (London: Tavistock, 1974), p. 16.

55. Dawson Clark, 'Painting and reality: the art and life of Velázquez', in *Velázquez* (London: National Gallery and Yale University Press, 2006), p. 48.

56. 'Representations of representation': Foucault, *The Order of Things*, p. 16; Thomas More, *The History of Richard III*, in *The Complete Works of Sir Thomas More*, ed. Richard Sylvester, 4 vols (New Haven: Yale University Press, 1963), vol. 2, pp. 80–1.

57. Chambers, *William Shakespeare*, p. 189.

58. Peter Thomson, *Shakespeare's Professional Career* (Cambridge: Cambridge University Press, 1992), p. 148.

59. Helen Hackett, *Virgin Mother, Maiden Queen: Elizabeth I and the Cult of the Virgin Mary* (New York: St Martin's Press, 1995), p. 176. See also Lisa Hopkins, 'The dark side of the moon: Semiramis and Titania', in Annaliese Connolly and Lisa Hopkins (eds), *Goddesses and Queens: The Iconography of Elizabeth I* (Manchester: Manchester University Press, 2007), pp. 117–35.

60. Frances Yates, *Astraea: The Imperial Theme in the Sixteenth Century* (Harmondsworth: Penguin, 1977), pp. 75–80.

61. Neale, *Queen Elizabeth*, p. 214; Walter Raleigh, 'The ocean's love to Cynthia', ll. 251–2, quoted in Hackett, *Virgin Mother*, p. 25.

62. 'Discourse of disrespect': Julia Walker, 'Introduction: The Dark Side of the Cult of Elizabeth', in *Dissing Elizabeth: Negative Representations of Gloriana* (Durham: Duke University Press, 1998), p. 1; Philippa Berry, *Of Chastity and Power: Elizabethan Literature and the Unmarried Queen* (London: Routledge, 1989), pp. 143–4.

63. Bodleian MS Rawl. 272, fols 11–12 (fol. 11v).

64. 'Phoenix of her age': Thomas Heywood, *The Fair Maid of the West: Part One*, quoted in Boas,

Queen Elizabeth in Drama, p. 20. Shakespeare's antagonistic imagery makes it highly unlikely that, as Fritz Levy proposes, the Princess of France in *Love's Labour's Lost* is a flattering representation of Elizabeth: 'The theatre and the court in the 1590s', pp. 283–4.

65. 'Pen-caricatures': Jennifer Woodward, *The Theatre of Death: The Ritual Management of Royal Funerals in Renaissance England, 1570–1625* (Woodbridge: Boydell, 1997), p. 89; 'deep unpopularity': Wallace MacCaffrey, *Elizabeth I: War and Politics, 1588–1603* (Princeton: Princeton University Press, 1992), pp. 160–1.

66. Edmund Spenser, *The Faerie Queene*, 'A letter of the author's', in Hugh Maclean, *Edmund Spenser's Poetry* (New York: Norton, 1982), p. 2; Woodward, *The Theatre of Death*, p. 90.

67. John Clapham, *Elizabeth of England: Certain Observations Concerning the Life and Reign of Queen Elizabeth*, ed. E. P. Read and C. Read (Philadelphia: University of Pennsylvania Press, 1951), p. 86.

68. 'Political misogynism': Christopher Haigh, *Elizabeth I* (London: Longman, 1988), p. 162; Leah Marcus, *Puzzling Shakespeare: Local Reading and Its Discontents* (Berkeley: University of California Press, 1988), pp. 51–105, esp. p. 53.

69. Andrew Hadfield, *Shakespeare and Republicanism* (Cambridge: Cambridge University Press, 2005), pp. 114, 174 et passim.

70. Ibid., p. 7.

71. Steven Mullaney, 'Mourning and misogyny: *Hamlet, The Revenger's Tragedy*, and the final progress of Elizabeth I, 1660–1607', *Shakespeare Quarterly*, 45 (1994), pp. 150–2. For Gertrude as the projection of male anxieties and phobias provoked by the ageing Elizabeth, see also Bruce Thomas Boehrer, *Monarchy and Incest in Renaissance England: Literature, Culture, Kinship, and Kingship* (Philadelphia: University of Pennsylvania Press, 1992); Lisa Hopkins, '"Ripeness is all": the death of Elizabeth in drama', *Renaissance Forum: An Electronic Journal of Early Modern Literary and Historical Studies*, 4 (2000), <http:/www.hull.ac.uk/renforum/> (last accessed August 2015); and Leonard Tennenhouse, 'Violence done to women on the Renaissance stage', in Nancy Armstrong and Leonard Tennenhouse (eds), *The Violence of Representation: Literature and the History of Violence* (London: Routledge, 1989), pp. 77–97. In *Rewriting Shakespeare, Rewriting Ourselves* (Berkeley: University of California Press, 1991), Peter Erickson not only reads Gertrude as 'a degraded figure of Queen Elizabeth', but sees the Queen portrayed in 'strong women' throughout the plays (p. 75).

72. See Hackett, *Virgin Mother*, for the 'favourite conceit' that acclaimed James as the sun rising after the moon, and thereby demoted Elizabeth to secondary, temporary status.

73. Quoted in Michael Graves, *Thomas Norton: The Parliament Man* (Oxford: Blackwell, 1994), p. 174.

74. Wendy Wall, '*The Merry Wives of Windsor*: unhusbanding desires in Windsor', in Richard Dutton and Jean Howard (eds), *A Companion to Shakespeare's Works. Vol. 3: The Comedies* (Oxford: Blackwell, 2003), p. 386; Barbara Freedman, 'Shakespearean chronology, ideological complicity, and floating texts: something is rotten in Windsor', *Shakespeare Quarterly*, 45 (1994), 190–210: 'why would anyone composing a personal compliment to Elizabeth represent her in the person of Mistress Quickly?'

75. 'Stick with which to beat the Stuart': Walsham, '"A very Deborah?"', p. 159.

76. Jennifer Woodward, 'Images of a dead queen', *History Today*, 47 (1997), 18–23.

77. Hackett, *Virgin Mother*, p. 227. For the Marian connotations of the cult of Elizabeth, see Yates, *Astraea*, and Strong, *The Cult of Elizabeth*.

78. Ibid., for a comprehensive commentary on this appropriation of Marian symbolism. Hackett is sceptical of the myth that Elizabeth deliberately absorbed the cult of the Virgin Mary. And this scepticism is echoed by Susan Doran, 'Virginity, divinity and power: portraits of Elizabeth I', in Doran and Freeman, *The Myth of Elizabeth*, ch. 7.

79. Paul Yachnin, '"Courtiers of beauteous freedom": *Antony and Cleopatra* in its time',

Renaissance and Reformation, 27:1 (1991), p. 11: 'It is as if Shakespeare had used what he knew of Elizabeth in order to work towards an understanding of Cleopatra' (p. 12). For the theory that Cleopatra is Shakespeare's ambiguous portrait of Elizabeth, see also Helen Morris, 'Queen Elizabeth "shadowed" in Cleopatra', *Huntington Library Quarterly*, 32 (1969), 271–8; and Keith Rhineheart, 'Shakespeare's Cleopatra and England's Elizabeth', *Shakespeare Quarterly*, 23 (1972), 81–6.

80. Ben Jonson, *Conversations with Drummond of Hawthornden 1619* (New York: New York University Press, 1966), p. 15.

81. The ballad is reproduced and discussed in John Murphy, *Darkness and Devils: Exorcism and 'King Lear'* (Athens: Ohio University Press, 1984), pp. 179–80 and 231–4.

82. See Willy Maley, 'Postcolonial Shakespeare: British identity formation and *Cymbeline*', in Jennifer Richards and James Knowles (eds), *Shakespeare's Late Plays* (Edinburgh: Edinburgh University Press, 1999), pp. 145–7; and Richard Danson Brown and David Johnson, *Shakespeare in 1609: 'Cymbeline' and the Sonnets* (Basingstoke: Macmillan, 2000), p. 34. But J. Mikalachki stresses that the death of a powerful female figure is the precondition of masculine reconciliation in a number of similar Jacobean dramas set in Roman Britain, in 'The masculine romance of Roman Britain: *Cymbeline* and early modern English nationalism', *Shakespeare Quarterly*, 46:3 (1995), 303.

83. Neale, *Queen Elizabeth*, p. 390.

84. Thomas Ferrers to Humphrey Ferrers, 25 March 1603, quoted in Mark Nicolls, *Investigating Gunpowder Plot* (Manchester: Manchester University Press, 1991), p. 119.

85. The Earl of Northumberland to James I, late spring 1602; quoted in P. M. Handover, *The Second Cecil: The Rise to Power, 1563–1604, of Sir Robert Cecil, Later First Earl of Salisbury* (London: Eyre and Spottiswoode, 1959), p. 284.

86. Quoted in William McElwee, *The Wisest Fool in Christendom: The Reign of James I and VI* (London: Faber and Faber, 1958), p. 136.

87. Anon. (Thomas Tresham), *A Petition Apologetical, Presented to the King's Most Excellent Majesty by the Lay Catholics of England in July Last* (Douai: 1604), p. 8.

88. *Calendar of State Papers Venetian*, vol. 10, p. 21; James I quoted in McElwee, *The Wisest Fool in Christendom*, p. 117.

89. Sandeep Kaushik, 'Resistance, loyalty and recusant politics: Sir Thomas Tresham and the Elizabethan state', *Midland History*, 21 (1996), 37–72, here 62.

90. For the 'unignorable' evidence that 'clinches the case' for Sonnet 107 as Shakespeare's commentary on the death of Elizabeth and the release of Southampton, see the authoritative note to the New Penguin edition by John Kerrigan, *Shakespeare: The Sonnets and 'A Lover's Complaint'* (Harmondsworth: Penguin, 1986), pp. 313–20. See also Katharine Duncan Jones's 'Introduction' to the Arden edition, *Shakespeare's Sonnets* (London: Thomas Nelson, 1997), pp. 21–4.

91. Helen Hackett, *Shakespeare and Elizabeth: The Meeting of Two Myths* (Princeton: Princeton University Press, 2009), p. 142.

92. *Calendar of State Papers, Venetian, 1592–1603*, pp. 562–3.

93. Swithun Wells quoted in Christopher Devlin, *The Life of Robert Southwell, Poet and Martyr* (London: Longmans, 1956), pp. 238–9.

94. Peter Millward, *Shakespeare's Religious Background* (Chicago: Loyola University Press, 1973), p. 191.

95. Quoted in Kenneth Fincham and Peter Lake, 'The ecclesiastical policy of James I', *Journal of British Studies*, 24 (1985), p. 184, n. 64.

4 No Enemy But Winter: Shakespeare's Rogue State

OLD CUSTOM

When Celia proposes to disguise herself 'in poor and mean attire,/And with a kind of umber smirch' her face, and Rosalind announces she will sport a 'gallant curtal-axe' upon her thigh, a 'boar-spear' in hand, the heroines of *As You Like It* flee the court, they imagine, to 'live like the old Robin Hood'. They say they will join the banished Duke Senior with his 'many merry men' in the Forest of Arden, where 'many young gentlemen flock to him every day, and fleet the time carelessly, as they did in the golden world' [1,1,100–3; 1,3,105–12]. So, with blacked-up faces and greenleaf garb, the 'blackamoor' and 'shemale' of Shakespeare's comedy tie its plot to the rough music, wild justice and ritual poaching of the Robin Hood tradition. Indeed, as I wrote in *Will Power*, 'until the 1900s no one doubted the affinity of *As You Like It* with the Robin Hood legend', nor that its wrestling champion, Orlando *de Boys*, was an Elizabethan avatar of a folkloric Robin of the Wood.[1] In particular, Shakespeare's teenage 'hoodies' were allied, I argued, to the real Silviuses and Williams of pre-Civil War England, the youth gangs of the Warwickshire Forest of Arden, and similar wood-pasture regions such as the Forest of Dean, who, disguised in cagoule, mask or woman's dress, rioted against the sale of royal forests to capitalist farmers, like the play's Oliver, under cover of 'skimmington' games and aliases like Lady Dorothy and Captain Pouch, Maid Marion and Robin Hood. The 'liberty' in which *As You Like It* was invested, according to this ideological criticism, was the delimited zone of carnival, in which 'brothers' mocked the 'others' that they feared.

My guide in this reading was the historian David Underdown, whose *Revel, Riot, and Rebellion* defined the moral economy of woodland rioters as 'a combination of rebelliousness and conservatism', driven 'more by localism than class', and emphasised how long traditions behind the foresters' forcible defence of common rights yoked their festive violence firmly to the status quo. Thus, 'in the Dean the name "Robin Hoods" had been applied' by the Earl of Northampton to arsonists in anti-enclosure attacks that swept the Forest in 1612, Underdown observed, but the leaders defiantly assumed the poacher's name to restore the subverted moral order by inverting it again: 'The customary world had been turned upside-down by enclosers; the protesters symbolically turned it upside down again (dressing as women, parodying their social superiors) in order to turn it right-side-up'.[2] The reason critics were able to play down the social violence of Shakespeare's bitter Arcadia, I therefore concluded, was that 'the old Robin Hood of England' [1,1,101] had himself been such a retrograde character, whom the dramatist co-opted for the revanchism that made every social bandit and primitive rebel non- or counter-revolutionary, in the analysis of the Marxist historian Eric Hobsbawm, and so, at the end of the day in the forest, unthreatening to traditional authority:

> Indeed, the legend frequently shows the sovereign pursuing the bandit and then asking him to court and making peace, thus recognising that his and the sovereign's interest is the same. . . . The peasant societies in which it occurs know rich and poor, powerful and weak, rulers and ruled, but remain . . . tenaciously traditional. . . . This is no doubt the reason why England, which has given the world Robin Hood, the archetype of the social bandit, produced no notable example of the species after the 16th century. . . . The social brigand appears only before the poor have reached political consciousness or acquired more effective methods of social agitation. The bandit is a pre-political phenomenon.[3]

Though peasants such as the play's old Adam bravely protect him, the outlaw's fall will always be by betrayal, Hobsbawm explained. And in *Will Power* I described Shakespeare's fraternisation with Robin Hood as just such an act of symbolic treachery, with his de Boys brothers personifying the bad faith of the propertied regarding the enclosure of royal forests, disafforestation and the resistance of sylvan society. With Anthony Munday's Robert Earl of Huntingdon plays, *As You Like It* belonged to a genre of Robin Hood dramas that in the 1590s pastoralised the poacher, or even elevated him to the nobility, as the discursive equivalent, I proposed, of the asset-stripping of the forests by London finance, a manoeuvre effected by the circumscription of Orlando's virility within Rosalind's 'sheep-cote fenc'd about with olive trees' [4,3,76–7]: 'For far from valorising the archaic greenwood as a locale of freedom, the play breaks up "the skirts of this wild wood" [5,4,148] to reinscribe it in private ownership'. Rosalind's fence enclosing 'antique' oaks [2,1,31] was a fitting symbol for this operation, I argued, since it is within its pale that depopulation and clearance occur: 'Pastoral discourse, which promises Arden woodlanders "measure heaped in joy" [5,4,168], will conceal the real revolution in the forest, which was invariably towards cereal production'.[4]

The poachers who might have figured freedom are disarmed by the shepherds in this account of *As You Like It*, which in reading the play's escapism as a form of ideology typified the hermeneutic of suspicion in historicist criticism in the 1990s. So the last song of the play takes us to an arable landscape thick with crops, I noted, where the labourers are permitted to frolic 'between the acres of the rye' and 'o'er the green cornfield', and 'think it a plenteous crop / To glean the broken ears after the man/That the main harvest reaps', because this is the deforested farmland of the agricultural revolution, in which 'pretty country folk' sport 'In spring time, the only pretty ring time' as guilelessly as the lads who after the 1607 Midland Rising were roped into Robert Dover's patrimonial Cotswold Games [3,5,102–4; 5,3,16–20]. With its ancient oaks defaced by graffiti, Arden's future belongs, my 1993 essay concluded, with speculators like Orlando's enclosing brother, or 'old Carlot' [3,5,109], the 'churlish' landlord of Corin, whose 'flocks, and bounds of feed/Are now on sale' [2,4,75–9]. And the foresters' passivity towards this revolution foretold the effective end of agrarian revolt in England. This was an anti-climactic interpretation in line with the New Historicist wisdom in the subversion/containment debate of the time, that there was 'subversion, no end of subversion', in such artworks, in Stephen Greenblatt's Kafka-esque formula, 'but not for us'.[5] It complemented the eco-critical and feminist objection that, as Jeanne Addison Roberts complained in The Shakespearean Wild, Shakespeare's 'gradual suppression' of the green world is archetypically patriarchal, and ends by denaturing Mother Earth.[6] And my critique of the play as a 'version of pastoral', sentimentalising what William Empson called 'a beautiful relation between rich and poor' by creating 'the illusion that ruling class interests do not exist', also chimed with the contention of scholars of 'rogue literature', that the theatrical appropriation of the outlaw narrative by a capitalist elite was a ruse, and a part of the 'reformation of popular culture' by the synthetic 'politics of mirth':[7]

> There is a marked dissociation between the fascination with the figure of the rogue in the theater and the genuine alarm the Tudor government felt. . . . But the rogue found himself welcome in the theater. There the audience could indulge, in safety from his vermin and pilfering, the curiosity and fascinated ambiguity always accompanying the figure of the rogue. . . . The ideological and fantastic character of the investment of the figure of the beggar can be gauged from the fact that . . . plays distinguish sharply between real peasants, who are treated with contempt, and the spiritual nobility of the vagabonds. . . . The genre is, in short, a branch of pastoral.[8]

Shakespeare's pastoralising of Robin Hood in As You Like It could be likened, on this view, to the de-politicising of the poaching scenario in earlier adaptations of the 1590s, such as George a Greene and Peele's Edward I, where, as Edwin Davenport showed, the rites of violence were disallowed by endings that insulate the hero from resistance, 'co-opting his constituency to the side of loyalty and monarchy by criminalizing traditional politics'; for as Edward Berry similarly observed in Shakespeare and the Hunt, the 'gentrification of the Robin Hood materials drained away their subversive potential'.[9] Thus Shakespeare, who opens The Two Noble Kinsmen with a Chaucer who decries 'the witless chaff of such a writer,/That blasts my bays and my famed works makes lighter/Than Robin Hood' [Pro.,19], seemed always to expose the anachronism of the greenwood saga. And when he had Justice Silence burst into song at the news that the old King is dead, with a refrain from the ballad 'Robin Hood and the Pinder of Wakefield' – 'And Robin Hood, Scarlet, and John'

[2 *Henry IV*, 5,3,96] – the irony was that for Falstaff and his 'good fellowship' of 'Gallants, lads, boys, hearts of gold', not to mention his 'Maid Marian', Doll Quickly [1 *Henry IV*, 3,3,103], last glimpsed being marched away to Bridewell, there would never be the 'merry' reconciliation of the outlaw legend between the King and 'Diana's foresters', those 'knaves in Kendal green' [1,2,22; 2,5,206; 255]. Instead, the King's epoch-marking repudiation – 'I know thee not old man' – appeared to signal Shakespeare's own disenchanted acceptance that, so Lois Potter concluded, 'the old-fashioned kind of robber' was now doomed.[10]

In this 1990s rewriting of Shakespeare's greenwood, the incoming ruler's proclamation that 'I have turned away my former self,/So will I those that kept me company' [2 *Henry IV*, 5,5,45–57] foretold the sorry Restoration volte-face analysed by Stephen Knight, the godfather of outlaw studies, when in a tableau staged at Nottingham for the coronation of Charles II, *Robin Hood and His Crew of Soldiers*, Robin swears he is 'quite another man' from the rogue who formerly captained 'this gallant attempt we've boldly followed' – the Good Old Cause – and now that the King is the Merry Monarch, 'like any repentant Roundhead' he can lead his soldiers (no longer brigands) in singing 'A Health unto our King'.[11] Thus, if the heartless expulsion of Falstaff as a 'fool and jester' [46] repeats the scapegoat rite of the 'trial of Carnival', when Shakespearean drama moves, in C.L. Barber's schema, 'Through Release to Clarification', the problem for critics, as the critic himself conceded, was that this theatrical 'reformation' [1 *Henry IV*, 1,2,191] appeared to be offered as an actual agenda for an England that would soon enough turn its revolutionary world back the 'right way' up.[12] Revelling in waylaying 'pilgrims going to Canterbury with rich offerings', or in pillaging 'traders riding to London with fat purses', Falstaff had joked that his 'amendment' would be 'from praying to purse-taking' [90–1; 112–13]. But Hal's formal suppression of such roguery seems, on this view, to anticipate the cruel experience of defeat in Christopher Hill's melancholy last book, *Liberty Against the Law*, a study of Robin Hood in actual counter-revolution England, the dispiriting coda of a history come full circle that was epitomised by *A Jovial Crew*, Richard Brome's 1636 updating of *As You Like It*, where the sisters and their lovers abscond to the woods, like Shakespeare's cousins, yet then 'quit, disillusioned not with the beggars . . . but recognizing the realities of life for outcasts exposed to the savagery of upper-class law':

Sir John Falstaff made a jest of highway robbery being his 'vocation' [Hill quoting 1 *Henry IV*, 1,2,92]. Shirley's *The Sisters*, played in 1642, the year of the breakdown, contains a gang of thieves who have their own kingdom and repudiate laws ('Hang laws/And those that make 'em'). The world had changed by the time of *The Beggar's Opera*. Late seventeenth-century governments . . . are busily suppressing pirates, highwaymen and robbers. 'Farewell to all my jovial crew', are dying words attributed to a condemned robber: 'The life which once I had/By Law is now controlled.' The Black Act of 1723 turned the judicial system into a ruthless engine for crushing poachers. It was all part of a single policy of making the world safe for English merchants and landlords to increase in wealth and so to contribute to the new power of the English state.[13]

In *The World Turned Upside Down* Hill had lauded the Forest of Arden as a 'nursery of sedition', which harboured the historical Coventry Ranters as well as Shakespeare's lovers.[14] Like Hobsbawm and the other Marxist historians who made such a cult of Robin Hood in the early pages of *Past and Present*, he was doubtless guilty here of that Whiggish idealisation of the peasant economy which Kathleen Biddick has witheringly diagnosed as a phantasmatic reaction to Britain's post-war loss of empire, the narrative substitute for a postcolonial historiography that shifted historical discourse away from the trauma of decolonisation and onto a pastoral non-place safely planted under English oaks. Thus Hill's nostalgia for the forest as an immemorial terrain of revolutionary resistance may well have typified the Old Left's discredited liberal humanism.[15] But in his last sad text Hill himself demoted his woodland redoubt of sturdy Saxon freemen to a mere figment of urban fantasy, a symptom of the helplessness of modern city workers. Thus 'The Robin Hood ballads were about a lost world of apparent freedom', the historian now lamented, 'hence their appeal to those trapped in the increasingly disciplined world of wage-labour'.[16]

In his swansong Hill still keyed the appeal of the wild woods as a reserve of 'imagined freedom' to Saxon resistance to the Norman yoke, since 'Robin Hood and his men preferred the freedom of the forest to the tyranny of a law in whose making they had no share', and 'in Robin Hood's day to be free meant escaping from a law imposed on the native English'. But the story Hill now told was of the disenchantment with the forest world, as 'the power of royal government was put behind enclosure', the game laws criminalised customary rights and 'the Robin Hood spirit' was crushed, when in 1660 'the propertied classes gained control'. 'Robin Hood still lives', he maintained, in legends like that of Marcos, the hero of Mexican peasant revolt. But the Marxist historian closed his life's work with a picture of the homeless sleeping rough in Thatcher's London, and the acid reflection that 'Some may see evidence of progress in the fact that we no longer flog the impotent poor out of town'.[17] As David Norbrook insists, Hill's idealisation of Anglo-Saxon liberties does not entirely disqualify his 'grand narrative' of the English struggling heroically for their freedoms.[18] But the confusion in *Liberty Against the Law* arose from the religious blind spot he shared in the 1990s with radical critics of Shakespeare. Dazzled by Puritan MPs opposed to Charles I who styled themselves 'Robins' and their leader 'Robin Hood', Hill could not perceive that one reason why Elizabethan dramatists resurrected the greenwood scenario was that its traditional anti-clericalism could be rekindled to bait his beloved Puritans, *in defence of the stage*.[19]

The anti-clerical thrust of the Robin Hood scenario made it an obvious subject for the 'religious turn' in criticism after 2000, with liberating consequences for the evaluation of *As You Like It*. In fact, the changing fortunes of Robin epitomise the way that the larger shift in criticism away from the ideological and towards the aesthetic has been enabled by a revisionist focus on post-Reformation religion. But this new take on the comedy also underlines how, far from toxic religion and poisonous politics being dissolved by the aesthetic demands of the play, in Shakespeare the play provides the symbolic means for these to be expressed. For if Robin's devotion to Maid Marian recalled the cult of the Virgin, critics noted how the greedy Abbot resurfaced in Elizabethan religious politics as the stooge Puritan, Martin Marprelate.

Thus, as Michael Shapiro emphasised in an essay on Marian, the actors who staged the rogue plays that Hill praised for Leveller sympathies were interested parties in the culture wars the historian described, invested in the very games and customs that were inimical to the Protestant nationalism to which they themselves subscribed.[20]

In Shakespearean London the professional theatre masqueraded as a form of liminal festivity of the kind that marked calendar time in Catholic societies, Shapiro argued, even as it evolved into one of the '*liminoid*' institutions that ushered in the economic time of Protestant change.[21] This ambivalence explains why it was the nationalist Admiral's Men at Henslowe's Rose who performed one after another Robin Hood drama during the 1590s; but also why their repertoire was torn, as Jeffrey Singman showed, between theatre's legacy of lawlessness and their Protestant programme.[22] Like Prince Hal, Peele, Munday and Chettle all repudiate the old Robin in the end, and disavow his roguery with the rover's return to the court. But it is precisely this Protestant renunciation of the play world, now we revisit it in light of critical interest in political theology following 9/11, that makes Shakespeare's meta-theatrical revival of the 'old custom' of the outlaw brotherhood in the woods appear so much more *worldly* or agonistic than that of his contemporaries:

> Now, my co-mates and brothers in exile,
> Hath not old custom made this life more sweet
> Than that of painted pomp? Are not these woods
> More free from peril than the envious court?
>
> [*As You*, 2,1,1–4]

THE POLITICS OF FRIENDSHIP

'All the world's a stage,/And all the men and women merely players' [2,7,138–9]: the Elizabethan Robin Hood texts legitimate the theatre's own roguery with the play metaphor. Yet as Andrew Barnaby complained, in an acute rebuttal of my essay on *As You Like It*, the materialist readings of the text systematically ignored its performative aspect and signifying capacity as 'a purposeful, socially engaged activity', and overlooked the historical conditions of its writing and reception. Such ideological criticism thus denied Shakespeare any 'critical distance' or 'capacity to comprehend [his] own situation'.[23] And read under the sign of its agonistic song about the essential and eternal enmity of 'winter and rough weather' [2,5,39], the contrast between his work and the Rose reruns of the bandit story confirms this objection. For whereas *George a Greene* affirms its loyalty to the establishment by having the rebel Earl of Kendal shamed by a true Robin; and *Edward I* attests its patriotism by killing off the Welsh prince Lluellen, who modelled his rebellion on 'the book of Robin Hood'; while *The Downfall of Robert Earl of Huntingdon* advertises its royalism by framing itself as a Robin Hood game devised for Henry VIII; only Shakespeare's version awards the renegade kingdom equal force to 'painted pomp', or validates its fugitives above 'the envious court'.[24] Thus the athletic 'gamester' [1,1,139] Orlando gives a new twist to the old story, and a confrontational *agôn* to Shakespeare's theatre, when he turns antagonism to sport, enemies to adversaries, by flooring the royal wrestler Charles, and thereby shows how, rather than irreconcilable difference being contained, here play becomes the arena in which that difference is *acted out*:

CHARLES: Come, where is this young gallant that is so desirous
                   to lie with his mother earth?
ORLANDO: Ready, sir; but this will hath in it a more modest
                   working.
DUKE FREDERICK: You shall try but one fall.
CHARLES: No, I warrant your grace you shall not entreat him to
                   a second that have so mightily persuaded him from a
                   first.
ORLANDO: You mean to mock me after; you should not have
                   mocked me before. But come your ways.

                                                            [1,2,166–74]

While the Rose adaptations of Robin always end with reintegration of the rogue state into an authoritarian order, in line with the official plotline, 'from law to outlawry to law', *As You Like It* seems to declare an adherence to the confessional pluralism of the former Strange's Men, now Chamberlain's Men, when it concludes with the radical reversal of a counter-insurgent militia *surrendering to the insurgency*, as Duke Frederick musters 'a mighty power' to corner the bandit captain and 'put him to the sword', only to meet 'with an old religious man', and be 'converted/Both from this enterprise and the world', before he can penetrate the 'skirts of this wild wood' [5,4,143–51].[25] No episode in Shakespeare's plays has therefore seemed more pertinent to those claiming the dramatist for the Old Religion than the sensational news that Frederick has 'put on a religious life/And thrown into neglect the pompous court' [170–1]. Yet, with a fast-forward to *Measure for Measure*, what this volte-face illustrates, as it hangs in the forest air, is how Shakespeare's agonistic playfulness also ushers in the new dispensation when a penitent sovereignty accedes to religious difference, and retreats from the space of the stage. In fact, *As You Like It* offers an instance of a theme explored in a 2006 volume, *Rogues and Early Modern English Culture*, where the essays move beyond identifying 'the compatibility of in-law and out-law worlds', to reconsider how, with their linguistic energy and social dexterity, unreconstructed outlaws become harbingers for differentiated forms of society, exemplars for those, like the Bankside players, 'exploiting the politics of privilege at court or surviving by their wits'.[26]

'Ah, rogue! i'faith, I love thee' [2 *Henry IV*, 2,4,195], Doll Tearsheet tells Falstaff; and the endearment suggests how Shakespeare exploited contemporary ambivalence towards the 'cogging' and 'cozening' of the 'insinuating rogue' [*Othello*, 4,2,135–6]. So in *As You Like It* he took his ending, where traitors trounce the law enforcers, from his primary source, the 1590 romance *Rosalynde*, which Andrew Hadfield reads as 'a plea for toleration and acceptance of differences', by the crypto-Catholic Thomas Lodge.[27] It is telling, then, that the 'skirt' trope not only ties Frederick to the Sheriff of Nottingham, with other Shakespearean rapists like Tarquin, Angelo and the Governor in *Pericles* who is repulsed by Marina, but also figures his priestly calling when he spares the sacred wood. Jacques duly follows, reflecting that 'I am for other than for dancing measures' [*As You*, 5,4,182]. As Linda Woodbridge remarks, in this melancholic's tears over the slaughtered deer something *green* is salvaged from the *maquis* in 'Shakespeare's premier countryside comedy': seeds of fertile forces that will spring up again in Birnam Wood. Anxious to fence romantic ecology from the politics of religion, Woodbridge ties this green matrix to a Celtic heritage that she likens to the Italian ancestor cult of the *benandanti*, excavated by Carlo Ginzburg.[28] Yet Puck's antics with holy water in the Athenian wood illustrate how pagan spirituality and Christian liturgy coexist in the 'night battles' of Shakespeare's Robin Goodfellow, whose rogue state, we now recognise, has as much to do with a utopia to come, via the *Ardennes* of Elizabethan Catholic *émigrés*, as with a dystopian present in the recusant Forest of Arden. Modern political theorists might recognise this theatre, then, as the dialectical space of agonistic pluralism. For while other Elizabethan dramatists neutralise or depoliticise 'the old Robin', sublimating sectarian conflict in aesthetic closure, what is lost in adversity is restored for Shakespeare, it emerges, in the *agôn* of those lapidary 'sermons' and 'books' of which his characters speak, as a form of *pharmakon* or provocation. Thus, when Duke Senior sermonises on enmity, he sounds uncannily like the philosopher of democratic pluralism, Chantal Mouffe:[29]

Sweet are the uses of adversity,
Which, like the toad, ugly and venomous,
Wears yet a precious jewel in his head;
And this our life, exempt from public haunt,
Finds tongues in trees, books in the running brooks,
Sermons in stones, and good in everything.

[2,1,12–17]

'I would not change it' [18], echoes Amiens, whose name specifies a painful context for this sermonising, in Catholic exile and the recusant fines exacted by the 'ugly toad' Robert Cecil. Thus Shakespeare's most topical correction to the Tudor Robin, his Platonising pun on 'good/God' insists, was to make his rebels' roguery more pious than 'the pompous court'.[30] The theological graffiti carved into Shakespeare's textual thickets may seem too cryptic now to be decoded. But the idea that rogue literature might have been created to signify the complexities of England's separation from Rome has been floated by Jeffrey Knapp, who, in *Shakespeare's Tribe*, argues that as the Protestant elite began to connect the vagrancy crisis of the 1590s with the Reformation disruption of social relief, 'the demonization of rogues provided a splintered England with a valuable common enemy'. A myth of a secret criminal underworld embodied the worst Protestant fears of schism, Knapp points out. So metropolitan writers like Thomas Dekker and Robert Greene evolved a vagrancy discourse to displace these anxieties, by 'stigmatizing vagabonds as the culprits, not casualties', and as the 'promoters of national disintegration rather than the passive victims' of Protestant reform. To exorcise self-accusation, it was not sufficient, however, to vilify Catholics as 'wandering Romanists', or 'holy thieves', whose papal allegiance made them a Fifth Column within the realm. England's divorce from Rome had itself to be differentiated as a virtuous form of truancy: a manoeuvre enacted in the *Faerie Queene* when Spenser portrayed the true church as an '*Errant damozell*', reduced to 'wandring in woods and forests'.[31]

Norbrook has described pastoral symbolism as the voice of Protestant aspiration under Elizabeth and of Protestant disaffection under James.[32] So it is not necessary to go as far as poet Ted Hughes, who believed a crypto-Papist 'Jacques-Pierre' portrayed himself as 'a kind of Hermes' in the mourning garb of 'melancholy Jacques' [2,1,26], to see how Shakespeare's Catholic legacy may have darkened his reaction to this Protestant pastoralism, a complication he marked with the name of a sylvan setting whose eponymous alignment with his persecuted Arden relations he may 'have associated with the Mother Forest that guards the mouth of the other world'.[33] For whenever the young Shakespeare crossed London Bridge to Bankside, biographers point out, he walked beneath the impaled heads of his 'old religious uncle' [3,2,311], Edward Arden of Park Hall, and the fanatic son-in-law of this 'uncle in the Forest of Arden' [1,3,101], John Somerville, condemned after the 1583 Warwickshire Throckmorton Plot, and was thus reminded of his own terrifying proximity to Catholic revolt.[34] With such a haunted family romance, the treason of Arden's rogue state was no mere theatrical trope. But that makes Shakespeare's wishful political theology, in this forest clearing, where virtues 'Are sanctified and holy traitors' [2,3,13] and 'kissing is as full of sanctity as the touch of holy bread' [3,4,12], sound all the more irenic, or *Anglican*, compared with the reproving Protestant narrative of the reformation of outlawed rogues. Certainly, the language of the play suggests that religion will be more here than the dwarf forced to hide under the table of the modern state, in Walter Benjamin's famous allegory of political theology:[35]

> True it is that we have seen better days,
> And have with holy bell been knolled to church,
> And sat at good men's feasts, and wiped our eyes
> Of drops that sacred pity hath engendered.
> And therefore sit you down in gentleness,
> And take upon command what help we have
> That to your wanting may be ministered.
>
> [2,7,119–25]

Shakespeare's sacred wood is a broad church, much like the Church of England, since 'This wide and universal theatre/Presents more woeful pageants than the scene/Wherein we play' [136–8]. There is a tradition that this meta-theatrical reference to the expansiveness and hospitality of the Globe 'Wherein we play' records Shakespeare's own performance as Orlando's 'venerable burden' Adam, whose last gasp is to wheeze, 'I scarce can speak to thank you for myself', and that the poet doubled this 'Last scene of all' [2,7,162–6] with that of the tongue-tied shepherd William, who is commanded by Touchstone to 'tremble, and depart' [5,1,52]. That the author should have played the 'good old man' [2,4,57] in 'a long beard', and 'so weak he was carried to a table at which he was feasted', struck the eighteenth-century editor Edward Capell as plausible in light of another legend, that he was no great actor, and 'took no parts upon him but such as this'.[36] And if he did act the part of the faithful old retainer, James Bednarz has explained, he would have been entering an intertextual thicket of pastoral self-portraiture that ran from Virgil's Tityrus to Sidney's Philisides and Spenser's Colin Clout.[37] Thus Anthony Munday would bob up in *England's Helicon* as 'shepherd Tony'. Yet given the Protestant cast of such cameo parts, what is striking about Shakespeare's auto-representation as the 'good old man' of *As You Like It* is how he turns Protestant pastoralism back on itself, by aligning with those superannuated elders who are 'not for the fashion of these times', when 'No night is now with hymn or carol blessed' [*Dream*, 2,1,102]. 'Now almost fourscore', the persona he adopts is that of a stalwart survivor of the 'merry' or 'golden world', before the Reformation Fall. For like the Old Shepherd of *The Winter's Tale*, who is similarly 'a man of fourscore-three' [*Winter's*, 4,4,441], it is aged Adam's presumed birth sometime in the 1520s, so before the break with Rome, that makes him a living link to 'The constant service of the antique world, / When service sweat for duty, not for meed' [*As You*, 1,4,57–72].

'Master, go on, and I will follow thee / To the last gasp of truth and loyalty' [70–1]: although Knapp never mentions *As You Like It*, the words about Adam's service to Orlando that Shakespeare may have spoken seem crucial to the changes he describes, when Anglican writers such as John Fletcher depict 'rogues as neutralizers of religious controversy', moving beyond the stereotyping of Catholics as thieving 'Fraters' or 'roguing Jesuits', to retell the old story as a tale of persecuted victims, who 'return to their society and right its wrongs only by first impersonating rogues', and then regain their former places while staying proudly in their roving guise. In play after play of the 1620s, Knapp shows, the rovers' return restores a solidarity worthier than the broken communities they deserted, while so magnanimous do outlaws become in works like Fletcher's *The Beggar's Bush* that 'they happily accept strangers such as exiled aristocrats into their company'. And it is this open-handed 'Anglican' welcome that distinguishes these rogues from the 'precise' Puritans who are their foils. Thus the rogue plays of pre-revolutionary London dare to imply that 'the charity for which they beg includes toleration as well as alms', and to reconcile the renegades at the same time as they rehabilitate the Gothic ruins and haunted forests of England's Catholic past. So, when the token on which *A Jovial Crew* revolves turns out to be 'The *Agnes Dei* my mother gave me', the Robin Hood scenario constitutes the virtual template for a new freedom of confession, Knapp concludes.[38] Theatre has become more than spilt religion here: it is a vessel through which religion flows. But it would not have provided such a compelling instrument for the weak 'enforcement' of the Church of England's 'gentleness' if the author of *As You Like It* had not *himself* stepped into the agonistic frame, as such a 'mouldy rogue' [2 *Henry IV*, 2,4,105], and played upon the violence of the antagonism:

If ever you have looked on better days,
If ever sat at any good man's feast,
If ever from your eyelids wiped a tear,

And know what 'tis to pity, and be pitied,
Let gentleness my strong enforcement be. . . .

[*As You*, 2,7,112–17]

AMBITIOUS FOR A MOTLEY COAT

'Let me go with you,/I'll do the service of a younger man/In all your business and necessities' [2,3,54–6]: if Shakespeare did play the part of old Adam, the words he wrote for himself read like a meta-dramatic declaration of the role he played in the factionalism of the 1590s. So if *As You Like It* was first staged, as its Arden editor, Juliet Dusinberre, speculates, for the actual court in the Great Hall of Richmond Palace on Shrove Tuesday 1599, before being launched upon 'the wide and universal' Globe, this pastoral angle on political theology, and the edge it gives to the satire on Marprelate Puritans, with Touchstone's teasing of its Friar Tuck, Sir Oliver, as 'a most vile Martext' [5,1,5], would seem to place this drama under the wing of the Essex party, whose project for toleration under a future King is that of its exiled Duke: 'First, in this forest let us do those ends/That here were well begun, and well begot./And after, every of this happy number/That have endured shrewd days and nights with us/Shall share the good of our returned fortune' [5,4,159–63].[39] With this revanchist prospectus, Shakespeare's specific '*here*' appears to situate 'these woods' within the timbered Globe, and to exploit this new Bankside locus to affirm the distance of his playhouse from the palace. If so, Essex's rebels must have known what they were doing when they launched their rising at carnival-time in 1601 with a paid performance on Shakespeare's stage. For in contrast to the Protestant fundamentalism of Rose scenarios, this 'Anglican' version of 'returned fortune' concludes in 'rustic revelry' [166], with an unabashed celebration of the exiles' bandit kingdom as a nursery for national regeneration, where illicit relationships and illegal activities that have been 'well begun' will prove 'well begot'.

As Helen Cooper comments, the innovation of Shakespeare's outlaw story is that here it is 'the country restoring wholeness to the court'.[40] It may not, then, be chance that the oldest script of *As You Like It* is the 1694 Douai text drafted for the Jesuit college in the Ardennes, where it is nominally set, as this pederastic play has an unparalleled six parts for boys.[41] Significantly, its songs were set to music by Thomas Morley, for choristers of William Byrd's crypto-Catholic Chapel Royal.[42] But whatever Shakespeare's own nostalgia for 'Bare ruined choirs where late the sweet birds sang' [Sonnet 73], what the recovery of its religious politics restores to his comedy is its agonistic performativity, the Anglican emphasis on ritual with which Duke Senior asks us to 'begin these rites/As we do trust they'll end' [186]. If 'all the men and women are *merely* players', this 'proceeding' implies, it does not matter what they believe. So, in an epilogue that Dusinberre suggests succeeded these lines at court, the aged Queen was flattered that 'Like the dial day by day,/You may lead the seasons on/Making new when old are gone', with a sly echo of Touchstone's bawdy pun, as 'he drew a dial from his poke', that so 'from hour to hour we rot and rot' [2,7,20–7]. The allusion was perhaps to a floral clock at Richmond.[43] But if so, the conceit must have reminded courtiers how deluded Orlando had been to assume 'There's no clock in the forest'. For beside a palace of rotting 'whores', this wilderness where Orlando is taught the time by the 'pretty youth' Ganymede, who has supposedly been educated by that 'old religious uncle' with 'Sermons in stones' [3,2,275–313], is more likely to be 'making new when old are gone':

> That the babe which now is young
> And hath yet no use of tongue
> Many a Shrovetide here may bow
> To that Empress I do now,
> That the children of these lords
> Sitting at your council boards
> May be grave and aged seen
> Of her that was their fathers' Queen.
>
> [Court Epi., 9–16]

Flattering Elizabeth as a perpetual clock produces such a 'claustrophobic sense of being trapped in time', writes James Shapiro, that this bowing to 'the fading Cleopatra' seems truly forced.[44] Once before, Shakespeare had ironised his subjection with an exaggerated bow, when at the close of Henry IV Part 2 the actor knelt 'but to pray for the Queen' [Epi. 30]. That this forelock-touching was printed with a different speech recited by the clown Will Kemp, whose jig, according to that text, compensates for the words, only heightens the ambiguity about what is being said to whom, in words pitched at both 'gentle creditors' in the 'assembly', who revel in Falstaff's guying of the Puritan martyr Sir John Oldcastle, and at the Queen, who is begged to 'acquit' the offence [10; 15]. The accidental printing of both epilogues to Henry IV Part 2 exposes Shakespeare's Janus-mask in playing to separate audiences, and so sheds light on the shadowboxing of As You Like It. For though we can never know what went on behind the scenes, the duplicity helps to explain why, in 1596, Oldcastle's descendant, the testy Lord Chamberlain, William Brooke, Lord Cobham, notorious for shaking his staff at the actors, surprisingly let the company stage all six plays performed at Christmas for the court.[45] As Pierre Bourdieu observed, 'struggles at the heart of the political field may best serve the interest of writers concerned about literary independence'.[46] And sure enough, a first sign of Shakespeare's autonomy after his Oldcastle retraction was that the name of Brooke was yet again taken in vain, when an unrepentant Falstaff bounded back in The Merry Wives of Windsor, facetiously toasting the benevolence of all 'Such Brookes . . . that o'erflows such liquor' [2,2,135].[47]

The impertinence of Falstaff's return to the stage in The Merry Wives may account for the smokescreen that it was Elizabeth who commanded a sequel with 'Sir John in love'.[48] In such a client system, as Andrew Gurr explains, 'courtiers constantly played status games', so players had to manoeuvre to ensure they did not suffer. But in the end it was a royal warrant which trumped every civic, noble or religious obstruction.[49] The two-faced cultural politics of Shakespeare's Windsor farce, where the greatness of the Queen was travestied 'I' th' posture of a whore' [Antony, 5,2,217], under her own royal oak, therefore furnished an object lesson in the ploy of playing competing audiences against each other. Yet what such impudence also underlines is the disingenuousness of the poet's protest at having his 'art made tongue-tied by authority' [Sonnet 66]. As Gurr emphasises, 'loyalty to the patron was an annual requirement at court, but loyalty to the multitudes who went to the plays throughout the year, including the court's factions, was a much more basic determinant'.[50] Thus, while Munday reconfigured the Robin Hood tale as the romance of an earl to please 'a real contemporary earl, his company's patron', the Lord High Admiral, Charles Howard Earl of Nottingham, for Shakespeare, by contrast, solidarity with the court jester in the servile bowing and scraping at the palace would always be a liberating cloak:[51]

> O, that I were a fool,
> I am ambitious for a motley coat. . . .
> It is my only suit,
> Providing that you weed your better judgements
> Of all opinion that grows rank in them
> That I am wise. I must have liberty
> Withal, as large a charter as the wind,
> To blow on whom I please, for so fools have.
>
> [*As You*, 2,7,43–9]

Jacques' 'suit' to Duke Senior for a royal charter, to license him 'To blow on whom I please' like a kept fool, may have been inserted into the text after *As You Like It* was 'stayed' from publication in line with the 1599 Bishops' Ban prohibiting printing of satire.[52] If so, his plea can stand for the opportunism with which dramatists flaunted a parti-coloured cloak of Sherwood green to assert the extra-legality of the literary field, and thus lead both churchmen and politicians on a merry dance. As editors observe, there is some literally fancy footwork behind Jacques' tribute to the 'motley fool' Touchstone as 'A worthy fool' [34], because it seems to herald the arrival in the Lord Chamberlain's troupe of Robert Armin, the 'wise wit' known for playing 'Tutch', and the exile of the 'clownish fool' [1,4,124] Kemp, who (with a parting shot at 'Shakerags') departed at this time on a mad stunt to dance 'out of the world' or Globe, and become 'Emperor of Germany' by reprising his previous Danish success.[53] Dusinberre thinks Shakespeare had intended Touchstone for that 'roynish clown' [2,2,8].[54] The fool's repining, therefore, that 'When I was at home I was in a better place; but travellers must be content' [2,4,13], sounds like an in-house joke about Kemp's *faux pas*, when his scheme to 'dance to France' and 'go along over the wide world' [1,3,126] came unstuck.[55] As *Hamlet* discloses, Shakespeare had no illusions about the fool's paradise in continental courts to which his fellow performers were flocking to escape London's censors and theatre wars. Jacques seems instead to envy a household clown such as Armin, who had been retained by Lord Chandos, and who exemplified the paradox of weak power already grasped by Quince, that free speech is to be found in a 'marvellous convenient' place near home: 'At the Duke's oak', a Speakers' Corner 'exempt from public haunt', just outside the City walls, yet close enough to the seat of power to baffle the censorship imposed on 'satire, keen and critical' by the 'usual manager of mirth' [*Dream*, 1,2,89; 5,1,35–54].[56]

'He uses his folly like a stalking-horse, and under the presentation of that he shoots his wit' [5,4,96]: Duke Senior's last word on Touchstone caps a train of analogies in *As You Like It* between two kinds of 'game': that of the theatre and the chase. The metaphor of the clown hiding his point under a show of folly like a poacher's decoy is one of the clearest statements of the agonistic 'method' in Shakespeare's 'antic disposition' [*Hamlet*, 1,5,173; 2,2,203], the passive-aggressive Brutus gambit, 'Wherein deep policy did him disguise', and by means of which he 'clothed his wit in folly's show': to be 'esteemed/As silly jeering idiots are with kings,/For sportive words and utt'ring foolish things' [*Lucrece*, 1809–15]. At such moments, the 'antique world' of this comedy sounds the most indebted of Shakespeare's settings to Erasmus's praise of folly, with its Socratic philosophy that 'The fool doth think he is wise, but the wise man knows himself to be a fool' [5,1,33].[57] Yet the hunting imagery reminds us of the rules of this dangerous game, which, as the Catholic critic Richard Simpson observed, meant 'the poor despised player' was granted 'as much licence on matters of state as Motley' by those who 'might have him hanged'.[58] So, 'The truest poetry is the most feigning' [3,3,15], avers Touchstone, after Sidney. As Hugh Grady comments, 'In Shakespeare's age and our own, the aesthetic is a licensed discourse precisely because it is deemed to be in a special zone exempt from the truth-claims implied by ordinary discourse'.[59] But the fact that Duke Senior looks straight through this cover could be one reason why there is such empathy in this forest between the poachers and their prey, and why, with their jesters' caps and harlequin coats, the creaturely deer, trapped only to be hunted 'in their own confines', are themselves so pointedly described as liveried and licensed fools:

And yet it irks me the poor dappled fools,
Being native burghers of this desert city,
Should in their own confines with forked heads
Have their round haunches gored.

[2,1,22–5]

If the 'poor sequestered stag' is seen as a 'velvet friend' in this drama which affiliates bestiality with sovereignty, that might be less because Shakespeare is preaching animal rights than because the 'hairy fool' is the brother of the player in the 'liberty' of his 'assigned and native dwelling place' [33–63]. Here, agonism is always liable to slip back to antagonism. This was a connotation Ben Jonson developed in *The Sad Shepherd, Or, A Tale of Robin Hood*, where the slaughtered deer is 'a scapegoat, a sacrificial animal sent out into the countryside to be hunted', which is associated, via Robin, with 'the vulnerability of the playwright'.[60] Richard Dutton terms the 'assigned' reserve of the actors, where 'authority blended with self-policing privilege', a 'charmed circle', inside which a velvet livery trumped the Privy Council, so long as the protector of the fraternity had the power of an earl.[61] This extramural zone may have been a legal non-place, a 'green world' in Northrop Frye's typology, which, as Bottom exults, afforded a similar asylum to the 'merry men' as to poachers, in their freedom to 'rehearse most obscenely and courageously' [*Dream*, 1,2,88].[62] But the hunting and enclosure imagery of all this song and dance over the fraught 'place of brother' [1,1,20] reminds us how such a liberty implied endless contestation; for, as Grady notes, Shakespeare's 'green world' consists of two realms, 'a utopia and a dystopia', and 'to the extent that the idea of the aesthetic is concerned with the relation between the human and the natural', aesthetic autonomy is always tinged with 'the ideology of male supremacy', and with the violent actuality of economic ownership and political domination.[63]

Anthropologists point out that it is precisely societies whose family structures do *not* treat brothers as equals, like the one depicted in *As You Like It*, that incline to a differentialist vision of humanity of the kind the play seems to endorse, rather than imposing universality. Thus, in the enclosed forest of Shakespearean comedy, 'the answer to the question of how to achieve harmony seems to be: in our dreams'.[64] So, with its stratified levels of players and fairies, jesters and 'poor dappled' deer, Shakespeare's 'green world' is a dream land that has inscribed within it what Grady terms the 'impure aesthetic' of the dialectic between theatre and reality. And the coarse aggression of the hunting metaphor suggests that this was not a relation based on the old latitude, that at Liberty Hall 'There is no slander in an allowed fool' [*Twelfth*, 1,5,80], but the pugilism of the prickly type of fool Shakespeare would script for racy Armin, starting with the 'cobblers' of the 'naughty knave' who bad-mouths politicians as a curtain-raiser at the Globe [*Julius*, 1,1,15]. As the Countess sighs of Lavatch, by taking such liberties this new type of rogue stretches the customary laxity, 'which he thinks a patent for his sauciness, and runs where he will' [*All's Well*, 4,5,54–6]. Thus, Feste goes too far for Lady Olivia when he abuses her steward Malvolio 'most notoriously' [*Twelfth*, 5,1,366]; the Gravedigger is so 'absolute' he can call the Prince of Denmark insane to his face [*Hamlet*, 5,1,126]; Thersites exploits his 'privilege' to deride all lords as 'fools' [*Troilus*, 2,3,51]; and Apemantus 'drops down/The knee' to his oligarchic patron in mockery of the old feudal obsequiousness, only to revile such 'Serving of becks and jutting-out of bums' as sycophantic grovelling to congenital dolts:

> I doubt whether their legs be worth the sums
> That are given for 'em. Friendship's full of dregs.
> Methinks false hearts should never have sound legs.
> Thus honest fools lay out their wealth on curtseys. . . .
> No, I'll nothing. For if I should be bribed
> too, there would be none left to rail upon thee. . . .
>
> [*Timon*, 1,2,229–37]

'Not only, sir, this your all-licensed fool,/But other of your insolent retinue/Do hourly carp' [*Lear*, 1,4,175–7]: as Goneril objects, Shakespeare's Jacobean fools act out a far more antagonistic patronage relation than the buffoons of old, in which the creature bites the hand from which it feeds. These altered relations are also seen in the reactions of the nobility, such as Lear's daughter, who can no longer share a joke with performers who are their social inferiors. What put the entertainer on his defences, we are told, was a new refinement about humour that now required the elite to regulate laughter more strictly, or refrain from laughing altogether.[65] So it is undeniable that a cold wind blows through the Boar's Head when Falstaff fails to 'turn all to merriment', after he is overheard calling Hal 'a shallow fellow' who would make 'a good pantler'. And in bidding 'Falstaff, good night' [2 Henry IV, 2,4,212; 272; 335] the Prince anticipates the ultimate dismissal of his companion. Peter Burke relates this elite recoil from popular culture to 'the advance of learning'; and Keith Thomas ties it to the 'new etiquette' marking social distinctions.[66] But after the wrestling match in As You Like It has introduced a new adversarialism, the alienation of Shakespeare's fools also demonstrates how such mutual estrangement was a necessary function of the autonomisation of the play. For what this stand-off defines, when, to flaunt his maturing self-assurance, a fool's head fronts a clown's misrule, as though that 'little tiny toy' were but 'a foolish thing' [Twelfth, 5,1,378], is the agonistic exchange between art and power, the creature and the sovereign, when each lays claim to absolute power.[67]

'I am better than thou art now', his jester lectures King Lear, since 'I am a fool' [Lear, 1,4,169]. For Dutton this 'all-licensed' foolhardiness means 'each depends on the other for validation'. Indeed, he assumes that the King's Men became such indispensable appendages of the Stuart dynasty that they were bound to suffer the same fate: no king, no fool.[68] Yet as Jane Rickard details in her study of James's own risky writings, by publishing a folio 'the Wisest Fool in Christendom' would inadvertently authorise the transfer of symbolic sovereignty to his 'insolent retinue'. So the editors of the 1623 Folio would never need to mention that this 'fool' had been one of the King's Men: Shakespeare's aesthetic autonomy was separated from political authority, and this was the severance which had been foolishly mandated by the King himself, when he asserted the authority of authorship.[69] With a restored monarch of the glen who loves to hunt the stag beside his clown, As You Like It looks, then, as if it had always been intended for the clowning that welcomed this 'wisest fool' into his long-delayed English inheritance, beside his ribald Scottish jester Archie Armstrong.[70] But if Shakespeare did conceive his knock-about comedy about 'new-fallen dignity' [5,4,165] with an eye to the royal gala which eventually took place at Wilton over Christmas 1603, such premeditation only confirms how early he had taken the measure of this 'folio' king as his friendly adversary, not to mention the impertinence of the original performance, when he wished a racked old queen the torture of a 'stretch'd-out life' [Troilus, 1,3,61]:

Once I wish this wish again
Heaven subscribe it with amen.

[Court Epi., 17–18]

YOUR ONLY PEACEMAKER

'Last scene of all that ends this strange, eventful history,/Is second childishness and mere oblivion': Elizabeth would expire four years after hearing these lines in As You

Like It, if the Arden editor is correct, writhing, 'sans teeth, sans eyes, sans taste, sans everything' [2,7,162], on the floor of the hall at Richmond, where the actor had archly wished her so many returns.[71] For, of course, Shakespeare never did 'wish this wish again', if, like others, his Epilogue was said just once.[72] Instead, by cueing 'their exits and their entrances', when Orlando disrupts the feast with the 'venerable burden' of a dying Adam [140], and littering his play of beginnings and endings with tributes and epitaphs to contemporaries like the 'Dead shepherd' Marlowe [3,5,81], Shakespeare adapted the Robin Hood genre into a pastoral elegy for an entire epoch, a *memento mori* in the last winter of the Tudor century, on the theme of *Et in arcadia ego*. And he did this by playing upon the motto of the Globe – *Theatrum mundi* – that granted his world in the wood an equal status to the moribund court. So what the identification of the Ardennes with the Jesuit seminaries, and the merry men with Christian 'brothers in exile', returns to *As You Like It*, in counterpoint to the Warwickshire Arden, is a sacred geography for the political imaginary, or utopian hope, that runs through this play, the counter-intuitive prospectus that, in the anti-pastoral lines of the Jesuit poet and martyr Robert Southwell, 'Time goes by turns': 'The lopped tree in time may grow again. . . . Not always fall of leaf, nor ever spring. . . . The saddest birds a season find to sing'.[73]

'Out of these convertites/There is much matter to be heard and learned' [5,4,173–4]: however we decipher the Catholic graffiti in the wood, and whether or not they refer to real contemporary conversions, like that of France's Henri IV, they lend force to Amiens's carol to the winter wind about the pessimism of the intellect and optimism of a free will: 'Hey-ho, sing hey-ho, unto the green holly./Most friendship is feigning, most loving mere folly./Then hey-ho, the holly,/This life is most jolly' [182]. And they add topical bite to a quality in this elegiac *fin-de-siècle* drama that recent critics have picked up, which is its hospitality, trumpeted in the title, to what Anne Barton called the pacifying properties and powers of the counter-factual 'if': a word that is repeated, Shapiro points out, once a minute in the play, and that 'excites our hope', Kiernan Ryan concurs, 'that these dreams of release from the coercions of history might one day be realized'.[74] As Touchstone testifies towards the end, there is 'much virtue in "if"', for 'Your "if" is your only peacemaker' in this fencing type of language game: 'I knew when seven justices could not take up a quarrel, but when the parties were met themselves, one of then thought but of an "if". As "If you said so, then I said so", and they shook hands and swore brothers' [5,4,87–92].

Touchstone's conjectural handshake is the performance of a white lie, a convenient fiction of sworn brotherhood. Here the play's shifting textual provenance and performance history may be crucial. For this moot thinking would have been anchored in hopes attending the arrival of King James if, as seems possible, these lines, and the unprecedented masque of Hymen that follows them, were added, like a rehearsal for the theophanies of the late plays, for the Christmas performance of the comedy before the new regime at Wilton.[75] Shakespeare was musing much around this time upon the aporetic promise of 'Incertainties' that 'crown themselves assured', when 'peace proclaims olives of endless age' [Sonnet 107]. Thus Hymen's marriage ceremony is conditional, as the strange god affirms, 'If truth hold true

contents'. But this return to the *contentedness* of romance, 'improvised in the key of
if', does seem to spring, like hope eternal, from the big 'if' of 1603, the great year of
contingency, that 'Incertainties' are now 'assured':[76]

DUKE SENIOR:	If there be truth in sight you are my daughter.
ORLANDO:	If there be truth in sight, you are my Rosalind.
PHOEBE:	If sight and shape be true,
	Why then, my love adieu!
ROSALIND [to the DUKE]:	I'll have no father if you be not he.
[to ORLANDO]:	I'll have no husband if you be not he.
[to PHOEBE]:	Nor ne'er wed woman if you be not she.

[5,4,107–13]

'If I were a woman I would kiss as many of you as had beards that pleased me'
[Epi.,14]: when the boy costumed as Rosalind who speaks the Epilogue, which may
not have been recited at both Wilton and the Globe, rubs the faces of his conjectural 'brothers' in the artifice of this release of repressed desires, by offering to
prostitute himself, the 'naughtiness' of 'the old Robin Hood' makes this last 'if' the
most roguish provocation of all. For a Protestant like Munday, female impersonation
could be allowed only if unacknowledged, and he solved the unmanning conun-
drum of Maid Marian by consigning her to a nunnery.[77] But it took Stephen Orgel
to recognise what the film *Shakespeare in Love* suppressed (and feminists obscure, by
theorising that both 'A male actor *and* female character is speaking'), which is that
'the play insists the wife is *really a boy*, and this too may be a way of offering Orlando
(or any number of spectators) what he "really" wants'.[78] Shakespeare had upped the
homoerotic stakes with a profusion of boy brides in *The Merry Wives*.[79] But here
the bristling *frisson* that the 'lady' has 'a beard coming' [*Dream*, 1,2,40] is pushed
further, to seal the difference of this conditional realm from the royal court, as the
agonistic place where the impossible does happen and, as Ryan applauds, 'we expect
the reverse of what passes for normal to prevail', in an agonistic moment 'committed
to envisaging forms of life liberated from whatever forbids the free play and shared
satisfaction of justified desires'.[80] Jacques Derrida had something to say about this
virtual space and time in *The Politics of Friendship*, the book of about brothers and
others, inspired by Montaigne, which comes closest to the homo-fraternal 'if' of *As
You Like It*. Here, the philosopher wrote, 'We would hesitate on the edge of a fiction':

The world would be hanging on a sort of elementary, borderless hypothesis: a
general conditionality that would spread over all certainties. The virtual space
and time of the 'perhaps' would be *in the process* of exhausting the force of our
desires, the flesh of our events, the uttermost of our lives. No, they would not
be *in the process* of exhausting us, for the very *presence* of such a process would
be reassuring and still too effective; no, they would be on the verge of success,
and this imminence would suffice for their victory. . . . From this virtuality
they could never escape. . . . The modality of the possible, the unquenchable
perhaps, would, implacably, destroy everything. . . .[81]

The essence of democracy, with its liberty, equality and fraternity, Derrida theorised, is that it 'remains to come'.[82] And so, in the final twist of the Shakespearean cringe towards the powerful, the bearded 'lady' laughs that if she curtsies to them the men 'will for my kind offer bid me farewell' [Epi.,18]. Shakespeare had ended *Love's Labour's Lost* with a similar separation between the harsh 'words of Mercury' and euphoric 'songs of Apollo', when the actor told the audience 'You that we, we this way'. There the play-world had been dashed 'like a Christmas comedy' [5,2,462; 903–4]. But this outlaw overture instead lays claim on behalf of the stage to the Robin Hood game of a world turned upside down. For we can, of course, never know whether males in the audience agree that one can never 'desire too much of a good thing', and follow Orlando in falling for Ganymede's 'coming-on', 'his' shirt-lifting suggestion that 'the cleanliest shift is to kiss' [4,1,66–105]. As Orgel notes, this last 'if' is unique in Shakespeare.[83] It plays on a Puritan's worst fear that theatre was, as Philip Stubbes alleged, a place for homosexual liaison, where 'every mate brings another home and in their secret conclaves they play the Sodomites or worse'.[84] And if it was not expressly written for the royal pederast at Wilton, then it can only have been made possible by the move to the Globe in the Liberty of Southwark, the extramural *banlieu* where 'the spectacle of the outcast and the marginal held sway', and where the 'place of the stage' was literally outside the place of the state.[85] For with this indecent proposal to steal forbidden kisses made by a boy bandit, Shakespeare crosses the line that makes his roving 'co-mates and brothers' in the playhouse identical to the outlaw fellowship in the woods. Now we grasp that Robin Hood's rogue state, the land of 'if', where 'liberty plucks justice by the nose' [*Measure*, 1,3,29], fraternity turns sovereignty inside out and equality puts the iron law of economics upside down, will indeed be the wooden 'nought' of the Globe itself:

> Under the greenwood tree
>   Who loves to lie with me,
>   And turn his merry note
>   Unto the sweet bird's throat,
> Come hither, come hither, come hither.

> [2,5,1–5]

TO CALL FOOLS INTO A CIRCLE

'Now go we in content, / To liberty, and not to banishment' [1,3,131–2]: auspicating the timbered Globe as a sacred grove, the exiles' farewell to the City in *As You Like It* promotes life 'Under the greenwood tree' in Southwark as the reverse of Elizabethan political reality, in an agonistic no-place where 'Who doth ambition shun' will crave only 'the food he eats', yet be 'pleased with what he gets'. 'Leaving his wealth and ease', as Jacques warns, whoever is foolish enough to join these 'merry men' must be motivated by 'A stubborn will to please' [2,5,31–5]. 'Stubborn Will', the author, professes the same freedom from material calculation in his very last lines for the Globe, when he has his magus, Prospero, admit that, without praise, 'my project fails, / Which was to please' [*Tempest*, Epi.,12]. So, if this plan to please has not achieved the autonomy of the aesthetic, it has the relative autonomy of the 'impure aesthetic' which Grady sees as a 'place-holder' for what is repressed, and as a playground for religious conflict, when it appears that 'art, not any specific confessional faith', will bring about a 'new cultural community'.[86] Art does not sublimate religious difference, on this view: it becomes *the means to make such difference possible*. And certainly, Jacques makes the mad method of a 'stubborn will to please' sound like a premonition of this pluralistic project, when, using a 'Greek invocation to call fools into a circle' [2,5,53], like Prospero, he conjures the foolhardy to enter a ring, and then 'stand spell-stopped' [*Tempest*, 5,1,61], and thereby inaugurates the inclusive roundness of this 'Wooden O' [*Henry V*, Pro.,12] with a parodic grace:

Ducdame, ducdame, ducdame.
  Here shall he see
  Gross fools as he,
An if he will come to me.

[2,5,48–51]

'What's that "ducdame"?' Amiens reasonably demands [52]. For editors gloss the pseudo-solemn 'ducdame' as a secret gypsy palmist's incantation meaning 'I foresee'. This fits a legend that Jacques was played by the 'sun-burnt gypsy' Jonson, who raided travellers' argot for his own plays.[87] It accords with the 'blacking' adopted by the exiles; and with the wanton boy who would 'conjure' men to kiss [5,4,10–12; Epi.,9]. Shakespeare had already had Mercutio confuse gypsies with Egyptians [*Romeo*, 2,3,37] and would present Cleopatra as 'a right gypsy' [*Antony*, 4,13,28] by making the gift economy of the Romany potlatch the spring of his tragedy of 'a gypsy's lust'. His African queen combines the Romany stereotypes of fortune-teller and feckless, dirty, thieving tramp. But the hospitality of her 'Egyptian bacchanals' transforms the image of the gypsy as a homeless beggar into that of a 'dangerously attractive' Lady Bountiful who trumps 'the quick comedians' at their own game [1,1,9; 2,7,98; 5,2,12].[88] Likewise, by beating the bounds and blessing the house with mock solemn vagabonds' cant, Jacques affiliates the suburban place of the stage with the one community whose 'defiance of the wage-labour system', as well as 'singing, dancing, sleight of hand, and fortune-telling', kept them on the margins of the Protestant state.[89] As Paul Yachnin stresses, though Jacques bemoans that 'All the world's a stage', and stalks from 'This wide and universal theatre', the play's answer to such anti-theatricality is 'not a denial of theatricality but an exploration of the liberating possibilities of intensified versions' of the theatre itself.[90] So it is a farrago of Romany salacity and slang that here 'sanctifies' the stage, where religious dissidence is not so much subordinated as suborned. Perhaps this translation of supernaturalism from one sacred precinct into another was what Dryden suspected when, in 1667, he attributed Shakespeare's authorial freedom to some occult power inherited from the 'old priesthood' that 'works by magic supernatural things':

. . . Shakespeare's magick could not copied be,
Within that circle none durst walk but he.
I must confess 'twas bold, nor would you now
That liberty to vulgar wits allow. . . .
Those legends from old priesthood were receiv'd
And he then writ, as people then believed.[91]

Of all rogues catalogued in the moral panic of the 1590s, it was gypsies, 'attracting people with the strangeness of their attire', who were viewed as 'the most theatrical', Paola Pugliatti points out.[92] Thus, their apparel was 'odd and fantastic', Dekker complained, with 'scarves of calico hanging their bodies like morris-dancers with bells and other toys', while their women wore 'rags and filthy mantles uppermost', exposing fancy underwear.[93] In 1607 John Cowell dismissed all gypsies as Welsh frauds, who, 'framing an unknown language, wander up and down, and under pretence of telling fortunes, abuse ignorant common people by stealing all that is not too hot or too heavy for their carriage'.[94] Yet Shakespeare accepted the clandestine affinity, it seems, between these royal thieves and his own 'co-mates' who in 1599 had just illegally dismantled the theatre in Shoreditch and carried its timber to re-erect the oak in a magic circle on Bankside. This was a different sort of felony to Robin's robbing of the rich to help the poor. But the notion that, as just such a mimic monarch, Shakespeare might identify with these pearly kings and queens, and revel in the vagrancy laws that lumped 'common players and minstrels' alongside bearwards, jugglers and charlatans, idle rogues and masterless men, is what distinguishes him from his respectable contemporaries. By 1600 Marlowe and Shakespeare had correlated the itinerancy of players with issues of 'religious as well as social errancy', Knapp argues, so that their successors, such as Brome, could envision playing as a means 'not only of elucidating English vagrancy but of celebrating it too'. Now that they had settled out of bounds, the players had legitimated their roving. Thus, with increasing daring, actors 'urged audiences to view themselves as members of a better "rogue" society, one that was more civil and godly than the vagabonds but less strict and intolerant than the puritans'.[95] And it was in As You Like It that the surprise superiority of this agonistic yet ever-widening 'universal theatre' over the antagonism of contemporary society was first proclaimed:

Meantime, forget this new-fallen dignity
And fall into our rustic revelry.
Play, music, and you brides and bridegrooms all,
With measure heaped in joy to th'measures fall.

[5,4,165–8]

Recent historians have emphasised how to acquire legitimacy early modern thieves and pickpockets imitated the 'new fallen dignity' of city gilds in their initiation rites.[96] But in As You Like It the confraternity of players seems to be returning the compliment of this underworld imitation, by *dressing down* in 'rustic revelry'. For as 'vagabonds on principle', who enjoyed 'a liberty poor Englishmen and women lacked', gypsies in particular 'raised a standard of libertarianism' that was asking to be emulated, Hill maintained.[97] At a time when even consorting with Roma was a capital offence (a sentence exacted on five citizens of Durham in 1592, with nine gypsies themselves hanged at York in 1595), to circumscribe the Globe as a gypsy liberty, turning enclosure inside out, was therefore paradoxically liberating.[98] As Ania Loomba relates, since the defining characteristic of gypsies was their artificiality, 'a complex web of connections between gypsies, stage actors, Moors, as well as local tricksters' made them equally suspect and exciting as agents of 'disguise, trickery, and conversion': 'The legislation concerning gypsies reveals a fear of contamination that might pass from "real" to "false" gypsies . . . at the same time suggesting that all gypsies were counterfeit'.[99] The rogue emerged in the political imaginary of London's early modern middle classes in a conflicted 'double bind of sympathy and disgust, admiration and fear', historians have shown.[100] But Jacques' gypsy incantation suggests that the ambivalence of this fictionalised complicity was exactly as they liked it.

In *Becoming Criminal*, his study of 'transversal performance and cultural dissidence', Bryan Reynolds takes the fantasies of the ever-expanding circulation of the 'Egyptian' sign seriously enough to argue that there were in fact no actual gypsies at all in Shakespeare's England, but only 'rogues and vagabonds' disguised by the strategy of 'becoming gypsy'. With 'smirch[ed]' face and 'poor and mean attire' [1,3,105–6], 'gypsyism' was the fetishised signifier, according to this analysis, of 'transversal anti-state concepts of heterogeneity, mutability, expansion, nomadism, performance, and indeterminacy'.[101] With such a weight of Deleuzean baggage, this definition risks making the journey to Arden more wearisome than even Touchstone finds it. But it does suggest how the itinerancy and mobility of the gypsy identity might make it synonymous with the playground of theatre, when at the start of the play Celia organises the migration by blacking herself to look even 'browner than her brother' [4,3,87].

As a concrete sign of agonistic confrontation, 'blacking' has provoked scandal in recent times on account of its imputed racism; but as E. P. Thompson showed, in early modern England the notion of 'an army of Blacks' sworn to serve 'their Mock Monarch' in poaching and trespass was often equally misinterpreted, as a conspiracy 'for establishing the Kingdom of Darkness'.[102] Feminist critics have thus stressed how by adopting the guise of such 'assailants' [1,3,108], Celia and Rosalind expand the circle of theatrical transgression to the limits Elizabethan outlawry. For it is Celia's adoption of the name of Aliena as 'Something that hath reference to [her] state' [121] and decision to darken her skin 'browner' than even the prostitute boy that mark the play with indelible alterity. By identifying with the despised 'Egyptian', Celia-as-Aliena reminds the audience of 'a potential transversal presence in their very midst'.[103] That this migrant magic will not be washed away is proved when Oliver falls in love with 'the poverty of her' upon 'but seeing' Celia in 'dissembling colour' [3,4,6; 5,2,2–6]. Shakespeare would link gypsy lore with the danger of such erotic 'giddiness' [5] by having Othello claim 'an Egyptian charmer' wove the demonic charge of her handkerchief to 'subdue' men to love [*Othello*, 3,4,54–8]. Yet by drawing actors and audience amorously beneath the ring of oak, introducing them to noxious horse thieves, con men, card sharps and fortune tellers, and thereby 'evoking the concept of a supernatural art coincident with nature', what the Romany wanderers of As You Like It are also conjuring is a time to come when 'the circle of this forest' will share the global reach of that Merlin-type sorcerer, 'most profound in his art and yet not damnable' [5,2,54], who already appears like the 'obscured' yet worldly author of the play, Shakespeare himself:[104]

DUKE SENIOR: I do remember in this shepherd boy
               Some lively touches of my daughter's favour.
ORLANDO: My lord, the first time that ever I saw him
               Methought he was a brother to your daughter.
               But my good lord, this boy is forest-born
               And hath been tutored in the rudiments
               Of many desperate studies by his uncle,
               Whom he reports to be a great magician
               Obscured in the circle of this forest.

                                                   [5,4,26–34]

Elizabethan statutes forbade all 'charms, sorcery, enchantment, invocations, circles, witchcrafts or any like crafts or imaginations'; and the 'dead shepherd's' Faustus had proved the mortal peril of a theatre of necromantic 'Lines, circles, scenes, letters, and characters'.[105] But by casting cod Romany spells 'to call fools' into a ring, Shakespeare reconfigured the Robin Hood scenario to claim for his wooden circus the liberty from law that was the magical birthright of 'Egyptian kings and queens'.[106] Thus, Jacques' circle describes the vagrant 'O' of Shakespeare's *worldly* world. For as Knapp points out, such *Romany* affiliation was itself a spell-binding conjuration to coexistence, considering 'Protestants habitually maligned English Catholics as "Egyptians"', and gypsy caravans were suspected of carting priests in disguise.[107] In fact, there is a chain of *Moorish* puns connecting the 'tribe' of Thomas More with Arabs, Egyptians and Moors in texts like A Midsummer Night's Dream and Othello that turns 'moral' exorbitance into an anagrammatic appeal for *Roman* emancipation.[108] As Celia quips, there is always 'more in it' when a Shakespearean character brandishes a relic like Orlando's 'bloody napkin' [4,3,137; 158]. And it was Jonson, a Catholic who 'spent a lifetime defining a position for himself – and for the artist – on the margins of courtly society', who learned enough from As You Like It to draw this subtext out, composing his masque The Gypsies Metamorpos'd for another papist, Francis Manners, Earl of Rutland (for whom Shakespeare devised a shield), as a vehicle for 'Romany' players to present themselves as vagrant rogues, whose rehabilitation 'transforms gloom into happiness' when it creates 'a space for tolerance'.[109]

The religious turn in twenty-first-century Renaissance studies has worked to dispel the hermeneutic of suspicion that in the 1990s viewed Shakespeare's aesthetic investment in a play like As You Like It as merely a version of ruling-class ideology. Thus it is the open secret of confessional coexistence that complicates the postco-lonial view of theatrical 'blacking' as a pernicious travesty, in which aristocracy and royalty like Celia and Rosalind 'besmirch' themselves as gypsies, Moors or negroes simply to reinforce paranoia about contamination.[110] As Lynda Boose and others have established, racial difference was always inscribed at this time 'within cultural and religious categories'.[111] When the 'beautiful and refined' African noblewomen present themselves to the 'British' men in Jonson's 1608 *Masque of Blackness*, for instance, it is as representatives of liberty, who rule the sea, in celebration of a vagrancy that is 'written *by* an outlaw *for* an outlaw': the Catholic Queen Anne.[112] 'Romany' religion is not sublimated into art through such a performance so much as it is the substance of the art itself. Likewise, in *As You Like It* the contested forest of religion provides both timber for the Globe theatre and the leaves from which its folio is made. So, it is the recent critical interest in religious politics that allows us to grasp that it is as provocateurs of creative freedom that gypsies are conjured into Shakespeare's magic circle, where these 'gentlemen of the shade', nomadic 'minions of the moon' [*1 Henry IV*, 1,2,22–3], play 'fast and loose' [*Antony*, 4,13,28], as forerunners of the lawless cheat of playing, who must be allowed to go 'in content,/To liberty, and not to banishment' [1,3,130–1].

The song that concludes *As You Like It* marries the lovers 'in faith', but also in sodomy, 'like two gypsies on a horse' [5,3,12]. This is a rapport that therefore locates the playhouse on the side of the illicit camaraderie that lies in that big 'if' of Hymen's promise to the King, to 'bar confusion' in some time 'When earthly things made even/Atone together' [5,4,98–114]. But it is underwritten by Shakespeare's fidelity to his own extramural liberty, as home to 'an honourable kind of thievery', where the outlaws swear, as they do in *The Two Gentlemen of Verona*, to do no outrages, 'By the bare scalp of Robin Hood's fat friar' [4,1,35–70]. Thus the dramatist restored to 'the old Robin Hood' the inverted logic of 'solidarity and contempt for financial concerns'.[113] And when he adapted the legend of the king disguised, to have Prince Hal 'drink with any tinker in his own language' [*1 Henry IV*, 2,5,16], the effect, as Stephen Greenblatt observes, was not to criminalise the rogue state, but to confirm the sinister thesis that the real state itself rests on a hypocrisy so deep 'the hypocrites themselves believe it'.[114] For as our own 'melancholy Jacques' reminded us in his book *Rogues*, the idea of the rogue state that began at the city walls with the challenge, 'What is the *banlieu?*' – the *without-law* – meets its *aporia* in the Shakespearean admission of 'what a rogue and peasant slave am I!' [*Hamlet*, 2,2,527]. Here 'there are no longer anything but rogue states, and there are no rogue states', Derrida assured us. And with its concern for the dark intimacy of the sovereign and the beast, and for the impossible aporetic politics of friendship, forgiveness, hospitality, justice, legacy, mourning, terrorism and the democracy to come, all the philosopher's signature themes are in this play with the deconstructionist title of *As You Like It*; but none more insistently than that of the late essay he called 'The rogue that I am': that the 'rogues and degenerates', those 'others of brothers', who are the 'excluded or wayward, outcast or displaced, left to roam' outside the city walls, are always also our fellow travellers, citizens and compeers, our 'co-mates and brothers in exile'.[115]

NOTES

1. Richard Wilson, 'Like the old Robin Hood: *As You Like It* and the enclosure riots', in *Will Power: Essays on Shakespearean Authority* (Hemel Hempstead: Harvester, 1993), pp. 66–87, here p. 70. The essay was first published in *Shakespeare Quarterly*, 43:1 (spring 1992), 1–19.

2. David Underdown, *Revel, Riot, and Rebellion: Popular Politics and Culture in England, 1603–1660* (Oxford: Oxford University Press, 1985), pp. 110–11.

3. Eric Hobsbawm, *Primitive Rebels: Studies in Archaic Forms of Social Movement in the 19th and 20th Centuries* (revised edn, Manchester: Manchester University Press, 1971), pp. 22–3; and see Eric Hobsbawm, *Bandits* (Harmondsworth: Penguin, 1985), p. 42: 'His role is that of a champion, the righter of wrongs, the bringer of justice and equity. His relation to the peasants is one of solidarity and identity . . . he is not the enemy of the king . . . but of the local gentry, clergy, or other oppressors'.

4. Wilson, 'Like the old Robin Hood', pp. 79–81.

5. Stephen Greenblatt, 'Invisible bullets: Renaissance authority and its subversion, *Henry IV* and *Henry V*', in Richard Wilson and Richard Dutton (eds), *New Historicism and Renaissance Drama* (Harlow: Longman, 1992), p. 108.

6. Jeanne Addison Roberts, *The Shakespearean Wild: Geography, Genus, and Gender* (Lincoln: University of Nebraska Press, 1991), p. 25.

7. William Empson, *Some Versions of Pastoral* (London: Chatto and Windus, 1935), pp. 11–12. 'the illusion that ruling class interests': Eliot Krieger, *A Marxist Study of Shakespeare's Comedies* (Basingstoke: Macmillan, 1979), p. 5; Peter Burke, *Popular Culture in Early Modern Europe*; and Leah Marcus, *The Politics of Mirth: Jonson, Herrick, Milton, Marvell, and the Defense of Old Holiday Pastimes* (Chicago: Chicago University Press, 1986). For New Historicist scepticism towards pastoral, see the important essay by Louis Montrose, 'Eliza, Queene of Shepheardes', *English Literary Renaissance*, 10 (1980), 153–82. And for an excellent overview of this critique, see also Michael Dobson, 'Cold front in Arden', *London Review of Books*, 31 October 1996, p. 24.

8. Jonathan Haynes, *The Social Relations of Jonson's Theater* (Cambridge: Cambridge University Press, 1992), pp. 102–3; see also Dennis Brailsford, *Sport and Society: Elizabeth to Anne* (London: Routledge and Kegan Paul, 1969), pp. 103–16.

9. Edwin Davenport, 'The representation of Robin Hood in Elizabethan drama: *George a Grene* and *Edward I*', in Lois Potter (ed.), *Playing Robin Hood: The Legend as Performance in Five Centuries* (Newark: University of Delaware Press, 1998), p. 60; Edward Berry, *Shakespeare and the Hunt: A Cultural and Social Study* (Cambridge: Cambridge University Press, 2001), p. 164.

10. Lois Potter, 'The Elizabethan Robin Hood plays', in Potter, *Playing Robin Hood*, p. 22 and n. 3, p. 25. Cf. J. C. Holt, *Robin Hood* (London: Thames and Hudson, 1989), p. 158. See also Erika T. Lin, 'Popular festivity and the early modern stage: the case of George a Greene', *Theatre Journal*, 61 (2009), 271–97.

11. Stephen Knight, 'Quite another man: the Restoration Robin Hood', in Potter, *Playing Robin Hood*, pp. 167–81; 'Like any repentant Roundhead': Underdown, *Revel, Riot, and Rebellion*, pp. 282–3. See also Stephen Knight, 'Robin Hood and the royal restoration', *Critical Survey*, 5 (1993), 298–312. The text of 'A Health unto our King' is reprinted in R. B. Dobson and J. Taylor, *Rymes of Robin Hood: An Introduction to the English Outlaw* (London: Heinemann, 1976).

12. C. L. Barber, *Shakespeare's Festive Comedy: A Study of Dramatic Form and Its Relation to Social Custom* (Princeton: Princeton University Press, 1959), pp. 6–10 and 216–21.

13. Christopher Hill, *Liberty Against the Law: Some Seventeenth-Century Controversies* (London: Allen Lane, 1996), pp. 5 and 9.

14. Christopher Hill, *The World Turned Upside Down: Radical Ideas During the English Revolution*

(Harmondsworth: Penguin, 1975), pp. 43–7. A significant variation on this account has recently been aired by Chris Fitter, in 'Reading Orlando historically: vagrancy, forest, and vestry values in Shakespeare's *As You Like It*', *Medieval and Renaissance Drama in England*, 23 (2010), 114–41, which interprets the comedy as a 'protest play' against the inexorable encroachment of Puritan attitudes on the 'vestry values' of 'merry England' (p. 114).

15. Kathleen Biddick, *The Shock of Medievalism* (Durham: Duke University Press, 1998), pp. 64–8. For a wry discussion of the poststructuralist assault on the empiricism and essentialism of Hill and other Old Left thinkers such as E. P. Thompson and Raymond Williams, see David Norbrook, 'Afterword', in *Poetry and Politics in the English Renaissance* (revised edn, Oxford: Oxford University Press, 2001), pp. 276–83: 'Whatever Hill's limitations, he had read far more of the literature of the period than any other historian and probably than any other literary critic, and . . . he was the most serious of empiricists in grounding his generalizations about the culture' (p. 283).

16. Hill, *Liberty Against the Law*, p. 56.

17. Ibid., pp. 72, 78, 81, 85, 96–8, 332 and 341.

18. Norbrook, *Poetry and Politics*, pp. 282 and 304–7.

19. For the West Country party known as the 'Robins' in the 1640 parliamentary elections, see Underdown, *Revel, Riot, and Rebellion*, pp. 134–6.

20. Michael Shapiro, 'Cross-dressing in Elizabethan Robin Hood plays', in Potter, *Playing Robin Hood*, pp. 86–7.

21. Ibid.

22. Jeffrey Singman, 'Munday's unruly earl', in Potter, *Playing Robin Hood*, pp. 63–76: 'By ennobling the outlaw hero, Munday appears to co-opt him and his actions on behalf of the official hierarchy. But in fact he has only succeeded in creating two Robins. . . . Between his fatuous Earl and the cunning outlaw of tradition there is an unbridgeable gulf' (p. 73).

23. Andrew Barnaby, 'The political conscious of Shakespeare's *As You Like It*', *Studies in English Literature*, 36 (1996), 373–95, here 377 and 392.

24. George Peele, *Edward I*, scene 7, 1176–7, in *The Dramatic Works of George Peele*, ed. Charles Tyler Prouty, 3 vols (New Haven: Yale University Press, 1952–70), vol. 1, p. 113. For meta-drama in the Robin Hood plays, see Lois Potter, 'Introduction' in Potter, *Playing Robin Hood*, p. 17.

25. 'From law to outlawry to law': Singman, 'Munday's unruly Earl', p. 70

26. Craig Dionne and Steve Mentz, 'Introduction', in *Rogues and Early Modern English Culture* (Ann Arbor: University of Michigan Press, 2006), pp. 1 and 5.

27. Andrew Hadfield, *Shakespeare and Republicanism* (Cambridge: Cambridge University Press, 2005), pp. 72–3.

28. Linda Woodbridge, *The Scythe of Saturn: Shakespeare and Magical Thinking* (Urbana: University of Illinois Press, 1994), pp. 188–94; Carlo Ginzburg, *The Night Battles: Witchcraft and Agrarian Cults in the Sixteenth and Seventeenth Centuries*, trans. John Tedeschi and Anne Tedeschi (London: Routledge and Kegan Paul, 1983). For the fertility symbolism of the walking wood in *Macbeth*, see John Holloway, *The Story of the Night: Studies in Shakespeare's Major Tragedies* (London: Routledge and Kegan Paul, 1961), p. 66: 'To a contemporary audience . . . the single figure . . . pursued by a whole company of others carrying green branches, was a familiar sight as a Maying procession, celebrating the triumph of new life over the sere and yellow leaf of winter'.

29. Richard Wilson, *Secret Shakespeare: Studies in Theatre, Religion and Resistance* (Manchester: Manchester University Press, 2004), pp. 104–25 et passim.

30. For the Platonising pastoralism of Duke Senior's speech, see Richard Cody, *The Landscape of the Mind: Pastoralism and Platonic Theory in Tasso's 'Aminta' and Shakespeare's Early Comedies* (Oxford: Oxford University Press, 1969), p. 49.

31. Jeffrey Knapp, *Shakespeare's Tribe: Church, Nation, and Theater in Renaissance England*

(Chicago: Chicago University Press, 2002), pp. 67 and 73; Edmund Spenser, *The Faerie Queene*, 1,2,9; 1,7,50; 2,1,19; and 3,1,24.

32. Norbrook, *Poetry and Politics*, p. 175.

33. Ted Hughes, *Shakespeare and the Goddess of Complete Being* (London: Faber and Faber, 1992), pp. 101–2 and 115.

34. For 'Shakespeare and the tragedy of Arden', see in particular Wilson, *Secret Shakespeare*, pp. 104–25.

35. Walter Benjamin, 'Theses on the philosophy of history: I', in *Illuminations*, trans. Harry Zohn, ed. Hannah Arendt (London: Jonathan Cape, 1970), p. 255.

36. 'A long beard': William Oldys; 'took no parts': Edward Capell, both quoted in Samuel Schoenbaum, *William Shakespeare: A Documentary Life* (Oxford: Oxford University Press, 1975), p. 149.

37. James Bednarz, *Shakespeare and the Poet's War* (New York: Columbia University Press, 2001), pp. 117 and 123.

38. Knapp, *Shakespeare's Tribe*, pp. 71–3 and 77–8; Richard Brome, *A Jovial Crew: or, The Merry Beggars*, ed. Ann Haaker (Lincoln: Nebraska University Press, 1968), 5,1,432.

39. Juliet Dusinberre (ed.), 'Introduction', in *As You Like It* (London: Arden Shakespeare/Thomson, 2006), pp. 36–46. For the sectarian pastoralism of the Robin Hood plays and its appropriation by poets such as Sidney and Spenser, see Helen Cooper, *Pastoral: Medieval into Renaissance* (Ipswich: Boydell and Brewer, 1977), pp. 193–5.

40. Cooper, *Pastoral*, p. 174.

41. Ibid., appendix 4, 'The Douai manuscript', pp. 374–87; James Shapiro, *1599: A Year in the Life of William Shakespeare* (London: Faber and Faber, 2005), p. 251. For dramatic performances at Douai, see A. C. F. Beales, *Education Under Penalty: English Catholic Education from the Reformation to the Fall of James II* (London: Athlone Press, 1963), p. 134.

42. Dusinberre (ed.), *As You Like It* (Arden Shakespeare), pp. 77–9. The song 'It was a lover and his lass' was first published in 1600 in Thomas Morley's *The First Book of Ayres*.

43. For the authenticity of this epilogue and its relation to a first Shrovetide performance of *As You Like It*, see Dusinberre (ed.), *As You Like It* (Arden Shakespeare), appendix 1, pp. 349–54. The text is reproduced on pp. 351–2. Shapiro connects the epilogue to a 1599 revival of *A Midsummer Night's Dream* but is less convincing: Shapiro, *1599*, pp. 84–8. The text was first published and its Shakespearean authorship mooted by William Ringler, Jr, and Steven May, in 'Epilogue possibly by Shakespeare', in G. Blakemore Evans (ed.), *The Riverside Shakespeare* (Boston: Houghton Mifflin, 1974), pp. 1851–2.

44. Shapiro, *1599*, p. 86.

45. For recent discussions of this surprise outcome, see Andrew Gurr, *The Shakespeare Company, 1594–1642* (Cambridge: Cambridge University Press, 2004), pp. 169–70; and Paul Whitfield White, 'Shakespeare, the Cobhams, and the dynamics of theatrical patronage', in Paul Whitfield White and Susan Westfall (eds), *Shakespeare and Theatrical Patronage in Early Modern England* (Cambridge: Cambridge University Press, 2002), pp. 64–89. See also Gary Taylor, 'William Shakespeare, Richard James and the house of Cobham', *Review of English Studies*, 38 (1987), 334–54.

46. Pierre Bourdieu, *The Rules of Art: Genesis and Structure of the Literary Field*, trans. Susan Emmanuel (Cambridge: Polity Press, 1996), p. 52.

47. See Janet Clare, *'Art Made Tongue-Tied by Authority': Elizabethan and Jacobean Dramatic Censorship* (Manchester: Manchester University Press, 1990), pp. 79–80: 'The death of William Brooke in 1597 may have convinced Shakespeare that it was safe to take greater liberties; Henry Cobham, his heir . . . did not possess the same influence . . . and the players may well have considered that . . . the suppression of "Brook" was a piece of censorship which they could safely override'.

48. The legend was first recorded by John Dennis in 1702; see Park Honan, *Shakespeare: A Life* (Oxford: Clarendon Press, 1993), p. 223.

49. Gurr, *The Shakespeare Company*, p. 170.

50. Ibid., p. 177.

51. Donna Hamilton, *Anthony Munday and the Catholics, 1560–1633* (Aldershot: Ashgate, 2005), p. 130.

52. See Alan Brissenden, 'Introduction', in *As You Like It* (Oxford: Clarendon Press, 1993), p. 2; and Cyndia Susan Clegg, 'Liberty, license, and authority: press censorship and Shakespeare', in David Scott Kastan (ed.), *A Companion to Shakespeare* (Oxford: Blackwell, 1999), p. 478.

53. William Kemp, *Nine Days' Wonder*, ed. G. B. Harrison (London: John Lane, Bodley Head, 1923), p. 3; 'Shakerags': quoted in Honan, *Shakespeare*, p. 271.

54. Dusinberre (ed.), *As You Like It* (Arden Shakespeare), pp. 45–6.

55. 'Dance to France': Weelkes, *Airs* (1608), quoted in David Wiles, *Shakespeare's Clown: Actor and Text in the Elizabethan Playhouse* (Cambridge: Cambridge University Press, 1987), p. 37.

56. Ibid., pp. 136–8. For the arrival of Armin as a shift from public performer to licensed wit, see also T. W. Baldwin, 'Shakespeare's jester', *Modern Language Notes*, 39 (1924), 447–55; Austin Gray, 'Robert Armine, the Foole', *PMLA*, 42 (1927), 673–85; Charles Felver, 'Robert Armin, Shakespeare's fool: a biographical essay', *Research Studies 5, Kent University Bulletin*, 49 (1961), 39–48; and Bas Van Es, *Shakespeare in Company* (Oxford: Oxford University Press, 2013), pp. 163–94.

57. See, in particular, Walter Kaiser, *Praisers of Folly: Erasmus, Rabelais, Shakespeare* (London: Gollancz, 1964), p. 87 et passim; and Bednarz, *Shakespeare and the Poet's War*, pp. 105–7.

58. Richard Simpson, 'What was the religion of Shakespeare? Part III', *The Rambler*, 9 (1858), 237.

59. Hugh Grady, *Shakespeare and Impure Aesthetics* (Cambridge: Cambridge University Press, 2009), p. 29.

60. Tom Hayes, *The Birth of Popular Culture: Ben Jonson, Maid Marian and Robin Hood* (Pittsburgh: Duquesne University Press, 1992), p. 132.

61. Richard Dutton, *Licensing, Censorship and Authorship in Early Modern England: Buggeswords* (Basingstoke: Palgrave, 2000), pp. 23, 26 and 29.

62. Northrop Frye, *Anatomy of Criticism: Four Essays* (New York: Atheneum, 1968), p. 182.

63. Grady, *Shakespeare and Impure Aesthetics*, pp. 67 and 76. For the interplay of family and inheritance structures with universalist and differentialist conceptions of humanity, see the work of Emmanuel Todd, in particular *The Origin of Family Systems. Volume 1: Eurasia* [*L'origine des systèmes familiaux. Tome 1: L'Eurasie*] (Paris: Gallimard, 2011). For a recent discussion, see Anne-Julia Zwierlein, 'Negotiating primogeniture, succession, inheritance and "spiritual legitimacy" in Shakespeare's plays', in *Drama and Cultural Change: Turning Around Shakespeare* (Trier: Wissenschaftlicher Verlag Trier, 2009), pp. 65–85.

64. Grady, *Shakespeare and Impure Aesthetics*, p. 77.

65. Chris Holcomb, *Mirth Making: The Rhetorical Discourse on Jesting in Early Modern England* (Columbia: South Carolina University Press, 2001), p. 176.

66. Peter Burke, *Popular Culture in Early Modern Europe* (London: Maurice Temple Smith, 1978), pp. 280–1; Keith Thomas, 'The place of laughter in Tudor and Stuart England', *Times Literary Supplement*, 21 January 1977, p. 80.

67. For the fool's head or *marotte* as a phallic symbol of theatrical misrule, see Wiles, *Shakespeare's Clown*, pp. 182–4.

68. Dutton, *Licensing, Censorship and Authorship*, p. 39.

69. Jane Rickard, *Authorship and Authority: The Writings of James VI and I* (Manchester: Manchester University Press, 2007), p. 207. Cf. Leah Marcus, *Puzzling Shakespeare: Local*

Reading and Its Discontents (Berkeley: University of California Press, 1988), p. 106: 'nowhere in the First Folio is it mentioned that Shakespeare . . . or any of the others included in "The Names of the Principall Actors" belonged to a company called the King's Men'. For James's underwriting of the printing of poetry with the publication of his own, see also Steven May, 'Tudor aristocrats and the mythical "stigma of print"', in A. Leigh Deneef and M. Thomas Hester (eds), *Renaissance Papers 1980* (Durham, NC: Southeastern Renaissance Conference, 1981), pp. 16–17.

70.   Alvin Kernan, *Shakespeare, the King's Playwright: Theater in the Stuart Court, 1603–1613* (New Haven: Yale University Press, 1995), p. xx.

71.   For the famous scene when Queen Elizabeth 'turned her face to the wall' in the Great Hall at Richmond, see J. E. Neale, *Queen Elizabeth* (London: Jonathan Cape, 1934), p. 390.

72.   For the theory that Shakespeare's prologues and epilogues were written to be spoken only once and at court, see Tiffany Stern, '"A small-beer health to this second day": playwrights, prologues, and first performances in early modern theatre', *Studies in Philology*, 101 (2004), 172–99.

73.   Robert Southwell, 'Time goes by turns', in *The Poems of Robert Southwell S.J.*, ed. James McDonald and Nancy Pollard Brown (Oxford: Clarendon Press, 1967), ll. 1 and 13–15, pp. 57–8.

74.   Anne Barton, 'Livy, Machiavelli and Shakespeare's *Coriolanus*', in *Essays, Mainly Shakespearean* (Cambridge: Cambridge University Press, 1994), p. 137; Shapiro, *1599*, p. 256; Kiernan Ryan, *Shakespeare*, 3rd edn (London: Palgrave, 2002), pp. 119 and 121.

75.   Adam Nicolson, *Earls of Paradise: England and the Dream of Perfection* (London: Harper Press, 2008), pp. 148–9.

76.   'Improvisation in the key of If': Maura Slattery Kahn, 'Much Virtue in "If", *Shakespeare Quarterly*, 28 (1977), 40–50.

77.   See Shapiro, 'Cross-dressing in Elizabethan Robin Hood plays', p. 83; and Singman, 'Munday's unruly earl', p. 73.

78.   Catherine Belsey, 'Disrupting sexual difference: meaning and gender in the comedies', in John Drakakis (ed.), *Alternative Shakespeares* (London: Methuen, 1985), p. 181; Stephen Orgel, *Impersonations: The Performance of Gender in Shakespeare's England* (Cambridge: Cambridge University Press, 1996), pp. 63–4.

79.   Wendy Wall, '*The Merry Wives of Windsor*: unhusbanding desires in Windsor', in Richard Dutton and Jean Howard (eds), *A Companion to Shakespeare's Works. Vol. 3: The Comedies* (Oxford: Blackwell, 2003), p. 386.

80.   Ryan, *Shakespeare*, p. 121.

81.   Jacques Derrida, *The Politics of Friendship*, trans. George Collins (London: Verso, 1997), p. 75.

82.   Ibid., p. 306.

83.   Orgel, *Impersonations*, p. 63.

84.   Philip Stubbes, *The Anatomie of Abuses* (London: 1583), facsimile edition, ed. Arthur Freeman (New York: Garland, 1973), N8r–v.

85.   See Stephen Mullaney, *The Place of the Stage: License, Play, and Power in Renaissance England* (Chicago: Chicago University Press, 1988), pp. 26–7 et passim.

86.   Grady, *Shakespeare and Impure Aesthetics*, p. 21.

87.   See Dusinberre (ed.), *As You Like It* (Arden Shakespeare), appendix 3 (pp. 368–73), and note to 2,5,48 (p. 213); Thomas Dekker, *Satiromastix*, in *The Dramatic Works of Thomas Dekker*, ed. Fredson Bowers, 4 vols (Cambridge: Cambridge University Press, 1953–61), vol. 1, 1,2,367. See Hill, *Liberty Against the Law*, p. 135. For Jonson's use of gypsy cant, see *Ben Jonson*, ed. C. H. Herford and Percy and Evelyn Simpson, 11 vols (Oxford: Clarendon Press, 1925–52), vol. 7, p. 615.

88.   See Geraldo de Sousa, *Shakespeare's Cross-Cultural Encounters* (London: Palgrave, 2002),

pp. 146 and 158; 'dangerously attractive': Stephen Orgel, 'Marginal Jonson', in *The Authentic Shakespeare and Other Problems of the Early Modern Stage* (London: Routledge, 2002), p. 198. For Cleopatra's blackness, see Janet Adelman, *The Common Liar: An Essay on 'Antony and Cleopatra'* (New Haven: Yale University Press, 1973), pp. 184–8.

89. Hill, *Liberty Against the Law*, pp. 131–2. For Cleopatra's reversal of stereotypes about gypsies and hospitality, see Janet Adelman, *Suffocating Mothers: Fantasies of Maternal Origin in Shakespeare's Plays* (London: Routledge, 1991), pp. 175–6; and Richard Wilson, *Shakespeare in French Theory: King of Shadows* (London: Routledge, 2007), pp. 254–5.

90. Paul Yachnin, *Stage-Wrights: Shakespeare, Jonson, Middleton, and the Making of Theatrical Value* (Philadelphia: University of Pennsylvania Press, 1997), p. 150.

91. John Dryden, 'Prologue to *The Tempest, or the Enchanted Isle*', A4r, reprinted in C. E. Hughes, *The Praise of Shakespeare* (London: Methuen, 1904), pp. 66–7.

92. Paola Pugliatti, *Beggary and Theatre in Early Modern England* (Aldershot: Ashgate, 2003), p. 146.

93. Quoted Lee Beier, *Masterless Men: The Vagrancy Problem in England, 1560–1640* (London: Methuen, 1985), p. 61.

94. Quoted in de Sousa, *Shakespeare's Cross-Cultural Encounters*, p. 143.

95. Beier, *Masterless Men*, p. 96; Virginia Gildersleeve, *Government Regulation of the Elizabethan Drama* (1908; reprinted New York: Burt Franklin, 1966), p. 287; Knapp, *Shakespeare's Tribe*, p. 65.

96. Craig Dionne, 'Fashioning outlaws: the early modern rogue and urban culture', in Dionne and Metz, *Rogues and Early Modern English Culture*, pp. 33–61.

97. Hill, *Liberty Against the Law*, pp. 131–2.

98. Robert Winder, *Bloody Foreigners: The Story of Immigration in Britain* (London: Little, Brown, 2004), p. 42.

99. Ania Loomba, *Shakespeare, Race, and Colonialism* (Oxford: Oxford University Press, 2002), pp. 128–9.

100. Dionne and Metz, *Rogues and Early Modern English Culture*, p. 8.

101. Bryan Reynolds, *Becoming Criminal: Transversal Performance and Cultural Dissidence in Early Modern England* (Baltimore: Johns Hopkins University Press, 2002), pp. 25–6.

102. *Whitehall Evening Post*, 30 April 1723, quoted in E. P. Thompson, *Whigs and Hunters: The Origin of the Black Act* (Harmondsworth: Penguin, 1990), p. 81.

103. Jenna Segal, '"And browner than her brother": "Misprized" Celia's racial identity and transversality in *As You Like It*', *Shakespeare*, 4 (2008), 9–21, here 11.

104. 'Evoking the concept of a supernatural art': Bednarz, *Shakespeare and the Poet's War*, p. 128. For the literary association of gypsies with the supernatural, see also Dale Randall, *Jonson's Gypsies Unmasked: Background and Theme of 'The Gypsies Metamorphos'd'* (Durham, NC: Duke University Press, 1975), p. 154.

105. 'Charms, sorcery, enchantments': 1559 statute quoted Randall, *Jonson's Gypsies Unmasked*, p. 129; 'Lines, circles, schemes': Christopher Marlowe, *The Tragical History of Doctor Faustus*, 1,53, in *Christopher Marlowe: The Complete Plays*, ed. Frank Romany and Robert Lindsey (London: Penguin, 2003), p. 348.

106. For gypsy 'royalty' see Beier, *Masterless Men*, pp. 59–60.

107. Knapp, *Shakespeare's Tribe*, p. 76.

108. Gāmini Salgādo, *The Elizabethan Underworld* (London: Dent, 1997; reprinted Stroud: Alan Sutton, 1992), p. 157. For 'Moorish' Catholic subtexts see Wilson, *Secret Shakespeare*, pp. 74–6; and Patricia Parker, 'What's in a name: and More', *Sederi*, 11 (Universidad de Huelva: 2002), 101–49, esp. p. 117.

109. 'Spent a lifetime ... transforms gloom': Hayes, *The Birth of Popular Culture*, p. 62 and 70; 'a space for tolerance': Marcus, *The Politics of Mirth*, p. 107. See also Randall, *Jonson's Gypsies Unmasked*.

110. Loomba, *Shakespeare, Race, and Colonialism*, pp. 132–3.
111. Lynda Boose, '"The getting of a lawful race": racial discourse in early modern England and the unrepresentable black woman', in Margo Hendricks and Patricia Parker (eds), *Women, 'Race', and Writing in the Early Modern Period* (London: Routledge, 1994), p. 36. For a similar argument, see also G. K. Hunter, 'Elizabethans and foreigners', in Catherine Alexander and Stanley Wells (eds), *Shakespeare and Race* (Cambridge: Cambridge University Press, 2000), pp. 37–63.
112. Hayes, *The Birth of Popular Culture*, pp. 40–1.
113. Hill, *Liberty Against the Law*, p. 72.
114. Stephen Greenblatt, 'Invisible bullets: Renaissance authority and its subversion in *Henry IV* and *Henry V*', in Richard Wilson and Richard Dutton (eds), *New Historicism and Renaissance Drama* (Harlow: Longman, 1992), p. 105. For the originality of Shakespeare's adaptation of the Robin Hood story in *Henry V* see also Anne Barton, 'The king disguised: Shakespeare's *Henry V* and the comical history', in Barton, in *Ben Jonson, Dramatist*, pp. 212–14; and Richard Helgerson, *Forms of Nationhood: The Elizabethan Writing of England* (Chicago: Chicago University Press, 1992), pp. 231–2.
115. Jacques Derrida, *Rogues: Two Essays on Reason*, trans. Anne-Pascal Brault and Michael Naas (Stanford: Stanford University Press, 2005), pp. 23, 63 and 106.

5   Fools of Time:
Shakespeare and the Martyrs

'To be or not to be' [*Hamlet*, 3,1,56]: for 400 years, Shakespeare's most quoted words were understood as a question simply about suicide, as if Hamlet's threat that he might 'his quietus make/With a bare bodkin' [75–6] was targeted only at himself. Even in 2011, this reading could prompt the nihilist idea, in Marius von Mayenburg's directionless version, of a psychotic Prince of Denmark rolling in mud. In the 1996 film, however, 'having whipped out a dagger on "bare bodkin", Kenneth Branagh for a moment unknowingly points it right at Claudius, who is hiding behind a two-way mirror', and this stage business registers the far more distressing realisation that the soliloquy is about mutual destruction as much as self-destruction, so that 'To be or not to be' is a question that takes us right into the mind of what we would now call a suicide bomber: 'Whether 'tis nobler in the mind to suffer/The slings and arrows of outrageous fortune,/Or to take arms against a sea of troubles,/And by opposing end them' [57–60].[1] *Hamlet*, we now perceive, is a play about the Manichean mentality that deems 'self-slaughter' an act of revenge [1,2,132]. Our time of terror has therefore put the ending of this play into an atrocious light, when the English Ambassador reels from the 'dismal sight' of 'so many princes' struck 'at a shot/So bloodily', and Fortinbras calls the bloodbath carnage.[2] 'This quarry cries on havoc', the inheritor exclaims, which editors gloss to mean that such an indiscriminate slaughter is a massacre [5,2,308–11].[3] This imaginary atrocity may well have inspired the drug-crazed Crown Prince of Nepal, who, in 2001, machine-gunned to death the entire Nepalese royal family.[4] Certainly, the 'havoc' Hamlet wreaks demonstrates how violent enmity is at the heart of Shakespeare's dramaturgy.

No wonder Hamlet fears 'what a wounded name,/Things standing thus unknown, shall live behind me' [286–7], as those wounds he begs Horatio to explain to an 'unknowing world' [323] are outrages the world will surely need to know about. Nor that Horatio's excuse for this butchery, as a case of 'purposes mistook' [328], rings so false, as he quibbles that his friend 'never gave commandment' [318] for the liquidation of Rosencrantz and Guildenstern, when we know Hamlet laughingly told him how he primed the letter-bomb that 'struck off' [5,2,26] both their heads. Here terror abuses, as it does on today's Facebook, the realm of the symbolic. So it is hardly necessary to believe, with Jacques Derrida, that the letter kills, to discern in this Black Prince an uncanny herald of our postmodern panic about Armageddon, when we see his monument all around us in the corpses of innocent victims.[5] As Ewan Fernie writes, in our permanent state of emergency 'Hamlet seems disturbingly like a contemporary terrorist' and the most alarming image in Sulayman Al-bassam's 2004 staging at Riverside Studio was 'the Prince's appearance in robes of Islamic fundamentalism'.[6] What the recent 'religious turn' towards political theology in Shakespeare criticism therefore confirms is that 'Hamlet's messianic casting of himself as a scourge and minister' inscribes this tragedy in an apocalyptic scenario with which we are all too familiar.[7] Like those who thought the burning of the Twin Towers 'the greatest work of art', Hamlet would have us view his suicidal mayhem as a theatre of cruelty.[8] 'From this time forth/My thoughts be bloody' [4,4,9], he there-fore posturises, after he has called his 'heavenly guards' to 'hover o'er me with your wings' [3,4,94]. Post 9/11, however, we begin to see this religious maniac through the eyes of his potential victims:[9]

> O heavy deed!
> It had been so with us had we been there.
> His liberty is full of threats to all.
> To you yourself, to us, to everyone.
> Alas, how shall this bloody deed be answered?
>
> [4,1,11–15]

'A rat, a rat!' [9]: Hamlet's extermination of Polonius and his family no longer seems so funny to us when terrorists likewise condemn random victims as vermin; and his argument that his college mates brought death on themselves by making love to the security services, so 'They are not near my conscience', sounds all the more chilling now that we are similarly told collateral fatalities are inevitable because ''Tis dangerous when the baser nature comes/Between the pass and fell incensèd points/Of mighty opposites' [5,2,58–63]. Though Terry Eagleton surprisingly never mentions *Hamlet* in *Holy Terror*, his book on religious violence, it is strikingly rele-vant to Shakespeare's character, therefore, when he observes how 'Suicide bombing is the last word in passive aggression. It is vengeance and humiliation in a single gesture. By actively consenting to be nothing, the suicide aims to become something of great price. . . . [But] like a number of tragic protagonists the suicide bomber is not notable for his fastidiousness about how many innocent victims he takes with him'. And when Eagleton adds that the suicide attacker defies death 'by freely submitting to it, becoming victor and victim', it is difficult not to think of the way Hamlet turns his 'powerlessness into a public spectacle', by embracing self-annihilation: 'If it be not now, yet it will come. The readiness is all. Since no man has aught of what he leaves, what is't to leave betimes?' [159–61].[10]

Hamlet's existentialist 'freedom-toward-death' is uncomfortably like the Islamist cult of martyrdom that resurged in the Iranian Revolution through thinkers such as Ali Shariati, who interpreted the 680 Karbala massacre of the grandson of Muhammad, Hussein, and his clansmen as 'an invitation to generations in all ages' to sacrifice themselves in a *jihad* against infidels, and extolled martyrdom as 'the only reason for existence. . . . If you cannot kill your oppressor, then die'.[11] Significantly, for the interpretation of *Hamlet*, the slaughter of Hussein is commemorated annually by Muslims in the Ta'ziyeh ritual, a mourning drama similar to the Christian Passion plays by which it was influenced. But Shariati scorned these flagellating mimetic sacrifices, and instead preached that 'the key point in the story was Hussein's existential choice . . . to remain silent and allow oppression to continue, or to choose death, and create the possibility of authentic Muslim living' for those believers who will come after.[12]

For Shariati, the sacrifice of the martyr is 'as beautiful as the "necklace" around the neck of a young girl'; and 'the martyr is under no obligation to give an account of himself on Judgement Day', because 'martyrdom is a pass into heaven'.[13] As Michel Foucault reported from Iran in 1979, there were eerie echoes in this fortified Shiite zeal for martyrdom of the militancy of the Counter-Reformation, for Islamist fundamentalists were resurrecting 'those old dreams which the West had known' in the sixteenth century, 'when it wanted to inscribe the figures of spirituality on the earth of politics'. In 'their hunger, their humiliations', and above all in their belief in 'sacrifice and the promises of the millennium', Shiite militants were restaging the tragic spectacles of the Catholic League, Foucault proposed.[14] And in Shariati's case this was not surprising, as, besides imbibing Marxism, the preacher had studied Catholic theology at the Sorbonne. The elective affinity of Islamist fundamentalism with reactionary Catholicism has recently been sardonically explored, and in the setting of the Sorbonne, by Michel Houellebecq in his dystopian novel *Soumission*.[15] But to anyone who lived through the IRA hunger-strikes and bombing campaigns in Britain, it will seem more than coincidence that after Hamlet begs Heaven, in the First Quarto, to receive his soul with his dying breath, the same Counter-Reformation glorification of martyrdom as the fast track to Paradise returns with Horatio's reading from the Latin burial service:

Now cracks a noble heart. Good night, sweet prince,
And flights of angels sing thee to thy rest.

[5,2,302–3]

Horatio's vision of his friend winging skywards will be replicated in the hyper-realist murals of Iranian cities, 'displaying portraits of martyrs whose names drip with blood'.[16] But if Hamlet's dilemma, 'Whether to suffer the slings and arrows . . . or to take arms', anticipates the break with Shiite quietism which sent hundreds of thousands of young Iranians to death in war with Iraq, and authorised the suicide bombers of the *intifada* who blew themselves up on Israeli buses, notice his imagery is that of sixteenth-century Catholic martyrology: specifically that of Sebastian, the youth pierced by 'slings and arrows' whose morbidly haemophiliac cult made him a poster-boy for the Roman Baroque. Historians note that the Counter-Reformation thirst for martyrdom coincided with the duelling craze, and with the 'obsession with blood' that Shakespeare incorporated into not only *Hamlet* but also *Twelfth Night*, his dark comedy featuring a Sebastian who fights back.[17] Horatio and Fortinbras both move quickly to claim the play's 'best violence' [243] for the successor regime, 'lest more mischance/On plots and errors happen' [138–9]. But given that the heady language in which the aspiration to be 'more an antique Roman than a Dane' [283] is here glorified chimes so well with Catholic resistance doctrine, and Jesuit apologetics for tyrannicide, it was logical that the Catholic lawyer turned Fascist ideologue Carl Schmitt should romanticise Hamlet as a great decider and precursor of the guerrillas he valorised for escalating enmity 'to the point of complete annihilation', when their elemental violence blasts through the parliamentary impasse of the modern liberal state to assert the archaic affinity of the sovereign and the beast.[18] For this unrepentant Nazi, far from being the prince of indecision, Shakespeare's protagonist was like some anti-colonialist partisan, in reaffirming the 'old blood rite' of sacred kingship with the revanchism of his 'dying voice' [298].[19]

Art historians confirm an intensification of violence in Catholic martyrology in the 1580s, when, instead of depicting the early Christians serenely enduring 'outrageous fortune', artists illustrated the agonies and death throes of their contemporaries with a pornographic realism intended to appal.[20] This contrasted with the woodcuts illustrating John Foxe's earlier *Book of Martyrs*, which sentimentalised Protestants 'clapping hands in the flames', where 'a victim defeated punishment by demonstrating joy'. In Foxe's iconography the role of martyr 'demanded suffering patiently the torments inflicted on the body'.[21] But the frescos painted in 1583 at the English College in Rome detailed the racking, hanging, disembowelling and dismemberment that were the realities for persecuted priests in England, as if to ensure 'there would be no mistake about the future that awaited them'.[22] Engraved in Richard Verstegan's 1587 *Theatre of Cruelties*, these lurid images of gibbets and cauldrons reveal the affinity of sacred art with anatomical dissection.[23] Their ideological alliance looks equally unholy, however, for what such extreme horror also attests is the desensitising of the Catholic Church militant as its missionaries trained for effective suicide, and 'mental impregnability' towards physical suffering was instilled in novices to condition them to actively court whipping and flaying, a death drive by which pious youths avidly internalised the martyrological ideal.[24] In *The Body in Pain* Elaine Scarry remarks that this ideal was, of course, the logic of the cross, which reverses the weapon of execution, so that 'one person's pain is not a sign of another's power'.[25] Like those photographs of the 'beautiful and seductive' Chinese boy ecstatically undergoing the 'Death of a Hundred Pieces' Georges Bataille carried, he said, 'to ruin in me that which is opposed to ruin', these hideous images do seem designed, then, to anaesthetise emotion.[26] As such, they illustrate the dehumanising process the play also records, as Hamlet wrestles with the problem that obsessed Catholics such as the head of the English Colleges, William Allen, 'about the value of martyrdom and the extent to which it should be sought', and, tellingly, by invoking the identical imagery of bodily dismemberment:[27]

> O that this too too solid flesh would melt,
> Thaw, and resolve itself into a dew,
> Or that the Everlasting had not fixed
> His canon 'gainst self-slaughter!

[1,2,129–32]

So many of his students died in his holy war, declared Philip II, that Cardinal Allen's hat 'might be said to have been dyed with blood of the martyrs he educated'.[28] In fact, 135 or 27% of 471 seminary priests known to operate in Elizabethan England were executed.[29] And indeed, 'no martyrdom can be more grievous than long sickness', Allen had rejoiced after the execution of his hero Edmund Campion in 1581, since 'he that departeth upon the pillow hath as little ease as he that dieth upon the gallows, block or butcher's knife'.[30] This was, however, the emotional numbness that also led the Cardinal to insist that those who shed their blood for Protestantism 'can be no martyrs but damnable murderers of themselves' and which let him slide from martyrdom to murder when he called upon all Catholics to join the Armada against Elizabeth – 'the Enterprise of England' – assuring them 'it is as lawful, godly and glorious for you to fight, as for us Priests to suffer and die', since to battle either way 'is always in the sight of God a most precious death and martyrdom'.[31] Catholic priests retreated behind a smokescreen of equivocation when interrogated on 'the Bloody Question' of treason.[32] But the historian Emmanuel Le Roy Ladurie contends that such Counter-Reformation zealots did share many characteristics with Shiite clerics, and that the Iranian Ayatollah Khomeini was a 'lethargic, dangerous equivalent of these hysterical preachers of the 1580s'.[33]

'Pious terrorists' is how the Catholic historian John Bossy describes Cardinal Allen's missionaries.[34] And lest we idealise Catholic Leaguers, Le Roy Ladurie cautions, we should recall that their missions were operations 'resurrecting fundamentalism in its most fanatical forms'. Zealous monks and preachers spearheaded the organisation, but it was 'totalitarian in the modern sense', a popular mass movement directed by mullahs: 'Perhaps in light of recent events we can understand how reactionary Catholicism and a revolutionary spirit formed their odd couple'.[35] And this unholy alliance was, perhaps, never stranger than in Shakespeare's play, where the slippage from martyrdom to massacre, and from suicide to assassination, so 'puzzles the will' [3,1,82]. For as Fortinbras states, the moment of *Hamlet* was precisely that of 'the Bloody Question' of Catholic terrorism, and its plot would 'so jump upon this bloody question' [5,2,319], that there can have been few in the audience who did not relate its protagonist's predicament – 'prompted to revenge' by both 'heaven *and* hell' [2,2,562] – to 'the Enterprise' of the Armada, when 'enterprises of great pitch and moment . . . their currents turn[ed] awry,/And los[t] the name of action' [88–90]. 'Enterprise' is Shakespeare's word for invasion – in his Trojan War 'the enterprise is sick' [*Troilus*, 1,3,103] – and Hamlet's use of the term keys his problem to 'the Enterprise of England', its 'great pitch and moment' turned awry in 'a sea of troubles', but at the time of the play still 'jump upon this bloody question' of whether to suffer oppression, like some medieval saint, or to take arms like a modern martyr, in suicidal resistance:

> Now whether it be
> Bestial oblivion, or some craven scruple
> Of thinking too precisely on th'event . . .
> I do not know
> Why yet I live to say 'This thing's to do',

Sith I have cause, and will, and strength, and means,
To do't.

[4,4,9:29–36]

If Hamlet hesitates over his suicide mission, that could be because the play stalls upon the distinction that Catholic martyrs were desperate to maintain between words and deeds, or 'the spiritual sword', as Allen put it, and 'the material sword of the soldier'.[36] So, though the Cardinal told missionaries his 'student matters' would not stop him praying for them to join 'the martyred saints and legions', modern historians have been in as much denial over Church involvement in terrorism as critics are over Hamlet's.[37] Eamon Duffy concedes, however, that the Cardinal 'was economical with the truth' in protesting that his priests died only for faith, as 'by any Elizabethan standard, Allen was a traitor'.[38] And Bossy alleges that 'there can be no reasonable doubt' that it was English Jesuits who persuaded the Pope that 'Elizabeth's life was the obstacle to the Enterprise, so permission ought to be given to arrange her assassination'.[39] The fatal summit took place in Paris in the summer of 1583, attended by Allen, the Ultra Duke of Guise, and the papal nuncio, who carefully minuted: 'As to putting to death that wicked woman, I will not write to the Pope because though he would be glad God should punish His enemy, it would be unfitting His Vicar should procure it. But there is no doubt that whoever sends her out of the world not only does not sin but gains his holy benediction'.[40] Elizabeth's 1570 excommunication had, in fact, already placed the Queen under a papal *fatwa*. But Allen was right when in September 1583 he wrote to Rome that 'now was the time for acting, there had never been a like opportunity, nor would such a chance ever recur'.[41]

Shakespeare was coming to political consciousness at the true date of dates for the Catholic *reconquista* of England. For on 25 October 1583 the marksman primed to murder Elizabeth set out for London, having told relatives 'he must die for the commonwealth', since 'it was necessary the Queen of England should be killed as she was the bane of the Church'.[42] At a Northampton inn, however, the gunman also reportedly informed drinkers that 'he hoped to see her head upon a pole, for that she was a serpent and a viper', and the bar soon 'filled with startled auditors'.[43] These reports sound disingenuous, the cover for a scene repeated across Europe as a result of the new doctrine of tyrannicide or justified murder proclaimed by Allen: a form of mass hysteria in which 'because people expect an attack fear creates its own object', and witnesses who dismiss the terrorist as mad secretly share his hope, or, were he successful, 'would voice their approval'.[44] As one such secret-sharer, Sir John Harington famously joked, 'Treason doth never prosper. . . . For if it prosper, none call it treason'.[45] Elizabeth's sworn killer was part of a Catholic terror campaign which scored spectacular hits with the assassination of William the Silent, at a second bloody attempt, the Huguenot commander Admiral Coligny, and Henry III and Henry IV of France, all knifed or gunned down by suicidal monks or Jesuit-inflamed fanatics. So this Midland jackal was no lone lunatic. In fact, John Somerville belonged to one of Warwickshire's foremost Catholic families, as he had married an Arden. Most importantly, for the context of *Hamlet*, his wife is believed by biographers to have been a cousin of Shakespeare's mother, Mary Arden.

'O what a noble mind is here o'erthrown! ... The observed of all observers, quite, quite, down!' [3,1,149–3]: in a now-familiar reflex, Hamlet's portrayal as insane was prefigured by Somerville's Arden relations, who assured magistrates he had been driven mad by jealousy of his wife. In fact, the twenty-three-year-old had been disgusted, he claimed, by Elizabeth's liaison with the Earl of Leicester. And like Hamlet, his sexual hang-ups, arrogance, asceticism, misogyny, intolerance and, above all, belief that indifference to his own survival 'established the Christ-like purity of the assassin', all add up to the identikit portrait of a suicide attacker.[46] In her book on early modern assassinations, *The Awful End of Prince William the Silent*, Lisa Jardine considers that 'in heavily policed London Somerville's plot seems far-fetched'. Yet she also records the widespread rumour that the condemned traitor was 'suicided' in custody, hours before his execution, to stop him naming his accomplices: 'Somerville was hanged to avoid a mischief'.[47] And while she thinks the Midlander and the copycats who imitated him were exploited by ministers 'to tighten their stranglehold by fear, surveillance, sudden arrests and interrogations, all in the name of "Homeland Security"', Jardine admits that, just as in our time, 'the idea that followers of one faith are convinced suicide bombing or hostage executions are sanctioned, causes consternation', so Protestants reacted with horrified indignation to the notion that murder could be promoted by priests in Jesuit propaganda such as 'Doctor Allen's book'.[48]

Catholic historians have slowly come round to categorising the liberation theologians of Shakespearean England as terrorists. It is now too easy, then, simply to echo the Cardinal's purported contempt for Elizabeth's government as paranoid, when Allen protested that 'there is not a poor priest can enter the realm to say Mass but they imagine he brings destruction; there is not a ship on the coast but it is for invasion'.[49] The truth is that this panic locked into Allen's very real threat that 'If the invasion be not carried out, I give up all hope in man'.[50] Somerville himself told his interrogators he had decided to act in reprisal 'after he heard his father-in-law say the Queen doth execute all good Catholics'.[51] And when the Ardens were arrested, they duly revealed a resistance network that stretched from Mary Queen of Scots to Midland homes such as Shakespeare's, where the dramatist's father had apparently signed the Jesuit pledge of faith.[52] Hastily, John Shakespeare hid the incendiary Testament in the rafters of the Henley Street Birthplace (where it would lie a guilty secret until 1757); and when the inspectors called on 5 November they had to report that unless confessions were extracted by torture, 'it will not be possible to find out more ... for the papists of this country greatly work upon ... clearing their houses of all show of suspicion'.[53] Shakespeare was just nineteen at the time. But as biographers are now realising, when he shortly became an actor he would have walked under the impaled heads of his kinsmen Somerville and Edward Arden whenever he crossed to the playhouses over London Bridge.[54] And the conflicting signals about martyrdom and murder he received from those tarred skulls must have reminded him every time how dangerously close he had come himself to a traitor's death.

In *Will in the World: How Shakespeare Became Shakespeare* Stephen Greenblatt comments that the hysteria after the Somerville plot 'provides a glimpse of

something rarely reported . . . Catholic families scurrying to burn or bury incriminating evidence . . . while the government agents hammer at the doors'.[55] And if
this traumatic scene was indeed a part of how Shakespeare became Shakespeare it
supplies a terrifying subtext for all those moments in the plays that recall Catholic
executions, as when a Jesuitical Antony retrieves another fatal Roman testament:
'Here's a parchment . . . I found it in his closet. . . . Let but the commons hear this
testament. . . . And they would go and kiss dead Caesar's wounds, / And dip their
napkins in his sacred blood' [*Julius*, 3,2,125–30]. We can never know whether
the dramatist was present at Smithfield to watch Edward Arden hanged, drawn
and quartered; or witnessed the mêlée at Tyburn when Campion was 'chopped to
pieces', and in the confusion a spectator was quick enough to cut off a thumb and
carry it away.[56] But as the Victorian Catholic critic Richard Simpson argued, 'we
cannot suppose Shakespeare was less moved than the rest of the London crowds
at these harrowing barbarities'.[57] So, as Gary Taylor concludes, while the evidence
might well suggest that 'for much of his life Shakespeare was a church papist', or
occasional conformist to the Church of England, and that 'once he began dividing
his life between Stratford and London, he might have become a recusant', absenting
from Anglican services, one thing his writing does tell us is that, 'like a majority of
English Catholics, he had no appetite for martyrdom'.[58]

Shakespeare, we can safely infer, did not share the sado-masochistic bloodlust
of 'so many smiling Romans', who 'Came smiling' to the blood of the victim, as in
Julius Caesar, 'and did bathe their hands in it' [2,2,77–86]. Carrion 'crows' is what
he called the Jesuit body-snatchers. So it is telling that his earliest allusion to a
'recusant' martyrdom occurs, in *The Comedy of Errors*, as a fate to be averted, when
the end turns on a reprieve of the *Syracusan* merchant Egeon from the scaffold, in
'The place of death and sorry execution / Behind the ditches of the abbey' [5,1,122],
which editors identify with Holywell, adjacent to the Theatre in Shoreditch, where
the missionary William Hartley (a friend of Stratford's Jesuit teacher, Simon Hunt)
was hanged.[59] Likewise, in *Titus Andronicus*, the text in which the word 'martyr'
occurs more than any other, the scene where a petitioner is ordered to be hanged
might refer to the foolishness of Richard Shelley, a Catholic left to rot in gaol
after begging Elizabeth for toleration; but the play then shows the futility of the
martyrdom that the old Roman Titus brings upon himself and his family by butchering the Goths, who are presented as analogous to the reformers martyred under
'Bloody Mary'.[60] The poet and priest Henry Walpole, himself destined for the scaffold, believed Campion's execution had converted 10,000; and drawing upon the
mystical notion of blood as semen, Catholics exulted that the martyrs' blood sows
'dragon's teeth'.[61] But it was the nightmare of this interminable cycle of bloodshed
that Shakespeare seems to question in *Hamlet*, when the Ghost rises up from the
torture chamber crying for revenge.

GHOST: My hour is almost come
              When I to sulphurous and tormenting flames
              Must render up myself.
HAMLET: Alas, poor ghost!

GHOST: Pity me not, but lend thy serious hearing
          To what I shall unfold.
HAMLET: Speak, I am bound to hear.
GHOST: So art thou to revenge when thou shalt hear.

[*Hamlet*, 1,5,3–10]

In all Shakespeare's world 'there is one portrait one sadly misses', Graham Greene regretted, for 'while the kings speak, the adventurers speak, the madmen and the lovers, the soldiers and the poets, the martyrs are quite silent. We come out of the world of the pilgrims into the silence of Hamlet's court'.[62] Yet if, as Greenblatt concludes in *Hamlet in Purgatory*, Shakespeare 'was probably brought up in a Roman Catholic household in a time of official suspicion and persecution', what strikes critics today is how his theatre *does* echo to the ghosts of that repressed and demonised past, pleading for a hearing.[63] Thus, in the midst of some tomfoolery, as in *Love's Labour's Lost*, we are suddenly in death, pulled up by 'The shape of love's Tyburn that hangs simplicity', and the memory of priests cruelly carted to the scaffold 'wearing papers' in the form of dunces' three-cornered caps, or 'pierced' like their leader 'Master Parson', the so-called 'pierce one' Robert Parsons [4,2,76–7; 4,3,43–9].[64] But just as the Shia metaphor for martyrdom is as a kind of commerce, where martyrs sell their souls to Allah, so missionaries came disguised as jewel importers, 'merchants of Venus'; and in *The Merchant of Venice* Shakespeare takes this romantic code at face value, to exchange death for life in a scene of sacrifice contrived to have 'no jot of blood' [4,1,301]. Thus, his dramatic tactic is the one devised by the actors in *A Midsummer Night's Dream*, to make a mockery of martyrdom, complete with a mantle 'stained with blood', by arranging to 'leave the killing out, when all is done', knowing that to 'do it too terribly were enough to hang us all' [1,2,61; 3,1,14; 5,1,272].

'Commend thy grievance to my holy prayers', Proteus begs his friend, when Valentine sails away to Milan, the capital of Catholic fundamentalism; but the only sacrifice in *The Two Gentlemen of Verona* is the puppy 'stolen by the hangman boys' in place of the mongrel Crab [1,1,17; 4,4,48]. Likewise, although Beatrice orders Benedick to 'Kill Claudio' to avenge the martyred Hero, and their story is 'saturated with references to burning at the stake, blinding, and hanging', these topical horrors are 'present merely as jokes', as Shakespeare converts the paranoid 'noting', or surveillance, of the Elizabethan 'war on terror' into *Much Ado About Nothing* [4,1,285].[65] The comedy ends preparing the dungeon for Don John, the villain named after the Spaniard who had longed to wipe England off the map. But 'Think not on him till tomorrow', Benedick laughs, 'I'll devise thee brave punishments for him. Strike up, pipers' [5,4,121]. The dramatist knew well enough the 'brave punishments' inflicted at Tyburn, having with *Venus and Adonis* created an entire poem to warn the young Catholic Earl of Southampton of the risks in resisting the Queen, with the nightmare of a boar 'nuzzling in his flank' as the 'swine' cuts into 'his soft groin' to castrate and disembowel Adonis [1115–16]. In fact these gruesome details read like an eyewitness report of the execution of the Earl's confessor, the 'beautiful English youth' and Jesuit poet Robert Southwell, carried obscenely by the executioner 'in his own arms to the place where he was to be quartered'.[66] So, if he did 'leave the killing out' of his plays, when it came to the 'eternal blazon' of the martyrs, that must have been because Shakespeare sensed its true horror, to speak of which even Hamlet's Ghost is forbidden:

> But that I am forbid
> To tell the secrets of my prison-house,
> I could a tale unfold whose lightest word
> Would harrow up thy soul, freeze thy young blood,
> Make thy two eyes like stars start from thy spheres,
> Thy knotty and combined locks to part,
> And each particular hair to stand on end
> Like quills upon the fretful porcupine.
> But this eternal blazon must not be
> To ears of flesh and blood.
>
> [Hamlet, 1,5,13–22]

The Catholic Greene complained that the squeamish decision to 'leave the killing out' means there is one scene we miss in Shakespeare, who seems aloof 'from the routine of the torture chamber'. Francis Bacon, the novelist observed, had been one of the attorneys sitting quietly taking notes while priests were racked, 'So for one moment would like to follow the Baconian heresy, and believe it was Shakespeare who faced the martyrs on their examination in the Tower'.[67] Greene had clearly not noticed how, when Gloucester is tortured and blinded to divulge 'Wherefore to Dover?' in the Quarto King Lear, the question is printed 'Wherefore to Douai?': the training school for missionaries founded by Allen [3,7,52]. Nor that the text answers Rackmaster Norton's threat to extend a prisoner 'a foot longer than God made him', with Kent's retort that 'He hates him much/That would upon the rack. . . Stretch him out longer' [5,3,312–14].[68] But Greenblatt speculates that Shakespeare did, in fact, meet Campion, and pictures 'the sixteen-year-old poet and forty-year-old Jesuit' together in Lancashire, when 'Will may have registered a powerful inner resistance. . . . Campion was a fanatic, or more accurately, a saint'. And Shakespeare, whose Joan of Arc is a whore, and Henry VI a holy idiot, 'did not entirely understand saints, and what he did, he did not like'.[69] Enough critics now endorse John Dover Wilson's insight, in any case, that in Hamlet 'the Ghost is Catholic', because 'he comes from Purgatory' [1,5,11–13], to make the strange nocturnal meeting on the battlements a symbolic encounter between Shakespeare and the faith of his fathers.[70]

Once we take Greenblatt's point that in Hamlet a distinctly Protestant student from Luther's Wittenberg is stalked by 'a distinctly Catholic ghost', we grasp why this witness to the days of Elizabethan persecution, demanding some bloody retribution, might appear to the protagonist in such a dubious and 'questionable shape' [1,4,24].[71] In 1600 Catholic plans for revenge included a plot to blow the Queen up with fireworks 'on the Thames in her barge', which would be the signal for a massacre, when 'whosoever gave not the watchword "Jesus Maria" should be slain'. Priests denied 'any such cunning in fireworks'.[72] But they could not deny the facts of the

Renaissance 9/11: the 1572 St Bartholomew's Day holocaust that gave the world the very word 'massacre', when, obeying firebrand sermons that vilified Protestants as 'a cancerous limb', French Catholics slaughtered over 10,000 Huguenots, to shrieks of 'Cut them down, burn them, kill them without a qualm'.[73] As the historian Natalie Zemon Davis dryly comments, 'in bloodshed, the Catholics were the champions'.[74] So, it is not surprising that, just 'as it was about to speak', the Ghost 'start[s] like a guilty thing' [1,1,128–9; 1,5,12]. Evidently, this ghost is made guilty by its own cries for blood, rather than any crimes it has to purge. Thus, if the logic of this call to sectarian violence is followed, what *Hamlet* stages is Shakespeare's own recoil from the martyrs, his resistance to the resistance of his father, and desperation, when all is said and done, to 'leave the killing out':

> What if it tempt you toward the flood, my lord,
> Or to the dreadful summit of the cliff
> That beetles o'er his base into the sea,
> And there assume some other horrible form
> Which might deprive your sovereignty of reason
> And draw you into madness? Think of it.

[1,4,50–5]

'What if it tempt you toward the flood'? This Doomsday scenario was inserted into the 1604 Quarto of *Hamlet*, with an extra warning that 'The very place puts toys of desperation,/Without more motive, into every brain/That looks so many fathoms to the sea/And hears it roar beneath', later cut from the Folio. Its spooky similarity to Edgar's vertiginous description of Dover Cliff for his blind father in *King Lear* shows how insistently Shakespeare associated the abyss of self-destruction with some 'horrible form' of 'madness' upon the Channel coast. It had been beneath Dover Cliff that Campion's suicide mission beached in 1580, *en route* for Stratford and that resistance cell where John Shakespeare signed the Jesuits' oath. Edgar has himself been disguised like a hunted priest, ranting about satanic fiends in the very words used in exorcisms by Shakespeare's own doomed Stratford schoolmate, the Jesuit Robert Debdale.[75] But during Gloucester's suicide attempt, 'Poor Tom' steps out of this role, and looks back on the disembarking martyrs with horrified compassion, as halfway down the cliff he imagines 'one that gathers samphire', condemned by his 'dreadful trade' to hang beside crows and jackdaws 'that wing the mid-way air'. Samphire is a corruption of Saint-Pierre; for this salty seaweed is St Peter's herb, with a leaf symbolising martyrdom, being the saline dressing in which body parts were preserved. Perhaps that is why Edgar gasps, 'Methinks he seems no bigger than his head' [4,6,11–24]. For we recall how, when the hangman at Tyburn shouted 'Behold the head of a traitor!', there was said to be never a sound from the crowds that witnessed a martyr's terrible end.[76]

In *King Lear* the 'tradesman' of death harvests the leaves for his embalmment, for when he falls the samphire he collects now will be the bed for his own 'shivered' remains; while those 'fishermen' who follow Peter on the beach will die 'like mice', Edgar perceives, after their 'tall anchoring bark', the Church of Rome, has sailed on its way. Arriving straight from Prague, Campion had climbed this Dover Cliff, and on 'a great rock fell upon his knees to commend to God his cause'.[77] But a quarter century later we see how he will also hang in the air, as those Jesuit 'crows' and Anglican 'jackdaws' circle around his corpse. So, Edgar's uncanny retrospective of the martyr clinging to Peter's rock is a trick perspective that foresees him executed at Tyburn. No wonder Edgar winces, 'I'll look no more, / Lest my brain turn and the deficient sight / Topple down headlong' [23–7]. Feste had mocked Campion as 'the old hermit of Prague' in *Twelfth Night* [4,2,11]. But it is when the son tricks his father to fall flat on his face with this verbal *trompe l'oeil* that Shakespeare reveals his disillusion with the 'deficient sight' of the suicide 'merchant' who, in Gloucester's words, imagined he 'could beguile the tyrant's rage / And frustrate his proud will' [63–4] by self-annihilation:

> I do remember now. Henceforth I'll bear
> Affliction till it do cry out itself
> 'Enough, enough,' and die. That thing you speak of
> I took it for a man; often 't would say
> 'The fiend, the fiend' – he led me to that place.
>
> [4,6,75–9]

'I will have such revenges. . . I will do such things – / What they are yet I know not; but they shall be / The terrors of the earth' [2,4,275–7]: Lear's plot to unleash global terror is cued by what the Book of Revelation (16: 18) says about Armageddon: 'there were thunders and lightnings, and there was a great earthquake such as was not since men were upon the earth'.[78] It is an apocalyptic prophecy like the curse uttered by the old nobility of the Histories: 'Let the vile world end / And the premised flames of the last day / Knit earth and heaven together!' [2 *Henry VI*, 5,3,40–3]. But there is an egomania to Lear's imagined detonation of 'All the stored vengeances of heaven' that puts the mad King himself at the epicentre of a universal disaster: 'You sulphurous and thought-executing fires, / Vaunt couriers to oak-cleaving thunderbolts, / Singe my white head!' [2,4,155; 3,2,4–6]. Histrionically, Lear places his own body in the eye of the storm that he invokes, making his own self-obliteration the instrument for 'Vengeance! plague! death! confusion!' as he 'tears his white hair, / Which the impetuous blasts, with eyeless rage, / Catch in their fury, and make nothing of' [2,4,89; 3,1,7–9]. Later he encounters in Edgar the figure of the 'bare, forked, animal' who has lived through such 'fire and flame', and realising that 'the thunder would not peace at my bidding', demands of this blasted survivor, 'What is the cause of thunder?' But Lear has known all along that the source of the 'all-shaking thunder' he hopes will 'Smite flat the thick rotundity of the world' is the Roman god Jupiter [3,2,7; 3,4,52,99,143; 4,6,100]. So, like the 'ear-deafening voice o'th'oracle / Kin to Jove's thunder' in *The Winter's Tale* [3,1,9–10], and the 'thunder, that deep and dreadful organ pipe', in *The Tempest* [3,3,98], Lear's fantasy weapons of mass destruction originate in Rome, and belong to the same symbolic sign system as all those bulls and excommunications, not to mention armadas and assassinations, sent to avenge the martyrs by the Pope.

The text of *King Lear* is 'crossed' by thoughts of the 'side-piercing site' of lacerating martyrdom. The King himself says that he cannot get 'crosses' out of his eyes; and allusions to St Lucy's 'poor old eyes', St Catherine's 'wheel of fire' and St Juliana's boiling in 'molten lead' are straight out of the *Theatre of Cruelty* of Catholic hagiography [3,7,57; 4,6,85; 4,7,47–8; 5,3,277].[79] This is a tragedy that advertises how it was first performed at court in 1605 on 26 December, the Feast of St Stephen, the martyred preacher whose stoning made him a 'pattern of all patience' [3,2,36].[80] Yet the Whitehall audience would surely have been right to detect in Lear's incendiary plans to 'Spit, fire!' and raise 'wind, thunder, fire', not Christian patience, but a smell of sulphur from nearby Westminster. For what would have made his persecution mania alarming to those lawyers and politicians, and still has the power to disturb today, is how such a martyr complex turns self-sacrifice towards mass murder, and revenge into a gunpowder plot that targets 'Such sheets of fire, such bursts of horrid thunder,/Such groans of roaring wind', against Lear's 'great image of authority', the 'robes and furred gowns' in those massed ranks of legislators who have been summoned to sit in Parliament [3,2,44–5; 4,6,159]:

> Let the great gods,
> That keep this dreadful pother o'er our heads
> Find out their enemies now. Tremble, thou wretch,
> That hast within thee undivulged crimes,
> Unwhipped of justice. Hide thee, thou bloody hand;
> Thou perjured; and thou simular of virtue
> That art incestuous. Caitiff, to pieces shake,
> That under covert and convenient seeming
> Hast practised on man's life. Close pent-up guilts
> Rive your concealing continents, and cry
> These dreadful summoners grace.
>
> [3,2,47–57]

'Child Roland to the dark tower came,/His word was still – Fie, foe, fum,/I smell the blood of a British man' [3,4,170–2]: Edgar's recital of the sinister rhyme at this point in the play gives the boy *the ogre's speech*, editors note, and alters 'English' to 'British', to match the proximity of the Whitehall performance to the Palace of Westminster, the 'dark tower' of King James's 'British' empire. So, coming from an outlaw, at Christmas 1605 this twisted song about a giant-killer lured into a dungeon by scent of British blood must have resonated with the discovery just weeks before of Catholic desperadoes in the cellars of Parliament, especially if it came with the Fool's Jesuitical prediction that churches will be rebuilt when 'the realm of Albion' has 'Come to great confusion' [3,2,89]. This is an apocalyptic moment, therefore, like the uncanny 'witching time of night' when Hamlet claims he 'could drink hot blood,/And do such bitter business as the day/Would quake to look on' [3,2,360–2]. Lear has invited certain 'high engendered' powers to 'Rumble [their] bellyful' and 'Let fall [their] horrible pleasure' in thunder and fire, while Cordelia has rallied the exiles in France, so that the 'injuries the king now bears will be revenged home'.

The 1605 plotters likewise imagined an invasion force striking out to aid them from Dover.[81] But the text now trails the treachery of those November days, when Gloucester warns his son that 'There is some strange thing toward . . . pray you . . . be careful'. The old duke locks the conspirators' plan in his closet, as Edmund quietly slips Cornwall the intelligence that 'from France there comes a power' with 'secret feet' in 'our best ports, at point' to strike, when 'something deeper' has exploded [3,2,13–34; 3,3,10]. As Guy Fawkes lamented, after he was arrested in the vault, 'giving warning to one overthrew us all'. He was referring to the mystery message warning Lord Monteagle that 'they shall receive a terrible blow this parliament'.[82] Evidently, if the letters that go back and forth in *King Lear* are so opaque they infuriate the critics, this may well be because the secrets on which they were based were so compromising.[83]

As Shakespeare's tragedy of intercepted letters must have been written 'i'the heat' [1,1,305] of these shattering events, the biographical question sparked by such coincidences is, of course, how much he knew about the Gunpowder Plot, considering that 'the great arc of Plotters' houses' converged on Stratford: at Lapworth, the home of Robert Catesby, where the dramatist's father may have signed that Jesuit pledge; and Norbrooks, the farm of John Grant, another distant relative, where Arden and Somerville had planned their earlier attack. Both here and at the Mermaid Tavern, where Catesby dined, the Plot was laid, as Antonia Fraser recounts, in 'Shakespeare country'.[84] Rumours of 'a huge conspiracy among local Catholics' had, in fact, been rife in Stratford for months; and in September Ambrose Rookwood, who procured the explosives, rented the nearby Clopton House as an arsenal.[85] On 12 November, officers would seize 'copes, crucifixes, chalices and other massing relics' at Rookwood's mansion; for this was where the Jesuit 'crows' had made 'wing to th'rooky wood' as 'Light thickened' during the fateful autumn [*Macbeth*, 3,2,31]. And the man arrested for concealing these incriminating 'relics' was none other than the playwright's Henley Street neighbour, George Badger.[86] All through his career we sense Shakespeare studiously writing his plays in a room next-door to the competing theatre of Catholic martyrdom, with its lurid and sensationalist repertoire of secret chapels, priest-holes, exorcisms, icons and grisly relics. But in Stratford in November 1605 our picture of him just a wall away from the martyrs' chamber had a literal truth; and judging by the drama he wrote next, the suspicion of what went on in there filled him with foreboding and repulsion:

> Thrice the brinded cat hath mewed,
> Thrice, and once the hedge-pig whined.
> Harpier cries, ''Tis time, 'tis time.'
> Round about the cauldron go,
> In the poisoned entrails throw.

> [*Macbeth*, 4,1,1–5]

'Fire burn, and cauldron bubble' [21]: stirring their relics of mummy, tooth, stomach, gullet, liver, gall, nose, blood and entrails into the cauldron of hate, for audiences after 5/11 the chanting Witches in *Macbeth* would have had a ghoulish resemblance to those other bearded 'women' [1,3,43] of the time, the Jesuits who haunted scaffolds after executions 'and scraped up the ashes where bowels had been burnt', searching 'for some lump of flesh'.[87] And the similarity of the 'weird women' [3,1,2] to those priestly necrophiles does look compelling, when they produce their wonder-working relic: 'Here I have a pilot's thumb,/Wrack'd as homeward he did come./A drum, a drum. Macbeth doth come' [1,3,28–30]. The so-called 'pilot' of the 1580 mission, Campion, had stayed with the Catesbys in Stratford, where he converted many of the Gunpowder Plotters.[88] But after his death his racked thumb became notorious as the macabre fetish circulated between Debdale and other Jesuit exorcists, reputedly to be inserted into 'the most secret part' of menstruating girls, so as to expel 'the devil that did reside in that place'. Thus, the Black Mass sung in *Macbeth*, where 'thumb' is made to rhyme with 'drum', has pornographic echoes of the actual Mass allegedly said by Father John Gerard at the Blackfriars Gatehouse that Shakespeare later weirdly purchased, at which the Plotters swore their secrecy.[89] The prosecution allegation was that this was indeed a 'Jesuit treason', in which, as Attorney-General Edward Coke fumed, the evil priests who pulled the strings were 'more to blame than all the actors'.[90] And the dramatist of the King's Men duly paid lip service to this official script, when he exonerated Duncan's assassin as but 'a poor player/That struts and frets his hour upon the stage' [5,5,23].

Macbeth blames the Jesuitical 'juggling fiends' for leading him astray [5,10,19]. And the peculiarity of this strange tragedy is how it thereby creates empathy for its villain, as if the killer can be separated from the 'secret murders sticking on his hands' [5,2,17]. When we recall, however, that Shakespeare 'had known Catesby and Grant from childhood, that Francis Tresham and the Winter brothers were connected [to him] by marriage, and that his friend Jonson dined with Catesby and Winter a few days before the explosion' was timed to go off, then his villain's dissociated hand looks uncannily symbolic, with Campion's thumb, of the dramatist's own mental disavowal of 'night's black agents', those 'secret, black, and midnight hags' [3,2,54; 4,1,64], the missionaries who worshipped such blood-soaked relics.[91] Certainly, no one could regard Shakespeare as a practising Catholic who accepts his authorship of the Porter scene in this tragedy, which answers the opening question, 'What bloody man is that?' [1,2,1] with the savage burlesque of Father Henry Garnet, who 'hanged himself' by colluding with the Plotters, knocking on Hell's door, as a poor fool 'who committed treason enough for God's sake, yet could not equivocate to heaven' [2,3,4–10]. Though pious Catholics pointed to the uncorrupted flesh of Garnet's skull on London Bridge as proof of his innocence, a play that opens by defiling Campion's thumb as a devil's dildo wastes no tears on napkins dipped in Jesuit blood. For as Macbeth's Porter objects, after the executions of so many innocents alongside the guilty, Shakespeare's England had seen 'napkins enough' [5].

Whenever some Elizabethan Catholic climbed the scaffold, the ritual was to throw a handkerchief into the crowd, 'whereupon some said: that will be taken up for a relic'.[92] Thus, the 1605 conspirators even had scarves 'significantly embroidered', so they could be 'dressed for martyrdom'.[93] But a year before the Plot, Shakespeare seems to have made the foolishness of relic worship the theme of *Othello*, his most sustained meditation upon such persecution mania. The figure of the holy fool was

Christ's, but had been adopted by the original Tudor martyr, Thomas More, who was proud that his name was an anagram of *Rome* and version of *morus*: the Latin for fool. More's martyrological symbol was a mulberry (from *morum*), which critics see encoded in the bloody fate of Thisbe, 'tarrying in mulberry shade' [*Dream*, 5,1,147], and of Desdemona, 'sighing by a sycamore' [*Othello*, 4,3,38].[94] And since More's heraldic crest was a moor's head, in homage to the black Doge from whom he claimed descent, it may be that 'The Tragedy of the Moor of Venice', which was partly based on this historic figure, critiques the *murmuring* worshippers who *immured* the martyr's *momenti mori*, like his bloodstained handkerchief, with all the *moroseness* that makes Othello such a 'fool, fool, fool!' [5,2,307]. Shakespeare's texts are littered with *morbid* napkins, of which there is said to be too much supplementary affect, ever '*more* in it' [*As You*, 4,3,158]. But he may have already presented More as a holy idiot, when he had Thisbe drop her mantle 'stained with blood', or mulberry juice, at 'old Ninny's tomb' [*Dream*, 5,1,252–72].[95] Thus a sacrilegious joke about the excess of the *mortuary* cult of the self-proclaimed 'old Ninny' suggests Shakespeare's last word on the misguided *mourners* of this Roman fool was 'Lord, what fools these *mortals* be!' [3,2,115].

Shakespeare, it seems, was no devotee of the Catholic work of mourning. Certainly, it is suggestive how the poet associated martyrdom with the *moronic* in the one text where he speaks openly of the impatience of the 'fools' who fall into the 'thralled discontent/Whereto th'inviting time our fashion calls'. The disavowal in his 'holy' Sonnet 124 of 'the fools of time' who put their heads in the noose by opposing 'fortune's bastard', Elizabeth, when with patience they might have survived to see 'the child of state . . . unfathered', would be as close as Shakespeare ever got to confessing membership of 'our fashion' – presumably the Catholic faith of his fathers – or expressing a view on that 'bastard' daughter of Anne Boleyn. But quoting the missionaries' metaphor for martyrs as flowers, his devotion, he claims here, is beyond the kind of 'accident' that swept up saints with sinners in the Tyburn harvest, as 'Weeds among weeds or flowers with flowers gathered'. Instead, he affirms his faith as a house 'builded far' from all changes of religion, unlike the mansions of those who 'suffer . . . in smiling pomp', or the ruins bequeathed by suicidal resisters. 'Politic' was the term adopted by Catholics who hoped, in face of terror, for a limited measure of religious toleration, like that in contemporary France; but in some of the most self-revealing lines Shakespeare ever wrote, he claims that his own patience is more 'politic' than even that of these self-styled 'politiques':

> It fears not policy, that heretic
> Which works on leases of short-numbered hours,
> But all alone stands hugely politic.
>
> [Sonnet 124]

Catholic priests suffered patiently, boasted Southwell, as 'God Almighty's fools'.[96] The Jesuit poet was invoking the Christians martyred in the Colosseum. But by imagining the 'bloody stage' of martyrdom [2,4,6] as 'this great stage of fools' [*Lear*, 4,6,177], Shakespeare took this suicidal *serio ludere* earnestly enough to create a counter-drama to the scaffold, showing how literally the martyrs had been fooled. So in *Macbeth* the 'horrid deed' of the Gunpowder Plot is blown back into the eyes of its perpetrators by the figure of Christ, 'like a naked new-born babe,/Striding the blast' [1,7,21]. The topical allusion is to the grim poetic justice when the Plotter Grant was blinded by his own explosives; but the judgement falls on all who followed the Jesuits, as the retort is also to Southwell's most celebrated poem, in which a 'babe all burning bright/Did in the air appear' like some incendiary device.[97] Shakespeare had exposed the masochism of pseudo-martyrdom in characters such as Isabella, who declares how she will wear 'Th'impression of keen whips . . . as rubies' and strip herself 'to death as to a bed' [*Measure*, 2,4,10].[98] But in this drama of 'dire combustion and confused events/New-hatched to the woeful time' [*Macbeth*, 2,3,54], he now projected the nightmare scenario of the incendiaries' *success*, when Macbeth accomplishes the 'bloody piece of work' that Catesby planned, and as the earth shakes and chimneys fall, 'strange screams of death' resound throughout 'the livelong night' [*Macbeth*, 2,3,51–6; 2,4,124].

Like the self-exonerating Lear, the Plotters had hoped to target only the guilty, saving 'as many as were Catholics or so disposed', and Catesby had guaranteed that 'tricks' would protect his friends; 'but when it came to the crunch his low opinion of others meant that he would rather see them all blown to perdition'.[99] Contemporaries were therefore horrified that the Plot had involved a massacre of innocents, including the young princes, eleven-year-old Henry and four-year-old Charles, whose fate *Macbeth* shadows in its murdered 'little ones' [4,2,69], like the 'bloody child' [stage direction 4,1,92], and Macduff's young son. Not until 1979 would Catholic terrorists succeed in assassinating any of the 'little ones' of the British royal family, with the murder of the aged Lord Louis Mountbatten and his grandson. But though apologists maintain that it is absurd to compare the 1605 conspirators to al-Qaeda, or to depict their Jesuit confessors as 'preachers of hate', and Antonia Fraser has even asked us to envision the Golden Age that would have ensued if only the explosives in the 'dark tower' at Westminster had gone off, Shakespeare had been exposed to the 'slaughterous thoughts' of these suicide bombers long enough to predict how they would have 'supped full of horrors' [5,5,13] if they had succeeded in striking down 'so many princes at a shot'.[100] As it was, the Gunpowder terrorists died not patiently, like 'the Roman fool' [5,10,1], Thomas More, but like Macbeth, hoping to take with them as many lives as possible, and imagining that their violent ends would be followed by Armageddon.[101]

'Hoist with his own petard' [*Hamlet*, 3,4,185:5], or blown up by his own weapon of mass destruction, in Shakespeare's plays the suicide attacker dies, like the real Plotters of 1605, who set fire to their own explosives, challenging his intended targets to 'Kill me and I will kill thee if I can!'[102] Critics have traditionally excused this indifference to the 'casual slaughters' [5,2,326] of innocent victims by mistaking the tragic hero for 'the true victim, even when he happens to be a murderer', thereby 'condoning the most monstrously thoughtless actions'.[103] Yet in our own time of terror, when we have learned to distrust the way collective murder is justified by religion, we have come to realise that, as Derrida insisted, 'A suicide bomber is always a criminal, both to himself and to those killed'.[104] 'The bloodboltered shambles in act five' of *Hamlet*, James Joyce considered, 'is a forecast of the concentration camp'.[105] The author of the most life-affirming 'yes' in all literature saw how Shakespeare could create a drama out of irremediable negativity. But now the Catholic critic René Girard asks us to imagine a contemporary terrorist like the Prince of Denmark 'with his finger on the nuclear button', and reasons that Hamlet's hesitation has never been more vital than it is today, when 'the sole religious law is to renounce revenge . . . or else'.[106]

Shakespeare's entire agonistic theatre, we can at last see, moves towards the instant in *The Tempest* when Prospero abandons the popish 'trash' that has been preserved as the relics of 'Mistress Line', who is identifiable as Anne Line, the martyred landlady of the Gunpowder Plotters, and decides that 'The rarer action is/In virtue than in vengeance' [4,1,222–33; 5,1,27–8].[107] More than any earlier generation, we can grasp that while his rivals revelled in violent revenge, and other European dramatists wrote 'martyr plays' glorying in bloodshed, Shakespeare's theatre is the best critique of such sacrifice ever composed. And we appreciate this because we too live in an age of massacres, hijackings, ethnic cleansing and 'humans not regarded as humans', and so have come to appreciate that 'precarious life' is best saved by 'tarrying with grief', in the words of Judith Butler, and not by 'endeavouring to seek a resolution for grief through violence'.[108] We understand that while his contemporaries relished their grisly theatre of cruelties, for Shakespeare, whenever the killing came, it would be premature, untimely and anachronistic. Happy to let the Protestants believe that their hero, the Lollard rogue Sir John Oldcastle, 'died a martyr' [2 *Henry IV*, Epi.,27], his own religion seems simply to have been to 'leave the killing out'. For the word *martyr*, Shakespeare noted in his 'holy sonnet', originally meant *witness*; and what he thought the Elizabethan martyrs would witness, if only they could come back, is that by living for death they had always died too soon:

> To this I witness call the fools of time,
> Which die for goodness, who have lived for crime.

NOTES

1. Note to *Hamlet* 3,1,76–82, in Robert Hapgood (ed.), '*Hamlet: Prince of Denmark*': *Shakespeare in Production* (Cambridge: Cambridge University Press, 1999), p. 180.
2. See Jacques Derrida, *Philosophy in a Time of Terror: Dialogues with Jürgen Habermas and Jacques Derrida*, ed. Giovanna Barradori (Chicago: Chicago University Press, 2003).
3. Note to *Hamlet* 5,2,308, in Stephen Greenblatt, Walter Cohen, Jean Howard and Katharine Eisaman Maus (eds), *Norton Shakespeare*, ed. Stephen Greenblatt, Walter Cohen, Jean Howard and Katharine Eisaman Maus (New York: Norton, 1997), note 6, p. 1755: 'All this slaughtered game ("quarry") proclaims a massacre'.
4. On 1 June 2001, Crown Prince Dipendra burst into a weekly meeting of the Nepalese royal family at the palace in Kathmandu and, as described in *Keesing's Record of World Events*, 'shot his father King Birenda, his mother Queen Aishwarya, and other relations, including his sister Princess Shruti, with automatic weapons, before turning a gun on himself. Eight

members of the royal family, including the king and queen, died on the spot, whilst Dipendra and the king's brother Dhirendra Shah both died in hospital on June 4. It was reported that the massacre was a result of a long-standing dispute over Dipendra's choice of a prospective bride'.

5. Jacques Derrida, *Specters of Marx: The State of the Debt, the Work of Mourning, and the New International*, trans. Peggy Kamuf (London: Routledge, 1994). And see the brilliantly timely reading in the context of the 'anthrax letters' by Russell Samolsky, 'Ghostly letters: *Hamlet*, Derrida and apocalyptic discourse', *Oxford Literary Review: Angles on Derrida*, 25 (2003), 79–101.

6. Ewan Fernie, 'The last act: presentism, spirituality and the politics of *Hamlet*', in Ewan Fernie (ed.), *Spiritual Shakespeares* (London: Routledge, 2005), p. 209.

7. Samolsky, 'Ghostly letters', p. 83.

8. The composer Karlheinz Stockhausen, quoted in Frank Letricchia and Jody McAuliffe, *Crimes of Art and Terror* (Chicago: Chicago University Press, 2003), p. 6.

9. See, in particular, Graham Holderness and Brian Loughrey, 'Rudely interrupted: Shakespeare and terrorism', *Critical Survey* (2007), 19:3, 107–23; and Matthew Biberman and Julia Lupton (eds), *Shakespeare After 9/11: How a Social Trauma Reshapes Interpretation* (Lewiston: Edwin Mellen, 2011).

10. Terry Eagleton, *Holy Terror* (Oxford: Oxford University Press, 2005), p. 90.

11. Ali Shariati, 'Jihad and shahadat' (1970), in Mehdi Abedi and Gary Legenhausen (eds), *Jihad and Shabbadat: Struggle and Martyrdom in Islam* (Houston: Institute for Research and Islamic Studies, 1986), pp. 213–14. Shariati owed the concept of 'freedom-toward-death' to his study of Heidegger in Paris.

12. Janet Afary and Kevin Anderson, *Foucault and the Iranian Revolution: Gender and the Seductions of Islam* (Chicago: Chicago University Press, 2005), pp. 44 and 62.

13. Shariati, 'Jihad and shahadat', pp. 177 and 214.

14. Michel Foucault, 'Is it useless to revolt?', originally published as 'Inutile de se souvenir?' in *Le Monde*, 11 May 1979, and subsequently in *Religion and Culture by Michel Foucault*, trans. James Bernauer, ed. Jeremy Carette (Manchester: Manchester University Press, 2000), p. 132.

15. Michel Houellebecq, *Soumission* (Paris: Flammarion, 2014).

16. Gilles Kepel, *Jihad: The Trail of Political Islam* (London: I. B. Tauris, 2002), p. 117.

17. François Billacois, *The Duel: Its Rise and Fall in Early Modern France*, trans. Trista Selous (New Haven: Yale University Press, 1990), p. 199: 'Why was there a sudden peak in the number of duels? We can answer by noting that the craze for duelling coincided with an obsession with blood. French tragedy was, like Elizabethan theater, a "theatre of blood, sensuality and death"; medical science . . . was discovering the repellent idea of the circulation of the blood; and in the Catholic Church, the chosen objects on which devotion was focused were the Five Wounds and the Sacred Heart.'

18. Carl Schmitt, *The Theory of the Partisan*, trans. and quoted in Jan-Werner Müller, *A Dangerous Mind: Carl Schmitt in Post-War European Thought* (New Haven: Yale University Press, 2003), p. 148.

19. Carl Schmitt, *Hamlet or Hecuba: The Intrusion of the Time into the Play*, trans. David Pann and Jennifer Rust (New York: Telos, 2009), p. 56.

20. See Pierre Janelle, *The Catholic Reformation* (Milwaukee: Bruce, 1963), pp. 166–8.

21. John Knott, *Discourses of Martyrdom in English Literature, 1563–1694* (Cambridge: Cambridge University Press, 1993), pp. 8–9 and 13.

22. Michael Williams, 'Campion and the English continental seminaries', in S. J. Thomas McCoog (ed.), *The Reckoned Expense: Edmund Campion and the Early English Jesuits: Essays in Celebration of the First Centenary of Campion Hall (1896–1996)* (Woodbridge: Boydell, 1996), p. 293.

23. Jonathan Sawday, *The Body Emblazoned: Dissection and the Human Body in Renaissance Culture* (London: Routledge, 1995), esp. pp. 117–25.

24. Alison Shell, *Catholicism, Controversy, and the English Literary Imagination, 1558–1660* (Cambridge: Cambridge University Press, 1999), p. 226.

25. Elaine Scarry, *The Body in Pain: The Making and Unmaking of the World* (Oxford: Oxford University Press, 1985), p. 214: 'It is not an accident that the image of the cross comes to have such a central place. The weapon becomes the primary sign because the entire religion is at its heart an alteration in the reading of this sign. . . . It is not that the idea of power is eliminated, and it is certainly not that the idea of suffering is eliminated: it is that the earlier relation between them is eliminated.'

26. George Bataille, *Inner Experience*, trans. Leslie Anne Boldt (Albany: SUNY Press, 1988), p. 120; discussed in Michel Surya, *Georges Bataille: An Intellectual Biography*, trans. Krzysztof Fizalkowski and Michael Richardson (London: Verso, 2002), pp. 93–5.

27. Williams, 'Campion and the English continental seminaries', p. 290.

28. Memorandum to Pope Sixtus V, quoted in Michael Williams, 'William Allen: the sixteenth century Spanish connection', *Recusant History*, 22 (1994), 133.

29. Eamon Duffy, 'William, Cardinal Allen, 1532–1594', *Recusant History*, 22 (1995), 276.

30. William Allen, *An Apology and True Declaration of the Institution and Endeavours of the Two English Colleges* (1581), quoted in Duffy, 'William, Cardinal Allen', p. 291.

31. William Allen, *A True, Sincere, and Modest Defence of English Catholics* (1581); and *An Admonition to the Nobility and People of England* (1587), quoted in Duffy, 'William, Cardinal Allen', pp. 269 and 285.

32. Elizabeth Hanson, *Discovering the Subject in Renaissance England* (Cambridge: Cambridge University Press, 1998), pp. 48–9.

33. Emmanuel Le Roy Ladurie, 'L'Iran de 1979 et la France de 1589', *Le Nouvel Observateur*, 22 January 1979, quoted in Afary and Anderson, *Foucault and the Iranian Revolution*, p. 105.

34. John Bossy, *Under the Molehill: An Elizabethan Spy Story* (New Haven: Yale University Press, 2001, p. 31.

35. Emmanuel Le Roy Ladurie, *Carnival at Romans: A People's Uprising at Romans, 1579–1580*, trans. Mary Feeney (Harmondsworth: Penguin, 1979), pp. xv-xvi.

36. William Allen, *A Modest Defence* (1581), p. 196, quoted Duffy, 'William, Cardinal Allen', p. 284.

37. William Allen, 'The copy of a letter by Doctor Allen concerning the yielding up of the city of Daventry' (1587), quoted in Williams, 'Campion and the English continental seminaries', p. 132.

38. Duffy, 'William, Cardinal Allen', p. 266.

39. John Bossy, 'The heart of Robert Persons', in McCoog (ed.), *The Reckoned Expense*, p. 150.

40. Quoted in Alison Plowden, *Danger to Elizabeth: The Catholics Under Elizabeth I* (London: Macmillan, 1973), pp. 207–8.

41. Quoted ibid., p. 209.

42. Quoted by Charlotte Carmichael Stopes, *Shakespeare's Warwickshire Contemporaries*, rev. edn (Stratford-upon-Avon: Shakespeare Head, 1907), pp. 75–81.

43. *Calendar of State Papers Domestic: 1581–90* (henceforth *CSPD*), p. 126: 'Examination of diverse persons taken before John Doyley of Merton touching certain speeches against the Queen's Majesty supposed to have been spoken by John Somerville'.

44. Roland Mousnier, *The Assassination of Henry IV: The Tyrannicide Problem and the Consolidation of the French Absolute Monarchy in the Early Seventeenth Century*, trans. Joan Spencer (London: Faber and Faber, 1973), pp. 48–9.

45. Sir John Harington, *Epigrams*, quoted in Lacey Baldwin Smith, *Treason in Tudor England: Politics and Paranoia* (London: Jonathan Cape, 1986), p. 1.

46. Stephen Holmes, 'Al-Quaeda, September 11, 2001', in Diego Gambetta (ed.), *Making Sense of Suicide Missions* (Oxford: Oxford University Press, 2005), p. 147.

47. *CSPD*, p. 295: 'Further secret intelligence from one at Exeter'.

48. Lisa Jardine, *The Awful End of Prince William the Silent: The First Assassination of a Head of State with a Handgun* (London: Harper Collins, 2005), pp. 106, 112 and 115; 'Doctor Allen's book': A *True and plain declaration of the horrible Treasons practised by William Parry the Traitor against the Queen's Majesty* (London: 1585), p. 5, quoted ibid., p. 112.

49. Allen (1588), quoted in Baldwin Smith, *Treason in Tudor England*, p. 178.

50. Allen (1584), quoted Duffy, 'William, Cardinal Allen', p. 282.

51. Stopes, *Shakespeare's Warwickshire Contemporaries*, p. 93.

52. See Richard Wilson, 'Shakespeare and the Jesuits', *Times Literary Supplement*, 19 December 1997, 11–13.

53. *CSPD*, pp. 129 and 135.

54. See Michael Wood, *In Search of Shakespeare* (London: BBC, 2003), pp. 92–6; Stephen Greenblatt, *Will in the World: How Shakespeare Became Shakespeare* (London: Jonathan Cape, 2004), pp. 157–60 and 172–3; Richard Wilson, *Secret Shakespeare: Studies in Theatre, Religion and Resistance* (Manchester: Manchester University Press, 2004), pp. 104–25; and Peter Ackroyd, *Shakespeare: The Biography* (London: Faber and Faber, 2005), pp. 94–5.

55. Greenblatt, *Will in the World*, p. 160.

56. Robert Parsons quoted in Richard Simpson, *Edmund Campion* (London: John Hodges, 1896), p. 455. For the later history of Campion's thumb, which is now divided into two pieces located in Rome and Roehampton, see Dom Bede Camm, *Forgotten Shrines: An Account of Some Old Catholic Halls and Families in England and of Relics and Memorials of the English Martyrs* (London: Macdonald and Evans, 1910), pp. 363 and 377–8. See also Wilson, *Secret Shakespeare*, ch. 8.

57. Simpson, *Edmund Campion*, p. 237.

58. Gary Taylor, 'Forms of opposition: Shakespeare and Middleton', *English Literary Renaissance*, 24 (1994), 298.

59. See T. W. Baldwin, *William Shakespeare Adapts a Hanging* (Princeton: Princeton University Press, 1931).

60. See John Klause, 'Politics, heresy, and martyrdom in Sonnet 124 and *Titus Andronicus*', in James Schiffer (ed.), *Shakespeare's Sonnets: Critical Essays* (New York: Garland, 1999), pp. 225–6.

61. Simpson, *Edmund Campion*, p. 462. The idea of blood as seed could also be applied to women. Thus John Mush relates how as the Catholic Margaret Clitherow 'cast the seed of her blood to the generation of many, so now she fighteth with blood to save those she hath borne, that the lily roots being watered with the fruitful liquor of blood . . . by how much more abundantly such sacred streams flow among them'. See Claire Cross, 'An Elizabethan martyrologist and his martyr: John Mush and Margaret Clitherow', *Studies in Church History*, 30 (1993), 278.

62. Graham Greene, 'Introduction', in *John Gerard: The Autobiography of an Elizabethan*, trans. and ed. Philip Caraman (London: Longmans and Green, 1951), p. x.

63. Stephen Greenblatt, *Hamlet in Purgatory* (Princeton: Princeton University Press, 2001), p. 249.

64. The entire hunting interlude in *Love's Labour's Lost*, during which the schoolmaster Holofernes and curate Sir Nathaniel debate whether the 'deer' was legally killed, and whether or not its crime ''twas treason', is riddled with allusions to 'our parson' Robert Parsons (or Persons) [4,3,190], and reads like a coded satire on the Elizabethan war on terror. See John Phelps, 'Father Parsons in Shakespeare', *Archiv für das Studium der neueren Sprachen und Literaturen*, 133 (1915), 66–86. Phelps presumes that 'The picture of the "piercing" of this arch-traitor [Father Parsons] would be richly enjoyed by an audience

accustomed to mock and ridicule the heads of traitors exposed on pikes' (p. 81). But if so, Parsons defied this gallows humour by escaping to Rome.

65. Stephen Greenblatt, 'Introduction' to *Much Ado About Nothing*, in Greenblatt et al. (eds), *Norton Shakespeare*, p. 1384.

66. Quoted by Arthur Marotti, 'Southwell's remains: Catholicism and anti-Catholicism in early modern England', in Cedric Brown and Arthur Marotti (eds), *Texts and Cultural Change in Early Modern England* (Basingstoke: Macmillan, 1997), p. 52.

67. Greene, 'Introduction', p. xi.

68. Thomas Norton to Francis Walsingham, 27 March 1582, quoted in Michael Graves, *Thomas Norton: The Parliament Man* (Oxford: Blackwell, 1994), p. 275.

69. Greenblatt, *Will in the World*, pp. 108–10.

70. John Dover Wilson, *What Happens in 'Hamlet'* (Cambridge: Cambridge University Press, 1935), p. 70.

71. Greenblatt, *Hamlet in Purgatory*, p. 240.

72. Quoted in Simpson, *Edmund Campion*, p. 428.

73. Quoted in Barbara Diefendorf, *Beneath the Cross: Catholics and Huguenots in Sixteenth-Century Paris* (Oxford: Oxford University Press, 1991), pp. 78 and 150. See also Mark Greengrass, 'Hidden transcripts: secret histories and personal testimonies of religious violence in the French Wars of Religion', in Mark Levine and Robert Roberts (eds), *The Massacre in History* (New York: Berghahn, 1999), pp. 69–88.

74. Natalie Zemon Davis, 'The rites of violence', in *Society and Culture in Early Modern France* (Oxford: Polity Press, 1987), p. 174.

75. See Peter Millward, *Shakespeare's Religious Background* (London: Sidgwick and Jackson, 1973), p. 54; and Stephen Greenblatt, '*King Lear* and the exorcists', in *Shakespearean Negotiations: The Circulation of Social Energy in Renaissance England* (Oxford: Clarendon Press, 1988), pp. 116–21.

76. Christopher Devlin, *The Life of Robert Southwell: Poet and Martyr* (London: Longmans and Green, 1956), p. 324; Philip Caraman, *Henry Garnet and the Gunpowder Plot* (London: Longmans, 1964), p. 439.

77. Simpson, *Edmund Campion*, p. 171.

78. See Joseph Wittreich, '*Image of the Horror': History, Prophecy, and Apocalypse in 'King Lear'* (San Marino: Huntington Library, 1984), p. 96.

79. See Julia Reinhard Lupton, *Afterlives of the Saints: Hagiography, Typology and Renaissance Literature* (Stanford: Stanford University Press, 1996), pp. 62–4, 114–16 and 211.

80. For the association of *King Lear* with St Stephen, see Roy Battenhouse, *Shakespearean Tragedy: Its Art and Its Christian Premises* (Bloomington: Indiana University Press, 1969), p. 144; Chris Hassel, *Renaissance Drama and the English Church Year* (Lincoln: University of Nebraska Press, 1979), pp. 100–3; and Wittreich, '*Image of the Horror*', pp. 11, 16–18, 114–19.

81. Mark Nicholls, *Investigating Gunpowder Plot* (Manchester: Manchester University Press, 1991), p. 7.

82. Quoted ibid., pp. 6 and 9.

83. For *King Lear* as an epistolary drama that problematises early modern technology of written communication, see Lisa Jardine, 'Reading and the technology of textual affect: Erasmus's familiar letters and Shakespeare's *King Lear*', in *Reading Shakespeare Historically* (London: Routledge, 1996), pp. 90–7; and Alan Stewart, *Shakespeare's Letters* (Oxford: Oxford University Press, 2008), pp. 193–230.

84. Antonia Fraser, *The Gunpowder Plot: Terror and Faith in 1605* (London: Weidenfeld and Nicolson, 1996), pp. 114–15.

85. Sandeep Kaushik, 'Resistance, loyalty and recusant politics: Sir Thomas Tresham and the Elizabethan state', *Midland History*, 21 (1996), 48–9.

86. Edgar Fripp, *Shakespeare: Man and Artist*, 2 vols (Oxford: Oxford University Press, 1938), vol. 2, p. 640.

87. Bede quoted in Camm, *Forgotten Shrines*, p. 362.

88. James Travers, *Gunpowder: The Players Behind the Plot* (London: National Archives, 2005), p. 23.

89. Samuel Harsnett, *A Declaration of Egregious Popish Impostures* (London, 1603), reprinted in Frank Brownlow, *Shakespeare, Harsnett, and the Devils of Denham* (Newark: University of Delaware Press, 1993), p. 297.

90. Quoted in Caraman, *Henry Garnet and the Gunpowder Plot*, pp. 397–8.

91. Leslie Hotson, *I, William Shakespeare* (London: Jonathan Cape, 1937), pp. 197–8.

92. Quoted in Ceri Sullivan, *Dismembered Rhetoric: English Recusant Writing, 1580 to 1603* (London: Associated University Press, 1994), p. 104.

93. Travers, *Gunpowder*, p. 93.

94. See Patricia Parker, 'What's in a name', *Sederi*, 11 (Seville: Universidad de Huelva, 2002), 101–49, esp. 117. For John Donne's similar 'praise of folly' by way of 'mad' religious play on the name of (his ancestor) More, see Thomas Docherty, *John Donne, Undone* (London: Methuen, 1986), pp. 198–207.

95. See 'Dyed in mummy: *Othello* and the mulberries', in Wilson, *Secret Shakespeare*, pp. 170–85.

96. Quoted in Devlin, *The Life of Robert Southwell*, p. 321; see also Peter Milward, *Shakespeare's Religious Background* (Chicago: Loyola University Press, 1973), p. 60.

97. Robert Southwell, 'The burning babe', in *The Poems of Robert Southwell, S.J.*, ed. James McDonald and Nancy Pollard Brown (Oxford: Clarendon Press, 1967), p. 15, ll. 7–8.

98. See Lupton, *Afterlives of the Saints*, pp. 110–40.

99. Nicholls, *Investigating Gunpowder Plot*, p. 41.

100. Michael Barnes, 'Terror, treason and plot', *The Tablet*, 5 November 2005, 4; Antonia Fraser, 'The Gunpowder Plot succeeds', in Brenda Buchanan (ed.), *Gunpowder Plots: A Celebration of 400 years of Bonfire Night* (London: Allen Lane, 2005), pp. 34–48.

101. Robert Winter, quoted in Travers, *Gunpowder*, p. 133: 'God will raise up seed to Abraham out of the very stones, our deaths will be sufficient justification of it. And it is for God's cause.'

102. Thomas Winter to his captors, quoted ibid., p. 93.

103. R. S. White, *Innocent Victims: Poetic Injustice in Shakespearian Tragedy* (London: Athlone Press, 1986), pp. 126–7. My reading of Shakespeare's 'suicide attackers' is much indebted to this eloquent and moving account of 'the disastrous and murderous consequences for innocent people' of the inhuman actions of Titus, Hamlet, Lear, Othello and Macbeth.

104. Jacques Derrida, 'Epoché and faith: an interview with Jacques Derrida', in *Derrida and Religion: Other Testaments*, ed. Yvonne Sherwood and Kevin Hart (London: Routledge, 2005), p. 41.

105. James Joyce, *Ulysses* (Harmondsworth: Penguin, 1968), p. 187.

106. René Girard, 'Hamlet's dull revenge', *Stanford Literature Review*, 1:2 (1984), 197–9.

107. For Shakespeare's allusions to the execution of Anne Line, see Wilson, 'Shakespeare and the Jesuits', pp. 12–13, 201 and 298; and the important article by John Finnis and Patrick Martin, 'Another turn for the turtle: Shakespeare's intercession for love's martyr', *Times Literary Supplement*, 18 April 2003, which argues that 'The phoenix and the turtle' was written to be set to music by the Catholic composer William Byrd as the requiem for the Jesuits' London 'mistress', who was martyred in 1601.

108. Judith Butler, *Precarious Life: The Powers of Mourning and Violence* (London: Verso, 2005), p. 30.

6 Veiling an Indian Beauty: Shakespeare and the Hijab

Thus ornament is but the guilèd shore
To a most dangerous sea, the beauteous scarf
Veiling an Indian beauty; in a word,
The seeming truth which cunning times put on
To entrap the wisest.

[*Merchant*, 3,2,97–101][1]

THE BEAUTEOUS SCARF

Bassanio's suspicion of the 'beauteous scarf/Veiling an Indian beauty' as an object of both danger and desire appears to explain why in *The Merchant of Venice* he prefers the casket of 'meagre lead' to 'pale and common' silver or 'gaudy gold'. This reversal of the traditional Epiphany scene that welcomes gifts from the East seems to belong to an Orientalist discourse in which the Muslim hijab alternates as a symbol of eroticism or violence. Devised, perhaps, for a New Year performance, the 'casket scene' thereby typifies carnival aggression, with its three kings no longer present-bearing strangers but recipients of what Jacques Derrida called Europe's 'hostipitality'.[2] So Bassanio's rejection of ornament plays to the prejudice of Portia's test, which ends when '*The curtain is drawn aside*' [stage direction 3,2,1;101], and a true Caucasian beauty is disclosed with the same eye-to-eye logic as that with which the Duke commands Shylock to 'stand before our face' [4,1,15]. Despite their masked charades, these Christians long for the face-to-face openness of a gift culture that is fast being destroyed by self-interest, for which a Jewish banker can be blamed. Discovered inside the lead casket, 'Portia's counterfeit' portrait is thus an epitome of lost transparency, with hair woven in 'A golden mesh', to publish, rather than hide, what this 'fairest creature northward born' claims: 'You see me, Lord Bassanio, where I stand, such as I am' [2,1,4; 3,2,115; 149].

During Elizabethan masques the ladies of the court were draped, liked Portia, in veils of such translucent gauze their true racial identities were never in doubt. Yet

here the travel conceit with which Bassanio envisages the hijab veiling a 'dangerous sea' reminds us how, to play this guessing game, he has had to avail himself of a
veil identical to that of the soiled Indian houri: the 'over-weather'd ribs and ragged
sails' of his lover Antonio's 'scarfèd barque', now 'Vailing her hightop lower than
her ribs', as the effeminised merchantman is 'Hugged and embraced', only to be
'rent and beggared by the strumpet wind' [1,1,28; 2,6,14]. And what the similarity of
sails to veils reveals is the unmanning rub that this belly dance is all in favour of the
East. As Ros Ballaster explains in *Fabulous Orients*, the 'Dark Lady' *topos* emerges in
this period when 'the veiled and hidden woman of the seraglio' begins to embody
both the superficial ease of Indian commerce and its underlying risk, and the subcontinent comes to be sexualised as an emasculating harem: 'a kind of abyss' in the
report of Colbert's commercial agent, 'for a great part of the gold and silver of the
world, that finds many ways to enter there, and almost none to issue hence'.[3] So, if
the Muslim veil should ever be 'rent', we are warned in Shakespeare's multi-layered
text, that 'dangerous sea' will expose the 'tradeful merchants' to the hidden violence
of the 'dark lady', and thereby reveal the treachery of their oriental desires, at a time
when 'India's economy is more productive', Europe's technological lead is 'limited
to ships', and it is Europe that is becoming dependent on Asian manufactures, not
the reverse:[4]

> Should I go to church
> And see the holy edifice of stone
> And not bethink me straight of dangerous rocks
> Which, touching but my gentle vessel's side,
> Would scatter all her spices on the stream,
> Enrobe the roaring waters with my silks. . . .
>
> [*Merchant*, 1,1,29–34]

If the 'beauteous' veil of Bassanio's 'dark lady' is some 'rich scarf' [*Tempest*, 4,1,82]
of silk, like those carried in the belly of Antonio's caravel, the confusion it causes
repeats the unease at illicit desires, and the sense of insidious *velleity*, that silk provokes throughout these plays, where a sensuous relish for the sheen of the deluxe
fabric cues disgust at the 'taffeta punk' [*All's Well*, 2,2,19], as opposed to native
'russet yeas, and honest kersey noes' [*Love's*, 5,2,413], whenever the 'simple truth'
is 'abused/With silken, sly insinuating' lies [*Richard III*, 1,3,51–2]. This elision
of 'changeable taffeta' [*Twelfth*, 2,4,75] with 'silken terms precise,/Three-piled
hyperboles' [*Love's*, 5,2,406–7] was keyed to the inflated price of silk, not farmed in
England until 1604, when it cost fourteen shillings a yard.[5] But it was the pliability
of its sinuous fibre that also made it synonymous with the oriental harem, as 'Silk
could be spun into thread of varying thickness and woven in fabric of different
appearances, from finest gauze (*cyprus*, *sarcenet*, used in linings, and *tiffany*, used for
puffs), to *taffeta*, which was not so fine, *velvet*, *plush* (a deeper pile than velvet), and
satin'.[6] Not for nothing, then, was Shakespeare's father a glover, whose silk linings
supplied a metaphor for linguistic duplicity – 'A sentence is but a cheveril glove to
a good wit' [*Twelfth*, 3,1,10–12] – and his Stratford friend Richard Quiney a draper,

selling taffeta, ribbon, scarves, skeins of silk and silk buttons; for his texts flaunt an appreciation of silk's versatility in all its polychromatic variations of 'sad cypress' [Twelfth, 2,4,52], 'green sarcenet' [Troilus, 5,1,26], 'flame-colour'd taffeta' [1 Henry IV, 1,2,9], 'peach-colour'd satin', or 'three-piled velvet' [Measure, 1,2,33; 4,3,9].[7]

Shakespeare was an old hand at all the duplicitous dodges of the rag trade. Indeed, in his book The Lodger Charles Nicholl situates the playwright at the very heart of London's multicultural silk industry, in the rooms he rented in the 1600s from Christopher Mountjoy in Silver Street, Cripplegate, writing directly above the atelier where the Huguenot haberdasher supervised the spinning wheels on which filaments of silk were twisted into thread known as 'sleaves', that were then braided with wires upon other wheels, to form the gold 'tissue' from which arose 'tires' or 'toys for the head' [Winter's, 4,4,317]. Trained in Crécy, a mecca, like Arras, for silk weaving, Mountjoy was a master of the mystery of working such 'Venice gold' [Taming, 2,1,346], the 'sweet commixture' [Love's, 5,2,296] of 'red and mingled damask' [As You, 3,5,124], also named from Damascus, where the techniques of damascene 'cloth a' gold . . . lac'd with silver' [Much Ado, 3,4,19] had been developed. It was in Silver Street, therefore, that Shakespeare would have observed the exorbitantly decorated and multi-decked 'ship-tire, the tire valiant, the tire of Venetian admittance' [Wives, 3,3,48], which literalised masculine insecurity about the veiled lady as a ship of war. So, though Nicholl peers into the Mountjoy house to catch him with seductive French Marie as his 'Dark Lady', the synaesthetic ambiance of exotic sensations, smells and sounds in which we are encouraged to imagine the writer weaving his own tissues of lies to the rhythm of the loom is here heady enough to account for Shakespeare's hypersensitivity to the subtle secrecy of silk:

> In one part of the shop an apprentice sits at a bench, drawing wires of gilded silver through die-holes to make the fine wire suitable for gold thread. There are hammers and rollers to flatten the wire into strips ready for spinning into thread. In another part of the shop bundles of raw silk are being separated into 'sleaves'. A third person is working the 'twisting wheel', turning those sleaves into silk thread, and silk thread into sparkling Venice gold. . . . Metal fumes hang in the close air of the workshop, the smell of glues and dyes. . . . Just outside . . . is a well-dressed gentleman of middle age who might be a merchant or mercer, but who is in fact the tiremaker's lodger . . . he is a shadow in the doorway, a footstep on the stairs . . . [but] what he sees and hears is stored away . . . to be used in turn as raw material in the manufacturing of metaphors . . . in 'Sleep that knits up the ravelled sleave of care' [Macbeth, 2,2,36].[8]

'For her own person, / It beggared description. She did lie / In her pavilion – cloth of gold, of tissue' [Antony, 2,2,203–5]: Shakespeare's report of the Nile cruise of the ultimate 'Dark Lady' echoes Marlowe, whose Dido likewise had galleons with 'tackling made of riven gold'. Both sovereigns are seen as 'tailors of the earth' in this Orientalist sartorial discourse, comforting their courtiers 'that when old robes are worn out there are members to make new' [1,2,149–50]. But whereas the Queen of Carthage boasted 'sails of folded lawn', the Egyptian surpasses linen with her dyed 'purple sails' of sleek 'silken tackle', which swell with 'touches of those flower-soft hands' [199; 215].[9] A whole crisis in European textile production lies behind this switch during Shakespeare's lifetime from wool to silk as the gold standard of economic prowess, a revolution Marlowe foretold with his Jew of Malta's 'argosy from Alexandria . . . Laden with riches and exceeding store/Of Persian silks'.[10] And the historian of globalisation Fernand Braudel provided a worldly context for this ambiguous nexus of danger and desire, sails and veils, swirling about an emasculating 'Indian beauty', when he noted how during the 1590s almost 'every single letter from Venetian merchants carried some reference to silk', and interpreted this fixation as an index of collective psychic insecurity, when the value of heavy bulk goods exported to the East, such as English lead, tin and woollen textiles, was outshone by the quality of the silk, chintz and other light fabrics imported in return.[11] Thus, there was a crisis of *super-demand* as 'the rich forsook gold and silver for silk, which as it became available to more people emerged as a symbol of social mobility' and the transcendental signifier for the disturbing changes of an emerging consumer society.

With mass marketing of Indian, Persian and Chinese silks, Braudel recorded, 'quick changes in fashion created artificial but imperative "needs" that might vanish overnight only to make way for other equally frivolous passions', for while 'people still spun and wove at home', the sudden ubiquity of silk meant that 'it was now fashion and the luxury trade that dictated demand'. European governments legislated to protect their textile industries from this alien incursion, Braudel related, 'but all in vain. Nothing worked', not banning all Asian silks from England in 1700, the prize of 500 livres put up by Paris clothiers 'to strip any woman wearing Indian fabrics' naked in the street, nor a French scheme to dress prostitutes in Indian silks and publicly undress them in disgrace.[12] For while Puritan defenders of the sumptuary laws such as Philip Stubbes raged that 'impudent insolvency is now so grown that everyone, though very poor, will not stick to have silk', the insatiable European demand for this suave and shimmering tissue ensured silk became what Bassanio makes it, and what Troilus evokes as he reminds the Trojans that their 'breath bellied his sails' when Paris abducted Helen, and that 'We turn not back the silks upon the merchant/When we have spoiled them' [*Troilus*, 2,2,68–73], a superlative example of the *objet petit a* that generates its own desire:

Kate, eat apace; and now, my honey love,
Will we return unto my father's house,
And revel it as bravely as the best,
With silken coats, and caps, and golden rings,
With ruffs, and cuffs, and farthingales, and things,
With scarves, and fans, and double change of bravery,
With amber bracelets, beads, and all this knavery.
What, hast thou dined? The tailor stays thy leisure,
To deck thy body with his ruffling treasure.

[*Taming*, 4,3,52–60]

MASTER SMOOTH, THE SILK MAN

In *Impersonations*, his dazzling study of cross-dressing, Stephen Orgel describes the fetish allure of female apparel for Renaissance males, and their proto-Lacanian awareness of what one Tudor moralist pinpointed as the tendency of 'the imagination of a desirable thing to stir up the desire'.[13] And feminists notice how, in episodes like Petruchio's cruel *fort/da* game with Kate's trousseau, where he scorns her fashionable toque in culinary terms, as 'A custard coffin, a bauble, a silken pie' [4,3,82], Shakespeare's women shift from being producers or consumers of textiles to being identified with the cloth itself, a reification testifying how 'In early modern England it is the material of subjectivity itself'.[14] Marina confirms this process by weaving 'sleided silk' so adroitly 'Her inkle, silk, twin with the rubied cherry' [*Pericles*, 15:21; 20:8]. Thus, as the object of Bassanio's erotic desire slides from the concealed face to its superficial veil, the real 'Indian beauty' the Venetians covertly crave, this travail metaphor insists, is the cargo of 'silks' and 'spices' that their 'argosies with portly sail' deliver from the 'dangerous' East [*Merchant*, 1,1,9–31]. And judging by the keenness of the sexual imagery of conception, pregnancy and expectation he employs, it could be that Shakespeare was himself among those investors who 'laughed to see the sails conceive/And grow big-bellied with the wanton wind', when some heavy freighter blown by the 'spicèd Indian air' laboured westward 'from a voyage, rich with merchandise' [*Dream*, 2,1,124; 134].

There is a slippery etymological connection, from the Latin *velum*, and *velle* (to will or wish), retained in the French *voile* and *voila*, between *veil* and *sail* as simultaneously opaque and open membranes, that enacts, so Hélène Cixous and Derrida suggest in their insinuating confection *Veils*, the slithering recession of volition, veil and value, travail and travel, and self and silk: of *soi* and *soie*. There can be no end, in this serial homonymy, to the Penelopean labour of 'unveiling as veiling'.[15] But in his own dance of veils, set in the capital of carnival, Shakespeare appears to fret over the travailing sailcloth, as a figure 'Marking the embarkèd traders on the flood' [127] as liable to be neutered by their veiled commerce with strangers, such as Muslims and Jews, and to be alarmed enough about the metonymic relation of their vessel's 'bellied sails' [*Troilus*, 2,2,74] to the Islamic hijab to wonder who in the end will *prevail*: those of other faiths who modestly refuse to 'thrust their head into the public street/To gaze on Christian fools with varnished faces' [*Merchant*, 2,5,31–2], or those cross-dressed clowns who travesty their Christianity by harassing strangers with grotesque masks. So, with even his 'wisest' investors 'trapped' by their circuit of veiled Indian transactions, or enmeshed in the bonds of paper credit necessary to float it, Shakespeare seems to intuit what Patricia Fumerton analyses in her essay 'The Veil of Topicality', that in dazzling masquerades like those that Portia stages, and that teasingly allude to the 'strange body' of overseas trade, Renaissance theatre is posing a crucial existential question for the European self as it enters the global market of exchangeable identities and dangerous desires:

> How to dress up in ornaments the foreign trade and bourgeois barbarousness in which it was involved, so as to sustain the fiction of gift culture while allowing

business to continue as usual? How, that is, to dress up cannibals and bankers so as to mask the fact that the 'private' self was the embodiment of such greedy consumption?[16]

'Nay, what are you, sir? O immortal gods, O fine villain, a silken doublet, a velvet hose, a scarlet cloak, and a copintank hat': though his father is supposedly a 'sail-maker in Bergamo', when he is got up in his silken garb Tranio imagines that he passes for a gentleman [*Taming*, 5,1,54–65]. Thus, as their speculative business goes global, Shakespeare's characters are alive to the reversal in world trade that literally *disorients* England's gift culture in such ways, when the export economy that had been grounded in continental demand for English wool is inverted into an import economy fuelled by English consumption of 'ornamental' luxuries from overseas. Secreted in darkness by slithering worms, silk is thus metonymic in these texts of the representational crisis when 'steel grows soft as parasite's silk' [*Coriolanus*, 1,9,45]. For in this moral panic about semblance and substitution, sericulture is truly the medium of a *serial* national betrayal. Thus, while the diplomats in Shakespeare's report of the Field of the Cloth of Gold seemingly 'make Britain India' with their imported silks, Britain's native cloth manufacturers are forced to 'put off/The spinsters, carders, fullers, weavers, who in desperate manner are all in uproar' [*Henry VIII*, 1,1,21; 1,2,32–7]. Likewise, what enrages the Kentish clothier Jack Cade are the 'silken-coated slaves' at court [2 *Henry VI*, 4,2,115]. Poins's delinquency is therefore measured by his 'peach coloured' silk stockings, as Hal's is by 'new silk and old sack' [2 *Henry IV*, 1,2,180; 2,2,14], until the Prince finally abandons his 'silken dalliance in the wardrobe' and resolves instead to fly his 'silken streamers' [*Henry V*, Pro.2,2; Pro.3,6] against the French, who are themselves led disastrously by a 'cockered silken wanton' [*John*, 5,2,70].

Shakespeare was no spokesman for England's textile industry, and in the Cade scenes of 2 *Henry VI* satirised the chauvinism of the clothiers' champion Thomas Deloney.[17] Yet when it came to silk, he was still capable of voicing protectionism. Thus, for Antipholus of Syracuse the height of oriental devilry is when 'a tailor called me in his shop,/And showed me silks' [*Comedy*, 4,3,5–6]. Timon's flatterers likewise reveal their decadent Athenian luxury when they 'wear silk, drink wine, lie soft' [*Timon*, 4,3,206]; as do Cymbeline's fops by 'rustling in unpaid silk' [*Cymbeline*, 3,3,24]. By the time of *The Winter's Tale*, however, the inventory of Autoclycus, the Dionysian pedlar who swamps the sheep-shearing fair with imported 'lesser linen', like 'inkles, caddises, cambrics, ribbons of all colours', and 'golden coifs and stomachers', registers an awareness not only of the commodity fetishism that historians term 'The Great Reclothing', the 'bondage of certain ribbons and gloves' in a fashion system where 'You would think a smock a she-angel', and they flaunt 'plackets where they should bear their faces' [4,4,202–15; 228–36], but recognition of the futility of any prophylactic to protect wool communities from the Asian market, given the universal penetration of textiles shipped from Bengal, Ceylon, Madras or Persia by 'the miracle of overseas trade'.[18] So, 'My traffic is sheets', leers this 'Master Smooth, the silk man' [2 *Henry IV*, 2,1,29], promoting his pornographic chapbooks, constituted from remnants of coarse woollen bedding, as well as advertising the luxurious 'white sheet bleaching on the hedge' that this mercenary cuckoo stains or steals in turn. And the 'fantastical' taste for modish oriental 'enfoldings' Autolycus passes on to his avid country customers, to have them refashion themselves as 'gentlemen born', is as much a metropolitan makeover in this rags-to-riches story of serial redressing as is the sexual availability he proclaims:

> Will you buy any tape,
> Or lace for your cape,
> My dainty duck, my dear-a?
> Any silk, any thread,
> Any toys for your head
> Of the new'st and fin'st wear-a?

> [Winter's, 4,4,318]

'If you bargain with Mr Shakespeare, or receive money therefore, bring your money home if you may. I see how knit stockings be sold; there is great buying of them at Evesham': the only surviving letters naming the dramatist place him as just such a 'Master Smooth', in the thick of the Midland garment trade as a backer of Quiney, albeit in a deal to make a killing in worsted 'knit hosings'.[19] Yet, like the itinerant pedlar who 'wore three-pile' velvet suits to wait on Prince Florizel [4,3,5; 4,4,710; 5,2,124], or indeed Shakespeare himself, who was issued yards of scarlet cloth by the Master of the Wardrobe to parade as a Groom of the Chamber before King James, his actors acquired their 'cut-rate wardrobe' of shining silk second-hand from the court.[20] This meant 'players appeared in clothes that might have belonged to members of the audience'; but Anne Jones and Peter Stallybrass argue that by recycling such hand-downs, the stage also became a catwalk for crowds to copy, a theory substantiated when the Citizens elbow into *Julius Caesar* flaunting their Sunday 'best apparel' [1,1,8].[21] Shakespeare's early plays turn upon the trick of cast-offs fitting 'As if the garment had been meant', as Julia says [*Two Gentlemen*, 4,4,155]. But his later works amplify elite concern over the self-fashioning that was suddenly available when, as Stubbes protested, 'all persons dress indiscriminately in silks, velvets, satins, damasks, and taffetas', as they also echo the actors' tiring-house anxiety that 'our strange garments cleave not to their mould' [*Macbeth*, 1,3,143].[22]

The cultural alarm about the link between usurpation and the upstart whose expensive but ungainly borrowed clothes 'Hang loose about him like a giant's robe/Upon a dwarfish thief' [5,2,21–2] is clinched in *The Tempest*, where Caliban's slave revolt terminates in a 'frippery', or second-hand shop, before Prospero disowns as popish 'trumpery' the 'rich garments, linens, stuffs' that have been the signifiers of his rule [1,2,164; 4,1,186; 224]. So, of the seventy instances in Shakespeare of the word 'garment', fifty are in his Jacobean texts, with fifteen in *Cymbeline* alone, the quick-change cross-dress tragicomedy that, as Stallybrass shows, questions more than any other play the fetishising of 'senseless linen' in a regime that judges a man by 'His mean'st garment' [1,3,7; 2,3,128].[23] 'I do not like the fashion of your garments', Lear tells Poor Tom: 'You will say they are Persian; but let them be changed'. The beggar raves against 'rustling of silks' himself. But the mad King's only answer to such 'gorgeous' oriental 'sophistication' is to 'unbutton' his 'lendings', and strip even 'looped and windowed raggedness' to the 'bare and unaccommodated' flesh, until 'Thou owest the worm no silk' [Lear, 2,4,269; 3,4,88–99; 3,6,73].[24] The historian Christopher Hill thought that the Quakers, who likewise streaked stark naked down Cheapside in the 1650s, were inspired by the nudism of Shakespeare's Lear.[25] But 'the pedlar's silken treasury' [Winter's, 4,4,350] also supplies the playful solution English consumers preferred to the bare life of such an apocalyptic divestment, which was to flaunt the seductiveness of new textiles, and front private desires with the public face of shamelessness itself:

> Lawn as white as driven snow,
> Cypress black as e'er was crow,
> Gloves as sweet as damask roses,
> Masks for faces, and for noses.

[Winter's, 4,4,214–17]

'Masks will be more hereafter in request,/And grow more dear': Shakespeare's 'cloth-driven theatre' is quick to pick up the agonistic ruse, reported here by Thomas Combe, whereby Londoners separated private faces from public spaces, which was to transport masks from fancy dress to street wear.[26] Stowe shuddered how 'Women's masks came into England about the time of the Massacre of Paris'; and Stubbes listed among obstacles to social order women walking with 'visors made of velvet wherewith they cover all their faces, having holes made in them against their eyes, wherewith they look'.[27] But by 1600 the game of seeing and enjoying, without being seen to enjoy, was taking the form of 'masks for noses', or half-masks known as vizards, which covered only the upper face, as though desires and identities were now to be read 'in quotes' as if *under erasure*. Initially adopted as functional accessories to protect the complexion, like the 'sun-expelling mask' Julia has discarded ever 'since she did neglect her looking-glass' [Two Gentlemen, 4,4,150], vizards were defined by John Cleveland in a 1647 poem, 'The King's Disguise', as articles 'such as Ladies wear/When they are veiled on purpose to be seen'.[28] Thus, in a new epoch of coexistence, elite women will learn to wear veils as empty signifiers, proclaiming that they conceal nothing of their essential selves, but *hide in full view*. And the ritual aggression of an identity that is simultaneously asserted and denied, as though in parenthesis, sets a precedent for our own multicultural societies, in which an identitarian politics has also come, as it were, face to mask, in panic over the hijab and 'the sorry affair of the *foulard*'.[29]

DEGREE BEING VIZARDED

All the arguments in current debates about the veil proceed on the assumption that the hijab functions as an obstacle to the transparency that is taken by both its adherents and its enemies to be the precondition of Enlightenment, and hence of a modern secular society. Thus, in *The Politics of the Veil*, Joan Wallach Scott has critiqued the 2004 French legal ban on the veil, together with other 'conspicuous signs' of religious affiliation, for a postcolonial blindness to the way in which *laïcité* converges with the exposure of female bodies in the exploitative spectacle of the market.[30] Then, in his recent *Saeculum: Culture, Religion, Idéologie*, Etienne Balibar has responded to this critique by asserting that equality before the law and capitalist commodification are not equivalent abstract universals, and by objecting to Scott's particular obliviousness to the way in which the Islamic veil functions to reproduce the structures of sexual difference in a monotheistic and patriarchal social order.[31] What both these opposed thinkers can agree, therefore, is that the *affaires des foulards* is symptomatic of the travails of Western modernity, and thus indicative of the impasse of a radical Enlightenment. But the surprise of the Shakespearean prehistory of this controversy is that the veil has not invariably intruded as a symbolic obstruction to Enlightenment, and that in seventeenth-century English society this ritual face of aggression functioned as Enlightenment's facilitator and mediator.

In the sexually relaxed and multi-confessional society of seventeenth-century London, the mask would become the paradoxical signal of danger and desire. Wycherley's Pinchwife will therefore miss the point when he exclaims that such a visor 'makes people inquisitive and is as ridiculous a disguise as a stage-beard'; for according to Christoph Heyl, in a contribution to *Masquerade and Identities*, this virtual disguise was *intended to be penetrated*: 'It was easy to recognise the wearer. But this must have been sufficient to introduce new opportunities for playing with anonymity', as these masks 'both obscure their wearers and attract attention'. Heyl therefore interprets the seventeenth-century vogue for half-masks as a version of incognito ritual, in which, if you signal you are invisible, people who recognise you are constrained to behave as though you are in fact unknown, a *performance* of suspended disbelief that can be compared to the theatrical aside in Restoration comedy. As Heyl explains, the vizard negotiated the separation of public and private spheres by turning its wearer into a threatening outsider, but entirely 'in brackets': a hazardous bluff in the face-to-face community where a stranger was either hosted or expelled, but a knowing wink of complicity in a metropolis 'populated by people who were and remained strangers to one another', yet who were 'more at ease with anonymity than ever'.[32]

The mask is the symbolic form in Shakespearean London of the freedom the dramatist claims 'to offend / But with good will' [*Dream*, 5,1,108–9]. A perambulating quotation mark, it therefore functioned according to the 'closet epistemology' defined by D. A. Miller and Eve Kosofsky Sedgwick as the means whereby the 'oppositions between public/private, inside/outside, subject/object are established' on the tacit understanding that 'we know perfectly well that the secret is known ... nonetheless we persist in guarding it'. Such is the agonistic strategy of hiding in plain view that Paul Hammond identifies in Shakespeare's Sonnets, in which a sexual interpretation is at once solicited and disallowed, when a term is cancelled 'but remains legible through the cancellation'.[33] 'Degree being vizarded', Shakespeare's spymaster Ulysses thus bemoans, 'The unworthiest shows as fairly in the mask' [*Troilus*, 1,3,83–4]. Yet according to this analysis, the relaxation of such sexual, social and religious discrimination was precisely the rationale of going 'veiled on purpose to be seen':

> This apparently bizarre pattern of behaviour demonstrates that the privacy of strangers or of people who now wanted to be treated as strangers had become something to be respected. Something which would have been regarded as a masquerade in most other countries was here being taken for granted as a part of everyday life. This points to a level of tolerance in urban English society which was indeed remarkable.[34]

'My visor is Philemon's roof. Within the house is Jove', explains Don Pedro [*Much Ado*, 2,1,80], alluding to the theme of the King and the Beggar that provided a pretext for the live-and-let-live rule practised by Charles II, his uncle Christian IV, and his grandfather Henri IV, in their escapades of clowning with the poor. The jest hints how, even in the masquerades of his Elizabethan plays, Shakespeare was attuned to a coming order that would depend not on revelation and unveiling, but on what the Spaniard Don Armado learns is better than wars of religion: a discreet veil drawn over 'Most maculate thoughts . . . masked under such colours' [*Love's*, 1,2,83]. Of course, no one was fooled by the emperor's new clothes when the Merry Monarch went slumming with the orange-seller Nell Gwyn, when his uncle slipped unheralded into London under the *nom de guerre* of Captain Frederickson, or when his madcap grandfather, got up as a 'whistling' doorman, swept the stage at the Louvre to 'make place for the rascal players'. Henri took dressing down so far that Louis XIII joked that you could always recognise his father by his goatish stench.[35] And New Historicism has long seen through Prince Hal's 'veil of wildness' [*Henry V*, 1,1,65]. Their peasant togs enact the same *faux naïveté* as the Mannerist court dresses distressed by artful 'slashing' to look 'new-fangled ill' [Sonnet 91], an affected *sprezzatura* that Petruchio deconstructs the instant he glimpses his wife's ballgown: 'O, mercy God, what masquing stuff is here? . . . Here's snip, and nip, and cut, and slish and slash,/ Like to a scissor in a barber's shop' [*Taming*, 4,3,87–9]. Yet as Eric Santner has proposed in *The Royal Remains*, by theatricalising 'the uncanny proximity' of the sovereign and the beast, this Baroque bohemianism was a form of *investiture crisis*, and an imposture of 'bare life' that marked 'the emergence of popular sovereignty'.[36]

Santner alerts us to the feral 'remnant of violence' when kings 'play bo-peep' [*Lear*, 1,4,154] in these dangerous games. But though no subject was deceived by the pretence when monarchy dressed down, Anne Barton noted how the persistent popularity of the 'disguised king' genre testified to the collective fantasy of 'harmony, good fellowship, and mutual understanding', and confirmed the enabling *agôn* of *good will* that was replacing face-to-face antagonism.[37] So when Rosaline mocks 'that visor, that superfluous case,/ That hid the worse and showed the better face', Navarre has no need to complain 'We were descried' [*Love's*, 5,2,387–9]; for what these exchanges likewise prove is the immunity granted by the incognito rule. François Laroque has analysed the interplay of light and dark, blindness and vision, in the masque in *Romeo and Juliet*.[38] But Ronald Knowles points out that Shakespeare changed the story of this lovers' meeting, which in the sources occurs when 'All did unmask', because 'for Romeo to have unmasked would have cancelled the hospitality' he exploits.[39] Thus, it is eye-to-eye contact that here becomes taboo. As Capulet affirms, when Romeo asks for 'a case to put my visage in', and dons 'A visor for a visor' to gatecrash the ball, confident that whatever 'curious eye doth quote deformity,/Here are the beetle brows shall blush for me', the virtue of going 'covered with an antic face' in this euphemised aggression is not so much the release from identity conferred upon the wearer, as the blind eye of obliviousness demanded of the suspicious viewer, whenever some spoilsport like Tybalt guesses the underlying truth [1,4,29; 1,5,53]:

> Content thee, gentle coz, leave him alone.
> A bears him like a portly gentleman,
> And, truth to say, Verona brags of him
> To be a virtuous and well-governed youth.
> I would not for the wealth of all this town
> Here in my house do him disparagement.
> Therefore be patient, take no note of him.
>
> [Romeo, 1,5,62–8]

'To be in a mask bringeth with it a certain liberty and licence', theorised Baldassare Castiglione, in an early statement of the closet epistemology of urban space, 'and if he were in a mask and though it were so all men knew him, it skilleth not'.[40] The Latin for mask, persona, meant that Roman law took a mask at face value; so the notion of persona as personality had licensed medieval mumming, which actually assumed that a 'vizard serveth to small effect when the Mummer is known'.[41] As Meg Twycross and Susan Carpenter relate in Masks and Masking, when Duke Ercole of Ferrara went 'guising' at New Year, looking for egg fights and erotic trysts, the blurring of social categories therefore depended upon 'the presence of the masker's identity'. Here 'the importance of masking is, and is acknowledged to be, a game' of both give and take.[42] This is the kind of playful moratorium that gives Henry VIII its nervous rictus, when, taking their cue from his disguise as a shepherd at Wolsey's ball, his victims humour the King by pretending not to recognise the 'one amongst 'em' [1,4,81] who has all the power. So it is significant that whenever Shakespeare includes such guising, he stretches the closet rules of this reverse blind-man's bluff, like actual London 'geezers' taking liberties by wearing their vizards in public around the town.

With each of his masked balls Shakespeare tests the limits of mutual toleration, either to destruction, as when Romeo and Juliet fail to make their masked encounter endure, or to triumph, as when the Princess and her Ladies put Navarre and his Lords to such shame that they must 'ever but in visors show their faces' [Love's, 5,2,271]. Whatever the outcome, this adjustment of focus, from display to concealment, reflects a new development in the mask–face equation, 'deliberately flirting with an identity that is teasingly hidden, but now never quite denied'.[43] The shift was from Queen Elizabeth's belief in princes 'set on stages in the sight and view of all the world', to King James's paranoia that 'all the beholders' were 'bent to look and pry' into his 'secretest drifts'.[44] And so, even as Stuart masques were illuminating the Apollonian perspective that put absolute power on spectacular display – when the 'deep truth about the monarchy' was *unveiled*, in Orgel's words, as 'the fiction opened outward to include the court' – Shakespeare was devising a far more demo-cratic theatre of coexistence, in which the monarch's mood to go masked and pass as 'a common man' was matched, as the soldier Williams reminds King Harry, by the subject's equally available privilege to speak in private without giving offence:[45]

> Your majesty came not like yourself. You appeared to me but
> as a common man. Witness the night, your garments, your
> lowliness. And what your highness suffered under that shape
> I beseech you take it for your own fault, and not mine for had
> you been as I took you for, I made no offence.
>
> [*Henry V*, 4,8,47–50]

'The King's first going abroad was privately to visit his Houses, for naturally he did not love to be looked on': when James toured his new capital 'secretly' in 1603, his cover was blown by the 'swarms' who shouted 'God save the King' to 'his great offence', whenever he emerged into the street.[46] Yet the very fact that the sly ruler's peculiar desire for privacy was respected by those in the know may be connected to the virtual blind spot whereby, as Orgel points out, there are hardly any 'instances in which anyone sees through a disguise in English Renaissance drama', for in this theatre of dissimulation 'clothes really do make the man'.[47] Thus, 'The soul of this man is in his clothes' [*All's Well*, 3,5,85], sniffs the snob Lafeu at Paroles, the 'jack-an-apes with scarfs' who has 'the theoric of war in the knot of his scarf' [4,3,138]. 'A snipped-taffeta fellow' [4,5,1], the braggart's persona is tied up with his slashed 'scarves and bannerets': 'So, my good window of lattice,' Lafeu snipes, 'I look through thee' [2,3,197–205]; and 'You are undone, Captain – all but your scarf, that has a knot on't yet', his captors sneer [4,4,300].

In *All's Well That Ends Well* Paroles will be tolerated so long as he wears his identity on his sleeve. With his French comedy Shakespeare was responding to the multi-confessional society that the real King of France was helping to introduce, where it would be possible to live and let live. So one of the sartorial twists that makes this story so unsettling is Paroles' resolve that if a silk cravat is his undoing, 'Simply the thing I am / Shall make me live' [311]. His muffler has been so much part of his old panache that, after he is blindfolded with it, the 'saffron' drape [*All's Well*, 4,5,2] does seem a window into his soul. 'Muffled' [4,3,112] by the scarf that blinds him, the man of words is therefore as much a victim as the puritanical Malvolio, in his yellow stockings, of the constricting bondage of costume and identity in the early modern fashion system, the tight fit between 'the superficiality of clothing and the depth of the superficial'.[48] In this world the clothes really do make the man. Yet when he confesses 'Captain I'll be no more' [308], what we glimpse in Paroles, as he unties his strangulating stock, is an inwardness not reducible to external matrices, a person behind the *persona*, or private face behind the public mask; as if, in the deep weariness of *All's Well*, this pilgrim play about the travails of travelling, Shakespeare was anticipating Derrida's boredom with the postmodern shibboleth of 'truth as a history of veils':

> Voilà, fatigued like truth, exhausted from knowing it, for too long, that history of the veil, and all the folds, explications, complications, explicitations of its revelations and unveilings . . . when they are to do not only with opening onto this or that but onto the veil itself, a veil beneath the veil, like the thing itself to be buried. I am weary, weary, weary of this opposition that is not an opposition, of revelation as veiling. *Fed up with vails and sails.*[49]

AN ENSHIELD BEAUTY

In *All's Well* Paroles' loosened scarf seems to flag his philosophy that 'There's place and means for every man alive' [4,4,316]. Likewise, in *Measure for Measure*, where the Duke who adopts a Franciscan habit is 'honest in nothing but his clothes', the old tag that '*Cucullus non facit monachum*' [5,1,259], the cowl does not make the monk, ironises Angelo's criticism of 'these black masks' that 'Proclaim an enshield beauty ten times louder/Than beauty could be displayed' [2,4,79–80]: the visors worn by Isabella and Mariana at the close, when Lucio '*pulls off the friar's hood and discovers the Duke*' [stage direction 5,1,347]. Angelo reads such a visor as an incitement, like the mask that Cressida carries 'to defend [her] beauty' [*Troilus*, 1,2,242], or the 'virtuous visor' the mother of Richard III fears hides a 'deep vice' [*Richard III*, 2,2,28]. But according to Andrew Gurr, the separation of public and private spheres in this comedy depends on the very ambiguity when its masked women are, as Posthumus will rail, either 'for preservation cased, or shame' [*Cymbeline*, 5,5,21]. Here the Duke rejects Lucio's excuse that he spoke, like the soldier Williams, 'according to the trick' [*Measure*, 1,4,12] when he defamed the monarch in private. But a comedy that spares its heroine the religious veil, and releases her from the convent rule that 'if you speak, you must not show your face;/Or if you show your face you must not speak' [1,4,11–12] still concludes by having Isabella wait behind a visor until the Duke offers her what he calls a 'destined livery' as his bride [5,1,498].

The half-masks in *Measure for Measure* solve 'the problem of finding a middle way between freedom and law', Gurr infers, by shielding the heroine from political intimidation: 'Disguise becomes a means to everyone's uncasing', as for the whole of the finale we see Isabella 'dressed in a gentlewoman's face mask, with all the freedom that it offered'. Hoods, masks, scarves and veils have received too little attention in Renaissance studies, the theatre historian rightly complains.[50] For whether or not Shakespeare was familiar with the Poor Clares, or had an aunt named Isabella who became a prioress, his comedy does seem to defer to the Greek, Roman, Byzantine, Hindu and Islamic, as well as Catholic, convention that respects the veil as a sign of privilege and power. *Measure for Measure* dates from a time when nuns like Mary Ward were adjusting the veil to variable degrees of seclusion; others, like the Venetian nuns whose transparent lace 'attracted rather than deflected the male gaze', were testing 'how permeable convent walls, grilles and doors could be'.[51] So in Shakespeare's part of this comedy, that we know to be finished by the coercive Middleton, the visor seems, like the modern hijab, a means 'to negotiate a sphere of social freedom'.[52] For once Isabella is fitted out in one of the fashionable silk half-masks of the 1600s, her enigmatic silence at the close is keyed to the epochal phe-nomenon that the play explores, the aversion to being studied by 'millions of false eyes' [4,1,59] in the metropolis, where even the King now claimed a 'safe discretion' for his private desires and 'secret drifts':

> I love the people,
> But do not like to stage me to their eyes.
> Though it do well, I do not relish well
> Their loud applause and *aves* vehement;
> Nor do I think the man of safe discretion
> That does affect it.
>
> [*Measure*, 1,1,67–72]

'Among all parts of the world, only England has not seen masked beasts', reported Polydore Vergil in the 1490s, 'nor does it want to, because among the English there is capital punishment for anyone who wears masks'.[53] As an Italian immigrant, Vergil had good reasons for exaggerating a City by-law against 'feined beards, painted visors, disformed or coloured visages, in any wise'.[54] But the Tudor resist-ance to street masking, culminating in a 1511 Act outlawing any who 'disguised and apparelled' themselves, or 'covered their faces with Visors in such manner that they should not be known', makes it yet more striking that Shakespeare's theatre revolves around the kind of 'mask'd and vizarded' imbroglio that brings *The Merry Wives of Windsor* to the boil, with 'vizors' for the children and a veil for the Queen of Fairies [4,6,40]. As Arden's 'hoodies' show when they dress up like Robin Hood, and with 'umber smirch' their faces, this is a stage in which those who 'outface it with their semblances' advance 'To liberty, and not to banishment' [*As You*, 1,3,106–32]. Equally notable, however, is that with the single exception of Snug's tragic lion mask, from the lady's vizard in which Flute plays Thisbe [*Dream*, 1,2,41] to the highwaymen's visors upon visors that 'inmask' Hal and Poins [*1 Henry IV*, 1,2,159], or the cagoules that 'mask' Caesar's assassins [*Julius*, 2,1,73–81], what intrigues Shakespeare is not the 'absolute mask' of antiquity – the fixed *persona* whose 'face is vizard-like, unchanging' [*3 Henry VI*, 1,4,117] – but the tantalising half-mask, which always teases with what Roland Barthes termed 'the theme of the secret', as if in this game the mask is purposely inviting Falstaff's response: 'By the lord, I knew ye as well as he that made ye' [*1 Henry IV*, 2,5,246].[55]

Shakespeare understands the liberating purpose of the ancient actor's disclaimer that 'I advance behind my mask', and he significantly shares this awareness with Descartes, whose adoption of the classical expression has been connected to his own religious heterodoxy, and regarded as one of the theological origins of modernity.[56] For, as Jean-Luc Nancy comments, it is the very function of such a mask to draw attention to itself, since its paradox is a 'self-showing that withdraws. Monstration occurs in concealment, and from out of that concealment or disappearance'.[57] Thus, for Heyl, the dialectical function of the half-mask, as both solicitation and repellent, is allied to the 'virtual disguise' of the literary pseudonym, as the kind of blind eye that was turned towards its open secret is essential to the 'striptease' of modern authorial anonymity. It may not therefore be chance that in the drama which, from the instant when the Ghost materialises with its 'beaver up' [Hamlet, 1,3,228], demonstrates more than any other the 'visor effect', as Derrida termed it, by which we pretend 'we do not see who is looking at us', this spectacular show of secrecy is associated throughout with what Heyl maintains was a perception unique to the public sphere of early metropolitan London, the revolutionary recognition that 'dress and outward appearance were no longer an infallible guide to status':[58]

> 'Tis not alone my inky cloak, good mother,
> Nor customary suits of solemn black. . .
> That can denote me truly. . .
> I have that within which passeth show,
> These but the trappings and the suits of woe.
>
> [Hamlet, 1,2,78–86]

Hamlet's 'antic disposition' [1,5,72] might be seen as a supreme instance of the inky textual cloak as functional equivalent of the Jacobean black mask: a ruse that only 'pretends to disguise', and 'instead of making one inconspicuous, makes onlookers more inquisitive'.[59] And in *Secret Shakespeare* I suggested such a 'masked imagination' relies on the same closet subjectivity as paintings by Caravaggio, where, as Leo Bersani and Ulysse Dutoit decode it, the invitation to interpret is itself its own concealment, for secrecy is here *performed* by a body 'at once presenting and withdrawing' its availability. Thus in Caravaggio's depictions of boys the coy homoerotic pose promotes unreadability into a 'wilful reticence, as if we were being solicited by a desire determined to remain hidden'.[60] *Putting secrecy on display* in such 'quotes', Caravaggio creates an inscrutability like that of the half-mask, in this account, signalling 'Don't ask, don't tell'. Likewise, what Shakespeare stages, I argued in *Secret Shakespeare*, is not some secret about his own sexuality or religion, but *the act of secrecy* itself. It may not, then, be chance that his carnival comedy opens trailing Antonio's tease, 'I know not why I am so sad' [Merchant, 1,1,1], a mystification that critics decipher, as they do these pictures, as nudging towards a modern gay identity that dares not speak its name. For unlike court masques, which culminate in the grand unveiling of the discovery scene, where illicit desires are displaced onto excluded strangers, in this drama the failure to scapegoat Shylock means that those 'fools with varnished faces' can never quite unmask their secret selves.[61]

The Merchant of Venice ends as it begins, in smooth talk about masked 'pageants of the sea', with 'woven wings' and 'portly sail' [1,1,9–11; 5,1,286–7]. So, while Bassanio thinks that 'golden locks,/Which makes such wanton gambols with the wind', are wigs as false as prosthetic beards on boys, he calls his own gamble a quest for 'golden fleece', and to marry into gold fakes a 'beard of Hercules' himself [1,2,170–1; 3,2,83–94]. Here a mask of masculinity is fashioned, we see, like the household livery Lancelot exchanges when he deserts the Jew, in contradistinction to the look of the 'little scrubbed boy', who 'will ne'er wear hair on's face' [2,2,139; 5,1,157–61].[62] While a happy ending to this game of open secrets also depends, as Orgel observes, on the 'pederastic fantasy' of 'girls turning into men' [3,5,79], since these females are in reality boys, the 'seeming truth' thus disguises an even deeper untruth: that in these 'cunning times' of 'masked balls' there will be mask on mask and veil on veil.[63] The latest 'Indian beauty' to be an object of such passionate desire in both men and women, we remember, was indeed Oberon's enigmatic and 'lovely Indian boy' [Dream, 2,1,22; 3,2,375]. In this play Bassanio pretends to prefer Portia's 'golden mesh' to a 'beauteous scarf'. Yet in a reversal of her own entry test, his bride will cross-dress, and name herself after Balthazar, the black magus who brought the gift of myrrh from the East. A Moorish complexion and sexual masquerade thus combine to throw English masculinity in doubt. So, it would be nice to think that Shakespeare had heard how early modern European travellers to the Indian subcontinent were startled when the beguiling figure who emerged at a Muslim wedding wearing a golden veil, and with a silk handkerchief covering the mouth, turned out to be the groom.[64]

A TWIST OF ROTTEN SILK

'Mislike me not for my complexion,/The shadowed livery of the burnished sun' [2,1,1–2]: as the only actual Muslim in The Merchant of Venice, Morocco's plea that his skin is but another mask gains a further layer of pathos if, as Patricia Parker deduces, a 'Moorish' or 'Indian' complexion is 'shadowed livery' in Shakespeare for the Catholic 'tribe' of the martyred fool Thomas More: a rumour heard when Morocco finds a momento mori preserved, as if in myrrh, inside the golden box.[65] 'The black man', as More was called, claimed descent from the negro Doge Moro, on whom Shakespeare based Othello, and so mounted a blackamoor on his crest. Morocco's death's-head looks, then, to clinch a network of crypto-Catholic murmurs running, by way of Latin puns on 'That black word death' [Romeo, 3,3,27], from the mural concealing Thisbe to the sycamour Desdemona sings. What knits them all, Parker proposes, is Ovidian moralising on the moro: the indelible mulberry darkened by the blood of Pyramus on which the silkworm feeds. Critics have long seen the silk handkerchief in Othello as 'more than just a symbol of marriage', like 'wedding sheets' by 'lust's blood spotted', in a play obsessed by 'lawn, gowns, petticoats and caps', in which the heroine dies because her husband doubts the innocence of 'her fan, her gloves, her mask, nor nothing' [4,1,105; 4,2,10; 4,3,72; 5,1,44].[66] For whenever Shakespeare brings a Moorish mask or silken handkerchief onto this stage, as Celia quips of Orlando's bloodied napkin in As You Like It, 'There is more in it' [4,3,158].

Othello's spotted handkerchief once seemed to have only sexual significance. But now we are reminded that the reason why 'There's magic in the web of it' is that 'The worms were hallowed that did breed the silk', because they were sanctified by feasting on the 'More tree'. This is why the cloth is said to have been 'dyed in mummy which the skilful/Conserved of maidens' hearts', like those of the

Tudor martyrs; and why it has been preserved by a *Romany* priestess [3,4,54–73]. The morbid facecloth thereby morphs into a relic to be placed beside veils like Veronica's, as a signifier of mourning for proscribed religion, and so joins Thisbe's mantle, the original Indian veil, presumably woven by Bottom, the weaver named after a skein of silk, in a true sericulture of veiled effusions of maudlin faith.[67] Being Venetians, these 'Christian fools in varnished faces' are, of course, themselves of 'the tribe of More', as Morocco hints, when he begs them to acknowledge 'This thing of darkness' [*Tempest*, 5,1,278] theirs. Shakespeare's play upon the name of More thus seems to work like a verbal mask, and to predict the 'qualified intolerance' that allowed early modern Londoners to 'judge without prejudice' the 'agreement of the Customs of the Indians with those of the Jews', in an agonistic pluralism that relativised Catholics under cover of a sense of 'analogy, shared history, and sameness'.[68] As this truly overdetermined veil of topicality unfolds, modern readers might find such a 'Moorish' subtext rebarbative, just as Morocco assumes we 'mislike' his negroid skin. The violent charisma of the veil means that it always presents itself in the form of such a ritual threat. But as Derrida reflects, when he ponders the warp and woof of his Jewish tallith in his essay 'A Silkworm of One's Own', however much a softer culture might deplore it, we will never get to 'the bottomless bottom' of the history of violence which colours such 'a twist of rotten silk' [*Coriolanus*, 5,6,95]:

> I would like to sing the very solitary softness of my tallith, a softness softer than softness, entirely singular, calm, acquiescent, a stranger to anything maudlin, to effusion or to pathos, in a word to all 'Passion.' And yet, before ever having worn a tallith, or even dreamed of having my own, I cultivated silkworms. . . . In truth, they needed lots of mulberry, too much, always too much, these voracious little creatures. . . . This philosophy of nature was for him, for the child I was, but that I remain still, naïveté itself, doubtless, but also the time of infinite apprenticeship, the culture of the rag trade . . . [so] the word mulberry was never far from ripening and dying in him, the mulberry whose colour he warded off like everyone in the family, a whole history and war of religions.[69]

'If you have tears, prepare to shed them now./You all do know this mantle' [*Julius*, 3,2,164] declares the martyr's memorialist, Antony; and Jones and Stallybrass consider all items of early modern clothing to be such emotive mnemonic materials, a 'second skin' that 'inscribed conflict' and had violence written into it, like the napkin embroidered with 'conceited characters' that the maid wrings in 'A Lover's Complaint': 'Laund'ring the silken figures in the brine'.[70] Thus, when Hero's wedding dress is compared to the infamous gown of 'cloth o' gold, and cuts, laced with silver, set with pearls, down sleeves, side sleeves, and skirts round underborne with a bluish tinsel', worn by Mary Tudor in her role as 'Duchess of Milan' at her marriage to Philip II of Spain [*Much Ado*, 3,4,14–19], the stains of sectarian violence could not be more overt.[71] But Shakespeare's texts string out a veritable washing-line of such memorial cloaks, mantles, masks, scarves, shawls, shrouds, veils and vestments, all tear-soaked or matted 'in harmless blood' [3 *Henry VI*, 2,1,63], from the souvenir dishcloth Armado was 'enjoined in Rome' to wear 'next to his heart' [*Love's*, 5,2,696], to the popish 'glistening apparel' hung out by Ariel to trap the morons mourning 'Mistress Line', the Jacobean Catholic martyr Anne Line [*Tempest*, stage direction 4,1,194; 233]. With such loaded sartorial allusions, this is a writing that would appear to do exactly what the Jesuitical Iago despises, and wear its heart on its sleeve [*Othello*, 1,1,64].

Shakespeare knows the martyr will always have devotees to 'dip their napkins in his sacred blood' [*Julius*, 3,2,130]; and in episodes such as Antony's inflammatory unveiling of Caesar's shroud, provoking mass hysteria over the 'place', 'rent' and 'unkindest cut', where 'the blood of Caesar followed', alerts us to the category confusion which idolises 'the mantle muffling up his face', as though it was 'Caesar's vesture' that was 'wounded' [181–90]: the 'strong madness in a silken thread' [*Much Ado*, 5,1,25] for an age that has seen 'napkins enough' [*Macbeth*, 2,3,6]. So Bianca fails to 'take out' the 'work', a 'sybil' in all 'her prophetic fury sewed' into the fatal Romany veil [*Othello*, 3,4,68–70; 174; 4,1,145]; and Stephen Greenblatt is perhaps wrong to say these plays are haunted by religious signifiers that have been '*emptied out*', if by that evacuation we mean their 'prophetic fury' has been laundered in the cathartic solution of theatre.[72] Shakespeare's characters cannot help inhabiting 'a worn world', clad in second-hand cast-offs from the Wars of Religion that have been fabricated in Italy, from silk shipped out of Africa and bought in India with American gold.[73] And as the action of *The Tempest* suggests, it is just when they imagine there is 'On their sustaining garments not a blemish,/But fresher than before' [1,2,219–20], that their tangled history of religious violence becomes most obvious:

> our garments being, as they were,
> drenched in the sea, hold notwithstanding their freshness and
> glosses, being rather new-dyed than stained with salt water . . .
> . . . as fresh
> as when we put them on first in Afric, at the marriage of the
> King's fair daughter Claribel to the King of Tunis.
>
> > [*Tempest*, 2,1,62–70]

From Muslim, to Catholic, to theatrical possession: 'What is at stake in the shift from the old religion' into the playhouse, asks Greenblatt, when 'a bit of red cloth' like a cardinal's silk berretta is recycled on a stage which both 'mocks and celebrates' its violent charisma?[74] The answer, Bassanio's 'Indian veil' suggests, is a *masking* or ritualisation of antagonism as the precondition of racial, religious, sexual and artistic freedoms. English Catholics are today uneasy about the analogy between their historic situation and that of contemporary Islamists; but the 'Moorish' mask of alienation was one their ancestors were happy to adopt. 'Unseen to see those she feign would know', the 'masked lady in the pit' of the playhouse was herself a player in this agonistic game of coexistence, Gurr shows.[75] And the 'Moorish' hieroglyphics of a text like the *Masque of Blackness*, acted by crypto-Catholic Queen Anne to outface those who thought black faces a 'very loathsome' sight, confirm how audiences would indeed penetrate Shakespeare's coded moral about his own dark materials, as he wove a tissue of terror and toleration out of a mortal 'thread of silk' [*Dream*, 5,1,341].[76]

In loaded episodes such as the veiling of the 'Madonna' Olivia in *Twelfth Night*, when the 'dark lady' covers with her mantilla, so 'like a cloistress she will veiled walk' [1,1,27], Shakespeare's plays seem to highlight the *morbid* risk of an antagonistic religious interiority apt 'to take dust', like 'Mistress Mall's' or the Virgin Mary's icon, curtained in a sequestered recusant house [1,5,43–137]. Doubtless the poet's own 'masked imagination' dreams of some grand unveiling of identity, when 'the curtain is drawn aside', like the face-to-face discovery scenes Prospero controls: 'The fringed curtains of thine eye advance / And say what thou seest yon' [*Tempest*, 1,2,412]. But in our present stand-off, this most secretive of writers seems to admit, the function of the hijab 'veiling an Indian beauty' must be to offend 'with good will', as Alain Badiou similarly reflects: 'Brecht says the end is with us when figures of oppression no longer need masks', but until that happens 'it is necessary to rethink the relation between violence and the mask. The mask is a symbol of a question erroneously designated in the century of the lie. The question is better formulated as follows: What is the relation between the passion for the real and a necessity of semblance?'[77] Or, as Derrida decides at the end of his essay on sails and veils, the secretion of the silkworm, this repellent 'slime from slugs', inscribes the precious secret of the secret itself:

> What I appropriated for myself was the operation through which the worm itself secreted its secretion. It secreted it, the secretion. . . . It secreted absolutely . . . this little silent finite life was doing nothing other than this: preparing itself to hide itself, liking to hide itself, with a view to coming out and losing itself . . . wrapping itself in white night.[78]

NOTES

1. All quotations of Shakespeare in this chapter are from the *Norton Shakespeare*, based on the Oxford edition, edited by Stephen Greenblatt, Walter Cohen, Jean Howard and Katharine Eisaman Maus (New York: Norton, 1997), except for quotations of *King Lear*, which are from the conflated text.
2. Jacques Derrida, 'Hostipitality', trans. Barry Stocker and Forbes Morlock, *Angelaki*, 5:3 (2000), 3–18. The Revels accounts record two performances of *The Merchant of Venice* during Shrovetide 1605, the second commanded by King James himself. For the Carnival connections, see Chris Hassel, *Renaissance Drama and the English Church Year* (Lincoln: Nebraska University Press, 1979), pp. 113–18. For a recent discussion of the ambiguity of the veil as a sign of both eroticism and violence, see Faegheh Shirazi, *The Veil Unveiled: The Hijab in Modern Culture* (Gainesville: University of Florida Press, 2001). But for a proposed emendation of Bassanio's lines, see Lisa Hopkins, '"An Indian beauty?" A proposed emendation to *The Merchant of Venice*', *Shakespeare Newsletter*, 50 (2000), 27. Hopkins argues for a punctuation of the lines as 'the beauteous scarf / Veiling an Indian; beauty – in a word, / The seeming truth. . .'. But this emendation diminishes the Orientalist 'dark lady' metaphor.
3. Ros Ballaster, *Fabulous Orients: Fictions of the East in England, 1662–1785* (Oxford: Oxford University Press, 2005), pp. 18–19, 69, 89 and 267–8; 'Letter to Lord Colbert' quoted ibid., p. 268. Cf. Lisa Jardine and Jerry Brotton, *Global Interests: Renaissance Art Between East and*

West (London: Reaktion, 2000), pp. 184–5: 'In the fifteenth and sixteenth centuries, East and West met on much more equal terms. . . . East met West in strenuous and constructive competition'. For the politically charged semiotics of silk, see also Roze Hentschell, 'Treasonous textiles: foreign cloth and the construction of Englishness', *Journal of Medieval and Early Modern Studies*, 32 (2002), 543–70.

4. 'Tradeful merchants': Edmund Spenser, *Amoretti*, 15:1; Philip Curtin, *Cross-Cultural Trade in World History* (Cambridge: Cambridge University Press, 1984), p. 149. For the connection between the 'dark lady' conceit and colonial economic encounters, see also Kim Hall, *Things of Darkness: Economies of Race and Gender in Early Modern England* (Ithaca: Cornell University Press, 1995), pp. 70–1 and 80–1; and Joel Fineman, *Shakespeare's Perjur'd Eye* (Berkeley: University of California Press, 1986), p. 34.

5. Percy Macquoid, 'Costume', in anon. (ed.), *Shakespeare's England: An Account of the Life and Manners of His Age*, 2 vols (Oxford: Clarendon Press, 1916), vol. 2, p. 101. For more recent histories of fashion in early modern England, see John Brewer and Roy Porter, *Consumption and the World of Goods* (London: Routledge, 1993), pp. 274–301; Elizabeth Kowaleski-Wallace, *Consuming Subjects: Women, Shopping, and Business in the Eighteenth Century* (New York: Columbia University Press, 1997); Beverly Lemire, *Dress, Culture, and Commerce: The English Clothing Trade Before the Factory, 1660–1800* (Basingstoke: Macmillan, 1997); Lena Orlin (ed.), *Material London, ca. 1600* (Philadelphia: University of Pennsylvania Press, 2000); Daniel Roche, *The Culture of Clothing: Dress and Fashion in the Ancien Regime*, trans. Jean Birrell (Cambridge: Cambridge University Press, 1994); Susan Vincent, *Dressing the Elite: Clothes in Early Modern England* (Oxford: Berg, 2003); and Lorna Weatherhill, *Consumer Behaviour and Material Culture in Britain 1660–1760* (London: Routledge, 1996). For an important discussion of women and consumer society, see also Karen Newman, 'City talk: women and commodification in Jonson's *Epicoene*', *English Literary History*, 3 (1989), 503–18.

6. Liza Picard, *Elizabeth's London: Everyday Life in Elizabethan London* (London: Weidenfeld and Nicolson, 2003), p. 154.

7. Edgar Fripp, *Master Richard Quyny Bailiff of Stratford-upon-Avon and Friend of William Shakespeare* (Oxford: Oxford University Press, 1924), pp. 83–4.

8. Charles Nicholl, *The Lodger: Shakespeare on Silver Street* (London: Allen Lane, 2007), pp. 164–5 and 247.

9. Christopher Marlowe, *Dido Queen of Carthage*, 3,1,115–24, in *Christopher Marlowe: The Complete Plays*, ed. Frank Romany and Robert Lindsey (London: Penguin, 2003), pp. 31–2. For imagery of re-clothing in *Dido Queen of Carthage*, see Richard Wilson, 'Tragedy, patronage, and power', in Patrick Cheney (ed.), *The Cambridge Companion to Christopher Marlowe* (Cambridge: Cambridge University Press, 2004), pp. 208–12.

10. Christopher Marlowe, *The Jew of Malta*, 1,1,44–5; 84–7; *Christopher Marlowe: The Complete Plays*, pp. 251 and 252.

11. Fernand Braudel, *The Mediterranean in the Age of Philip II*, trans. Siân Reynolds (London: Harper Collins, 1992), p. 402. For the London end of this transcontinental traffic, see in particular G. D. Ramsay, 'The undoing of the Italian mercantile colony in sixteenth century London', in N. B. Harte and K. G. Ponting (eds), *Textile History and Economic History: Essays in Honour of Miss Julia de Lacy Mann* (Manchester: Manchester University Press, 1973), pp. 22–49, esp. p. 24.

12. Fernand Braudel, *The Wheels of Commerce* (*Civilization and Capitalism: 15th–18th Century*), trans. Siân Reynolds (London: Collins, 1982), p. 178.

13. Stephen Orgel, *Impersonations: The Performance of Gender in Shakespeare's England* (Cambridge: Cambridge University Press, 1996), pp. 34–5; 'stir up the desire': John Rainoldes, *The Overthrow of Stage Plays* (London: 1600), p. 97.

14. 'The material of subjectivity': Edith Snook, 'The Greatness in good clothes: fashioning

subjectivity in Mary Wroth's *Urania* and Margaret Spencer's Account Book (BL. Add. MS 62092)', *The Seventeenth Century*, 22 (2007), 225–42, here 242. For the 'silencing' of women in this reification, see Susan Frye, 'Staging women's relations to textiles in *Othello* and *Cymbeline*', in Peter Erickson and Clark Hulse (eds), *Early Modern Visual Culture: Representation, Race, and Empire in Renaissance England* (Philadelphia: University of Pennsylvania Press, 2000), pp. 215–50.

15. Jacques Derrida, 'A silkworm of one's own', in Hélène Cixous and Jacques Derrida, *Veils*, trans. Geoffrey Bennington (Stanford: Stanford University Press, 2001), pp. 39 and 58.

16. Patricia Fumerton, *Cultural Aesthetics: Renaissance Literature and the Practice of Social Ornament* (Chicago: Chicago University Press, 1991), p. 173.

17. See Richard Wilson, 'A mingled yarn: Shakespeare and the cloth workers', in *Will Power: Essays in Shakespearean Authority* (Hemel Hempstead: Harvester, 1993), pp. 23–46.

18. Margaret Spufford, *The Great Reclothing of Rural England: Petty Chapmen and the Wares in the Seventeenth Century* (London: Hambledon Press, 1984), esp. pp. 88–105; 'miracle of overseas trade': Braudel, *The Wheels of Commerce*, pp. 582–601, and for penetration of rural England, see pp. 64–7; cf. Walter Cohen, 'The undiscovered country: Shakespeare and mercantile geography', in Jean Howard and Scott Shershow (eds), *Marxist Shakespeares* (London: Routledge, 2001), p. 144.

19. Abraham Sturley to Richard Quiney, 30 October 1598, reprinted in E. K. Chambers, *William Shakespeare: A Study of Facts and Problems*, 2 vols (Oxford: Clarendon Press, 1930), vol. 2, pp. 102–3.

20. Samuel Schoenbaum, *William Shakespeare, A Documentary Life* (Oxford: Oxford University Press, 1975), p. 196; Stephen Greenblatt, 'Resonance and wonder', in *Learning to Curse: Essays in Early Modern Culture* (London: Routledge, 1990), p. 162.

21. Stephen Greenblatt, *Shakespearean Negotiations: The Circulation of Social Energy in Renaissance England* (Oxford: Clarendon Press, 1988), p. 9; Anne Jones and Peter Stallybrass, *Renaissance Clothes and the Materials of Memory* (Cambridge: Cambridge University Press, 2000).

22. Philip Stubbes, quoted in Macquoid, 'Costume', p. 103.

23. Peter Stallybrass, 'Worn worlds: clothes and identity on the Renaissance stage', in Margreta de Grazia, Maureen Quilligan and Peter Stallybrass (eds), *Subject and Object in Renaissance Culture* (Cambridge: Cambridge University Press, 1996), pp. 308–10. For the acquisition of clerical vestments by actors, see also Greenblatt, *Shakespearean Negotiations*, pp. 112–14.

24. For Lear's suicidal mania for undressing, see Margreta de Grazia, 'The ideology of superfluous things: *King Lear* as period piece', in de Grazia, Quilligan and Stallybrass (eds), *Subject and Object in Renaissance Culture*, pp. 24–5.

25. Christopher Hill, *The World Turned Upside Down: Radical Ideas During the English Revolution* (Harmondsworth: Penguin, 1975), p. 279.

26. 'Masks will be more hereafter in request': Thomas Combe, *The Theatre of Fine Devices* (London: 1592), Emblem VI, sig. B; 'Cloth-driven theatre': Stallybrass, 'Worn worlds', p. 300.

27. John Stowe quoted in M. Channing Linthicum, *Costume in the Drama of Shakespeare and His Contemporaries* (Oxford: Clarendon Press, 1936), pp. 271–2; Philip Stubbes, *The Anatomy of Abuses* (London: 1583), sig. G.2.

28. John Cleveland, 'The King's Disguise', in *The Character of a London-Diurnal: With Several Select Poems* (London: 1647), p. 33.

29. Alain Badiou, *Saint Paul: The Foundation of Universalism*, trans. Ray Brassier (Stanford: Stanford University Press, 2003), p. 8.

30. Joan Wallach Scott, *The Politics of the Veil* (Princeton: Princeton University Press, 2010).

31. Etienne Balibar, *Saeculum: Culture, Religion, Idéologie* (Paris: Éditions Galilé, 2012).

32. Christoph Heyl, 'The metamorphosis of the mask in seventeenth- and eighteenth-century

London', in Efrat Tseëlon (ed.), *Masquerade and Identities: Essays on Gender, Sexuality and Marginality* (London: Routledge, 2001), pp. 114–34, here pp. 119–20 and 128. This important essay is reprinted as 'When they are veyl'd on purpose to be seen', in Joanne Entwistle and Elizabeth Wilson (eds), *Body Dressing* (Oxford: Berg, 2005), pp. 121–42.

33. D. A. Miller, 'Secret subjects, open secrets', in *The Novel and the Police* (Berkeley: University of California Press, 1988), pp. 192–220, here pp. 195 and 207. Cf. Eve Kosofsky Sedgwick, *The Epistemology of the Closet* (Berkeley: University of California Press, 1990); Paul Hammond, *Figuring Sex Between Men from Shakespeare to Rochester* (Oxford: Clarendon Press, 2002), p. 70.

34. Heyl, 'The metamorphosis of the mask', pp. 119 and 128.

35. John Gade, *Christian IV, King of Denmark and Norway: A Picture of the Seventeenth Century* (London: Cassell, 1928), pp. 80–4; Leeds Barroll, *Anna of Denmark, Queen of England: A Cultural Biography* (Philadelphia: University of Pennsylvania Press, 2001), p. 143; Sir Robert Dallington (1604), quoted in Desmond Seward, *The First Bourbon: Henry IV, King of France and Navarre* (London: Constable, 1971), p. 164.

36. Eric Santner, *The Royal Remains: The People's Two Bodies and the Endgames of Sovereignty* (Chicago: University of Chicago Press, 2011), pp. 47 and 78. For the slashing vogue, which peaked at the time of Shakespeare's romances, see Aileen Ribeiro, *Fashion and Fiction: Dress in Art and Literature in Stuart England* (New Haven: Yale University Press, 2005), pp. 32–3.

37. Santner, *The Royal Remains*, p. 19; Anne Barton, 'The king disguised: Shakespeare's *Henry V* and the comical history', in *Essays, Mainly Shakespearean* (Cambridge: Cambridge University Press, 1994), p. 212.

38. François Laroque, '"Cover'd with an antic face": les masques de la lumière et de l'ombre dans *Romeo and Juliet*', *Études Anglaises*, 45 (1992), 385–95.

39. Ronald Knowles, 'Carnival and death in *Romeo and Juliet*', in Ronald Knowles (ed.), *Shakespeare and Carnival: After Bakhtin* (Basingstoke: Macmillan, 1998), p. 44; see also Geoffrey Bullough, *Narrative and Dramatic Sources of Shakespeare*, 7 vols (London: Routledge and Kegan Paul, 1964), vol. 1, p. 290.

40. Baldassare Castiglione, *The Book of the Courtier*, trans. Thomas Hoby, ed. J. H. Whitfield (London: Dent, 1974), pp. 99–100 and 105.

41. Jacques Yver, *Le Printemps d'Iver* (Paris: Jean Ruelle, 1572), p. 202. Translated in Meg Twycross and Susan Carpenter, *Masks and Masking in Medieval and Tudor England* (Aldershot: Ashgate, 2002), p. 61.

42. Twycross and Carpenter, *Masks and Masking*, pp. 67–8.

43. Ibid., p. 188.

44. Elizabeth I and James VI and I quoted in Christopher Pye, 'The sovereign, the theater, and the Kingdome of Darknesse: Hobbes and the spectacle of power', in Stephen Greenblatt (ed.), *Representing the English Renaissance* (Berkeley: University of California Press, 1988), p. 279.

45. Stephen Orgel, *The Illusion of Power: Political Theater in the English Renaissance* (Berkeley: University of California Press, 1975), p. 39. For the Apollonian optic of the court, see Martin Jay, *Downcast Eyes: The Denigration of Vision in Twentieth-Century French Thought* (Berkeley: University of California Press, 1993), pp. 87–90.

46. Sir Roger Wilbraham and Arthur Wilson, reprinted in Robert Ashton, *King James By His Contemporaries* (London: Hutchinson, 1969), pp. 62–4.

47. Stephen Orgel, *Impersonations*, p. 102.

48. Jones and Stallybrass, *Renaissance Clothes and the Materials of Memory*, p. 3.

49. Derrida, 'A silkworm of one's own', pp. 38–9. See Katharine Eisaman Maus, *Inwardness and Theater in the English Renaissance* (Chicago: Chicago University Press, 1995), for a sustained critique of the idea that 'the individual derived sense of the self from external matrices' in Shakespearean England (p. 2).

50. Andrew Gurr, 'Measure for Measure's hoods and masks: the Duke, Isabella, and liberty', English Literary Renaissance, 27 (1997), 89–105, here 91 and 102–3.

51. Jutta Gisela Sperling, Convents and the Body Politic in Late Renaissance Venice (Chicago: Chicago University Press, 1999), p. 141. For Mary Ward and the debate about the clausura, see Elizabeth Rapley, The Dévotes: Women and Church in Seventeenth-Century France (Montreal: McGill-Queen's University Press, 1990), pp. 28–9 and 54–6.

52. John Bowen, Why the French Don't Like Headscarves: Islam, the State, and Public Sphere (Princeton: Princeton University Press, 2007), p. 71.

53. Polydore Vergil, Beginnings and Discoveries: Polydore Vergil's 'De inventoribus rerum', trans. Beno Weiss and Louis Përez (Nieukoop: De Graaf, 1997), p. 329.

54. Proclamation of 1418, London: Guildhall Letter Book I, folio 223r, quoted in Twycross and Carpenter, Masks and Masking, p. 331.

55. Roland Barthes, 'The face of Garbo', in Mythologies, trans. Annette Lavers (London: Vintage, 1993), p. 56.

56. Michael Allen Gillespie, The Theological Origins of Modernity (Chicago: University of Chicago Press, 2008), p. 297.

57. Jean-Luc Nancy, 'The masked imagination', in The Ground of the Image, trans. Jeff Fort (New York: Fordham University Press, 2005), p. 96.

58. 'Visor effect': Jacques Derrida, Specters of Marx: The State of the Debt, the Work of Mourning, and the New International, trans. Peggy Kamuf (London: Routledge, 1994), p. 7; Heyl, 'The metamorphosis of the mask', p. 128.

59. Heyl, 'The metamorphosis of the mask', p. 128.

60. Richard Wilson, Secret Shakespeare: Studies in Theatre, Religion and Resistance (Manchester: Manchester University Press, 2004), pp. 35 and 298; Leo Bersani and Ulysse Dutoit, Caravaggio's Secrets (Cambridge, MA: MIT Press, 1998), pp. 8–9.

61. See Stephen Orgel, The Jonsonian Masque (Cambridge, MA: Harvard University Press, 1967), pp. 87–8.

62. For beards as signifiers of masculinity, see Will Fraser, 'The Renaissance beard: masculinity in early modern England', Renaissance Quarterly, 54 (2001), 155–87. But for the prosthetic construction of masculinity in false facial hair, see Mark Albert Johnston, 'Prosthetic absence in Ben Jonson's Epicoene, The Alchemist, and Bartholomew Fair', English Literary Renaissance, 37 (2007), 401–29.

63. Orgel, Impersonations, p. 77.

64. Meer Hassan Ali, Observations on the Mussulmauns of India Descriptive of Their Manners, Customs, Habits and Religious Opinions (London: Humprey Milford and Oxford University Press, 1832; reprinted 1917), p. 204: 'The dress of the bridegroom is of gold-cloth, with an immense bunch of silver trimming that falls over his face, and answers to the purpose of a veil . . . and to his mouth he keeps a red silk handkerchief closely pressed to prevent devils entering'.

65. Patricia Parker, 'What's in a name: More', Sederi XI: Revista de la Sociedad Española de Estudios Renacentistas Ingleses (Huelva: Universidad de Huelva Publicaciones, 2002), 101–49, esp. 131–5; Wilson, Secret Shakespeare, pp. 155–85, esp. p. 178.

66. Dympna Callaghan, 'Looking well to linens: women and cultural production in Othello and Shakespeare's England', in Howard and Shershow (eds), Marxist Shakespeares, p. 61.

67. For Thisbe's veil as a feature of a Babylonian love story and so the prototype of the hijab, see Shirazi, The Veil Unveiled, pp. 3–4.

68. John Tolland, The Agreement of the Customs of the East Indians With Those of the Jews and Other Ancient People (London: 1705; reprinted New York: AMS Press, 1999), p. ii; 'Qualified intolerance': Antony Milton, 'A qualified intolerance: the limits and ambiguities of early Stuart anti-Catholicism', in Arthur Marotti (ed.), Catholicism and Anti-Catholicism in Early Modern English Texts (Basingstoke: Macmillan, 1999), p. 105.

69. Derrida, 'A silkworm of one's own', pp. 61, 84 and 90–1.
70. Jones and Stallybrass, *Renaissance Clothes and the Materials of Memory*, p. 32; 'Shared history': Ballaster, *Fabulous Orients*, p. 18.
71. See Wilson, *Secret Shakespeare*, pp. 96–7.
72. Greenblatt, *Shakespearean Negotiations*, pp. 119 and 126.
73. Stallybrass, 'Worn worlds'.
74. Greenblatt, *Shakespearean Negotiations*, pp. 161–3. The fact that Greenblatt was mistaken in identifying Wolsey's actual hat with that of the actor who played the Cardinal in *Henry VIII* does not negate his point about the circulation of charisma.
75. John Lane (1600) and 'T.M.' (c.1620), quoted in Andrew Gurr, *Playgoing in Shakespeare's London* (Cambridge: Cambridge University Press, 1987), pp. 66 and 73.
76. 'Very loathsome': Dudley Carleton, cited in C. H. Herford, and Percy and Evelyn Simpson, *Ben Jonson*, 11 vols (Oxford: Clarendon Press, 1925–52), vol. 10, p. 449. For Anne's defiant 'drama of feminine blackness', see Sophie Tomlinson, 'Theatrical vibrancy on the Caroline court stage', in Clare McManus (ed.), *Women and Culture at the Courts of the Stuart Queens* (Basingstoke: Palgrave, 2003), pp. 194–5.
77. Alain Badiou, *The Century*, trans. Alberto Toscano (Cambridge: Polity Press, 2005), p. 47.
78. Derrida, 'A silkworm of one's own', pp. 89–90; 'slime from slugs': ibid., p. 91.

7 When Golden Time Convents: Shakespeare and the Shah

At the British Museum, the grand exhibition entitled 'Shah 'Abbas: The Remaking of Iran' that opened beneath the mosque-like dome of the former Reading Room on 19 February 2009 was kept dark, to protect the delicate parchments and textiles on display, but the incidental effect was to perpetuate the cliché of a seductive oriental mystery. As *The Times* excitedly reported, 'The spectator – like some traveller arriving along one of the East–West trade routes – is led into a strange, elaborate and shadowy land of men with drooping moustaches and shadowy designer stubble, of worshipping dervishes and Islamic-style dandies, of Indian ambassadors bringing exotic gifts, of prancing Arab stallions and hooded hunting hawks'. The result, gasped Rachel Campbell-Johnston, was that 'Weaving your way through it can feel a bit like picking your way through the labyrinth of one of the carpets. This world is intricate, complex, luxurious, and rare. It can also be difficult'. But *The Times* reporter was in no doubt of the urgency of the challenge, now that Iran looks 'stubbornly unapproachable, nurturing its hardline fundamentalism and nuclear programme'.[1] The question this prompted, of course, is how this 'shadowy' Islamic world would relate to the British Reading Room in Bloomsbury, which was so close to the sites of the 7 July 2005 Islamist terrorist bombings. Would it appear to be miraculous or monstrous; alien, or all too familiar?

The 'Shah 'Abbas' exhibition was praised by the press for reminding us of a time when envoys were sent to Iran 'by Elizabeth I from a desire to build trading relations' and because of her 'view that Iran was an equal on the international stage'.[2] The museum's director, Neil MacGregor, encouraged this response when he asserted that while he found the smiles of the current Iranian leadership 'delphic', the aim of the show was 'to make it easier for people to start thinking about that complexity'. MacGregor proposed that to understand 'Shah 'Abbas' we need only recall the 'key parallel' of his contemporary, 'our own nation-shaping Elizabeth I', who broke with Rome just as his Shi'ite state warred with the Sunni Ottomans. 'In a strange way', the director told the press, Elizabethan England became 'the only other state to have such a close formal link between the state structure and state church'.[3] So, to underline the elective affinity between Elizabeth's England and the Shah's Iran, and to guide us through the Shia maze, the organisers had laid a trail of helpful literary clues. Repeated throughout the display, quotations from *The Merchant of Venice* and *Twelfth Night* reassured visitors that the Safavid ruler he called 'the Sophy' had been as familiar and impressive to Shakespeare as Gloriana herself:

> SIR TOBY: Why, man, he's the very devil, I have not seen such a
> virago. I had a pass with him, rapier, scabbard, and all, and
> he give me the stick-in with such a mortal motion that it is
> inevitable, and on the answer, he pays you as surely as your
> feet hits the ground they step on. They say he has been a fencer
> to the Sophy.
>
> [*Twelfth*, 3,4,243–8]

At the British Museum Shakespeare's allusions to 'the Sophy' served to underline the director's philosophy that the 'rapier, scabbard, and all' on display were artefacts to 'provoke people from one part of the world to think about the world itself'. MacGregor is an influential figure in the vexed debate over the global antiquities market brought to a head by America's pillage of Iraq. Thus the words of the Globe dramatist authorised the universalism the director claims as the rationale for his 'encyclopaedic museum': the ideal that the great metropolitan museums hold collections 'in trust' for 'the whole world' and for 'all time', a claim he insists 'has nothing to do with national ownership', even if it has been 'aided by a past of national wealth and imperial power'. Shakespeare's supposedly universal genius was being mobilised, in fact, in a culture war about who owns the past that pits the museums' cosmopolitan dream of 'the world under one roof' against UNESCO-backed restrictions on the traffic in cultural property, and the opposing view that an object ripped out of its historical or religious context is, as the Italian Ministry of Culture asserts, a mere 'dead thing'.[4] Shakespeareans like Stephen Greenblatt who begin 'with the desire to speak with the dead' might be surprised by the way the Bard's global status has become a trump card for universalists in this battle for possession of actual corpses.[5] Yet as Professor Robert Foley of Cambridge University's Duckworth Laboratory of Human Osteology insists, repatriating the estimated 61,000 Australian aborigine body parts currently hoarded in British collections to their desecrated ancestral burial grounds would be 'like saying we no longer need the texts of Shakespeare'.[6]

In laboratories and museum halls where it is as if New Historicism had never happened, Shakespeare remains the test of timeless truths about mankind, an imperial measure 'Of all that insolent Greece, or haughty Rome / Sent forth, or since did from their ashes come', in Ben Jonson's words, since he seems himself indisputably 'not of an age, but for all time'.[7] Thus, citing the Bard clinches the circular logic that, as the Anglo-Ghanaian philosopher Kwame Anthony Appiah affirms in *Whose Culture?*, a book based on an internationalist symposium organised by James Cuno, director of the Arts Institute of Chicago, the British Museum serves the interests 'not of Britain but of the whole world', because 'the interests in question are the interests of all of humankind'.[8] The cosmopolitanism Appiah and these curators invoke is defiantly that of the Enlightenment, with a pre-theoretical faith in plays and poems as models for the encyclopaedic collection, on the principle that 'Homer sang not for the Greeks alone but for all nations, and for all time'.[9]

In contemporary museology, the expansiveness of Shakespeare's 'wide and universal theatre' [As You, 2,7,131] has become a paradigm for the cosmopolitanism of the wide and universal collection. This writer so embedded in the earthy actuality of Elizabethan England thereby becomes paradoxically *kulturlos*: beyond or without culture. And the literary analogy that equates postcolonial museum holdings with canonical texts does look all the more impressive now that technology is overriding traditional controls on movement of information, and 'Just as the Enlightenment created the Universal Museum, the digital age is spawning the Universal Library'.[10] For there is indeed an undeniable affinity between what Cuno calls 'the promise of museums' and the universal appeal we like to ascribe to a text such as Shakespeare's, which, in Salman Rushdie's words about *The Satanic Verses* that Appiah quotes in his own book *Cosmopolitanism: Ethics in a World of Strangers*, and that preface *Whose Culture?*, we have learned to interpret as an antidote to the poison of racism, and as a celebration of 'hybridity, impurity, intermingling':

> the transformation that comes of new and unexpected combinations of human beings, cultures, ideas, politics, movies, songs. It rejoices in mongrelization and fears the absolutism of the Pure. Mélange, hotchpotch, a bit of this and that is how newness enters the world. It is the great possibility that mass migration gives the world, and I have tried to embrace it.[11]

When Barack Obama flew to Moscow in 2009 his speech on universal human values was said to be 'pressing the reset button' in Washington's Moscow relations by quoting Pushkin, 'the national icon and Russia's favourite author'.[12] In fact, the verses the President recited about the universality of geometry and poetry sent a less Slavophile signal about global interconnectedness. For as every Russian knows, Pushkin was a great-grandson of the slave named Hannibal brought by Peter the Great from the seraglio of Sultan Ahmed III, who was originally from Abyssinia, close to Obama's father's region of Kenya, and who thus figures as an eternal refutation of Saul Bellow's supremacist taunt, 'No African Tolstoy'. With their famed hospitality to migrant meanings, Pushkin and Shakespeare therefore provide perfect e-books for the globalised Facebook generation, who, according to Cuno, look to international cultural institutions for the tall order of helping them both to understand 'the world's diversity and interrelatedness', and to 'feel that they are a part of this world, they and everyone else with whom they are connected by virtue of their humanity'.[13] Thus, the shock of the new and unexpected coalition of Shakespeare and the Shah served a global need, according to this consensual programme, reminding the Museum's visitors of its director's paradox that only in such a grand imperial space is there the 'possibility of allowing people – all of us – to think and imagine different histories from those with which we were raised. . . . And it is surely more important now than ever to insist that the world is one'.[14]

Slavoj Žižek has connected the tolerant liberal multiculturalism of which the British Museum is a temple to the ersatz tendency of late capitalism to generate placebos as risk-free substitutes for dangerous experiences or stimulating substances, 'a whole series of products deprived of their malignant property: coffee without caffeine, cream without fat, beer without alcohol', and rages that this 'history lite', purveyed under the logo of the united colours of humanity, belongs with online sex or drone warfare, 'as an experience of the Other deprived of its Otherness'. So, with its reification of symbolic capital into the merchandised junk of its souvenir industry, the globalisation of history into a universal shopping mall currently being effected by London's museum emporia seems a triumphant instance of the 'culturalisation of politics' Žižek deplores.[15] Certainly, the animadversions of the Slovenian Thersites appear to be borne out by the mission statement of the 'encyclopaedic museum', which, as MacGregor declares, is the Enlightenment project envisioned by Diderot, 'to shape the citizens of "that great city, the world"', as well as by the rationale of its 'trusteeship', that 'objects from other cultures tell us not only about distant peoples but about ourselves'. For the project of his museum, the director unashamedly states, is to reveal the 'oneness of the world: that all societies think and behave the same way'.[16]

Itself the beneficiary of the disconnection from national identities and tax bases of the global elite, the international museum establishment's quest for essential universal human sameness is the exact opposite of Claude Lévi-Strauss's definition of anthropology as 'the view from afar'.[17] MacGregor, who read modern languages at Oxford, is of course alert to the postcolonialist critique that such collections as his own are merely the spoils of victory carried away in imperial triumph. But he responds with the tautology that what Yeats called these 'ingenious lovely things' were *themselves* the 'butchering tools' that 'let us conquer the world and build great cities such as London, where visitors to the British Museum are able to see the truth that humanity is one'.[18] The colonial slavery and suffering that created and filled Bloomsbury's marble halls reassuringly turn out, in this self-serving and short-circuited 'Enlightenment' thinking, to be necessary preconditions of our own benevolent cosmopolitan world order.

In Bloomsbury Shakespeare underwrote the inclusionary idea of 'a universal museum aimed at a universal audience, for the use of the whole world'.[19] But the 'Shah 'Abbas' exhibition was, in fact, the third British Museum blockbuster unashamedly celebrating empire as the essential engine of globalisation, following 'Hadrian' and 'Qin Shihuang', of the terracotta army, and with 'Montezuma' following in 2009. It was this last exhibition that brought MacGregor's cultural relativism to a dead-end, however, with much hand-wringing over the array of Aztec 'butchering tools' used to flay human skin, daggers to rip out hearts and boxes to collect the entrails of sacrificed children. For these artefacts were no longer merely the 'famous ivories/And all the golden grasshoppers and bees' that museum frequenters like the poet have long accepted as the pay-off for the history of human violence.[20] As Philip Hensher complained in *The Independent*, 'It does no good to pretend these objects are morally neutral; they are disgusting and barbaric. I hope we never come to the point where the instruments of genocide of the Nazis or Khmer Rouge are offered in aesthetic mitigation'.[21]

The unintended effect of globalisation in the triumphal procession of empire exhibitions at the British Museum was to highlight the dialectical difference between the *globe* of the capitalist masters of the universe and the *world* of its peoples, and thereby to pluralise its history. Thus, for many commentators, the curators of 'Montezuma' had pushed Walter Benjamin's truism that 'There is no document of civilization which is not a document of barbarism' too far, with a display that appeared to regret that the Aztecs had not been left to go on crafting such exquisite items for their sacrificial victims: 80,400 over four days in 1484, according to the records.[22] Aztec 'barbarism places them on the far side of a line that divides civilisation from its opposite', Hensher protested.[23] So, though Benjamin had seen the world's cultural treasures as a procession in which the victors marched on implacably over the corpses of the vanquished, it was the Aztecs' monstrous jewel-encrusted skulls that made the Museum's imperial parade seem not quite such a universal human triumph after all.

THAT'S ALL ONE

If all human societies are 'effectively, the same', as the British Museum maintains, the fact that the Elgin marbles ended up in its kitsch art deco cinema hall, looking as if they had been arranged by Hitler's architect Albert Speer, is mere chance. It so happened that London met the conditions for conserving the Parthenon frieze, MacGregor maintains, but it could just as easily have been any other capital city.[24] 'The fragments, scraps, the bits and greasy relics' [*Troilus*, 5,2,159] of a supposedly democratic Greece, identified with the dawn of Europe, yet at the intersection of so many later empires, the Parthenon frieze has become a supreme prize in the war between universalism and cultural differentialism. But as the Cambridge classicist Mary Beard reminds us, it is no accident that these sculptures commemorating the Greek victory over Persia are today key pawns in the custody dispute between global culture and national patrimony, universalism and particularism, for their successive histories within an Athenian temple, Byzantine church, Islamic mosque, Turkish ammunition dump and British museum are what constitute their universality, and 'That can't belong to one country'.[25]

It is as the fractured jigsaw of multiple contexts, a fusion of so many antagonistic and competing histories which make us recognise the contingency of our historical perspective, Beard proposes, that the fraught legacy of imperial history comes down to us, to make as much sense of as we can, from our incompatible subjective positions. This is close to Alain Badiou's proposal that a postcolonial world is required to animate its cultural and racial differences in order that a true universality may be constructed, and that this new *worldliness* will need 'to expose itself to all differences and show, through the ordeal of their division, that they are capable of welcoming the truth that traverses them'.[26] And it is at least arguable that to strive in just this way, to make one from the many in the teeth of so much antagonistic difference, was indeed also Shakespeare's project. For as he has his fool Feste sagely sing at journey's end in *Twelfth Night*, the play mentioning the Shah of Persia that is located exactly where East meets West, precisely in that liminal or oxymoronic 'Middle Eastern' space of the Parthenon, known for so long as the Levant, 'A great while ago the world begun,/With hey, ho, the wind and the rain,/But that's all one, our play is done/And we'll strive to please you every day' [5,1,392–5].

Shakespeare can easily be made to endorse the theme of the British Museum's all-inclusive but patronising programme of tolerant 'history lite', that, at the end of globalisation's contemporaneous day, 'that's all one'. For it is true that the dramatist's awareness of the great wheel of world commerce does create what Walter Cohen terms a 'global feel', and that his generation's experience of globalisation as a spatialisation of the world might well explain why his Globe theatre was so named.[27] Shakespeare is certainly invested in the idea that contemporaneity is the temporality of globalisation; and when this global poet had his most unified play, *The Comedy of Errors*, turn upon a voyage 'bound/To Persia' [4,1,3–4], he started something that is indisputably more of a Romantic absolute than the Orientalism of rivals such as Marlowe. For there, despite all the fascination with 'the stranger in a strange land', 'your merchants of Persepolis' shrink to racist stereotypes of the 'slavish Persian', as Tamburlaine rides in 'triumph through Persepolis', and the Jew of Malta, whose profits from 'the Persian ships' make him a wish fulfilment of the encyclopaedic desire to cram 'infinite riches in a little room', is exterminated, for all his 'exceeding store of Persian silks'.[28]

Shakespeare shares Marlowe's excitement about the Persia of the Shahs, as a 'gateway through which luxury goods arrive from the east', along the fabled Silk Road.[29] But what makes his plays so ripe for the British Museum to co-opt is the universalist vision that does assuredly run through them: that, in the words of *Twelfth Night*, all these global journeys might some day converge to 'end in lovers' meeting', in some Kantian 'golden time' of perpetual peace, when, as Orsino, his Duke of Illyria, prophesies, 'A solemn combination shall be made/Of our dear souls' [2,1,39;5,1,370].[30] For in Shakespeare we never cease to be tantalised that 'The time of universal peace is near' [*Antony*, 4,6,4], and nor are we allowed to abandon that defining humanist dream of 'the world under one roof'. But neither are we ever permitted to forget that a democratic world order has not yet arrived, nor to ignore the paradoxical fact that globalisation's human cost is the privation of the world that actually exists. In these plays the global story is never 'history lite'.

'This is the economy, stupid', MacGregor assured the *Financial Times*: Shakespeare knew about the Shah because 'Abbas opened Iran to English traders, and the multicultural and tolerant society he is said to have created in Isfahan arose from that 'economic expediency'.[31] All the images of this 'enlightened despot' drinking with foreigners therefore have less to do with the 'rapier, scabbard, and all', they feature so prominently, we were told, than with the 'soft power' of porcelain diplomacy. The plate's the thing, in reified British Museum terms, to catch the conscience of the King. A cult of such worldly goods replaces historical analysis in much of the virtual shopping that passes for current Renaissance studies. But reviewers noticed how this consumerist commodity fetishism minimised the Shah's monstrosity. Indeed, just two lines in the sumptuous and exhaustive exhibition catalogue touch upon his 'acts of extreme cruelty', such as 'having two of his sons blinded and another killed', cutting out the tongues of his critics, or garrotting the dervishes who had prophesied his death.[32]

There was no mention in the Shah 'Abbas exhibition of how one evening the Persian monarch 'went out dressed as a peasant and bought some bread and meat, only to find he had been sold short. He had the baker thrown into an oven and the meat-seller roasted alive'.[33] Tactfully ignored, too, were his habits of boiling prisoners in oil, or enthusiastically castrating his favourite catamites, albeit with such surgical despatch that it was said that 'very few boys died under his hands'.[34] And nowhere in this glittering showcase for 'The Art of Museum Diplomacy'[35] was any reference made to 'Abbas's own brand of cultural diplomacy, as when he received the first embassy from the Emperor Rudolf II in 1603, and the ambassador, Georg Tectander, 'had an unnerving experience':

> An Ottoman prisoner was brought in and Abbas called for two swords, which he then proceeded to appreciatively examine. He chose one, tested its blade, and then sliced off the prisoner's head. Tectander feared the Shah had heard the Emperor Rudolf was making peace with the Ottomans and would use the second sword on him. Instead Abbas turned to Tectander with a smile and said that was how the Christians should treat the Turks.[36]

The earliest European travellers to Iran were awed by the Shah's spectacular New Year presents, but also advised that the gifts he loved to receive in return were human heads, 'those of distinction enveloped in a silk turban, the others bare, and each thrust through with a lance'.[37] So, when Sir Anthony Sherley, the first English emissary to Iran, met 'Abbas in 1598, he was saluted by a thousand lancers waving the heads of neighbouring Uzbeks impaled on spears, with 'their ears on strings and hanged about their necks'. The Shah did not waste any time, Sherley admiringly reported, with small talk of 'apparel, building, beauty of our women, or such vanities', but only wanted to hear 'of our proceeding in our wars, of our usual arms, of the commodity of our fortresses, and of the use of artillery'.[38] Since Anthony's father Sir Thomas was Elizabeth's Treasurer of War, what interested 'Abbas was how 'his new model army could be equipped with the most up-to-date weaponry'.[39] So the Englishman 'presented to the King a number of girdles and pistols he had brought from Aleppo'.[40] His reward was a contract to retrain the Shah's gunners.[41] In view of the Iran–Contra arms-for-hostages scandal, and current nuclear stand-off, this was not the kind of Anglo-Iranian exchange to feature in the exhibition.

The British Museum employed the words of the Bard to help guide visitors around the awkward facts of past and present Anglo-Iranian encounters. The problem with the quotations it was led to install, however, was that if they were meant to help to rehabilitate a pariah state, they were equally militaristic. Thus, the organisers posted without comment Sir Toby's menacing warning, shortly before Sebastian impales his skull, that his assailant is rumoured to be Shah 'Abbas's fencing-master; and highlighted without explanation the Sunni Prince of Morocco's bloodcurdling war-cry that the shining scimitar he sports is the one with which he 'slew the Sophy and a Persian prince/That won three fields of Sultan Suleiman' [Merchant, 2,1,24–7].

As Ladan Niayesh has observed in an essay on 'Shakespeare's Persians', the blade of Morocco's scimitar not only reflects the unexpected antagonisms of Muslims towards each other, but subverts the Orientalist binarism 'between the "West" and the "Rest"'.[42] So, perhaps Toby really does compare the chimerical 'devil' 'Abbas with the transvestite 'virago' Elizabeth. For despite MacGregor's glance at the Protestant Reformation, suppressed in the Museum's anodyne narrative of the irresistible triumph of global capitalism were the violent contradictions not only of the Shah's schismatic Iran, but of Shakespeare's England itself.[43]

Shakespeare's references to the Shah of Persia are anything but innocuous. Thus, in the quotation that introduced the 2009 exhibition, 'They say he has been a fencer to the Sophy', Sir Toby's solemn asseveration that 'he pays you as *Shahly* as your feet hits the ground', sounds as if it is a sinister multiple pun on the reports from the Sherley mission of the deadly war-game with which 'Abbas trained his troops, and with which a 1607 play, *The Travels of the Three English Brothers*, begins: 'He ran in among them with his sword drawn and gave four of them their death's wound . . . cutting off the arms from divers of them. One gentleman which did but only smile . . . the King gave him such a blow in the middle, that one half of his body fell from the other'.[44] For as is well known, these terrifying warnings about the Sophy's savage swordsman refer to Sir Anthony's younger brother Robert Sherley, whose dazzling portrait beside that of his Iranian wife, Teresia, the daughter of a Circassian chief, Ishmael Khan, and a relation of the Shah, formed the brilliant focus of the show.

Stylistically, the masque-like paintings of the Sherley couple resemble those mass produced for the early Jacobean court, and must date from 1611, when, as the catalogue noted, 'Teresia gave birth at the Sherley home in Sussex to a son, Henry, probably the first child born in England of Iranian descent'.[45] Although she is shown wearing an elaborate veil, the most alienating feature of Teresia Sherley's portrait, however, is the bejewelled flintlock pistol which she brandishes with her finger on the trigger. Misdating the picture, the Museum connected this firearm with a romantic legend about her later rescue of her husband from the Portuguese. But a loaded firearm in Jacobean Sussex hints at an antagonism barely registered in Bloomsbury: 'She eventually reached Rome, living out her days at the Carmelite convent of Santa Maria della Scala', where she is buried alongside her husband.[46] The Sherleys resided opulently in Rome on rights to sell relics and rosaries, and, most lucratively, to nullify illegitimacy, granted by the Pope.[47] This primed gun was therefore an assertion of a militant religiosity, and a disputed Catholic universalism, that Europeans tend to forget whenever they prejudge Islam. But the *Guardian* inferred that the parallels between Shakespeare's world and the Shah's were much less comfortable than the British Museum, with its self-interested Blairite investment in 'soft power', was caring to admit:

Iran has provoked fascination and fear in western Europe for more than two millennia. This fearful incomprehension has only increased since the Iranian Revolution. Shia rituals of self-flagellation, saintly relics, and martyrs can alienate in a Europe that is now rapidly forgetting its own version of such rituals in the Catholic tradition.[48]

In its culturalist fixation on the shimmering surfaces of the silk fabrics that were Iran's main exports to the West, the Shah show did not explore the ulterior purposes of the weapons offered in exchange. This might have been to avoid offending Iran's enemies in Istanbul. But the superficiality was also due to the fact that the Museum's idea of Shakespeare's England was too simplistic to explain what these Sherley brothers were doing on a mission that 'ran completely counter to the foreign policy of Elizabeth I's government, which was seeking friendship with the Ottomans on the principle that "my enemy's enemy is my friend"'.[49] Thus, while the catalogue describes the gorgeous silk robes, turban and sash that Robert wears in his picture as the ceremonial suit in which he was dressed by his hosts, when he and his brother were formally received by the Shah at Qazvin, there is no mention of the Catholic politics that brought these Englishmen to Persia, and explain the fact that, contrary to the information at the Museum, 'The Sherley mission had no sanction whatever from the English government'.[50]

Nothing was made at the British Museum of the fact that the unauthorised nego-tiations between the Sherleys and the Shah were viewed with justified alarm by Elizabeth's ministers. By coincidence, however, another exhibition opened at the same time in London, also starring portraits of Robert and Teresia Sherley, and this exposed the disingenuousness of the message that these East–West encounters were about nothing but innocent trade. 'Van Dyck' at Tate Britain centred on a pair of equally extravagant images of the silk-swathed couple, but in these the great painter portrayed them blazing in their true colours, with Teresia in her Roman garden, and Robert, again flaunting the Persian turban he liked to top with a cross, 'to show he is a Catholic', as the Shah's ambassador to the Pope.[51] Like a 1609 engraving of Islam's English envoy kissing the papal foot, this was therefore a picture that revealed com-peting narratives of the universal church, and the dark irony of the cry that echoes through *Twelfth Night*: 'For the love o'God, peace' [2,3,77].

JOURNEYS END

The irony of the British Museum's floating of *Twelfth Night* as a warrant for its detoxified brand of 'history lite' is that this drama is, in fact, one of Shakespeare's heaviest and densest texts about tolerance as an ideological category, and a record of the fact that modern liberal universalism emerged out of the violence of Europe's Wars of Religion. No Shakespearean play is in truth more laden with the baggage of its own sectarian origins, nor more in need of such heavy annotation. Thus the Museum's slogans, 'he pays you *Shahly*', and 'I will not give over my part of this sport for a pension of thousands to be paid from the Sophy' [2,5,156], are topical allusions to Sir Anthony Sherley's Contra-style funding of the Earl of Essex out of the 30,000 crowns annual commission he pocketed from upgrading the Persian army. So, as they persecute Malvolio as 'a kind of puritan' [2,3,135], it is in fact profoundly worrying that Shakespeare's Illyrians liken their religiously motivated violence to the Shah's.

The Oxford Shakespeare footnotes Fabian's interjection about kickbacks of thousands by explaining that 'In 1599 Sir Robert Sherley returned from an embassy to the Shah and boasted of the rewards he had received'.[52] In fact, Robert would not leave Persia until bound for Rome in 1608, when he was made a papal count, not knight, and was in no position at the time of the play to boast about anything. Given the wildness of contemporary intelligence about the lookalike Sherley siblings and their money-laundering schemes, however, textual editors can be relied on to get the brother wrong. The same sibling confusion may even have prompted Shakespeare's own updating of his Plautine plot about interchangeable identical twins. For the renegade brothers' deliberately obfuscated activities in Isfahan were more significant, and this offshore 'pension from the Sophy' more pertinent, to *Twelfth Night*, than any editor as yet admits.

What the heavy historical luggage of Shakespeare's Epiphany play about 'these wise men' [1,5,75] in the East reveals is the manic political and religious context out of which the text has been composed. The dramatist signals this topicality when he has Viola explain, in another meta-theatrical aside, that the professional performer who is 'wise enough to play the fool' has to 'observe their mood on whom he jests,/The quality of the persons, and the time', which is 'a practice as full of labour as of art' [3,1,53–9]. And certainly, no Shakespearean text is more laboured in its attentiveness to 'the persons, and the time' than this one about 'wise men, folly fall'n' [61] in the Orient; for all these allusions hint that, in reality, the Sherley brothers were sent to Persia by the Earl of Essex as part of a complex manoeuvre *against* the Queen. Later, when it was safe to do so, the brothers admitted they were sent East to 'get money' to ease the succession of their 'future sovereign, James VI and I'.[53] But it looks as if, under cover of a decoy tour of Italy, their secret mission was also to induce the Shah to attack the Ottomans, thereby freeing Spain to threaten England and compel Elizabeth to purge her own Malvolio, the lawyerly minister Robert Cecil, and name as her successor the King of Scots, then vowing to usher in the 'golden time' of reinstated 'convents' and religious reconciliation [5,1,169] the play's Duke is still pledging at the end.[54] Such were the two-faced politics of Catholic toleration in 1601. Thus, far from diminishing Shakespeare's interest in universality, restoring *Twelfth Night* to its violent historical contexts turns out to be one way in which Shakespeare's investment in the dream of the world under one roof, and his awareness of its limits, can be properly understood.

The universalism that is hourly expected in *Twelfth Night* can doubtless be appreciated without referring to its contemporary context in Catholic conspiracies to see that 'These sovereign thrones are all supplied, and filled . . . with one self king' [1,1,37–8], or to King James's own deluded mirage of 'a general Christian union'. But without the play's Epiphany theme that 'Journeys end in lovers meeting', it is hard to appreciate what 'every wise man's son' [2,3,39] knew in 1601 about the hopes of toleration arising from the East.[55] For because Essex also had Puritan support, his Catholic backing has been underplayed. And since the insurgency ended in disaster, the Sherleys spent the rest of their lives obfuscating what Sanjay Subrahmanyam has described as 'the ultimate paradox in early modern diplomacy', with a smokescreen that makes it as hard for historians as contemporaries to grasp why these young Englishmen 'should be working for the Shah to drum up an alliance against the Ottomans, when everyone knew that Elizabeth was pursuing a *pro*-Ottoman policy'.[56]

The British Museum made no reference to their religion, but in Sussex the Sherley family were known to be diehard recusants; and the brothers, who, like John Donne, were educated in Oxford at Hart Hall when the college was a secret seminary for Jesuits, formally converted on arriving in Italy.[57] They thus typified the crypto-Catholic gentry at the heart of the Essex conspiracy: 'premature Jacobeans' activated by the Earl's promise of a *politique* toleration, like that of Henri IV's recent Edict of Nantes.[58] It was while arms-running for the French King that Anthony was dubbed a Knight of the Holy Order of St Michael, for which temerity he was gaoled in the Fleet Prison. But if the irenic dream of 'A solemn combination' of 'our dear souls' lay behind the delusions about the universal love of God which supporters of the Sherley brothers projected onto 'the very devil' in Iran, the violence of the divisions within both Christianity and Islam may also explain why *Twelfth Night* seems to fear that all this fooling with 'the love of God' will *surely* be paid in blood:

SIR ANDREW: For the love of God, a surgeon – send one presently
                 to Sir Toby.
OLIVIA: What's the matter?
SIR ANDREW: He's broke my head across, and has given Sir Toby
                 a bloody coxcomb too. For the love of God, your help!
                 I had rather than forty pound I were at home.
OLIVIA: Who has done this, Sir Andrew?
SIR ANDREW: The Count's gentleman, one Cesario. We took him
                 for a coward, but he's the very devil incardinate.
                                      [5,1,168–76]

'Bloody as the hunter', the 'interceptor' in Shakespeare's comedy, who is written off as a mere 'knight dubbed with unhatched rapier and on carpet consideration', unexpectedly turns out to be a 'devil incardinate', whose 'incensement . . . is so implacable that satisfaction can be none but by pangs of death and sepulchre' [3,4,196–213]. If the wordplay on being *surely* paid alludes to its being funded through the Sherleys by the Shah, then this '*sepulchral*' and '*incardinate*' '*incensement*' also points to the papal incitement of Essex's *coup d'état*. The traumatic volte-face on which *Twelfth Night* turns, when the harmless 'eunuch' [1,2,52] with the Roman diminutive, Cesario (really Viola in disguise), is confused with 'his' twin, the mercenary Sebastian does seem keyed to the shock of the plot.[59] For Jonathan Bate maintains that because Shakespeare was 'over half-way an Essex man', his *Richard II* was undoubtedly the play the rebels paid to be acted at the Globe on 7 February 1601, to rally their uprising next day.[60] The first recorded performance of *Twelfth Night, or What You Will* came one year later, at Candlemas, the feast of the Purification of the Virgin, 2 February 1602, in the conspirators' headquarters of Middle Temple Hall. And whatever Shakespeare might once have wished, his dark drama about purging desires, with the title of the post-Christmas reality-check, now looks set to count the cost of 'What You Will'.

'For the love of God, a surgeon! Send one presently to Sir Toby': when Sir Andrew Aguecheek staggers bleeding onto stage after his assailant has 'broke his head across, and has given Sir Toby a bloody coxcomb too', Shakespeare's winter comedy comes very close indeed to the violence of its historical moment. As Anne Barton senses, something more than a fool's coxcomb is severed with this irruption, for 'Surgeons belong to the reality of death and disease outside the limits of festivity'.[61] In fact, this play is punctuated with references to the 'unhatched rapier' operating with the precision of 'a Lucrece knife/With bloodless stroke the heart [to] gore' [2,5,95–6]. Thus, if the anaemic Aguecheek 'were opened and you find so much blood in his liver as will clog the foot of a flea', jests Sir Toby Belch, uneasily, 'I'll eat the rest of the anatomy' [3,3,53–5]. And the castration anxiety behind all this surgical fencing about being treated *Shahly* becomes explicit when the dyspeptic Belch warns Sebastian that he 'must have an ounce or two of this malapert blood from you' [4,1,39], only to be referred himself in the end to the drunken mercies of one 'Dick Surgeon' [5,1,190].

With its hunting and medical symbolism of blooding and bloodletting, *Twelfth Night* appears to dramatise, perhaps more than any other play, the surprising and ironic violence out of which the project of religious toleration was emerging at the beginning of the seventeenth century. For strung out upon a series of mock duels, until the brutal climax when Sebastian plays cruel 'havoc' [5,1,195] with the knights by paying them so *Shahly*, Shakespeare's New Year play pushes its moral to be careful what you wish for so heartlessly that it suggests its author may well have shared in the general horror when Essex led his mêlée of 'angry young men in a hurry' in the stampede across London they had planned to be 'the bloodiest day that ever was'.[62] Certainly, the 'strange regard' which Olivia and the other characters throw on the brother who looks to have made a self-immolating 'division of [him]self' [215] mirrors the consternation with which onlookers greeted these 'Rash, inconsiderate, fiery voluntaries,/With ladies' faces and dragon's spleens' [*John*, 2,1,66–7], when journey's end for these androgynous young 'viragoes' turned out to be not some 'lovers' meeting', but a bloody duel to the death:

I am sorry, madam, I have hurt your kinsman,
But had it been the brother of my blood
I must have done no less with wit and safety.
You throw a strange regard upon me, and by that
I do perceive it hath offended you.

[5,1,201–5]

'He will not now be pacified' [3,4,250]: as a New Year offering *Twelfth Night* is curiously unsatisfying, its 'dark house' [4,2,30] unenlightened, and its 'pestilence' [1,1,19] unpurged, when Orsino swears that until Malvolio is reconciled 'We will not part from hence' [5,1,371].[63] For although Fabian continues to hope that its 'sportful malice' will 'rather pluck on laughter than revenge' [354–5], the unprecedented aggression of *Twelfth Night* leaves the Duke's universalist project for a 'solemn combination' of Christian souls stalled, hanging on some legal 'suit' [269] prosecuted by Malvolio against the master of the ship carrying the twins that was wrecked before the start. Orsino gives orders to 'Pursue him, and entreat him to a peace'. But the steward's angry and uncompromising last words, 'I'll be revenged on the whole pack of you', do not augur well when it is remembered that 'He hath not told of us of the captain yet' [365–8].

As it seems that the 'maid's garments' which 'Cesario' dimly recalls wearing, when 'The captain did first bring me on shore', cannot be recovered until the prisoner is freed from 'durance' [267–9], the pageboy's equivocal sexuality, the 'blank' 'he' ascribes to an imagined sister [2,4,109], thereby becomes a screen for all the frustrated desires of this disappointing time of gifts. In *Twelfth Night*, the quest for the impossible object of desire that Lacanians term 'the Real' is therefore quite literally projected onto a blank page. In fact, it is tempting to view Malvolio's inexplicable court 'action' [5,1,268] as figuring the legal suits that remained unresolved after the *coup d'état*, with many of the indicted rebels, including Shakespeare's patron, the Earl of Southampton, detained at the Queen's pleasure in legal limbo at the Tower, pending an expected amnesty from the presumptive heir, the pederastic King of Scots. Since the Puritan steward is to be 'both the plaintiff and the judge' [343] in the proceeding case, it looks likely 'there shall be no more cakes and ale' [2,3,104]. But in no other Shakespearean play is the promise of 'the present hour' [5,1,346] stalemated by such a paralysing sense that 'What's to come is still unsure' [2,3,45].

With its Epiphany scenario, *Twelfth Night* seems written as if in fulfilment of Viola's mission: 'I hold the olive in my hand. My words are as full of peace as matter' [1,5,185–6]. And with Feste singing 'There dwelt a man in Babylon' [2,3,71], or swearing by St Anne that 'ginger shall be hot in the mouth' [305], Shakespeare's Illyrians therefore struggle to deliver the gifts of the Day of Kings, which they still expect to come from the East. Thus, the jape to crown Malvolio the season's king of beans has him smiling like 'the new map with the augmentation of the Indies' [3,2,67–8]. Yet the unfinished lawsuit with the sailor puts a question mark over the eastern journey that initiates this plot, reminding us how the swashbuckling Sebastian had refused to disclose his journey's end when his friend Antonio begged to 'know of you whither you are bound': 'No, sooth, sir. My determinate voyage is mere extravagancy' [2,1,8–10]. We never do learn where the identical siblings were headed when their ship sank off the coast of Illyria, nor why its master is liable to be accused and imprisoned by, of all people, Malvolio. But if the steward is in fact a stand-in for an intolerant Protestant regime, and the journey's end to which the characters of the play are headed the religious toleration that was a justification of the Essex Revolt, then the eastern Mediterranean setting acquires a truly freighted topicality in light of the government's pro-Turkish anti-Catholic strategy, and the Sherleys' treasonous operations to subvert this with their mission to the Shah.

CHANGEABLE TAFFETA

Seen in the topical context of the calamity of the Essex Revolt, the stalemate of *Twelfth Night* can be read as if it were a Yeatsian recoil from the political tragedy of those its author had assumed 'But lived where motley is born', a belated realisation, 'now/That winds of winter blow', that 'we were crack-pated when we dreamed'.[64]

And it is in tune with such a reaction that the dramatist appears to suspend judgement on those silken presents promised from the East. Constance Relihan has in fact remarked how Shakespeare seems to deliberately *repress* the Orientalism of his main literary source, Barnaby Riche's romance 'Apollonius and Silla', which is set in Constantinople and Cyprus.[65] For the trial of the Captain makes the outcome contingent on a voyage as indeterminate as that of the brothers who had altered their tale so often about their true business in Iran. Thus, when the Shah asked Sir Anthony to lead a return embassy to his purported patron, Elizabeth, who wanted never to see him again, in a scam worthy of the Iran–Contra operation Sherley persuaded 'Abbas to fund him instead as a roving ambassador 'to all Christian princes', so that he could then bribe Europe's rulers into supporting Essex with chests of Persian silks; and it seems that it is the 'extravagancy' of this two-faced diplomatic suit, ostensibly about 'nothing', yet on-going 'everywhere and nowhere' as Shakespeare wrote, upon which the denouement of *Twelfth Night* hangs:

FESTE: Now the melancholy god protect thee, and the tailor
make thy doublet of changeable taffeta, for thy mind is a very
opal. I would have men of such constancy put to sea, that their
business might be everything, and their intent everywhere, for
that's it that always makes a good voyage of nothing.

[2,4,72–6]

In *Twelfth Night* everything quibbles upon the *Shahly* payment for a silk suit. Thus, at the outset, 'the suit from the Count' [1,5,93] is blocked, because Olivia 'will admit no kind of suit' [1,2,41]; but after the presentation of many 'another suit' [3,1,100], with even Antonio arrested 'at the suit of Count Orsino' [3,4,292], it turns out that, in the end, Sebastian does not after all go 'suited to his watery tomb' [5,1,227]. By the time this highly suitable show was paraded before the suited legal silks of the Inns of Court, Sherley had altered the case for his reversible suit to the Shah so suavely, due to the breaking news of the Essex fiasco, that his agent in Italy was complaining that 'if we were to go for dinner I would end up paying the bill'; and the factor of the Levant Company that had sponsored him to *open* up the silk road into Turkey was writing from Aleppo that the double-crossing knight was 'a warning to know how to trust such slippery gentlemen'.[66] So it may not be chance that, as the latest Arden editor, Keir Elam, points out, in *Twelfth Night*, 'as in no other play, material – the textile, weave and colour of fabric – determines not only distinctions between characters and their respective social status but the events themselves'.[67]

No other play of Shakespeare's is more literally *invested* in the business of dress and dressing, according to this editor, than *Twelfth Night*. This fixation on the transformative power of textiles – running from the 'flax on a distaff' worked by 'spinsters and knitters in the sun' [1,3,85; 2,4,43] to the cypress crepe of Olivia's veil [3,1,113], the damask of Viola's fantasy sister [2,4,111] and the velvet gown [2,5,43] draped over Malvolio in his dreams – continually reminds us of the suitability of silk clothing for self-conversion.[68] But as with Sir Andrew's 'divers-coloured stock' [1,4,114], or the cross-gartered 'yellow stockings' [2,5,174] that trip the steward up, such silken objects of refashioning prove treacherous, as if the strange body of alien beliefs and practices had now penetrated 'inside England's stately home', along with the 'changeable taffeta' and Persian rugs.[69] Thus, 'We have no great opinion of his wisdom', the English ambassador dryly reported, when Robert Sherley turned up in Madrid in 1609, 'for coming with a turban on his head'.[70] If *Twelfth Night* does efface the 'East' that is its violent referent, that might be because, as Patricia Fumerton writes, silk suits like those flaunted by the Sherley boys were truly *disorienting*, as they suggested the monstrous strangeness of the Islamic Orient had now arrived and come inside the English house itself:

> Something strange was happening to England's wealth, and no one knew where exactly to point the finger . . . to reify the trouble 'out there', to embody strangeness in particular foreign nations, peoples, or events that could be quarantined from the home trading body. For the paradox was that whenever the English actually fingered an embodied culprit responsible for trouble, it turned out that the English were involved. Strangeness 'out there' was also 'in here'.[71]

Robert Sherley 'very much affected to appear in foreign Vests . . . and accounted himself never ready till he had something of the Persian habit about him', scoffed Thomas Fuller.[72] So, even when he was presented to King James, Robert was reported to be reluctant to take off his turban. Likewise, 'My Lady's a Cathayan' [2,3,68], explodes Sir Toby, when his niece determines to immure herself 'like cloistress' and 'veilèd walk' [1,1,27]. Though he brags he will fight 'To the gates of Tartar' [2,5,179], on the Shah's Uzbek frontier, like the Sherleys, any impaled head, however, will be the knight's own, for in *Twelfth Night* the Orient 'resembles nothing more than England' itself.[73] Thus, the very word 'Cathayan', we learn, connotes not a 'lying Chinese', as editors have glossed it, but a European 'going native' in the East.[74] What Richard Marienstras wrote about Sebastian and Antonio in *The Tempest* applies equally to their murderous namesakes here, that when they reveal they are 'the degenerate product of civilisation' by being so 'ready to kill for power', we grasp how disparate geographical localities are actually interrelated and how gross 'violence shows itself at the heart of what had been considered as the highest virtue'.[75]

In *Twelfth Night* it is said by Maria that the splenetic violence of the humour does not merely make you 'laugh yourselves into stitches', but is enough to see a Christian 'turned heathen, a very renegado, for there is no Christian that means to be saved by believing rightly can ever believe such impossible passages of grossness' [3,3,59–61]. 'Renegado', editors explain, was the contemptuous Spanish term for a Christian convert to Islam. Nowhere is the play's relativising of Christian and Islamic violence more pointed, therefore, than in the incarceration of Malvolio, a revanchist replay of the treason trial of Edmund Campion, 'the old hermit of Prague, that never saw pen and ink', in the words of a famous Catholic poem, as, despite the best efforts of the Rackmaster, Thomas Norton, author of *Gorboduc*, the Jesuit was never tortured into signing any confession for that 'niece of King Gorboduc' [4,2,12–15], the Queen.[76] This cruel mock trial leaves its victim 'more puzzled than the Egyptians', or gypsy Roma, 'in their fog' [44]. But Feste's Inquisitorial roles in it are those of 'Sir

Topaz' and 'Master Parson', the priests Henry Garnet and Robert Parsons, and it is these Roman disguises that tie the Jesuitical interrogation in Shakespeare's Illyria directly to the Sherleys and the Shah.

References to 'the old hermit of Prague', 'Sir Topaz' and 'Master Parsons' bemuse editors; but they acquire loaded significance from the religious politics of the Essex Revolt. For Sir Anthony had arrived in Rome, on his supposedly innocent mission, via Moscow and Prague, in April 1601, and was immediately debriefed at the Spanish embassy by Father Parsons, when their talk was about a concerted 'attack on London'.[77] The priest guessed the reason the Shah's envoy was plotting against England was 'maltreatment' of a third brother, the 'notable pirate' or 'salt-water thief' [5,1,63] Thomas Sherley, by Cecil, 'in taking his wife and keeping her openly' as his mistress (as Malvolio plans). But the Spanish ambassador minuted that it was because he was 'bound to the Count of Essex'.[78] So the code for Feste's charade, as a phantasmagoria of turning tables, may have come to Shakespeare via the clown Will Kemp, with whom Anthony gossiped in Rome.[79] For 'it is common knowledge the City is extremely alienated from the Queen', Sherley reminded the ambassador, 'because of the death of the Count'. So, 'Strike at London', he advised Parsons, 'and you strike at England's heart'.[80] He was right. Londoners were shocked by Essex's execution, which occurred just as the Persian delegation crossed the Alps. Such was the apparent 'wreck past hope' [5,1,73] to which the fantasy of a 'golden time' of peace and harmony had been reduced by the real time of *Twelfth Night*. But that Shakespeare was still able to welcome newness into this world was perhaps thanks to the Sophy after all. For in a veritable Iran–Contra arms-for-hostage deal, 'Abbas was holding the youngest of the Sherley brothers as security in Iran.

THAT OLD AND ANTIC SONG

'He hath had wonderful great entertainment of the [Shah] with many exceeding rich gifts', marvelled the English consul in Aleppo when Sir Anthony began his treasonous return embassy, before adding ominously: 'His brother remaineth in Persia until his return. God grant his voyage return good'.[81] Robert Sherley was, in fact, now the Shah's personal 'slave', according to Vatican informants, and the eighteen-year-old boy travelled about in luxury as 'a favourite of the King, who generously gave him everything he needed'. He had 'gained the goodwill of the King by whom he is greatly liked', ran the papal despatches, 'because he renders services' according to the particular local 'habits and customs, in things far from edifying'.[82] Just what these unedifying services might have amounted to is suggested by other memoirs. As a connoisseur of Persian verse, and an adept 'composer of rhapsodies and part-songs' himself, the Shah frequented coffeehouses where 'boys performed lascivious dances to the accompaniment of flutes', one scandalised Spaniard complained.[83] Sir Thomas Herbert, who accompanied Robert on his final embassy in 1628, recalled how 'youthful pages' played music while 'Abbas was served at table by other 'Ganymede boys'.[84] And John Thaddeus, a Carmelite monk, related that provincial governors would send such beautiful youths as gifts, that he 'kept more than two hundred boys' in his harem, and that he was attended 'by forty naked boys whenever he went to the baths'.[85]

The fresco of Robert Sherley painted in Rome's Quirinale Palace for Pope Paul V still depicts him in 1611, aged thirty, as a handsome full-lipped youth in feathered turban, crimson fur-trimmed cape and green silk coat. No wonder King James wrote urgently to the Shah from Scotland inquiring about his fate.[86] That Persia's court culture of pederasty and poetry was governed by eunuchs 'Abbas had castrated with his own knife must have added piquancy to news circulating in 1600, with the *True Report of Sir Anthony Shirley's Journey,* that the younger of the English brothers had been left behind to 'render services' to his benefactor. To the reported discomfort of London's Islamic clerics, the British Museum highlighted a highly suggestive portrait of 'the 56-year-old Shah 'Abbas caressing a beardless, round-cheeked, almond-eyed pageboy, who is holding an exaggeratedly phallic wine flask between his knees', in its publicity, however.[87] The 'old and antic song' [2,4,3] inscribed on this picture, we were informed, compares 'the lips of the beloved' to 'the lips of the cup', and the 'flowing wine to love'.[88]

On London's buses and tubes in the spring of 2009, the advertising for the Shah show depicted 'Abbas inviting his adolescent cupbearer to be 'quick and fresh' with the 'spirit of love', and 'give me excess of it' [1,12,9]. And in the display itself, other steamy lyrics about the aphrodisiac 'food of love' [1] illustrated the long and sexually explicit Persian literary cult of spiritualised pederasty. These poems were tactfully left untranslated; and when the Museum director came up with his own bestseller about the Bard, to cash in on yet another universalising exhibition in 2012, this time on 'Shakespeare Staging the World', no less, MacGregor made no mention of Persia or the Shah.[89] But if the dramatist was intrigued by the scandalous implications of the Sherley antics, it seems he would not be the last to exploit the coercive homoeroticism of Shah 'Abbas's musical banquets in a narrative about antagonistic religious extremes. In a work that opens with Eucharistic imagery and the metaphor of music as an emetic purge, administered so the sexual appetite 'may sicken and so die' [1,1,3], we are never served anything non-stimulating, in any case, nor without the violent cathartic content its history prescribes:

ORSINO: Give me some music. Now good morrow, friends.
           Now, good Cesario, but that piece of song,
           That old and antic song we heard last night;
           Methought it did relieve my passion much . . .
           Come hither, boy. If ever thou shalt love,
           In the sweet pangs of it remember me;
           For such as I am all true lovers are,
           Unstaid and skittish in all motions else
           Save in the constant image of the creature
           That is beloved. How dost thou like this tune?
VIOLA: It gives a very echo to the seat
           Where love is throned.

                                  [2,4,1–21]

Viola's troubling ploy to 'serve this duke' by convincing the Captain 'it may be worth thy pains' to 'present me as an eunuch to him', so as to sing 'And speak to him in many sorts of music' [1,2,53–4], is often explained as an authorial false start.[90] But Elam establishes that the real 'pains' of the eunuch continue to haunt this play, in Sir Andrew's impotence [1,3,64], for instance, the 'C', 'U' and 'T' [2,5,78] of the Letter Scene, or Malvolio's musing on being 'born great' [126–7], which parodies Christ's theological discrimination between those born sterile and those 'made Eunuchs' (Matthew 19:12).[91] Stephen Orgel further proposes that when played by an adolescent boy, the part of Orsino's abbreviated 'little Caesar' insinuated 'a world of possibilities that were, to a Protestant society (perhaps temptingly) illicit'. These historicist critics relate the little Roman's musical offerings to opera in the seventeenth-century Vatican, where teenage castrati excited fantasies that were 'simultaneously heterosexual and homosexual'.[92] But as Relihan points out, the play's extended flirtation with risky homosexual desire is also 'linked to its delicate negotiation between eastern cultures and English values'.[93] And that negotiation was precisely what concerned Cesario's real-life avatar, the young 'fencer to the Sophy', Robert Sherley, at the time of the play.

The political correctness of gay and gender criticism has had the unintended side-effect of confirming how decidedly *Twelfth Night* is set down in the East. Bruce Smith indeed interprets the play as a systematic rewriting of the Renaissance 'Myth of the Shipwrecked Youth', which ordinarily introduced same-sex desire in a Muslim setting to reinforce existing cultural prejudices. Thus, when Shakespeare has the Duke praise his page because the 'Dear lad' still has a 'small pipe' like a 'maiden's organ . . . And all is semblative a woman's part' [1,4,29–32], he challenges the ways in which this familiar hostage narrative operated to police 'the dangerous fact of desire between a man and adolescent boy', Smith proposes, and this literal disorientation is more than simply sexual, for 'If we have undergone a rite of passage, it is a journey toward another country, not a return trip to the shores we left behind'. 'Getting outside oneself, experiencing the world through somebody else's eyes', according to this multiculturalist revaluation, 'is central to the comic vision' of *Twelfth Night*.[94]

Getting a bit outside of oneself is all very well, of course, so long as we do not dwell too much upon the Shah's penchant for the 'delicate negotiations' of surgical emasculation. Thus, Elam likens the 'sanctity' of Antonio's 'devotion' to Sebastian [4,1,326], and Orsino's concluding teasing of Viola-as-Cesario that he will love 'him' as long as 'he' remains a man [5,1,372], to the ritualisation of same-sex unions that attracted later English sexual outlaws like Byron to the historical Illyria, modern Albania.[95] What this connection avoids bringing out, however, is the precariousness of Byron's predicament when, plying him 'with almonds and sugar sherbet like a child', and praising his 'small ears, curling hair, and little white hands', the Albanian warlord Ali Pasha expected *him* to 'turn Turk' and play the passive 'part of young Caesar in Bithynia'.[96] Julius Caesar never lived down his reputation as the Bithynian King Nicomedes' 'fancy's queen' [5,1,375]. Yet though they do relate the infantilised form of Cesario to *caesus*, the Latin for 'cut', which gave the Roman, born by Caesarean section, his name, critics tend to agree that whenever the castration theme surfaces in the play – as it does in Sir Andrew's impotent 'dry jest' [1,3,64]; Sir Toby's sodomitic joke that 'If thou hast her not i'th'end, call me cut' [2,4,165]; or throughout the 'notorious abus[ing]' [5,1,366] of Malvolio – the dramatist is simply 'having fun'.[97]

The eunuch trope of *Twelfth Night* has critics in just such stitches of laughter as Maria foresees. For Orgel, therefore, Cesario's comedic career goes to show what 'good arguments could be produced in favour of castrating your son. Castration had the disadvantage of being irreversible, but the advantages, in terms of income and security, were correspondingly large'.[98] Feminists who would be horrified if the 'comic vision' of Shakespeare's play centred on the Muslim rite of female circumcision, or if its plot troped the practice of clitoridectomy, are merely tickled by the possibility of the castration of an adolescent male. Thus, the violent Islamic and Catholic actuality of emasculation, and the fierce religious antagonism that lurks beneath this story, are all foreclosed, in the interests of the 'radical challenge to patriarchal values' which, as Catherine Belsey explained in a much-cited essay, requires we forget the painful truth of the dramatic situation, and 'derive pleasure (in this case a certain titillation) from the dangers which follow from the disruption of sexual difference'.[99]

The knives that featured so disturbingly in the Shah 'Abbas exhibition, and shadow Shakespeare's comedy, may not look quite so barbarous as the sacrificial tools of the Aztecs, but they raise similar questions about context and universality. For under the sway of the Shah's scimitar, in *Twelfth Night* the real dangers are, in fact, as much those that *accompany*, as follow, the disruption of sexual difference, since we can never cease worrying about Cesario's presumed masculine status, 'as a squash before 'tis a peascod, or a codling when 'tis almost an apple', and thus about the vulnerability that would make 'his' 'small pipe' so 'very comptible, even to the least sinister usage' [1,5,140; 156]. Gary Taylor has contested the myth, derived from Freud's *Kastrationkomplex*, and perpetuated in *S/Z*, Roland Barthes's study of Balzac's story about an operatic castrato, *Sarrasine*, that equates castration with male loss, and reminded us that prior to psychoanalysis, 'castration could produce a powerful voice, a powerful intimate of women, a powerful spirituality'.[100] And it is true that the *escape* from the seraglio would become a signature only of a later Orientalism. With *Twelfth Night*, however, the ambiguity as to whether Viola is presented at court 'as an eunuch' [1,2,52], as planned, or as the pubescent boy the Duke desires, creates an insecurity that aggravates the complex about the unmanning effect of *waiting* to perform for another that runs throughout Shakespeare's work, and that will here cause the Fool to bring down the curtain regretting that 'when I came to wive . . . By swaggering' like an actor, 'could I never thrive' [5,1,383–5]:

Away, my disposition, and possess me
Some harlot's spirit. My throat of war be turned,
Which choired with my drum, into a pipe
Small as an eunuch. . . .

[*Coriolanus*, 3,2,111–14]

The last words of *Twelfth Night*, 'We'll strive to please you every day', tie its eunuch trope with the *attentisme* it stages, the suspense of waiting on command. Editors note that the 'eunuch' is in fact a toy flute that makes no sound of its own; and for Shakespeare it seems to figure an even more traumatic loss of agency than he associates with the recorder [*Hamlet*, 3,2,316–41]. So whatever the author was himself expecting from Robert Sherley's dangerous game of *playing the part* of the Shah's lover, Viola's charade of acting 'as an eunuch' appears keyed to his own fear that, as a performer, his 'foolish thing was but a toy' [5,1,378]. When in the duel the false page admits 'A little thing would make me tell them how much I lack of a man' [3,4,268–9], the absence of a male 'weapon' is so emphatic, in any case, that we cannot ignore what it would mean for a boy to be made to be paid *Shahly*, and become his 'master's mistress' [5,1,314], nor the 'sinister usage' to which the blades of 'the Sophy' will be put in this culture of 'rapier, scabbard, and all', where the test of manhood is to 'strip your sword stark naked . . . or forswear to wear iron about you' [223]. For if Cesario's 'little thing' is its veritable *objet petit a*, the lack at the centre of its psychic economy, or empty 'blank' beneath its silken suit, it seems that in *Twelfth Night* Shakespeare conflates the duel with the castration that was so frequently its physical outcome, because both practices are presented as being 'as uncivil as strange' [225], monstrous customs outside the boundaries of civilisation, 'Fit for the mountains and the barbarous caves,/Where manners ne'er were preached' [4,1,44]. Yet each is imagined as a form of sanctified violence, a *rite de passage* on which 'what's to come' that's 'still unsure', in the phallic imagery of the play, will surely depend:

> Cesario, come –
> For so you shall be while you are a man;
> But when in other habits you are seen,
> Orsino's mistress, and his fancy's queen.
>
> [5,1,372–5]

WHAT'S TO COME

As a New Year commencement, *Twelfth Night* is full of quibbles about travelling in terms of *pleasure* and *assurance*. But if it was written in the aftermath the Essex Revolt, when hopes for universal peace turned on what was *Shahly* paid to a young English hostage held as *surety* in Isfahan, then its presentiments about a future in which an Inquisition interrogates suspected heretics on its crazed theology, in a kind of forecast of Abu Ghraib, while the fundamentalist vows revenge, suggest that when Shakespeare looked into the heart of Christian universalism he found in it a 'hideous darkness' [4,2,27]. In locating this heart of darkness within the very emancipatory politics of toleration, Shakespeare's castrating Levantine comedy thus comes as close as his circumcising Venetian one to unmasking the hidden violence of these 'Christian fools with varnished faces' [*Merchant*, 2,5,32]. Indeed, the plot of *Twelfth Night* prefigures what Žižek writes about the violent irruptions of the 'universality-in-becoming', when he remarks of the systemic violence which 'remains foreclosed in the all-inclusionary/tolerant' project, that the only way for this universality to come into existence, 'is in the guise of its very opposite, of what cannot but appear as an excessive "irrational" whim. These violent *passages à l'acte* bear witness to *antagonism* that can no longer be symbolized'.[101] Thus, the unanswerable question posed by Malvolio about such antagonism, 'Tell me why?' [5,1,333], will receive nothing more than Fabian's shrugging confession of 'some stubborn and uncourteous parts/We had conceived' [350–1], as though Shakespeare is challenging us to consider with this unending ending what Žižek writes about the qualified intolerance that would finally serve to separate these feuding Christians:

> Let us not forget that liberalism emerged in Europe after the catastrophe of the Thirty Years War between Catholics and Protestants. It was an answer to the question of how people who differ in their fundamental religious allegiances could ever coexist. It demanded from citizens more than a condescending tolerance of diverging religions, more than tolerance as temporary compromise. It demanded that we respect religions not *in spite of* our innermost religious convictions but *on account of* them – respect for others as a proof of true belief. This attitude is best expressed by Abu Hanifa, the great eighth-century Muslim intellectual: 'Difference of opinion in the community is a token of Divine Mercy'.[102]

After *Twelfth Night*, the question 'Tell me why?' will never again be satisfactorily answered on Shakespeare's stage. 'Demand me nothing', Iago will therefore snarl, when Othello reiterates Malvolio's bafflement, 'What you know you know./From this time forth I never will speak word' [*Othello*, 5,2,309–10]. Instead, by rendering so palpable the violence that sustained the dream of universal brotherhood, and disclosing his own anxious professional involvement in that violence so reflexively, Shakespeare responded to the politics of toleration with a dramaturgy that echoes to the unappeased cry of the persecuted: 'you wrong me, and the world shall know it' [5,1,292]. Thus Olivia, who begins the play veiled as a nun, in a display of fundamentalist self-exclusion, ends it shaken into regretting how this 'extracting frenzy' has 'banished' her capacity to empathise with the self-excluding 'frenzy' of the other [5,1,274–5]. But the complex *worldliness* of *Twelfth Night* is a *grounded* universality that transcends this familiar liberal recognition of the contingency of each particular cultural position. By giving the puritanical zealot Malvolio the implied last word, Shakespeare instead inaugurates this New Year of a new century with the prospect of a 'universality-in-becoming' that arises not in spite of antagonisms, but *because* of them, and with a dialectical rigour of which Žižek might approve:

> The key moment of any theoretical – and indeed ethical, political, and even aesthetic – struggle is *the rise of universality out of the particular lifeworld*. The commonplace according to which we are all grounded in a particular, contingent lifeworld . . . needs to be turned around. The authentic moment of discovery, the breakthrough, occurs when a properly universal dimension *explodes*

from within a particular context. . . . This universality is not simply external to or above a particular context: it is inscribed within it.[103]

Perhaps the most elementary hermeneutic test of the universality of a work of art is its ability to survive being torn from its original context, Žižek concedes. But the reason 'there is a romantic Shakespeare and a realist Shakespeare' is not simply that 'each epoch reinvents and rediscovers' these dramas in its own image, but that Shakespeare himself abstracts universality from the 'historical trivia' of his own grounded historical situation: 'For it is not only that every universality is haunted by a particular content that taints it; it is that every particular position is haunted by its implicit universality, which undermines it'.[104] Thus, at a time when relations between East and West were determined more by internecine Christian schism than any anti-Islamic crusade, with its cruel mutilations of eunuch slaves, veiled wives and 'mute' guards [1,2,58], the perfumed garden of the harem offered the dramatist a cultural scenario to turn a menacing hostage crisis into a play about the struggle called globalisation in which we are 'all one' in 'qualified intolerance', like 'the wind and the rain' [5,1,377]. Or as Žižek puts it, rather than dramatising a bland tolerant multicultural inclusiveness, in the commercialised mode of the British Museum, Shakespeare seems to show us how to 'share our *intolerance*, and join forces in the same struggle'.[105]

If the imaginary 'Persia' of his 'Sophy' is a pretext for Shakespeare's Illyria, one trivial pursuit might be to connect the 'shared intolerance' of this quarrelsome dukedom with the ethnic and religious antagonisms of the actual Illyria, on the frontier between Christendom and Islam, where the Hegelian ancestry of Žižek himself can be traced to James VI's favourite Catholic, Marco Antonio De Dominis, Archbishop of Split. Improbably, it was this Croatian controversialist, who settled in London and was satirised as the 'Fat Bishop of Spalato', forever apostasising in Thomas Middleston's *A Game at Chess*, whose agonistic theories offered 'the most systematic treatment' of the dialectical Christian union of opposites the King espoused.[106] De Dominis thought he had discovered a model for such agonism in the refractions of the rainbow. And to Shakespeare, 'the golden window of the east' [*Romeo*, 1,1,112] was likewise the symbolic frame for such a becoming-universality. For of his fifty references to 'the East', over half invoke sunrise at 'the first op'ning of the gorgeous east' [*Love's*, 4,3,219], a heliotropic turn towards the 'grey-eyed morn . . . Chequ'ring the eastern clouds with streaks of light' [*Romeo*, 2,2,1] that reverses the Virgilian *translatio imperii*, and appears to align what Robert Weimann calls 'the commodious thresholds' of Shakespeare's stage away from the West's sunset world and towards renewal from the Orient.[107]

Shakespeare would inscribe the perilousness of the Sherley brothers' Eastern journeys in quest of religious reconciliation in the broken odyssey of *Pericles*, it has been claimed.[108] And certainly, the chill dawn that recurs like a signature in every Shakespearean genre reminds us how often these plays are initiated, as befits texts so often acted at Christmas or Twelfth Night, during the liminal hours of New Year, when ''Tis bitter cold' [*Hamlet*, 1,1,6] in a Europe that feels old, and the watchmen on the walls await whatever it is that 'Walks o'er the dew of yon high eastward hill' [149]. As François Laroque notes, the daybreak of this 'festival *par excellence*' witnessed 'a veritable myth of universal fraternity', fuelled by a notion of *hospitalitas* which dictated that houses should be open to all-comers.[109] So, there is an elective affinity between the *arrivance* and hermeneutic openness of the Shakespearean text and seasonal customs, like the wassail bowl or New Year gifts, enacted to welcome humankind in whatever migrant form it may turn up, a concrete universality, in Žižek's terms, constituted agonistically by 'those who have no place within the social Whole which generates them'.[110] Shakespeare's Eastern deportment was thereby structurally keyed to the 'journey's end' of the Magi, and its staging in the annual advent of the Mummers, or in those virtual embassies from 'The Prince of Purple' and 'The Prince of Love', confrontations that taught the lawyers of the Inns the silken suits of immunity, *but of the hostages*, not of the hosts.[111]

LIKE AN ICICLE ON A DUTCHMAN'S BEARD

'Twelfth Day [6 January 1663] . . . we met with Major Thomson . . . who doth talk very highly of Liberty of conscience. He says that if the King thinks it good, the papists may have the same. . . . After dinner to the Dukes house and there saw *Twelfth Night* acted well, though it be but a silly play and not relating at all to the name or day':[112] Samuel Pepys's blithe contempt for Shakespeare's comedy gains irony from his failure to connect it with either the Epiphany theme of 'journey's end' or his own gossip about religious toleration. But his diary entry does provide historical perspective on the play's hope to 'let no quarrel nor no brawl to come/Taint the condition of this present hour' [5,1,345–6]. For 'what's to come' by way of the universality of *Twelfth Night* is still taking centuries to arrive, though it cannot be chance that in the winter of 1609 the other Sherley play, *The Three Brothers*, was toured in 'the wind and the rain' of remote country houses in the Yorkshire Dales to recusant audiences that included the orphans and widows of the executed Gunpowder Plotters, by a company of outlawed Catholic players, soon prosecuted for sedition, alongside *Pericles* and *King Lear*.[113]

'I do not like the fashion of your garments', Lear tells Edgar; 'You will say they are Persian; but let them be changed' [3,6,73–4]. By the time of the Gunpowder Plot Shakespeare had grown wary of these 'surely' promises that came in such treacherous Persian disguise. Yet the anonymous play called *The Three Brothers* seems to share his enduring hopes for the 'golden time' of a universality to come, because it ends with all the Sherley brothers reunited, and the Shah agreeing to build a church 'Wherein all Christians that do hither come/May peaceably hear their own religion'.[114] This was a universalism that even the Calvinist Thomas Middleton could endorse, when, in yet another extravagant Sherley public relations exercise, he recounted how it had not been young Robert's 'garments embroidered thick with gold' that so 'dazzled' the Persians and the Pope, but the 'excellent music of his tongue', which had sued so well that it had converted Shah 'Abbas himself into 'confessing and worshipping' Christ.[115]

'Would you undertake another suit', Olivia likewise assures Cesario in Shakespeare's comedy of silken embassies, 'I had rather hear you to solicit that/Than music of the spheres' [3,1,100–2]. In truth, the Sherley brothers would never be reunited, and Robert would soon be reporting 'the hatred ['Abbas] bears all Christians, burning and pulling down all Churches'.[116] Yet in Shakespeare's Illyria, plans for universal toleration are still hopefully suspended on the caesura of whatever is covered by Cesario's silken suit. Sir Anthony had left Isfahan with thirty-two chests of silks as the gifts from the Shah to Europe's rulers, with which he intended to generate the backing for Essex's putsch. These chests were last seen at Archangel, where in the aftermath of the disastrous plot, Sherley instead stowed them with the captain of a Dutch ship bound for England from Russia, before sailing off 'into the north of my lady's opinion', to 'hang like an icicle on a Dutchman's beard' [3,2,22]. Editors read this metaphor as an allusion to Barents's 1597 Arctic voyage. But whatever its exact historical referent, the image of frozen assets seems apt enough for the harsh political climate in which *Twelfth Night* was first performed.

One should recognise 'the hugely liberating aspect of the violence' between warring Christians that generated the project of toleration around 1600, writes Žižek.[117] But the figure of hope hanging on such a cold coming suggests how hard Shakespeare found it to suspend his disbelief. Someone who might have kept the dramatist *au courant* with the Shah's presents was the errant brothers' uncle Sir Thomas Sherley, the Treasurer of Middle Temple. For after the Essex disaster, it was Sir Thomas who was in charge of the lawyers' feasting for this frosty New Year. He had 'a strong motive to stage a prestigious entertainment', and so commissioned the Lord Chamberlain's Men, and expensive musicians, to present a play.[118] The comedy they acted was *Twelfth Night*. So it would be satisfying to think that the proceeds from Shah 'Abbas's missing silks paid for Shakespeare's comedy; and that contrary to Edward Said's dualism of European production and Oriental seduction, this New Year gift from Persia was a musical offering to a London hungry for 'the food of love' [1,1,1].[119] We learn, however, that the Shah's wise men continued to pursue Sherley through the High Court, because they claimed the knight had sold their silk presents for 'a great price'. The go-between in all these complicated global transactions, according to Father Parsons, had indeed been his absent 'friend the captain'.[120] And only the missing Dutchman knew the truth about the 'Sophy's suit'.

NOTES

1. Rachel Campbell-Johnston, 'Shah 'Abbas: the remaking of Iran at the British Museum', *The Times*, 14 February 2009.
2. James Mills, 'Back to the future with Iran diplomacy', *The Tribune*, 24 February 2009.
3. Peter Aspden, 'Vaster than empires', *Financial Times*, 7 February 2009.
4. 'World under one roof': Neil MacGregor, 'To shape the citizens of "that great city, the world"', in James Cuno (ed.), *Whose Culture? The Promise of Museums and the Debate Over Antiquities* (Princeton: Princeton University Press, 2009), pp. 39–54, here pp. 39 and 54; 'dead thing': anonymous spokesperson, Italian Ministry of Culture, quoted in Philippe de Montebello, '"And what do you propose should be done with those objects?"', ibid., pp. 55–70, here p. 65.

5. Stephen Greenblatt, *Shakespearean Negotiations: The Circulation of Social Energy in Renaissance England* (Oxford: Clarendon Press, 1988), p. 1.

6. Robert Foley, quoted in Claire Scobie, 'The long road home', *Observer Magazine*, 28 June 2009, 32–7, here 37.

7. Ben Jonson, 'To the memory of my beloved, the Author', reprinted in Stephen Greenblatt, Walter Cohen, Jean Howard and Katharine Eisaman Maus (eds), *The Norton Shakespeare* (New York: Norton, 1997), pp. 3351–2.

8. Kwame Anthony Appiah, 'Whose culture is it?', in Cuno (ed.), *Whose Culture?*, p. 82.

9. Montebello, '"And what do you propose should be done with those objects?"', p. 55.

10. Michael Brown, 'Exhibiting indigenous heritage in the age of cultural property', in Cuno (ed.), *Whose Culture?*, p. 146.

11. Salman Rushdie, *Imaginary Homelands: Essays and Criticism, 1981–1991* (London: Granta, 1991), p. 394, quoted in Kwame Anthony Appiah, *Cosmopolitanism: Ethics in a World of Strangers* (New York: Norton, 2006), p. 112, and in Cuno, 'Introduction', in *Whose Culture?*, p. 27.

12. Shaun Walker, 'Obama plays the perfect guest', and 'Pushkin: the way to a Russian's heart', *The Independent*, 8 July 2009, 19.

13. Cuno, 'Introduction', p. 17.

14. MacGregor, 'To shape the citizens', pp. 39 and 54.

15. Slavoj Žižek, *The Puppet and the Dwarf: The Perverse Core of Christianity* (Cambridge, MA: MIT Press, 2003), p. 96; 'culturalization of politics': 'On Tolerance as an Ideological Category': in *Violence: Six Sideways Reflections* (New York: Picador, 2008), p. 119.

16. MacGregor, 'To shape the citizens', pp. 47–8 and 50.

17. 'The view from afar': Claude Lévi-Strauss quoted and discussed in Anthony Tatlow, *Shakespeare, Brecht, and the Intercultural Sign* (Durham, NC: Duke University Press, 2001), pp. 3 and 230–1.

18. MacGregor, 'To shape the citizens', pp. 40 and 44; 'ingenious lovely things': William Butler Yeats, 'Nineteen hundred and nineteen', in *The Variorum Edition of the Poems of W. B. Yeats*, ed. Peter Allt and Russell King Alspach (London: Macmillan, 1987), p. 428.

19. Ibid., p. 40.

20. 'Famous ivories': Yeats, 'Nineteen hundred and nineteen'. For an extended and culturally acute discussion of these lines, see Michael Wood, *Yeats and Violence* (Oxford: Oxford University Press, 2010).

21. Philip Hensher, 'The art of death on a mass scale', *The Independent*, 28 September 2009, 33.

22. Walter Benjamin, 'Theses on the philosophy of history', in *Illuminations*, trans. Harry Zohn (London: Fontana, 1970), p. 258; the figure 80,400 is from Tzvetan Todorov, *The Conquest of America*, trans. Richard Howard (New York: Harper, 1984), p. 143.

23. Hensher, 'The art of death on a mass scale', 33.

24. MacGregor, 'To shape the citizens', pp. 40 and 44.

25. Mary Beard, quoted in Stephen Moss, 'Our goal is to have the best museum in the world', *The Guardian*, Arts section, 16 June 2009, 6–9, here 8.

26. Alain Badiou, *Saint Paul: The Foundation of Universalism*, trans. Ray Brassier (Stanford: Stanford University Press, 2003), p. 106.

27. Walter Cohen, 'The undiscovered country: Shakespeare and mercantile geography', in Jean Howard and Scott Shershow (eds), *Marxist Shakespeares* (London: Routledge, 2001), p. 132.

28. 'Stranger in a strange land': Stephen Greenblatt, *Renaissance Self-Fashioning: From More to Shakespeare* (Chicago: Chicago University Press, 1980), p. 194; Christopher Marlowe, *Tamburlaine the Great: Part One*, 1,1,37; 2,5,49–54; and 4,3,68; *The Jew of Malta*, 1,1,2; 37; and 88, in *Christopher Marlowe: The Complete Plays*, ed. Frank Romany and Robert Lindsey, pp. 76, 100, 131, 250–1 and 253. For Elizabethan dramatic representations of Persian luxury, see Emily Bartels, *Spectacles of Strangeness: Imperialism, Alienation, and Marlowe*

(Philadelphia: University of Pennsylvania Press, 1993), pp. 9–13 and 65–9; and Paulina Kewes, 'Contemporary Europe in Elizabethan and early Stuart drama', in Andrew Hadfield and Paul Hammond (eds), *Shakespeare and Renaissance Europe* (London: Thomson Learning, 2005), p. 163.

29. Daniel Vitkus, *Turning Turk: English Theatre and the Multicultural Mediterranean, 1570–1630* (Basingstoke: Palgrave Macmillan, 2003), p. 71. See also Jonathan Burton, *Traffic and Turning: Islam and English Drama, 1579–1624* (Cranbury, NJ: Associated University Press, 2005); Matthew Dimmock, *'New Turkes': Dramatizing Islam and the Ottomans in Early Modern England* (Farnham: Ashgate, 2005); Mark Hutchings, 'The "Turk" phenomenon and the repertory of the late Elizabethan playhouse', *Early Modern Literary Studies*, 16 (2007), 1–39; Linda McJannet, 'Islam and English drama: a critical history', *Early Theatre*, 12:2 (2009), 183–93; and Daniel Vitkus, 'Adventuring heroes in the Mediterranean: mapping the boundaries of Anglo-Islamic exchange on the earl modern stage', *Journal of Medieval and Early Modern Studies*, 37:1 (2007), 75–95.

30. Emmanuel Kant, 'Towards perpetual peace', in *Practical Philosophy*, trans. and ed. Mary Gregor (Cambridge: Cambridge University Press, 1996), pp. 328–31. For Shakespeare and Kant see Richard Wilson, 'Making men of monsters: Shakespeare in the company of strangers', in *Shakespeare in French Theory: King of Shadows* (London: Routledge, 2007), pp. 242–60, in particular p. 50.

31. Aspden, 'Vaster than empires'.

32. Sheila Canby, 'Introduction', *Shah 'Abbas: The Remaking of Iran* (London: British Museum Press, 2009), p. 19.

33. David Blow, *Shah Abbas: The Ruthless King Who Became an Iranian Legend* (London: I. B. Tauris, 2009), p. 162.

34. Ibid., pp. 133 and 173–4.

35. William Lee Adams, 'The art of museum diplomacy', *Time*, 19 February 2009.

36. Blow, *Shah Abbas*, p. 77, quoting Georg Tectander, *Eine Abenteuerliche Reise Durch Russland Nach Persien, 1602–1604* (Tulln: Herausgegeben von Dorothea Mueller-Ott, 1978), p. 58.

37. Pietro Della Valle, quoted in Blow, *Shah Abbas*, p. 167.

38. Anthony Sherley, letter to Anthony Bacon, 12 February 1600, quoted ibid., pp. 54 and 56.

39. Ibid., p. 37.

40. Abel Pinçon, quoted in D. W. Davies, *Elizabethans Errant: The Strange Fortunes of Sir Thomas Sherley and His Three Sons, As Well in the Dutch Wars as in Muscovy, Morocco, Persia, Spain, and the Indies* (Ithaca: Cornell University Press, 1967), p. 108.

41. R. Savory, 'The Sherley myth', *Iran: Journal of the British Institute of Persian Studies*, 5 (1967).

42. Ladan Niayesh, 'Shakespeare's Persians', *Shakespeare*, 4 (2008), 127–36, here 128–9. See also Jane Grogan, '"A warre . . . commodious": dramatizing Islamic schism in and after *Tamburlaine*', *Texas Studies in Language and Literature*, 54 (2012), 45–78.

43. These contradictions were also airbrushed from the highly sanitised book that originated at the same time as the exhibition from the Iranian exile lobby in Washington: *Shakespeare, Persia and the East*, by Cyrus Ghani (Washington, DC: Mage, 2008).

44. George Manwaring, quoted in Blow, *Shah Abbas*, p. 159. For representations of the Sherley brothers in Shakespearean literature, see especially Ton Hoenslaars, 'The Elizabethans and the Turk at Constantinople', in C. C. Barfoot and Theo 'D'Haen (eds), *Oriental Prospects: Western Literature and the Lure of the East* (Amsterdam: Rodopi, 1998), pp. 9–26; and Kate Arthur, 'You will say they are Persian, but let them be changed: Robert and Teresa Sherley's embassy to the court of King James', in Gerald Maclean (ed.), *Britain and the Muslim World: Historical Perspectives* (Newcastle: Cambridge Scholars, 2011), pp. 37–51.

45. Canby, 'Introduction', p. 57.

46. Ibid.

47. Davies, *Elizabethans Errant*, p. 228.

48. Madeleine Bunting, 'Empire of the mind', *Guardian*, 31 January 2009.

49. Blow, *Shah Abbas*, p. 53. See also Matthew Dimmock, *New Turkes: Dramatizing Islam and the Ottomans in Early Modern England* (Aldershot: Ashgate, 2005), pp. 137, 139 and 141; and Sanjay Subrahmanyam, 'The perils of realpolitik', in *Three Ways To Be Alien: Travails and Encounters in the Early Modern World* (Waltham: Brandeis University Press, 2011), pp. 73–132.

50. Blow, *Shah Abbas*, pp. 53–4.

51. Giovanni Mocenigo, Venetian Ambassador in Rome, to the Doge and Senate, 3 October 1609, *Calendar of State Papers Venetian, 1607–10*, XI, p. 361. The cross in Van Dyck's portrait has evidently been painted over at a later date, but it appears in the engraving by Diego de Astor depicting Count Robert's audience with the Pope: reprinted in Davies, *Elizabethans Errant*, p. 227. See *Van Dyck and Britain*, exhibition catalogue, ed. Karen Hearn (London: Tate, 2009), pp. 52–5; Christine Riding, 'The Orientalist portrait', in *The Lure of the East*, exhibiton catalogue (London: Tate, 2008), p. 49; and Aileen Ribeiro, *Fashion and Fiction: Dress in Art and Literature in Stuart England* (New Haven: Yale University Press, 2005), p. 236.

52. William Shakespeare, *Twelfth Night, or What You Will*, ed. Roger Warren and Stanley Wells (Oxford: Oxford University Press, 1994), p. 151.

53. Sir Thomas Shirley, quoted in Davies, *Elizabethans Errant*, p. 72.

54. For the false hopes of Catholic toleration James raised before his succession, see William McElwee, *The Wisest Fool in Christendom* (London: Faber and Faber, 1958), pp. 117–19: 'English Catholics were convinced . . . that James had pledged himself . . . to remit all fines for recusancy and tolerate their worshipping in private. . . . In Ireland it was almost universally believed that the king was himself a Catholic' (p. 118).

55. For James's plan for 'a general Christian union', see W. B. Patterson, *King James VI and I and the Reunion of Christendom* (Cambridge: Cambridge University Press, 1997), pp. 34–43, here p. 36.

56. Blow, *Shah Abbas*, p. 62; Subrahmanyam, 'The perils of realpolitik', p. 97.

57. Philip Caraman, *The Autobiography of an Elizabethan: William Weston* (London: Longmans, 1955), p. 187, n. 2: 'Throughout Elizabeth's reign Hart Hall was a refuge for Catholics. . . . Perhaps for this reason it flourished as did no other College in this reign'; Davies, *Elizabethans Errant*, pp. 5, 135, 167 and 257.

58. 'Premature Jacobeans': Mervyn James, 'At the crossroads of the political culture: the Essex Revolt, 1601', in *Society, Politics and Culture: Studies in Early Modern England* (Cambridge: Cambridge University Press, 1986), p. 426. Essex was 'wont to say that he did not like any man be troubled for his religion': *Calendar of State Papers Domestic*, pp. 649–9.

59. See Richard Wilson, 'Bloody as the hunter: *Twelfth Night* and the French duel', in *Shakespeare and French Theory: King of Shadows* (London: Routledge, 2007), pp. 202–26.

60. Jonathan Bate, *Soul of the Age: The Life, Mind, and World of William Shakespeare* (London: Penguin, 2007), p. 272.

61. Anne Barton, '*As You Like It* and *Twelfth Night*: Shakespeare's sense of an ending', in Malcolm Bradbury and D. J. Palmer (eds), *Stratford-upon-Avon Studies: 14. Shakespearean Comedy* (London: Edward Arnold, 1972), p. 174.

62. Lawrence Stone, *The Crisis of the Aristocracy, 1558–1641* (Oxford: Clarendon Press, 1965), pp. 482–3.

63. For the play's ritual associations with the lights of Twelfth Night and purification of Candlemas, see Chris Hassel, *Renaissance Drama and the Church Year* (Lincoln: University of Nebraska Press, 1979), pp. 77–101.

64. 'But lived where motley': 'Easter 1916'; 'now/That winds of winter': 'Nineteen Hundred and Nineteen', in *The Variorum Edition of the Poems of W. B. Yeats*, pp. 200 and 430.

65. Constance Relihan, 'Erasing the East from *Twelfth Night*', in Joyce Green MacDonald (ed.), *Race, Ethnicity, and Power in the Renaissance* (Madison: Fairleigh Dickinson University Press, 1997), pp. 80–94, here p. 80.

66. Quoted Davies, *Elizabethans Errant*, pp. 113 and 132.

67. Keir Elam, 'Introduction', in *The Arden Shakespeare: Twelfth Night* (London: Cengage Learning, 2008), pp. 42–3.

68. Anne Jones and Peter Stallybrass, *Renaissance Clothing and the Materials of Memory* (Cambridge: Cambridge University Press, 2000), p. 18.

69. Patricia Fumerton, *Cultural Aesthetics: Renaissance Literature and the Practice of Social Ornament* (Chicago: Chicago University Press, 1991), pp. 194–5.

70. Francis Cottington to William Trumbull, 20 December 1609, quoted in Davies, *Elizabethans Errant*, p. 228.

71. Fumerton, *Cultural Aesthetics*, pp. 174–5.

72. Thomas Fuller, *The Worthies of England* (1662), ed. John Nichols, 2 vols (London: 1811), vol. 2, p. 393.

73. Elam, 'Introduction', p. 75.

74. Timothy Billings, 'Caterwauling Cataians: the genealogy of a gloss', *Shakespeare Quarterly*, 54 (2003), 1–28.

75. Richard Marienstras, *New Perspectives on the Shakespearean World*, trans. Janet Lloyd (Cambridge: Cambridge University Press, 1985), p. 6.

76. For the background to this scene, which oddly defeats editors, see Michael Graves, *Thomas Norton: The Parliament Man* (Oxford: Blackwell, 1994), pp. 250–65. Like Malvolio, Norton had the tables turned when he was himself imprisoned in the Bloody Tower: pp. 394–403.

77. The Duke of Sessa to Philip III, 10 April 1601, quoted in Davies, *Elizabethans Errant*, p. 135.

78. Ibid.; Robert Persons to Ralph Eure, 30 April 1601, quoted ibid., pp. 72–3.

79. See David Wiles, *Shakespeare's Clown: Actor and Text in the Elizabethan Playhouse* (Cambridge: Cambridge University Press, 1987), pp. 36–7.

80. The Duke of Sessa to Philip III, 10 April 1601, quoted in Davies, *Elizabethans Errant*, p. 135.

81. Richard Colthurst to John Sanderson, 26 July 1599, quoted ibid., p. 126.

82. *Chronicle of the Carmelites in Persia and the Papal Mission of the XVIIth and XVIIIth Centuries* (London, 1939), I, pp. 143–4; and Alfonso de la Cueva, Spanish ambassador in Venice, to Philip III, 12 March 1608, quoted ibid., pp. 168 and 212.

83. Don Garcia Figueroa, *L'Ambassade de D. Garcia de Silva Figueroa en Perse* (Paris: 1667); and Antoine De Gouvea, *Relation des Grandes Guerres et Victoires par Le Roy Perse Chah Abbas* (Rouen: 1646), quoted in Blow, *Shah Abbas*, pp. 120 and 169.

84. Thomas Herbert, *Travels in Persia, 1627–9* (London: 1928), quoted in Blow, *Shah Abbas*, pp. 166–7.

85. *Chronicle of the Carmelites*, quoted ibid., p. 172.

86. Davies, *Elizabethans Errant*, p. 139.

87. Paul Levy, 'A new look at the old Iran', *Wall Street Journal*, 27 February 2009.

88. Canby, 'Introduction', p. 251; Farah Neyeri, 'Iran's fidgety, cruel Shah Abbas in British Museum show', *Bloomberg News*, 17 February 2009.

89. Neil MacGregor, *Shakespeare's Restless World* (London: Allen Lane and the British Museum, 2012).

90. See T. W. Craik, 'Introduction', in *The Arden Shakespeare: 'Twelfth Night*, ed. J. M. Lothian and T. W. Craik (London: Methuen, 1975), p. 10.

91. Elam, 'Introduction', pp. 57–68, here p. 60; and Keir Elam, 'The fertile eunuch: *Twelfth Night*, early modern intercourse, and the fruits of castration', *Shakespeare Quarterly*, 47

(1996), 1–36. See also John Astington, 'Malvolio and the eunuchs: texts and revels in *Twelfth Night*', *Shakespeare Survey*, 46 (1993), 23–4.

92. Stephen Orgel, *Impersonations: The Performance of Gender in Shakespeare's England* (Cambridge: Cambridge University Press, 1996), pp. 53–7.

93. Relihan, 'Erasing the East from *Twelfth Night*', p. 91.

94. Bruce R. Smith, *Homosexual Desire in Shakespeare's England: A Cultural Poetics* (Chicago: Chicago University Press, 1991), pp. 151–6.

95. Elam, 'Introduction', pp. 73–5; John Boswell, *The Marriage of Likeness: Same-Sex Unions in Pre-Modern Europe* (London: Harper Collins, 1995), pp. 269–70.

96. Louis Crompton, *Byron and Greek Love* (London: Faber and Faber, 1985), pp. 133–9, here p. 137.

97. Orgel, *Impersonations*, pp. 53–4. For Malvolio's humiliation as a 'displaced gelding', see Astington, 'Malvolio and the eunuchs', p. 20.

98. Orgel, *Impersonations*, p. 55.

99. Catherine Belsey, 'Disrupting sexual difference: meaning and gender in the comedies', in John Drakakis (ed.), *Alternative Shakespeares* (London: Methuen, 1985), pp. 166–90, here pp. 180 and 184–5.

100. Gary Taylor, *Castration: An Abbreviated History of Western Manhood* (London: Routledge, 2002), pp. 43 and 116; Roland Barthes, *S/Z*, trans. Richard Miller (New York: Hill and Wang, 1974), p. 36.

101. Slavoj Žižek, *The Ticklish Subject* (London: Verso, 2000), p. 204.

102. Slavoj Žižek, *Violence* (London: Picador, 2008), p. 146.

103. Ibid., p. 152. Original emphasis.

104. Ibid., pp. 152 and 155.

105. Ibid., p. 157; 'Qualified intolerance': Antony Milton, 'A qualified intolerance: the limits and ambiguities of early Stuart anti-Catholicism', in Arthur Marotti (ed.), *Catholicism and Anti-Catholicism in Early Modern English Texts* (Basingstoke: Macmillan, 1999), p. 105.

106. Patterson, *King James VI and I*, p. 220.

107. Robert Weimann, *Author's Pen and Actor's Voice: Playing and Writing in Shakespeare's Theatre* (Cambridge: Cambridge University Press, 2000), ch. 8.

108. H. Neville-Davies, '*Pericles* and the Sherley brothers', in E. A. J. Honigmann (ed.), *Shakespeare and His Contemporaries: Essays in Comparison* (Manchester: Manchester University Press, 1991), pp. 94–113.

109. François Laroque, *Shakespeare's Festive World: Elizabethan Seasonal Entertainment and the Professional Stage* (Cambridge: Cambridge University Press, 1991), pp. 148–50.

110. Slavoj Žižek, 'King, rabble, sex, and war in Hegel', in Jamil Kader and Molly Anne Rothenberg (eds), *Žižek Now: Current Perspectives in Žižek Studies* (Cambridge: Polity Press, 2013), p. 189.

111. See Meg Twycross and Susan Carpenter, *Masks and Masking in Medieval and Tudor England* (Aldershot: Ashgate, 2002), pp. 92–100.

112. Samuel Pepys, *The Diary of Samuel Pepys: IV. 1663* (London: G. Bell, 1971), pp. 5–6.

113. C. J. Sisson, 'Shakespeare Quartos as Prompt-Copies', *Review of English Studies*, 18 (1942), 136–8; and Richard Wilson, *Secret Shakespeare: Studies in theatre, religion and resistance* (Manchester: Manchester University Press, 2004), pp. 271–93.

114. Anon., *The Travels of the Three English Brothers*, in *Three Renaissance Travel Plays*, ed. Anthony Parr (Manchester: Manchester University Press, 1995), p. 131: xiii, 179–80. See also Anthony Parr, 'Foreign relations in Jacobean England: the Sherley brothers and the "Voyage of Persia"', in Jean-Pierre Macquerlot and Michèle Willems (eds), *Travel and Drama in Shakespeare's Time* (Cambridge: Cambridge University Press, 1996), pp. 14–31.

115. Thomas Middleton, 'Sir Robert Sherley, his entertainment in Cracovia', ed. Jerzy Limon and Daniel Vitkus, in *Thomas Middleton: The Collected Works*, ed. Gary Taylor and John

Lavagnino, 2 vols (Oxford: Clarendon Press, 2007), vol. 2, pp. 674–5: ll. 89–90 and 230–41. For the context, see Chloe Houston, 'Turning Persian: the prospect of conversion in Safavid Iran', in H. Hendrix, T. Richardson and L Stelling (eds), *The Turn of the Soul: Representations of Religious Conversion in Early Modern Art and Literature* (Leiden: Brill, 2011), pp. 85–108.

116. Robert Sherley to Sir Anthony Sherley, 1605, quoted in Davies, *Elizabethans Errant*, p. 169.
117. Žižek, *Violence*, p. 146.
118. Anthony Arlidge, *Shakespeare and the Prince of Love: The Feast of Misrule in the Middle Temple* (London: Giles de la Mare, 2000), pp. 56–8 and 114 et passim.
119. Edward Said, *Orientalism: Western Conceptions of the Orient* (Harmondsworth: Penguin, 1985), p. 71.
120. Davies, *Elizabethans Errant*, p. 123.

8 Like an Olympian Wrestling: Shakespeare's Olympic Game

THIS SHORT-GRASSED GREEN

The opening ceremony of the 2012 Olympic Games began on the evening of Friday 1 June with a massed choir singing 'Songs of Welcome' by folk artist Eliza Carthy, based on traditional English melodies but also inspired, it was stated, by 'the values of the modern Olympic and Paralympic movements', before the spectacular entry of an actor dressed in historic royal costume. Courtesy of the Palace, the gimmick of representing the sovereign as a good sport was doubtless intended to symbolise the hopeful inclusiveness celebrated in Carthy's signature refrains, 'We're all together again, singing all together again', and 'I wish that the wars were all over'. In fact, as Leah Marcus has pointed out, King James originally gave permission for this mimicry, and donated his 'Hat and Feather and Ruff' to his impersonator, 'purposely to grace him and consequently the solemnity', as part of the patriarchal 'politics of mirth', the calculated campaign to co-opt traditional holiday pastimes to 'the symbolic language of Stuart power'.[1] 'A substitute shines brightly as a king' [*Merchant*, 5,1,101], however; and as Shakespeareans know, seventeenth-century English sovereigns started something they could not easily control when they played with 'the cease of majesty' [*Hamlet*, 3,3,15] by allowing their regalia to be used in sport.

The merry monarch who inaugurated the Midsummer Games of 2012 wore a get-up more in keeping with Shakespeare's Globe than any sporting fixture, because this was, of course, not London 2012, into which Queen Elizabeth II was represented leaping by a parachutist wearing her signature pink dress, but the Cotswold Olympics, founded in 1612, on the site of much older summer rites at Chipping Campden in Gloucestershire, by the lawyer Robert Dover, whose friend the courtier Endymion Porter arranged for him to preside over these Games of wrestling, stick-fighting, pole-vaulting, leap-frogging, javelin-throwing, jumping, hammer-tossing, gymnastics, and shin-kicking, as well as hunting, horse- and greyhound-racing, dicing, dancing, chess (for the gentry), and drinking, in front of a toy mock-up of Dover Castle, in the royal clothes. Previously the Whitsun wake took place there, Michael Drayton recorded in his 1622 poem *Polyolbion*, under the lead of a 'Shepherd King', whose flock had 'chanc'd that year the earliest lamb to bring'.[2] London 2012 had proudly cited its Jacobean precursor, however, in its bid to host the Games, and commenced on 27 July with the actor Kenneth Branagh, posed as the King of Engineers, Isambard Kingdom Brunel, reciting lines from *The Tempest*, a play exactly contemporary with Dover's Games, that were clearly meant to signal the same pastoral message about 'this green land' [*Tempest*, 4,1,143], that 'on this grass plot, in this very place' [69], there was for this special time nothing of which to be afraid:

Be not afeard; the isle is full of noises,
Sounds and sweet airs, that give delight and hurt not.

[3,2,134–5]

What frightened London's panoptic Olympic organisation, LOCOG, was the threat of an Islamist terrorist attack. But by winding the athletes' parade around one of the 'turfy mountains', complete with maypoles and 'nibbling sheep' [69], mentioned in Prospero's masque, a 'wanton green' like those into which the ancient Britons had supposedly cut 'the quaint mazes' that by Shakespeare's day were already said 'for lack of tread' to be 'indistinguishable' and 'filled with mud' [*Dream*, 2,1,98–9], the director Danny Boyle led his two billion TV audience a merry dance, to which Fox News was unable to provide a clue. So the outrage of the right-wing media was provoked as much by bemusement at its initiation into the semiotic labyrinth of 'this short-grassed green' [*Tempest*, 4,1,90] as by the subsequent pageant of Britain's National Health. Yet, 'How does your fallow greyhound, sir?' Shakespeare's Slender needles Page, 'I heard say he was outrun on Cotswold' [*Wives*, 1,1,72], prompting enthusiasts to cite the Bard himself as an eyewitness to the importance of the events on Dover's Hill.[3] The 'hilltop of Sports and Merriments', one of the wags calls the site of 'Dover's Olympicks' in Richard Brome's *A Jovial Crew*.[4] And sports historians do, in fact, trace the modern Olympics in part to a visit paid in 1890 by their instigator, the French Baron Pierre de Coubertin, to the Wenlock Hills in Shropshire, where for forty years Dr William Penny Brookes convened an athletics festival inspired by the ancient Greek Olympics that took off from Dover's Games.[5]

Official Olympic history might prefer the heroics admired by the French aristocrat in the proto-fascism of Thomas Arnold's Rugby School, but by setting London's 'Olympic village' down upon the hallowed turf of a 'nine-men's Morris' [*Dream*, 2,1,98], in the timeless springtime of an actual English village green, then planting the nations' flags on Fortune's 'high and pleasant hill' [*Timon*, 1,1,74], Boyle looked to be idealising a disarmingly alternative genealogy, and a bucolic rather than heroic sporting culture that had lingered on Dover's Hill until 1851, when, having become a 'trysting place of the lowest scum of the population which lived between Birmingham and Oxford', the Cotswold Games were officially suppressed.[6] The director had done his homework, for historian David Underdown has indeed correlated the English Civil War with a fault-line running through these parts, between the chalk country that played the bloody melée of football, and rallied to the King, and the cheese country, which preferred more mediated bat-and-ball

games such as cricket, and sided with Parliament.[7] By hurling Her Majesty's lookalike into the air at the start, and then ending the Paralympic revels on 2 September
with the Shakespearean knight Sir Ian McKellen as an abdicating Prospero, London
2012 thus appeared to be nodding not only to those summer kings who wore the
monarch's clothes, but to a vision Shakespeare also worked into *The Tempest*, of an
island unperturbed by power, a pastoral place in a utopian time with 'no sovereignty'
[2,1,160]:[8]

> Had I a plantation of this isle . . .
> In the commonwealth I would by contraries
> Execute all things; for no kind of traffic
> Would I admit; no name of magistrate.
>
> [*Tempest*, 2,1,146–53]

Gonzalo's dream of an isle exempt from sovereignty is shot down by the cynics
with brutal logic: 'No sovereignty. Yet he would be king on't' [148]. Sovereign is he
who decides the exception, however.[9] So when the self-mocking Queen 'welcomed
all, served all' [*Winter's*, 4,1,7] at the Olympic feast, she exemplified one of the
contortions inherent in the Olympic ideal which Boyle struggled to negotiate: that,
as Steven Connor observed in a timely sprint through the philosophy of sport, the
exception of sport is set off from the sovereign decision 'by an act of pure decision,
by the simple decision to mark out a space in which to decide' the game on its own
terms.[10] For in contrast to the immemorial festive world of the 'Shepherd King',
which François Laroque has shown to have been deeply integrated into both profane
and sacred calendars, sport 'comes into being in the antagonism between absolute
and immanent time', and is always governed by the desire 'to take the time to which
one is subject and convert it into a time of which one is the subject', an ambition
that saw its mad apogee in the timeless test-matches of pre-war cricket.[11] It is this
transcendence of real time that makes sport more than a pastime, Connor proposes.
But what renders the Olympic concept truly exceptional, ever since Hercules, legendary founder of the Olympics, was said to have enforced the Sacred Truce, the
ekecheiria or 'staying of hands', for an interregnum of sixteen days, is the invocation
of sovereignty to suspend sovereignty, and so to subsume absolute time to play time
absolutely, for the time of the Games.[12]

'Who durst assemble such a Troop as he', wondered one of Dover's admirers, 'But
might of insurrection charged be?'[13] In fact, the 'Cotswold Hercules' said he could
not recall where he got his idea of reviving the Olympics: 'Nor can I give account to
you at all,/How this conceit into my brain did fall'.[14] So it is not surprising that the
contributors to *Annalia Dubrensia*, his 1636 Festschrift, were divided as to whether
his politics amounted to subversion, encouraging shepherds to rise against the
'bad owners of enclosed grounds', or containment, bowing 'To's King'.[15] Nor that
Dover's encomiasts were confused over whether his plan was to rehabilitate 'country
Wakes', the 'Palm and rush-bearing, harmless Whitsun ales' of Old England, or
introduce the Olympic spirit of the sporting festival as a transcendent event, in
which case, someone predicted, 'those two days of thine will (perhaps) stir/Some

Saints to wrath, cut out of the Calendar'.[16] Dover's modern editor, Christopher Whitfield, calls the Cotswold Games 'a little local makeweight put in on the side of compromise' in religion; yet Phebe Jensen is surely right to infer that the effect of the *Annalia* was to insulate sport from the contentiousness of religion altogether, 'by implying that English festivity originated not with the medieval church, but Grecian sports'.[17] In his *Sport, Politics and Literature in the English Renaissance*, Gregory Semenza goes further: 'the invention of sport' in this poets' symposium, itself a panegyric competition, was also the inception of a liberal society with an autonomous aesthetic.[18] Dover's jostling cheerleaders concurred, affirming that his ulterior purpose in assembling 'Such multitudes' from so many classes, conditions and confessions, in this 'Great Instauration' of the Games, was precisely 'to advance true love and neighbourhood', as Ben Jonson toasted, in a zone of innocent neutrality:

> His Soldiers, though they every one dissent
> In minds, in manners, yet his Merriment
> Ones them: Lords, Knights, Swains, Shepherds, Churls, agree,
> To crown his sports, Discords make Harmony.[19]

FLORAL WARS

New Historicists insist that while Renaissance writers like Sir John Harington recognise play as a defining human activity, 'whose only end is delight of the mind or the spirit', they ground their defence of sport in the prerogative of the gentleman, rather than any Kantian disinterestedness.[20] And to be sure, Dover's Olympics were as much a rich man's club as our own so-called Olympic 'family'. Yet read against the backdrop of the Wars of Religion, *Annalia Dubrensia* amounts to a universalist manifesto in which Gloucestershire's Olympic Committee legislates the rules of the game of neutralisation a century and a half before an affectless Kantian aesthetic issued in the Enlightenment project of perpetual peace. For Dover's Games would indeed be applauded by Shakespeare's Stratford relation John Trussell (author of a poem on Helen) as a universal truce, when 'scorn/And pride' were 'wholly at that time forborne', as contestants strove 'to excel. . . . In love and courtesy'. 'For though . . . thy sports most man-like bee,/Yet they are linked with peace and modestie', attested another of the poets: 'Here all in th'one and self-same sphere do move,/Nor strive so much to win by force as love'.[21] So on Dover's Hill, according to this moralising, a different ethic of sportsmanship to that of the country meets of old was emerging, which affirmed that what mattered was not the win or loss, but how the game was played:

> . . . where men meet not for delight,
> So much as for delight to meete,
> And where, to make their pastime right,
> They make it not so great, as sweete;
> Where love doth more than gain invite,
> Hands part at last as first they grete,

And loosers none, where all that's plaid,
With friendship won, may not be weighed.[22]

'The Pythian, Grecian, and the Trojan plays/Are hardly match to those that thou dost raise', affirmed Dover's cousin John Stratford, for 'Thy sports are merely harmless'. Thus, they would teach 'each man how to master passion', sermonised the lawyer Sir William Denny. Likewise, Michael Drayton enthused how the Cotswold Games restored 'The golden Age's glories. . . . As those brave Grecians in their happy dayes/On Mount Olympus. . . . Where then their able Youth Leapt, Wrestled, Ran', purely 'for the garland'.[23] It cannot be coincidence, then, that so many of Dover's reconcilers were Catholics, nor that he had himself trained with the Jesuits in the 'concentration camp for Catholics' at Wisbech Castle in Norfolk.[24] For these Pindarics extol his Games as a template for exactly the kind of 'Westphalian' system of coexistence that would, during the seventeenth century, displace the passions of sectarian conflict into what Carl Schmitt contemptuously termed a *theatre* of war: a war in form, whereby 'war became analogous to a duel, a conflict of arms between *personae morales* who contended on the basis of the *jus publicum Europaeum*'. The Cotswold project was indeed typical of all those 'masonic lodges, conventicles, synagogues, and literary circles' Schmitt blamed for sabotaging Hobbes's leviathan state with a myth of power as 'a plant, a growing tree, or even a flower', which 'left nothing to remind people of a "huge man"', and whose pacifism he identified not only with 'the restless spirit of the Jew' but also 'the humanist-rational superiority' of Shakespeare's Prospero:[25]

> The Grecians next (a nation of great fame)
> To stout Alcydes make the Olympic game,
> Which Games each lustrum they with great expense
> Perform'd with state, and true Magnificence.
> Mycenae, and Argos, and prow'd Sparta hight,
> From thence each Spriteful Lord and Active Knight
> Went up Olympus Mountain Top, to try
> Who in their Games could win the Victory.
> Wrestling, Running, Leaping, were games of Prize,
> Coursing with Chariots, a prime exercise.
> Contention there, with Poets and Musicians,
> Great emulation amongst the Rhetoricians;
> And crown'd with garland from the Olive Tree
> He was, in those Games, that won the Victory;
> And to those Games came Nations far and nigh. . .
> But when those noble games the Grecians left, they fly,
> To ease, to Lust, from Lust to Luxury.
> Then stepp'd the Soldier in, with Conquering Blade,
> And in a moment of Greece Conquest made.[26]

It is the Catholicism of Dover's Olympians that exposes his disingenuousness in disclaiming any intellectual source. For the very first Renaissance study of the

Olympic Games had recently been produced in an analogous culture of Christian humanism, with an identical subtext of ecumenical *détente*. Modern sports specialists are thrown by the 'muscular Catholicism' of the *Agonisticon*, published in 1592 by another French aristocrat, Pierre du Faur, or Petrus Faber, and describe its 360 pages of Latin as 'disorganized, repetitive, and unclear'.[27] But du Faur's attempt to align gymnastics with Carlo Borromeo's spiritual exercises, and his moralisation of the ancient Olympics as the foundation for a European peace, become intelligible within the Erasmian and Platonising networks of the French Academies in which he moved, where, as Frances Yates recounted, the programme of rationed toleration that would be sealed in the Edict of Nantes was thrashed out by the moderate Catholic 'politique' party to which most Academicians belonged.[28] Born in 1550 in Toulouse, and President of its Parliament, du Faur was in fact a leading light of the world's oldest surviving literary society, the city's august Académie des Jeux Floraux. So, if the modern Olympics have any single taproot, it is in the Floral Games played since 1323 by the troubadours of the Languedoc, in which flowers are awarded to the champions of the variegated literary forms, du Faur himself winning the junior prize of a carnation in 1572. For as chancellor of this so-called 'gay science', the pink champion wrote his treatise on the Olympics, he stated in its dedication, in order to continue these floral wars by other means:

> I started this my *Agonisticon* a year ago, when the law had fallen silent in a city that had given itself over to war, and I had retired to my small estate on the outskirts, where I could not sit idly by on the side-lines, however, without using my experience to aid my fellow citizens.[29]

'In all our games', rejoiced one of du Faur's Academicians, 'the fighting spirit of the Greeks is revived. Since fame is our only ambition, we do not aspire to win a crown, but limit ourselves to flowers'.[30] Thus, centuries before Jacob Burckhardt attributed Greek civilisation to the 'agonistic spirit' of athletics, but in their fatigue with the Wars of Religion, these Renaissance Games-makers had evolved the Neo-Platonic notion of competitive sport as a demonstration that, since 'Discords make harmony', religious pluralism could produce a complementary coincidence of opposites. Henceforth, sport would consume man's 'conflicts, joys, and agonies', as Roland Barthes put it, 'without ever letting anything be destroyed'.[31] Rather than modern liberal pluralism, what the civic humanism of these Catholic Olympic gamesmen seems, in fact, to have prefigured is the 'agonistic pluralism' advocated by Schmitt-inspired thinkers of our own time, like Chantal Mouffe, whereby the precondition of a democratic politics becomes not the elimination of conflict and division, but their legitimation, in a system that renounces the illusion that we can ever free ourselves from force and violence, and seeks instead to transform enemies into adversaries, or *antagonism* precisely into *agonism*:

> This requires providing channels through which collective passions will be given ways to express themselves over issues that, while allowing enough possibility for identification, will not construct the opponent as an enemy but as an

adversary. An important difference with the model of 'deliberative democracy' is that for 'agonistic pluralism', the prime task of democratic politics is not to eliminate passions from the sphere of the public, in order to render a rational consensus possible, but to mobilize those passions to democratic designs.[32]

Modern political theorists who advocate 'agonistic pluralism' as a means to acknowledge the tension between the opposing constitutive elements of a multi-confessional and multicultural society, and to harness its violence in productive ways, help us to understand how appealing a programme like du Faur's Olympic Games might have been to Elizabethan Catholics. Dover probably studied the *Agonisticon* during his Wisbech internment. But it seems unlikely, in any case, that he and his English *Pléiade* were unfamiliar with this *politique* Olympianism, as they confabulated on how 'These Cotswold to th'Olympicke Games compare', considering how Shakespeare caught its cult of agonistic strife so accurately in the 'little academe' of Navarre in *Love's Labour's Lost*, where fame is the spur to a war waged not against enemies, but 'the huge army of the world's desires' [1,1,1–15], and similarly sublimated in the *Discordia concors* of 'Very reverend sport' [4,2,1].[33] The Bard knew as well as Samuel Beckett the importance of 'a very good bowler' [5,1,100]. And whether or not the Cotswold Olympians had read the French tome, their fellow West Midlander certainly associated the glory that was Greece with the ethical turn the *Agonisticon* described, when the Grecian 'Soldier with Conquering Blade' returned from the wars to institute an age of peace and toleration in the garlanded *agôn* of the playing field, as Theseus, having slain the Minotaur and renounced his kingship in favour of democracy, was said to have founded the Isthmian Games 'In glory of [his] kinsman Hercules' [*Dream*, 5,1,47]:

> Go, Philostrate,
> Stir up the Athenian youth to merriments,
> Awake the pert and nimble spirit of mirth. . .
> Hyppolita, I wooed thee with me my sword,
> But I will wed thee in another key,
> With pomp, with triumph, and with revelling.
>
> [1,1,12–19]

In *A Midsummer Night's Dream* the Queen of the Fairies complains to the King that 'never, since the middle summer's spring,/Met we on hill, in dale, forest or mead. . . . But with thy brawls thou hast disturb'd our sport' [2,1,81–7]; yet in Athens the Duke hangs up his sword in a gesture that annuls such sovereign spoil-sporting in the spirit of the Grecian Games. Editors warn us that whenever Shakespeare uses the term 'sport' it is in the earlier sense of the freakish or gratuitous act, the animal instinct to play that Roger Caillois distinguished from *ludus*, the regulation of rule-bound games, and that Gloucester seems to associate with the sadism of the Roman circus when he bewails that 'As flies to wanton boys are we to the gods:/They kill us for their sport' [*Lear*, 4,1,36]. So when in 1588 Montaigne mused that if I play with my cat, 'how do I know she is not playing with me?', he was reflecting an urgent new anxiety in the humanist mind about the danger to the aesthetic realm of that amoral and arbitrary *playfulness* that Marlowe, by contrast, perversely relished when he dreamed of classical life as one long orgy of 'heady riots, incests, rapes'.[34] Of course, Andreas Höfele has recently reminded us how difficult even Shakespeare found it to separate 'fencing, dancing, and bearbaiting' [*Twelfth*, 1,3,86], or indeed theatre itself, from aristocratic blood sports such as hunting, 'the sport of kings', in which the game of killing game is a 'playing with life – a playing with forces that might otherwise make you their plaything'.[35] So the stakes, in every sense, could not be higher as these plays turn persistently to a Greece where modernity is being defined as a paradigm shift from the tragic necessity of such sacrifice, through the proclamation of something approaching the agonistic give-and-take of the 'Olympic Game', and an Olympianism that Shakespeare can even imagine, like Dover's poets, relocated to the English Midlands, in his case, to the Warwickshire Forest of Arden:

> ROSALIND (*to* ORLANDO): Now Hercules be thy speed, young man!
> CELIA: I would I were invisible, to catch the strong fellow by the leg.
> [CHARLES and ORLANDO] *wrestle*
> ROSALIND: O excellent young man!
> CELIA: If I had a thunderbolt in mine eye, I could tell who should down.
> [ORLANDO throws CHARLES] *Shout*
> DUKE FREDERICK: No more, no more.
> [*As You*, 1,2,175–81]

FOOL'S PLAY

Clifford Leech long ago noticed how Greek settings 'gave Shakespeare special liberty' and that 'he felt curiously free' when he sailed in his imagination to 'these golden shores' [*Wives*, 1,4,70], as if he liked to believe that because 'we came into this world together' we could still go 'hand in hand' [*Comedy*, 5,1,426–7] and again 'think ourselves for ever perfect' [*Timon*, 1,2,82], as Timon imagines, for all the flaws of that 'imperfect man', the Athenian 'who dreamt of human brotherhood'.[36] So when the Trojan champion Hector fights Greek Ajax in Shakespeare's version of the Troy story, and the entire war is displaced onto a match to test which of them is most like Pythagoras's son-in-law, the 'Bull-bearing Milo' [3,1,233] of Croton, a six-time Olympic wrestling champion, and five-time winner of the grand slam of all four panhellenic Games, it is what Achilles derisively calls 'A maiden battle' [4,6,89] without blood.[37] The 'order of the field' is that referees must decide if 'the knights/Shall to the edge of all extremity/Pursue each other, or be divided' [68–9]: 'either to the uttermost/Or else a breath'. But as King Agamemnon smiles, 'The combatants being kin/Half stints their strife before their strokes begin' [92–3]; and the flexing musclemen are no sooner in action than the umpires stop the fight, to finish it 'As Hector pleases' [4,7,3]. This interruption is so abrupt the Oxford editor,

Gary Taylor, splits the scene in two to allow the bruisers to continue '*fighting*', as they do in Chapman's 1598 *Iliad*, until 'out gusht the blood'.[38] But that seems a misreading. For what is truly at stake here is the question on which both *Troilus and Cressida* and the Olympic movement turn, and that Homer gave to a war-weary Achilles at the end of his poem, of whether 'strife' can ever be 'stinted' 'among the men and gods'.[39]

As Shakespeare's most sustained imaginative engagement with the Greeks and their Games, *Troilus and Cressida* stages Schmitt's observation in his book *Hamlet or Hecuba* that while 'children and frisky cats play with special intensity, delighting in the fact that they do not play according to fixed rules but in perfect freedom', there is in 'the rules of the game . . . a fundamental negation of the critical situation': the 'unplayability' (*Unverspielbarkeit*) of the tragic 'ends where such play begins'.[40] So it is no wonder that Aeneas nudges the two joshing jocks that 'There is expectation here from both sides / What further you will do' [30–1]; or that Hector explains to his opponent that the reason why 'I will no more' is that 'The obligation of our blood forbids / A gory emulation 'twixt us twain . . . the just gods gainsay / That any drop thou borrowed'st from thy mother, / My sacred aunt, should by my mortal sword be drained' [6–19]. Achilles had joked about the sweaty amorousness of this match, confessing his 'woman's longing. . . To see great Hector in his weeds of peace' [3,3,230–2]; and it is because Ajax is 'A cousin-german to great Priam's seed' [4,7,5] that 'The issue is embracement' [32] all round, so this war can be a *civil* one in every sense. But it is old Nestor, famed for the garrulousness of his own 'stretched-out life' [1,3,61], who recalls that this is how Hector has always operated, since 'the order of their fight' [4,6,93] permits these 'huge men' to 'stint' their 'strife' by treating their encounters as bloodless and unheroic extensions of the Olympic Games:

> I have, thou gallant Trojan, seen thee oft,
> Labouring for destiny, make cruel way
> Through ranks of Greekish youth, and I have seen thee
> As hot as Perseus spur thy Phrygian steed,
> And seen their scorning forfeits and subduements,
> When thou hast hung th'advancèd sword i'th'air,
> Not letting it decline on the declined,
> That I have said to some my standers-by,
> 'Lo, Jupiter is yonder, dealing life!'
> And I have seen thee pause and take thy breath,
> When that a ring of Greeks have hemmed thee in,
> Like an Olympian, wrestling.
>
> [4,7,67–78]

Nestor's anachronistic memory of Hector halting amid Greeks with 'high blood chafed' [Pro.,2], to take breath like the great Olympic wrestler Milo, is prefigured in *Henry VI, Part 3*, when Clarence promises his troops 'such rewards / As victors wear at the Olympian games' [2,3,52]. Semenza considers that warfare is 'stinted' into chivalric 'sport royal' in all Shakespeare's Histories.[41] What we glimpse in this locker-room posturing is something newer, however, that implicitly anticipates the disarmament Schmitt dreaded in all such schemes for a Christian Union or United Nations. For in Shakespeare's Olympics sport is already what George Orwell called it: a mock 'war without the bullets'.[42] So, whether or not the Bard ever frequented them personally, what Dover's classicised Cotswold Games provide is a discursive context for the humanist ideal to which *Troilus and Cressida* keeps returning: of Hector's Olympian pause as a literal *breathing space*, a life-dealing amnesty or moratorium from the deadliness of armed struggle, when 'during all question of the gentle truce' [4,1,13] sectarian 'strife' is sublimated into the godlike mutuality of live-and-let-live, an evacuation of pathos of the kind that Johann Huizinga maintained always underpins the rules of the game. Anthropologists now consider Huizinga's notion of *Homo ludens* to be founded on an untenable distinction between play and reality, seriousness and sport; but in this drama that puts the grace of the 'Olympian' ideal under such pressure, it is what inspires the two parliaments of Shakespeare's Greeks and Trojans to dream of the internationalised zone of 'free play' as their soothing substitute for the murderous 'unplayability' of a tragic war:

> standing quite consciously outside 'ordinary' life as being 'not serious,' but at the same time absorbing the player intensely and utterly. It is an activity connected with no material interest, and no profit can be gained by it. It proceeds within its own boundary of time and space in an orderly manner and according to fixed rules.[43]

Since our knowledge of the Olympic truce comes largely from reports of its breach, classicists doubt the *ekecheiria* was as universal as modern Olympians think; and Schmitt, whose concept of *total war* as *Ernstfall*, or 'serious event', was developed partly in killjoy opposition to Huizinga's notion of warfare as a kind of game, even cited Pindar for the realpolitik that the victor will be the one who cheats or violates the peace.[44] But the first lines of Shakespeare's drama suspend the action inside the 'fair play' of just such an unsovereign-like demobilisation, when Troilus commands: 'Call here my varlet. I'll unarm again./Why should I war without the walls of Troy/That find such cruel battle here within' [1,1,1–3]. Editors of *Troilus and Cressida* are stumped by the inconsistency of this 'dull and long-continued truce' [1,3,259], with its constant 'news from the field' and the 'war without the walls' [1,1,2; 104]. The preening parade of 'the flowers of Troy' as they are 'coming from the field' [1,2,164–71] is at odds with reports that in the stalemate they are 'resty grown' [1,3,260]. Yet Dover's Olympians show how early modern readers could appreciate ancient civilisation as a permanent *ludus* of such 'pale and bloodless emulation' [134]. What seems to trouble the dramatist, however, as it did Montaigne, is the tension between the level playing field of this rule-bound agonistic contest and the daylight robbery of chance, as his 'armed' Prologue [Pro.,23] ominously sets the scene for 'sport abroad' [1,1,111] by relating how 'expectation, tickling skittish spirits/On one and other side, Trojan and Greek,/Sets all on hazard', in the aleatoric capriciousness of a throw of dice: 'Like or find fault; do as your pleasures are;/Now good or bad, 'tis but the chance of war' [Pro.,20–31]. So there is wishful thinking when Aeneas says the reason for 'the gentle truce' [4,1,13] is that this 'sportful combat', in which so much 'opinion dwells' [1,3,329–30], is precisely *not* to be a life-or-death struggle, but rather a friendly fixture the home team is just itching to play: 'Hark, what good sport is out of town today . . . But to the sport abroad' [1,1,109–11].

Play and sport are neglected topics in current Shakespeare studies.[45] Yet what must have intrigued the dramatist in his source is how Chaucer's *Troilus and Criseyde* performs its own game theory by constantly alluding to sporting events, like the 'queynte pley' in 'tyme/Of Aperil', when despite the siege Trojans insist 'Palladiones feste for to holde'.[46] For throughout Shakespeare's drama, its characters struggle to hold a similar line between cruel chance and competitive sport, *alea* and *agôn*, as we are told how 'Hector in his blaze of wrath subscribes/To tender objects' [4,6,108–9]; or that Diomedes will 'let Aeneas live,/If to [his] sword his fate be not [his] glory' [4,1,26].[47] As on Dover's Olympic hill, the 'Contention' of 'the Soldier with Conquering blade' can be appeased so long as the lethal passion of 'gory emulation' is subsumed into the innocuous agonistics of a 'pale and bloodless' sport. Thus, according to Troilus, even those elemental enemies 'The seas and winds, old wranglers, took a truce' to assist Paris to 'do some vengeance on the Greeks', supposing the rape of Helen to be yet another playful charade, when 'for an old aunt whom the Greeks held captive/He brought a Grecian queen' [2,2,72–8]. But if this war is one long siesta, the impatient stripling jeers, 'Let's shut our gates and sleep' [46]. Instead, he prides himself that he 'cannot sing,/Nor heel the high lavolt . . . Nor play at subtle games' [4,5,86–8]. For as he portentously lectures his brother Hector, merely to 'play the hunter' [4,1,19] in this trivialising way, with sword suspended in a perpetual amnesty, 'Not letting it decline on the declined', may be sportsmanlike, but such an unsovereignly and passionless 'vein of chivalry' [5,3,31] can never distinguish friend from foe, nor who is truly 'for Hector's match' [5,4,23]:

TROILUS: Brother, you have a trick of mercy in you,
　　　　　Which better fits a lion than a man . . .
　　　　　When many times the captive Grecian falls,
　　　　　Even in the fan and wind of your fair sword,
　　　　　You bid them rise and live.
HECTOR: O, 'tis fair play.
TROILUS: Fool's play, by heaven, Hector . . .
　　　　　　　For th'love of all the gods,
　　　　　Let's leave the hermit Pity with our mothers,
　　　　　And when we have our armours buckled on,
　　　　　The venomed vengeance ride upon our swords,
　　　　　Spur them to ruthful work, rein them from ruth.
HECTOR: Fie, savage, fie!
TROILUS: Hector, then, 'tis war.

[5,3,37–49]

FUNERAL GAMES

If the phenomenon of Renaissance pacifism that crystallised around 1600 in the Olympic revival 'is neither an anachronistic concept nor an ephemeral aberration', it is *Troilus and Cressida*, Stephen Marx has noted, that marks the turning point in Shakespeare's thinking, as he 'mounts an attack on classical war heroes and on the very arguments for going to war he had supported earlier'.[48] For here he pits the disarmament of the Olympic idea against the blood and guts of Chapman's *Iliad*, as he toys with the game when 'fair play' lets peace catch breath, and allows the mimicry of war to blunt the 'edge of steel', as if 'The time of universal peace' promised by Tudor and Stuart propagandists is truly 'near' [*Antony*, 4,6,4]. The equilibrium of this 'good sport' is in itself nothing new, for, as Kiernan Ryan remarks, these plays are full of footloose warriors *killing time*: demobbed veterans 'spinning things out, keeping this breathing space open and holding time at bay'.[49] But what the universalism of the contemporary Olympic movement gave the author of *Hamlet*, it seems, was a cue to conceive an anti-tragic work in which *the entire history of the world* would be stalled 'in the fan and wind' of a tied 'time of pause' [4,5,34], 'this extant moment' [4,7,53] of deadlocked gamesmanship amid the anarchic destructiveness of 'pelting wars' [4,7,151], presided over by a 'honey-sweet queen' [3,1,131] of 'I spy' [3,1,86], the interminable and pointless nursery game of deliberate displaced mimetic desire, Helen herself.[50] Tragedy is Freud's '*fort/da* game for grown-ups', Catherine Bates has brilliantly suggested.[51] Yet by endlessly toying with the question of whether 'to keep Helen still', or 'To have her back returned' [2,2,185–90], it is as though Shakespeare's ancients have extended the whole of human history into an anti-tragic version of the *fort/da* game, in which the infantile illusion of cheating death through repetition is perpetually sustained:

> Sweet Helen, I must woo you
> To help unarm our Hector. His stubborn buckles,
> With these your white enchanting fingers touched,
> Shall more obey than to the edge of steel
> Or force of Greekish sinews. You shall do more
> Than all the island kings: disarm great Hector.
>
> [3,1,138–45]

Shakespeare is always fascinated by the playhouse as a place to catch breath, and by performance as an inspirational 'breathing time' [*Hamlet*, 5,2,156], a means to 'eat the air, promise crammed' [3,2,92], in which players and playgoers are recharged by 'the animating and generative force of breath'.[52] By inserting so many speechless 'periods in the midst of sentences' [*Dream*, 5,1,96], this 'master of ellipsis' appears to be experimenting with something like 'the queer art of failure' Judith Halberstam has identified on the faces of Olympic *losers*, the paradox implicit in Danny Boyle's anti-triumphalism, that 'all our failures combined might just be enough to bring the winner down'.[53] If 'seeing the world as an aesthetic phenomenon' is one definition of camp, in Susan Sontag's famous formulation, then in its perverse undoing of male striving for paramountcy *Troilus and Cressida* might even be considered the original 'campy' work of art.[54] What marks its 'stretched out' *détournement*, however, is that here these poetics of unsuccess succeed so well that, like one of those sporting fixtures that absorb time into themselves by ineluctably generating a timed-out draw, 'After seven years siege' [*Troilus*, 1,3,11], 'Yet Troy walls stand', as if 'The wise and fool, the artist and unread,/The hard and soft seem all affined and kin' [1,3,12;24–5]. In this tragicomedy, written, editors think, during the inactive interregnum between two dynasties, 'policy' has displaced war, but not without being subjected to the scathing contempt of who those who 'Forestall prescience and esteem no act/But that of hand' [199–200]. For this neutralising of distinctions between friend and enemy, 'when degree is shaked' [101] by the anodyne power of weakness, the impasse Caillois terms a 'convulsion of simulation', and René Girard an epidemic of 'undifferentiation', is analysed within the drama itself with a rigour that anticipates Schmitt's acid critique of parliamentarianism in *The Concept of the Political*, when the arch-politician Ulysses winces that 'when degree is shak'd . . . right and wrong,/Between whose endless jar justice resides . . . lose their names, and so should justice too' [110–18]:[55]

> A world in which the possibility of war is utterly eliminated, a completely paci-fied globe, would be a world without the distinction between friend and enemy, and hence a world without politics. It is conceivable that such a world would contain many very interesting antitheses and contrasts, competitions and intrigues of every kind, but there would be no meaningful antithesis whereby men could be required to sacrifice life, authorized to shed blood, and kill other human beings.[56]

Arrested 'in pause' [*Hamlet*, 3,3,42], during the hiatus of indecision between the end of the Tudor century and the arrival of the Stuarts, which was also the time of the Globe, 'something new' emerges in Shakespeare, according to the critics, a mental crisis about performance, as the author weighs up what happens when the actor loses the plot: the seizing up of mental operations before the order to do something 'dreadful' which Brutus first invokes, when he reflects on how 'Between the acting of a dreadful thing/And the first motion, all the interim is/Like a phantasma' [*Julius*, 2,1,63–5]. This seizure was the distantiation and delay of Hamletian interiority that persuaded even Schmitt 'to acknowledge (more or less unwillingly) the irreducibility of the play *as play*'.[57] But in *Troilus and Cressida* we hear that the men of action call the endless *attentisme* of this brinkmanship 'bed-work', 'mapp'ry', 'closet war' [205]; and the neutrality concept it instantiates is indeed personified by a veritable *Homo ludens*, who promises with his queer art of substitution a per-petual block on all existential decision-making. Like the Kantian philosopher Ernst Cassirer in the famous debate at Davos with the Nazi Martin Heidegger, Pandarus looks always to language to find 'common ground'.[58] A deconstructive figure of Derridean indeterminacy, like the assimilated Jew Schmitt despised, Cressida's uncle is therefore a kind-hearted fool 'who wants to make the bed for every couple', Jan Kott considered; but for Girard, in his voyeuristic desire for the universal mediation of indiscriminate 'Love, love, nothing but love' [3,1,105], he is more specifically a playwright, since 'all playwrights are panders . . . *Troilus and Cressida* is written and staged by Pandarus'.[59]

'What would the depoliticization Schmitt denounces in modernity reveal?' asks Derrida in *The Politics of Friendship*; and answers, the lesson that 'The less politics there is, the more there is'.[60] In Shakespeare, the figure for this hyperbolisation is a compere of theatre as camp, a *flâneur* whose pointless playfulness insinuates into tragedy what Schmitt derided as the 'baroque theatricalization of life' that comes with the triumph of technology, liberalism and culture over politics. Pandarus is a ludic personification of the neutralisation that arose out of 'despair and nausea' at the Wars of Religion but ended, according to Schmitt, by erasing 'all conceptions of truth'.[61] His creator admits as much, giving him rights to address the playhouse as 'Pander's hall' [5,11,46] and to sell his niece to join 'the daughters of the game' [4,6,64]. Thus Cressida learns from her uncle what it means to teasingly 'play the tyrant' [3,2,108], becoming a model for 'what is, and is not' when 'a thing inseparate/Divides' [5,2,146-9] into the original and fake. 'Populuxe' is Paul Yachnin's Baudrillardian term for the pathological 'madness of discourse' [142] Pandarus thereby disseminates with the contagion of his 'diseases' [5,11,31].[62] For what this poseur poses is the crisis of indistinction prompted by the purposelessness of the aesthetic, the promiscuous representationalism similarly personified by 'Achilles' male varlet' [5,1,15] Patroclus, who prostitutes theatre to pure 'sport and pleasure' [2,3,100] by caricaturing heroism in the queer histrionics of a 'pale and bloodless' simulacrum of 'mere oppugnancy' [1,3,111], making 'paradoxes' of 'Excitements to the field or speech of truce', until 'at this sport/Sir Valour dies' [175-82]. As Heather James acutely comments in her study of Shakespeare's Troy, in presenting this scandalous play world as symptomatic of 'the problem of "emulation" or rivalrous imitation', *Troilus and Cressida* thereby anticipates Walter Benjamin's worryingly Schmittian thesis in 'The Work of Art in the Age of Mechanical Reproduction', that the copy loses the *aura* of immediacy, since 'the presence of the original is the prerequisite to the concept of authenticity':[63]

> . . . like a strutting player whose conceit
> Lies in his hamstring, and doth think it rich
> To hear the wooden dialogue and sound
> 'Twixt his stretched footing and the scaffoldage.
>
> [1,3,153-6]

The 'poor player/That struts and frets his hour upon the stage' haunts Shakespeare's Jacobean dramas as a figure for the false autonomy of the play as 'a tale/Told by an idiot, full of sound and fury, signifying nothing' [*Macbeth*, 5,5,23-7] in 'someone else's words'.[64] So what distances *Troilus and Cressida* from the plays that it contains is how Shakespeare suddenly calls the ethical turn into question 'in terms of the morality of morality', by stressing that 'what is forgotten by the moralizing moralists', as Derrida conceded in his meditation on the sacrifice of Isaac, is how such universalism unbolts the door to the 'universal wolf' [1,3,121] of sovereign violence.[65] It would be hard to imagine quicker footwork than Derrida's sudden discovery that caring for *someone* is incompatible with caring for *everyone*, quips Jacques Rancière, knowing the philosopher was himself an old footballer.[66] Likewise, the play seems abruptly to recall how, despite wearing his Olympic garland into battle, the golden athlete Milo was eventually eaten by a wolf.[67] For its neutralising of friend and enemy in the endless substitutability of indifference to difference will finally be exposed as 'fool's play' when Hector encounters Achilles in a 'blaze of wrath', but, 'scorning forfeits and subduements', hangs his sword in the air, just as he has his mortal foe at bay, to apply his usual 'trick of mercy' and allow the other to 'Pause if thou wilt' [5,6,15]. All the text's 'Olympian' idealism is focused in this last 'staying of hands', which repeats as it predicts the 'interim' opened by Pyrrhus in *Hamlet* [5,2,73], when Achilles' son stood stalled 'as a painted tyrant', in an epitome of the aesthetic as pointed pointlessness, as his sword which was 'declining on the milky head/Of reverend Priam, seemed i'th'air to stick . . . And like a neutral to his will and matter/Did nothing' [*Hamlet*, 2,2,457–62]. This is the ultimate Shakespearean play-within-the-play, which is itself a word picture of the suspense when the 'speechless' actor freezes during a performance at the Globe:[68]

> . . . as often we see against the storm
> A silence in the heavens, the rack stand still,
> The bold winds speechless, and the orb below
> As hush as death. . . .
>
> [*Hamlet*, 2,2,463–6]

As pretty as a picture, Shakespeare's image of Pyrrhus' blade hanging as if 'painted' evokes the countless depictions of Damoclean swords or emasculated warriors in actual Baroque paintings, where the mimicry of blood in paint inspires the redemptive idea of art as 'an antidote to violence', which would be most searchingly explored by Rembrandt in his own *The Sacrifice of Isaac*.[69] There the 'virtuoso of interruption' reveals the mediation when the angel stays the hand of Abraham to be a paradigm of the aesthetic as a transcendence of the imperative to sacrifice.[70] All the liberalism that caused Spinoza to be excommunicated by the rabbis is foretold in this hiatus. Likewise, in their episodes of indecision Shakespeare's killers seem to represent the caesura of representation as 'a dream of passion' [2,2,529], a stalemate we might be relieved to think is indeed taking 'the time to which one is subject' and converting it into 'a time of which one is the subject', by 'signifying nothing'. The queer effect produced by beautifying these violent incarnations of sacrificial masculinity into such a 'painted' immobility is perhaps comparable to that of the photographs by Jewish artist Collier Schorr of young Nazi soldiers cradling flowers or fruit, which in Halberstam's view deconstruct the fascist equation of eros with terror.[71] Yet behind all these Shakespearean pauses hovers the hungry ghost of Marlowe, whose Aeneas recites Troy's holocaust story to Dido, and whose 'entire absorption in the game' carried him inexorably to the nihilistic irresponsibility of '*absolute* play', in Stephen Greenblatt's words, and an atrocious death in Deptford.[72] So in *Troilus and Cressida* the Marlovian Achilles will refuse to humour Hector's gentlemanly game, snarling 'I do disdain thy courtesy, proud Trojan' [5,6,16]. As Caillois writes, the ethical turn ends and 'the corruption of the *agôn* begins at the point where no referee is recognised'.[73]

In his interregnum play, Shakespeare dramatises a scenario he had never envisaged before, the power vacuum, as even existential enemies take a truce, when the big 'if' of the democratic state is finally instituted, but the antagonism eradicated 'when degree is shak'd' then reappears 'In beastly sort' [5,11,5], with the emergence of the one 'who decides on the exception'. For instead of the Levinasian ethic of 'fair play' Rembrandt could depict a generation later, in Shakespeare's Trojan War 'The bull has the game', as Thersites gleefully snipes: 'Now, bull! Now, dog!' [5,8,2–3]. *Homo homini lupus*: by descending into the havoc of a bare Hobbesian life, in which man becomes 'the universal prey' [1,3,123], *Troilus and Cressida* trashes the Olympic ideal to reassert the terrifying affinity of the sovereign and the beast. Critics connect the resulting mayhem to the shock and awe of the Essex Revolt, and the intrusion of what Schmitt called 'historical time' into the time of the play.[74] Whatever its context, *Troilus and Cressida* thereby simply confirms over the length of an entire play Montaigne's dark foreboding that 'players may be played; that as an object in the game, the player may be its stake'.[75] So when Hector ribs his nemesis that 'like a book of sport thou'lt read me o'er', Achilles' response is truly unsporting: 'Tell me, you heavens, in which part of his body/Shall I destroy him?' [4,7,123–7]. For, as the decisionist prince Troilus warns Cressida, if we mistake life for some Olympian 'book of sport' we will 'suddenly' discover that the irrational arbitrariness of 'chance . . . jostles roughly by/All time of pause' [4,5,32–4]. A 'venomed vengeance' is the action on which this disillusioned romantic therefore decides, as 'Distinction with a loud and powerful fan . . . winnows the light away' [1,3,26–7] and the solitary decider's words about the discriminating fall of his 'prompted sword' are almost exactly those of the avenging son of Achilles:

> Not the dreadful spout
> Which shipmen so the hurricano call,
> Constringed in mass by the almighty sun,
> Shall dizzy with more clamour Neptune's ear
> In his descent than shall my prompted sword
> Falling on Diomed.
>
> [5,2,178–83]

'The end crowns all', Hector believed, hoping for at least a sporting chance to receive 'such a reward as victors wear at the Olympian games' from 'that old common arbitrator Time' [4,7,107–9], when the final 'trumpets sound' and 'stickler-like, the armies separate' [5,9,16–18]. For even in sport, 'Everything is time', observes Connor, and 'All the time, the time is running out'.[76] In *Troilus and Cressida*, however, Father Time is a 'stickler', or umpire, who carries 'a wallet at his back' crammed with 'scraps' [3,3,140] of the scorecards he ignores. Thus, 'After so many hours, lives, speeches spent' [2,2,1], Hector has to decide whether to call time by returning Helen, or to fight in earnest. He likens warmongers to callow youths 'Aristotle thought/Unfit to hear moral philosophy' [2,2,165–6], for confusing war with a game. Aristotle *before* Homer? This insane anachronism is Schmitt's 'real time' intruding into 'the time of the play', to prove the difference between the seriousness of Shakespearean tragedy and sport: a shot at the Inns of Court, where the play was staged shortly after the students backed Essex's doomed rebellion, letting their 'hot passion' overrule a 'true decision' [168–72].[77] So, 'Hector's opinion/Is this in way of truth' [187–8]. Yet merely for the puerile sensation of a shock 'to shriek amazement' [209], like that of the cat's claw Montaigne feared, the champion gamesman elects to indulge the childlike fantasy of the *fort/da* game by deciding 'to keep Helen still' [190], and so goes down to 'ugly night' [5,9,6] at the hands of Achilles and his storm-troopers. No wonder Karl Jaspers said that, faced by Nazism, German thinkers 'no longer had any inclination to read Goethe, but seized on Shakespeare'.[78] For such a catastrophe is 'but the chance of war'; yet the *Blitzkrieg* of Myrmidons, with 'balls of wildfire in their murderous paws,/Which made the funeral flame that burnt fair Troy', might have been scripted by the pyromaniac Marlowe, or even by Schmitt himself:[79]

HECTOR: I am unarmed. Forego this vantage, Greek.
ACHILLES: Strike, fellows, strike! This is the man I seek.
[The Myrmidons kill Hector]
        So, Ilium, fall thou. Now, Troy, sink down.

                                                                    [5,9,9–11]

'Troy's lofty towers, which once ore-topped the clouds,/And menaced heaven, Helen's beauty shrouds/In cinders', but 'This turret swells as proud', proclaimed his Olympians of Dover's wooden castle.[80] It was Aeneas himself who had 'Revived those games. . . . Amongst his wearied Trojans' who were 'now transferred over/Into out Cotswold by thee, worthy Dover', to endure for all time, these poets fantasised.[81] Of course, it was not to be. By 1643 ignorant armies were clashing 'Over the Cotswold Downs, where Dover's Games were', as the real fortress of nearby Campden House, 'which was so fair', burned to the ground.[82] 'Be not afeared', the Cotswold Olympians had poeticised. But even they could not hide their own fear of the Puritans. And in Shakespeare's Olympic story, too, what makes us truly afraid is the exception of the man who will not play the game, but instead turns agonism back to antagonism and sport to sacrifice. 'We know from the Hellenic context that it is common for sports to evolve to competitions from sacrificial displays and back again (think of Olympic wrestling)', comments Justin Smith, for 'it has long seemed that sports would be far more interesting if the losing team were truly punished'. The philosopher cites the Mayan ball game in which the losers were slaughtered by being trussed and bounced down from on high as the balls of their own match.[83] And such is the unplayability of *Troilus and Cressida* that Achilles proves the point, as 'in fellest manner' [5,7,6] he returns the sacred turf of 'this short-grassed green' to something more truly 'sportive' or sovereign, with the potlatch of the oldest form of athletic display, the Homeric funeral game, when 'at the murderer's horse's tail/In beastly sort', the loser's body is dragged about 'the shameful field' [5,11,4–5], on the winner's lap of honour:

Come, tie his body to my horse's tail;
Along the field I will the Trojan trail.

                                                                    [5,8,21–2]

NOTES

1. Leah Marcus, *The Politics of Mirth: Jonson, Herrick, Milton, Marvell, and the Defense of Old Holiday Customs* (Chicago: Chicago University Press, 1989), p. 5; 'purposely to grace him': Anthony à Wood, *Athenae Oxonienses*, reprinted in Christopher Whitfield, *Robert Dover and the Cotswold Games: 'Annalia Dubrensia'* (London: Henry Sotheran, 1962), p. 18. See also Dennis Brailsford, *Sport and Society: Elizabeth to Anne* (London: Routledge and Kegan Paul, 1969), pp. 103–16; Francis Burns, 'Robert Dover's Cotswold Olimpick Games: the use of the term "Olimpick"', *Olympic Review*, 210 (1985), 231–6; Celia Haddon, *The First Ever English Olimpick Games* (London: Hodder and Stoughton, 2004); and Peter Stallybrass, '"Wee feaste in our Defense": Patrician Carnival in Early Modern England and Robert Herrick's "Hesperides"', *English Literary Renaissance*, 16:1 (1986), 234–52.

2. Michael Drayton, *Polyolbion*, 14th Song, 1:162.

3. See, for example, Peter Levi, *The Life and Times of William Shakespeare* (London: Macmillan, 1988), p. 28: 'I think the greyhound . . . must have been in the unreformed version of the Cotswold Whitsun meeting . . . and that Shakespeare knew these country sports. . . . The key that fits this door is Robert Dover. Shakespeare knew him as a boy from Barton in the Heath, and probably later at the Inns of Court'. But Whitfield points out that the reference in *The Merry Wives* occurs only in the Folio, and suggests Shakespeare 'attended the games during the last few years of his life' as 'one of a gathering of kindred, neighbours, cousins, and friends': Whitfield, *Robert Dover and the Cotswold Games*, pp. 23 and 29.

4. Richard Brome, *A Jovial Crew, or the Merry Beggars*, ed. Ann Haaker (London: Edward Arnold, 1968), p. 39.

5. John Findling and Kimberly Pelle (eds), *Enclopedia of the Modern Olympic Movement* (Westport: Greenwood, 2004), p. 457.

6. E. R. Vyvian (ed.), 'Introduction', in *Cotswold Games: Annalia Dubrensia* (Cheltenham: Williams, 1878; reprinted London: Tabard Press, 1970), p. ix.

7. David Underdown, *Revel, Riot, and Rebellion: Popular Politics and Culture in England, 1603–1660* (Oxford: Oxford University Press, 1985), pp. 73–6.

8. For Dover's games and 'summer kings', see Sandra Billington, *Mock Kings in Medieval Society and Renaissance Drama* (Oxford: Clarendon Press, 1991), pp. 63 and 80–5.

9. Carl Schmitt, *Political Theology: Four Chapters on the Concept of Sovereignty*, trans. George Schwab (Chicago: Chicago University Press, 2005), p. 5.

10. Steven Connor, *The Philosophy of Sport* (London: Reaktion, 2011), pp. 52–3.

11. François Laroque, *Shakespeare's Festive World: Elizabethan Seasonal Entertainment and the Professional Stage*, trans. Janet Lloyd (Cambridge: Cambridge University Press, 1991); Connor, *The Philosophy of Sport*, p. 83.

12. Nigel Spivey, *The Ancient Olympics* (Oxford: Oxford University Press, 2004), pp. 76–7 and 189–90; Connor, *The Philosophy of Sport*, pp. 78–82.

13. Nicholas Wallington, 'To the great inventor and champion of the English Olympicks', reprinted in Whitfield, *Robert Dover and the Cotswold Games*, p. 150.

14. Robert Dover, 'A congratulatory poem to my poetical and learned noble friends'; 'Cotswold Hercules': Richard Wells, 'To his worthy friend Mr Robert Dover concerning his Dover Castle and Cotswold Olympicke', reprinted ibid., pp. 205 and 223.

15. Shackerley Marmion, 'To Mr. Robert Dover, upon his annual sports at Cotswold', and Nicolas Wallington, 'To the great inventor', reprinted ibid., pp. 150 and 210.

16. John Trussell, 'To my noble friend, Mr. Robert Dover'; and Richard Wells, 'To his worthy friend, Mr. Robert Dover', reprinted ibid., pp. 105 and 205.

17. Whitfield, *Robert Dover and the Cotswold Games*, p. 2; Phebe Jensen, *Religion and Revelry in Shakespeare's Festive World* (Cambridge: Cambridge University Press, 2008), p. 203. See also Laroque, *Shakespeare's Festive World*, pp. 163–5.

18. Gregory Colón Semenza, *Sport, Politics and Literature in the English Renaissance* (Newark: Delaware University Press, 2003), p. 116.

19. Dover, 'A congratulatory poem to my poetical learned noble friends'; Ben Jonson, 'An epigram to my jovial good friend, Mr. Robert Dover, on his great instauration of his hunting and dancing at Cotswold', reprinted in Whitfield, *Robert Dover and the Cotswold Games*, p. 134; Wallington, 'To the great inventor'.

20. John Harington, 'A treatise on play', in *Nugae Antiquaae*, ed. Henry Harington, 3 vols (1779; reprinted Hildesheim: Georg Olms, 1968), vol. 2, p. 173; Louis Montrose, *The Purpose of Playing: Shakespeare and the Cultural Politics of the Elizabethan Theatre* (Chicago: Chicago University Press, 1996), pp. 41–2.

21. John Trussell, 'To the noble and disposed ladies and gentlewomen assembled in Whitsun-week upon Cotswold'; John Mosson, 'To his worthy friend Mr Robert Diover, on his famous yeerely assemblies upon Cotswold', reprinted in Whitfield, *Robert Dover and the Cotswold Games*, pp. 172 and 199.

22. William Basse, 'To the noble and fayre assemblies. . . and their jovial entertainer, my right generous friend, Master Robert Dover, upon Cotswold', reprinted ibid., pp. 166–7.

23. John Stratford, 'To my kind cosen and noble friend Mr Robert Dover on his sports upon Cotswold'; William Denny, 'An encomiastick to his worthy friend Mr Robert Dover on his famous annual assemblies at Cotswold'; Michael Drayton, 'To my noble friend Mr. Robert Dover on his brave annuall assemblies upon Cotswold', reprinted ibid., pp. 102, 118 and 179.

24. Ibid., p. 6.

25. Carl Schmitt, *The Nomos of the Earth in the International Law of the Jus Publicum Europaeum*, trans. G. L. Ulmen (New York: Telos, 2006), pp. 141–2; Carl Schmitt, *The Leviathan in the State Theory of Thomas Hobbes*, trans. George Schwab (Chicago: University of Chicago Press, 2008), pp. 60–3.

26. Stratford, 'To my kind cosen and noble friend, Mr. Robert Dover'.

27. 'Muscular Catholicism': Spivey, *The Ancient Olympics*, p. 240; 'disorganized, repetitive': Hugh Lee, 'Politics, society, and Greek athletics: views from the twenty-first century', *Journal of the History of Sport*, 12 (2003), 168.

28. Frances Yates, *The French Academies of the Sixteenth Century* (London: Routledge, 1988), pp. 68–76. For the religious politics of the *Agonisticon*, see Maurizio Zerbini, *Alle Fonti Del Doping* (Rome: Bretschneider, 2001), p. 44.

29. Pierre du Faur (Petrus Faber), *Agonisticon* (Lyons: Franciscus Faber, 1592), 'Dedication', p. 1. My translation.

30. Quoted in Isabelle Luciani, 'Floral Games and civic humanism in the 16th-century city', in Nathalie Dauvois (ed.), *Humanism in Toulouse, 1480–1595* (Paris: Honoré Champion, 2006), pp. 301–35, here pp. 319–20. See also John Charles Dawson, *The Floral Games of Toulouse in the Renaissance: Etienne Dolet, 1532–1534* (New York: Columbia University Press, 1921).

31. Roland Barthes, *What Is Sport?*, trans. Richard Howard (New Haven: Yale University Press, 2007), p. 61.

32. Chantal Mouffe, *The Democratic Paradox* (London: Verso, 2005), p. 103.

33. William Bellas, 'To the heroick and generous-minded gentleman Mr Robert Dover, on his yeerely assemblies upon Cotswold', reprinted in Whitfield, *Robert Dover and the Cotswold Games*, p. 162.

34. Roger Caillois, *Man, Play and Games*, trans. Meyer Barash (Urbana: University of Illinois Press, 2001), pp. 30–6; Michel de Montaigne, 'Apology for Raymond Sebond', in *The Complete Essays*, trans. M. A. Screech (Harmondsworth: Penguin, 1991), p. 505; Christopher Marlowe, 'Hero and Leander', 1,144, in *The Collected Poems of Christopher Marlowe*, ed. Patrick Cheney and Brian Striar (Oxford: Oxford University Press, 2006),

p. 200. See Robert Logan, 'Edward II, Richard II, the will to play, and an aesthetic of ambiguity', in Shakespeare's Marlowe: The Influence of Christopher Marlowe on Shakespeare's Artistry (Aldershot: Ashgate, 2007), pp. 83–116.

35. Andreas Höfele, Stage, Stake, and Scaffold: Humans and Animals in Shakespeare's Theatre (Oxford: Oxford University Press, 2011); Connor, The Philosophy of Sport, p. 32.

36. Clifford Leech, 'Shakespeare's Greeks', in B. W. Jackson (ed.), Stratford Papers on Shakespeare (Toronto: McMaster University Press, 1963), pp. 1–20, here pp. 18–19.

37. Harold Arthur Harris, Greek Athletes and Athletics (London: Hutchinson, 1952), pp. 110–13.

38. Stephen Greenblatt, Walter Cohen, Jean Howard and Katharine Maus (eds), Norton Shakespeare (New York: Norton, 1997), pp. 1833–4 and 1893; George Chapman, The Iliad, ed. Allardyce Nicoll (Princeton: Princeton University Press, 1998), 7,232, p. 160.

39. Homer, The Iliad, 18,107.

40. Carl Schmitt, Hamlet or Hecuba: The Intrusion of the Time of the Play, trans. David Pan and Jennifer Rust (New York: Telos Press, 2009), p. 40.

41. Semenza, Sport, Politics and Literature, p. 83. The allusion to Milo of Croton was noted as being among the most conspicuous of the anachronisms of the play as early as 1712 by John Dennis, in 'Letter II' of An Essay on the Genius and Works of Shakespeare with Some Letters of Criticism to The Spectator, reprinted in William Shakespeare: The Critical Heritage. Volume 2: 1693–1733 (London: Routledge, 1974), p. 286.

42. George Orwell, Collected Essays, Journalism and Letters, ed. Sonia Orwell (Harmondsworth: Penguin, 1970), pp. 61–4.

43. Johann Huizinga, Homo Ludens: A Study of the Play Element in Culture, trans. anon. (New York: Roy Publishers, 1950), p. 13. For Schmitt's equally problematic distinction between 'normal life' and the state of exception, see David Pan, 'Carl Schmitt on culture and violence in the political decision', Telos, 142 (spring 2008), 49–72, especially pp. 56–7.

44. Spivey, The Ancient Olympics, p. 3; Schmitt, The Leviathan in the State Theory of Thomas Hobbes, pp. 69–77; discussed in Giorgio Agamben, Homo Sacer: Sovereign Power and Bare Life, trans. Daniel Heller-Roazen (Stanford: Stanford University Press, 1998), pp. 30–4. The citation is of Pindar, Fragment 169 (Heidegger's favourite), which refers to Hercules as law-founder despite his theft of Geryon's cattle. For Schmitt's valorisation of 'total war' as a response to Huizinga's Homo ludens, see Carlo Galli, 'Hamlet: representation and the concrete', in Graham Hammill and Julia Lupton (eds), Political Theology and Early Modernity (Chicago: University of Chicago Press, 2012), pp. 60–83.

45. A singular exception is Catherine Bates, Play in a Godless World (London: Open Gate, 1999). But this penetrating Nietzschean study contains only one chapter on Shakespeare.

46. Geoffrey Chaucer, Troilus and Criseyde, ed. Barry Windeattt (London: Penguin, 2003), 1,48–168.

47. For the distinction between games of chance and competition, see especially Caillois, Man, Play and Games, pp. 14–19.

48. Stephen Marx, 'Shakespeare's pacifism', Renaissance Quarterly, 45:1 (1992), 49–95, here 55 and 59.

49. Kiernan Ryan, Shakespeare (Basingstoke: Palgrave, 2004), pp. 123–4. See also Marx, 'Shakespeare's pacifism', pp. 71–5.

50. Chaucer, Troilus and Criseyde, 1,148–68; 1,866–8; 4,1629; 5,304.

51. Bates, Play in a Godless World, p. 176.

52. See Carolyn Sale, 'Eating air, feeling smells: Hamlet's theory of performance', Renaissance Drama, 35 (2006), 145–68, here 163.

53. 'Master of ellipsis': Harold Bloom, The Anatomy of Influence (New Haven: Yale University Press, 2011), p. 49; Judith Halberstam, The Queer Art of Failure (Durham, NC: Duke University Press, 2011), pp. 120–1.

54. Susan Sontag, 'Notes on camp', in *Against Interpretation: And Other Essays* (New York: Farrah, Straus and Giroux, 1966), p. 277.

55. Caillois, *Man, Play and Games*, pp. 88–9; René Girard, *A Theatre of Envy: William Shakespeare* (Oxford: Oxford University Press, 1991), pp. 157–8.

56. Carl Schmitt, *The Concept of the Political*, trans. George Schwab (Chicago: University of Chicago Press, 1996), p. 35.

57. 'Something new': Stephen Greenblatt, *Will in the World: How Shakespeare Became Shakespeare* (London: Jonathan Cape, 2004), p. 301; see also James Shapiro, *1599: A Year in the Life of William Shakespeare* (London: Faber and Faber, 2005), p. 152; 'to acknowledge': Katrin Trüstedt, 'Hecuba against Hamlet: Carl Schmitt, political theology, and the stake of modern tragedy', *Telos*, 153 (2010), 109.

58. Edward Skidelsky, *Ernst Cassirer: The Last Philosopher of Culture* (Princeton: Princeton University Press, 2008), p. 215.

59. Jan Kott, *Shakespeare Our Contemporary*, trans. Boleslaw Taborski (London: Methuen, 1964); Girard, *A Theatre of Envy*, p. 158.

60. Jacques Derrida, *The Politics of Friendship*, trans. George Collins (London: New York, 1997), p. 129.

61. Schmitt, *Hamlet or Hecuba*, p. 41; 'despair and nausea': Schmitt, *The Leviathan in the State Theory of Thomas Hobbes*, pp. 42 and 45.

62. Paul Yachnin, '"The perfection of ten": populuxe art and artisanal value in *Troilus and Cressida*', *Shakespeare Quarterly*, 56 (2005), 306–27.

63. Heather James, *Shakespeare's Troy: Drama, Politics, and the Translation of Empire* (Cambridge: Cambridge University Press, 1997), pp. 97–8.

64. Thomas Betteridge, *Shakespearean Fantasy and Politics* (Hatfield: University of Hertfordshire Press, 2005), p. 142.

65. Jacques Derrida, *The Gift of Death*, trans. David Wills (Chicago: Chicago University Press, 1995), pp. 68–9.

66. Jacques Rancière, 'Should democracy come? Ethics and politics in Derrida', in Pheng Cheah and Suzanne Guerlac (eds), *Derrida and the Time of the Political* (Durham, NC: Duke University Press, 2009), pp. 274–90, here pp. 286–7.

67. Michael Poliakoff, *Combat Sports in the Ancient World* (New Haven: Yale University Press, 1987), pp. 117–19 and 182–3.

68. The classic reading of the pause is Clifford Leech, 'The hesitation of Pyrrhus', in *The Morality of Art: Essays Presented to G. Wilson Knight* (London: Routledge and Kegan Paul, 1969), pp. 41–9. Christopher Pye views it as a 'model of autochthonic subjectivity' in *The Vanishing* (Durham, NC: Duke University Press, 2001), pp. 110–17; and for its Lacanian decoding as a mirror of Hamlet's hesitation, see Philip Armstrong, 'Watching *Hamlet* watching: Lacan, Shakespeare and the mirror/stage', in Terence Hawkes (ed.), *Alternative Shakespeares: 2* (London: Routledge, 1996), pp. 223–6. But for antecedents, see Catherine Belsey, 'Senecan vacillation and Elizabethan deliberation: influence or confluence?', *Renaissance Drama*, 6 (1973), 65–88.

69. 'An antidote to violence': Svetlana Alpers, *The Vexations of Art: Velázquez and Others* (New Haven: Yale University Press, 2007), p. 129. See also Leo Bersani and Ulysses Dutoit, *Caravaggio's Secrets* (Cambridge, MA: MIT Press, 1998), pp. 98–9.

70. 'Virtuoso of interruption': Simon Schama, *Rembrandt's Eyes* (London: Allen Lane, 1999), p. 605. For the redemptive interpretation of Abraham's suspended knife and the face of the other in Rembrandt's 1635 painting, see Steven Shankman, 'Justice, injustice, and the differentiation of the monotheistic worldview: reflections on Genesis 17, 20, and 22', in *Differentiation and Integration of Worldviews: International Readings in Theory, History and Philosophy of Culture*, 19 (St Petersburg: Hermitage, 2004), 201–12.

71. Halberstam, *The Queer Art of Failure*, pp. 162–71.

72. Stephen Greenblatt, *Renaissance Self-Fashioning: From More to Shakespeare* (Chicago: Chicago University Press, 1980), p. 220.

73. Caillois, *Man, Play and Games*, p. 46.

74. Schmitt, *Hamlet or Hecuba*, pp. 23–5, 44–5, et passim.

75. Jacques Ehrmann, 'Homo ludens revisited', *Yale French Studies*, 41 (1968), 31–57, here 55.

76. Connor, *The Philosophy of Sport*, p. 77.

77. Schmitt, *Hamlet or Hecuba*, p. 51. For the anachronistic allusion to Aristotle, see W. R. Elton, 'Aristotle's *Nicomachean Ethics* and Shakespeare's *Troilus and Cressida*', *Journal of the History of Ideas*, 58 (1997), 331–7; reprinted in *Shakespeare's 'Troilus and Cressida' and the Inns of Court Revels* (Aldershot: Ashgate, 2000), pp. 183–9.

78. Karl Jaspers, *Unsere Zukunft und Goethe* (Bremen: Storm, 1948), p. 18, quoted in Skildelsky, *Ernst Cassirer*, p. 6.

79. Christopher Marlowe, *Dido Queen of Carthage*, 2,1,217–18, in *Christopher Marlowe: The Complete Plays*, ed. Frank Romany and Robert Lindsey (London: Penguin, 2003), p. 257.

80. William Durham, 'To my noble friend Mr Robert Dover, on his dauncing assembly upon Cotswold', reprinted in Whitfield, *Robert Dover and the Cotswold Games*, p. 109.

81. Stratford, 'To my kind cosen and noble friend, Mr. Robert Dover'.

82. Richard Symonds, *Diary of the Marches of the Royal Army* (London: Camden Society, 1859), p. 133.

83. Justin Smith, 'Who better to punish than the innocent?', *Cabinet*, 46 (2012), 80–4, here 81.

9   As Mice by Lions: Political Theology and *Measure for Measure*

I'll come right out and say it: the King of Kings preferred bad ministers. And the King of Kings preferred them because he liked to appear in a favourable light by contrast. How could he show himself favourably if he were surrounded by good ministers? The people would be disoriented. . . . There can be only one sun.[1]

TO ENFORCE OR QUALIFY

'A substitute shines brightly as a king,/Until a king be by' [*Merchant*, 5,1,93–4]; and the editorial story of *Measure for Measure* in the twenty-first century has been just such a comedy of substitution, in which we have watched the play's 'demigod authority' [1,2,100] make way for a 'new deputy' [134], whose 'commission' [1,1,13], 'so to enforce or qualify' the work 'as to [his] soul seems good' [65], has strangely reinforced its theme, that 'if power change purpose' we shall see 'what our seemers be' [1,3,53], thus proving 'the hood does not make the monk': '*Cucullus non facit monachum*' [5,1,259]. Of course, one of the most striking features of this play, to which its critics keep returning, is that its characters always seem to be standing in like this for someone else, be it God, King James I, or their creator himself, so that its stage threatens to open up into an infinite recession. But this chapter is concerned with how the evidence for its co-authorship adds yet another level to the *mise en abime* that is *Measure for Measure*. For whether or not Thomas Middleton appreciated the irony when he was contracted the original author's 'absence to supply' [1,1,18], by revising Shakespeare's 1604 comedy of split personalities and substitute sex in the city for the 1623 Folio, the recent reassignment of much of the extant text to this deputising dramatist has uncannily paralleled its plot, where, in the sovereign's 'remove' [43], his 'place and greatness' [4,2,56] are likewise delegated to a 'precise' lieutenant [1,3,50]: a stand-in promoted as 'one that can' the master's 'part in him advertise' [1,1,41], whose over-zealous interpretation of his scope to 'borrow place of him' [5,1,354] simply goes to expose his failure to measure up to his precursor, the 'old fantastical Duke of dark corners' [4,4,147], who is thereby reinstated in his pomp.

Shakespeare and Middleton seem such strange bedfellows, the one with so many suspect Catholic connections in Stratford, the other an official of the City of London Protestant elite, that their alliance in the aftermath of the 1605 Gunpowder Plot, initially on *Timon of Athens* and *Macbeth*, hints at a shotgun marriage. It is as if a Roundhead teamed up with a Cavalier. Yet 'Young Charbonne the puritan and old Poisson the papist, howsome'er their hearts are severed in religion', smiled Shakespeare indulgently in *All's Well That Ends Well* at this time, 'their heads are both one, they may jowl horns together like any deer i'the'herd' [1,3,45]. So perhaps 'old Poisson' was forced to hand over to 'Young Charbonne' as someone more conformable and rigorous in the panic following the Plot. But however these improbable partners were made to bang heads together, reading the composite 'genetic text' of *Measure for Measure*, produced for the 2007 2,016-page Oxford edition of the so-called 'collected works of Thomas Middleton', where the presumed original lines are printed in grey and the proxy's in bold type, we reprise the same suspicion of some 'sinister measure from his judge' [3,1,465] as we sense when we see the novice 'figure dressed' in the Duke's 'ample grace and honour' [1,1,17–20], as though Middleton had been set up as a fall guy, or that Shakespeare's 'true meant design' [1,4,54] was that this play about ghosting, which opens with an old hand entrusting a play-script to an understudy, 'From which', he warns, 'we would not have you warp' [1,1,13], would prove to be a hard act to follow, completed with similar ineptitude, to make him appear in the most favourable light:

> Therefore, indeed. . . .
> I have on Angelo imposed my office,
> Who may in the ambush of my name strike home,
> And yet my nature never in the fight
> T'allow in slander.
>
> [1,3,39–43]

Although Dr Johnson believed that 'there is not one of Shakespeare's plays more darkened' than *Measure for Measure* by the 'unskillfulness . . . distortions of phrase, or negligence' of its Folio transcription, to his Oxford supporters the aptly named Middleton's 'deputation' as a mediator of the text we now possess proves he succeeded to 'all the organs' of his master's 'power' [1,1,20].[2] As early as 1636 the younger playwright was regarded as 'Shakespeare's true heir', Gary Taylor points out; and the monumentally weighty 'Middleton Folio' is designed to crown him at last as a legitimate inheritor, 'Our other Shakespeare . . . that we can carry to our private desert islands'.[3] Clearly, if any 'be of worth/To undergo such ample grace and honour' [22–3], it is the author of *The Changeling*, *A Chaste Maid in Cheapside*, *Women Beware Women*, and according to this count, *The Revenger's Tragedy*, a masterpiece Middleton wrote at twenty-six, 'Shakespeare's age when he churned out *Henry VI, Part Two*', Taylor jibes.[4] The Middletonians have an axe to grind about the Bard. But such scholarship has revolutionised our understanding of the collective habits of English Renaissance playwrights, who are now more than ever seen as hired hands, journeymen 'who often did piecework, writing "new additions" to a valuable old property – as Middleton did to Shakespeare's', in Taylor's words, publishing 'in the ambush of his name', and so 'Upon his place, / And with full line of his authority' [1,4,54–5].[5]

Textual revisionism has established *Measure for Measure* beyond question as a 'posthumous collaboration', and guaranteed that as far as this play is concerned we can never go back to the idea of the sovereign Shakespeare. But this revolution raises other questions about Middleton's role as intermediary between the dead author and the King's Men, who late in 1621 required a rewriting.[6] For the 'world's media get excited by any attempt, however weak, to take something away from Shakespeare', bemoaned Brian Vickers in the *Times Literary Supplement*, after Laurie Maguire published an article intriguingly claiming co-authorship of *All's Well That's End Well* for Middleton as well.[7] So, if he is to be acknowledged not only as a part author of *Macbeth* and *Timon of Athens*, but also of *Measure for Measure*, this veritable middleman's 'enforcing or qualifying' of the work he inherited as 'Shakespeare's "double" and "other"' creates similar problems as Angelo's stand-in for the absent Duke: 'What figure . . . think you, he will bear' in this complicated act of succession [16]; and is the great originator's 'world as it was' after such a prosthetic makeover?[8] What are the consequences of the substitution of the *deus absconditus*, as it were, by his earthly vicar? For Middleton's revision of *Measure for Measure* may well be 'a fascinating example of how a text takes on a markedly different hue when its context changes', but just how did the updated drama differ 'in the collaborative environment of the playhouse' of the 1620s from the play Shakespeare was alive to supervise in 1604?[9] 'Which is the way? Is it sad or few words? Or how? The trick of it?' [3,2,303–5].

If we accept that *Measure for Measure* has come down to us via Middleton, acting as the sorcerer's apprentice, as it now seems that we must, it is appropriate that this reallocation should prompt so many editorial questions about how much he 'enforced' or 'qualified' his assignment, seeing as its Biblical title demands that we make just such comparisons: 'Haste still pays haste, and leisure answers leisure; / Like doth quit like, and measure still for measure' [5,1,402–3]. With its allusion to the sacrificial economy implicit in the symbol of the scales of justice, the title in fact highlights how the action will comprise the auditioning of a parade of underwhelming seconds-in-command, as one after another clueless yet conscripted placeman strives to live down the Duke's condescending slight on his deputy's deputy Escalus, who, 'Though first in question, is thy secondary' [1,1,46], the viceroy is assured. The headless city of this famously inconclusive comedy seems indeed to be entirely franchised out to vice-principals, with the favourite, Angelo, deputising for Duke Vincentio, Escalus for Angelo, Friar Peter for Friar Thomas, Isabella for Claudio, Mariana for Isabella, Mistress Overdone for Kate Keepdown, Mistress Elbow for Mistress Overdone, Master Froth for Pompey, Pompey for the headsman Abhorson, Barnardine for Claudio, and the actual head of Ragusine, yet another substitute of a substitute, for Barnadine's. The sacrificial premise of this macabre prevision of Schnitzler's *La Ronde* is that Isabella must yield her maidenhead to Angelo to save her brother Claudio's head. But *per capita*, it turns out that *everybody* in this decapitated capital 'must change persons with' some missing head [5,1,333], as the Duke tells Lucio, and as Friar Peter says he represents his Father Superior Ludowick, who is actually the truant sovereign in disguise: 'To speak, as from his mouth, what he doth know/Is true and false' [154–5].

HEADING AND HANGING

Conscripted as yet another safe pair of hands into the hangman's 'mystery', Pompey wonders 'What mystery there should be in hanging' [4,2,40]. But as with all the Duke's caretakers, the pimp is keen, he says, to hear a head man unfold 'the properties' of government [1,1,1]: 'I hope, if you have occasion to use me for your own turn, you shall find me yare', with 'your block and your axe' [4,2,42–7]. What he learns is, in fact, the 'discourse' [1,1,4] of abjection expounded by theorists of sacrificial violence like Joseph de Maistre and Georges Bataille: that by his wielding of 'the sword of law', all 'greatness, all power, all subordination rests on the executioner. He is the terror and the bond of human association'.[10] The abject headsman stands for the sublime King, according to this political theology, for death row is the headquarters, and capital punishment the headway made by every state in the Old Order, where, as Michel Foucault gruesomely recounted, power put itself on display in savage rites of violence, a 'scaffold spectacle' literally *capped* in England at the instant of sentencing to death, when the judge donned the infamous 'black cap'.[11] Heads roll in order that a head can rise in a sacrificial system, where 'it is but heading and hanging' [2,1,211], a paradox enshrined in the legend of the martyr carrying his own head to the Abbey named after Saint Denis that then became the Capitol of sacred royalty in France. The *ancien régime* always demands such a satisfactory 'heading', as Jacques Derrida put it: 'The word "cap" (*caput, capitis*) refers to the head or the extremity, the aim and the end . . . ordered by the *man* who decides the heading, from the advanced point that he himself is, the prow, at the head. . . . It is *he* who is the headman . . . and oftentimes, he is called the *captain*'.[12]

Measure for Measure* knows the executioner is 'the king's sword'.[13] But in Shakespeare's text this power has hung 'like unscoured armour' [1,2,144] these fourteen years. So, in the play's Vienna, starting with the Duke's symbolic self-decapitation, when he cuts off his own 'absolute power' to condemn to death in favour of 'the life removed' [1,3,8–13], a self-subordination encapsulated in his syntactically perverse announcement that his function will precisely *not* now be 'Of government, the properties to unfold' [1,1,2], the buck is for ever passed to someone else. With its worldly-wise maxim that 'If you head and hang all that offend . . . you'll be glad to give out a commission for more heads' [2,1,213], this capsized metropolis seems indeed a prototype of Bataille's ideal of the headless republic, where a powerless power deposes itself, and sovereignty cuts off its own head, by renouncing violence. More specifically, critics have long perceived that if '*Measure for Measure* is a play about substitution, replacement – and thus, re-presentation', this catches the 'combination of absence and presence' by which King James himself operated. But they have been less quick to connect the fact that for most of the plot the Duke's only 'power lies in withdrawing', with the tragicomic pathos of the 'douce and crafty' King of Scots.[14] It had always frustrated James, however, that the monarch was a mere member and not head of the Church in Scotland; and the 1604 drama might have seemed like a nightmare version of the new King's old kingdom, with its self-governing Presbyterian system, of which the notional leader snapped that 'Presbytery agreeth as well with monarchy as God with the Devil'.[15] For the anoma-lous situation in which a nominal ruler 'More mocked becomes than feared' [1,3,27] is precisely that which James blamed on 'the reformation of religion in Scotland' having proceeded not 'from the Prince's order' but from 'a popular tumult':

> wherein . . . some fiery spirited men of the ministry got such a guiding of the people at that time of confusion, as finding the gust of government sweet, they [began] to fantasy to themselves a democratic form of government . . . and after usurping the liberty of the time . . . settled themselves so fast upon that imag-ined democracy as they fed themselves with the hope to become *Tribuni plebis*: and so in a popular government by leading the people by the nose, to bear the sway of all the rule.[16]

Like the Scottish King who had just succeeded to the English throne at the time of the original performance, Shakespeare's Duke is almost as hapless as the monarch in a German *Trauerspiel*, so disrespected he can be called 'a fleshmonger, a fool, and a coward' [5,1,328] to his face. As Jonathan Goldberg remarks, 'in these re-presentational procedures, the play offers an image of its own relation to sover-eign power'.[17] For such *lèse-majesté* could surely only be risked during the headless interregnum at the outset of the new reign, when James delayed his entry into his southern capital for a year after he had deserted his northern one, where, he com-plained, every 'Jack, and Tom, and Will, and Dick' would 'meet and censure me and my council'.[18] With its 'headstrong weeds' [1,3,20], and head of state who 'is very strangely gone' [1,4,49], the city of *Measure for Measure* must indeed have looked uncomfortably like the Scottish one the King had just escaped, 'where beardless boys would brave us to the face'.[19] Thus, in a jest that enacts the displacement from sovereignty and sacrifice to divestment and deferral the play seems to have consid-ered funny, Pompey jokes how he cannot 'cut off a man's head . . . if he be a married man', because a husband is 'his wife's head, and I can never cut off a woman's head' [4,2,1–4]. For in the devolved constitution of this acephalic state, a heady dukedom has deliberately beheaded itself by ensuring that there is always 'another prisoner saved,/Who should have . . . lost his head' [5,1,481]. So there may be a trace of some suppressed 'Scottish' dimension, with Angelo the stereotypical Presbyterian, when early on Pompey reassures the madam Mistress Overdone she should not fear any 'change in the commonwealth', with the deputy's proclamation that fornication is to be a capital offence, as she will never 'lack clients. Though you change your place, you need not change trade' [1,2,76–89].

Measure for Measure may have been rewritten for the same reason that *Edward III* was excluded from the Folio: allusions to the travails of the King of Scots. Referring to the Porter's comparison of Scotland to Hell in Macbeth, Andrew Hadfield suggests that, given that James's aim from the day he came south was to unite his two kingdoms, 'such reminders of the problems he had left behind in Scotland were potent warnings of a troubled future'.[20] Its first audiences must, in any case, have been thrown by a play about regime change that marked the coronation of Queen Elizabeth's successor with speculation as to 'Whether the tyranny be in his place, / Or in his eminence that fills it up' [139–40], and then made the incoming placeholder a 'scarecrow' [2,1,1]. For under the 'motion unregenerative' [3,1,356] of this 'ungenitured agent' [406], and with its insistent linking of attenuated 'scope' [1,1,64; 1,2,119; 1,3,35] to gelding and beheading, the inverted visual economy of Measure for Measure can be compared to that in the paintings of Caravaggio, where in execution pictures such as David and Goliath the exactly contemporary artist deconstructs the very possibility of sovereignty by portraying his own wide-eyed yet disembodied head. 'There is no getting rid of the head' in this castrating art, conclude Leo Bersani and Ulysse Dutoit, but Caravaggio's self-topping seems a recognition that there are 'life-sustaining ways of losing your head'.[21] And as it 'deliberately cedes the reforming powers of the artist', the script Middleton reconstituted seems once to have been similarly intent on decapitating any kind of sovereignty that is headed by capital punishment or power over life and death.[22] As Julia Lupton remarks in Afterlives of the Saints, in its circulation of beheading imagery through all its 'saucy' equivalences in 'stamps that are forbid' [2,4,45], with clipped heads of state, heads on coins and maidenheads, Measure for Measure transposes the self-headed sovereignty of the execution scaffold into the decentred universalism of a post-Christian modernity:

> In Measure for Measure, the relentless circulation of severed heads converts the coinage of martyrological beheading into the common currency of sex and politics. The exchange of heads and maidenheads in particular emblematizes the play's climactic substitution of the martyred saints of hagiography for martyred heroines of romantic comedy, a generic transaction that installs Shakespeare's play as the afterlife of the Catholic saints. This use of decapitation as a principle of secularization – like castration in psychoanalytic theory – represents the gesture of symbolization *par excellence*. . . . The play uses the hagiographic motif of decapitation in order to decapitate hagiography itself. . . .[23]

Like the executioner, according to the economy of sacrificial substitution, the martyr is a captor, literally the *witness*, of truth: 'someone who renders an authoritative account'.[24] For in cultures of sacrificial violence grounded in scapegoat rites of capital punishment, such as Jacobean England, Revolutionary France, or the United States, such suffering, specifically by hanging or beheading, is imposed to capture meaning as a caesura or capstone of representation, Julia Kristeva explains in The Severed Head: Capital Visions, a grimly captivating history of decapitation: 'The thoroughly displayed beheading signals the end point of the visible. The show is over, ladies and gentlemen, move on! There is nothing more to see!'[25] Thus, with the beheading of Charles I and Louis XVI in mind, Maistre lauded martyrdom as the *point de capiton* of order that sees the victim victorious.[26] But in desiring an ever 'more strict restraint' [1,4,4], on this view, Isabella merely mimes an *impression* of such a 'capital vision', a word the nun applies to herself that keys into capitalist metaphors of coining, counterfeiting and printing, and thereby betrays her inauthenticity, when she boasts how she will flaunt the 'impression of keen whips . . . as rubies,/And strip myself to death as to a bed' [2,4,101–2]. So in this drama of insatiability we are forever promised a *capitonnage*, as it is reported of the condemned that 'within these three days his head is to be chopped off' [1,2,60]; and the suspense remains that his 'head stands so tickle' on his shoulders 'a milkmaid in love may sigh it off' [149]. Yet preferring the 'devilish mercy' of saving 'a head/To cleave a heart' [3,1,59–60], the Duke contrives that even the execution of Barnardine, planned to put a cap upon displacement, is indefinitely deferred when he agrees to 'omit/This reprobate till he were well inclined,/And satisfy the deputy with the visage/Of Ragusine' [4,3,65–8]. As Stephen Greenblatt remarks, here 'Substitution reigns' because this representational system is echoing 'the root condition' of theatre, for 'How else could theatre, which depends upon a low-born actor convincingly miming a prince, thrive?'[27]

If Shakespeare's subjection of 'place and greatness' to the 'thousand escapes of wit' in his theatre of representation [4,2,56] predicts the 'consensus politics' described by Jacques Rancière and Slavoj Žižek, whereby the sovereign becomes 'the subject *par excellence*' by splitting from himself, or Bataille's project to sacrifice sacrifice by miring sovereignty in its own waste, all the insecurities of the Enlightenment are also foretold in the Duke's implausible ruse to 'satisfy' his deputy with a mock execution and simulacrum of a decollated head.[28] As Robert Darnton relates in *The Great Cat Massacre*, early moderns would devise many such mimetic practices, involving the execution of animals or, in England, burning of effigies of papists, like the Gunpowder Plotter Guy Fawkes, to slake the communal thirst for catharsis.[29] In Vienna, neither prince nor public will ever be satisfied, however; because if it started out as Shakespeare's *Capital*, the idea in this rumination on the economy of desire seems to have been that the show can *never* be *caput*, since it is only by capitalising on 'an accident that Heaven provides', when the 'notorious pirate' Ragusine dies of gaol fever [62–8], that the sacrificial logic of substitution can be brought to any kind of head. For as anyone who has read Foucault will recognise, this regime has long perfected 'the experiment of abandoning public violence in return for private discipline', thereby negotiating 'that crucial shift in the economy of punishment whereby the ancient right to take life was replaced by a new power to foster life'.[30] But what frustrates the 'strict deputy' [1,2,158] who must pick up this legacy of 'too much liberty' [1,2,105], and suggests his affinity with the stringent subaltern who follows an easy-going Shakespeare, is the problem of closure in such a headless state or pointless play, for, as Angelo exclaims to his own seconder:

This will last out a night in Russia,
When nights are longest there. I'll take my leave,
And leave you to the hearing of the cause,
Hoping you'll find good cause to whip them all.

[2,1,122–5]

In a Viennese courtroom poised like Jacobean London's Chancery between the normative rule of common law and the arbitrariness of royal prerogative, an adjutant 'Whose settled visage and deliberate word/Nips youth i'th'head' [3,1,88–9], itches to foreclose these temporising games of amnesty and derogation by flexing his imperative 'scope of justice' [5,1,231]. Reneging on his promise of a pardon, Angelo will therefore have 'Claudio's head sent' to him 'by five' [4,2,114]. Acting on this executive order at 'an unusual hour' and without 'a special warrant' [5,1,549] will cost the Provost his job. But like President Bush, who loved to declare 'I am the decider', the acting CEO has learned enough about political theology from Hobbesian fables, such as the tale his master tells about the mice unfazed by the 'o'ergrown lion in a cave/That goes not out to prey' [1,3,23], to grasp the realpolitik that, in the 'sensual rein' and 'sharp appetite' of their absolute 'will', the criminal, beast and sovereign are all brothers 'outside the law'.[31] 'My place i'th'state', Angelo therefore brutally lectures Isabella, means 'my false o'erweighs your true' [2,4,156–70]. For 'after all this fooling' [1,2,62], what the Duke's lieutenant seems to share with Shakespeare's decisionist successor is exasperation that when the toothless old lion devolved power to his 'secondary', ostensibly to be as 'full' as himself [42], he simply triggered an avalanche of insubordination, as all the substitutions so crucial to this story are, 'in various ways, unsatisfying'.[32]

GOD IN MY MOUTH

Like some post-Reformation monarchy, after its 'supreme head' has been disconnected from the Church, in Shakespeare's dukedom, where everyone stands for some missing head, it seems that the 'mad fantastical trick' of the sovereign 'to steal from the state' [3,1,140] merely formalises the regime's long withdrawing 'remove' from government, the dis-antagonising of the state that allows its subjects to contentedly 'run by the hideous law/As mice by lions' [1,4,62–3]. Thus, Elbow explains that 'as they are chosen' democratically themselves, representatives of 'the generous and gravest citizens' [4,5,14] are 'glad to choose' him as Constable [2,1,238]. 'Our city's institutions and the terms/For common justice' [1,1,10] thrive on such a Presbyterian subsidiarity, this deputy believes. But the drama we have is a tale of two cities with clashing concepts of *election*, a term that, as Lupton notes in relation to its importance in *All's Well*, 'conceptualizes the simultaneously divine and popular legitimacy of preliberal politics'.[33] And in the city of popular legitimacy, Escalus is unimpressed by this Dad's Army of reserves: 'Look you, bring me in the names of some six or seven, the most sufficient in your parish' [2,1,242]. Since the whole of the existing play will involve just such a 'leavened and prepared choice' [1,1,51], to identify from 'the most sufficient' of 'our city' the truly *elect*, an incorruptible Cromwell or Robespierre figure 'of stricture and firm abstinence' [1,3,12], 'whose blood/Is very snow-broth' [1,4,55–6], or whose 'urine is congealed ice' [3,1,355], to halt the endless polling of substitutes by his monopolisation of 'absolute power and place' [1,3,13], Elbow's quest for this great decider, who can pronounce categorically that 'We are definitive' [5,1,424], looks doomed. For not only does the 'pernicious caitiff deputy' [5,1,88] vitiate his own secondment by his insubordination, but, as Alexander Leggatt observes, all these disappointing surrogacies, each a simulacrum or approximation that fails to duplicate the original, unhinge the very concept of vicariousness on which a Christian society is built:

> God acts on man through a series of substitutions: the Incarnation, the Eucharist, and the priesthood – represented here by the Duke who dresses up as a Friar and goes around hearing confessions in a manner that would produce a major scandal in an actual Catholic community. In every case the substitution, as it appears in Measure for Measure, is in some way clouded in irony. . . . For Angelo and Elbow have this in common: they fail to perform adequately in the roles assigned to them.[34]

In Shakespeare's Vienna the Duke's devolution generates a legitimacy crisis that extends to the most vicarious of substitutions, the transubstantiation symbolism of the body and blood of Christ. For Vincentio's 'leavened' preparation aligns his chosen one with the predestined elect of Calvin, who, in a defining Reformation dispute, insisted on leavened bread for the Host. 'When I would pray and think, I think and pray/To several subjects', Angelo thus laments, with 'Heaven in my mouth,/As if I did but only chew his name' [2,4,1–5]. Of course, this Eucharist reference must once have read 'God in my mouth'; so it is especially ironic that reference to the sacrament is expurgated by Middleton's alteration of God to 'Heaven' throughout the Folio, in obedience to the 1606 Act of Abuses banning theatres from taking the name of God in vain. 'He who eats and drinks unworthily, eats and drinks damnation to himself, not discerning the Lord's body', writes St Paul (1 Corinthians 11:29); for Christ's sacrifice is 'given without measure', according to John 3:34. So in the earlier text Angelo's masticating on Christ's 'name' linked him directly with Reformers like Calvin, who measured, or, like Zwingli, denied, the real presence in the consecrated bread. Middleton had been born into such a demystifying Protestantism; yet the purpose of taking the word of God out of actors' mouths was to resacralise the host they swallowed as a transcendental signifier of the body of Christ. The implications for a play set in a headless city of recapping the community in this Anglican way, as 'one mystical body the head of which is Christ', go beyond censorship; for as Ernst Kantorowicz explained in The King's Two Bodies, the political theology of sacred kingship – the belief that a king 'represented and "imitated" the image of the living Christ'[35] – was bound up with this substitution doctrine of 'the real presence of both the human and divine Christ in the Eucharist'. Authority, in such a system, was always referred to God:

> Here, at last, in that assertion of the 'Lord's Two Bodies' – in the bodies natural and mystic, personal and corporate, individual and collective of Christ – we seem to have found the precise precedent of the 'King's Two Bodies'.[36]

If Angelo is one of the elect, he is surely God's mistake. But according to the revelatory Oxford editor, John Jowett, in 1604 he literally bid the retiring Duke *adieu*, saying 'The Lord give safety to your purposes'; while in 1621 he commended him only to 'the heavens' [1,1,74]. Likewise, 'God keep your honour', Isabella greeted the deputy, before this was moderated to 'Heaven' [2,2,42]. Such euphemisms often wreck Shakespeare's imagery, as when the nun tells the judge he might pardon Claudio, 'And neither *heaven* nor man grieve at the mercy' [2,2,51]. Likewise, Lucio's meek 'indeed', instead of a conjectured *in faith* [3,1,338], banalises a character we hear speak 'much more, much worse' [5,1,335]. The Folio Lucio is an inconsistent character, half court jester, half police informer, who has to be told twice about Claudio's arrest [1,2,57; 104]. But the loss of such presumed profanities as *'Sblood* and *fore God* tames his sacrilege, while a tepid 'On my trust' for *on my faith* [5,1,146] simply sounds inane. These adaptations were imposed in deference to the blasphemy law; yet, like the reviser's imposition of acts and scenes, they are indicative not only of the urge of the succeeding generation to introduce decorum, but of the seriousness with which it came to consider Shakespeare's farce of derogation, which in its endless insubordination must have worked precisely by taking the name of God, along with His avatars and vicars, including His living image, the King himself, in vain. 'By eliciting a longing for certainty that is perpetually deferred', the first half of this play encourages audiences 'to view both the world they inhabit and the fictional world of the play as representations'.[37] Middleton's most telling alteration, in this light, was therefore to give the kindly magistrate Escalus a wholly uncharacteristic, indeed Girardian, *obiter dictum* on the communal necessity of the scapegoat mechanism of sacred violence, which signals the implacable recuperation of the force of law:[38]

> ESCALUS: It grieves me for the death of Claudio,
>   But there's no remedy.
> JUSTICE: Lord Angelo is severe.
> ESCALUS: It is but needful.
>   Mercy is not itself that oft looks so;
>   Pardon is still the nurse of second woe.

[2,1,249–54]

The moralising captiousness of Middleton's newly identified intrusions adds an extra dimension to what Leggatt considers the ultimate substitution in this work: that of *Measure for Measure* itself for the play Shakespeare would have preferred.[39] Thus the Folio Lucio not only swears meekly, he is raised to the role of confidant that formerly belonged to the Provost, when he abets Isabella's plea for Claudio's life with interjections like 'Thou'art in the right girl. More o'that' [2,2,132]. Many of the changes in the earlier scenes of the surviving play were in fact introduced to build this fool up as the Duke's foil, who in the later alterations can then be knocked down. Thus, as the Oxford editor footnotes, the clown's 'marrying a punk' is unnecessary to the ending, but when inserted in 1621 it awards the Duke the last word: 'Slandering a prince deserves it' [5,1,515–17].[40] And nowhere is this deference to princely power more crucial than in the rearrangement of the one speech that directly invokes the doctrine of divine right, the Duke's rhyming couplets about 'the sword of heaven', which he originally spoke as a self-critical aside while Isabella plotted the bed trick with Angelo's jilted Mariana onstage, thus associating what he calls 'my vice' with this shady 'Craft', but that in the Folio is moved forward, isolated from the now unseen intrigue by an act division, and then followed by a sentimental song about lips that 'sweetly were forsworn', from a hit of 1618 called 'Rollo, Duke of Normandy', to become the sacred and sublime fulcrum of the entire play. Moreover, the introduction of the unique aubade bathes the scenes that precede and follow it in numinous light and, as Jowett remarks, accentuates the importance of Mariana by imposing a fresh two-part structure on the play: 'The act-interval moats the grange from Vienna; the song that follows it reinforces that separation and affirms the new turning point' with 'a prospect that a spirit of romantic tragicomedy might perhaps prevail'.[41] But it also elevates the Duke's soliloquy to providential stature as a statement of regalian political theology:

> He who the sword of heaven will bear
> Should be as holy as severe,
> Pattern in himself to know,
> Grace to stand, and virtue go,
> More nor less to others paying
> Than by self-offences weighing.
> Shame to him whose cruel striking
> Kills for faults of his own liking!
> Twice treble shame on Angelo,
> To weed my vice, and let his grow.
>
> [3,1,480–90]

As holy as *severe*: the Duke's prescription for the heaven-sanctioned ruler as an ultimate concrete deciding presence sounds so unlike the dramatist who wrote 'The quality of mercy is not strained' [*Merchant*, 4,1,179], and so inapposite to the irenic spirit of 1604 that we might suspect the entire speech to be a Middletonian insertion. Its emphasis on the calculated measuring out of grace, self-interest, vice and payment certainly sounds like homage to the complex religious identity of James, who 'remained at heart a regal Calvinist'.[42] But its fierceness also adds to the impression of grinding gears. For 'Here comes a man of comfort, whose advice/Hath often stilled my brawling discontent' [4,1,8–9] announces Mariana unconvincingly to the chorister who has been singing of deceitful kisses in the daybreak scene, once attributed to John Webster but now definitively assigned to Middleton, which was interpolated to edify the Duke's commanding position at this mid-point of the Folio text. Its author could not resist a censorious, and very un-Shakespearean, disclaimer about the danger of music provoking 'good to harm' [15]; but Jowett connects the operatic intermission to the fashion for Fletcherian tragicomedy in the 1620s. The new turning point radically changed Shakespeare's comedy into Middleton's tragicomedy, according to this analysis. For there had surely been no such interlude of Mariana and her watery grange in the pre-existing city comedy, nor any hint that the Duke ever visited her in such a pastoral retreat. Yet the episode would become one of the most frequently illustrated in all English literature after it inspired 'Mariana', Tennyson's lachrymose poem of 1831, where 'In sleep she seems to walk forlorn, / Till cold winds wake the grey-eyed dawn, / About the lonely moated grange'.[43] And this Middleton-influenced afterlife would have a profound impact on the twentieth- and twenty-first-century Christological interpretations of *Measure for Measure* as a play about authoritarian sovereignty, in which 'Shakespeare seems to be endorsing a conservative political position' that specifically underwrites King James's supposed assertion of 'the king's priestly aura in the teeth of papal and presbyterian claims that rulers are mere laypersons and hence subject to the church'.[44]

LIKE POWER DIVINE

Lugubrious pictures by the Pre-Raphaelite artists John Everett Millais and Dante Gabriel Rossetti cemented Middleton's pseudo-Shakespearean rendezvous between Mariana and the Duke into the Victorian imagination as a quintessential locus of romantic longing, and modern theatre directors have heightened its seductiveness by breaking for an interval after the 'sword of heaven' speech. The effect during the twentieth century was to infuse the Duke's soliloquy with the spiritual aura that was presumably in the adaptor's mind when he transformed it from a confession of human fallibility into an assertion of sovereign violence and heavenly retribution. The weapon to which Shakespeare alluded in 1604 was doubtless Curtana, the broken sword of Edward the Confessor carried at English coronations to symbolise mercy, which was just then preceding the new King into Westminster Abbey. But in Middleton's reconstruction it became something altogether more pointed. In its pivotal position, the severing sword of justice came to prove how, in the words of the New Penguin editor, 'a thoroughly irresponsible ruler belatedly learns his business and ends by conforming to the pattern of the ideal prince'.[45] Thus the picturesque décor Middleton supplied for Shakespeare's play worked not only to update it for the candlelit indoor musical theatre of the 1620s, but also to put the cap on its farrago of substitutions. For in the Folio, the buck stops decisively with 'He who the sword will bear', the divinely appointed autocrat who is now ready to be what G. Wilson Knight called him in 1930, 'the prophet of a new order of ethics, like Jesus', and whom a craven Angelo indeed proclaims at the end of the existing play:[46]

> O my dread lord,
> I should be guiltier than my guiltiness
> To think I can be undiscernible,
> When I perceive your grace, like power divine,
> Hath looked upon my passes.
>
> [5,1,358–62]

It was Middleton's *recapitulation* of Shakespeare's text, the Oxford collection makes us realise, that transformed it from a drama of demonic substitution, focused on an 'outward-sainted deputy' [3,1,93], like its Elizabethan source, George

Whetstone's play *Promos and Cassandra*, into an allegory of divine sovereignty, idealising the monarch as a *deus ex machina*. In Whetstone, old King Corvinus of Hungary is the ineffectual recluse we glimpse in the first half of *Measure for Measure*, the over-indulgent 'father of much fast', who 'held in idle price to haunt assemblies' [1,3,9], and let his people go their way, 'Like rats that ravin down their proper bane' [1,2,129], by having 'the strong statutes/Stand like forfeits in a barber's shop,/As much in mock as mark' [5,1,315–18]. Whetstone's senescent king does not preach morals, hide in disguise, match-make or engineer the happy end, which comes about only because the gaoler takes it on himself to swap the head of an executed man for that of a condemned one. Perhaps the Provost played the same representative role before being side-lined by Middleton. For though *Promos and Cassandra* reflects political conditions in 1578, when England was a republic in all but name, its dispersal of power may still be close to the delegated authority that was the cause of comedy before Middleton made the Duke into such a 'meddling friar' [5,1,127]. The overdetermined 'problem play' that resulted from this totalitarian concentration of 'absolute power and place' in one man used to be attributed to Shakespeare's gamesmanship: he 'built up the problems for the sheer joy of resolving them', it was said.[47] But if the Oxford editors are correct, the real problems of *Measure for Measure* reflect the contradiction of Jacobean ideas about election and divine right, and the regression of Tudor parliamentarianism into Stuart personal rule, the mark of which, in an influential book of 1966, *'Measure for Measure' as Royal Entertainment*, Josephine Bennett was able to pinpoint precisely to this moment of the play:

> The whole character of Duke Vincentio was created . . . to please and flatter the King. For this purpose Shakespeare used the King's own picture of himself as it appears in his most successful and timely literary effort . . . the *Basilikon Doron* . . . the 'king's book'. . . . At the end of the third act in *Measure for Measure* the Duke steps out of his disguise and addresses the audience, to explain his principles of government and his plan for correcting Angelo. This soliloquy turns King James's concept of kingship into tetrameter verse:
> > *God gives not Kings the style of Gods in vain,*
> > *For on his throne the Scepter they do sway:*
> > *And as their subjects ought them to obey,*
> > *So Kings should fear and serve their God again.*[48]

Bennett noticed how the politics of *Measure for Measure* hinge on the prominence of the 'sword of heaven' speech, which she connected to a Christmas performance at court in 1604. But critics have been reluctant to grasp the implications of co-authorship for the notion that the soliloquy therefore confirms Shakespeare's endorsement of sacred monarchy. This is the interpretation still recycled by Debora Shuger, for instance, in her acclaimed *Political Theologies in Shakespeare's England*, where we read that it is 'high Christian royalism' that 'makes sense of Shakespeare's Duke, who acts as a priest', in accord with 'the sacerdotal nature of royal authority, and thus what it means to bear "the sword of heaven"'. In Shuger's account, *Measure for Measure* differs from dramas such as 'Marlowe's *Edward III*' [*sic*] in upholding the royal prerogative exercised in the Star Chamber, which, *pace* the Whig history of 'Maccauly' [*sic*], contemporaries venerated as a court of equity, where the King sat 'as God's deputy-judge upon earth'. Specifically, according to this Christianising recuperation, the text 'bears witness to a cultural moment in which Duke Vincentio makes sense': that of the January 1604 Hampton Court conference on religion, where James proclaimed himself a 'priest-king'.[49]

'The king sat in his furs in the cold weather as the fire roared up the great chimneys of Hampton Court', revelling in speaking 'with freedom to men of learning. At last he had found the bending hierarchies' for which he longed. The transcript of the conference shows, however, that he did no such thing as present himself as a priest, since the 'sacerdotal element' of kingship 'was not so much repellent to King James as wholly alien', which is why he was so sceptical about the royal touch.[50] But Shuger views the entire scenario of *Measure for Measure* as a premonition of the state of emergency as defined in the decisionist maxim that 'sovereign is he who decides on the exception' by the Nazi jurist Carl Schmitt in *Political Theology*, which is 'the only modern work', she thinks, 'to focus on the crucial role of the exception'.[51] Apparently this Fellow of the august Berlin Wissenschaftskolleg is unfamiliar with the writings of Giorgio Agamben, Étienne Balibar, Walter Benjamin and Jacques Derrida. But more damagingly, although her book appeared in 2001, almost a decade after Jowett and Taylor had established his co-authorship, she never mentions Middleton once. This is, however, scarcely surprising, when we appreciate how the Schmittian thesis about the theocratic Shakespeare of 1604 is exploded by the evidence that the *Measure for Measure* we possess was actually finished by an altogether different writer, in 1621.

CRUEL STRIKING

The textual disintegration of *Measure for Measure* is fatal to the myth of Shakespeare as a mystic royalist, which can be sustained only by critics deaf to irony and oblivious of the play *as theatre*. Thus, when Middleton broke the back of the original comedy of clemency and commutation by having the Duke extol 'the sword of heaven' in solitary eminence, he had to shift the monarch's melancholy meditation on the 'millions of false eyes' stuck on 'place and greatness' back to the end of the new act, to cover Isabella's intrigue with Mariana, where its inappropriateness to a moment when the ruler is applying his omniscient 'Craft' underlined the drastic change of scene. Until this moment, it would seem, sheer 'inventiveness allowed Shakespeare to think beyond the absolutism of Jacobean rule', as *Measure for Measure* developed his signature theme of 'the great eclipse' of monarchy marking the eve of liberal constitutionalism, the deconsecration when the King 'carded his state,/Mingled his royalty with cap'ring fools' and 'Had his great name profanèd with their scorns' [*1 Henry IV*, 3,2,63].[52] The Shakespearean Duke indulges this 'permissive pass' as a Brueghel-like holiday, when 'Liberty plucks justice by the nose', since monarchy is now too implicated in its subjects' lives to 'unloose' the 'tied-up Justice' that goes with 'absolute power'. With his Calvinist notion of election, Middleton would tip this merry moratorium into Hogarthian morality, however, by stigmatising its low-life with deterministic names like 'Madam Mitigation' [1,2,40]. 'It is a bitter deputy' [4,2,70] who populates the prison scenes with Middletonian inmates such as 'young Drop-hair that killed Lusty Pudding' [4,3,12]. But Vincentio still sounds as though he has been enjoying the Elizabethan Bankside, because the mayhem he depicts, when 'the threatening birch' is stuck up 'for terror, not to use', is the entropic carnival scenario of all Shakespeare's previous comedies, where, symbolically at least, 'The baby beats the nurse,/And quite athwart/Goes all decorum' [1,3,13–38].

Beginning in that midsummer dawn when Duke Theseus startles his subjects by agreeing to 'overbear' the 'ancient privilege of Athens' [Dream, 1,1,41;4,1,176], up to now Shakespearean monarchy had been progressively absorbing the Kantian lesson that, as his Viennese counterpart admits, "Twould be my tyranny to strike and gall them/For what I bid them do' [Measure, 1,4,36]. In particular, Shakespeare's aestheticising project had been to disrupt the sacrificial cycle by dramatising the Abrahamic moment when the sword 'seemed i'th'air to stick' [Hamlet, 2,2,459]. Thus, with their 'decrees/Dead to infliction' [1,3,26–7], 'In the delaying death' [4,2,160], and making 'privily away' with 'safe discretion', the rulers of his earlier plays were well on the way to becoming the bicycling royals of modern democracies, who 'love the people,/But do not like to stage' themselves 'to their eyes', and no longer 'relish well/Their loud applause and aves vehement' [Measure, 1,1,66–71]. As Meredith Anne Skura writes, 'The Duke claims to have no need of approval. The whole problem in Vienna has arisen because he disdains (rightly, we think) the gaudy public display which is inherent in a duke's role'.[53] It therefore makes it seem 'downright schizophrenic' when, half way through the story he took up, Middleton switches the Duke from being 'absolute for death' [3,1,5] to being 'absolute' for 'place and power', from 'a shy fellow' [3,1,372] of 'dark corners' who detests spectacles 'Where witless youth and bravery keeps' [1,3,10], disdains 'the public ear' [4,2,100] and confesses his failings to a friar, into the histrionic showman who brazenly faces down Lucio's acute report that it was his 'feeling of the sport' that 'instructed him to mercy' [3,1,384], with a stagey sequence of 'fantastic tricks' [2,2,124] or 'bringings-forth', that not only puts his power on vainglorious display 'to the envious' as 'a scholar, a statesman, and a soldier' [3,1,364–84], but melodramatises the show trial of his fallen favourite 'in the street' [4,4,9]:[54]

> O, your desert speaks loud, and I should wrong it
> To lock it in the wards of covert bosom,
> When it deserves with characters of brass
> A forted residence 'gainst the tooth of time
> And razure of oblivion. Give me your hand,
> And let the subject see, to make them know
> That outward courtesies would fain proclaim
> Favours that keep within.
>
> [5,1,9–16]

'Bid them bring the trumpets' [4,5,9], orders the Duke, when he returns in the published text; and in lurching from autonomy to 'dependence on its actor-manager', authorial absenteeism to authoritarian absolutism, after giving its scape-goat rope to hang himself, Middleton's *Measure for Measure* would teach the Stuarts a lot about the theatrics of raising and disgracing over-mighty ministers, such as Francis Bacon, whose fall coincided with the revision.[55] For what we now witness is the counter-revolution, when, as Žižek writes, 'the State regresses to the level of Substantiality', since 'this *coup de theatre* is also a political coup', as, with Angelo on his right and Escalus 'on our other hand', like scales of justice or the 'good support-ers' of an arch [17], Vincentio's re-entry into Vienna has the triumphalist heraldry of one of James's own parades.[56] And this is not surprising, given that it was actually Middleton who orchestrated the King's long-delayed procession into London on 15 March 1604, with a moral pageant performed in Fleet Street, in which the figure of Zeal preached that all classes were burning with 'holy zeal' to see the new ruler govern with 'Justice in causes, Fortitude 'gainst your foes,/Temp'rance in spleen, and Prudence in all those'. By identifying puritanical 'zeal' with 'joys on every subject's face', Middleton thus allayed any fears that London's Protestants were as hostile as their Edinburgh co-religionists to the advent of 'absolute power'. Instead, 'The Whole Royal and Magnificent Entertainment', as it was styled, expressed the conformity of the Puritan leaders, who at the Hampton Court Conference two months earlier had declared they were 'grave men and obedient to the laws', when it ushered in the Scottish monarch as a reformer whose all-seeing 'regal eye' would advance 'new faces and new men': 'So with reverberate shouts our globe shall ring,/The music's close being thus: God save our King!'[57]

Ever since Margot Heinemann anachronistically affiliated him with the 'par-liamentary Puritan opposition' to Charles I, it has been usual 'to sketch a scene in which the subversive Middleton undermines the conservative Shakespeare'.[58] Yet this construction of a more 'modern Middleton', who 'took the part of the "people"', flies in the face of the facts that, as Paul Yachnin objects, his canon is so 'often royalist and orthodox', while the 'strain of zealous English Protestantism running right through it' is less deeply contrarian than Shakespeare's irony.[59] Thus, his paean about 'our globe' ringing across the Thames 'with reverberate shouts' that applaud the entrance of a new caesar, on another ides of March, itself echoed the 'replication' of the 'universal shout' with which Shakespeare inaugurated the Globe of 1599 in *Julius Caesar*. There the reverberations of Caesar's triumph made the river 'tremble', in apprehension [1,1,45], however, whereas no such foreboding disturbed Middleton's panegyric. Instead, his annexation of the Globe as a mainstay of impe-rial power was built into the arch he underwrote, which was topped by an actual sphere that revolved to disclose figures representing 'all the degrees and states that are in the land', a device that was quickly incorporated by Inigo Jones into the court masque *Hymenaei*.[60] This would prove a prophetic prelude to all of Middleton's Shakespeare appropriations. For though his admirers have always known how his processional dramaturgy was shaped by the programmatic civic pageantry into which he had been initiated by a privileged upbringing in a mansion adjacent to London's Guildhall, they have been less ready to accept that with his masques for the City and Inner Temple, or tyrannical fixation on the 'light–darkness and sight–blindness' dualism and absolutist symbolism of the eye, the Calvinist deviser of Lord Mayor's Shows, such as *The Triumphs of Truth*, in which Zeal flays Error with a 'scourge of fire' to expose his moral ugliness, was literally *at home* in the epicentre of Stuart power.[61]

A LOOKER-ON

Editors have long recognised how the masque-like song and dance interludes Middleton inserted into *Macbeth* 'form the core of the operatic development of the play which held the stage' in the later seventeenth century.[62] In fact, *all* the younger writer's additions to Shakespeare functioned to square the pre-existing texts with the ceremonialism of the triumphal entry, thereby eliding the contradiction between plays originally conceived for the open platform of a public amphitheatre and their revival in the increasingly pictorial frame of the private playhouse. A far more decisive and processional dramaturgy is therefore functioning in these insertions than in Shakespeare's theatre of crab-wise circumspection. As Scott McMillin explains in the Oxford volume: 'To visualize Middleton's plays visualize costumed actors standing out as full-dimensioned figures ... his stage does not "stand" for something else so much as it allows different figures to be set forth in its own repeated space'.[63] It is therefore not surprising that the effect of the musical add-ons to *Macbeth* was 'to shift the emphasis on to the witches as being in command'.[64] For all the focus of these pageant-like embellishments is on the recuperation of power, and Hecate's irritation is revealing, as she berates her earthly representatives for daring 'To trade and traffic with Macbeth', when she, their sovereign, has played no part in displaying 'the glory of our art'. In Middleton's phantasmagoria, of course, the deputies make certain that this Shakespearean dereliction of authority is quickly corrected: 'Come, let's make haste. She'll soon be back again' [*Macbeth*, 3,5,4–9; 74].

Power strikes back again in all Middleton's rhymed adaptations of Shakespeare, to ensure that after the infliction of such cruel pains, the successor 'shall share the i'th'gains' [4,1,40], a 'hegemonic conservatism' Kevin Quarmby connects to the 'medievalism' of his morality play design, but that Gail Kern Paster aligns with a 'political theory customarily required of princes'. By always 'magnifying the importance of the men and the entertainments' he stages, she notes, Middleton provides them 'with the same ethical justification' used for masques at court.[65] In his determination to assert authorial control, and 'the glory of our art', we might add, this legatee displays all the hubris of the survivor. Since the older dramatist was active until as late as 1615, it has been argued that Shakespeare must have agreed in advance any changes made by his accessory.[66] Yet 'The moon's an arrant thief/And her pale fire she snatches from the sun', reads the Shakespearean section of *Timon of Athens* [4,3,430–1], suggesting that Middleton's senior partner was fully alive to the Oedipal aspect of these appropriations, the parasitism which John Davies of Hereford poeticised when in 1610 he assured the doyen that 'honesty thou sow'st, which they do reap;/So, to increase their Stock which they do keep'.[67]

The substitution scenario of *Measure for Measure* implies that Shakespeare had long anticipated and discounted his ideological and stylistic supersession by his patricidal successor, and wrote this castration anxiety into his legacy by booby-trapping his bequest. The absolutist implications of such a Baroque takeover are evident, in any case, in the triumphalist denouement of the earliest Middletonian collaboration, which sees Timon's inheritor Alcibiades command trumpets to 'Sound to this coward and lascivious town/Our terrible approach' [5,5,1–2]. Likewise, the *Measure for Measure* Middleton rewrote for the Folio compilers ends with the Duke ordering the Provost to 'Proclaim' his royal justice 'round about the city' [5,1,505]. Yet this public ostentation is so at odds with the earlier Shakespearean scenes which decry 'man, proud man,/Dressed in a little brief authority' [2,2,120–1] that it makes one wonder what 'this good deputy' [4,1,24] would have done if he had been able to produce a drama with the same plot without the old master's complicating res-ervations about the actual authorities. And we do not need to look far to find out, because as a matter of fact he did.

Middleton wrote his first play, *The Phoenix*, for the choirboys of St Paul's some time in 1604, in the same months as the King's Men were preparing *Measure for Measure* for the Globe, and it seems possible the twenty-four-year-old tyro devised it after studying a copy of Shakespeare's script. James attended performances of both plays. But the title of *The Phoenix* implies it was composed to trump the older dramatist's peculiar take on kingship, as it refers to the myth of the bird reborn from its ashes that Elizabeth adopted, and her successor embraced, to the extent of writing an elegy with the same title in memory of his favourite, Esmé Stuart, as an image of the political theology of 'The King's Two Bodies', that the sovereign never dies. Pointedly, then, Middleton's Duke of Ferrara has reigned for forty-five years, the same as the Queen when she passed away, while Phoenix is the actual name adopted by his heir as he awaits the succession in disguise. Clearly, *The Phoenix* was devised to be more royalist than the King. But the possibility that it was also written to be more royalist than *Measure for Measure* is reinforced by hints that Shakespeare's drama, with its Italian names, was once set in Ferrara too, and that it was the reviser who changed its location to Vienna, in honour of James's schemes to avert the Thirty Years War 'despite of all controversy' [1,2,24]. In 1621 Middleton had just produced *The World Tossed at Tennis*, and his topical updating of the Shakespearean text, with soldiers rooting for a continental war over 'the King of Hungary' [2], is of a piece with the rapturous praise of James as a politician and poet he stuffed into that earlier masque:

> And I'll settle
> Here, in a land of most glorious peace
> That ever made joy fruitful, where the head
> Of him that rules, to learning's fair renown,
> Is doubly decked, with laurel and a crown. . . .[68]

Critics who assume that being 'most strait in virtue' [2,1,9] made the evangelis-ing Middleton more 'oppositional' than Shakespeare have clearly not appreciated how his 'absolutist fantasy of despotism-as-providence' locked into his hyperbolic endorsement of 'The blessedness, peace, honour, and renown,/This kingdom does enjoy, under the crown/Worn by that royal peace-maker, our king', in the words of his 1623 pageant, *The Triumphs of Integrity*.[69] This was a writer who in his satire *The Nightingale and the Ant* could salute James on his succession as a 'manly lion' who 'now can roar/Thunder more dreaded than the lioness' Elizabeth.[70] Nothing could sound less like the 'o'ergrown lion' of the Shakespearean half of *Measure for Measure* than this decisionism. When he reconstructed the dead writer's agonistic comedy of crowds and power, in any event, the author of *The Phoenix* had form as a royal cheerleader, and had even ghosted, with Bacon, *The Peacemaker*, a pamphlet on the *Rex Pacificus*, published in 1618 in the King's name.[71] By the time he adapted the old play about election, Middleton had also risen to be the City's archivist, as well as the stage manager of its mayoral shows, whose official business made him its true 'looker-on' [5,1,314]. So when he again took on Shakespeare, what the successor transferred from text to text, with such confusing consequences for criticism, was the authoritarian ideal that runs throughout his canon, of the great dictator, a head man like Prince Phoenix, whose power, according to his father, comes from the 'regal eye' that sees the 'character' in a life 'That to th'observer doth [its] history/Fully unfold' [1,1,27–8]:

> State is but blindness; thou hadst piercing art
> We only saw the knee, but thou the heart.
> To thee then power and dukedom we resign;
> He's fit to reign whose knowledge can refine.[72]

'My business in this state/Made me a looker-on here in Vienna', echoes the Folio Duke, 'where I have seen corruption boil and bubble/Till it o'errun the stew' [314–18]. The image of this panoptic overseer peering over the city uncannily prefigures Hobbes's *Leviathan*, with its famous frontispiece of the 'mortal god who brings peace and security', and 'on the basis of its sovereignty determines what the subjects of the state have to believe to be a miracle'.[73] Yet if Shakespeare editions have been slow to absorb the news from Vienna that the schizophrenia of *Measure for Measure* is a result not of 'authorial despair, haste, forgetfulness, or despondency', but of its having been constructed by different dramatists of distinct attitudes and generations, working seventeen years apart, they have nonetheless always registered resistance in the play to this totalitarian project of putting power on display.[74] The bare life of Barnardine, the recidivist prisoner who will take no 'advice' from his supreme head about being 'absolute for death', and 'will not die today for any man's persuasion' [4,3,57], has therefore come to exemplify a deep Shakespearean obstruction to the political theology of royal supremacy, with its sacrificial logic of the headsman. For Barnardine's withholding of 'consent to die this day' [48] drives as much of a wedge between the fictive and personal dimensions of the body politic as the execution of Charles Stuart would do to separate the King's Two Bodies.[75] So, long before textual revisionism called the authorship of the ending of this play into question, this criminal's incorrigible refusal of foreclosure was recognised for what it is: a Shakespearean affirmation of the license to offend, albeit 'a most unlikely emblem of artistic freedom'.[76]

If the author of the original *Measure for Measure* had had his way, the new bibliography suggests, the recalcitrance of a shuffling Barnardine would have ensured the perpetuation of 'our good will' in an endless round of fictionalising substitutions and parliamentary postponements. To Middleton's promoters, of course, it is the claim that *Measure for Measure* belongs in his 'Collected Works' that makes the play more accessible, democratic and modern. And it has even been argued that this metropolitan moraliser of 'filthy vices' [2,4,42], whose radical Protestantism was of such 'stricture and firm abstinence' [1,3,12], would make a more inclusive or politically correct candidate for the title of Bard of Britain than the shifty, procrastinating immoralist from Stratford. Yet canonised now among Middleton's complete plays, *Measure for Measure* emerges as a drama about the impossibility of ever completing what was left so provocatively 'to be continued'. The text that survives has a head grafted onto the trunk of Shakespeare's acephalic comedy. But in his own absolutism, our 'leavened and prepared choice' to cap in this way the 'very superficial, ignorant, and unweighing fellow' [3,2,132] whom we know all too well as the 'old fantastical' author of the plays we love, has himself come to look, the closer we study his 'cruel striking', less like some 'radical alternative', and more and more like one of those 'seemers' with something dark to hide, 'Though angel on the outward side' [3,2,260].[77]

NOTES

1. Ryszard Kapuściński, *The Emperor: Downfall of an Autocrat*, trans. William Brand and Katarzyna Mroczkowska-Brand (New York: Vintage Books, 1984), p. 33.
2. Samuel Johnson, '*Measure for Measure*', in *Samuel Johnson on Shakespeare*, ed. H. R. Woudhuysen (Harmondsworth: Penguin, 1989), p. 173.
3. Gary Taylor, 'Thomas Middleton: lives and afterlives', in *The Collected Works of Thomas Middleton*, ed. Gary Taylor and John Lavagnino (Oxford: Oxford University Press, 2007), p. 58.
4. Ibid., p. 55.
5. Ibid., p. 37.
6. 'Posthumous collaboration': Mark Hutchings and A. A. Bromham, *Middleton and His Collaborators* (London: Northcote/British Council, 2008), p. 64.
7. Brian Vickers, '*All's Well That Ends* Well: an attribution rejected', *Times Literary Supplement*, 11 May 2012, 8–9, here 8.
8. '"Double" and "other"': James Bednarz, 'Collaboration: the shadow of Shakespeare', in Suzanne Gossett (ed.), *Thomas Middleton in Context* (Cambridge: Cambridge University Press, 2001), pp. 211–34, here p. 234.
9. 'A fascinating example': Hutchings and Bromham, *Middleton and His Collaborators*, pp. 64–5.
10. Joseph de Maistre, *Les Soirées de Saint-Pétersbourg, ou Entretiens sur le gouvernement de la Providence*, 2 vols (Paris: Editions de Maisnie, 1980), vol. 1, p. 34, trans. and quoted in Jesse Goldhammer, *The Headless Republic: Sacrificial Violence in Modern French Thought* (Ithaca: Cornell University Press, 2005), pp. 99–100.
11. Michel Foucault, *Discipline and Punish: The Birth of the Prison*, trans. Alan Sheridan (Harmondsworth: Penguin, 1977), pp. 32–69.
12. Jacques Derrida, *The Other Heading: Reflections on Today's Europe*, trans. Pascale-Anne Brault and Michael Naas (Bloomington: Indiana University Press, 1992), p. 14.
13. Foucault, *Discipline and Punish*, pp. 51 and 53.

14. 'Combination of absence and presence': Jonathan Goldberg, *James I and the Politics of Literature* (Stanford: Stanford University Press, 1989), p. 235; 'douce and crafty': David Mathew, *James I* (London: Eyre and Spottiswoode, 1967), p. 72.

15. James VI and I, Hampton Court conference, 14–17 January 1604, *State Trials*, vol. 2, p. 83, quoted in Mathew, *James I*, p. 126.

16. James VI and I, *Basilikon Doron*, in *Political Works of James I*, ed. Charles Howard McIlwain (Cambridge, MA: Harvard University Press, 1918; reprinted New York: Russell and Russell, 1965), p. 23.

17. Goldberg, *James I and the Politics of Literature*, p. 233.

18. James VI and I, Hampton Court conference, 14–17 January 1604, *State Trials*, vol. 2, p. 83, quoted in Mathew, *James I*, p. 126.

19. Ibid., p. 124.

20. Andrew Hadfield, *Shakespeare and Republicanism* (Cambridge: Cambridge University Press, 2005), p. 192.

21. Leo Bersani and Ulysse Dutoit, *Caravaggio's Secrets* (Cambridge, MA: MIT Press, 1998), p. 99.

22. Huston Diehl, '"Infinite space": representation and reformation in *Measure for Measure*', *Shakespeare Quarterly*, 49 (1998), 393–410, here 410.

23. Julia Reinhard Lupton, *Afterlives of the Saints: Hagiography, Typology, and Renaissance Literature* (Stanford: Stanford University Press, 1996), p. 139.

24. Goldhammer, *The Headless Republic*, p. 21.

25. Julia Kristeva, *The Severed Head: Capital Visions*, trans. Jody Gladding (New York: Columbia University Press, 2012), p. 89.

26. Joseph de Maistre, *Eclaircissement sur les sacrifices* (Paris: Pocket, 1994), quoted in Goldhammer, *The Headless Republic*, pp. 109–10.

27. Stephen Greenblatt, *Shakespeare's Freedom* (Chicago: University of Chicago Press, 2010), p. 11.

28. 'Consensus politics': Jacques Rancière, *Dissensus: On Politics and Aesthetics*, trans. Steven Corcoran (London: Continuum, 2010), p. 100; 'the subject *par excellence*': Slavoj Žižek, *The Sublime Object of Ideology* (London: Verso, 1989), p. 221; Georges Bataille, *The Accursed Share: An Essay on General Economy*, trans. Robert Hurley (New York: Zone Books, 1993), p. 106. For the obstruction of this process, see Eric Santner, *The Royal Remains: The People's Two Bodies and the Endgames of Sovereignty* (Chicago: Chicago University Press, 2011), pp. 105–7.

29. Robert Darnton, *The Great Cat Massacre, And Other Episodes in French Cultural History* (Harmondsworth: Penguin, 1985).

30. Richard Wilson, *Shakespeare in French Theory: King of Shadows* (London: Routledge, 2007), pp. 97 and 103, quoting Michel Foucault, *The History of Sexuality. Volume 1: Introduction*, trans. Robert Hurley (Harmondsworth: Penguin, 1980), pp. 137–81, here p. 139. See also Daniel Cadman, '"The very nerves of state": biopolitics and sovereignty in Shakespeare's Vienna', in Guillaume Winter (ed.), *Lectures de 'Measure for Measure'* (Rennes: Presses Universitaires de Rennes, 2012), pp. 159–72.

31. 'I am the decider': quoted in Hal Foster, 'I am the decider', *London Review of Books*, 17 March 2011, 31–2; Jacques Derrida, *The Sovereign and the Beast. Volume 1*, trans. Geoffrey Bennington (Chicago: Chicago University Press, 2009), p. 17. For the pessimistic anthropology of animal fables, see also pp. 43–5; and Carl Schmitt, *The Concept of the Political*, trans. George Schwab (Chicago: Chicago University Press, 1996), pp. 51–3.

32. Alexander Leggatt, 'Substitution in *Measure for Measure*', *Shakespeare Quarterly*, 39 (1988), 342–59, here 344. See also James Black, 'The unfolding of *Measure for Measure*', *Shakespeare Survey*, 26 (1973), 119–28, esp. 124–5; and Nancy Leonard, 'Substitution in Shakespeare's problem comedies', *English Literary Renaissance*, 9 (1979), 281–301.

33. Julia Reinhard Lupton, *Thinking With Shakespeare: Essays on Politics and Life* (Chicago: University of Chicago Press, 2011), p. 114.
34. Leggatt, 'Substitution in *Measure for Measure*', p. 344.
35. Ernst Kantorowicz, *The King's Two Bodies: A Study in Medieval Political Theology* (Princeton: Princeton University Press, 1997), p. 87.
36. Ibid., pp. 196 and 199.
37. Diehl, '"Infinite space"', p. 403.
38. For sacrificial substitution as a mechanism for quelling intracommunal violence, see René Girard, *Violence and the Sacred*, trans. Patrick Gregory (Baltimore: Johns Hopkins University Press, 1992).
39. Leggatt, 'Substitution in *Measure for Measure*', p. 359.
40. John Jowett, '*Measure for Measure*: a genetic text', and note to 5,1,476, in *The Collected Works of Thomas Middleton*, ed. Taylor and Lavagnino, pp. 1543 and 1584. See also Gary Taylor and John Jowett, *Shakespeare Reshaped, 1606–1623* (Oxford: Clarendon Press, 1993), pp. 123–40.
41. Jowett, '*Measure for Measure*: a genetic text', p. 1546.
42. Mathew, *James I*, p. 127.
43. Alfred Tennyson, 'Mariana', in *The Poems of Tennyson*, ed. Christopher Ricks (London: Longman, 1987), pp. 205–6.
44. 'Shakespeare seems to be endorsing': Tina Krontiris, 'The omniscient "auctor": ideology and point of view in *Measure for Measure*', *English Studies*, 80, 293–306, here 305; 'the king's priestly aura': Debora Kuller Shuger, *Political Theologies in Shakespeare's England: The Sacred and the State in 'Measure for Measure'* (Basingstoke: Palgrave, 2001), p. 59.
45. J. M. Nosworthy, 'Introduction', in William Shakespeare, *Measure for Measure* (Harmondsworth: Penguin, 1969), p. 23.
46. G. Wilson Knight, *The Wheel of Fire; Interpretations of Shakespearean Tragedy* (Oxford: Oxford University Press, 1930), p. 88.
47. Nosworthy, 'Introduction', p. 15.
48. Josephine Waters Bennett, '*Measure for Measure*' as Royal Entertainment (New York: Columbia University Press, 1966), pp. 81 and 85–6.
49. Shuger, *Political Theologies in Shakespeare's England*, pp. 38, 60, 90 and 110–11.
50. Mathew, *James I*, p. 127.
51. Shuger, *Political Theologies in Shakespeare's England*, pp. 79–80; 'Sovereign is he who decides': Carl Schmitt, *Political Theology: Four Chapters on the Concept of Sovereignty*, trans. George Schwab (Chicago: Chicago University Press, 2005), p. 5.
52. Paul Yachnin, 'Shakespeare's problem plays and the drama of his time', in Richard Dutton and Jean Howard (eds), *A Companion to Shakespeare's Works: The Poems, Problem Comedies, Late Plays* (Oxford: Blackwell, 2006), p. 66; Franco Moretti, 'The great eclipse: tragic form as the deconsecration of sovereignty', in *Signs Taken For Wonders: On the Sociology of Literary Forms* (London: Verso, 1993), pp. 42–82.
53. Meredith Anne Skura, *Shakespeare the Actor and the Purposes of Playing* (Chicago: Chicago University Press, 1993), p. 143.
54. 'Downright schizophrenic': Darryl Gless, '*Measure for Measure*', the Law, and the Convent (Princeton: Princeton University Press, 1979), p. 156.
55. 'Dependence on its actor-manager': Anthony Dawson, '*Measure for Measure*, New Historicism, and theatrical power', *Shakespeare Quarterly*, 39 (1988), 328–41, here 335.
56. Žižek, *The Sublime Object of Ideology*, p. 222; 'this *coup de théâtre*': Ifig Cocoual, 'The Duke is the King is the Prince: the virtuoso play of Machiavellian representation in *Measure for Measure*', in Guillaume Winter (ed.), *Lectures de 'Measure for Measure'* (Rennes: Presses Universitaires de Rennes, 2012), 137–58, here 152.
57. 'Grave men and obedient': quoted in William McElwee, *The Wisest Fool in Christendom*

(London: Faber and Faber, 1958), p. 139; Thomas Middleton, *The Whole Royal and Magnificent Entertainment*, ed. R. Malcolm Smuts, in *The Collected Works of Thomas Middleton*, ed. Taylor and Lavagnino, pp. 263–4, ll. 2156–7 and 2170–3.

58. Margot Heinemann, *Puritanism and Theatre: Thomas Middleton and Oppositional Drama Under the Early Stuarts* (Cambridge: Cambridge University Press, 1980); Hutchings and Bromham, *Middleton and His Collaborators*, p. 71.

59. 'Took the part of the "people"': Swapan Chakravorty, *Society and Politics in the Plays of Thomas Middleton* (Oxford: Clarendon Press, 1996), p. 194; Paul Yachnin, 'Reversal of fortune: Shakespeare, Middleton, and the Puritans', *ELH*, 70 (2003), 787–811, here 771.

60. *The Collected Works of Thomas Middleton*, ed. Taylor and Lavagnino, p. 261, ll. 2059–60.

61. 'Light–darkness': David Bergeron, 'Middleton's moral landscape: *A Chaste Maid in Cheapside* and *The Triumphs of Truth*', in Kenneth Friedenreich (ed.), *'Accompaninge the Players': Essays Celebrating Thomas Middleton, 1580–1980* (New York: AMS Press, 1980), pp. 133–46, here p. 138; 'scourge of fire': Thomas Middleton, *The Triumphs of Truth*, ed. David Bergeron, in *The Collected Works of Thomas Middleton*, ed. Taylor and Lavagnino, p. 971, l. 342.

62. Inga-Stina Ewbank, 'Introduction', *The Tragedy of Macbeth*, in *The Collected Works of Thomas Middleton*, ed. Taylor and Lavagnino, p. 1165.

63. Scott McMillin, 'Middleton's theatres', in *The Collected Works of Thomas Middleton*, ed. Taylor and Lavagnino, pp. 83–4.

64. Ewbank, 'Introduction', p. 1168.

65. Kevin Quarmby, *The Disguised Ruler in Shakespeare and His Contemporaries* (Farnham: Ashgate, 2012), pp. 39–58, esp. pp. 53–4; Gail Kern Paster, 'The idea of London in masque and pageant', in David Bergeron (ed.), *Pageantry in the Shakespearean Theater* (Athens, GA: University of Georgia Press, 2011), pp. 48–64, at p. 56.

66. Hutchings and Bromham, *Middleton and His Collaborators*, p. 63.

67. John Davies of Hereford, 'To our English Terence, Mr. Will. Shake-speare', reprinted in E. K. Chambers, *William Shakespeare*, 2 vols (Oxford: Clarendon Press, 1930), vol. 2, p. 214.

68. Thomas Middleton, *The World Tossed at Tennis*, ed. C. E. McGee, in *The Collected Works of Thomas Middleton*, ed. Taylor and Lavagnino, p. 1430, ll. 877–81.

69. 'Absolutist fantasy': Chakravorty, *Society and Politics in the Plays of Thomas Middleton*, p. 35; Thomas Middleton and Anthony Munday, *The Triumphs of Integrity*, ed. David Bergeron, in *The Collected Works of Thomas Middleton*, ed. Taylor and Lavagnino, p. 1771, ll. 272–4. For the theory of Middleton as more oppositional than Shakespeare, see Gary Taylor, 'Forms of opposition: Shakespeare and Middleton', *English Literary Renaissance*, 24 (1994), 283–314; and for the opposite argument, see N. W. Bawcutt, 'Was Thomas Middleton a Puritan dramatist?', *Modern Language Review*, 94 (1999), 925–39.

70. Thomas Middleton, *The Nightingale and the Ant*, ed. Adrian Weiss, in *The Collected Works of Thomas Middleton*, ed. Taylor and Lavagnino, p. 168, ll. 222–3.

71. See Rhodes Dunlap, 'James I, Bacon, and the making of *The Peacemaker*', in Josephine Bennett (ed.), *Studies in the English Renaissance Drama* (London: Peter Owen, 1961), pp. 82–94.

72. Thomas Middleton, *The Phoenix*, ed. Lawrence Danson and Ivo Kamps, in *The Collected Works of Thomas Middleton*, ed. Taylor and Lavagnino, 15.179–82.

73. Carl Schmitt, *The Leviathan in the State Theory of Thomas Hobbes: Meaning and Failure of a Political Symbol*, trans. George Schwab (Chicago: University of Chicago Press, 2008), p. 53.

74. Gless, *'Measure for Measure'*, *the Law, and the Convent*, p. 156.

75. Kantorowicz, *The King's Two Bodies*, p. 41.

76. Greenblatt, *Shakespeare's Freedom*, p. 13.

77. 'Radical alternative': Hutchings and Bromham, *Middleton and His Collaborators*, p. 71.

10 Incensing Relics: *All's Well That Ends Well* in Shakespeare's Spain

WITH SAINTED VOW

'I am Saint Jaques' pilgrim, thither gone': at the turning point of *All's Well That Ends Well* [3,4,4] the heroine, Helena, 'the daughter of Gerard de Narbonne' [1,1,33], writes to her mother-in-law, the Countess of Rousillon, to tell her that instead of remaining in Perpignan, she is taking the pilgrim road – El Camino – across Navarre and the Pyrenees to Pamplona, and by way of Burgos and Leon, to the greatest of Europe's Catholic shrines, at Santiago de Compostela. Helena's announcement astonishes the old lady, who declares that 'Had I spoken with her,/I could have well diverted her intents' [3,4,20–1]; and with good cause, since this is the only time in Shakespearean drama that a character declares an intention to go to Spain. It is the putative destination of this serious comedy in the holiest of Catholicism's sacred places that leads many critics to conclude that what Shakespeare is here staging for his sceptical countrymen is the 'reversion to a much older, quasi-magical mode of thought and worship that preceded the splitting of the faiths'.[1] But the characterisation of its heroine as a 'holy pilgrim' [3,5,36] on the road to Compostela also seems to play provocatively upon the political enmity of an England where, as Oliver Cromwell would comment, 'The papists have ever been accounted, since I was born, Spaniolized'.[2] So it is possible that with *All's Well That Ends Well* Shakespeare turned to the name of Santiago, and to the literal well-springs of theatre, for a true catharsis, in a therapeutic scenario that casts his exiled heroine in the role of *pharmakos*, and locates in the toxic site of an outlawed religion a model for his own agonistic theatre, as a poison that cures.

Rousillon was in Spanish hands when the play was written, around 1603–4, and would remain so until 1659; but it is its Galician horizon that sends *All's Well That Ends Well* in the direction of the romances. In *Afterlives of the Saints*, Julia Lupton observes how Shakespeare highlights aspects of his sources most rebarbative to Protestants, for 'his Venice, Verona and Navarre, as well as the strangely Italianate Vienna of *Measure for Measure*', belong to the Europe of pilgrimage routes, 'mapped by the medieval legends of the saints'.[3] And it is true that, for a supposedly patriotic

Protestant, this writer had a provoking trick of setting his happy endings in the Habsburg lands of the Mediterranean or Holy Roman Empire. But in *The Two Gentlemen of Verona* 'the Imperial's court' [2,3,4] is never quite linked to Spain, despite the boys joining a delegation 'to salute the Emperor' led by one Don Alfonso [1,3,39–41]; in *Much Ado About Nothing* Don Pedro's army seems more at home in Sicily than Aragon; in *As You Like It* the outlaws perhaps flee to the Warwickshire Arden, rather than the Ardennes of the seminaries funded by Philip II; in *Twelfth Night* Illyria floats free of any Habsburg coast; in *Measure for Measure* Vienna is spared Hispanic fanaticism; in *The Winter's Tale* Bohemia is as much a haven for refugees from Inquisition paranoia as it was under Rudolf II; and in *The Tempest* Milan is restored to its duke despite the fact that it was also occupied by Spain. Likewise, in *The Merchant of Venice* Belmont scorns the Prince of Aragon as 'a blinking idiot' [2,9,54]; and in *Love's Labour's Lost* the King of Navarre mocks the 'refined traveller of Spain' [1,1,161], Armado, for a penance 'enjoined in Rome' to wear his mistress's dishcloth 'next to his heart' [5,2,695]. So, it seems no accident that the Don is devoted to a girl named Jaquenetta. When Helena walks off barefoot 'To Saint Jaques le Grand' [*All's Well*, 3,5,31], her 'zealous fervour' [3,4,11] to worship at the shrine of the patron saint of Spain thus looks set to initiate an opening, in defiance of the 'black legend' of Iberian otherness Shakespeare wove into *Othello*, to the heartland of England's Catholic enemy:[4]

I am Saint Jaques' pilgrim, thither gone.
Ambitious love hath so in me offended
That barefoot plod I the cold ground upon
With sainted vow my faults to have amended.

[3,4,4–7]

On the Feast of Santiago, Saint James's Day, 25 July 1554, with a sermon on the name of James by Archbishop Gardiner, Queen Mary and King Philip of Spain had been married in Winchester Cathedral in a Mass which haunted Shakespeare's imagination, judging by the memory in *Much Ado* of the bride's wedding-dress of 'cloth o' gold' [3,4,17], as a familial solution to England's schism with Europe. Thus, from Don Pedro to Queen Catherine of Aragon, his plays are full of Spanish exiles whose sadness comes, as Benedick sighs, from disappointed love [5,4,117]. Perhaps only a worldly Shakespeare could personify the dreaded Armada in the 'sweet warman' Armado, who goes 'woolward for penance' [*Love's*, 5,2,647; 696]. But it is this very worldliness that makes Spanish settings such a conspicuous absence from his stage. Which is to say that the Europe Shakespeare represents is split by the same iron curtain as the fractured continent of his day. Spain is out of bounds to his characters because the central geopolitical fact of Counter-Reformation Europe was the sectarian wall that cut the pilgrim ways from England to Iberia and the shrine of Saint James. Historians calculate that at any time in the late Middle Ages, 'one tenth of Europe's population had been either on pilgrimage, or engaged in servicing the pilgrim trade'.[5] But within a few years in the sixteenth century, the Reformation had put this veritable travel industry, with its cosmopolitan resorts, hostels and ferries, entertainments, merchandising and protection rackets, out of reach of all but the most determined northern European Catholics.

In his *Reformation: Europe's House Divided*, Diarmaid MacCulloch recounts how, until the 1560s, it was 'the pilgrimage routes that still united Europe by sea and land'. Thus Bristol had been a 'national departure point for the Apostle's shrine on Spain's coast, and pilgrims sailing from the port would be able to enjoy the devotion to Saint James in the city-centre church'.[6] The voyage from Bristol to Galicia had taken five days; but the three-week journey across France, under the auspices of the Confraternity of St James, was preferred by penitents, as Helena suggests, keen to expiate their sins with a more punishing ordeal. So, for five centuries it was the multitudes on the Great Road of St James who fused Europe into a single narrative that 'transcended while affirming local allegiances': from Reading, where a hand of the saint donated by Queen Matilda was preserved; or Slovenia, where his pilgrims were exempted from tax; to Saragossa, where it was said he had been visited by the Virgin.[7] Even in the late sixteenth century, Fernand Braudel reminds us, the road to Spain from Paris, down the Rue St-Jacques, was still 'the most active thoroughfare in France'.[8] For 'while trips to Jerusalem and Rome became the privilege of the very rich, penitents continued to wend to Santiago' in such multitudes that, according to John Hale in *The Civilization of Europe in the Renaissance*, the age of Shakespeare was the 'high-point of cosmopolitanism': *for everyone except the English.*[9] So, when Helena vows to take the road to the Field of the Stars, she is reminding the audience of the Spain they have repressed, at the very instant when the power of pilgrimages and sacred shrines is being reaffirmed in countless Catholic miracle books, saints' lives, pilgrims' manuals and tourist guides:

> Calderon and other numerous dramatists joined the huge throngs in the festivals by writing spectacular pageants. For one of the great themes of Baroque literature was the pilgrimage. Cervantes, Meteo Alemán, and Baltasar Gracian each made pilgrimage the basis of the works they considered their masterpieces, and Lope de Vega poured into one of his most ambitious narratives, *El peregrino*, accounts of pilgrimages and shrines, and poems honouring wonderworking images of the Virgin.[10]

When Shakespeare's Arden relations were arrested in 1583, it was their copy of Luis de Granada's penitential *Prayers and Meditations* that the prosecution produced to see them hanged.[11] Clearly, the Stratford writer knew the toxicity of scenes like the one when Helena enters, after her 'sainted vow' to walk to Spain, and is identified by the pilgrim's costume she wears until the final seconds of the play: 'God save you, pilgrim! Whither are you bound?', to which she affirms that she is headed 'To Saint Jaques le Grand' [3,5,32–4]. As the Countess announces, a happy ending now depends on the power to work miracles with prayers 'heaven delights to hear / And loves to grant' [3,4,27–8]. But even Catholic critics concede that this scenario of 'pilgrimage to Spain, invocation of Saint James, penitential practice of walking barefoot', and prayers for intercession, must have struck English audiences as offensively papist.[12] Predictably, therefore, the Arden editor states that the idea that the author himself takes this itinerary seriously is 'too Popish to be probable'.[13] Yet it is precisely in terms of such improbability that Helena dedicates herself to her journey, when she says her love for Bertram is such an 'idolatrous fancy' that she 'must sanctify his relics', since she is 'Indian-like,/Religious in [her] error' [1,1,95–6; 1,3,200].

POWERFUL TO ARAISE KING PEPIN

Like the Indian boy in A *Midsummer Night's Dream* [2,1,124] or the 'base Indian' of *Othello* [5,2,356], Helena's 'Indian-like' or Moorish figure puns, Patricia Parker explains, on English Catholics as the 'tribe' of Thomas More: the Tudor protomartyr.[14] And it suggests that, when Helena discloses how the hydrotherapy she practises as her inheritance has been 'sanctified/By th'luckiest stars in heaven' [*All's Well*, 1,3,231–2], the cathartic 'receipt' with which she cures the King of France of a lethal fistula has been consecrated by 'the great'st grace lending grace' [2,1,159] during her father's own pilgrimage to Compostela. Stellar imagery reinforces this cathartic connotation. Thus, the play opens with the 'poor physician's daughter' [2,3,115] wishing Count Bertram luck as 'a bright particular star' [1,1,81], but seeing herself among the unlucky, 'Whose baser stars do shut us up in wishes' [170]. And when, after being ennobled, her ascent is still not enough for her 'star' to accept her as his wife, she says she will 'With true observance seek to eke out that/Wherein toward me my homely stars have failed' [2,5,70]. The clown Lavatch believes Helena was born under 'a blazing star', however, and associates her with 'the surplice of humility' worn 'over the black gown of a big heart' [1,3,76–9]. And it is the pilgrim garb she flaunts that makes the audience assume she will be one those who, as the braggart Paroles jests, 'eat, speak, and move, under the influence of the most received star' [2,1,52]: to which she smiles that he was 'born under a charitable star' [1,1,177]. So all these wishes made upon 'most received', 'charitable', 'homely', 'base', yet 'sanctified', 'blazing' and 'luckiest' stars set Helena firmly towards the 'bright particular star' of Santiago, as if in one of those tall stories of miraculous healing told by wayfarers that make Protestants choke, as the old courtier Lafeu exclaims:

> I have seen a medicine
> That's able to breathe life into a stone,
> Quicken a rock, and make you dance canary
> With sprightly fire and motion; whose simple touch
> Is powerful to araise King Pepin. . . .

> [2,1,70–4]

Lupton comments how 'The France of *All's Well* is undergoing a crisis in sacral sovereignty', as the King's mortal body has been opened 'to dangerous flows and exchanges' that compromise the viability of the body politic. For if Helena has the skills to revive the King, this involves 'a transformation in kingship itself', exposing monarchy to its dependence on the managers of the modern state.[15] Lafeu's resurrection imagery therefore alludes to the older 'medicine' associated with King

Pepin: the Eucharistic wine and holy oil with which the founder of the Carolingian line had been anointed King of the Francs. This ceremony had been devised to efface the embarrassment that the last Merovingian, Childeric III, was still alive, and to dignify the papal diktat that 'It is better to give the name of king to him who possesses power, than him who does not, so that order is preserved'.[16] Thus, hapless Childeric was tonsured and sent to a monastery when in 754 Pope Stephen splashed Pepin and his son Charlemagne with the holy chrism, and 'to colour this usurpation' invented the doctrine vital to sacred monarchy, that 'kings were the Lord's Anointed' and received from the unction their power to heal by touch.[17] It was by this reversible logic that sufferers from king's evil, or scrofula, a tuberculosis contracted from milk, not only had their 'repulsive tumours' probed by the 'royal physicians', but, according to Marc Bloch, imbibed the water in which the kings were disinfected, for 'the healing fluid was thought to have been transferred from the royal hand'.[18] Despite such contaminating exchanges, it therefore seems as if Shakespeare takes the catharsis of the royal touch seriously enough to invert its therapeutic economy, when Helena is introduced as the oxymoronic 'Doctor She', whose contrasting 'simple touch' is 'powerful enough' to *erase* King Pepin:

> nay,
> To give great Charlemagne a pen in's hand
> And write to her a love-line.
>
> [2,1,74–6]

As his 'weakest minister' [2,1,135] tends the King, it is tempting to see a rehearsal of the scene in 1788 when Dr Willis cured the madness of George III, and sovereign power was displaced by the new disciplinary power identified by Michel Foucault. But the philosopher himself thought that what we witness in Shakespeare is a different scenario, of 'one sovereign power falling under another'.[19] Thus the touch of the hand of Charle-*main*, the liberator of Compostela from the Moors according to the twelfth-century Book of St James, connects this plot to the tales of royalty with which Cluniac monks paved the Pilgrim's Way. And one cue for the story is, indeed, a yarn about Gerard of Roussillon, who built the abbey of Vézelay, at the start of the Road, as his penance for refusing a bride chosen by Charlemagne.[20] There he enshrined relics of Mary Magdalene, who supposedly died at Marseilles, from where Helena will return as though from the dead. Other textual cues include a fable of a doctor's daughter, Christine of Pisano, who cured King Charles V, and Boccaccio's novella about Giletta, 'a poor physician's daughter of Narbonne' who 'healed the French king of a fistula'.[21] And in the background lies the Grail legend of the Fisher King, hinted in the allusion to Pepin. So, where these medieval trails converge is in posing the problem put by the heroine when she takes the hand of the dying King: namely, the power of 'royal blood', with its 'sceptre and its hopes of heaven' [191], in an age 'When miracles have by the greatest been denied' [139].

Recent critics alert us to the ways in which the French setting of *All's Well That Ends Well* implies 'both nostalgia for England's Catholic past and the religious uncertainties of contemporary France'.[22] Yet neither nostalgia nor uncertainty characterises the play's heroine, whose faith in wonders never ceases. Thus, when Helena confesses 'on my knee, before high heaven', that her love of the one she adores 'next unto high heaven' is like a vestal's 'sieve', the iconographic symbol of chastity, in which 'I still pour in the waters of my love/And lack not to lose still' [1,3,175–88], the expectations she prompts are those of the miracle books. And when she dedicates herself, with her 'sainted vow', to 'wish chastely and love dearly' [196], we are led to expect impossible returns, like the wonders of Our Lady of Rocamadour, who saw to it, we are told, that when the 'man tormented by a fistula was taking his bandages off the ulcers that gnawed his muscles, to his delight he found he was cured'.[23] This is a truly noxious drama of penitential 'posting day and night' [5,1,1], which, according to the Counter-Reformation crown of thorns its heroine says she covets [4,4,32], might indeed end in the dispensation of dubious 'waters of love' at the shrine of Saint James. Shakespeare habitually mocked such stories in episodes like the fake 'miracle' of Simpcox, the 'blind man at Saint Alban's shrine' [2 Henry VI, 2,1,66]. And that was hardly surprising, as it was precisely Protestant disgust at any such 'religious rite smacking of magic' that defined English attitudes to the European continent:

> It was on the Continent that Papists preserved their trust in pilgrimages and relics. It was the 'superstitious' character of popular devotion that therefore attracted the attention of English visitors . . . how in South Germany peasants flocked to get water blessed by the image of St. Francis Xavier; how in Rome the Virgin drove away pestilence; in Venice, St. Rock. So long as it was possible for a Catholic prelate, like the Bishop of Quimper in 1620, to throw an Angus Dei into a dangerous fire in hope of putting it out, the Roman Church could hardly fail to retain a reputation in England of laying claim to supernatural remedies.[24]

THAT WISHING WELL

Shakespeare was writing All's Well at the moment, it is said, when 'They had forgotten what enchanted springs were, what pilgrimage churches and places of power meant, and what curses lay upon silent corners'.[25] Yet 'How should I your true love know/From another one?' sings Ophelia, and gives a rebuke to Hamlet, who has come, not, as in the words of the old Catholic ballad, from Walsingham, still less Compostela, but from Luther's Wittenberg: 'By his cockle hat and staff,/And his sandal shoon' [Hamlet, 4,5,23–6]. For those who did return from the 'field of the star' – like the pilgrim buried in Worcester Cathedral 'with his staff and cockleshell by his side, his boots on his feet'; the fifteenth-century Sussex testator who left provision for five neighbours to go 'to St James in Galicia'; the Suffolk parishioner who in 1501 donated to his church 'scallops and signs of St James'; or the London families of the 1560s who 'cherished shells from Santiago as heirlooms passed from father to son'[26] – seeing was still believing, and the act of walking to Spain was rewarded by the relics they carried home.

Dante, who compared the candlelit procession on the *campus stellae* to the Milky Way, wrote that 'none are called pilgrims save those journeying to Saint James'.[27] So the shells of Santiago became proof that miracles do happen when 'the saint's aid was attained through exchange of gifts'.[28] In *All's Well* the 'triple eye' Helena's father bequeathed her [2,1,103] may be such a relic. And back in England the contract with Spain was renewed each Feast of St James by the custom of decorating shrines with shells, a ritual that gave the date its name of Grotto or Oyster Day. Thus, Londoners danced on 25 July at springs like Clerkenwell; and folklorists describe the grottoes erected by East End children to collect coins as late as July 1914 as 'the last faint memory of the great medieval pilgrimages to the shrine of St James'.[29] So this is the pilgrim tradition that even the sceptical Paroles will be compelled to invoke at end of the play, when he begs 'a single penny' of Lafeu, from the 'unclean fish-pond' of his life [5,2,17–31].

Seashells are ancient talismans against evil; and the aphrodisiac connotations of the legend that Saint James's shells commemorate a bridegroom who rode into the sea to pull the saint's body ashore, and then returned to his bride covered in cockles, are perpetuated in the persistent fertility ritual of dropping coins in fountains.[30] Such is the apotropaic symbolism when Shakespeare has the 'fantastically dressed' Petruchio ride to wed Kate with a cockney rhyme: 'Nay, by Saint Jamy, / I hold you a penny, / A horse and a man / Is more than one' [*Taming*, 3,2,74–8]. It cannot, therefore, be chance that James is the male saint with most well dedications in Britain. Nor, for a play about 'holy wishes' that starts from Helena's macabre joke, 'I wish well. . . That wishing well had not a body in it' [1,1,52; 166], can it be immaterial to *All's Well* that the largest number of all well dedications is to the mother of Constantine, who united Britain with Rome, the first English pilgrim, Saint Helena.

Jonathan Gil Harris has argued that the name of this play quibbles on pregnancy in the trope that 'All Swell That End Swell'.[31] But from 'awl's swell' to 'all's well', the fecund implications of this punning title extend yet further, into the biopolitics of welfare itself. For, as with the debilitated kings of the *Trauerspiel* studied by Walter Benjamin, the vicissitudes of its 'melancholy' [1,2,56] monarch metonymise what Eric Santner terms the 'royal remains' of the 'strange material and physical presence' of the Prince, and the redistribution of this sacred 'body' into the body politic of the people.[32] Bloch showed how the accession of the sceptical James had, in fact, come near to ending the well cult, along with the royal touch, which the Calvinist-educated monarch 'had been instructed to view as sheer superstition and imposture'.[33] So once the title of this wishful-thinking comedy, with its imagery of bodily remains in well water, is taken literally, and its text is keyed to this moment of dispersal in English cultural history, when 'Holy Wells became wishing wells', Helena's wish fulfilment has a charged political theology:[34]

The water of St Thomas Becket – into which, it was said, Thomas' blood had been infused – was important for the relics for healing miracles . . . [but] equally important were the many holy wells associated with a particular saint – St Friedeswide in Oxford and Our Lady at Walsingham. . . . For the medieval Christian, the rituals upon reaching the shrine – venerating the relics, drinking holy water, or washing parts of the body in it – were central components of a tradition in which miracles of healing were experienced in relation to holy places, ritual, and sacred object.[35]

With a punning title and commoner healer, Shakespeare seems in *All's Well* to foresee how post-monarchical societies will be 'faced with the problem of *securing the flesh* of the new bearer of the principle of sovereignty, the People'.[36] For it was the London hospital that dispensed the waters of the saint that gave the court of St James its name, when a palace was built at the spring, and for centuries English kings sponsored the well as the thaumatological scene for their royal touch.[37] Even Henry VIII went on pilgrimage to the well at Walsingham, trudging with bleeding feet the last few miles.[38] As Keith Thomas detailed in *Religion and the Decline of Magic*, after receiving such royal patronage, wells became covers for Catholic resistance in Reformation England because they 'retained semi-magical associations, even though Protestants preferred to regard them as medicinal springs working by natural means'.[39] Thus, Mary Queen of Scots turned St Anne's well at Buxton, officially plugged in 1538, into a Mecca for recusants when she drank its 'milk-warm' water nine times during her captivity; and Bath was redeveloped in the 1590s by the knot of Catholic gentry who 'met at the Bath' to plan the Gunpowder Plot.[40] In fact, the Elizabethan regime lifted a 1539 ban drinking Bath's spring water only because of the exodus of dissidents to Spa in the Spanish Netherlands under the pretext of taking the cure. A starting point for the Grand Tour, Spa would remain 'a centre of Catholic intrigue', which 'the English government kept under strict surveillance' during the reign of James I, its colony of émigrés quaffing Spa water as an act of faith, as much as health.[41]

Given that wells were no longer only 'associated with the Catholic past' but 'masked recusant plots', it is telling that in *All's Well* the heroine equivocates about the magical or natural origin of the certain 'something' added to the remedy she gives the King, hinting only that 'Great floods have flown from simple sources' [2,1,137].[42] The chant with which she administers the purge specifies, however, that 'Ere twice in murk and occidental damp/Moist Hesperus hath quenched her flame. . . . Health shall live free' [162–7], and the invocation of sunset over western waters may indicate a 'simple source' in St Winifred's or Holywell in Flintshire. In the 1600s this 'Welsh Lourdes', with a chapel, built by Lady Margaret Beaufort in 1490, hung with crutches discarded by rheumatics, remained the most popular devotional site in Britain, and the authorities were powerless to prevent 'daily disorders around St. Winifred's Well' of 'confused multitudes' who went on 'superstitious pilgrimage there by pretending the waters to be beneficial'.[43] In 1629 an informer reported how the 'Papists and priests who assembled on St. Winifred's Day' comprised 'knights, ladies, gentlemen and gentlewomen of diverse countries to the number of 1,500'.[44] In 1687 James II and Catherine of Braganza would take the waters at Holywell as a defiant prelude to Catholic toleration. We can infer that the dramatist who set the climax of *Measure for Measure* at such a 'consecrated fount' [4,3,89] took an interest in this shrine, because among those who travelled to Holywell, and adopted Winifred as his patron, according to the Jesuit 'Testament' he may have signed, was his father John.[45] Yet as Lisa Hopkins points out, in *All's Well* this pre-Christian belief system seems to be deliberately introduced to shock, as though to agitate rival Christian confessions into troubled coexistence:

> This blending of past and present suggests that the ideological heart of *All's Well* is in a recent past whose troubles it thinks it can transcend by reference to a past still further back, in ways that will allow hope for the future. . . . In this play, the 'virgin birth' of Helena's child can be brought about and offer hope for the future because it is pitted against the idea of the pre-Christian past. In this context, differences of confession rather than differences of belief system are minimised. There may indeed have been trouble between the two sides in the past, as seen most recently in the French Wars of Religion, but it is not too late to hope for better in the future, because, after all, all's well that ends well.[46]

When Bertram forsakes Helena for Diana, he calls his new lover 'Fontibell' [*All's Well*, 4,2,1]: the name of a public fountain in Cheapside that featured a statue of Diana. As G. K. Hunter reasonably asked, 'Why should Bertram give his beloved the name of a fountain?'[47] The answer may be that *All's Well* follows the programme of the Court of St James on its saint's day, precisely by circling around a wish. Thus, when Helena cures the King of the disease that he says even her 'most learned' father would have wished to terminate in death – and 'I after him do after him wish too' [1,3,63–4] – this wishing-game follows the ambivalent scenario of a Stuart pilgrimage, where magic coexisted with tourism, and, as Lafeu observes, the confusion of 'the learned and authentic Fellows' allowed for the possibility of the 'hand of heaven' [2,3,12–31]. Sceptics like Camden were bemused when science seemed to confirm the curative power of waters 'famous in old wives' fables'.[48] But Shakespeare's comedy takes place precisely in the epistemological space opened by this embarrassment, when 'scientific discourse was the first to re-signify the old religious beliefs', those 'ensconcing' themselves 'in seeming knowledge' learned to be 'Generally thankful' for popish survivals [38], and far from being eclipsed by the new centres of healing, holy wells 'were instead incorporated within the spa establishments'.[49] So, dispensing her 'waters of love', Helena treads the same road as the pilgrims with their flasks of consecrated water, even as she disavows 'water in which relics were immersed'.[50] Her wish that her wishing-well 'had *not* a body in it' seems targeted, in fact, at those Catholic ultras who persisted in dispensing water infused with gruesome relics, and prepares for the twist in the story, when even though her wish is granted by the King, 'Doctor She' does *not* have this wish come true.

With each of Helena's suitors given a wish by 'Her that so wishes' [2,3,83], the well-wishing rites of *All's Well* are intended to intermix her 'merit', so Lafeu quips, with that of the 'one grape' whose 'father drank wine' as a Catholic, before the son lapsed [95]. Queen Elizabeth thought wine mixed into holy water a joke, and goaded Leicester to dilute his claret 'with as much sacred water' from Buxton 'as he lusteth to drink'.[51] But Spenser spelled out the Eucharistic implications of this lustration, by relating how the 'well of life' had flowed with Reformation 'virtues and med'cine good', like Bath or Wells, until the 'Dragon defiled those sacred waves' with toxic blood.[52] Granting Helena's wish, the King therefore explains, will dissolve such toxicity, since 'our bloods, / Of colour, weight, and heat, poured all together, / Would quite confound distinction' [2,3,114–16]. In *Shakespeare's Tribe* Jeffrey Knapp has claimed that the dramatist, who lodged at this time in Cripplegate with French Huguenot refugees, himself wished to disarm confessional enmities in the ecumenical or Gallican spirit with which Lavatch would like to knock together the hypocritical heads of 'young Charbonne the puritan and old Poisson the papist' [1,3,45–7].[53] And with his preaching to Diana that 'Love is holy' [4,2,33] it is possible to see Bertram as the portrait of just such a hypocritical young Puritan. Yet when the King inflicts a forced marriage on this 'proud scornful boy' [2,3,151], the involuntary 'recantation' [186] is as constrained as any of the actual King of France's wishful-thinking declarations of religious reconciliation, such as the recent Edict of Nantes:

> Good fortune and the favour of the King
> Smile upon this contract, whose ceremony
> Shall seem expedient on the now-born brief,
> And be performed tonight. The solemn feast
> Shall more attend upon the coming space,
> Expecting absent friends. As thou lov'st her
> Thy love's to me religious; else, does err.
>
> [2,3,173–9]

TO MAKE THE COMING HOUR O'ERFLOW

On the 'not coincidental' St James's Day, 25 July 1603, King James walked to Westminster for an 'expedient' coronation with 'all show and pomp omitted'.[54] The King thus 'lost no time retreating to uninfected air', for 'that week 1,103 persons died of plague'.[55] So, instead of Cheapside's 'Diana' gushing wine, the Jacobean reign was instituted with wells that were truly decorated to repel bad luck. But it was in this hiatus of 'coming space', with a 'solemn feast' delayed a year, 'Expecting absent friends', that Shakespeare's comedy was staged. After the funeral, the season of *All's Well* was, in fact, a time of genuine well-wishing, when the new King suspended anti-Catholic fines, peace with Spain was proclaimed and the court did await absent friends, in the form of an embassy from Philip III. Recent research locates Shakespeare in the orbit of Catholic unionists like the Earl of Worcester, who received Spanish pensions and had most to gain from the toleration they hoped to extract from a King who had himself been baptised in the Catholic faith.[56] So, with Spanish gold behind them, nothing was more apt than that the King's Men should present a play set on the Jacobean Road to Santiago that hangs on well-wishing promises, like those made by Bertram, to admit 'The great prerogative and rite of love' in 'due time. . . . Whose want and whose delay is strew'd with sweets / Which they distil now in the curbed time, / To make the coming hour o'erflow with joy / And pleasure drown the brim' [2,4,38–44]. As Shakespeare's first Jacobean tragedy, *Othello*, would respond to the King's epic poem *Lepanto*, so this coronation comedy strung along the royal road of Saint James would be a meditation on the meaning of the King's own name.

The well imagery announced in its title implies that Shakespeare devised *All's Well That Ends Well* to be a *Jacobean* play. For whether or not it was commissioned to be acted before the court of St James, this well-wishing comedy would return again and again to the trope suggested by the cult of Santiago, of the overflowing spring. So it may not be incidental to its hydrotherapeutic imagery that a likely venue for the play's premiere was Bath, a spa city with bright prospects as a theatrical venue, where Shakespeare's troupe acted on the 'King's Holiday', 25 July 1603, and pitched base, Leeds Barroll deduces, during the plague epidemic, when the entire court decamped to nearby Wilton.[57] The dramatist may have taken heart for his own waiting game, indeed, from the presentation of credentials there on 8 October by the Spanish envoy, Don Juan de Tassis, after a 'slow journey' through the West Country testing Catholic strength. On 12 October Tassis reported that any Gallican edict of toleration would depend on negotiated peace.[58] And scholars are intrigued by this diplomatic summitry, as when the Spaniards arrived in London in August 1604, Shakespeare and eleven fellow-actors from the King's Men were paid to wait on the Constable of Castile at Somerset House for eighteen days. Some have even speculated that though 'we are unable to say what form Shakespeare's "tip" may have taken', the dramatist was among those who shared the bribes distributed by the ambassador, possibly in the shape of the 'broad silver-gilt bowl' he bequeathed in his will to his daughter Judith.[59] So Shakespeare's Jamesian comedy might well register some personal investment in the anticipated decrees of toleration in speeches like the one in which the King declares he intends to waste 'Not one word more of the consumed time':

Let's take the instant by the forward top;
For we are old, and on our quick'st decrees
Th'inaudible and noiseless foot of time
Steals ere we can effect them.

[5,3,38–42]

'Let us from point to point this story know/To make the even truth in pleasure flow': at the close of *All's Well*, according to the King, 'The bitter past, more welcome is the sweet' [321–30], and the Jamesian figure of sweetened water promises benefits from swallowing sugared lies. Thus, it is in the spirit of Grotto Day that Lafeu throws pennies to Paroles, even though the old lord sees through the man of words as 'a vagabond and no true traveller', who makes 'tolerable vent' of his travels, but is not 'a vessel of too great a burden' [2,3,196–245; 5,2,17]. In fact, the humiliation of the 'Captain' seems to condescend to the anti-Spanish party, and may allude to the Winchester show-trial of its hero, Raleigh. Biographers link *All's Well* to the Herberts at Wilton, and a ploy by the Countess of Pembroke to entice James there, and 'cajole him in Raleigh's behalf', with the bait of 'the man Shakespeare'.[60] It was to Mary Herbert's husband that the Welsh doctor John Jones had dedicated *The Baths of Bath's Aid*; and to her son William the veteran Robert Barrett his *Theory of*

Practice of Modern Wars.[61] If this unionist circle was the patronage network in which Shakespeare was now also working, that might explain the shift of sympathy when Paroles, who 'has the whole theory of war in the knot of his scarf' [4,3,137], grovels to survive, as Raleigh did before his similar mock execution.

As Paul Yachnin remarks, from the instant Lafeu regrets that the King's illness is 'notorious' [1,1,32], *All's Well* is intensely 'newsy' in its awareness of the power of words to shape events, while spinning the 'cascade of letters' Helena posts about her travels as superior to 'odious ballads' [2,1,171].[62] So the hand of peace offered to the warmonger can be seen as part of the comedy's own well-wishing, and a sign of its investment in the advocacy Helena initiates when she enjoins the Countess to 'Write, write . . . that from the bloody course of war . . . your dear son, may hie' [3,4,8–9]. If *All's Well* does date from the Anglo-Spanish talks, it appears, moreover, to accept the policy of live and let live James was offering the Puritans, in Paroles' resolve to let his sword rust, on the *politique* understanding that 'There's place and means for every man alive' [4,3,316]. With the 'gallant militarist' [137] disgraced as a precondition for détente, the play can then locate itself exactly between 'an overture of peace' and 'a peace concluded' [39–40]. And if this topicality sounds excessively 'newsy', then that simply reflects the text's confidence in what Bertram, who will be trapped by them, unthinkingly says are 'The best wishes that can be forged' [1,1,68].

If *All's Well* was written in 1604 as a consciously Jamesian entertainment, to make the 'best wishes' come true for the Jacobean age, the bed trick Helena rigs to fool Bertram might have been devised to prepare audiences for the catharsis of swallowing similar white lies. For in this play we learn to distinguish, as Lafeu says, 'one that lies three thirds', and 'should be once heard and thrice beaten', like Paroles, from the 'good traveller' who is 'something at the latter end of a dinner' [2,4,27–30], because her forgeries are ultimately benign. Thus, by a coincidence worthy of Borges, this play about a miracle cure which draws on tales of chivalry to show the uses of enchantment was likely put on to welcome the first readers of the greatest fiction ever built upon that same 'ill-compiled' edifice of 'Knightly Books': *Don Quixote* itself.[63] Cervantes' masterpiece was at press when the Treaty of London was signed in August 1604; but the Don had smashed so many sales records by the time the negotiators returned to Spain to ratify the Treaty with their English co-signatories in June 1605 that the figure of Quixote starred in the pageant put on at Valladolid to celebrate the peace. And this was the occasion (the Cervantes scholar Astrana Marin speculated) when the creators of Hamlet and Don Quixote met face to face, Shakespeare having come to Spain in the train of Charles Howard, Earl of Nottingham.[64]

Since the moment of *All's Well That Ends Well* was the very time when Cervantes reflected upon Essex's 1587 raid on Cadiz with his story *La española inglesa*, in which a girl kidnapped by an English officer is raised honourably as his daughter in London, Hispanists are excited by the idea of 'a summit meeting of the giants of literature', with a show of mutual respect.[65] But, as Jean Canavaggio writes, 'Let us stop dreaming. Only one thing is certain. Howard and his compatriots, when they return to the banks of the Thames, are going to spread the word about Don Quixote'.[66] It is enough that the first English writer to quote Cervantes is Shakespeare's Catholic collaborator George Wilkins, who at the time of their *Pericles* in 1607 imagines 'tilting at windmills' in *The Miseries of Enforced Marriage*. That play used the *All's Well* plot of the coerced groom to allegorise papists bullied to conform, and was keyed to the scheming of the crypto-Catholic Howard clan for toleration.[67] So it is significant that when Shakespeare himself adapted *Don Quixote*, and at last set a play in Spain, the *Cardenio* he co-authored with John Fletcher was based upon Thomas Shelton's 1612 translation, dedicated to Theophilus, heir to Thomas Howard Earl of Suffolk. Equally moot is the fact that in *Cardenio* a forced marriage was played to advertise Howard ambitions during the divorce of Frances Howard from the Puritan Earl of Essex.[68] As England and Spain drew closer in the 1600s, what English Catholics discovered in the Cervantine story of arranged marriage, it seems, was a template for a system of toleration in conflict.

In the presumed transcript of *Cardenio* the hero leaps out to stop his lover marrying her detested groom Henriquez, who seems to satirise the Puritan Prince Henry. The episode expresses Catholic confidence in 1612–14, when Henry Howard, Earl of Northampton, was so powerful he was nicknamed 'El Cid'. But it also signals Shakespeare's most pointed revision of Cervantes, whose Cardenio goes mad after he dares not halt the wedding by preventing Luscinda answering in 'a languishing voice, "I will".'[69] The rewriting changes the basis of Cardenio's insanity; yet if it was to please the Howards, it looks like a riposte to Cervantes' report on England's secret Catholics, in *La española inglesa*, as too weak for armed revolt, 'even if spiritually ready for martyrdom'.[70] For though the Spanish novelist may never have read the English dramatist, he was an acute reader of Shakespeare's England, and his story of Isabela, the girl her namesake Elizabeth I admires for being 'star-like' in her Catholic faith, reflects badly on her captors, who are torn between the Queen and Pope. So, if *Cardenio* solves the 'Bloody Question' of allegiance by dreaming of a Catholic England so strong it can dictate its terms, Cervantes was true to the reality Shakespeare earlier figured in *All's Well*, when he projected his ending as one in which the Englishman Ricaredo goes on a pilgrimage, and is reunited with Isabela only as she is about to enter a convent in Seville.

Cervantes had been impressed during the peace conference when Charles Howard spoke Spanish (a facility the novelist fancifully attributed to Elizabeth) and attended Masses to celebrate the birth of Philip's heir, and even the election of a Pope, when other Spaniards mocked the cynicism of this 'Lutheran who swore / To the Treaty on Calvin's works'.[71] But the similarity between his novella and *All's Well* – in both of which the heroine comes close to immuring herself in a Spanish religious house – underlines the brinkmanship of this détente. The precariousness of Cervantes' fantasy of toleration helps explain Helena's dogged pursuit of Bertram, and the anxiety aroused in the comedy by fear of 'deadly divorce' [5,3,312] if the shotgun marriage should be prevented and the pilgrim allowed to go on her way. For feminist critics have noticed how Helena conforms to the type of 'holy anorexic' whose 'superhuman fasts and vigils' challenged patriarchy with fanaticism.[72] Holy wells, like Shakespeare's own local one at Shottery, which 'cured women's complaints', were chiefly 'a women's preserve', and the sorority that Helena ends up leading with

Diana and her mother does resemble some devotional female cult.[73] So in *All's Well That Ends Well*, as the Countess warns, the ending promised in the title hinges on hopes that the devotee 'will speed her foot' back from her holy business [3,4,37], before she really *does* achieve the sanctity she is said to have attained in Santiago:

> Sir, his wife some two months since fled from
> his house. Her pretence is a pilgrimage to Saint
> Jaques le Grand; which holy undertaking with most
> austere sanctimony she accomplish'd; and there
> residing, the tenderness of her nature became as a
> prey to her grief; in fine, made a groan of her last
> breath, and now she sings in heaven.
>
> [4,3,45–51]

LYING WITH SIMPLE SHELLS

Helena's Spanish 'Life', verified 'by her own letters, making her story true even to the point of her death', and her saintly 'death itself', which, since it 'could not be her office to say is come' is 'faithfully confirmed by the rector', no less, of Compostela [52–6], are fictions that echo the expectations of a generation of English Catholics who saw their daughters vanish into the convents of Toledo and Madrid. Shakespeare's daughters were both unmarried at this time, when English 'Poor Clares' were also recruiting for a new convent at Saint-Omer; and Susanna would soon be listed as a 'popishly affected' recusant.[74] So in his previous comedy, *Measure for Measure*, the writer had tested the conventual vocation even more intensely, by having Isabella take her vows among the 'votarists of Saint Clare' [1,4,5]. There even the rake Lucio paid lip-service to one 'enskied and sainted' by her 'renouncement' [33]. In fact, no other English dramatist accords anything near the respect given by Shakespeare to those who 'endure the livery of a nun/For aye to be in shady cloister mewed', and whose 'maiden pilgrimage' he has even the serial rapist Theseus salute [*Dream*, 1,1,70–5]. In *Troilus and Cressida*, for instance, it is Hector's awe at the 'strains/Of divination' in Cassandra that silences Troilus's contempt for a 'foolish, dreaming superstitious girl' [2,2,112; 5,3,82]. And even Hamlet's obscenity to 'Get thee to a nunnery' [*Hamlet*, 3,1,122] is purged in *Pericles*, by Marina's purification of the brothel and prayers beside the 'maiden priests' at 'Diana's altar' [5,1,226; 5,2,37]. As Robert Miola writes, 'as heir to Catholic traditions that celebrated celibacy as a victory over world, flesh and devil', in all his references to nuns Shakespeare 'portrays chastity as a moral virtue', like the 'barricado' Helena erects when she says she 'will stand for it a little, though I die a virgin' [*All's Well*, 1,1,2107; 126].[75]

As a 'votress' of the Virgin goddess, Marina is given a curriculum vitae to make her exemplary of the life among those sisters in Flanders or Spain that may in fact have inspired what Shakespeare's biographer Park Honan terms 'Henley Street piety', when 'She sings like one immortal', dances 'goddess-like', composes 'admired' hymns and teaches needlework so ardently 'That pupils lacks she none' [5,0,3–11].[76]

So critics who assume the dramatist shared Puritan disgust at the decision of those, like Olivia, to wall themselves in chantries, ignore the irony that he gives the Protestant critique of virginity to the roué Paroles [1,1,116–50].[77] They forget that what makes his image of the enclosed life so unlike that of any of his rivals is the cathartic return effect in his dramas between the communal and the claustral, meaning that if the cloister is tested in them by the world, the world is tested by the cloister. So it comes as no surprise that in 1619 *Pericles* was catalogued as the only secular text taught by the Jesuits at Saint-Omer; nor that in the 1640s the Second Folio was on their syllabus at Valladolid.[78] The Europe of the Counter-Reformation took this English dramatist seriously. And he returned the compliment, projecting the forbidden continent of pilgrimages and relics as a hypothetical destination in play after play, where the end so often draws towards some virtual shrine, like the 'monument' to the 'virgin knight' Hero before which Claudio swears a 'Yearly . . . rite' in *Much Ado About Nothing* [5,3,13; 23], or the pilgrim's tomb of cockleshells Pericles imagines for Thaisa:

> . . . a monument upon thy bones
> And aye-remaining lamps. . .
> Lying with simple shells.
>
> [*Pericles*, 3,1,60–3]

In *All's Well*, Helena's burial in Santiago is reported to her husband as a veridical fact, with 'the particular confirmations, point from point, to the full arming of the verity' [4,3,60]. The audience knows, however, this forgery to be yet another pilgrims' tale, and that instead of plodding from France to Spain, the heroine has turned up in Florence, where she changes direction again, and introduces herself to the Widow as one of the 'palmers' (so-called from the palms they carried) returning from Jerusalem [3,5,35]. Critics have long frowned at this false turn, starting with Dr Johnson, who dryly remarked that the Tuscan city 'was somewhat out of the road from Rousillon to Compostela'.[79] Helena's trip to Italy looks like an instance of Shakespeare's ignorance; or of the gap between European fact and English fiction that traps criticism in a law of diminishing returns, whereby the more facts scholars gather about the continent, 'the less this yields new insights into the plays'.[80] Helena has, however, travelled to Florence to shadow Bertram, while her detour fulfils her mother-in-law's wish to have 'diverted her intents'. So it is very much to the point that in Shakespeare's next play, *Othello*, the 'young and sweating devil' Iago [3,4,40] carries another name that affiliates him expressly with the road to Compostela, and the most fundamentalist face of St James, as the crusading defender of Christendom and slayer of the Moors.[81]

Critics have frequently viewed the character of Iago as a caricature of Jesuit sedition; and it was in fact the cult of the warrior saint as Santiago Matamoros that fired the Basque veteran and Jesuit founder Inigo de Loyola.[82] Rather than an exercise in the Black Legend, *Othello* can thus be decoded as an allegory of the politicising by Jesuits of the English 'tribe of More'; and the perversion of the Moor's 'pilgrimage' [1,3,152] into paranoia over a relic as a figure for the 'foolishness' of the 'Spanish faction' of Catholic fundamentalists who put their faith in bloody handkerchiefs. Santiago Matamoros is exposed in such symbolisation as the slayer of moronic English Catholics.[83] So this Jacobean tragedy, which plays dangerously with the name the King shared with his Jesuit foes, shows why the Jamesian comedy could never terminate in Santiago, and why its pilgrimage remains a feint. Having posited a Spanish religious exile as its last resort, *All's Well* swerves from the Pyrenees to disavow the ultras. In a London that would applaud Middleton's anti-Jesuit and Hispanophobic *Game at Chess*, what is remarkable, however, is not that Helena shies from Catholic Spain, but how long she keeps a counterfeit 'pretence' of being one of the *devotés*, the 'enjoin'd penitents. . . . To Great Saint Jaques bound' [3,5,93], and, when she is 'supposed dead' [4,4,11], has her mourners believe her 'incensing relics' are interred at Compostela [5,3,25]. Most startling of all is how, by calling on 'the saints to surety' [109], she allows her purported return from Spain, when she rises from 'oblivion' at the end [24], to be viewed by the King as a specifically popish plot, one of the exorcisms that made the Jesuits notorious:

> Is there no exorcist
> Beguiles the truer office of mine eyes?
> Is't real I see?
> HELENA: No, good my lord;
> 'Tis but the shadow of a wife you see. . . .
>
> [5,3,298–301]

'Who cannot be crushed with a plot?': Paroles' comment on his forced 'confession' as a spy to the interrogator 'he supposes to be a friar' [4,3,104; 301] is a question that also casts doubt on the Jesuitical trickery with which Helena corners the Count. Thus, in a chapter entitled '*King Lear* and the Exorcists' Stephen Greenblatt concludes that by the time of *All's Well*, 'Shakespeare had marked out exorcisms as frauds', and staged such rituals as 'popish impostures' that are now '*emptied out*'.[84] Yet this is surely to side too much with those 'philosophical persons' who, in the terms of the play, 'say miracles are past' and thereby 'make modern and familiar things supernatural and causeless', making 'trifles of terrors', when they 'should submit . . . to an unknown fear' [2,3,1–5]. It is to ignore how Shakespeare toasts 'absent friends' on this day of Jacobean rapprochement with Catholic Spain, and meets their faith half way. The audience knows Helena's pilgrimage to Compostela is only a traveller's tale. And they can see that, far from dying a martyr, 'she feels her young one kick' [5,3,299], from bedding Bertram. But her well ending depends on her husband's gullibility in fearing that he has killed his wife, and on his confessing 'high-repented blames' [37]. So, like the dedication of Hero's tomb to the 'goddess of the night' [*Much Ado*, 5,3,12], or the statue of Hermione by that 'rare Italian master' from the citadel of the Counter-Reformation, Giulio Romano [*Winter's*, 5,2,87], Helena's 'incensing' shrine at Santiago is a truly *cathartic* provocation, an antagonising piece of Catholic idolatry around which worldliness revolves.

His King of France pretends to have 'buried the incensing relics' of Catholic devotion 'deeper than oblivion' [5,3,26]. But by playing on the name of James,

Shakespeare seems in his coronation comedy to be toying with the Catholic associations of the ruler who, more than any other, lived out the political theology of the
King's two bodies, when he both 'insisted in his writings on the divine right of kings
secured in royal bloodlines', yet represented a 'shift in the very logic of representation' that located royalty as a *remainder* of the Catholic concept of sacral kingship.[85]
The wishful thinking ending of All's Well That Ends Well therefore comes perilously
close to itself looking like a popish imposture, and, together with these ambivalent allusions, makes it unlikely this chicanery was co-authored by a Protestant
like Middleton. In his final collaboration, with the Anglican John Fletcher, *All
Is True*, Shakespeare would set such white lies in a worldly context, when he had
Catherine of Aragon dream of the 'spirits of peace' who visit from her 'friends in
Spain' and her father Ferdinand, who was 'The wisest prince that there had reigned'
[2,4,46–53; 4,2,83]. 'My friends,/They that my trust must grow to, live not here',
grieves Shakespeare's devout Spanish Queen of England, 'They are (as all my other
comforts) far from hence/In mine own country' [3,1,87–9], but she dies in the arms
of the envoy of her nephew, Emperor Charles V. The 'Spectre of Spain', the demonised evil empire of flagellating penitents, holy wells and pilgrim shrines, would long
remain under erasure on the London stage. But no English dramatist was ever so
open as this one, who was, by his own account, 'reformed indifferently' [*Hamlet*,
3,4,32] to the return of the Catholic repressed. It may not be chance, therefore, that
the first recorded purchaser of the 1623 Folio was the Spanish ambassador, Count
Gondomar.[86] For the worldliness Shakespeare gave his Ferdinand of Navarre defines
an entire dramaturgy, when the King of the Basques swears the provoking crusader
tales Armado tells about St James and the Moors are of such 'enchanting harmony'
that the Don's tilting at windmills can be turned to art:

> This child of fancy that Armado hight
>   For interim to our studies shall relate
> In high-borne words the worth of many a knight
>   From tawny Spain lost in the world's debate.
> How you delight, my lords, I know not, I;
> But I protest I love to hear him lie,
> And I will use him for my minstrelsy.
>
>   [*Love's*, 1,1,160–74]

THE HELP OF BATH

'All's well that ends well; still the fine's the crown./Whate'er the course, the end
is the renown' [*All's Well*, 4,4,35–6]: Helena's rhyme, with its allusions to Catholic
fines, wells and relics, cheerfully accepts that in an age when 'They say miracles
are past' [2,3,1] the old lies pilgrims 'love to hear' can be turned to modern ends.
As Harold Gardiner noted in his classic study of the last days of Christian theatre,
Mysteries' End, 'dramatic artists, particularly in Spain', continued to work in religious forms in the 1600s, and plays like *All's Well That Ends Well* and *Measure for*

Measure indicate that 'English dramatists, too, might have given the people a dramatic fare devotional as well as secular, had they felt free to do so'.[87] Critics such as Louis Montrose have returned to Gardiner's insight that the place of the London stage was often literally the space occupied by shrines like Holywell, the location of the Theatre.[88] And in the two plays he wrote during the Anglo-Spanish talks of 1603-4 that spin on the Jesuitical bed trick, Shakespeare used the *mise-en-scène* of the holy well with a sense of the potential of the shrine as an intermediate space, where the waters 'were no longer credited by Episcopal bulls but chemical testing, and friars were replaced by doctors and chemists'. Seventeenth-century comedies set in Epsom, Tunbridge or Sadler's Wells would exploit the paradoxical status of the spa as a liminal contact zone for just such an accommodation. True believers who witnessed this performative medicine were often scandalised by the hypocrisy that 'the pretence of these waters brings vast numbers of people together that are in very good health'.[89] But by returning to the well-springs of theatre as a purging *pharmakon*, *All's Well That Ends Well* already affirms, with its homeopathic title, that the well's ending as a context for pilgrimage is its beginning as a therapeutic pretext, and that a multi-confessional society has everything to gain from the catharsis.

Bridewell, Camberwell, Ladywell: with their curative powers and fertility rites, the holy wells of early modern England were too valuable to an emerging culture of consent to be wholly terminated. As Alexandra Walsham explains, the reason well-wishing was 'allowed to linger on the fringes and margins' of society was that the Protestant state remained eager to appropriate a tradition of pilgrimage and healing, once it was shorn of its 'overtly "popish" components'.[90] Thus, in *All's Well That Ends Well* the holy well by which Helena heals the King, and has her wish, is a sign of a culture that does not evacuate the old Catholic sovereignty, but transports it into 'modern and familiar' contexts, so that 'the "St Francis"' [3,5,32] becomes the name of a hotel.[91] And there are two parallel texts that appear to confirm Shakespeare's acquiescence in this slippage. Sonnets 153 and 154 close his 'sugared sonnets' with a bittersweet coda that recounts how the 'sick' writer 'the help of bath desired,/And thither hied, a sad distempered guest'. Editors are reluctant to identify the 'cold valley-fountain' with Bath. But the account of the reformation of 'this holy fire' by 'A maid of Dian's' into 'a seething bath, which yet men prove/Against strange maladies a sovereign cure', is so close to *All's Well* as to suggest it also dates from the 1603 season at the spa. The poet, however, finds 'no cure' in this 'bath and healthful remedy', for his shrine 'lies/Where Cupid got new fire', in his 'mistress' eyes'. The bitter secular reading of this line is that the patient received no cure from his 'treatment for venereal disease'.[92] But the cathartic meaning is an insinuated Marian one: the cold water of Protestantism 'cools not love', because the pilgrim's 'heart' remains on fire.

'Yes, I have gained my experience': in *As You Like It* the traveller who has brought home no more than a dry biscuit is not called Jaques for nothing. As editors note, his name plays on 'jakes', the word for a latrine. And the pun suggests his experience has been that of a tourist in an age when the waters of Saint Jaques have been turned from holy wells to drains. With his Spaniolated melancholy, Jaques has returned from Santiago, Rosalind sighs, with only the experience to make him sad:

'to have seen much and to have nothing is to have rich eyes and poor hands . . . and to travel for it too!' [2,7,39; 4,1,10–26]. The very name Jaques thus sums up English disenchantment when the pilgrimage network centred on Compostela was discredited as, in the words of Reformers, 'a forsaking of the Fountain of living waters, to go to a broken Cistern'.[93] For Londoners, the breach had been celebrated in 1589, when Drake landed in Spain 'intent on destroying Santiago, the heart of "pernicious superstition"'.[94] On that occasion the saint's relics were saved from the English marauders by being buried. Yet Shakespeare ironised such iconoclasm by characterising the most famous of all English travellers to Santiago, John of Gaunt, as a barbaric vandal whose idea of chivalry is to spread desecration and sacrilege as far as 'the sepulchre, in stubborn Jewry' [*Richard II*, 2,1,52]. Similarly, by setting Henry IV's deathbed in the 'Jerusalem Chamber' of Westminster Abbey, the dramatist trumped Erasmus's Reformation joke that there was no point in going on pilgrimage to the Holy Land if you could be a pilgrim in your own room.[95]

Shakespeare's Protestant compatriots insisted they had time for neither holy wells nor pilgrimages. 'Sewer's End' was therefore their term for Santiago: an insularity canonised by Raleigh, who preferred his 'Scallop shell of quiet' to an embassy to Spain.[96] Tudor minds had been set in this Europhobic frame by the ex-monk and physician Andrew Boorde, when in the 1540s he reported that not only was there 'not one ear or bone of St James in Compostela', but the sacred waters of Santiago were so polluted that nine of his companions died from drinking them.[97] Shakespeare may well have read Boorde's 'modern and familiar' travelogue while writing *All's Well*, if the book stood in the library of his fellow graduate of Montpellier, Doctor John Hall, who settled in Stratford in 1600. Perhaps the doctor's presence was one reason why, on this welfare stage, the trail from magic to medicine takes the heroine towards Huguenot Montpellier, rather than Catholic Santiago, as, within a couple of years, the Puritan physician would marry Shakespeare's 'popish' daughter, Susanna. So, though the Gunpowder Plotters would make one last pilgrimage from Warwickshire to St Winifred's Well in 1605, to pray for the union of Catholic England with Spain, it might have seemed to the author of *All's Well That Ends Well* that, from farewell to welfare, well-wishing was well ended with his daughter's swelling.

NOTES

1. Lisa Hopkins, 'Paris is worth a Mass: *All's Well That Ends Well* and the Wars of Religion', in Dennis Taylor and David Beauregard (eds), *Shakespeare and the Culture of Christianity in Early Modern England* (New York: Fordham University Press, 2003), pp. 369–81, here p. 378.
2. Oliver Cromwell, quoted in Albert Loomie, *The Spanish Elizabethans* (New York: Fordham University Press, 1963), p. 3.
3. Julia Reinhard Lupton, *Afterlives of the Saints: Hagiography, Typology, and Renaissance Literature* (Stanford: Stanford University Press, 1996), p. 112.
4. For the 'blackening' of Spain by Elizabethan and Jacobean writers, see Eric Griffin, 'Othello's Spanish spirits, or, un-sainting James', in *English Drama and the Specter of Spain: Ethnopoetics and Empire* (Philadelphia: Pennsylvania University Press, 2009), pp. 168–206; and 'From ethos to ethnos: Hispanizing "the Spaniard" in the Old World and the New', *New Centennial*

Review, 2 (2002), 69–116; Gary Taylor, *Buying Whiteness: Race, Culture, and Identity from Columbus to Hiphop* (Basingstoke: Palgrave, 2005), pp. 132–9; and Barbara Fuchs, 'The Spanish race', in Margaret Greer, Walter Mignolo and Maureen Quilligan (eds), *Rereading the Black Legend* (Chicago: University of Chicago Press, 2007), pp. 88–98.

5. Nicholas Luard, *The Field of the Star: A Pilgrim's Journey to Santiago de Compostela* (London: Michael Joseph, 1998), p. 9.

6. Diarmaid MacCulloch, *Reformation: Europe's House Divided, 1490–1700* (London: Allen Lane, 2003), p. 18.

7. Walter Starkie, *The Road to Santiago: Pilgrims of St James* (London: John Murray, 1957), pp. 16, 60 and 68–9.

8. Fernand Braudel, *The Mediterranean and the Mediterranean World in the Age of Philip II*, trans. Siân Reynolds, 2 vols (London: Collins, 1972), vol. 1, p. 217.

9. François Lebrun, 'The two Reformations: communal devotion and personal piety', in Roger Chartier (ed.), *A History of Private Life: The Passions of the Renaissance*, trans. Arthur Goldhammer (Cambridge, MA: Harvard University Press, 1989), p. 89; John Hale, *The Civilization of Europe in the Renaissance* (London: Harper Collins, 1993), p. 164.

10. Alban Forcione, *Cervantes and the Humanist Vision: A Study of Four 'Exemplary Novels'* (Princeton: Princeton University Press, 1982), pp. 321–3.

11. Charlotte Carmichael Stopes, *Shakespeare's Warwickshire Contemporaries* (Stratford-upon-Avon: Shakespeare Head Press, 1907), pp. 75–6.

12. David Beauregard, '"Inspired merit": Shakespeare's theology of Grace in *All's Well That Ends Well*', *Renascence*, 51 (1999), 231.

13. G. K. Hunter (ed.), *All's Well That Ends Well* (Arden Shakespeare) (London: Methuen, 1959), p. 82.

14. Patricia Parker, 'What's in a name and more', *Sederi XI: Revista de la Sociedad Espanola de Estudios Renascentistas Ingleses* (Huelva: Universidad de Huelva, 2002), pp. 101–449, esp. p. 117. It is this Catholic/Moorish empathy that makes Eric Griffin's reading of *Othello* as a recycling of the Black Legend, in which 'Shakespeare played a part in its Hispanophobic generation', seem superficial: Griffin, 'Othello's Spanish spirits, or, un-sainting James', p. 208.

15. Julia Lupton, *Thinking With Shakespeare: Essays on Politics and Life* (Chicago: University of Chicago Press, 2011), pp. 112–13.

16. *Annales regni francorum*, ed. F. Kurze (Hanover, 1895), p. 8, trans. and quoted in Robert Folz, *The Coronation of Charlemagne: 25 December 800*, trans. J. E. Anderson (London: Routledge and Kegan Paul, 1974), p. 28.

17. Marc Bloch, *The Royal Touch: Sacred Monarchy and Scrofula in England and France*, trans. J. E. Anderson (London: Routledge and Kegan Paul, 1973), pp. 37–8.

18. Ibid., p. 53.

19. Michel Foucault, *Psychiatric Power: Lectures at the Collège de France, 1973–74*, ed. Jacques Lagrange, trans. Graham Burchell (London: Palgrave Macmillan, 2006), 14 November 1973, pp. 21–2.

20. Russell Fraser (ed.), *All's Well That Ends Well* (Cambridge: Cambridge University Press, 1985), p. 6.

21. William Painter, *The Palace of Pleasure* (London: 1566), quoted ibid., p. 7.

22. Lupton, *Thinking With Shakespeare*, p. 113.

23. Marcus Bull (ed.), *The Miracles of Our Lady of Rocamadour* (Woodbridge: Boydell, 1999), p. 143. For the sieve that does not leak as an iconographic symbol of virginity, an allusion to the vestal virgin Tuccia, see Gail Kern Paster, *The Body Embarrassed: Drama and the Disciplines of Shame in Early Modern England* (Ithaca: Cornell University Press, 1993), p. 50.

24. Keith Thomas, *Religion and the Decline of Magic: Studies in Popular Beliefs in Sixteenth- and Seventeenth-Century England* (Harmondsworth: Penguin, 1973), pp. 84–5.

25. Peter Sloterdijk, *Globes. Spheres II: Macrospherology*, trans. Wieland Hoban (South Pasadena: Semiotexte, 2014), p. 784.

26. Eamon Duffy, *The Stripping of the Altars: Traditional Religion in England, 1400–1580* (New Haven: Yale University Press, 1992), pp. 167 and 193; Starkie, *The Road to Santiago*, p. 71.

27. Dante, *Vita Nuova*, 40, commentary on Sonnet XXIII, quoted in Starkie, *The Road to Santiago*, p. 60.

28. Beauregard, '"Inspired merit"', p. 231.

29. Christina Hole, *A Dictionary of British Folk Customs* (London: Paladin, 1978), p. 119; and Christina Hole, *English Custom and Usage* (London: Batsford, 1942), p. 82.

30. Mortimer Wheeler, 'A symbol in ancient times', in Ian Cox (ed.), *The Scallop: Studies of a Shell and Its Influence on Humankind* (London: Shell, 1957), pp. 35–48; Horton Davies and Marie-Hélène Davies, *Holy Days and Holidays: The Medieval Pilgrimage to Compostela* (Lewisburg: Bucknell University Press, 1982), pp. 21–0.

31. Jonathan Gil Harris, 'All swell that end swell: dropsy, phantom pregnancy, and the sound of deconception in *All's Well That Ends Well*, *Renaissance Drama*, 35 (2006), 169–89.

32. Eric Santner, *The Royal Remains: The People's Two Bodies and the Endgames of Sovereignty* (Chicago: University of Chicago Press, 2011), pp. 10–11, 55 et passim; Michel Foucault, *Discipline and Punish: The Birth of the Prison*, trans. Alan Sheridan (Harmondsworth: Penguin, 1977), pp. 208 and 222–3. See also Giorgio Agamben, *Homo Sacer: Sovereign Power and Bare Life*, trans. Daniel Heller-Roazen (Stanford: Stanford University Press, 1998), pp. 176–8; Roberto Esposito, *Bios: Biopolitics and Philosophy*, trans. Timothy Campbell (Minneapolis: Minnesota University Press, 2008), pp. 39–41, 55–61, 166–7 et passim.

33. Bloch, *The Royal Touch*, p. 191.

34. James Rattue, *The Living Stream: Holy Wells in Historical Context* (Woodbridge: Boydell, 1995), pp. 70–1; 'Holy Wells became wishing wells': W. Addison, *English Spas* (London: Batsford, 1951), p. 3.

35. Jane Shaw, *Miracles in Enlightenment England* (New Haven: Yale University Press, 2006), p. 21.

36. Santner, *The Royal Remains*, p. xv.

37. Edwin Mullins, *The Pilgrimage to Santiago* (London: Secker and Warburg, 1974), p. 64.

38. Francis Jones, *The Holy Wells of Wales* (Cardiff: University of Wales Press, 1954), p. 58.

39. Thomas, *Religion and the Decline of Magic*, p. 80.

40. Phyllis Hembry, *The English Spa, 1560–1815: A Social History* (London: Athlone Press, 1990), pp. 22–4 and 33; Shaw, *Miracles in Enlightenment England*, p. 25.

41. Shaw, *Miracles in Enlightenment England*, pp. 40–1.

42. Ibid., pp. 4–5.

43. 'Welsh Lourdes': Frederick Alderson, *The Inland Resorts and Spas of Britain* (London: David and Charles, 1973), p. 20; 'daily disorders . . . confused multitudes': quoted in Hembry, *The English Spa*, p. 15.

44. Jones, *The Holy Wells of Wales*, p. 64.

45. Samuel Schoenbaum, *William Shakespeare: A Documentary Life* (Oxford: Clarendon Press, 1975), pp. 41–6, esp. p. 42.

46. Lisa Hopkins, 'Reformation and deformation', in *The Cultural Uses of the Caesars on the English Renaissance Stage* (Aldershot: Ashgate, 2007), p. 31.

47. Hunter (ed.), *All's Well That Ends Well*, p. 101.

48. Rattue, *The Living Stream*, pp. 114–15.

49. 'Scientific discourse was the first': Manuel J. Gomez Lara, 'Trotting to the waters: seventeenth-century spas as cultural landscapes', *Sederi XI: Revista de la Sociedad Española de Estudios Renascentistas Ingleses* (Huelva: Universidad de Huelva, 2002), p. 225; 'were instead incorporated': Rattue, *The Living Stream*, p. 122.

50. Carole Rawcliffe, 'Pilgrimage and the sick in medieval East Anglia', in Colin Morris and

Peter Roberts (eds), *Pilgrimage: The English Experience from Becket to Bunyan* (Cambridge: Cambridge University Press, 2002), pp. 121, 131 and 136.

51. Quoted in Reginald Lennard, *Englishmen at Rest and Play: Some Phases of English Leisure, 1558–1714* (Oxford: Clarendon Press, 1931), p. 9.

52. Edmund Spenser, *The Faerie Queene*, ed. A. C. Hamilton (London: Longman, 1977), I, xi, 29–30, p. 149.

53. Jeffrey Knapp, *Shakespeare's Tribe: Church, Nation, and Theater in Renaissance England* (Chicago: Chicago University Press, 2002), pp. 53 and 169.

54. David Cressy, *Bonfires and Bells: National Memory and the Protestant Calendar in Elizabethan and Stuart England* (Berkeley: University of California Press, 1989), p. 57

55. A. P. V. Akrigg, *Jacobean Pageant: The Court of King James I* (London: Hamish Hamilton, 1962), pp. 29–30.

56. John Finnis and Patrick Martin, 'Another turn for the turtle: Shakespeare's intercession for love's martyr', *Times Literary Supplement*, 18 April 2003, pp. 12–14; Caroline Bingham, *James VI of Scotland* (London: Weidenfeld and Nicolson, 1979), p. 22.

57. Leeds Barroll, *Politics, Plague, and Shakespeare's Theater* (Ithaca: Cornell University Press, 1991), pp. 107–9.

58. Quoted Antonia Fraser, *The Gunpowder Plot: Terror and Faith in 1605* (London: Weidenfeld and Nicholson, 1996), pp. 77–8.

59. Ernest Law, *Shakespeare as a Groom of the Chamber* (London: George Bell, 1910), pp. 59–60; Schoenbaum, *William Shakespeare*, p. 196.

60. The theory was first put forward by George Bernard Shaw. For Shakespeare and the Herberts see Michael Brennan, '"We have the man Shakespeare with us": Wilton House and *As You Like It*', *Wiltshire Archaeological Magazine*, 80 (1986), 225–7; Michael Brennan, *Literary Patronage in the English Renaissance: The Pembroke Family* (London: Routledge, 1989), pp. 105–7; Anthony Holden, *William Shakespeare* (London: Little, Brown, 1999), pp. 209–10; and Park Honan, *Shakespeare: A Life* (Oxford: Oxford University Press, 1998), p. 301.

61. See Brennan, *Literary Patronage*, pp. 100 and 223–4.

62. Anthony Dawson and Paul Yachnin, *The Culture of Playgoing in Shakespeare's England* (Cambridge: Cambridge University Press, 2001), pp. 201–3.

63. Miguel de Cervantes, *The History of Don Quixote of the Mancha*, trans. Thomas Shelton (London: Edward Blount, 1612; reprinted in 4 vols, London: David Nutt, 1896), 'To the Reader', vol. 1, p. 11.

64. Luis Astrana Marin, *Vida exemplar y heroica de Miguel de Cervantes Saavedra, con mil documentos hasta ahora ineditos y numerosas illustraciones y grabados de epoca*, 7 vols (Madrid: Instituto Editorial Reus, 1948–57), vol. 6, p. 37.

65. William Byron, *Cervantes: A Biography* (London: Cassell, 1979), pp. 383–4.

66. Jean Canavaggio, *Cervantes*, trans. J. R. Jones (New York: Norton, 1990), p. 222.

67. See David Lindley, *The Trials of Frances Howard: Fact and Fiction at the Court of King James* (London: Routledge, 1993), p. 41.

68. See Richard Wilson, *Secret Shakespeare: Studies in Theatre, Religion and Resistance* (Manchester: Manchester University Press, 2004), pp. 230–45.

69. Cervantes, *The History of Don Quixote*, vol. 1, pp. 271–2.

70. Miguel de Cervantes, *La española inglesa*, quoted in Ruth Safar, *Novel to Romance: A Study of Cervantes's Novelas ejemplares* (Baltimore: Johns Hopkins University Press, 1974), p. 153.

71. Sonnet attributed to Luis de Gongora, quoted in Canavaggio, *Cervantes*, p. 221; Thomas Hanrahan, 'History in *Española inglesa*', *Modern Language Notes*, 83 (1968), 267–71.

72. See Rudolph M. Bell, *Holy Anorexia* (Chicago: Chicago University Press, 1985), pp. 122 and 151–79.

73. Rattue, *The Living Stream*, p. 95.

74. See May Winefride Sturman, 'Gravelines and the English Poor Clares', *London Recusant*, 7

(1977), pp. 1–8. See also A. C. F. Beales, *Education Under Penalty: English Catholic Education from the Reformation to the Fall of James II* (London: Athlone Press, 1963), pp. 203–4; Patricia Crawford, *Women and Religion in England, 1500–1700* (London: Routledge, 1992), p. 85; and Marie Rowlands, 'Recusant women, 1540–1640', in Mary Prior (ed.), *Women in English Society, 1500–1800* (London: Routledge, 1985), pp. 168–74, esp. p. 169. For Susanna Shakespeare's listing as a recusant on 5 May 1606, see Hugh Hanley, 'Shakespeare's family in Stratford records', *Times Literary Supplement*, 21 May 1964, p. 441: the records are in the Act Books of Kent County Records Office, via the Sackville papers.

75. Robert Miola, '"An alien people clutching their gods?": Shakespeare's ancient religions', *Shakespeare Survey*, 54 (2001), 34–45, here 38.

76. Honan, *Shakespeare*, p. 309.

77. See, in particular, Juliet Dusinberre, *Shakespeare and the Nature of Women* (Basingstoke: Macmillan, 1996), pp. 5–7 and 30–51.

78. Willem Schrickx, '*Pericles* in a book-list of 1619 from the English Jesuit mission and some of the play's special problems', *Shakespeare Survey*, 29 (1976), pp. 21–32.

79. Quoted in Hunter (ed.), *All's Well That Ends Well*, p. 6.

80. Manfred Pfister, 'Shakespeare and Italy, or, the law of diminishing returns', in Michelle Marrapodi, A. J. Hoenselaars, Marcello Cappuzzo and L. Falzon Santucci (eds), *Shakespeare's Italy: Functions of Italian Locations in Renaissance Drama* (Manchester: Manchester University Press, 1997), p. 296.

81. See Barbara Everett, 'Spanish *Othello*: the making of Shakespeare's Moor', *Shakespeare Survey*, 35 (1982), p. 103.

82. See Robert Watson, '*Othello* as Protestant propaganda', in Claire McEachern and Debora Shuger (eds), *Religion and Culture in Renaissance England* (Cambridge: Cambridge University Press, 1997), pp. 234–57.

83. See Wilson, *Secret Shakespeare*, pp. 155–85.

84. Stephen Greenblatt, '*King Lear* and the exorcists', in *Shakespearean Negotiations: The Circulation of Social Energy in Renaissance England* (Oxford: Clarendon Press, 1988), pp. 114 and 119.

85. Santner, *The Royal Remains*, p. 152.

86. See Gary Taylor, 'Forms of opposition: Shakespeare and Middleton', *English Literary Renaissance*, 24 (1994), p. 315.

87. Harold Gardiner, *Mysteries' End: An Investigation of the Last Days of the Medieval Religious Stage* (New Haven: Yale University Press, 1946), p. 117.

88. Louis Montrose, *The Purpose of Playing: Shakespeare and the Politics of the Elizabethan Theatre* (Chicago: Chicago University Press, 1996), pp. 23–8, 30–1 and 58–61.

89. Henri Misson, quoted in Alderson, *The Inland Resorts and Spas of Britain*, p. 25; see also Lara, 'Trotting to the waters', p. 225.

90. Alexandra Walsham, 'Reforming the waters: holy wells and healing springs in Protestant England', in Diana Wood (ed.), *Life and Thought in the Northern Church, c. 1100 – c.1700: Essays in Honour of Claire Cross* (Woodbridge: Boydell and Brewer, 1999), pp. 236 and 244.

91. For a similar interpretation of the statue scene in *The Winter's Tale*, see Lupton, *Thinking With Shakespeare*, pp. 196–218.

92. William Shakespeare, *The Sonnets and A Lover's Complaint*, ed. John Kerrigan (Harmondsworth: Penguin, 1986), p. 387.

93. Thomas Hall, *Flora Floralia; Or, the Downfall of the May Games* (London: 1661), quoted in Thomas, *Religion and the Decline of Magic*, pp. 105–6.

94. Starkie, *The Road to Santiago*, p. 58.

95. Erasmus, *The Colloquies*, trans. C. Thompson (Oxford: Oxford University Press, 1964), p. 312, quoted in Wes Williams, *Pilgrimages and Narrative in the French Renaissance: 'The Undiscovered Country'* (Oxford: Clarendon Press, 1998), pp. 128–9.

96. Alderson, *The Inland Resorts and Spas of Britain*, p. 20; Walter Raleigh, 'The passionate man's pilgrimage', in *The Poems of Sir Walter Raleigh*, ed. Agnes Latham (London: Routledge and Kegan Paul, 1951), p. 49.

97. Andrew Boorde, *The First Book of the Introduction of Knowledge*, ed. James Hogg (Salzburg: Universitat Salzburg, 1979), pp. 9 and 87–8.

Epilogue:
Flower Power in Bohemia

A VILE PHRASE, 'BEAUTIFIED'

'There is an upstart Crow, beautified with our feathers': playwright Robert Greene's deathbed curse on the 'absolute Johannes factotum' who 'is in his own conceit the only Shake-scene in a country', is 'among the most famous' yet 'the bitterest lines ever written about Shakespeare', and a record of apparently irreconcilable antagonism.[1] As 'the king of the paper stage' drank himself to death in the tanners' quarter of London, he warned his 'fellow Scholars' from the universities, dramatists Marlowe, Nashe and Peele, never to trust the actor 'that with his *Tiger's hart wrapped in a Player's hide*, supposes he is as well able to bombast out a blank verse as the best of you'. The allusion was to *Henry VI, Part 3*, where Queen Margaret possesses a 'tiger's heart wrapped in a woman's hide' [1,4,137]; and biographers read this as a case of 'a drunk, a cheat, and a liar', in Stephen Greenblatt's opinion, finding 'something frightening in Shakespeare'.[2] 'I know the best husband of you will never prove a Usurer', Greene explained; and he capped the aspersion that Shakespeare had charged him interest on loans with the fable of the ant, a 'waspish little worm' who refuses the grasshopper relief: 'Use no entreats, I will relentless rest,/For toiling labour hates an idle guest'.[3] Greene died in shame at deserting his wife, 'too honest for such a husband', for the 'sorry ragged quean' who bore his bastard son Fortunatus.[4] But his infamous last words about a 'relentless' parasitic Shakespeare tarnished his rival's reputation forever. Thus, 'A deathsman of the soul Robert Greene called him', lectures Stephen in James Joyce's *Ulysses*: 'Not for nothing was he a butcher's son wielding the sledded poleaxe and spitting on his palm'.[5] This voice of hate echoing from beyond the grave therefore presents us with a challenge. What if Greene's implacable hostility was justified, and his suspicions of parasitism and plagiarism were not paranoid but true?[6]

Greene had been happy to be thought 'every quarter big with one pamphlet or another'; and his assault on Shakespeare was quickly published as *Greene's Groat's-worth of Wit, bought with a million of repentance*, an ugly specimen of the abuse pamphlets that Elizabethan writers liked to pass off as their bastard 'penurious brats'.[7] Its cheek was partly its reference to plumes, equating the player's piratical hat with a writer's purloined pen.[8] So, how did its victim respond to this offensiveness? 'The thrice-three muses mourning for the death/Of learning, late deceased in beggary', is how he archly 'beautified' Greene's 'satire, keen and critical', which Theseus considers 'Not sorting with a nuptial' in A *Midsummer Night's Dream* [5,1,54]. The Duke's suavity echoes that of certain unnamed aristocrats who, according to its publisher Henry Chettle, protested against the 'Shakes-scene' diatribe, vouching for their protégé's 'uprightness of dealing, which argues his honesty, and his facetious grace in writing, which approves his art'.[9] In 1603 the militant Protestant Chettle would out Shakespeare as a crypto-Catholic, for refusing to mourn Queen Elizabeth; and some think he ghosted Greene's attack.[10] But he was careful now to disavow any libel, squirming how he had 'seen his demeanour no less civil than he excellent in the quality' of acting.[11] Presumably, the printer had been intimidated by an actor armed with testimonials from such powerful friends; but the offensive imputation, that this carrion crow *beautified* his work with feathers stolen from his social and intellectual betters, evidently struck deep, for 'a vile phrase, "beautified"', the playwright would have his Polonius object [*Hamlet*, 2,2,111]. Thus its subject was still chewing over this insult long after the perpetrator's death, remarks Joseph Loewenstein in his study of early modern plagiarism. So, while it is true his accuser had impugned his very profession as a playmaker, along with 'his loyalty, his sincerity, and his taste', Shakespeare's disproportionate long-cherished grudge needs to be seen in the context of the clash between his own education in classical imitation and a literary culture that was beginning to be 'fervently committed to proprietary protections':

> The episode sheds light on . . . more than the old question of whether Shakespeare began his career . . . as a botcher of others' plays. Much in the development of that career can be understood as a ramifying reaction to the sting of Greene's remarks. Shakespeare can be seen flouting [them] in the brazen, ranting extravaganza of *Titus Andronicus* . . . the beastly bombast . . . of Bottom *factotum* responds to Greene with slightly drier wit. These are profound and ingenious responses, and they are only the earliest ones. Though Greene's insult is hardly some secret origin of all of Shakespeare's efforts at self-promotion, many of those efforts sustain a . . . flyting dialogue with the dead.[12]

In *Will in the World* Greenblatt proposes that it was the jobbing wordsmith who was the 'sleazy parasite', and that Shakespeare repaid Greene not with the money for which he begged, but in the character of Falstaff, for 'The deeper we plunge in the tavern world' of the Fat Knight, 'the closer we come to Greene'. Shakespeare's detractor was just such a 'grotesque figure', the critic infers, whose libels were returned with the 'incalculable gift' of literary immortality.[13] Yet recently there has been a spirited defence of Greene as Elizabethan England's first professional writer, whose abuse of the pushy 'upstart' was driven not by neurotic jealousy of a future literary king, but by a modern sense of 'proprietary protection', which was offended by his imitator's bastardisation of literary intention. Fighting for survival at the frenetic 'pamphlet moment' of Elizabethan literature, the author of *Friar Bacon and*

Friar Bungay was himself an inveterate plagiarist, known for selling plays such as his *Orlando Furioso* to the actors twice. And it was surely ironic that his defence of artistic originality was an imitation of Horace. Yet with 'multiple engagements in the literary field', this supposed hack 'with no moral compass', whose bibulous life was 'a shambles', in Greenblatt's scathing assessment, now emerges as a herald of 'authorial and literary sophistication, rather than bohemian disinterest or pecuniary desperation'.[14] It is arguable whether this makeover as a pioneer of authorial sovereignty helps Greene look any more attractive. But it does offer an institutional context for our embarrassment that the first mention of the Bard in show business is a denunciation of his unearned interest, an accusation of theft, and a record of the battle between the poet and the player over intellectual property and authors' rights. For just how deeply the dead man's words had wounded would emerge only after some sixteen years, when with *The Winter's Tale* Shakespeare conceived a drama of unintended consequences, a tragicomedy of broken hospitality, paranoid suspicion and slanders of illegitimacy, and as if deliberately defying the deathbed curse, shamelessly 'beautified' a story about repentance that he pilfered from Greene's romance *Pandosto, The Triumph of Time*:[15]

> I understand the business, I hear it. To have an open ear, a quick eye,
> and a nimble hand is necessary for a cutpurse. A good nose is requisite
> also, to smell out work for th'other senses. I see this is the time that the
> unjust man doth thrive. . . . Sure the gods do this year connive at us, and
> we may do anything extempore.
>
> > [*Winter's*, 4,4,653–6]

In *Pandosto*, paternal 'jealousy' curdles 'joy' into 'bloody revenge'; but Shakespeare's 'beautifying' supplies an unintended happy ending to this turbid tale – about a King of Bohemia who kills himself after wrongly accusing his wife, Bellaria, of adultery with his bosom friend King Egistus of Sicily – when the comic rogue Autolycus is transported into the story from another of Greene's pamphlets, his *Groat's-worth of Wit*. There the poet 'Roberto' is waylaid by a stranger on the road. This dandified highwayman turns out to be a player, who offers the unworldly writer a contract, boasting how 'men of my profession get by scholars their whole living'.[16] Editors relate the mercenary characterisation of the pedlar Autolycus as 'a snapper-up of unconsidered trifles' [4,3,25] to two more of Greene's publications, his brace of *Conny-Catching* guides to con men who cheat 'rabbits', or suckers, where the Curber is defined as 'he that with a Curb or hook, doth pull out of a window any loose linen; which stolen parcels they in their Art call snappings'.[17] Shakespeare's thieving magpie likewise 'traffics in sheets' [4,3,23] that he lifts. But when he also 'sings several tunes faster than you'll tell money', or 'utters them as he had eaten ballads', until 'all men's ears grew to his tunes', it is clear the sheets he filches include printers' proofs, and that these 'prettiest love-songs', which suit his adoring audiences so well 'no milliner can so fit his customers with gloves' [4,4,184–94], are metatheatrical references to the 'foul' sources of a play that is itself constructed out of the 'myriad forms' of such second-hand narration, and thus to its creator's own literary cuckoldry.[18] Greene's professional plagiarist is a 'Country Author' with a provincial accent. Thus, whether or not he was intended as a portrait of the son of the Stratford glover, all Shakespeare's anxieties of influence, belatedness and illegitimacy seem to have been stirred by his rival's acid tableau of the university-educated poet conned by the self-fashioning player into prostituting his art:[19]

> 'What is your profession?' said Roberto. 'Truly sir', he said, 'I am a player.' 'A player', quoth Roberto, 'I took you rather for a gentleman of great living; for if by outward habit men should be censured, I tell you, you would be taken for a substantial man'. 'So am I where I dwell', quoth the player, 'reputed able at my proper cost to build a Windmill. What though the world went hard with me, when I was fain to carry my playing Fardel a footback; *Tempora mutantur*; I know you know the meaning of it better than I, but I thus conster it: 'It is otherwise now'; for my very share in playing apparel will not be sold for two hundred pounds'.[20]

Greene's 'Windmill' is a gibe at London's moneymaking playhouse; and with its scorn for the 'playing Fardel', the conning of the guileless 'Roberto' rehearses the *agôn* of the poet and player that marked the birth of the author in early modern England. To Greene, players were merely the poets' 'puppets that spake from our mouths, antics garnished with our colours'.[21] Such antagonism therefore connected with the violent energies that were ripping early modern society apart over questions of presence and representation. As James Bednarz comments in *Shakespeare and the Poets' War*, this professional civil war over the ownership of words was suicidal, since without poets the players would be forced back into minstrelsy, yet 'without players poets would be denied the profits and prestige from the stage'.[22] Greene's bafflement therefore highlights the realisation of 'the *Poets* of these sinful times' that, as Thomas Dekker recorded, 'the *Players* have now got the upper hand'.[23] For trapped between a declining patronage system and a rising theatre public, this graduate of both Oxford *and* Cambridge had displaced all the bad faith of his dealings with publishers and their 'peddling chapmen' onto the roguish motley of his Pied Piper. What is disarming, then, about the villain's revisiting of the primal scene of literary enmity sixteen years later is that, despite all those outraged protests about his 'uprightness' of dealing, the allegations of parasitism and plagiarism are now cheerfully acknowledged in the rascally piracy of the feral Autolycus, whose very name, the latest Arden editor John Pitcher points out, makes him sound exactly like Greene's tiger or 'wolf in sheep's clothing', and whose capacious holdall affiliates him with the pretentious 'know-all' that the University Wits vilified as 'Johannes Shagbag'.[24] Thus, in *The Winter's Tale* it is as if Shakespeare at last comes clean, and exposes the personal and professional antagonism that underlies his art:

> What a fool honesty is, and trust – his sworn brother –
> a very simple gentleman! I have sold all my trumpery;
> not a counterfeit stone, not a ribbon, glass, pomander, brooch,

table-book, ballad, knife, tape, glove, shoe-tie, bracelet, horning
to keep my pack from fasting.

[4,4,584–8]

A FOUL GAP IN THE MATTER

Shakespeare's picking over the wounds of Greene's antagonism so near the end
of his career is an indicator of how dearly he must have loved his enemies. For by
incorporating his professional enmity in *The Winter's Tale*, Shakespeare seems at
last to be revealing his winning hand. Thus Autolycus proves the shepherds in the
play are right to worry that 'the wolf will sooner find' their sheep 'than the master'
[3,3,64]. The contents of this tinker's 'pack' in fact mark him out as one of the commercial travellers Margaret Spufford has described in *The Great Reclothing of Rural
England* as the truest agents of 'cultural revolution' in the Shakespearean era. For
though they sparked moral panic in the authorities, which in 1597 acted to outlaw
'all Jugglers, Tinkers, Pedlars, and Petty Chapmen wandering abroad', according to
this historian the inventory of Autolycus's haversack discloses how the itinerants
who brought these beauty products 'cannot have been as unwelcome and dubious'
to the 'humbler sort' as 'they appeared to legislators'.[25] The bag of a pedlar left on
Salisbury Plain in 1618 may have contained only needles, nails, cloth rags, stolen
purses and a comb, but when the ban was repealed in 1604 it was an indicator of the
irresistibly rising status of men who were more 'often making large sales' at gentry
houses.[26] So Autolycus breezes into Shakespeare's story 'When daffodils begin to
peer' [4,3,1], to 'come before the swallow dares, and take / The winds of March with
beauty' [4,4,120–1], as harbinger of the beautification of the world that in *Vermeer's
Hat*, his book about the shimmering dawn of globalisation, Timothy Brook describes
as the transformative effect of all the furs and fabrics, fruits and furnishings, which
were being carried into Europe along the new networks of world trade, and which
meant the rules of even courtship changed:

> Romance took over from cash-in-hand as the currency of love, and the home
> became the new theatre for acting out the tension between the genders. Men
> and women still negotiated over sex and companionship but the negotiation
> was now disguised as banter, not barter, and its object was a solid brick house
> with leaded window panes and expensive furnishings, not an hour in bed.[27]

While it is true that Autolycus was a linen thief, Spufford concedes, in return he
produced many more beautifying textiles from his self-fashioning bag: 'there were
cambrics, lawns' and a variety of haberdashery: 'Caddises for garters, ribbons in all
colours of the rainbow, trimmings like lace, and all the inkles, tape, points . . . pins
and thread in his pack were absolutely essential tools to the householder'. And this
nomad combined staples with sophistication, for as well as ready-made accessories,
such as hats and scarves, he sold cheap luxuries like 'the vital looking-glasses',
jewellery, mirrors and cosmetics, which tied rural communities into the leisure

and entertainment industries: 'there were maskings, perfumes and poking sticks for ruffs in his pack', and 'much of his success as a salesman was due to his singing of the ballads he sold'.[28] In *Late Shakespeare: A New World of Words*, Simon Palfrey therefore infers that this lone wolf is more than merely a figure for the individualism of 'printed texts, cash, and contract', for his 'pedlar's silken treasury' [4,4,347] is metonymic of the endless beautifying or morphing *re-creation* of the playhouse itself, and thus prefigures the advent of the purposelessness of the aesthetic:

> Autolicus' pack . . . evokes the bustle and litter of a public theatre's tiring-house:. . . As if the theatre's own resplendent book-keeper, Autolicus sings to the click of counted cash. . . . But his meta-dramatic potency extends beyond being some mascot of consumerism. . . . Indeed Autolicus' mimetic reflexiveness seems to have been plotted from his name. In Ovid's *Metamorphoses*, the infamous thief is the first of twins, one born of Mercury, the other Apollo. As an emblem and example of the medium's processes, then, the mercurial Autolicus challenges the play's nominally supreme justice and narrator, Apollo. . . . this minstrel is a challenge to our very definition of the Apollonian – or as so often in critical history, the Shakespearian – voice and progeny.[29]

'Littered under Mercury', the demonic recycler and Ovidian *bricoleur* of *objets trouvé*, with his 'unconsidered' appropriations Autolycus seems to personify the trope of *akrasia*, the irony of unintended consequences, as a figure not only for the 'strange bedfellows' [*Tempest*, 2,2,37] necessitated by the ironic cycles of world trade, but for the death of the author himself. Thus, this bastard begetter of bastards scandalises Greene's Apollonian dream of aesthetic purity and authorial intention, which Shakespeare subversively places at the centre of the story, when, in words lifted straight out of *Pandosto*, the god of light affirms through his Delphic Oracle that the queen is 'chaste', her friend 'blameless' and her 'innocent babe truly begotten' [*Winter's*, 3,2,131]. In fact, the serial seducer of desperate housewives seems to be invented as a *frère ennemi* to Apollonian reason precisely to justify the King's hermeneutic suspicion applied to his own wife's possible 'hermetic' dealings with Hermes, when Leontes insists 'There is no truth at all i'th'oracle' [138]. For Autolycus cheerfully brags that his pack conceals his 'sow-skin budget' [4,3,20], or toolbag, which editors inform us is slang for the scrotum; and that this expansive reticule contains gods and gloves 'for man or woman of all sizes' [4,4,193]. A 'glove' was a condom ('Your quondam wife swears still by Venus' glove' [*Troilus*, 4,7,63], gloats Hector to Helen's cuckolded husband Menelaus), and the 'gods' [205] by which Autolycus swears to give promiscuous satisfaction are in fact his phallic Herms, or leather dildos.

According to the ingenuous Servant who announces this gatecrasher's coming into the Bohemia of the play, the pedlar's 'love songs for maids', with such 'delicate burdens of dildos and fadings' as 'Jump her, and thump her', are prophylactic against 'bawdry', being guaranteed not to 'break a foul gap in the matter', or *mater*, when the 'stretched-mouthed rascal . . . makes the maid to answer, "Whoop, do me no harm, good man"' [4,4,195–9]. And equally credulous critics like to rest assured that, despite thus supplying 'What maids lack from head to heal' [223], 'Autolycus' manipulations are relatively harmless', because 'he has no intimate connections with the women in the play'.[30] But this is to underestimate the son of Mercury. For the textual desire throbbing through the 'foul gaps' of his provisions enacts the very puncture of 'proprietary protection' they are purchased to prevent; and as he discards his gloves and gods, the rogue therefore disseminates the semantic current that seeps throughout the play, between illegitimate printing and parenting. For like all of these late works, the stage of The Winter's Tale is literally littered with throwaway signifiers of the promiscuous hermeneutic relations of publishing, marks of the legitimacy crisis that connected sexual infidelity to the indelible stain of ink, and that was only intensified, Margreta de Grazia and Wendy Wall point out, by the suggestive pornographic machinery of the printing press itself, imaged as a bastardising whore, obscenely and repetitively 'performing virtual copulative acts'.[31]

'Behold, my lords,/Although the print be little, the whole matter/And copy of the father' [2,3,99–101]: when the matronly Paulina Shakespeare also invented for The Winter's Tale prefaces the baby Perdita for King Leontes, it is as though the dramatist's implacable antagonist Robert Greene haunts the story as its nominal parent in his own proprietary metaphor of textual reproduction. 'They say it is a copy out of mine', the King had earlier observed doubtfully, in the face of his son and heir: 'they say we are/Almost as alike as eggs. Women say so,/That will say anything' [1,2,124–33]. As feminist critics remark, there is a long and troubled Shakespearean history of sexualised anxiety over textual origins behind this print metaphor, and a deep disquiet about corrupt transmission, which Posthumus vents in Cymbeline, when he frets that his father 'was I know not where/When I was stamped' [2,5,4–5].[32] What is noticeable, however, is that up to this point all Shakespeare's print images are confidently patriarchal, and thus refer to handwriting, as when Speed purports to 'speak in print' from a letter [Two Gentlemen, 2,1,151]; to minted monetary coinage, like the 'metal' that has 'so great a figure . . . stamped upon it', to which the false deputy Angelo is compared [Measure, 1,1,49]; or to seals, like the father's stamp which makes the child, so Theseus preaches to Hermia, merely 'a form in wax/By him imprinted' [Dream, 1,1,49].[33] In short, before The Winter's Tale, printing always retains in these recuperative paternal images the illusion of self-presence of written speech.

In Coriolanus the protagonist is reminded by his mother that his son is 'a poor epitome of yours,/Which by th'interpretation of full time/May show like all yourself' [5,3,67–9]; and Leontes will reach for this time-honoured patriarchal trope of permanent 'imprinting' when he assures Florizel, the son of the friend he suspected of fathering Perdita, that 'Your mother was most true to wedlock, prince;/For she did print your royal father off/Conceiving you' [Winter's, 5,1,123–5]. But Polixenes had undermined his paternal security in being the owner and origin of his own meaning, and initiated the ensuing crisis of representation by promising at the start to act 'like a cipher' in 'rich place', and 'multiply' with one replicating press of friendship 'many thousands more' [1,2,6]. So now Leontes' manly compliment involuntarily refers to the 'royal' paper format, twenty inches by twenty-five, of printed folio volumes; and like the term for the author's 'royalty', the pun on 'prints'

thereby simply exposes the extent of paternal and sovereign unease at the untrust-
worthiness of all the multiple editions, epitomes, imitations, piracies, translations
and simulacra in this first age of mechanical reproduction, when supposedly timeless
authorial rights are increasingly asserted in denial of the evidential facts of promiscuous textual dissemination, claiming 'rights over printing that did not exist'.[34] For
as Shakespeare's Queen Hermione warns her husband, once 'published' there can in
fact be no retraction of the 'dangerous supplement' of the printed text in this frenzy
of irrrecuperable representation:[35]

> How will this grieve you
> When you shall come to clearer knowledge that
> You thus have published me? Gentle my lord,
> You scarce can right me throughly then to say
> You did mistake.
>
> [2,1,98–102]

Just prior to *The Winter's Tale* King James had reissued his 1607 *Apology for the
Oath of Allegiance* with corrections, but then rushed out a proclamation asking pur-
chasers to bring back 'all such Books as they have to our Printer, from whom they
shall have other copies' correcting the errors made in the corrections caused by 'the
rashness of the Printer'; and in her study of this self-cancelling 'royal author', Jane
Rickard notes how even as these repeated recalls and reissues 'attempt to impose
order, they form a striking public acknowledgement' of the ungovernable vagaries
of print.[36] Nothing would undermine James's sovereignty more, in this account,
than his foolishness in publishing a folio of his own literary 'works'. Likewise,
Leontes' attempt to assert the 'royalty' of a folio volume involuntarily concedes
there can be no return to the phallocentrism of the 'stamped coin' [4,4,704], which
even Autolycus admits that he prefers. So, if 'childbirth is the literal and symbolic
centre' of this play, it remains fraught with a publisher's anxiety about 'some foul
issue' [2,3,153], and racked by the determination that 'I'll not rear another's issue'
[193].[37] The word 'issue' indeed occurs fifteen times in *The Winter's Tale*: twice as
often as in any other Shakespearean text; and Helen Hackett explains how this
recurrence connects 'the issue of it' [5,2,8], as unforeseeable outcome, to the characters' concerns that they 'should not produce fair issue' [2,1,150], and the narrative's
'issued doubted' [1,2,259] to the 'fair issue' [2,1,150] of such progeny.[38] So Leontes'
sensation that 'I play a part, whose issue/Will hiss me to my grave' [1,2,189–90] is
provoked by the tension between playing and printing in a culture that was still
without copyright, yet already tyrannically fixated upon the author function. Hence,
the King will 'spend much of the play trying (and failing) to control his own language and the language of others'.[39] But when Paulina advises Leontes to 'Care not
for issue./The crown will find an heir' [4,1,46], the play also registers what Robert
Knapp terms a new 'bookish authority' in the later Shakespeare, where the kings and
fathers learn that all reproductive 'issues' must from now on be taken on trust, even
when 'the text is foolish' [*Lear*, 4,2,38].[40]

VERY TRUE, AND BUT A MONTH OLD

A play without an author is 'a Bastard without a Father', playwright Thomas Heywood had declared.[41] Yet Shakespeare's romances mark a major shift in this monological trope of printing and parenting, when they decide to 'weigh not every stamp', as Posthumus puts it in *Cymbeline*, but 'Though light, take pieces for the figure's sake' [5,5,118–19]. As Adrian Johns explains in *The Nature of the Book: Print and Knowledge in the Making*, a real 'print revolution' occurred at this time, when, with the realisation that patriarchy's 'print of goodness' would no longer 'take' [*Tempest*, 1,2,355], the credibility gap was bridged by a new 'intersubjective trust', as 'questions of credit took the place of assumptions of fixity'.[42] If the sixteenth century had been a time for the hermeneutic of suspicion, the seventeenth century would therefore be the heyday of unlimited credit. In *The Winter's Tale*, the King's justified distrust of the unverifiable is therefore met with the appeal, 'Beseech your highness, give us better credit' [2,3,147]; and we need not go quite so far as Louis MacNeice, whose poem 'Autolycus' reads into the 'master pedlar', with his 'confidence tricks,/Brooches, pomanders, broadsheets and what-have-you', the Bard's self-portrait in 'his last phase, when hardly bothering to be a dramatist', to perceive here a blithe disclaimer of both professional antagonism and authorial responsibility.[43] For by equivocating about how much the persons and incidents of this play are both like and yet *unlike* 'an old tale still, which will have matter to rehearse though credit be asleep and not an ear open' [5,2,55], Shakespeare turns his rival's story back against its putative owner, to dissolve suspicions of plagiarism and illegitimacy in a collective leap of faith, which 'Were it but told you, should be hooted at/Like an old tale' [5,3,117], because 'This news which is called true is so like an old tale that the verity of it is in strong suspicion' [25–6]:

AUTOLYCUS: Here's one to a very doleful tune, how a usurer's wife was
brought to bed of twenty money-bags at a burden, and how
she longed to eat adders' heads and toads carbonadoed.
MOPSA: Is it true, think you?
AUTOLYCUS: Very true, and but a month old.

[4,4,253–7]

As 'credulous to false prints' as their own 'complexions' [*Measure*, 2,4,128–9], female readers cannot get enough of Autolycus's ballads about mermaids and monsters, since they 'love a ballad in print', Mopsa exclaims, 'for then we are sure they are true' [251]. The truth of the ballad of the usurer's wife is indeed certified, Autolycus vouches, by the signature of the midwife, 'one Mistress Tail-Porter' [259]. The tell-tale name of the female tale-teller thereby mocks Paulina's story about Perdita, as if the play itself has such a 'deal of wonder . . . that ballad-makers cannot be able to express it' [5,2,22–3]. Like the excitement of Stephano and Trinculo over the 'monster' Caliban [*Tempest*, 2,2,29], this is therefore one of a spate of references in his final plays to the genre of 'monstrous birth' ballad, which imply that around 1610 Shakespeare became alert to the reflexive way that these popular broadsides projected anxieties about their bastard status, as stigmatised forms of print, onto the supposed 'deformed biological reproduction' of their own lower-class readers.[44] In *Illegitimate Power: Bastards in Renaissance Drama*, Alison Findlay argues that the strategy of *The Winter's Tale* was therefore to subvert the opposition between the natural and unnatural, by showing how society's efforts 'to displace illegitimacy (its own cultural construct)' onto nature are themselves unnatural. Natural yet unnatural, the bastard undoes distinctions between true and false, original and copy, speech and writing, in this analysis. Thus, when Leontes plots 'to make the murder of a bastard look natural' by exposing the baby in some 'remote and desert place' [2,3,176], he thereby merely confirms his own monstrosity.[45] Likewise, the implausible structure of Shakespeare's hybrid generic 'bastard' of a tragicomedy seems to be deliberately designed to confound all sovereign efforts to fix social differences between the discourses of the believable and unbelievable:

Lest barbarism, making me the precedent,
Should a like language use to all degrees,
And mannerly distinguishment leave out
Betwixt the prince and beggar.

[2,1,86–9]

Autolycus will be on his 'footpath way' [4,3,121] long before the issue of the 'summer songs' that he boasts he sings 'for me and my aunts, / While we lie tumbling in the hay' [11], becomes apparent. It will be 'Nine changes of the watery star' [1,2,1], as we were reminded at the start, before the unintended consequences of any 'foul gap' in the mother are delivered. But the breaches in his leaking goods are so like 'that wide gap' that leaves 'the growth untried' [4,1,6] in Shakespeare's own 'weak-hinged' [2,3,118] plot, they make us continue to doubt Apollo's oracle when at the end the King ominously repeats that he will 'Each one demand and answer to his part / Performed in this wide gap' [5,3,153] of time. Without a theophany to back it, Apollo's verdict on the Queen's chastity is like 'paper currency' without gold, smiles Howard Felperin.[46] Nor is our own trust advanced when Florizel lets slip that 'the fire-robed god' himself went disguised as 'a poor humble swain' [4,4,29–30], to seduce Alcestis. There are too many such foul gaps in the stretched fabric of *The Winter's Tale*, with its 'unprecedented obfuscation' over the reported death of Hermione, not to speculate what this latest interrogation will reveal.[47] Leontes estimates a 'tenth' of wives to be unfaithful [1,2,200]; and Jacobean England was indeed registering an actual illegitimacy crisis, with 'percentages of baptised children described as illegitimate' rising in 1610 to levels 'never again attained before 1750'.[48] Thus, 'I would there were no age between ten and three-and-twenty', repines the Old Shepherd, 'for there is nothing in the between but getting wenches with child' [3,3,58]. Littered by the errant god of commerce, Autolycus and the bastards he leaves behind after his part-songs with Mopsa and Dorcas have therefore surely been imported into Greene's story to make us wonder: suppose Leontes' suspicions of promiscuous slippage were true, and the baby born to the King was indeed the accidental issue of 'some scape', the technical term for a printing error, as the wise countryman who discovers this 'unconsidered' castaway of the litter logically infers, when, however small the print, he is confident he can read between the lines of any story that is purportedly 'very true, and but a month old'?:

> Sure some scape. Though I am not bookish, yet I can read
> 'waiting-gentlewoman' in the scape. This has been some stair-
> work, some trunk-work, some behind-door-work. They were
> warmer that got this than the poor thing is here.
>
> [3,3,69–72]

Critics have always assumed that Perdita's adoptive family is illiterate; yet while they know they are not 'bookish', Shakespeare goes out of his way to associate them with reading and writing, giving her brother her shopping-list for the sheep-shearing, and introducing her lover Florizel with her father's commendation that 'he'll stand and read, / As twere, my daughter's eyes' [4,4,174–5]. So, if the Shepherd thinks he can read the 'little print' of his foundling like a book, then that may be because he has been poring over such 'unconsidered trifles' as Greene's *Pandosto*, which return over and again in this period to the Cinderella narrative of the exiled princess, as if working out the professional dream of their literary legitimacy. What Shakespeare appears to have noticed in figuring Perdita as a cast-off volume, that is to say, is how much it matters to the writers of these retellings that the found-ling is *really* royal, as though her change of clothes validates their own proprietary claims to authorial sovereignty. As Catherine Belsey has commented, 'these stories clearly fulfilled in fantasy a desire to overcome social difference', yet reproduce the very hierarchy they aspire to transcend.[49] Thus Greene's shepherd is persuaded to save the baby only by his 'greedy desire' for the 'great sum of gold' deposited with it, when 'the covetousness of the coin overcame him', while the 'exquisite perfec-tion' of the child's 'natural disposition did bewray that she was born of some high parentage'.[50] If *Pandosto* thereby legitimates its folktale elements by asserting class distinctions, however, such hierarchies do not impress the Bohemian reading public in *The Winter's Tale*. For what Shakespeare instead stresses is the discerning literacy of Perdita's nurturing family, the 'lower messes' who, despite the social prejudices of the court, are quite as capable of deciphering a Cinderella story as 'finer natures' of 'headpiece extraordinary', like Camillo (who has, in fact, been 'reared' from the 'meaner' class himself [1,2,315–16]):

> Was this taken
> By any understanding pate but thine?
> For thy conceit is soaking, will draw in
> More than the common blocks. Not noted, is't,
> But of the finer natures? By some severals
> Of headpiece extraordinary? Lower messes
> Perchance are to this busy blind?
>
> [222–8]

With its promise to be 'Pleasant for age to avoid drowsy thoughts, and profitable for youth to eschew other wanton pastimes', *Pandosto* had been one of a line of Elizabethan works, like George Peele's *The Old Wives' Tale*, that evoked peasant customs and oral culture with a nostalgia for the community 'where nobody went beyond earshot' which anticipated Rousseau's romantic idealisation of the golden age of speech.[51] Thus Greene would sentimentalise the 'cloth breeches' of 'merry England' over the 'velvet' finery of a bastard age; but as Peter Burke relates, such patronising of popular culture was actually a sign of the withdrawal of the Elizabethan elite, which was learning to look down on wandering minstrels and traditional ballads 'with a mixture of curiosity, detachment and contempt'.[52] In his essay 'Peasants Tell Tales', Robert Darnton has confirmed how much the literary rewritings that date from this time are embarrassed by the cruel amorality of the folktales recited by wet-nurses and kitchen maids.[53] For as Greene's and Peele's efforts showed, 'an old wives winter's tale' too often turned out to be 'a heavy tale / Sad in thy mood and sober in thy cheer', like the 'winter's tales' of 'spirits and ghosts that glide by night', or the 'mere old wives tales' which Marlowe's Barabas and Faustus affect to despise as 'old women's words'.[54]

Shakespeare wrote *The Winter's Tale* when literary authors were for the first time starting to condescend to fairy stories and folktales, to Mother Goose and Old Mother Hubbard, as the voices of unvarnished truth.[55] Unlike Greene and other compilers of these *faux naïf* Elizabethan and Jacobean 'winter's tales', however, Shakespeare never succumbed to the Rousseauist vision of storytelling as a discourse of innocence. Thus, when Macbeth sees Banquo's ghost, his wife says his terror is such as 'would well become / A woman's story at a winter's fire / Authorized by her grandam' [3,4,63–5]. And the 'old tales' Shakespeare mentions are truly grim: like those 'tales of woeful ages long ago', or 'sad stories of the deaths of kings', recited 'In winter's tedious nights', recalled by Richard II [*Richard II*, 3,2,152; 5,1,40–2]; the 'old tale' whispered around Windsor about Herne the Hunter turning milk to blood as he 'shakes a chain / In a most hideous and dreadful manner' [*Wives*, 4,4,26–32]; or the spine-chilling legend of 'Bluebeard' itself, which Benedick cites for the murderer's denial to his victim of 'the story that is printed in her blood': 'it is not so, nor 'twas not so, but indeed, God forbid it should be so' [*Much Ado*, 1,1,175; 4,1,121]. As Darnton observes, the world of Mother Goose was in reality a cruel Hobbesian one of wicked stepmothers and abandoned orphans, with 'unending toil and brutal emotions', and its setting was a primitive surveillance society: the 'nasty village' of prying parents and nosy neighbours.[56] So when *The Winter's Tale* features just such a scare story, the tale defines Leontes' kingdom of Sicily, and the tragic world of *Pandosto*, as precisely the kind of closed, in-bred, suspicious and possessive community its characters will need to beautify in order to escape:

MAMILLIUS: A sad tale's best for winter. I have one
              Of sprites and goblins.
HERMIONE: Let's have that, good sir.
              Come on, sit down, come on, and do your best
              To fright me with your sprites. You're powerful at it.

MAMILLIUS: There was a man –
HERMIONE: Nay, come sit down, then on.
MAMILLIUS: Dwelt by a churchyard. . . .

[2,1,23–30]

Mamillius's winter's tale is interrupted by his father's cry of vindication: 'All's true that is mistrusted' [2,1,48]. But it will be picked up again when Hermione appears as 'the ghost that walked' [5,1,63] 'in pure white robes' to terrify Antigonus as 'with shrieks,/She melted into air' [3,3,21–36]. The prince who starts this uncanny chiller about a man living among corpses, whom the boy soon enough joins, is named after the heroine of Greene's first novel, *Mamillia*, a story of 'Two Maids Wooing a Man' [4,4,278] that belied its author's reputation as a 'Homer to women' with its misogynistic rant. When the eerie child precociously mocks the ladies' 'beautifying' cosmetics, the answer to their query 'Who taught this?' [12] would therefore have to be the gynophobic stories by the likes of Greene that Mamillius has been made to read. Thus, because 'Truth' will be legitimated as a 'Daughter of Time', so *Pandosto* affirms, only when she is 'most manifestly revealed', Greene's novel has been called a phantasmagoria of the suspicious male gaze frustrated by the 'limits of a man's knowledge', where 'desire and jealousy flourish at the margin of what is knowable, just beyond the limits of what can be seen'.[57] What this craving for visual possession in fact incubates is a sinister premonition of modern psychoanalytic decodings of Cinderella, when Pandosto develops a 'frantic affection' for his half-familiar daughter Fawnia. So, confronted by the 'chain and jewels' that prove the girl to be his child, Pandosto reacts like Oedipus, and 'calling to mind how he had betrayed his friend Egistus, how his jealousy was the cause of Bellaria's death, how contrary to the law of nature he lusted after his own Daughter, he fell into a melancholy fit, and to close up the Comedy with a Tragical stratagem, slew himself'.[58] The self-reflexiveness of this cursory conclusion thus betrays the desperation of its author's drive for sovereign proprietorial control. Confronted by the wildly miscellaneous contents of the magic fardel, Greene's insulated, incestuous and faithless world of fixed identities and stable signifiers can only destroy itself.

IN SO PREPOSTEROUS ESTATE

Shakespeare had already anticipated the Freudians by exposing incest as the dirty secret of Cinderella in *King Lear*; and began to map an exit in *Pericles*, where all the travels of the hero are made in order to escape this doom: 'Bad child, worse father, to entice his own' [1,27]. *The Winter's Tale* hints at the same incest, when the King ogles his daughter with an eye that 'hath too much youth in it', and confesses she so resembles her mother, 'I thought of her/Even with these looks I made' [5,1,224–7].[59] This is where the Pygmalion-like fixation upon producing offspring 'Almost as like' their parents 'as eggs' [1,2,132], to attest paternal ownership, has been leading all along. Shakespeare's later play avoids this deathly *cul de sac*, however, for Perdita will never be 'the whole matter/And copy' [2,3,98–9] of her natural father, because of her *nurture*. This daughter of the foul-mouthed, evil-minded King Leontes avoids the incestuous fate of Fawnia and Antiochus's daughter, after she is trained to accomplish 'anything' as 'featly' as she dances [4,4,177–8], by following her surrogate father's civil lessons in hospitality and openness. Nothing shows up royal incivility more, therefore, than the Old Shepherd's subsequent resolve that 'we must be gentle now we are gentlemen' [5,2,136]. And Perdita underlines this reversal when she rebuts the prejudice that her beauty is 'more than can be thought to begin from such a cottage' [4,2,38], with the urge to assure King Polixenes that 'the selfsame sun that shines upon his court/Hides not his visage from our cottage' [4,4,231–2]. So, though the Arden editor calls her adoptive father a 'gnarled, illiterate old peasant', who could not possibly be the tutor for the 'intelligence' and 'grace' with which Perdita discourses about art and nature, his instructions to his daughter establish that this is precisely what he is:[60]

> Pray you bid
> These unknown friends to's welcome, for it is
> A way to make us better friends, more known.
> Come, quench your blushes, and present yourself
> That which you are, mistress o'th'feast. Come on,
> And bid us welcome to your sheep-shearing,
> As your good flock shall prosper.

[4,4,64–70]

When Autolycus starts his bawdy ballad 'Two Maids Wooing a Man', it is the Shepherd's son who blushes, saying that 'We'll have this song out anon by ourselves' [297]. Throughout *The Winter's Tale* Shakespeare inverts the social logic and causality of *Pandosto*, beginning with the surprise that Bohemia is now the summer land of worldly hospitality, and Sicily the winter wasteland of insular suspicion. So, contrary to the notion that in *The Winter's Tale* Shakespeare naturalises class and property, as Terry Eagleton has argued, by valorising 'the father child relationship as a paradigm of authentic individual possession', recent critics reread the play as a subversion of the 'natural aristocracy' of the Cinderella fantasy, and an affirmation of a dialectical relationship between 'high' and 'low' that demonstrates how they are implicated in each other.[61] In this revaluation, the gullibility of Autolycus' country customers not only re-enacts the prejudice that lets Leontes call Hermione 'A bed-swerver, even as bad as those/That vulgars give bold'st titles' [2,1,95–6], but puts into relief the vulgarity of the King and court. So, when the pedlar 'beautifies' himself in the finery of Prince Florizel, the naïvety of the shepherds in mistaking him for 'a great man', as he coaxes them into acknowledging 'the air of the court in these enfoldings' [4,4,710–30], merely mirrors the King's failure to distinguish his Queen from a 'flax-wench that puts to/Before her troth-plight' [1,1,279–80], as well as our own class bias in identifying Perdita as a princess on the mere evidence of the 'majesty of the creature' [5,2,32], as though this rewriting was setting out to generate the very social reversals and cultural mistakes Greene deplored, and that his characters so dread, 'And mannerly distinguishment leave out/Betwixt the prince and beggar':[62]

CLOWN: This cannot be but a great courtier.
SHEPHERD: His garments are rich, but he wears them not handsomely.
CLOWN: He seems to be more noble in being fantastical. A great
           man, I'll warrant. I know by the picking on's teeth.

[4,4,726–9]

By incorporating Greene's embittered antagonism in order to disarm it, and with a title taken from the greater rival poet Marlowe, *The Winter's Tale* becomes a lesson in the very courtesy that is nurtured by its own humble country characters. Whereas *Pandosto* had betrayed its author's frustrated ambition for social distinction and possessive ownership, this sequel therefore revisits the primal scene of Shakespeare's own beautification with all the worldly self-knowledge of a parvenu who, as one of the King's Men, had truly realised Autolycus's professional dream, to serve a prince and wear 'three-pile' [4,3,13]. Patricia Parker infers that the entire tragicomedy is, in fact, organised around the anachronicity of this preposterousness, a 'reversal of priority, precedence, and ordered sequence' which the young Clown explains in the final act, when he relates how 'I was a gentleman born before my father, for the King's son took me by the hand and called me brother; and then the two kings called my father brother', so that for these 'four hours' they have been in just such a 'preposterous estate' [5,2,114–32]. As they back into the limelight of their new celebrity, Shakespeare's rustics thereby exemplify their creator's lifelong strategy of minimising his own 'royalty', in order to disarm professional enmity and convert antagonism into agonism.

Editors gloss the young shepherd's description of his 'preposterous' social advance as a provincial's malapropism for 'prosperous'; but the anachronism of a world turned arsy versy, upside down, is the rule in this play, from the instant when a playwriting Time upturns his glass, 'To o'erthrow law, and in one self-born hour/To plant and o'erwhelm' [4,1,8–9]. And sure enough, thanks to their unearned 'fairy gold', its shepherds are very soon 'from very nothing, and beyond the imagination' of their neighbours, 'grown into an unspeakable estate' [4,2,38]. The contrariness of this revolution does not, moreover, only describe the rise of the gentry through the social mobility of new men such as the commoner Camillo, but, as Parker points out, the ascent of William Shakespeare himself, Greene's 'upstart crow', to the eventual status of the 'gentleman born', in the grant of arms he retroactively obtained for his father John.[63] Thus, if Shakespeare's Sicily is founded upon Greene's Elizabethan Gothic horror story, as an intolerant, paranoid and inward-looking kingdom, nostalgic for the sterile immobility of an age when 'We were as twinned lambs' that 'knew not the doctrine' original sin [1,2,69–72], his Bohemia is a far more tolerant land, like his contemporary Jacobean one, living out the unintended consequences and migrant meanings of its fortunate fall.

MAKE THE GREEN ONE RED

The learning curve of *The Winter's Tale* has taken us from a suspicious world where 'Intention stabs the centre' [1,2,137] to a tolerant one where we know enough to credit what 'Interpretation should abuse' [4,4,339]. From intention to interpretation, in Shakespeare's play the emancipated actor is truly, then, among 'things newborn', as the possessive author is among 'things dying' [3,3,110]. Critics often sentimentalise the Bohemia of the play as a lost organic community, in which 'the pastoral scene' yokes 'human growth, decay and rebirth with the vital rhythms of nature'. In such an agrarian society 'rooted in the soil', F.R. Leavis believed, 'People talked, so making Shakespeare possible'.[64] But though *The Winter's Tale* does invoke the archaic institution of the storyteller, the *veillée* where old wives laugh their 'sport o'er by a country fire' [*Wives*, 5,5,119], it leaves that haunted house with the dead Mamillius in Sicily, as the global winds of change blown by print and commerce sweep into the Bohemian sheep-shearing festivities, and convert a tragedy of confinement into Shakespeare's most truly *worldly* play. The Shepherd fondly recalls olden times, when a wife 'was both pantler, butler, cook,/Both dame and servant', who 'welcomed all, served all,/Would sing her song and dance her turn' [4,4,55–8]; but in Perdita's reign as 'queen of curds and cream' [161] these oppressive customs will be commercialised by Autolycus at her imperious command. In *Shakespeare's Festive World*, François Laroque has analysed sheep-shearing as a seasonal opportunity 'to display one's sense of hospitality and good-neighbourliness'; but he then compares Shakespeare's adaptation of the agricultural rite to the primitivism of modernist artists juxtaposing naïve totems or *objets trouvé* in montage.[65] This mercurial beautification of the festive world is never clearer, therefore, than in Perdita's shopping list, which, with its exotic luxuries, extends hospitality so far it opens up this insulated society to the intercultural exchanges of what Fernand Braudel called the true magic of the seventeenth century, 'the miracle of long-distance trade':[66]

> CLOWN:　Let me see, what am I to buy for our sheep-shearing feast? Three pound of sugar, five pound of currants, rice – what will this sister of mine do with rice? But my father hath made her mistress of the feast, and she lays it on. . . . I must have saffron to colour the warden pies; mace, dates, none – that's out of my note; nutmegs, seven; a race or two of ginger – but that I may beg; four pounds of prunes, and as many of raisins o'th'sun.
>
> 　　　　　　　　　　　　　　　　　　　　　　　　　　　　[4,3,34–45]

'Bohemia: a desert country *near the sea*' [stage direction 3,3,1]: like the grocery of the isolated Westmorland town of Kirkby Stephen that so impressed Braudel with its imported sugar, wine, soap, tobacco, lemons, almonds, raisins, pepper, mace and cloves, the marketplace that supplies Perdita with fruit and spices reveals that 'the timeless, bucolic green world' is in fact 'integrated into the international economy' and the cycles of world trade.[67] It can benefit from access to its sea coast due to the wool from the sheep raised with the 'fairy gold', a flock of 'fifteen hundred' which

yields the Shepherd £140 per year [30]. Thus there is all the poetic justice of unintended consequence when Perdita speaks against cultivating 'our carnations and
streaked gillyvors, / Which some call nature's bastards' [82], since the genus *Dianthus*,
with its flesh-tinted pinks and Sweet Williams, was prized as 'the Queen of delight
and of Flowers' for the dazzling diversity and fortuitousness of its hybridisation.[68]
'Solomon in all his princely pomp was never able to attain this beauty', exclaimed
the poet Barnabe Googe in 1577; and the zany permutations of carnation varieties,
with names like Painted Lady, fascinated contemporary gardeners such as John
Gerard, because 'every year every country bringeth forth new sorts' from the natural
cross-pollination Polixenes calls the 'art that nature makes' [91].[69] This spontaneous
'piedness share[d] / With great creating nature' [87] made carnations metonymic of
the very miscegenation which Perdita professes to abhor. So, like Autolycus doing
good deeds against his will, both the father and the foundling are personifications
of the irony of *akrasia*. For Shakespeare might have known that in the real Bohemia
the pioneer botanist Clusius, Charles de l'Écluse, was just then studying the freakish
flower as an emblem, like the bizarre anamorphic art of Arcimboldo, for the cosmopolitan 'confessional mosaic' of the Hapsburg Empire under Emperor Rudolf, and
that the patrons of his genetic research were Chancellor Lobkowicz and his formida-
ble wife Polyxena.[70] If the dramatist had heard of this, there is an entire ecological
politics of 'transculturation' behind the speech in favour of such beautification made
by King Polixenes, when he lives up to his own xenophile name, as the *unintention-
ally* worldly ruler of a Bohemian heterotopia:[71]

> You see, sweet maid, we marry
> A gentler scion to the wildest stock,
> And make conceive a bark of baser kind
> By bud of nobler race. This is an art
> Which does mend nature – change it rather; but
> The art itself is nature. . . .
> Then make your garden rich in gillyvors,
> And do not call them bastards.

[4,4,89–99]

The 'streaked' carnation commended for the garden of a future Queen of Bohemia
can stand as a living representation of Shakespeare's worldly dramaturgy because
it had already been invested with agonistic symbolism as an emblem of religious
pluralism. Emperor Rudolf would later prefer the tulip as a horticultural icon for the
'utopian allure' of ecumenical inclusiveness; but his project of tolerating the intolerant has been discerned behind *The Winter's Tale* by James Ellison, who keys this text
to the hopes for Christian unity excited by the wedding in February 1613 of James's
daughter Elizabeth to Frederick, Elector Palatine and future King of Bohemia.[72]
Perhaps this masque-like carnation interlude was added, therefore, for that grand
celebration, along with the resurrection of Hermione, which does not figure in
either Greene's novel or Simon Forman's report of the 1611 Globe performance. For
in another recent essay Amy Tigner suggests that 'the statue of our queen' [5,3,10],

'newly performed by that rare Italian master Giulio Romano' [5,2,87], may allude to the animated sculptures that featured in the Mannerist gardens of Rudolfine Prague.[73] Shakespeare inherited the Edenic garden metaphor from Greene, whose Bellaria cues Pandosto's jealousy by walking 'into the garden' with Egistus, as Hermione does with Polixenes.[74] It is a long way, however, from the grubby textual rivalry of Greene to Giorgio Vasari's Romano and masques at the Stuart court. So, as Pitcher says, it seems unlikely that Shakespeare returned to *Pandosto*, and 'the green-eyed monster' jealousy [*Othello*, 3,3,170], simply 'to prove his plays were a hundred times better than anything Greene ever wrote'.[75] In this romance of dynastic union, acted for the marriage of a princess who would become Bohemia's Winter Queen, Shakespeare's agonistic drama of worldly coexistence seems rather to have found in the pink carnation a symbol for his own living art of words made flesh.

Truly green with envy, Shakespeare's dying rival had called him an upstart and a bastard. But what these invented garden scenes offer is not only a *paragone* of how he could disabuse such professional 'jealousies . . . too green and idle/For girls of nine' [3,2,178–9]. His beautifying of his sickly green original, with blooms named for their blushing carnality, and a statue designed to 'verily bear blood' [5,3,64], reverses the myth of paternal origin which had driven 'the lives of the artists' from Pygmalion to Romano, by giving 'life to that which gave it life' in a triumph of the performative theatrical event over the marmoreal inertia of literary possession, since 'Who was most marble there changed colour' [5,2,87].[76] It is surely no accident, therefore, that to 'incarnadine' its bilious source, and 'make the green one red' [*Macbeth*, 2,2,59–60], this resurrection scene should require a tincture of carnation, the ground ingredient of cosmetics for 'women's faces' [2,1,12], and of the 'ruddiness' [5,3,81] of the painters' pigment, since, this veined sweet-scented flower was 'at the intersection of both the arts' of portraiture and performance with horticulture, Farah Karim-Cooper explains, as it generated the standard of worldly beauty 'that required fair faces, red lips, and "flesh-pink" cheeks'.[77]

To 'make the green one red': 'If this be magic, let it be an art/lawful as eating', like the Eucharist for which so much real blood had been shed [5,3,109–10], decrees a newly enlightened King Leontes, of the transubstantiation of marble and paint into the flesh and blood of an actor's performance at the end of *The Winter's Tale*. In this drama of metamorphosis and dissemination, which is so preoccupied with the dualism of 'changed complexions' [1,3,377], with gentlemen and genes, seeds and sex, and the toleration of the intolerable, the cross-fertilising carnations are in fact some of the many things that can never be seen on stage, and therefore in which 'It is required/You do awake your faith' [5,2,94–5]. For in the winter of 1613 Time would, of course, have made these 'fairest flowers o'th'season' [4,4,81], that in late summer had been 'the freshest things now reigning', as 'stale' as his tale now seems to them [4,1,13]. Yet such a symbolisation was, perhaps, the closest Shakespeare ever came to that union of transcendence and immanence which Christian theologians located in the *corpus mysticum* of the Church.[78] For with the cheeks of the boy player beautified by the carnation rouge, to make it appear as though 'The statue is but newly fixed; the colour's/Not dry' [5,3,47], and the 'tincture and lustre in her lip' [3,2,202] coloured crimson to suggest that 'the ruddiness on her lip is wet' [5,3,81], this agonistic flower power in Bohemia is truly an *incarnation* of Sweet William, the latest worldly flourish of our good will.

NOTES

1. 'There is an upstart Crow': Robert Greene, *A Groat's-worth of Wit, bought with a million of repentance* (1592), quoted in Park Honan, *Shakespeare: A Life* (Oxford: Oxford University Press, 1998), p. 159; and reprinted in Samuel Schoenbaum, *Shakespeare: A Documentary Life* (Oxford: Oxford University Press, 1975), p. 115; 'bitterest lines': ibid.
2. Stephen Greenblatt, *Will in the World: How Shakespeare Became Shakespeare* (London: Jonathan Cape, 2004), pp. 218 and 224.
3. 'The king of the paper stage': Gabriel Harvey, *Foure Letters*, ed. G. B. Harrison (London: 1922), p. 18; 'Waspish little worm': Greene quoted in Honan, *Shakespeare*, p. 160.
4. Harvey, *Foure Letters*, p. 20.
5. James Joyce, *Ulysses* (Harmondsworth: Penguin, 1968), p. 187.
6. One scholar who thinks Greene's hostility was justified – and that the grasping 'waspish little worm' gives an accurate picture of Shakespeare, is E. A. J. Honigmann, in *The Impact of Shakespeare on His Contemporaries* (Basingstoke: Palgrave Macmillan, 1982).
7. 'Big with one pamphlet': Thomas Nashe; 'penurious brats': Constantia Munda, both quoted in Maria Teresa Micaela Prendergast, 'Promiscuous textualities: the Nashe–Harvey controversy and the unnatural productions of print', in Douglas Brookes (ed.), *Printing and Parenting in Early Modern England* (Aldershot: Ashgate, 2005), p. 173.
8. For the ambiguity, presumably deliberate, see Katherine Duncan Jones, *Ungentle Shakespeare* (London: Arden Shakespeare, 2001), p. 47.
9. Henry Chettle, *Kind-Harts Dreame* (1592), reprinted in Schoenbaum, *Shakespeare*, p. 117. Critical opinion remains divided over the extent to which Chettle himself may have rewritten, or even forged, *Greene's Groat's-worth of Wit*. For the theory that he was the real author, see John Jowett, 'Johannes factotum: Henry Chettle and *Greene's Groat's-worth of Wit*', *Papers of the Bibliographic Society of America*, 87:4 (1993), 453–86; and for a defence of Greene's primary authorship, D. Allen Carroll, 'Introduction', in *Greene's Groat's-worth of Wit* (Binghampton: Medieval and Renaissance Texts and Studies, 1994), pp. 1–31.
10. Henry Chettle, *England's Mourning Garment* (1603), quoted on Honan, *Shakespeare*, p. 297.
11. Chettle reprinted in Schoenbaum, *Shakespeare*, p. 117.
12. Joseph Loewenstein, *Ben Jonson and Possessive Authorship* (Cambridge: Cambridge University Press, 2002), pp. 85–6.
13. Greenblatt, *Will in the World*, pp. 216, 219 and 225.
14. Ibid.; Kirk Melnikoff and Edward Gieskes (eds), 'Introduction', in *Writing Robert Greene: Essays on England's First Notorious Professional Writer* (Farnham: Ashgate, 2008), p. 24.
15. Lori Humphrey Newcomb has recently argued that instead of regarding Greene's romance as Shakespeare's pale source, we should 'think of the play as part of *Pandosto*'s reception': *Reading Popular Romance in Early Modern England* (New York: Columbia University Press, 2002), p. 117. Jonathan Baldo comments that Shakespeare is 'pilfering from his old rival in order to turn a profit': 'The greening of Will Shakespeare', *Borrowers and Lenders: The Journal of Shakespeare Appropriation*, 3:2 (2008), 1–28, here 12.
16. Greene, *A Groat's-worth of Wit*.
17. Robert Greene, *The Second Part of Conny-Catching*, reprinted in Geofffry Bullough (ed.), *Narrative and Dramatic Sources of Shakespeare. VIII: Romances* (London: Routledge and Kegan Paul, 1975), p. 215; Kenneth Muir, *The Sources of Shakespeare's Plays* (London: Methuen, 1977), pp. 275–6.

18. 'Myriad forms': W. R. Morse, 'Metacriticism and materiality: the case of Shakespeare's *The Winter's Tale*', *English Literary History*, 58:2 (1991), 283–304, here 297.

19. For the longstanding debate over the theory that Greene's unnamed player refers to Shakespeare, see in particular M. C. Bradbrook, *Rise of the Common Player* (London: Chatto and Windus, 1962), p. 85–6; A. L. Rowse, *Shakespeare the Man* (New York: Harper and Row, 1973), p. 60; D. Allen Carroll, 'The player-patron in Greene's *Groat's-worth of Wit* (1592)', *Studies in Philology*, 91 (1994), 301–10.

20. Greene, *A Groat's-worth of Wit*.

21. Ibid.

22. James Bednarz, *Shakespeare and the Poets' War* (New York: Columbia University Press, 2001), p. 230.

23. Thomas Dekker, *Jests to Make You Merry* (1607), quoted in Honan, *Shakespeare*, pp. 162–3.

24. John Pitcher, 'Some call him Autolycus', in Ann Thompson and Gordon McMullan (eds), *In Arden. Editing Shakespeare: Essays in Honour of Richard Proudfoot* (London: Thomson Learning, 2003), pp. 255–6; John Pitcher (ed.), 'Introduction', in *The Winter's Tale* (Arden Shakespeare) (London: Methuen, 2010), p. 9; Honan, *Shakespeare*, p. 163.

25. Margaret Spufford, *The Great Reclothing of Rural England: Petty Chapmen and Their Wares in the Seventeenth Century* (London: Hambledon Press, 1984), pp. 8 and 145–6.

26. Lee Beier, *Masterless Men: The Vagrancy Problem in England, 1560–1640* (London: Methuen, 1985), p. 90.

27. Timothy Brook, *Vermeer's Hat: The Seventeenth Century and the Dawn of the Global World* (London: Profile, 2009), pp. 27–8.

28. Spufford, *The Great Reclothing of Rural England*, pp. 88–9.

29. Simon Palfrey, *Late Shakespeare: A New World of Words* (Oxford: Clarendon Press, 1997), pp. 232–5.

30. Carol Thomas Neely, 'Women and issue', in Kiernan Ryan (ed.), *Shakespeare: The Last Plays* (Harlow: Longman, 1999), p. 180.

31. Margreta de Grazia, 'Imprints: Shakespeare, Gutenberg, and Descartes', in Brookes (ed.), *Printing and Parenting in Early Modern England*, p. 43; Wendy Wall, 'Reading for the blot: textual desire in early modern English literature', in David Bergeron (ed.), *Reading and Writing in Shakespeare* (Newark: Delaware University Press, 1996), pp. 131–50

32. For the ways in which the late plays 'represent infidelity through references to blackness and ink', see Wall, 'Reading for the blot', p. 137.

33. See Helen Smith, '"A man in print"? Shakespeare and the representation of the press', in Richard Meek, Jane Rickard and Richard Wilson (eds), *Shakespeare's Book: Essays in Reading, Writing and Reception* (Manchester: Manchester University Press, 2008), pp. 62–6.

34. Loewenstein, *Ben Jonson and Possessive Authorship*, p. 50.

35. 'Dangerous supplement': Jacques Derrida, *Of Grammatology*, trans. Gayatri Chakravorty Spivak (Baltimore: Johns Hopkins University Press, 1976), p. 144.

36. Jane Rickard, *Authorship and Authority: The Writings of James VI and I* (Manchester: Manchester University Press, 2007), p. 128.

37. Neely, 'Women and issue', p. 170.

38. Helen Hackett, '"Gracious be the issue": maternity and narrative in Shakespeare's late plays', in Jennifer Richards and James Knowles (eds), *Shakespeare's Late Plays: New Readings* (Edinburgh: Edinburgh University Press, 1999), pp. 25–39.

39. Lynn Enterline, '"You speak a language that I understand not": the rhetoric of animation in *The Winter's Tale*', *Shakespeare Quarterly*, 48:1 (1997), 17–44, here 27.

40. Robert Knapp, *Shakespeare: The Theater and the Book* (Princeton: Princeton University Press, 1989), p. 241; and see also David Bergeron, 'Treacherous reading and writing in Shakespeare's romances', in Bergeron (ed.), *Reading and Writing in Shakespeare*, pp. 160–77.

41. Thomas Heywood, 'Epistle prefatory' to *The English Traveller* (1633), quoted in Loewenstein, *Ben Jonson and Possessive Authorship*, p. 50.

42. Adrian Johns, *The Nature of the Book: Print and Knowledge in the Making* (Chicago: Chicago University Press, 1998), pp. 31, 35 and 58.

43. Louis MacNeice, 'Autolycus', in *Louis MacNeice: Poems*, ed. Michael Longley (London: Faber and Faber, 2001), pp. 79–80.

44. 'Deformed biological reproduction': Aaron Kitch, 'Printing bastards: monstrous birth broadsides in early modern England', in Brookes (ed.), *Printing and Parenting in Early Modern England*, p. 232.

45. Alison Findlay, *Illegitimate Power: Bastards in Renaissance Drama* (Manchester: Manchester University Press, 1994), pp. 135–6.

46. Howard Felperin, '"Tongue-tied our queen?": the deconstruction of presence in *The Winter's Tale*', in Patricia Parker and Geoffrey Hartman (eds), *Shakespeare and the Question of Theory* (London: Routledge, 1993), p. 8.

47. 'Unprecedented obfuscation': Muir, *The Sources of Shakespeare's Plays*, p. 267.

48. Ralph Houlbrooke, *The English Family, 1450–1700* (Harlow: Longman, 1984), p. 82.

49. Catherine Belsey, *Why Shakespeare?* (Basingstoke: Palgrave Macmillan, 2007), p. 73.

50. Robert Greene, *Pandosto, The Triumph of Time*, reprinted in Pitcher (ed.), *The Winter's Tale*, p. 423.

51. Derrida, *Of Grammatology*, p. 168.

52. Robert Greene, 'A quip for an upstart courtier, or a quaint dispute between velvet breeches and cloth breeches' (London: 1592), quoted in J. J. Jusserand, *The English Novel in the Time of Shakespeare* (London: Fisher Unwin, 1891), p. 189; Peter Burke, *Popular Culture in Early Modern Europe* (London: Temple Smith, 1978), p. 277.

53. Robert Darnton, 'Peasants tell tales', in *The Great Cat Massacre, And Other Episodes in French Cultural History* (London: Allen Lane, 1984), pp. 62–5.

54. 'An old wives winter's tale': George Peele, *The Old Wives Tale*, ed. Patricia Binnie (Manchester: Manchester University Press, 1980), line 99; Christopher Marlowe, *The Jew of Malta*, 2,1,24–6; *Doctor Faustus*, 5,136, in *Christopher Marlowe: The Complete Plays*, ed. Frank Romany and Robert Lindsey (London: Penguin, 2003), pp. 273 and 364.

55. Natalie Zemon Davis, *Society and Culture in Early Modern France* (Cambridge: Polity Press, 1987), p. 229.

56. Darnton, *The Great Cat Massacre*, pp. 29 and 55.

57. Greene, *Pandosto*, reprinted in Pitcher (ed.), *The Winter's Tale*, p. 406; Joel Davis, 'Paulina's paint and the dialectic of masculine desire in the *Metamorphoses*, *Pandosto*, and *The Winter's Tale*', *Papers on Language and Literature*, 39: 2 (2003); 115–30, here 22.

58. Greene, *Pandosto*, reprinted in Pitcher (ed.), *The Winter's Tale*, p. 445.

59. See Barbara Melchiori, 'Still harping on my daughter', *English Miscellany*, 11 (1960), 59–74.

60. Pitcher (ed.), *The Winter's Tale*, p. 56.

61. Terry Eagleton, *William Shakespeare* (Oxford: Blackwell, 1986), p. 92; Jennifer Richards, 'Social decorum in *The Winter's Tale*', in Richards and Knowles (eds), *Shakespeare's Late Plays*, p. 78.

62. Ibid., pp. 75–9; see also Anne Barton, 'Leontes and the Spider', in Ryan, op. cit. (note 30), pp. 22–42.

63. Patricia Parker, *Shakespeare From the Margins: Language, Culture, Context* (Chicago: University of Chicago Press, 1996), pp. 21 and 23.

64. F. R. Leavis, 'Shakespeare's late plays', in *The Common Pursuit* (London: Chatto and Windus, 1962), pp. 180–1; F. R. Leavis, 'Joyce and the revolution in the word', *Scrutiny*, 2:2 (1933), 200.

65. François Laroque, *Shakespeare's Festive World: Elizabethan Seasonal Entertainment and the Professional Stage* (Cambridge: Cambridge University Press, 1991), pp. 156 and 185.

66. Fernand Braudel, *The Wheels of Commerce (Civilization and Capitalism: 15th–18th Century)*, trans. Siân Reynolds (London: Collins, 1982), pp. 582–5.

67. Ibid., p. 66; Walter Cohen, 'The undiscovered country: Shakespeare and mercantile geography', in Jean Howard and Scott Cutler Shershow (eds), *Marxist Shakespeares* (London: Routledge, 2001), p. 144.

68. 'Queen of Flowers': John Parkinson, *Theatrum Botanicum* (London: 1629), quoted in Alice Coats, *Flowers and Their Histories* (London: Hulton, 1956), p. 71.

69. Barnabe Googe quoted ibid.; John Gerard, *The Herball or Generall Historie of Plantes* (London: 1597), quoted in C. Oscar Moreton, *Old Carnations and Pinks* (London: George Rainbird, 1955), p. 4.

70. Moreton, *Old Carnations and Pinks*; 'confessional mosaic': Karen Barkey, 'Empire and toleration', in Alfred Stepan and Charles Taylor (eds), *Boundaries of Toleration* (New York: Columbia University Press, 2014), pp. 203–32, here p. 220. See also R. J. W. Evans, *Rudolf II and His World: A Study in Intellectual History, 1576–1612* (Oxford: Clarendon Press, 1973), pp. 119–20, 207 et passim.

71. For the theory of 'transculturation' see Brook, *Vermeer's Hat*, pp. 21, 126 and passim; and Fernando Ortiz, *Cuban Counterpoint: Tobacco and Sugar* (1940; reprinted Durham, NC: Duke University Press, 1995).

72. 'Utopian allure': Alfred Thomas, *A Blessed Shore: England and Bohemia from Chaucer to Shakespeare* (Ithaca: Cornell University Press, 2007), p. 169; James Ellison, 'The Winter's Tale and the religious politics of Europe', in Alison Thorne (ed.), *Shakespeare's Romances* (Basingstoke: Palgrave Macmillan, 2003), pp. 171–204. For Rudolf and the beginning of the tulip craze, see Simon Schama, *The Embarrassment of Riches: An Interpretation of Dutch Culture in the Golden Age* (London: Collins, 1987), p. 351.

73. Amy L. Tigner, 'The Winter's Tale: gardens and the marvels of transformation', *English Literary Renaissance*, 36:1 (2006), 114–34; Evans, *Rudolf II and His World*, p. 121.

74. Greene, *Pandosto*, reprinted in Pitcher (ed.), *The Winter's Tale*, p. 408: 'Bellaria would walk with him in the garden, where they two in private and pleasant devices would pass the time to both their contents'.

75. Pitcher (ed.), *The Winter's Tale*, p. 265; see Duncan Jones, *Ungentle Shakespeare*, pp. 229–30.

76. Baldo, 'The greening of Will Shakespeare', p. 8.

77. Farah Karim-Cooper, *Cosmetics in Shakespearean and Renaissance Drama* (Edinburgh: Edinburgh University Press, 2006), p. 13; and see pp. 81, 139.

78. See Jennifer Rust, 'Political theologies of the *corpus mysticum*: Schmitt, Kantorowicz, and de Lubac', in Graham Hammill and Julia Lupton (eds), *Political Theology and Early Modernity* (Chicago: University of Chicago Press, 2012), pp. 102–24, at pp. 118–19.

Index